MODERN SOCIAL WORK THEORY

Also by Malcolm Payne:

*The Origins of Social Work: Continuity and Change**

*Teamwork in Multi-professional Care**

Anti-bureaucratic Social Work

What is Professional Social Work?

*Social Work and Community Care**

Writing for Publication in Social Services Journals

Linkages: Networking in Social Care

*Social Care in the Community**

*Working in Teams**

*Power, Authority and Responsibility in Social Services**

Citizenship Social Work with Older People

Social Work in End-of-Life and Palliative Care

*Humanistic Social Work: Core Principles in Practice**

*Social Care Practice in Context**

*Also published by Palgrave Macmillan

MODERN SOCIAL WORK THEORY

MALCOLM PAYNE | 4TH EDITION

palgrave
macmillan

First edition 1990
Second edition 1997
Third edition 2005
Fourth edition 2014
Published by
PALGRAVE MACMILLAN

Palgrave Macmillan in the UK is an imprint of Macmillan Publishers Limited, registered in England, company number 785998, of Houndmills, Basingstoke, Hampshire RG21 6XS.

Palgrave Macmillan in the US is a division of St Martin's Press LLC, 175 Fifth Avenue, New York, NY 10010.

Palgrave Macmillan is the global academic imprint of the above companies and has companies and representatives throughout the world.

Palgrave® and Macmillan® are registered trademarks in the United States, the United Kingdom, Europe and other countries.

ISBN: 978–0–230–24960–8   paperback

This book is printed on paper suitable for recycling and made from fully managed and sustained forest sources. Logging, pulping and manufacturing processes are expected to conform to the environmental regulations of the country of origin.

A catalogue record for this book is available from the British Library.

A catalog record for this book is available from the Library of Congress.

Typeset by Aardvark Editorial Limited, Metfield, Suffolk

Printed in China.

Brief contents

Contents

List of figures

Preface to the fourth edition

The aims of this book and its social construction perspective

It continues to be my aim in *Modern Social Work Theory* to present and review theories that currently inform the practice of social work. I want to show how these ideas can guide and enthuse us, enhancing social work practice so that it achieves the outcomes that policy and law, our professional imagination and our clients' needs and aims set for us.

I have completely rewritten this fourth edition in an attempt to make the text an easier read. In response to feedback, I have included and highlighted more case examples, increased the use of diagrams to help readers who find a visual presentation of ideas helpful, and reduced the complexity of tables summarizing the texts that have been reviewed. I am grateful to Emma Reith-Hall for providing two extended case studies in Chapters 2 and 6, which contribute to our understanding of the complex interaction between theory and practice in our agencies. I have also spread throughout the text opportunities for you to 'pause and reflect', applying your own thinking to crucial aspects of the argument.

One illustration of the pace of theory development in social work is that, although this edition is being published only eight years after the previous edition, most of my accounts of example texts, which show how social work writers have used theories to present comprehensive accounts of practice, are new. I have continued to include the bare bones of how each group of theories developed, with historical citations that I hope will continue to provide a bibliographical resource, but mostly I refer to current sources. About a third of the citations were published since the last edition, and about two-thirds since the millennium.

Part of the reason for this comprehensive change is an equally substantial change in my perspective. I have retained my social construction perspective because it makes clear that many different interests form our theory and practice. In particular, our clients, their families, carers and communities make demands on us and work in alliance with us. In doing so, they stretch us and our theory and practice to help and work with them better. But, as accountable professionals, our theory and practice are also influenced by political and social ideas and our professional learning, skill and experience.

More than a quarter of a century ago, however, when I was first writing *Modern Social Work Theory* in the late 1980s, we were coming to the end of what some (for example, Orme and Shemmings, 2010) have called the theory or paradigm 'wars'. Theories were opposed to one another; people argued that some were better than others and would supplant them, but it has not turned out to be so. Instead, reviewing theory as it is currently used, I increasingly find that there are shared ideas present in most practice theories. In Figure 1.7, I extract these principles, which I call the 'the shared value principles' of social work practice. They are present in the way in which most theory is used today in practice, and you will find them recurring as you read social work theory and practice texts. I have sometimes highlighted them in discussing particular theories, but if you bear them in mind you will find them leaping out at you elsewhere in the text.

This book is, therefore, an argument that, rather than being at war, social work theories are increasingly presented as contributors to the range of enterprises that social work engages with. Therefore, I have changed the structure of each chapter to say first: 'this is the special contribution to your practice that this group of theories makes'.

My decision to suggest these shared values as signs of agreement about practice theory might be criticized as taking a consensus view of the social phenomenon that is social work. But no, I think there is still plenty of principled disagreement in social work even if common modes of practice are emerging. I look forward to watching future developments.

The structure of the book and its chapters

The book is divided into two parts. Part 1 (Chapters 1–3) summarizes general debates about social work theory and how to apply it. Part 2 (Chapters 4–14) reviews the main groups of social work theories, derived from my analysis of leading texts in Chapter 2.

The structure of each chapter in Part 2 starts by defining:

- the theory's distinctive features that make up its *main contribution* to social work practice;

and then offers a summary account of:

- the *main points* that help us to understand that contribution;
- important *practice ideas* and concepts that this group of theories has contributed to social work; these cover only ideas used in practice, and this section is not a glossary of theoretical terms;
- *major statements* of this theory in current social work texts;
- a *debate summary* of the main points of contention about this theory.

The debate summary leads into a more detailed account of this group of theories, considering:

- *wider theoretical perspectives* that put the theory in context – where did it come from?;
- *connections* between this theory and other social work theories;
- *the politics* of the theory, showing how it is contested in social work debate;
- *values issues*: a brief comment on values issues raised by the theory.

Building on this account of the theory, I then provide an account of how it is put into action within social work, covering:

- *applications*: an overview of how the theory is applied in social work;
- *example text(s)* selected from book-length accounts of how a particular author has applied this group of theories in a social work text; the judgements that informed the selections are accounted for in the 'major statement' section earlier in the chapter;
- *conclusion: using the theory* sums up the main points about how this group of theories is used in social work practice.

Each chapter ends with:

- *additional resources*, which include further reading and specialized journals, and suggestions of websites that provide good access to internet resources.

From the lists above, the following are either a new section or in a new format in this edition:

- main contribution;
- debate summary;
- values issues:;
- applications;
- example text;
- conclusion: using the theory;
- additional resources.

I have continued to try to restrain the size of this volume, although it is again longer than its predecessor, and my accounts of a particular theory are only a starting point for a further exploration – hence the additional resources that I suggest. This means that, to anyone committed to a particular theory or point of view, my at times heavy condensation is disputable and disputed. My aim is to give access to a range of ideas and encourage readers to progress from this introduction to the comprehensive accounts you can find in the books and articles I have referred to. I find the social work literature full of stimulating ideas for practice and understanding. I am sure you will do so, too.

I hope that new generations of practitioners and students will continue to find this review of social work practice theories useful in constructing their practice.

MALCOLM PAYNE
Sutton, Surrey

The publishers would like to express their gratitude to Lyceum Books for their permission to use Figures 10.1 and 14.6 and to Policy Press for Figure 1.6.

About the author

Malcolm Payne is Emeritus Professor, Manchester Metropolitan University, and Honorary Professor in the Faculty of Health, Social Care and Education at Kingston University/St George's University of London, with further honorary academic appointments in Finland and Slovakia. From 2003 to 2012, he was Director of Psychosocial and Spiritual Care and Policy and Development Adviser, St Christopher's Hospice, London. He is the widely translated best-selling author and editor of many books and articles, including, recently, *What is Professional Social Work?*, *The Origins of Social Work: Continuity and Change, Social Care Practice in Context, Humanistic Social Work: Core Principles in Practice, Citizenship Social Work with Older People* and (with Margaret Reith) *Social Work in End-of-life and Palliative Care*. He is an active contributor to social media, including Twitter (@malcolmpayne) and blogs on older people and end-of-life care.

A note on terminology

'Clients' and other words for the people we work with

There are problems with putting people into categories. Many social workers dislike giving the people they work with category names like 'client', 'patient', 'resident' and 'user'. It sometimes leads to them being referred to as 'the clients' or 'the users' in a disrespectful way, and all these terms are unacceptable to some of the people to whom they are applied.

Different countries have varying preferences. Since this book has an international circulation, I have often used the term 'client' as being the most inclusive and generally understandable term for its wide range of readers. I use other terms where the circumstances are appropriate, for example 'patients' when referring to healthcare situations, 'residents' when referring to residential care, and 'users' when referring to people who are receiving packages of services or to services for people with learning disabilities, where this term has the widest currency.

Social development issues

In literature about international issues, people argue over how to refer to the economic and social development of particular countries. Should we say that a country is developed, underdeveloped or developing, which hides an assumption that development is a desirable end result? The term 'Third World', referring to political allegiance, derives from the Cold War period and has appropriately fallen out of use. Should we say that a country is a Western country, meaning a country with an industrialized developed economy, whose culture originates from European and North American models? Some writers refer to the North (the northern hemisphere) and the South, implying that most countries in the North are economically developed and most in the South are not. Some countries in the Southern hemisphere, such as Australia, are 'Northern' and 'Western' in their social and economic development and culture.

Some countries, however, do not fit into any such category. Examples might be countries such as China that are experiencing rapid economic and social change and development alongside substantial poverty and inequality, or Eastern European 'transition' economies, which are moving from being part of the Soviet sphere of influence to participation in European economic markets.

Bearing all this in mind, I have chosen in this book to refer to economically developed countries with a largely European or North American culture as Western countries. I refer to poorer nations with less industrially developed economies as 'resource-poor', a term that is current in the healthcare professions.

THINKING ABOUT SOCIAL WORK THEORY

The social construction of social work theory

1

Main contribution

This chapter aims to help practitioners feel confident in using theory in their practice. It discusses the different kinds of social work theory and the arguments around them, and explains how all of this may be useful in practice. It shows how social work theory in general, and practice theory in particular, is socially constructed in interactions between clients and practitioners in their agencies and in wider political, social and cultural arenas. This makes clear that we build both practice and theory through our experience operating in the real world; they are not given to us from on high. Social construction ideas also show that practice and theory are not separate, settled bodies of knowledge, but constantly evolve and influence each other. Change in social work, and in the lives of practitioners and clients, is possible through engagement in this process of evolution of ideas and practice.

Main points

- The main aim of the book is to review social work practice theories.
- Theories are generalized sets of ideas that describe and explain our knowledge of the world in an organized way.
- Theory is different from both knowledge and practice.
- All practice is influenced by formal and informal theories of what social work is, how to do social work and the client world.
- The four types of practice theory are perspectives, frameworks, models and explanatory theories; they often complement each other.
- Theory helps us understand and contest ideas, and the world around us, offers a framework for practice and helps us to be accountable, self-disciplined professionals.
- Social construction ideas emphasize that change for social institutions and individuals is always possible, although it may be slow, and social experience often reinforces stability rather than change.

- The social construction of social work forms a politics; this means that groups within the profession contend to gain influence over practice by getting support for particular theories.
- Three views of social work objectives (empowerment, social change and problem-solving) are derived from the aims of social work and from political philosophies. They form the context in which practice theories are socially constructed.
- Five shared value principles affect our use of all practice theories: alliance, aim, action sequence, critical practice and rights.
- Social work is socially constructed in three main arenas of debate and practice theories in the arena of relationships between clients, workers and social agencies.
- Clients make an important contribution to the construction of social work through their reflexive interaction with practitioners in social work agencies.

Theory and knowledge in social work practice

All over the world, at this moment, people are struggling into an office to see a social worker, or they are meeting a social worker in their home or working with a social worker in a building such as a residential care home or groupwork or day centre. How can the people using the social worker's services understand what is happening? How can the social worker decide what to do and explain it to them? You may have found that many statements about social work are generalized or idealistic and give no clue about what is supposed to happen when social work takes place. Yet social workers have to learn what to do and carry out what their profession expects of them. To do this, they rely on practice theories, that is, theories that provide an organized account prescribing what social workers should do when they practise.

The main aim of this chapter is to help you understand what theory is and what social work practice theories are, and to think through some of the debates about using them in practice. In this first section, I look at ideas about the various kinds of theory and knowledge available in social work and how theory and knowledge are connected but different.

What is theory?

One way to answer this question is to start from general ideas about theory. Sheldon and Macdonald (2009: 34) examine a dictionary definition of it and suggest that our understanding includes both scientific and everyday uses of the word. To a scientist, a theory is a general principle or body of knowledge, reached through accepted scientific processes, that explains a phenomenon. The everyday use of the word 'theory' refers to abstract thoughts or speculations. In its everyday use, therefore, people may think that theory is generally disconnected from reality. Many social work writers (for example, Howe, 2009; Sheldon and Macdonald, 2009; Thompson, 2010) focus on explanation and structure: a theory should explain some aspect of the world in an organized form. Others accept less exacting understandings of theory: Nash et al. (2005a) see theory as a 'map' interacting with practice. Fook (2012: 44) argues that there are many different meanings of theory, and that the important thing is to be inclusive so that we do not cut ourselves off from useful ideas.

Bringing these points together, I define a theory as a generalized set of ideas that describes and explains our knowledge of the world around us in an organized way. A social work theory is one that helps us to do or to understand social work.

There is a debate about whether practice theories, that is, those which tell us what to do in social work, or how to do it, are more important than theories about what social work is or where it fits into related services. Later in this chapter, I discuss practice theory in greater detail. Nash et al. (2005a) suggest that a fundamental requirement of social work theory is that it interacts with or is useful in some way in practice. D'Cruz (2009) similarly argues that social work is not interested in knowledge or theory that has no practical use. On the other hand, Sheldon and Macdonald (2009: 35) argue that British and American everyday thinking sees theory as too abstract. This is not a view shared with writers across the globe, for example in Europe, where philosophical argument is valued on its own merits.

These arguments demonstrate the following:

- Theory is different from knowledge – theory involves thinking about something; knowledge is a description of reality. Reality is a picture of the world that is accepted as true.
- Theory is different from practice – theory is thinking about something; practice involves doing something.

While we can distinguish theory from knowledge and from practice, it is also connected to them. First, if a theory is to explain the world, it must explain our knowledge of the world. The real is more than what is merely apparent; understanding a reality involves ensuring that the apparent is true, using some agreed process to check that what appears to be true actually is true. The real world exists independently of theories and ideas about it, but evidence about that real world has to be obtained in ways that are accepted as valid through the 'accepted scientific processes' that I mentioned above. Second, social work is an activity, something that we do, so theories about it must be explanations of the real world that connect with how we act as practising social workers.

Types of social work theory

There are different types of theory in social work. In Figure 1.1, I have collected a number of points that enlarge on Sibeon's (1990) distinction between formal and informal theory. Formal theory is written down and debated in the profession and in academic work. Informal theory consists of wider ideas that exist in society or that practitioners derive from experience. Sibeon (1990, p. 34) also distinguishes between three different types of theory:

▨ Theories of *what social work is* are part of a discourse about the meaning of social work. Discourses are disagreements between people, which you can see or hear in debates in articles and at conferences, but they are also reflected in the different ways people do social work. You can, therefore, take part in a discourse because of the way you do something, and not only in talk and writing. I consider theories about the meaning of social work briefly later in this chapter and more fully in Payne (2006). They offer different views of social work that, when you put them together, give you a fuller picture of what it is and what its aims are.

▨ Theories of *how to do social work* are the practice theories that this book explores. They build on theories of what social work is by saying: 'If social work is like this and these are its aims, here are some ideas about how to do that and achieve the aims.'

▨ Theories of *the client world* are about the social realities that social workers deal with. Much of this material is contested in the field it came from. For example, ideas in child development, or the sociology of families and organizations, are vigorously debated. It is useful to know about them as we deal within social work agencies with children in their families. However, using this material in social work means that we must transfer it from its original discipline into social work practice. In doing this, we have to remember that it is not final knowledge; there will still be continuing disagreement over it and research into it. In addition, agencies, child development and family sociology interact in a particular way in social work because social workers need this information for their particular purposes, which are different from those of, say, doctors. The practice theories that I discuss in this book connect knowledge from different disciplines to social work practice; they say: 'To practise in the way this theory proposes, you need these kinds of knowledge from other fields of study.' In this way, practice theories help us practise by organizing how we transfer knowledge into social work.

Figure 1.1 Types of theory

Types of theory	'Formal' theory	'Informal' theory
Theories of *what social work is*	Formal written accounts defining the nature and purposes of welfare (e.g. personal pathology, liberal reform, Marxist, feminist)	Moral, political and cultural values drawn upon by practitioners for defining the 'functions' of social work
Theories of *how to do social work*	Formal written theories of practice (e.g. casework, family therapy, groupwork); applied deductively; general ideas may be applied to particular situations	Theories inductively derived from particular situations; can be tested to see if they apply to particular situations; also unwritten practice theories constructed from experience
Theories of *the client world*	Formal written social science theories; empirical data (e.g. on personality, marriage, the family, race, class, gender)	Practitioners' use of experience and general cultural meanings (e.g. the family as an institution, 'normal' behaviour, good parenting)

Source: Sibeon (1991), Fook (2012) and Gilgun (1994).

You may, as you look at Figure 1.1, need an explanation of informal theories as being 'inductively derived'. *Induction* means generalizing from particular examples, that is, 'bottom-up' theorizing in which you start from a series of similar experiences and make up a theory that explains them. *Deduction*, on the other hand, means arriving at conclusions about the particular instance from a general theory, that is, 'top-down' theorizing in which you look at a theory that someone has formulated and work out how a case you are working on fits in. A case example may help to understand this distinction.

Case example: Using induction and deduction when working with dying people

This example considers people's emotional reactions to dying. Perhaps you have worked with several dying people who at first got angry, and then became depressed, and then accepting about their approaching death. By a process of induction, you might create an informal model of the progression of emotional reactions to impending death using your experience. Imagine that you then meet a dying person who is depressed. As a deduction from your model, you might work on the assumption that they will shortly become accepting. So induction allows you to take ideas from a particular case or a small number of cases and use them to create a general theory. In this way, induction enables practitioners to transfer ideas observed from practice experiences into more general theories. It also allows us to contribute to theory from our own practice. We can feed patterns that we observe into writing about social work or into discussion about practice in our agency.

Deduction, on the other hand, allows you to use general theories in practice. For example, in this same area of work, Kübler-Ross (1969) came up with a theory in an interview study of dying people that they went through five stages. First, they went through a stage of disbelieving their diagnosis; she called this the shock and denial stage. Second, they went through an anger stage – resentment that this was happening to them. Next, they went into bargaining behaviour, for example: 'If I eat more healthily, I'll be able to fight this illness and recover.' The fourth stage was depression, and finally they became accepting of their fate. If you knew about Kübler-Ross's work, you would not need to use induction to create your own theory. Instead, from day one in your job, if you came across a dying person who was angry, you would expect bargaining behaviour next. So knowing about her theory allows you to hit the ground running in your work, rather than having to work without any guidelines until you have built up experience from lots of different situations.

The problem with both deduction and induction is that they can lead you astray. Suppose, for example, you did not see enough examples. You might assume that something was a pattern, when, if you looked at more examples, you would find that there were many exceptions to your initial assumption. The answer to this problem is to treat all your inductive theories cautiously, constantly testing them out with new experience. In this way, you build up better evidence to support your work.

Deduction may also be unreliable, because you might also be led astray by the research that led to the theories you are making deductions from. Indeed, Kübler-Ross's theory has been refined to suggest that these reactions are quite common, but people do not go through all the stages in order, so, if a client misses one out, practitioners do not have to worry that they are not adjusting properly to their situation. Therefore, practitioners need to look at the evidence that underlies a theory and, on finding aspects of it that are not true, may need to adjust their deductions and contribute that experience to the literature to refine the theory. All professions build up knowledge to support their work in this kind of way. In addition, they need to keep an eye on new research that tells them when a theory has been modified. So whether working inductively or deductively, practitioners have to keep on learning.

Induction and deduction therefore go together and interact with each other: practitioners deduce how to practise from general theories and induce ideas from experience to contribute to the theory.

Types of practice theory

Practice theory covers four different approaches to thinking about how to practise, which I illustrate in Figure 1.2.

Opinion differs about whether all of these approaches are equally useful. *Perspectives* allow practitioners to make decisions according to general guiding principles. Lying behind a preference for using perspectives is a philosophy that human beings are immensely diverse and that precise rules about how to act do not allow you to respect that diversity. Instead, you deduce from your perspective how to act in the particular situation that you are facing. A preference for using perspectives also has the advantage of integrity: your perspective and your actions fit your personal value systems. *Frameworks* are more concrete and less value-based than perspectives, although there are usually some implied values that can be teased out from how they work. They can help us by setting out the range of situations that we typically have to deal with, and by identifying the range of methods available for us to select from, perhaps giving us some basis for making our selection. *Models* are frameworks that set out a clear sequence of actions to take when we are faced with a particular situation. *Explanatory theories* are models that are based on well-researched explanations of human and social behaviour, so the sequence of actions that you take is informed by knowledge about the reasons why this situation occurs and is backed up by evidence about the right actions to take to achieve the required outcome.

People prefer frameworks, models and particularly explanatory theories because they think it is wrong for their own personal values and preferences to intrude into decisions about professional actions. They think it is more ethical instead to concentrate on evidence that tells you what will be most effective in dealing with people and the problems they are facing; in that way, you may have a better chance of achieving what your agency or client wants. However, this sort of approach sees social work as a more technical matter of applying knowledge in a neutral way. People who use perspectives say that since social work is a human, interpersonal process, using a coherent set of ideas that is right for the human beings involved is more likely to be effective than using a non-human technical process.

1.2a **Perspectives** express ways of thinking about the world based on consistent values and principles. Perspectives help you to apply a coherent set of ideas to what is happening. Applying different perspectives can help you see situations from different points of view. Examples of perspectives are humanistic (Chapter 9) or feminist (Chapter 13) theories.

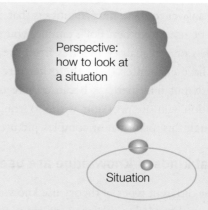

Perspective: how to look at a situation

Situation

Methods available

Situations dealt with in social work

1.2b **Frameworks** organize bodies of knowledge in a systematic way so that you can focus on and select useful knowledge required to practise in different situations. Systems theories (Chapter 7) are a good example.

1.2c **Models** extract patterns of activity from practice and describe what happens during practice in a structured form. This helps to give our practice consistency in a wide range of situations. Models help you to structure and organize how you approach a complicated situation. A good example is task-centred practice (Chapter 5).

| Situation | Action 1 | Action 2 | Action 3 | Outcome |

1.2d **Explanatory theory** accounts for why an action results in or causes particular consequences and identifies the circumstances in which it does so. Some writers reserve the word 'theory' for ideas that offer this causal explanation. To them, theories have to tell you 'what works' and why it works. Cognitive-behavioural theory (Chapter 6) is an example.

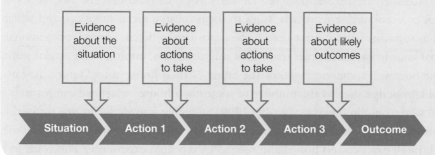

| Evidence about the situation | Evidence about actions to take | Evidence about actions to take | Evidence about likely outcomes |

| Situation | Action 1 | Action 2 | Action 3 | Outcome |

Figure 1.2 Approaches to practice. (a) Perspective. (b) Framework. (c) Model. (d) Explanatory theory

One answer to these uncertainties is that, to some degree, these different types of theory may be used together. For example, you might use a framework or perspective to select models or explanatory theories from the options available, depending on the situation you have encountered. In the other direction, you might prefer to use an explanatory theory, but find, perhaps because there is no relevant evidence, that it does not fit the situation you are working with, so you use an appropriate perspective to guide you through this unknown or complex picture.

What kinds of knowledge are useful in practice?

These different types of theory use knowledge in various ways, so this section looks at the kinds of knowledge that may inform practice. Jacobs (2009) summarizes various philosophical accounts of knowledge in practice, as follows:

- 'Knowing how' to do something is different from 'knowing that …' something is true or 'knowing about …' some aspect of the world.
- Technique is knowledge that is formulated in an organized way and is usually written down. Technique helps practitioners to do something, but it is different from practical knowledge, that is, the unformulated knowledge of how to do something.
- Tacit knowledge is also unformulated and is different from express knowledge, that is, formulated knowledge of facts, procedures and values.
- Knowledge about the world used in academic study of the natural or social world is worked out by rational deductions from confirmed observations. This is different from knowledge in practical fields like social work. In practical fields where knowledge is used to do something, practitioners use theories to help them understand how knowledge can support their decision-making. Their aim is not just to know more, but to use what they know. In practical fields of work, therefore, theory is about supporting reasonable judgements with thought-through arguments based on knowledge.

The implication of these distinctions is that you can know a lot about facts, procedures and values, and possess techniques for doing things, but knowledge about *how* to act may not be so easily formulated. Polanyi (cited by Jacobs, 2009) suggests that there are important facets of the professional use of knowledge in practice. The first is about priorities. A professional learns which issues to focus on in a given situation, and which can be left as subsidiary and do not need to be dealt with in detail. Second, professionals use personal knowledge that comes from their interpretation, intuition and similar skills, for example how well someone cares for the fabric of their house. In addition, they use impersonal knowledge such as the number of rooms in a house, which we can learn in a mechanical way. Toulmin (cited by Jacobs, 2009) adds that knowledge in practical fields often involves 'clinical' skills, which mean making timely decisions based on skills acquired through practice and honed and refined by repeated experience. This leads to a kind of practical wisdom. We develop this by a constant use of everyday practices, using local knowledge that allows for constant minor readjustments of formal rules by feel. The sociologist Garfinkel (1967; Roberts, 2006: 90) took this idea further and showed that we all develop 'practical theories' about the world by building up with people around us a shared wisdom and sense of what is reasonable and intelligible.

When a mass of knowledge about a situation has been built up, one of the uses of theory is to help you rise above what you can immediately observe and find patterns that are not obvious in the tangle of everyday life. Howe (2009: 1) describes how the first people to fly in balloons saw the landscape in a new way. He is suggesting that patterns and order already exist, and by looking more broadly than just at the situations you are faced with, you can identify aspects of them that are present but hidden from you. By providing you with organized descriptions of the world, a practice theory offers ideas about where to look.

Theory and practice in social work

Why use theory in social work practice?

This section deals with the second issue – the difference between theory and practice – and asks why we need to use theory in a practice activity at all. Why should a seemingly abstract idea connect with what you need to do in real life? Perhaps you find the difference between theory and practice so great that you feel uncomfortable about using any theory in your work. This might be because you see yourself as a practical person – doing rather than theorizing. Or maybe you have found theory difficult to digest or to connect with your practice experience in social work.

So why do practitioners use theory in social work? Figure 1.3 lists some of the advantages of doing so that have been identified by social work writers. These points are not exhaustive, some of them overlap, and not everyone would accept all of them. However, simply listing the potential advantages of using theory in social work practice shows that people make a big claim for the value of theory in practice.

> **Pause and reflect** *Summarizing the claims for theory*
>
> Look through the list in Figure 1.3. Why might it be important to get help with these areas of practice by looking at theory?

Some suggestions: the four main uses of theory

The list in Figure 1.3 contains a number of different ideas about the usefulness of theory in practice, but these may be summarized and grouped into four main points as follows:

▪ Theory helps us *understand and contest* ideas. This is important because theory can be *revelatory*: it reveals and makes clear things that might not be obvious.

▓ Theory offers *explanation and understanding*. This is important because it *orders* complexity. Social workers deal with complex human behaviour and social phenomena and need to think out what to focus on when they take action.

▓ Theory offers a *practice framework*. This is important because it organizes ideas and research that offer *guidance* about what to do in these complicated situations.

▓ Theory helps us to be *accountable, self-disciplined* professionals. This is important because clients, colleagues and agencies are entitled to expect that practitioners can justify and explain what they are doing and why.

Figure 1.3 Why use theory?

Reason	Theory helps you to	Four uses of theory
Accountability	... be accountable to agencies, clients and colleagues	Professional
Boundaries	... locate the limits of permitted and required practice	Professional
Causation	... understand causation	Explanation
Control	... control situations you are involved with	Practice framework
Critical	... be critical of and contest assumptions and ideas	Ideas
Cultural understanding	... understand how general cultural differences affect us	Explanation
Cumulation	... build experience from one situation to another	Explanation
Discourses	... identify debates about meaning in our lives	Ideas
Effectiveness	... decide what is most likely to be effective	Practice framework
Explanation	... explain human development and social phenomena	Explanation
Focus	... identify relevant and irrelevant factors	Practice framework
Framework	... organize practice consistently	Practice framework
Guide	... guide actions	Practice framework
Identification	... identify concepts and theoretical traditions	Ideas
Ideologies	... understand the impact of organized systems of thought	Ideas
Intervention	... identify potential interventions	Practice framework
Knowledge base	... use knowledge to inform your actions	Explanation
Mobilization	... get support for potential objectives	Professional
Neutrality	... avoid bias in making decisions	Ideas
Outcomes	... select intervention outcomes	Practice framework
Prediction	... predict outcomes	Practice framework
Professional	... behave professionally rather than as an amateur	Professional
Self-discipline	... avoid irrational responses	Professional
Simplification	... simplify complex phenomena	Explanation
Understanding	... understand behaviour and social	Explanation
Value positions	... avoid taking dogmatic value positions	Ideas

Source: Healy (2005), Hardiker and Barker (2007 [1991]), Fraser and Matthews (2008), Greene (2008b: 4–8), Gray and Webb (2009) and Walsh (2010).

Many writers about theory pick up ideas from the social sciences and, less commonly, from the humanities and sciences as well. For example, the first section of a recent book (Gray and Webb, 2013) does this by presenting chapters about particular social thinkers: Habermas, Giddens, Bourdieu, Foucault and Butler. Each chapter introduces their ideas, and analyses how various writers in social work have used these. This approach to theory might lead you to wonder whether some theory may be drawn directly from ideas in other areas of the social sciences rather than being interpreted through a practice theory. Such an approach asserts that ideas are useful in their own right without having to be interpreted specifically into practice formulations.

Why use practice theories?

If we accept that theory is, in general, useful in social work practice, why do we need to use practice theories to adapt ideas for use in social work? In this next Pause and Reflect question, I look at the different kinds of knowledge that are useful in a particular case example, and argue that practice theories allow practitioners to bring all these resources together in taking action.

Pause and reflect: A case example
Using practice theory in working with a bereaved son

At the hospice where I work, a man came to see me about his mother. She had died unexpectedly while he was abroad with his father, who was divorced from his mother; she had since remarried. He spoke calmly but said he was upset that this had happened while he had been away. I asked how I could help him. He had two main requests: he wanted help in finding out what had happened, and he wanted to know what he should do now. What would you do?

Some suggestions: theory is a useful framework

My starting point was to ask an open-ended question, letting the client take the lead and expressing my willingness to try to help with whatever he needed. In this situation, it is usual to appear sympathetic and express how sorry you are for the bereaved person's loss, but this does not come naturally to everyone; many people fear they may not be able to handle strong emotion, if it is expressed. Looking at this, some skills training in the right way to start interviews off, and experience and confidence that you can respond appropriately to whatever situation arises would be a good basis for starting social work. These skills are based on psychological and sociological communication theory, but they are also practical human behaviour that many people would have acquired through social experience. No need for a practice theory here, then.

The client's requests presented a legal and administrative problem. Information about his mother's medical care was private, so I had to obtain his stepfather's permission to allow him access to this information. I then arranged for him to meet a nurse who had cared for his mother so that he could hear the story of her last few hours. This required legal knowledge about access to confidential information, and administrative knowledge and organizational skills to know whom to contact and how to set up a meeting.

Finally, I needed to ask myself 'what should he do now?' We talked over his memories of his mother, and he completed a salt sculpture of his mother, a commonly used technique for making a physical memorial to someone (see Reith and Payne, 2009: 151 for a description of what to do). In another session, we discussed how he could help his stepfather with some practical tasks, including sorting out his mother's finances and property and keeping some items of hers that were important to him. After this, we talked about his feelings about losing his mother, and I gave him the telephone number of our bereavement service, also asking him whether we could call him every so often to offer further help. I needed a sound knowledge of practical technique and of theory about bereavement and loss here. It was clear that it would be some time before the man wanted to tackle his feelings of loss and bereavement, and that the repeated offer of a service would empower him to seek help if he needed it; most people, however, manage bereavement without professional help.

This case example illustrates some of the reasons why people often feel that using social work theory is not relevant to them, since:

- practitioners can rely on skills learned in ordinary human interaction (e.g. being warm and welcoming);
- practice relies on learned communication and interview skills (e.g. open-ended questions);
- practice is often guided by legal and administrative requirements (e.g. access to records and arrangements for referral to other professionals);
- practice is often informed by practical techniques built up in agencies and learned by their staff (e.g. the salt sculpture approach);
- practice is informed by theory about problems (e.g. bereavement and loss) rather than social work theory.

So why would we need a social work practice theory? Let's stand back and look at the whole process with this client. There is a framework that guided the events which took place, and this consisted of a number of elements:

- The agency (the hospice) had decided to employ social workers and give them particular roles and responsibilities, which came from some generalized view of what social workers might offer as part of a hospice service.
- In using my skills, I addressed issues that reflected the client's wishes as well as my own view about what it was important for me to deal with. That view came partly from the agency mandate (what social workers are expected to do in the hospice) and also from broader policy and social expectations (the expectations of social policy and the general public about what social workers do).
- My focus was on a combination of the client's personal emotional responses, practical tasks and social relationships. Combining work on different issues is characteristic of social work.

■ I drew together a range of knowledge about psychological reactions and social relationships in bereavement and loss, legal, administrative and practical issues and interpersonal skills, which is again characteristic of social work.

The framework of a social worker's practice in this particular instance is underpinned by knowledge and ideas about what social workers representing their profession, as opposed to, for example, doctors, should do for the best when faced with a situation like this. My medical colleagues, when asked to see someone like this, would check for physical and psychiatric symptoms and pass the client straight on to a social worker. Our agency and society in general say that someone with combined emotional, practical and relationship concerns coming from an event in their lives needs a social worker.

And this was not a big part of my week. I often deal with three or four such situations each day, all with different concerns. Therefore, questions such as 'what is my responsibility?', 'what skills do I need to act?', 'what should I focus on?' and 'what knowledge do I need?' come up repeatedly. Practice theory means that practitioners do not need to rethink social work every time they see a client: a set of ideas about social work describe and explain in an organized way the events in the world around them and provide general guidance on how to react. Practitioners may then adapt them to different scenarios.

As you look at the theories discussed in this book, you might identify some of the sources of my approach in this particular case. For example, ideas about attachment (Chapter 4) inform bereavement practice, and crisis intervention theory (Chapter 5) suggests an initial focus on feelings. Although both of these theories influence theory about bereavement, bereavement theories do not in general tell you how to approach and work with people in a social work agency and then bring to the surface and respond to the issues that bereavement theory tells us are important.

Figure 1.4 shows my analysis of the role of social work theory as a framework for deciding on and planning intervention in a social work agency. Practitioners gain information about clients and their feelings and attitudes, and about the social situations that clients experience. The practice theory framework enables practitioners to create interventions that bring the specific information about this client in this situation together with generalized social work skills and knowledge. You can see from the 'social work agency' boundary here that although all this is brought together in the agency, some knowledge and skills come from outside it, and the intervention itself also has effects outside the agency.

The knowledge and skills from outside the agency emerge from expectations taken up from the society that has created this agency and given it a mandate to operate. A society is the whole pattern of relationships between people, which form into social institutions that provide an organized and understood structure for people to manage the relationships between themselves.

Social work and social work agencies are examples of those patterns of relationships and the institutions in which they take shape. Therefore, people form or construct social work and its agencies by their demands and expectations, and social workers and their agencies are influenced to change by their experiences with the people they serve. In addition, practitioners, clients and agencies contribute to some extent to society's expectations and its political and social processes by their own thinking and doing. That is a process of social construction in which people who do things together and as part of the same social organizations come to share common views of the world that they see as a social reality. In this way, it is a circular process, with each element – agency, client, social worker – influencing the others, and all this occurring in the context of the social expectations that come from their wider social relations and the practical realities they all face. I will explain more about social construction in Chapter 8.

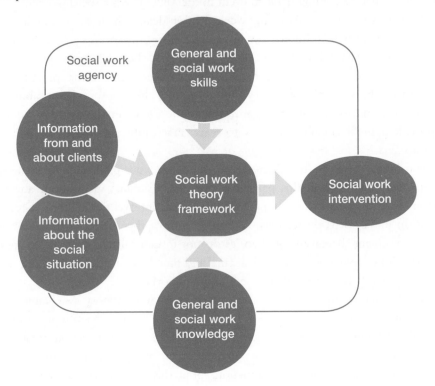

Figure 1.4 The role of social work theory

In the following case example, Angus had first gone to the people he saw regularly – the healthcare workers. They defined his problem as a housing issue, but when he went to the housing department, they saw it as a financial problem and sent him to the social worker. The social worker gave advice about social security and charitable grants, but also picked up the emotional elements of end-of-life care. Each stage of this pathway to the social worker had defined the problem differently, constructing for Angus a picture of the role of the next official he saw. He came to the social worker seeing her as a problem-solver, mainly in the area of financial difficulties, and she expanded the role, building on these initial expectations. Later, her identification of an end-of-life care situation and subsequent discussion with the healthcare workers might have reconstructed their assumptions about what else social workers can do.

Case example: A client's pathway to the service contributes to a shared construction of social work practice

Angus, a man in his seventies, was sent by a housing welfare officer from the local government housing office to a social services agency. He had arrears in payments for gas and electricity for his home. His wife had been ill and he had been using the heating more, but the house was also damp, and the housing welfare officer advised him that he needed better heating to prevent mould growing on the apartment walls. Angus's doctor and the district nurse who helped his wife had also advised him that he needed to make sure the house was suitable for caring for his wife. The social worker advised him about his social security entitlements, and also talked through the management of his income and the costs of his wife's illness. She agreed to apply for a charitable grant to help him. Visiting to complete the application form, she also discussed the pressures on him as a carer for his increasingly sick wife, and his fears that she was coming towards the end of her life.

The pathway to a particular worker and agency, and the forward pathway from a practitioner referring a client onwards, constructs a picture for clients and colleagues of the role of each service and each profession. They then share this with other colleagues and members of the community (Payne, 1993). In this case, there was a shared social construction of the profession. The practitioner influenced that social construction by doing something unexpected – picking up emotional and end-of-life care issues – when the client and other colleagues expected a practical response. The case example shows how social construction works, with practice actions contributing to a discourse about a profession and its role.

In summary, I argued above that perspective, framework, model and explanatory theory can be used together. Going further, I argued that for a social work practice theory to be useful, all of these elements are necessary. Because social work is practical action, practice theory must include a model of explicit guidance. Yet action is not entirely pragmatic because social work acts must be based on evidence about what is valid and effective, so any models should be backed up by explanatory theory and we need to evaluate the different kinds of knowledge that support it. Model and explanatory theory can only gain consistency over a wide range of social work and offer general usefulness if they offer a perspective that allows us to transfer ideas between one situation and another and be consistent in our work.

The social construction of social work

This section picks up again on theories of 'what social work is' (see Figure 1.1) and shows how social work is socially constructed by our practice, the people and organizations involved with us and the theories that inform our practice. The process is set out in Figure 1.5. I argued above that how we see the nature and aims of social work affects how we choose and use practice theories, whether they are formal written or informal unformulated theories. If we practise according to these theories, they will influence what we do. What we do then becomes a contribution to ideas and theories about social work, either through professional or social debate or more directly because, as we have seen, the social work that people see and experience influences their understanding of what it is. Practice theories are also part of the debate about what social work is because they give you an idea about what social workers are supposed to be doing, so there is a two-way interchange between practice theories and the nature of social work.

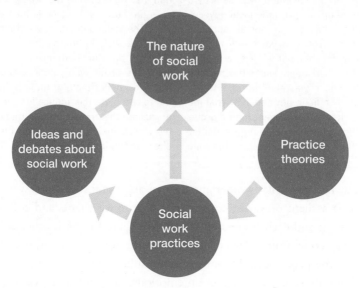

Figure 1.5 The social construction of social work

Social construction

Exploring ideas about social construction helps to explain how this works. The idea of *social construction* comes from the work of the sociologists Berger and Luckmann (1971). They say that, in social affairs (they are not talking about the natural world), what we call 'reality' is social knowledge that has been agreed between people because having a shared view about how things work between people helps us to live an ordered life. For example, I always drink beer from a glass because my mother taught me that this was polite and told me that the tops of bottles often had broken glass that might cut my mouth. However, we all have slightly different views of that social reality, because we all see and interpret what happens around us in slightly different ways, and this varies according to our life experience. Continuing the example, when I go into a bar with my son, he is always given the bottle, while the bartender looks at my greying hair and offers me a glass. This is evidence that a social change has taken place that we share awareness of: people often drink from the bottle nowadays. We arrive at agreed views of social reality and the circumstances affecting what is considered to be appropriate behaviour by sharing our knowledge with other people through various social processes that organize it and make it objective. How to go about shopping might be something we learn by example from our parents, while we might learn how a church service goes and how to behave there by watching other people who seem to know what they are doing.

Social activity becomes habitual, so our assumptions about how things should be come to be accepted as true. In addition, we behave according to social conventions based on that shared knowledge of what we have accepted as true. So these conventions become institutionalized, that is, we turn them into rules of behaviour because most people agree about the accepted way of understanding that aspect of society. These understandings also become legitimized, that is, accepted as morally right and appropriate, by a process that attaches 'meanings' that integrate these ideas about reality into an organized and plausible system. Social understanding is, in this way, the product of human understandings.

The social understandings of the humans involved are also objective because the knowledge of reality is widely shared. Since everyone grows up within those social under- standings to accept that they are a reality, people are in a sense the product of society. So there is a circular process in which individuals contribute through institutionalization and legitimization to the creation of social meaning within the social structure of societies, and in turn societies, through individuals' participation in their structures, create the conventions by which people behave. We can see a spiral of constantly shifting influence, creating and recreating structures, and these changing structures recreate the conven- tions by which people live within them. Looking back at the case example of Angus, his pathway to practice may have reconstructed a different reality of social work for him, his family and the healthcare professionals he worked with. It is this same circular process that you can see creating social work in Figure 1.5.

Social construction ideas have been widely used in social psychology to criticize tradi- tional psychology. Influential proponents of this view are Gergen (Gergen, 1994, 1999; Gergen and Gergen, 2003) and, in Britain, Parker (1998). To give you a flavour of what this might mean for social work, you might think that in reality we all have a personality, which is basic to our individual identity. Constructionist psychology casts doubt on this because we all have the possibility of making changes, and then we become a different person. Traditional psychology emphasizes the continuity of personal identity, so it might lead you to say that it is difficult or impossible to change someone's basic beliefs. Constructionist psychology emphasizes the possibility of change and might lead you to be optimistic about changing people's personalities.

A good reason for using social construction ideas in social work is this idea that social arrangements are not set in stone. The nature of social work, and any other social construction, changes as events in history or relationships in various social contexts alter. So you cannot define social work in one way for all time and across the whole world; it changes according to how societies, clients and practitioners use it. This is a cause for optimism as it tells us that everybody can make a difference to any social institution or social relationship – because by doing it or debating it, we can contribute to changing it. All social work practice, yours and mine, plays a part in creating social work. This is also a positive idea for practice since social construction tells us that people can reconstruct their lives and behaviour; we should not be gloomy about whether people can change.

A criticism of social construction identifies a consequence of this idea that the nature of social realities is always changing: it leads to a position where there are no certainties and we can have no security, because everything is always changing; this is called 'relativism'. There are two answers to this criticism (Archer, 1995). First, this process of social construction is a gradual one: things change slowly, morphing in a series of small changes until we become aware that a large change has occurred below the radar. We can keep up with this, and understanding the changes that we can see around us helps us to adjust to wider social change. Second, many things do not change, and much social experience reinforces current social constructions, so social construction often supports stability and security.

The politics of theory

Social construction creates what I call a 'politics of theory' (Payne, 1992, 1996, 1998, 2002) in which political debate and conflicts create change within a profession about the theory that profession uses. I call it *political* debate because groups of people gain an interest in a particular theory and support it in arguments with groups who support other theories. These groups are like the political parties supporting one policy or another in Parliament. This goes on in professions in the same way as in ordinary social life, as part of the constant interaction about what reality is.

The aim of each group is to gain wider acceptance within social work of the theory that they support. If they can achieve this, the support groups for particular theories shift our understanding of the nature and practice of social work. In this way, proponents and supporters of a particular point of view struggle to have it accepted, and they use practice theories that support their premises to ensure that it contributes more to the overall construction of social work and that it has a greater impact on practitioners' actions within social work.

So when, as a practitioner, you use a theory, you are contributing to the politics of theory, because what you do in social work is or becomes social work through the process of social construction.

Three views of social work objectives

A widely discussed construction of social work is contained in the International Definition of Social Work (International Federation of Social Workers, 2000); this is a good example of how social work is constructed from the variety of views on it. The definition proposes that social work has three main objectives, presented in Figure 1.6 as the corners of a triangle, the triangle itself representing a discourse between them. Discourses are interactions between what people or groups say or do that indicate important differences between them in the meanings they give to something. The important differences between these views of social work connect with different political views about how welfare should be provided. We can therefore see that each view represents a political position (Payne, 2006) in social work, connected with a political philosophy that would be recognized more widely in society.

Empowerment views

Dominelli (2009) calls these therapeutic helping approaches. These see social work as seeking the best possible well-being for individuals, groups and communities in society by promoting and facilitating growth and self-fulfilment. In this view of social work, practitioners help clients to gain power over their own feelings and their way of life. Through this personal power, they are enabled to overcome or rise above suffering and disadvantage. This view expresses in social work the social democratic political philosophy, that is, that economic and social development should go hand in hand to achieve individual and social improvement.

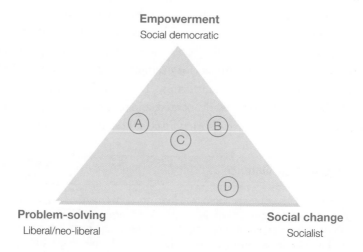

Figure 1.6 Three views of social work and their underlying political philosophies
Source: Adapted from Payne (2006).

The following case example illustrates how clients contribute to constructing social work: as practitioners gain experience of clients' lives, their views of what is possible and desirable in their practice shifts. Empowerment views of social work emphasize the importance of helping people lead a more fulfilling life by developing their skills and personal relationships. Humanistic and feminist theories are good examples of empowerment views. These views are basic to many ideas of the nature of social work, but the two other views modify and dispute it.

Case example: A drug user's life

Karim was a young man who had become a drug user from an early age, being offered drugs at school, becoming part of a gang of young men and earning money by supplying drugs to others. Several years on, a new practitioner, Ken, became Karim's social worker as part of a drug rehabilitation project. Ken was shocked by the way Karim lived in derelict houses in poor and unhealthy conditions. Although he knew a lot of theory about the effects of drugs and possible treatment methods, he had not appreciated until he spent time with Karim the urgency of Karim's need to get a regular fix, his lack of drive to make progress with his rehabilitation in spite of his unpleasant lifestyle and the influence of friends from his gang life, which meant that Karim could not keep to a daily routine involving activities not centred around drugs. When Karim failed to avoid drugs in a hostel placement, Ken was dispirited by his return to his old life and the failure of his treatment methods. He realized the importance of building a relationship with Karim, helping him to develop skills in social relationships and trying to provide a new social environment for him.

Social change views

These see social work as seeking cooperation and mutual support in society so that the most oppressed and disadvantaged people can gain power over their own lives. Social work facilitates this by enabling people to take part in a process of learning and cooperation that creates institutions which everyone can own and participate in. Elites accumulate and perpetuate power and resources in society for their own benefit. By doing so, they create oppression and disadvantage, which social work tries to supplant with more egalitarian relationships in society. Dominelli (2009) calls these 'emancipatory approaches' because they free people from oppression. Others (for example, Pease and Fook, 1999) call them transformational because they seek to transform societies for the benefit of the poorest and most oppressed. They imply that disadvantaged and oppressed people will never gain personal or social empowerment unless society makes these transformations.

Case example: Domestic violence

Ushi, the daughter of a Chinese family, married a violent man who often beat her. She accepted this as part of her husband's personality until he also began hurting their two daughters. Child protection concerns were reported by the girls' school, and the social worker helping the family picked up Ushi's increasing distress at the pattern of her husband's behaviour. The practitioner referred her to a woman's refuge, and the social worker there helped her to live in safety until legal action against her husband made it safe for her to return home with her daughters. In the process, Ushi became aware of her right to have positive expectations of her relationships with men, and her husband was forced also to shift his perceptions of acceptable behaviour by a men's violence project.

Value statements about social work, such as codes of ethics, represent this objective by proposing social justice as an important value of all social work. This view expresses socialist political philosophy, that is, that planned economies and social provision promote equality and social justice. Examples of social change views are anti-discriminatory or critical practice.

Problem-solving views

These see social work as an aspect of welfare services for individuals in societies that aim to meet individuals' needs and improve the services offered to them. Such views see social work as maintaining social order and the social fabric of society, supporting people during difficult periods so that they can recover their stability. This view expresses the liberal or neo-liberal political philosophy that supports personal freedom in economic markets, underpinned by the rule of law. This philosophy says that people should be free to make decisions about their lives, but if they have problems they should suffer the consequences of those problems. The role of social work is to help people adjust to this way of organizing society, smoothing the way through problems they cannot handle. A good example of problem-solving views is task-centred practice.

Case example: Mental illness

Bernard experienced considerable stress at work, which led to several periods of depression, and he eventually lost his job. After a period of hospitalization, a community mental health project involved him in a drop-in day centre, which reduced the sense of isolation he felt living in a small shared house. The project staff made sure Bernard's medication was continued and arranged for him to get help in applying for jobs, including putting him on a course to improve his job interview skills. They also persuaded him to take additional qualifications so that he could increase his job prospects.

Each of the views discussed above says something about the activities and purposes of social work in welfare provision in any society. Each criticizes or seeks to modify the others. For example, seeking personal and social fulfilment, as in empowerment views, is impossible to social change theorists because the interests of elites obstruct many possibilities for oppressed peoples unless we achieve significant social change. Social change theorists argue that merely accepting the social order, as empowerment and problem-solving views do, supports and enhances the interests of elites. Karim and Bernard might have been helped personally by engagement with their practitioners or by practical services, but the social pressures that make it hard for vulnerable youngsters to make their way in life still remain, so there will be a continuing flow of young men involved in cultures of drug misuse, or suffering from exploitation leading to mental ill-health. To social change theory, therefore, the empowerment and problem-solving views do not remove the barriers that obstruct opportunities for people who should be the main beneficiaries of social work.

To take another example, problem-solving theorists say that trying to change societies on a large scale to make them more equal or to enable personal and social fulfilment through individual and community growth is unrealistic in everyday practice. Chapter 10 includes an example of this argument in relation to social development. Midgley and Conley (2010a) argue that steps forward are made through more practical measures to empower people to solve their problems. They, and others, argue that social change ideas are unrealistic because most social work activity deals in small-scale change, which cannot lead to major social changes. In addition, stakeholders in the social services who finance and give social approval to social work activities mainly want to achieve a better fit between society and individuals rather than seeking to effect major changes.

However, these different views also have affinities with each other. For example, both the empowerment and social change views largely concern change and development, as we see in the cases of Karim and Ushi. In addition, empowerment and problem-solving views are about individual work rather than broader social objectives; indeed, many practitioners find these two perspectives complementary. Most conceptions of social work include elements of each of these views, or they acknowledge the validity of elements of the others. Social change views criticize unthinking acceptance of the present social order, which is often taken for granted in empowerment and problem-solving views. Nevertheless, most social change practice theories include helping individuals to fulfil their potential within current social systems. Such theories often see this as a stepping stone to a changed society by promoting a series of small changes aiming towards bigger ones.

Looking at Figure 1.6, if you or your agency were positioned at A (which is very common, especially for social workers at the start of their careers), your main focus might be providing assistance and therapeutic services as a care or case manager, or in child protection. You might do very little in the way of seeking to change the world, and by being part of an official or service system you are accepting the current pattern of welfare services. However, in your individual work, what you do may well be guided by eventual change objectives. For example, if you believe that relationships between women and men should be more equal, your work in families will probably reflect your views.

Position B might represent someone working in a refuge for women who have experienced domestic violence. Much of their work is concerned with helping the women therapeutically, but the reason for the existence of their agency is to change attitudes towards women, and you might do some campaigning work as part of your role there.

Position C is equally balanced – some change, some service provision, some therapeutic helping. My hospice job is like that: one aspect is to promote community development so that communities respond better to people who are dying or bereaved, but I also provide help for individuals and am responsible for liaison with other services so that our service system becomes more effective.

Position D is mainly about social change but partly about problem-solving. This reflects the reality that seeking social change is not, in the social services, about creating a revolution, but aims to make the service system more effective. Many community workers, for example, are seeking big changes in the lives of the people they serve by trying to foster improved cooperation and sharing, but they may also, as they do this, help local groups make their area safe from crime, provide welfare rights advocacy or organize self-help playgroups in the school holidays. Working on such issues allows people to gain the skills to achieve wider social change in their community (see Chapter 10).

Political aims in welfare, views of social work and particular practice theories link in complex ways. The links between, say, liberal political theory and problem-solving social work are clear, but the devisors of task-centred practice (Chapter 5) did not say to everyone 'we are neo-liberal theorists' and follow this up by devising a theory that expressed their political ideas. They did research, came up with an approach that seemed to work, and presented it to social workers to use. When we set this alongside other theories, we can see that it meets some of the aims and philosophies of social work but not others. The wider theoretical perspective and connections sections of the chapters in Part 2 of this book draw attention to some of the links and disagreements between theories that express these philosophies of welfare and views of social work.

Taking part in social work means that you will always, by the way you practise, express a view about your particular balance between these various aims – you will construct your own version of social work that will guide the actions you take. Thinking about the 'three views' of social work objectives helps you to clarify your own view.

Five shared value principles in social work theory

I argued in the previous section that all social work actions express a balance between the three views of social work's objectives. Agency policies also mean that agencies represent a balance between these views, as does the wider political debate about the objectives of social work within any society when it leads to new social laws and innovation in social services. This balancing of objectives is part of the social construction process through which social work constantly evolves, influenced by our clients and their social experiences and professional and academic knowledge about our societies.

If we see social work as a constantly changing balance of these objectives, how does this affect the diversity of practice theories? If the overriding broad objectives interact, so must the practice theories, because they are specific formulations of practice that meet those objectives. Thus, there is not only a politics in which different objectives vie to influence our view of social work, but there are also constructions that make connections between theories. This is why each chapter dealing with a specific practice theory in Part 2 identifies the politics of that particular theory and also the connections between that theory and other ideas in social work. Each practice theory influences the others, making a contribution to social work practice ideas as a whole. I explore this process further in Chapter 2 (see particularly Figure 2.1). The process of mutual influence has been continuing for some decades, to the point where it is possible to identify in the diverse formulations of social work theory some clear shared theoretical value principles, which inform all social work practice theories. I set these out in Figure 1.7.

Figure 1.7 The five shared value principles of social work theory

Element	Examples
Alliance	Informed consent, relationship, therapeutic alliance, dialogic relationship
Aims	Clearly specified and positive outcomes
Action sequences	Specified sequences of actions
Critical practice	Disruption, critique of current social assumptions
Rights	Human rights, cultural respect, equality, sustainability

The shared value principles of social work practice theories represent accepted ideas informing a wide diversity of practice. The first of these shared value principles is the concept of alliance between practitioner and client. Most theories are moving towards equality within this relationship, in which the client gives informed consent to the practice, influences the setting of the intervention's aims and engages in dialogue to arrive at a shared understanding of the situation and the actions taken.

As a corollary of this, interventions focus on clearly specified outcomes, the second principle, partly because this is most effective in gaining commitment from both the client and the practitioner to engage in the practice. It also means that the agreement between agency, practitioner and client is transparent. These aims are now stated in positive terms, rather than as deficits in the client or as problems to be solved. Consequently, the international definition (International Federation of Social Workers, 2000) is becoming inaccurate in presenting problem-solving as one of the objectives of social work; social work is now more about positive outcomes than the definition of the problems. This development also challenges cognitive-behavioural and task-centred practice, which emphasize a detailed specification of problems.

Theories increasingly present clear sequences of action for practitioners and clients to work on, the third principle. Again, this means that what social workers do is more openly and equally shared with clients, their families and communities than in the past. This is a balancing factor that supports cognitive-behavioural and task-centred practice in spite of their problem-solving impetus, since these theories also emphasize clear action sequences.

Exploring the shared value principles in this way can help to produce criteria for evaluating the contribution of theories to social work practice. By looking at the important elements in a particular theory, we can see how it might be especially relevant to social work within the welfare regime of a particular country, and see its value in discourse about social work and social work practice within the different arenas of debate that are discussed in the next section.

At the same time, all practice theories are concerned with being critical, the fourth principle, in the sense that individual practice often seeks to disrupt people's assumptions or expectations about behaviour. Critical practice also requires practitioners to question the social structures that contribute to clients' problems. Finally, the fifth principle of explicit concern for equality, respect for cultural diversity, social justice and human rights is increasingly integral to all theory of social work practice.

All practice theory incorporates these five elements as shared practice values more clearly than was the case when the different practice theories reviewed in this book first began to build separate theoretical identities. Social work practice theories are capable of mutual influence and shared development where these value elements are present, and their contribution is more likely to be questioned when they deviate from these shared values. You can see how deviation from the shared theoretical values leads to the questioning and rebalancing of views about the contribution of particular theories in my discussion of the role of cognitive-behavioural and task-centred practice in social work in the next section.

Arenas of social work construction

The final element to consider in the social construction of social work is how the politics of social work theory takes place across society. Three arenas of social construction are important for social work, as set out in Figure 1.8 (Payne, 1999a), and each arena influences the others. One is the *political–social–ideological arena*, in which social and political debate forms the policy that guides agencies and their purposes. Social workers engage in this through professional associations and other organizations and their involvement in social issues, as activists, voters or writers. Another is the *agency–professional arena*, in which employers and collective organizations of employees, such as trade unions and professional associations, influence each other over the more specific elements of how social work operates. The third is the *client–worker–agency arena*. This is the most important arena for the focus of this book on practice theory, since, as we saw in the case examples in this chapter, clients can influence how social work practice is constructed through their relationships with practitioners in the agency.

Client–worker–agency arena

Political–social–ideological arena

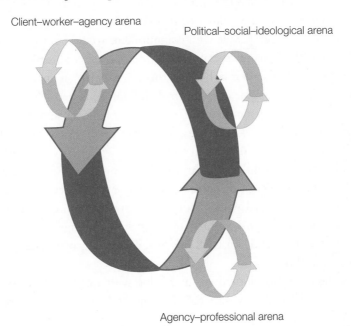

Agency–professional arena

Figure 1.8 Arenas of the social construction of social work

Clients can influence the political–social–ideological arena by, for example, their votes, by rioting and in many other ways. They can affect the agency–professional arena through their reaction to social work practice, influenced by their community and other agencies, as they follow the pathway to service. For example, they can change policy and practice by arriving at agencies in large numbers asking for service.

Changes are negotiated in many different places, and these three arenas are only a limited selection, indicating important centres of influence. For example, in the 1980s, when HIV/AIDS first became evident, pressure groups and specialist agencies started to appear to influence government and social debate; this is influence in the political–social–ideological arena. People with problems arising from HIV/AIDS came to social agencies and caused them to change their practice; this was change in the agency–professional arena.

Conclusion: using ideas about social work theory

This chapter shows how social work theory is connected with the real world in which social workers practise; it is not completely abstract or irrelevant. Social construction ideas show how theory is created in a variety of social arenas and how clients' interactions with practitioners in their agencies form an important arena in the construction. What you do in your practice is therefore important to theory. It is also important to the different groups engaged in the politics of theory. Debate about using theory is part of the political process by which people with commitments to different views of social work gain influence and seek to change social work in their preferred direction.

It works the other way round too, because theory provides a framework for action. All actions are based on theory, some of it informal and unformulated. Using theory in practice therefore relies on understanding different types of theory and how they connect. The social construction of social work suggests that its theory is constructed by the same social forces that construct the profession and its agencies. Theory for practice inevitably responds to current social realities, so that it is shaped by current interests and concerns. Yet it also reflects the histories of theoretical, occupational and service context. The social construction view is that social work theory is a representation of more or less agreed understandings about social work within various social groupings. The struggle between competing understandings and constructions of social work is manifested in the differing theories discussed in this book.

Social work theory is a construction, interacting with a real world of social relations, but because it is a construction, we are able to adapt and develop it as we practise, just as we can help clients to develop and adapt by our practice. To do so, we need to have ideas to direct, manage and inform what we do. These ideas are the social work practice theories reviewed in Chapters 4–14 of this book. However, to use them, we have to be able to make decisions about which theories to use, evaluate which will be most useful for different purposes, and integrate our practice with those ideas. The next two chapters focus, then, on putting theory into practice.

Additional resources

Further reading

Burr, V. (2003) *Social Constructionism* (2nd edn) (London: Routledge).

An accessible account of social construction theory in social psychology.

Jokinen, A., Juhila, K. and Pösö, T. (1999) *Constructing Social Work Practices* (Aldershot: Ashgate).

A useful collection of papers, many of them research-based, demonstrating how social construction ideas may be applied to social work, and how effective social construction research may be in researching practice.

Payne, M. (2005) *The Origins of Social Work: Change and Continuity* (Basingstoke: Palgrave Macmillan).

This book examines the development of social work and continuing themes in its social construction as a profession within different welfare regimes.

Payne, M. (2006) *What is Professional Social Work?* (2nd edn) (Bristol: Policy Press).

An extended discussion of the points summarized in this chapter about the social construction of social work within the three perspectives. It also examines the construction of practice from ideas about social work, its values and its organizational setting, and deals with issues such as globalization, power and professionalization.

What is Professional Social Work? and *The Origins of Social Work: Change and Continuity* are related to the present book and its account of how practice theory constructs social work. Together, they give an extended account of the social construction of social work as a social phenomenon, a practice activity and a profession.

Websites

http://ifp.nyu.edu/

Information for Practice is a regularly updated website with extensive resources about all forms of social work.

http://www.ifsw.org/

The International Federation of Social Workers website provides access to national associations of social workers and codes of ethics across the world, many of which have useful resources. It also contains the International Definition of Social Work and international codes of ethics.

http://www.socialworksearch.com/

Social Work Search is a useful directory of websites relevant for social work; it comes from American bases but has reasonable world coverage.

http://www.aasw.asn.au/acsw; http://www.collegeofsocialwork.org/

The Australian and England Colleges of Social Work may become a useful resource on social work, but their websites are still in development as I write.

Podcasts can be found on iTunes U (University), and this is likely to expand. Coverage of social work is included by Trinity College Dublin (Ireland), the Open University (UK), the Columbia University School of Social Work (USA) and Living Proof, the University of Buffalo School of Social Work (USA); this has an impressive and growing list of podcasts, a few of which are about issues of theory. Search iTunes for the institution and look for the school of social work in the 'see all' listing. If you do not have an iPod or equivalent device, you can view or hear podcasts on a desktop or laptop computer.

Evaluating social work theory

2

Main contribution

This chapter aims to enable practitioners to evaluate the range and usefulness of the practice theories available in social work.

Main points

- A stable range of theories, which can be divided into eleven main groups, have been accepted as making a contribution to social work practice. There are two main approaches to choosing which theories to use: selection and eclecticism.
- Most social work practice uses managed eclecticism – theories are combined through agency and team decisions.
- Interpretivist and positivist views of knowledge are the main alternative positions in debates about whether objective knowledge of a real world is possible.
- Evidence-based practice (EBP) is the main positivist position. It proposes that the main factor in making practice decisions should be empirical evidence of the effectiveness of different theories in achieving the desired outcomes; this should then provide for a systematic and accountable form of practice.
- Social construction, empowerment and critical realist views of knowledge are important interpretivist positions.
- Decisions about using practice theory are influenced not only by research evidence, but also by wider policy and the agency's decision-making processes.

Major statements

The major recent textbook reviews of social work indicate the range of social work practice theory that is available. These reviews are cited alongside each other in Figures 2.2 and 2.3, later in the chapter. They all have their merits and different approaches, which I discuss below.

It is essential for practitioners to understand and take a position in the debate on EBP. An authoritative and complex account of how to operate in accordance with evidence-based principles is Gambrill's US text (2006), which she applies to a very wide range of social services and social work practice. Sheldon and Macdonald (2009) offer a less comprehensive, more idiosyncratic but nonetheless wide-ranging UK text with a similar approach. Gray et al. (2009) is the major account of the critical position, providing a thoughtful and formidable, but not wholly negative, critique. There are several collections of essays that can present various positions and arguments about the debate. Otto et al. (2009) is the best, containing contributions from many American protagonists in the debate, as well as more philosophical and critical comment from European writers.

The main groups of practice theory

A wide range of practice theories is available for social work practitioners to choose from. In this chapter, I aim to help you do this, first by classifying the theories into groups using the broad ideas about theory that I discussed in Chapter 1. This classification divides up the ideas into a number of categories that we can realistically handle, relying on important differences between the theoretical ideas that underlie the different groupings. However, we do not have to separate theories completely in practice. Therefore, I move on to look at two important options: selecting from among the theories and combining aspects of different theories eclectically. To help you decide on appropriate combinations, I look at some of the general debates about ways of evaluating theories. The main focus of these debates is currently on what kinds of evidence we can use to inform our use of theories.

This section deals with the first of these tasks, classifying the main groups of theories available.

Until the 1970s, most theoretical debate in social work focused on various forms of psychodynamic theory (see Chapter 4); Roberts and Nee's (1970) review of social work theory looks mainly at alternative psychodynamic theories. From the 1970s onwards, other theoretical positions emerged, mainly in criticism of psychodynamic theory (Payne, 2005: Ch. 9). These alternatives became differentiated into a number of theoretical positions, each incorporating new ideas as it developed. I previously compared reviews of practice theories published in book form from 1970 to date (Payne, 2009a), finding that the range of theories remained stable for several decades. Recent reviews of theory mainly discuss eleven groups of theories: these form the basis of the theory chapters (3–14) in this book and are summarized in Figure 2.1.

Each column says something about the usefulness of these practice theories. In the first column, I list the eleven groups of social work theory; I have identified these by comparing recently published reviews of practice theories that have become widely accepted (see the next subsection). Different countries, agencies and practitioners use some more than others. The second column classifies these groupings according to the international definition of social work's three main objectives (see Figure 1.6). This

Figure 2.1 Groups of practice theories and their contribution to practice

Chapter	Theory group	Social work objectives	Contribution to practice
4	Psychodynamic	Problem-solving	Emphasizes the importance of people's internal feelings and conflicts in generating behaviour and in resolving the problems that they face
5	Crisis and task-centred		Focuses on brief, highly structured models of intervention with clearly definable problems that will respond to active efforts to resolve them
6	Cognitive-behavioural		Emphasizes the importance of rational management of behaviour in understanding the source of people's problems and managing it
7	Systems/ecological		Integrates interpersonal work with individuals with interventions with families, communities and social agencies
8	Macro practice/social development/social pedagogy	Problem-solving/ empowerment	Gives priority to the social and educational, engaging people with shared interests and concerns to work jointly to overcome them
9	Strengths/solution/ narrative	Empowerment	Recasts clients' and families' apparent problems, seeking strengths that enable them to build positively for the future
10	Humanistic/ existential/spiritual		Emphasizes personal development through shared experience as a source of individual and group empowerment
11	Empowerment/ advocacy	Empowerment/ social change	Creates experience and alliances that empower people to achieve a greater understanding of their lives and the changes in them
12	Critical	Social change	Offers critiques to the present social order that analyse and deal with social factors that underlie problems or social barriers
13	Feminist		Explains and responds to the oppressed position of women in most societies through collaborative dialogue and groupwork to achieve consciousness of issues affecting women's social relations
14	Anti-discriminatory/ multicultural sensitivity		Develops an understanding of cultural and ethnic barriers, conflicts and difference, and practice that respects people's individual and social identities

reflects long-standing debates about the objectives of social work (Payne, 2006). Two groupings of theory, macro practice/social development/social pedagogy, and empowerment/advocacy stand at the intersection of different social work objectives. In the third column, I set out that practice theory's 'claim to fame' – the distinctive contribution it makes to the range of social work practice ideas available to us. I expand these statements at the beginning of each theory chapter (4–14).

The theories' different objectives and their different contributions to practice overall are what make each group of theories different from the others. In the next subsection, I look in more detail at the comparison between reviews of practice theory that forms the basis of this analysis.

Reviews of practice theory

Several writers and editors have reviewed and compared a range of social work theories. Figures 2.2 and 2.3 summarize the coverage of some of these published since 2005, when the previous edition of this book was published. Column one of each table lists the coverage in this edition, so that you can compare other books with this one. Both tables list the main categories of theory covered by reviews of social work practice theories, excluding material that is not about specific practice theories. It also gives the national location of the authors or editors. By comparing them, we can see what theories different authors and editors select and how they classify them. This allows you to test out the judgements I have made in setting out eleven main areas of theory. Figure 2.2 contains listings of the theories in books that distinguish many different theories and hence provide a broader perspective (for example, Teater, 2010), while Figure 2.3, later in the chapter, covers books that take a more selective approach with more detailed reviews of particular theories (for example, Brandell, 2011). Both are set out across two pages.

Pause and reflect *Choosing theories as useful in your studies and practice*

Looking at Figures 2.2 and 2.3 allows you to think about how different authors and editors have classified and selected theories for coverage. What conclusions do you reach about choosing theories to focus on in your studies and in social work practice?

Some suggestions

Comparing the tables as part of this reflection task should allow you to reach five main conclusions. First, certain theories recur more than others. Three theories in particular feature in all the broad reviews and many of the selective reviews. These are psychodynamic, cognitive (or cognitive-behavioural) and systems (or systems and ecological) theories. From this, I conclude that these three theories form the basic foundation of social work theory and that understanding these theories offers practitioners a solid grounding. Other theories that are covered in 75% of broad reviews are task-centred and crisis, solution and related theories, humanistic, and person-centred and empowerment theories. Task-centred and crisis theories also have good coverage in the selective reviews. Understanding these as well would give practitioners a good awareness of the theories most widely discussed in the practice theory literature and most likely to be used in their agency.

Second, there is no universally accepted method of grouping ideas together. Theories that some academics group together are sometimes disaggregated by myself and others. The most disaggregated presentation is by Turner (2011); this covers thirty-five theories, some of which are mainly of historical interest. Most reviews collect theories into between ten and twelve groups. Among the theories most commonly disaggregated are psychodynamic, strengths and humanistic groupings and, to a lesser extent, systems and cognitive and behavioural theories.

Third, there are many occasional inclusions. These reflect particular theoretical perspectives (that a theory is important from a particular point of view) or editorial judgements (that a theory is relevant to a particular country or group of readers). Many of the ones that I cover are useful as examples of the application of a group of ideas. For example, mindfulness is a fairly new formulation of an ancient set of ideas, coming originally from Buddhist philosophy but nowadays used in cognitive and other forms of psychotherapy and in stress reduction education. Mindfulness is implemented mainly as part of cognitive therapies so this is where I discuss it in more detail, but it also has some implications for psychodynamic and humanistic ideas.

Fourth, the selective surveys (Figure 2.3) typically cover about half the number of groups of theories and are usually derived from a particular context. Healy (2005) and Nash et al. (2005b), for example, base their analyses on reviews of current service requirements in Australia. Lindsay (2009) and, from the broad reviews, Beckett (2006) select theories claimed to be practically useful in the British context, implying that other ideas are less so. Lehmann and Coady (2007), for example, in the broad reviews, present two metatheories as frameworks into which a wide range of theory and knowledge can be fitted: ecological systems theories and ideas about human behaviour. Gray and Webb (2013) focus mainly on critical sociological theories. Brandell (2011) covers four main theories and then provides accounts of practice with particular client groups. This variety of approaches suggests that once you have your broad overview of what is available, it may help you to concentrate on what people have found useful in your context.

The final point relates to the International Federation of Social Workers' analysis of the three roles of social work, which I considered in Chapter 1. Much of the coverage emphasizes psychological, individual problem-solving theories, often differentiating many different sub-theories, rather than empowerment or social change theories. In addition, except for feminism and empowerment, social change theories do not usually appear in books from North American sources. I therefore conclude from this and the previous point that there is disagreement over the usefulness of theories in particular national or service contexts, and that the main focus of practice theory is on psychological theory for problem-solving roles, although some empowerment theories are also valued.

Figure 2.2 Wide-ranging theory reviews

Payne (this book) – British	Beckett (2006) – British	Lishman (2007) – British	Lehmann and Coady (2007) – Canadian	Greene (2008a) – American
Psychodynamic	Psychodynamic	Psychodynamic Erikson's life cycle		Psychoanalytic Eriksonian – ego mastery
	Attachment	Attachment	Attachment Relational Self-psychology	
Crisis/task-centred	Crisis Task-centred	Crisis Task-centred	Crisis Task-centred	
Cognitive-behavioural	Cognitive-behavioural	Cognitive-behavioural	Cognitive-behavioural	Cognitive
Systems/ecological	Systems Family systems work	Family therapy and systemic		General systems Ecological
Strengths/narrative/ solution	Solution		Solution	
	Constructive Postmodernism		Constructivist Narrative	Social construction
Humanistic/existential/ spiritual	Client-centred		Client-centred Existential	Person-centred
Social/community development	Groupwork	Group care		
	Community work	Community development		
Critical		Structural		
Feminist			Feminist	Feminist
Anti-discriminatory/ cultural sensitivity				
Advocacy/ empowerment	Advocacy Empowerment	Empowerment and advocacy		
	Carers Other professionals/ agencies			
	Coercive roles			
				Genetics
				Risk/resilience
		Bereavement		

Howe (2009) – British	Walsh (2010) – American	Teater (2010) – British/ American	Turner (2011) – Canadian
Psychoanalytic

Attachment | Psychodynamic: object relations
Psychodynamic: ego psychology

Psychosocial | Psychosocial | Psychoanalysis
Ego psychology
Psychosocial
Relational
Attachment
Functional
Problem-solving |
| Task-centred | Crisis | Crisis intervention
Task-centred | Crisis
Task-centred |
| Cognitive-behavioural
Cognitive
Behavioural | Cognitive
Behavioural | Cognitive-behavioural | Cognitive-behavioural
Cognitive
Social learning |
| Systems
Ecological | Family emotional systems | Social systems/ecological | General systems
Life model
Social networks |
| | Structural family therapy | | |
| Solution
Strengths | Solution

Narrative | Solution
Strengths
Social constructivism | Solution
Strengths
Constructivism
Postmodern
Gestalt
Chaos
Narrative
Role
Self-efficacy
Strategic |
| Person-centred | | Person-centred | Client-centred
Meditation
Existential
Neurolinguistic programming
Transactional analysis
Transpersonal |
Critical			
Feminist		Feminist	Feminist
Anti-oppressive			Aboriginal/Cree
Empowerment		Empowerment/use of language	Empowerment
	Interpersonal
Motivational interviewing	Motivational interviewing	
Neuro-pyschological			Hypnosis

Figure 2.3 Selective theory reviews

Payne (this book) – British	Healy (2005) – Australian	Nash et al. (2005b) – Australian
Psychodynamic		Attachment
Crisis/task-centred	Task-centred	
Cognitive-behavioural		
Systems/ecological	Systems	Ecological systems
Strengths/narrative/solutions	Postmodern Strengths	Strengths-based
Humanistic/existential/spiritual		
Social/community development		Community development
Critical		
Feminist		
Anti-discriminatory/cultural sensitivity	Anti-oppressive	
Advocacy/empowerment		

In addition, social change theory is not considered central in the North American social work literature, but is debated (hotly and extensively) elsewhere.

Given the extensive range of different social work practice theories, how do students and practitioners make decisions about which theories they will study and use in practice?

Two suggestions have informed my treatment of this issue in this book. A professional practitioner in any field should have a wide understanding of the ideas in use in that field. Therefore, a broad coverage of the theories in contention is required, and I have given roughly equal coverage in the following chapters to the groupings of theory that are actively debated internationally. Each of them contributes to the ideas available in social work and to how we can understand it. This broader theoretical awareness enables us to use alternative ideas to criticize the conventions of our own practice. In this way, we can select particular aspects of the theories for specific purposes, as well as selecting a more limited range of ideas to use in our everyday work.

Second, most presentations of practice theory make a selection from the available range on grounds of usefulness in practice or theoretical or research support for a theory. Practitioners need, similarly, to come to a view about how they will narrow the range of theory they will use to manageable proportions. The rest of this chapter explores ways of evaluating theories for practice, and Chapter 3 moves on to look at how you make the links between the theories and ideas that you find useful and the decisions and actions you take in practice.

Gray and Webb (2013) – international	Lindsay (2009) – British	Brandell (2011) – American
	Psychosocial	Psychoanalytic
	Task-centred	
	Crisis	
	Cognitive-behavioural	Behavioural and cognitive
	Family therapy and systemic	Systems
Postmodernism	Life story and life review	
Critical		
Structural		
Feminist		
Neo-liberalism		
	Motivational interviewing	
	Mediational	
		Neurobiology

Using theory selectively and eclectically

There are two main approaches to helping practitioners find ways of using the theories available: selection and eclecticism.

To use theory selectively, you review the theories and then select one group of theories to use as the basis of practice. You might select a theory that is particularly relevant to a client in a particular case, or to the client groups you commonly work with, or to all of your practice, or to all of the practice in a particular agency. An important consideration in making a selection is evidence from research and scholarship about how particular theories help you achieve desired outcomes with your clients. The extent to which this is possible and desirable is, however, the subject of much controversy, as I will discuss later in the chapter.

Selectivity is common in specialized agencies, where the theory works well for the specialism. Although you might theoretically, for example, use crisis intervention (see Chapter 5) in a variety of situations, it is mainly used explicitly in agencies dealing with mental health emergencies, often involving psychiatrists, psychiatric nurses and others as well as social workers. This theory originated in mental health settings and may be particularly relevant in them. In the USA, other emergency services, such as the police, use it when dealing with disasters and emergency situations. Services dealing with emergencies with a strong emotional component, such as rape and domestic violence, also employ it. In this case, selecting one main theory means that workers coming from different professional backgrounds can share the same ideas in their different roles, speak the same theoretical language and understand each other's actions. Selectivity, therefore, often works well in multiprofessional agencies.

Eclecticism means taking ideas from several theories and combining them to produce a style of work that suits the agency and the capabilities and preferences of the individual practitioners. Some studies indicate an inexplicit, or what Olsson and Ljunghill (1997) call 'naive', use of theory, which is linked to the idea of tacit knowledge that we met in Chapter 1. Calling commonplace uses of knowledge and theory 'naive' or 'tacit' draws attention to the risk that we might use theory thoughtlessly, without fully understanding what we are doing. Similarly, if we pick up ideas from different places, we risk confusion.

It can be hard to disentangle the ideas we are using. One of the main uses of theory is to make us accountable as professionals so that we can explain what we are doing to clients, colleagues and the public. It is therefore important to be aware of the sources, values, methods and objectives of the theories we are borrowing from, and which combinations of ideas work well together (or do not). This is another reason for having a broad knowledge of the theories we use in social work.

Research and debate in social work has led to a wide acceptance that everyday practice is usually eclectic (Lehmann and Coady, 2007). In clinical psychology, eclectic practice is a model of practice, and Lehmann and Coady use the theoretical discussion and research underlying its use there as part of their argument for eclecticism in social work. A caution, however: theoretical eclecticism that works in counselling or clinical psychology practice might not transfer fully to the different context of social work.

Critics of an eclectic use of theory worry that it leads to practitioners making personal choices so that they feel comfortable with the ideas they practise with, when evidence might suggest that other alternatives might be better (Sheldon and Macdonald, 2009: 46). Theoretical inconsistency is another potential problem: practitioners might use theories in ways that are internally inconsistent or debase the full theory. This is because it is difficult to keep in mind the possible implications of all social work theories and to use them with credibility. It is also not practical to use many theories in depth without going into them in considerable detail, which requires considerable supervision and support in their application.

In many agencies, therefore, it makes sense for practitioners, managers and policy-makers to come to an agreement about combining points that are relevant to practice in that setting. Being eclectic is thus something that that we should do consistently, in a planned way. Testing out our decisions against agency policy and with a team of people working together is better than being eclectic on a casual or an individual basis (Epstein and Brown, 2002: 268–9).

Pause and reflect *How to use selection and eclectic practice*

From this discussion, look at your present work setting or, if you are a student, a setting you want to work in. Make notes about any preferred main group of theories that are relevant to it and other ideas that you might use eclectically alongside that group of theories.

This book aims to provide a starting point, allowing you to move thoughtfully on to literature on particular theories that are relevant to your particular practice. Each chapter starts with a section on 'the main contribution' that each theory makes to practice. This should help you compare and choose within the range of theories. Each chapter lists the major practice ideas and concepts relevant to each theory near the start of each chapter. This should help you to identify useful concepts to transfer into an eclectic practice. These starting points then move into a more detailed account of the theory, and additional resources listed at the end of the chapters help you to explore the idea in greater detail if you, your agency and your team want to do so.

Some suggestions

My suggestions for a reasonable approach by practitioners to the selection of theories and eclecticism are as follows:

- Start from the agency's and professional expectations and preferences.
- Connect these to the needs and preferences expressed by the clients using your agency.
- Build on these expectations, needs and preferences, in debate with team colleagues, adapting to new ideas as they become available and you have tested them out.
- Try to identify a theoretical model whose main contribution to social work is relevant to your setting.
- Identify practice ideas and concepts from different theories relevant to your setting that are used in or available for your setting.
- Specialist settings might use a realm of theory; for example, a women's refuge might explicitly use feminist theory. The agency might attract workers already committed to feminism, or workers might go there to develop this theoretical emphasis in their repertoire.
- Within general agencies, workers might decide to use a particular theory in greater depth with appropriate people. This would be backed up by team decisions, supervision, peer support and training.
- As many social workers now work in multiprofessional settings, you may need to use or at least understand the theories used by your colleagues. This makes it important also to be explicit about the theories you are using.

Throughout such a process, you need to evaluate the evidence for effectiveness in the practice you are concerned with, as well as looking at your own perceptions and feelings. It is also important to test your ideas against the needs and wishes of clients, their families and carers, because you are selecting ways of working with them and incorporating their objectives in what you are doing. It would be wrong to use theories that seem congenial to you, if they are unacceptable to clients.

The following case study of how a four-tier model of children's mental health services builds on an NHS Health Advisory Service Report (1995) shows how different tiers call for varying theories. Tier 1, universal services, deals with low-level emotional and behavioural difficulties. The case study writer works in Tier 2, community CAMHS, with mild to moderate mental health problems. Tier 3, specialist CAMHS, addresses more severe, complex or enduring disorders. Tier 4 includes specialist day units, hospital outpatient teams and inpatient units.

Case example: Selecting from theories to develop an eclectic agency practice
(The case study and associated text have been written especially for this book by Emma Reith-Hall)

The case study that follows is more extensive than the case examples used in many parts of the book; it explores in some detail how an agency arrived at its selection of theory, and the way in which different uses of theory are combined within the agency's organization to provide a comprehensive service using a range of theories of practice. It describes the theoretical organization of practice in a community child and adoles-cent mental health service (CAMHS) in a medium-sized city. It starts from the significance of attachment theory (see Chapter 4) as a basis for the service's practice and then goes on to explore possibilities for using other theories. The service deals with the mild to moderate mental health problems and emotional and behavioural difficulties of children and young people from infancy to the age of 18 years.

Throughout the 1970s and 80s, literature on attachment theory centred on work with babies and toddlers, revolutionizing Tier 4 services, that is, children's hospital and day-care provision (Belsky and Rovine, 1988). This did not, however, address the challenge of working with older children who present with attachment difficulties – the children typically referred to community CAMHS. Recent research and literature on attachment does address working with older children and adolescents, yet it focuses on fostered or adopted children, understandably so given that attachment difficulties in children are closely related to ineffective, neglectful or even abusive parenting practices.

In our city, this client group falls within the remit of our Tier 3 Specialist CAMHS Looked After Children Team, who provide consultation to professionals and carers around the mental health of children and young people in foster or adoptive care. Similarly, the more severe cases of attachment difficulties (a disordered or disorientated attachment pattern, no attachment pattern, or the DSM-V diagnosis of 'Reactive attachment disorder' [American Psychiatric Association, 2013]) would fall within the remit of the Tier 3 Specialist CAMHS Emotional Disorders Team.

However, I do not work with fostered or adopted children. Typically, the cases seen by Tier 2 Community CAMHS involve low to moderate attachment difficulties, and the children often remain with their birth parents or families. This is sometimes the context within which attachment difficulties have occurred. The prevalence of these cases is high, although exact numbers are hard to establish because referrals usually cite the behavioural or emotional presentation displayed by the child rather than the cause of the difficulties, which is often attachment-related. From clinical practice, I would estimate that one-fifth of the Tier 2 Community CAMHS cases involve attachment difficulties.

Although attachment difficulties often appear in children who remain with their birth parents, there is a dearth of research and literature on working with attachment difficulties within the birth family context. Hughes (2009), writing about the importance of attachment-focused work for all families, is one notable exception.

Attachment is one of the complex influences on children's development and the emotional, behavioural and social difficulties that are typical of those referred to Tier 2 Community CAMHS. Attachment difficulties can manifest in an internalized way, whereby children present with anxious or depressive symptoms and indulge in soothing behaviours such as rocking, biting or picking at their skin. Alternatively, these difficulties can manifest in externalized ways, with the children displaying anger, aggression and poor impulse control. 'Attachment theory provides a framework within which we can understand the children and the behaviours they are displaying' (Golding, 2008: 71). The Tier 2 service uses three levels of intervention, which will all be considered here. These include direct work with the child, direct work with the parent and consultation.

Direct work with the child is the intervention most often requested by referrers. Parents, carers and professionals often refer children assuming that they need direct work to 'fix' their emotional and behavioural problems. However, all types of direct work with the child alone have limited use where there are attachment difficulties, as supported by the literature on the subject. The idea that therapy can 'cure' children comes from a medical model, setting up the expectation that treatment can be used to make the child better. Therapies aimed at helping children modify their behaviour 'do not take into account core deficits they have in managing their emotion or in living within relationships' (Golding, 2008: 79–80). Attachment theory tells us that attachment difficulties lie within the parent–child relationship rather than within the child in isolation. Thus, working with the child alone, whatever intervention is used, is not only counterintuitive, but may also serve to compound the child's difficulties further. Locating the relational problem of attachment difficulties within the child further pathologizes them, and might have a detrimental impact on their already negative self-view. Until issues within the family environment are addressed and care-givers can provide emotional support, direct work with the child alone is not appropriate.

Services therefore increasingly recognize that therapeutic work should only take place when the child is in a safe, secure and contained environment (Golding et al., 2006). Harrington (2003: 51) argues that 'no treatment for the child is likely to succeed if basic needs such as security of family placement are not met'. Providing children with the message that their distress can only be managed by a therapist can be unhelpful as it suggests that their care-givers cannot bear or contain their hurt (Hunter, 2001). In addition, if a child has an anxious-avoidant pattern of attachment (see Chapter 4 for further information), it reinforces the child's existing view.

With attachment difficulties, then, cognitive-behavioural therapy (CBT) and other behavioural approaches, which seek to 'change' the child, present difficulties. CBT works on the premise that it is not a given situation that is problematic, but the child's response to it that causes difficulties. Yet for children with insecure attachments, the behaviours they display help them adapt to the environments in which they live; thus, it is the *situation* that needs to change, not the child's response to it. Using CBT to challenge the child's core belief will be ineffective and inappropriate while the relationship with the care-giver is uncertain and insecure, as the child's belief is adaptive to the situation.

Play therapy is another alternative approach, in which children are enabled to make sense of their situations through play. Golding et al. (2006) describe role-play scenarios from which 'children are able to explore simultaneously the feelings and actions of the adult, hear the child's responses from the therapist, and gain some mastery over a painful situation, perhaps by changing the outcomes of expressing their own story and previously hidden feelings' (Golding et al., 2006: 310). This might help looked-after children (the UK term for children in the care of the local council), but children who remain in the same family relationships from which their attachment difficulties have arisen find it difficult to make sense of the past when the difficulties remain in the present.

In the light of these difficulties, therapeutic approaches that address attachment difficulties within the context of the child–parent relationship may be more beneficial. Family therapy provides one such approach. The family is supported to view itself from a different perspective, to move away from entrenched behaviours and patterns of interaction towards identifying alternative solutions (Herbert, 1999). However, many of the children seen by the Tier 2 Community CAMHS do not meet the threshold of experiencing a 'severe and enduring mental health problem' that is required for working with the Tier 3 specialist family therapy team.

Interventions that focus on increasing the responsiveness and sensitivity of the care-giver are a key treatment approach for children with attachment difficulties (Bowlby, 1988; Hughes, 2006, 2009; Golding, 2008). They can also be implemented even when the child does not want any therapeutic input (Hunter, 2001). Community CAMHS provide attachment-based sessions to parents that are based on the Solihull Approach and House Model of Parenting. These, alongside parenting programmes (for example, Webster-Stratton, Triple P, Strengthening Families and 1-2-3 Magic), aim to teach parents how to manage the emotional and behavioural difficulties that children and young people display. Parenting interventions take time, patience and support. The literature on attachment difficulties suggests that the child must experience a secure and safe relationship with the care-giver *before* behaviour management techniques can be effective (Douglas and Brennan, 2004; Hughes, 2009). In fact, parents need to demonstrate availability and nurturing care *despite* any difficult behaviour displayed by the child if attachment difficulties are to be addressed. Therefore, parents need support to meet their children's emotional needs before attempting to address behavioural difficulties.

The Solihull Approach, developed in 1996, is a brief early intervention model that provides professionals with a framework for supporting parents to think about their children's emotional and behavioural difficulties within the context of the parent–child relationship. Parental emotions and anxieties are processed through *containment*, allowing problem-solving abilities to be restored. *Reciprocity* focuses attention on the attunement between parent and child, helping to foster a better emotional connection. The Solihull Approach uses these key concepts underpinning attachment to provide a theoretical focus for practical interventions in *behaviour management*, providing a resource pack for addressing this.

In a small-scale study with health visitors, the Solihull Approach was found to decrease parental anxiety by 66% and reduce the severity of children's difficulties after three sessions (Douglas and Brennan, 2004). The Solihull Approach has now been developed for use by other professionals and has been endorsed by our service. The training is being rolled out and the concepts integrated into our work. For example, our CAMHS mental health assessments now incorporate the Solihull Approach Assessment, enabling us to identify attachment difficulties from the outset, and influencing the treatment plan.

The House Model of Parenting (Golding, 2008) aims to help older children and caregivers build more secure attachments. It consists of:

- the ground floor – a secure base;
- the upper floor – parenting with playfulness, acceptance, curiosity and empathy (PACE; see later in the chapter);
- the roof – behaviour management.

For the ground floor, Golding (2008) describes five features conducive to building a secure base, which enables a balance to be attained between the child's attachment and exploratory systems. First, the parent will need to provide *empathy* for the feelings behind the child's behaviour. Conveying this back to the child ensures that their internal experience is accepted, even when their behaviour is not. Second, 'the experience of *attunement* with a responsive, sensitive parent is a pre-requisite for a secure attachment' (Golding, 2008: 115). Attunement is the emotional connection between child and parent, whereby enjoyable experiences are amplified and stressful experiences are contained. At times when children are disciplined, attunement will be broken; hence the emotional connection must be repaired. Parental reassurance shows the child that the relationship has not been damaged. Third, the adults in the household need to maintain a *positive family atmosphere* with consistent attitudes, values, rules and norms. Golding (2008: 128) suggests that 'living in a calm accepting atmosphere with a high level of empathy and support will gradually help the child to learn about the emotions she experiences and manage these in a self-regulating way'. Fourth, as parents control the emotional rhythm of the house, the child experiences a *sense of belonging*. Fifth, the importance of parental *self-care*, through rest, relaxation and support, is highlighted.

The upper floor of the house focuses on building a deeper relationship with the child. Parents are encouraged to adopt the PACE attitude (Hughes, 2009; Golding and Hughes, 2012). *Playfulness* emphasizes the importance of the parent and child enjoying each other's company and spending quality time together. *Curiosity* encourages parents to understand the child, to wonder about the meaning behind the behaviour displayed. *Acceptance* involves demonstrating to the child that their inner feelings are acknowledged and valued. The parent expresses *empathy* for the child's thoughts and feelings before implementing guidance and boundaries.

The roof of the house represents managing difficult behaviour. Different strategies are required for different problems and must take into account the age and stage of the child's development. Regardless of the strategies used, parents need to be interested, attentive and empathic to manage the child's behaviour difficulties. From this, parents need to provide routine, structure and firm consistent guidance and boundaries.

Consultation is a method of engaging the network around a child, and is increasingly receiving support from research into its effectiveness and flexibility (Golding, 2004). Consultation benefits consultees by providing them with a space to reflect on a child's difficulties and how to address these, and to consider the impact the child has on them both personally and professionally. Consultation benefits CAMHS practitioners as it helps to contain the anxieties of professionals within the network, builds the capacity and skills of other professionals, moves away from seeing the CAMHS staff as having an 'expert' role, supports multiagency working and informs the intervention plan.

Consultation is an effective intervention for children with attachment difficulties, and it has therefore become a primary intervention used with looked-after children. 'The most effective way to change a child's behaviour in the short term is to change the context. This can be accomplished in various ways, such as parent training programmes, but for children who are looked after, consultation has emerged as a particularly effective way of making changes in the network' (Dent and Golding, 2006: 170). Consultation recognizes the importance of strengthening the relationships between the child and the people already involved in their lives, rather than expecting children with relationship struggles to develop a new relationship with a therapist.

Consultation is also being adopted as the model of choice for mental health practitioners working in school settings (Dickinson, 2000). It can help networks around the child, including family members, social workers and school staff, to consider the child's behavioural difficulties in the context of their attachment relationships. This helps the adults to understand the child's feelings that underpin their challenging behaviour. In turn, this can foster helpful changes within the network. Supporting school staff is crucial for CAMHS work, since the school context plays a key role in children's emotional health and well-being. For example, a school teacher who recognizes and implements aspects of PACE within the school context, such as expressing empathy for the child's feelings before implementing school rules, can make a big difference. 'Feeling understood and experiencing empathy is the starting point from which children develop trust and new ways of relating to people' (Golding, 2008: 71). Consultation can help professionals to build more positive relationships with a child who is struggling with trusting and relating to adults, and to gain an understanding of how these children can be helped to overcome attachment difficulties.

One model of consultation used in Tier 2 CAMHS Teams is a solution-focused consultation. This invites the network to identify their goals by identifying what a preferred future would look like. Scaling questions and tools are used 'to establish progress already achieved, to allow for the exploration of what the consultee has done that is useful and to establish detailed pictures of the way forward' (George, 2005: 60). A solution-focused consultation is particularly suited to large professional networks, helping them to consider the past, present and future implications of complex decision-making (Bremble and Hill, 2004).

This case study shows how local managers adopted locally the structure for this service, which had been presented in a national report, and then selected theories relevant to their practice from each part of the structure. A new practitioner appointed to a job in the service might see this as a given, but it is always possible to see where the structure and theoretical decisions came from. Over a period, practitioners can see theoretical ideas being picked up and adapted by managers and colleagues to be used in the local context.

Theory in different forms of social work: group, macro, residential care and family therapy practice

The case study just presented is an example of how managed eclecticism in the use of practice theory emerges in a social work service. Another aspect of eclecticism arises when theory is adapted so that it is relevant to particular forms of practice.

Many writers distinguish three forms of social work, called 'modalities' in the USA: work with individuals and families, usually called casework until the 1970s, groupwork and community or macro work. In most practice settings, as in the case study of CAMHS above, work with individuals and families is the main form of practice, other forms of practice sometimes being added to it. In the USA, using several modalities together is called 'integrated practice'. In addition to this, many practitioners work in residential care, and some do specialist kinds of work such as family therapy, counselling or psychotherapy. Others work in particular settings such as education or school social work, or practise using ideas built up in particular countries, such as in social pedagogy or social development. In the USA, organizing and managing agencies is also often treated as a form of practice; in other countries, management is seen less as a practice and more as a responsibility of people in promoted posts, requiring separate training and education that is often based on business school or public administration education. The existence of these different forms of practice raises the question of whether there are particular theories designed to be used in these forms of practice, and of how social work and its theories are connected with or separated from them.

Most analyses of groupwork start from Papell and Rothman's (1966) ground-breaking article. This offers three approaches, depending on the groups' aims:

▪ In the *remedial* model, groups bring together individuals who have problems, often of how they function in social roles, aiming to help them change their undesired patterns of behaviour. Any groupwork that aims to change behaviour is remedial in approach. A contemporary approach is, for example, implementing solution-focused therapy in groups (Sharry, 2007). Encounter groups are normally regarded as a separate humanist and gestalt form of groupwork concerned with personal growth; Glassman (2009) developed a broader humanistic approach to groupwork (see Chapter 10). Groupwork is also possible using CBT methods.

▪ The *reciprocal* model emphasizes self-help and mutual support according to a programme devised by group members alongside practitioners. For example, hospices run groups for people who are caring for family members who are dying (Reith, 2011).

▪ The *social goals* model, associated with social pedagogy or youth and community work, uses groupwork to pursue external goals, such as arts, community or education activities. For example, hospices also use arts activities to maintain dying people's hope and interest in life and stimulate family interaction (Hartley and Payne, 2008).

Recent developments in groupwork are more pragmatic (Trevithick, 2012). For example Brown and colleagues (Brown et al., 1982; Brown, 1992) developed time-limited groups aimed at meeting agency objectives to achieve individual change in clients, using shared activities and discussion focused on issues that the group members have in common, for example caring responsibilities for frail relatives. These may involve elements of remedial, reciprocal and social goals objectives. Heap (1992) argued that groupwork became more multidisciplinary and less central to social work practice, and this is a worldwide trend. He also pointed out the growing importance of self-help and mutual-support groups in healthcare work with people with mental illness and long-term conditions. Supporting and stimulating such groups has become a major focus of groupwork development and has begun to merge with community work and empowerment practice.

Many practice theories reviewed in this book and other similar reviews of theory can be transferred or adapted to be used in group, residential or day-care settings. Garvin et al. (2004), in an edited collection, draw on an eclectic range of ideas concerned with evidence about group functioning, different client groups and many of the practice theories discussed in reviews of social work theory, as adapted to groupwork practice. Alternatively, elements of the theories can be applied across these settings. For example, task-centred practice has also been used and researched in group and family practice (Epstein and Brown, 2002; Tolson et al., 2003). Many practitioners therefore transfer and adapt ideas that they are confident in applying in one part of their practice to other aspects of their work.

Community work, an element of what is now often called macro practice in the USA, similarly has its range of objectives. York (1984) suggested that several conceptualizations of community work divide it into three types. As with Papell and Rothman's (1966) analysis of groupwork, these are linked with the aims of the community practice:

- organizing community agencies;
- developing local competences;
- political action for change.

These objectives are reflected in many recent analyses of community work practice. In addition, feminist practice and work with black and minority ethnic groups are also often seen as separate theoretical positions, because they focus on responding to the particular needs of groups who might be excluded from community concerns.

While some writers include family therapy within social work theory (see Figure 2.2 earlier in the chapter), this trend of the 1980s has receded. In this practice, all or several members of the family are treated together on the assumption that their problems arise from interactions between them all. Family therapy is a multidisciplinary area of practice in which several occupational groups operate and to which several professions, including social work, have made contributions. Some social workers use or borrow from family therapy and contribute to the development of family therapy theory and practice. Many social workers see themselves as practising social work with special relevance to families, and taking into account the family context as part of working with clients in their situation or social environment. In doing so, they often use systems ideas, which is the source of much family therapy.

Similar points might be made about counselling and psychotherapy. These are, along-side clinical psychology, separate professions whose role overlaps with that of social work, particularly in healthcare or similar clinical roles. Many social work practice theories have been adapted from clinical psychology, counselling, psychiatry and psychotherapy, and social work overlaps with work in these fields, particularly in the USA, where social workers are involved in private clinical and counselling practice. Since this book focuses on theory that is formulated as part of social work practice, I do not differentiate the many counselling and psychological theories directly used in US social work that some-times appear in North American texts. Counselling and psychotherapeutic knowledge also influence social work skills, in particular communication (Bellinger and Fleet, 2012).

Residential care is mainly a setting in which other treatment theories are used, rather than being a distinct form of social work activity justifying theories of its own. Clough's (2000) typology of theory in residential care is as follows:

- Theories of the resident world are like theories of the client world.
- Theories of function and task in residential care are like theories of the nature of social work.
- Theories of intervention are like social work practice theories.
- Theories of residential homes as systems refer to the specific characteristic of residential social work practice that it needs so it can take account of the social organization of the location in which it operates. It would, and perhaps should, be worthwhile for practitioners in other settings to think more about the influence on their practice of the social organization of their location.

Social pedagogy is a key European perspective that has important relationships with groupwork, especially with children and with residential work. This is a general theory of social work that concentrates on social work as an educational and developmental process (see Chapter 8).

Using evidence to support practice theory

Positivist and interpretivist uses of knowledge

The major area of debate about social work theory, from the 1990s to the present, has been epistemological; that is, it is about how we organize our knowledge and thinking about human beings to back up the theories that we use. One position in this debate – EBP – is that we should base our practice on knowledge that comes from empirical evidence about what is effective in achieving our objectives. Because a group of social work writers is pushing for us to accept their view of how practice should be, this debate is an example of what I called in Chapter 1 a politics: people forming into groups as a way of influencing what social work should be like. Similar debates are also taking place in medicine, nursing, clinical psychology and other professions, so EBP is an interdisciplinary movement of professional politics.

EBP has become influential, particularly in the USA, supported by important and powerful arguments. However, there is equally strong opposition to it. This contestation is important for thinking about theory because some arguments for EBP reject theory as being useful in social work, saying that theory is simply ideas, not knowledge that comes from evidence. This is a special case of the arguments that we met in Chapter 1, first, that the term 'theory' means insubstantial ideas unrelated to reality, and second, that it should be reserved for explanatory theory rather than being used more broadly, as I use it in this book.

As Webb (2001) points out, this is a long-standing philosophical debate that dates back to the 1700s. The debate is between positivism and interpretivism (Brechin and Sidell, 2000):

- *Positivists* believe that the world is orderly and that how it works follows natural rules that we can come to understand. The world exists independently of human beings, and we can stand outside it and observe it objectively. Being objective means that we can observe it independently of our own feelings and beliefs and we can check that we are right. Other people can also observe it, and we can compare observations to make sure that we are all seeing reality in the same way. Human beings are like objects to a positivist; they are animals in a natural world and behave according to rules that apply to objects of the human kind. If we observe them systematically, we can understand the rules that affect the inhabitants of the human world, just as we can understand the natural world. We can then apply that knowledge to create the desired changes. In doing so, we can be effective, because we can explain how one action causes another. Human beings are complicated, so it will be difficult, but positivists believe that it must be possible.

- *Interpretivists* believe that human beings are independent, free to follow their will as part of the world, in relationships with other human beings, so they cannot be objective. Because we participate in human relationships, we inevitably influence the world we are studying, and in turn our understandings about the world will influence how we behave; that is, we are subjective. Interpretivists believe that human beings are subjects, meaning that they can freely take command of their thinking and their actions. Although their actions affect others, in acting they also change themselves. This is so even though they may be constrained by the natural and social order of the environment around us. This view says that it is just not possible to collect all the necessary information to understand the rules of human life, so it is better to think about the world in a more flexible way.

Case example: Shouting at the children

Baz shouted at his children because they ran away from him and he was frightened they would get onto the road and be involved in an accident. They were upset because they thought he was being angry with them. Seeing this, he was angry with himself for seeming aggressive rather than helping them to understand his concern. When they got home, he explained why it was important to be careful. The next time they went out, he reminded them that it was sensible to stay together and keep away from the traffic.

The positivist observes the behaviour and the reaction: does Baz keep the children out of danger? Yes, so his behaviour is effective. But interpretivists do not accept that people can be objective, that is, stand outside their actions. Baz is doing more than standing outside himself and looking at his behaviour objectively, because he does not just take for granted what happened; instead he questions it. In questioning what happened, he shows that how people act and how others react to their actions will always affect each other in a circle of interactions; this is called reflexivity.

The interpretivist notes that whether the behaviour is effective depends on the question you ask. Yes, in this instance, it is effective at keeping the children out of danger this time. But ask a different question: does this behaviour mean that Baz develops his relationship with his children so that they love and trust him and he is able to influence them success-fully to keep them safe in the long term? Doubtful; if we look at the later behaviour, the evidence might be that reasoning and advance reminders are more effective than shouting.

The interpretivist view is therefore that social workers enter into relationships with people and engage in mutual exploration of what is happening to gain a full and complex appreciation of the situations we are engaged in. People's social objectives and values in their relationships are always a factor. Baz was affected by his children's reaction: he did not want to be the kind of father that made his children fearful. So his social assumptions about how a father should act, drawn from interactions with other people in his experi-ence of life, and his perception of his children's reaction caused him to adapt his behav-iour. His behaviour was influenced by values and predispositions: Baz had a specific idea of how a 'good' father should behave, and of ways of fathering that would be helpful or unhelpful in realizing that vision. In contrast, another father may think differently. Someone else may believe that it is all right to use his size, loud voice and status as a father to manage his children's behaviour by dominating them. Since this father's starting point would be different, he might consider the upset reactions of Baz's children to be a satisfactory and appropriate response: perhaps they would remember to behave next time. So the assumptions, perceptions and interpretations – not the behaviour – are important in understanding what happened.

The development of EBP

How do these ideas affect discussions of theory? To start with, why is this an issue for social work and its practitioners? Pragmatically, many practitioners in general social work settings have picked up ideas according to their interest or use. But, apart from your own feeling that some ideas are valuable, how can you tell whether one is more useful than another? Social work is used across the planet for a widening range of social purposes. Of course, more does not necessarily mean better. Social work has critics and detractors, but so too have doctors, journalists, lawyers, politicians or priests, all of whom are universal. We live in a less deferential, more critical age, and this pushes us to be alert to improve our performance. But this leads us back to how we think about theory. Positivists would say we can find the rules that will tell us what treatment is effective to achieve our aims, while interpretivists ask instead how we can understand and work within a complex of human interactions and a variety of potential aims.

Early evaluations of social work in the 1950s and 60s took the positivist route. They found that it did not achieve its aims, or that it produced uncertain results (Mullen and Dumpson, 1972; Fischer, 1973, 1976; Reid et al., 2004: 72). It seemed that nothing worked. So researchers in the 'empirical practice movement' tried to find what would work. The most important developments from this were task-centred practice and accumulating evidence of the effectiveness of cognitive-behavioural methods. Using behavioural models, practitioners were encouraged to use single-case or single-system research designs (Kazi, 1998; Royse, 2008: Chapter 4) as they practised. These start from a baseline at the beginning of a piece of intervention, and check for improvement in the intended directions during and after the intervention. This is a practical way for individual social workers or teams to examine whether their practice is successful.

As a result of these developments in theory and how we thought about practice, several advances were made: social work objectives in individual cases became more highly specified and testable; goals were more limited; assessment was more thorough; evaluation gave better feedback to practitioners; intensive and focused activities were used; clients rehearsed behaviour instead of just being counselled and supported; special projects and developments were tested instead of there being evaluations focusing on routine services; attempts were made to restrict outside interference that limited projects' effectiveness; and services were located to encourage clients to come early for help (Sheldon, 1987). All these led to clear evidence, mostly from the USA, of demonstrable success in well-designed agency programmes or individual work (Reid and Hanrahan, 1982; Thomlison, 1984; Rubin, 1985; Videka-Sherman, 1988; Macdonald and Sheldon, 1992; Gorey, 1996). This led to an emergence of the 'aims' and 'action sequence' elements of the shared value principles (see Figure 1.7). The first states that we should be clear about our objectives as we practise, and the second that we should follow clearly identified and transparent procedures in what we do.

Most interventions in this research were cognitive-behavioural, but about half the investigations of ordinary casework, non-behavioural groupwork and much family therapy were also successful (Macdonald and Sheldon, 1992). American surveys of groupwork (Tolman and Molidor, 1994) and residential care (Curry, 1995) show that research techniques have been less strong in these areas, but some positive results have been achieved. A number of studies have shown that service developments including or focusing on social work have been successful (Goldberg, 1987). Many studies looking at specific aspects of service or practice with particular client groups have been published and collected into accounts of practice that are supported in some way by research. One example is the two-volume *Handbook of Empirical Social Work Practice* (Wodarski and Thyer, 1998). The first volume summarizes studies related to a wide range of mental disorders, the second studies related to particular social problems. More recent texts summarize evidence of useful practice techniques and service provision for a range of common problems experienced by various client groups (for example, Roberts and Yeager, 2004), sometimes in the context of a broader account of social work practice (for example, Gambrill, 2006; Sheldon and Macdonald, 2009).

Reid et al. (2004) examined a range of small-scale experiments and evaluations that compared different interventions or looked at the contribution of different elements of an intervention, and found that there was evidence of their effectiveness. Reviewing effectiveness research, Lehmann and Coady (2007) judge that the research into many models of interpersonal work in counselling, psychotherapy and social work confirms the impression that well-designed and rigorously implemented interventions according to a wide range of theoretical models, including psychodynamic practice and solution-focused practice, have been shown to be effective. It is not that 'everything works', but rather that research has identified important 'common factors' (Reid et al., 2004: 72) other than the theoretical model used in helping people. Important examples are the quality of the relationship between practitioners and clients and the organization of the agency service in which practitioners work. Zimmerman et al. (2003) similarly found that social engagement was an important factor in successful service provision in residential care and assisted living in the USA. These points emphasize another of the 'shared elements' of all social work theories that I identified in Chapter 1: the 'alliance' between practitioner and client.

Should we just forget about theory, then, and concentrate on skills and knowledge about the social issues we are asked to intervene with? This takes us back to the debates we reviewed in Chapter 1: practitioners find practice theory useful for organizing their work, in addition to the other kinds of knowledge and theory that they call on.

What is EBP?

Arising from these developments, an EBP movement emerged in the USA and elsewhere (Gray et al., 2009), which has promoted a policy of following empirical evidence to decide on practice actions. There are two approaches to EBP:

- The first is the principle that evidence should determine how social work should be provided and organized. This is a 'top-down' approach. It looks in general at what kinds of practice have been found to be effective with particular client groups for whom a service is provided, and it organizes services to practise in that way.
- The second is a system of practice in which individual practitioners, together with their clients, evaluate the most effective methods to help with the problems faced by their clients.

The first approach suggests that services should reflect the best research in existence, so that the agencies are providing services that will achieve the best outcomes possible in meeting their own and their clients' objectives. To support this, research information is disseminated to practitioners and agencies and combined with legal and professional knowledge to achieve an agreed 'best practice' (Jones et al., 2007). This is done by collecting:

- systematic reviews of research about particular problems or interventions;
- information about effective agency services or intervention programmes;
- practice guidelines setting out intervention protocols (Jenson, 2005).

The second approach puts the responsibility on practitioners to work with clients, groups or community organizations, to identify the aims of their intervention and to review possible options for achieving these aims and the research supporting each option. The practitioners would decide what they do according to the research evidence.

Bellamy et al. (2009) propose six practice steps, set out in Figure 2.4.

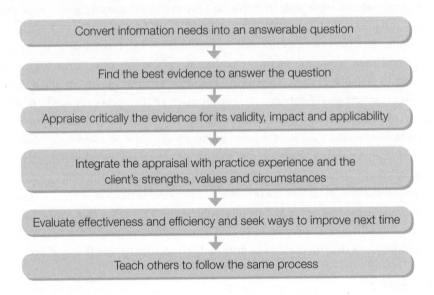

Figure 2.4 EBP: six steps

Source: Bellamy et al. (2009); for a practice critique of this process, see McCracken and Marsh (2008).

In practice, there are short cuts. For example, as in the case study on CAMHS earlier in the chapter, most practitioners work within agencies or in private practices that deal with specific problems, and as a result similar problems will arise again and again. Practitioners will therefore develop standard patterns of service and guidelines for practice that reflect the best evidence. In addition, the accumulation of evidence would suggest certain approaches that are typically successful for the main objectives of social work, so these would gain wide currency. Less successful approaches, or approaches that did not gain research support, would fall out of use.

Arguments for EBP

Arguments for EBP as the main form of practice are as follows:

- It provides for a planned and systematic form of practice.
- It is ethical to use methods that are proven to be effective and to avoid other methods.
- It is unethical to prefer methods on the grounds of practitioners' personal preferences or personal and professional theories and values, rather than methods that are proven to be effective.

- EBP is accountable to clients. This is because if the practice method (the second approach) is used, clients are involved in decision-making and can influence the problems to be tackled, as well as the choice of outcomes and methods.
- EBP is accountable to agencies and more broadly to the mandate of social work, because it sets clear objectives, prescribes methods that have been demonstrated to be most likely to achieve those objectives and focuses on measuring the outcomes of the work, rather than on ideological or theoretical preferences.

Arguments against EBP

The arguments against EBP fall into four main areas. I have adapted these points to a social work context from House and Loewenthal's (2008) discussion of CBT in psychology, which succinctly summarizes the main aspects of the debate. Most critiques of EBP expand on these points.

- *Paradigmatic.* EBP relies on a positivist worldview that cannot be integrated with the alternative interpretivist worldview. Promoting EBP therefore leads to division and sterile argument that can never be reconciled.
- *Practical.* The aims and practices of social work are broad. Often, they cannot be defined in ways that will allow research to provide enough guidance to make decisions that respond to the diversity and complexity of behaviour, personality and social relations that practitioners deal with. In addition, that complexity interacts with the equally unresearchable personality and skills of diverse practitioners. Moreover, it assumes that practice will be mainly about behavioural change rather than broader social issues.
- *Epistemology and research.* EBP gives priority to the certain kinds of knowledge, produced by certain kinds of research, and disparages other knowledge. EBP prefers research showing evidence that practitioners' interventions have made a difference to a pre-existing state, and research in which external factors that might interfere with the clarity of findings are controlled. Thus, random controlled trials are preferred, especially those that compare one intervention with another and find which is more successful (Reid et al., 2004). Circumstances like this are rare in practice, so the findings of such studies are limited in practice.
- *Cultural and political.* In its research, EBP explores, and therefore by implication accepts, the present social order, including its existing political and cultural assumptions, and therefore prescribes practice that encourages behaviour change so that people adapt to a society in which there are widespread inequalities and injustices. It may, therefore, 'blame the victim' by seeking to change individuals, families and communities, rather than working to deal with inequalities in society. In this view, EBP accepts Western cultural assumptions rather than the alternatives available in diverse cultures and ethnicities. Feminists argue similarly that EBP promotes male ways of thinking about reality as a set of certainties, rather than female preferences for exploring and accepting diverse ways of thinking and acting. Moreover, social work is part of government, or is otherwise used on behalf of existing social structures in which most clients are relatively

powerless, and a model of practice that accepts those structures is inappropriate to the values and objectives of social work. In reality, the aims of social work agencies are set by economic and political factors rather than by decisions about practice that are made by practitioners, so EBP makes false assumptions about how practice works.

These arguments are connected. If you take an interpretivist view of knowledge, you are also likely to accept that the diversity and complexity of behaviour and practice raise barriers to EBP. Similarly, an interpretivist is also likely to value a diverse epistemology and a wide range of research methods, and to acknowledge the importance of cultural and political influences on decision-making.

The politics of EBP

The politics of EBP pit an international group of supporters against other groups who are critical of the research priorities implied by EBP and the possibility of implementing it in practice or through social work education. In addition, groups concerned with using evidence to support policy innovations in social services, including politicians and civil servants, and managers seeking greater effectiveness in practice are also important players. Gray et al. (2009) review the international development of the EBP movement and its opponents.

These arguments about EBP have been played out in social work debate in three phases. The first was early articles seeking to establish empirical research evidence as a basis for practice, contested by writers supporting interpretivist understandings of knowledge development, who were often described as constructionist (Witkin, 1992; Atherton, 1993, 1994; Thyer, 1994). The second was a phase of debate about the validity of EBP; two important articles, the second replying to the first, express this debate very fully (Webb, 2001; Gibbs and Gambrill, 2002). The third phase has been a body of work concerned with introducing EBP into the social work curriculum, particularly in the USA, where using EBP to achieve wider change in the rigour of social work education has been an important trend since 2005 (Jenson, 2007). It is connected with political trends towards managerialism or the new public management, which emphasize the managerial and political control of professional discretion in practice. A positivist stance that emphasizes evidence similarly questions professional judgement as the basis of practitioners making practice decisions. There is, consequently, also a significant move to incorporate EBP into the regulation of social work agencies, particularly in Europe, where governments have sought to identify and disseminate effective practice methods, through organizations such as the Social Care Institute for Excellence in the UK (Walter et al., 2004) and the National Institute for Health and Welfare in Finland (Sociaaliportti, 2009).

Rubin and Parrish (2007) identify the main areas of contention in these debates:

- reductionism – can complex human, individual and personal issues be expressed in empirical research?;
- the meaning of EBP – does it mainly mean the first (top-down) or second (every-case) of the approaches that I identified in the section 'What is EBP?';

■ evidentiary standards – does it include all empirical research, including small-scale and qualitative studies, or is research acceptable only if it provides causal explanations that define effective practice?

These issues partly point to a discussion about the extent to which different research methods can appropriately and successfully provide guidance in undertaking social work practice. There are many other methods of research that can deal with complexity more effectively than EBP does, such as decision trees (Hudson, 2009) or naturalistic decision-making through ideas such as 'recognition-primed decision-making' (van de Luitgaarden, 2009). 'Soft' evidence such as clients' accounts, explanations and interpretations of their lives, arguments between people and non-verbal communication can all be evaluated in rigorous ways and contribute helpful knowledge to practitioners (Murdach, 2010). Such concerns about using different research methods in social work lead in turn to questions about whether EBP can be adequately incorporated into social work education, even though most social work academics in the USA view it favourably (Rubin and Parrish, 2007).

In addition to the research challenges, there continue to be questions about whether it is feasible to implement EBP in practice decisions that are affected by many factors other than research evidence and at every step of Bellamy et al.'s six practice steps (see Figure 2.4) (McCracken and Marsh, 2008). Some of the difficulties identified by Webb (2001) arise from the fact that social work is:

■ mediated by organizations, the availability of resources, communication and social relations between individuals within and outside agencies;
■ situated in complex decision-making environments;
■ provisional, since most social situations cannot be fully understood;
■ pragmatic, arising from an interaction between clients', agencies' and social workers' understandings of particular situations rather than being concerned with formal, therapeutic decision-making.

Consequently, research may not tell you enough about the situations your agency is responsible for for the research to be relevant to your practice, as this case example shows.

Case example: CBT in residential care

A Campbell Collaboration paper (Armelius and Andreassen, 2007) examines CBT for antisocial behaviour in residential care, a crucial topic for many practitioners dealing with that small group (about 5%) of adolescents who present serious antisocial behaviour. The paper brought together twelve studies covering 4,500 young people from the USA, Canada and the UK. Generally, placing young offenders in institutions is not effective in itself in reducing their subsequent criminal behaviour; it may even have a negative effect on their behaviour. Therefore, family and community interventions are often preferred. However, it is sometimes impossible to retain serious offenders in the community, so they go into institutions. Since CBT has a very good record in achieving changed behaviour, researchers asked if it could achieve better results than residential care without CBT.

▸

The collected studies showed that CBT achieved a 10% reduction in recidivism (meaning a return to crime after treatment or punishment) over twelve months after the adolescents had been released from the institutions, compared with young offenders in institutions who did not receive CBT. This sounds good until you work out the figures: you have to treat nine young offenders with CBT before you will find one whose recidivism improves. In addition, there is some indication that several other structured forms of treatment are just as effective as CBT in achieving this uninspiring result, but there were not enough studies on these to find out whether any other treatment was better or worse than CBT.

The client group in this case example, young offenders, is very important politically and in practice. Yet all the study tells you is that if you put young offenders in an institution and actively do something organized about changing their behaviour, a small reduction in their reoffending rate might be achievable, which is not a particularly insightful conclusion. If EBP cannot tell you anything useful in a fairly well-researched, politically important area, it is likely to be even less useful in less clear areas of study. This makes many practitioners doubt its practical use.

One of the strongest arguments for EBP is ethical: that clients should benefit from the best knowledge available. Furman (2009), however, points to an ethical counterargument, viewing the privileging of some research methods as an ethical rather than a pragmatic issue. He argues that it is a value decision to focus on knowledge about outcomes rather than the value of relationships and effective interpersonal skills; he also proposes that it is a value decision to focus on developing quantitatively measurable methods of practice over improved practitioner education and a focus on broad social change or qualitative improvements in people's lives. For example, Manthorpe et al. (2008) report a study of older people's views about social workers in which older people, while recognizing the value of fair assessment and an efficient delivery of services, expressed regret that this was given priority over building a relationship that acknowledged their feelings about the changes occurring in their lives.

Interpretivist and realist evidence

There are three main research approaches that use evidence in different ways from the EBP approach: the social construction, empowerment and realist views.

Social construction views argue for an interpretivist view of knowledge and theory in social work. I take this position and argued for it in my account of the social construction of social work theory in Chapter 1; here, we are meeting it applied to social work knowledge more broadly. Empowerment views argue that clients' needs and preferences should be the main source of our decisions. Realist views emphasize the need to use research in ways that reflect the different social contexts in which it is used.

Social construction is an interpretivist, postmodernist set of ideas proposing that understandings about the world come from interactions between people as part of many interchanges in a social, cultural and historical context. Knowledge is therefore constructed within cultural, historical and local contexts through the language used to interpret social experiences. This comes to form and represent how people understand their social experiences. In social work, this position is represented most directly in the work of a group of Finnish researchers (Jokinen et al., 1999; Karvinen et al., 1999; Hall et al., 2003) and Parton (1996; Parton and O'Byrne, 2000). Their work has been increasingly influential since the 1990s, particularly in ideas such as solution, narrative and strengths-based practices (see Chapter 9).

The social and historical context in which situations develop and knowledge is researched must have an important impact on our understandings of individuals, society and research as a source of knowledge. Social construction therefore has a distinctive approach to research, which tries to engage people who are the subjects of research in an equal relationship with researchers. As a result, complex human understandings about the situation are explored from different points of view, and the outcomes represent a full picture of intricate human situations. Social construction research often uses detailed analysis of human interaction, particularly conversation analysis, relying on video- and audio-taped records of interactions, so it is particularly relevant to social work practice. These taped records are systematically analysed to reveal patterns of communication and behaviour that may be hidden. These patterns also often show the covert exercise of power and provide research support for empowerment practice. Social constructionists argue that the results of EBP do not reflect this rich, complex reality. EBP's narrow research base is naive, and a wider range of methods that examine how people make sense of the social situations they face is more helpful (White, 1997).

Social construction ideas therefore not only propose an alternative worldview, but also make it clear that there are alternative, valid ways of researching social work practice.

Empowerment views argue that knowledge primarily comes from clients and that, to be ethical, social workers should use knowledge according to clients' wishes in order to empower them further. In social work, these ideas are most clearly represented in Beresford and Croft's work (1993, 2001) and are particularly associated with social and community development, empowerment and advocacy theories (see Chapters 8 and 11 respectively).

Empowerment views of knowledge argue two things:

■ The purposes of social work require practitioners to seek social justice, and therefore to empower people by responding to their knowledge and understanding of the world.
■ Clients (in this view often called consumers or service users) often have the best knowledge about their circumstances and objectives, which should therefore be followed. They are expert carers, clients, patients or users whose expertise should direct practice, rather than ideas held by the practitioner doing this.

Since service users are often oppressed, disadvantaged and marginalized, empowerment views of knowledge argue that understanding their situation should guide social work practice. Such views partly rely on 'epistemic privilege', the view that the person or social group that creates knowledge or experiences particular aspects of life has an advantage in understanding and describing their knowledge or experience. This view is also espoused in relation to people from minority groups; it is claimed that only they have the experience of oppression that gives them the full understanding of it. Empathy from professionals is not enough. In democratic societies, professionals and governments should respond to the social demands of the citizens.

Empowerment views suggest that it is neither ethical nor practical to pursue activities contrary to service users' wishes. Many approaches to knowledge, including EBP, emphasize the social worker as an expert whose knowledge of research results should set the direction of work, and this diminishes their valuation of their client's knowledge. A better way of using research is through working in a dialogue that incorporates service users' views as a critique of professional knowledge (Sellick et al., 2002). Feminist social workers argue that social workers reinforce the oppression of women through the role of social work in the surveillance and enforcement of conventional patriarchal relationships (Dominelli, 2002a).

This approach also produces a useful research perspective. Action research proposes a technique for evaluating social projects as they develop, the results influencing how the project progresses as it goes along. Because of its interpretivist view, this can be criticized for its lack of rigour by positivists, although it has proved practically useful in evaluating experimental projects. It was also criticized by empowerment writers for viewing projects from the point of view of the funders or professionals involved in the projects. This led to the development of participative action research in resource-poor countries (Whyte, 1991). More individual work also produced alternative research approaches. De Shazer and Berg (1997), for example, emphasize the importance of whether solution-focused therapy meets clients' objectives rather than the agency's purposes.

Realist views are a fairly new perspective and argue that evidence of reality is not always available to empirical observation, so that knowledge emerges or is generated from human interpretations of successions of events that can be captured empirically. In social work, these ideas are represented in the work of Houston (2001), Morén and Blom (2003) and Kazi (2003). Although this view is often described as 'realist' for convenience, many writers prefer to talk about 'critical realism' because this particular view of realism seeks to question taken-for-granted assumptions about theory and research, and this connects the ideas to critical social science theory, which tries to achieve this critical position. This research approach contributed another of the 'shared elements' of practice theory that I identified in Chapter 1: critical practice. EBP is realist in another way, because it assumes that there is a reality that we can research.

Realist views argue that it is true that social phenomena exist beyond social constructions (Houston, 2002), but that it is nevertheless important to understand those constructions. Their current importance originates from the work of contemporary social scientists, in particular Bhaskar (1979, 1989) and Archer (1995) and researchers such as Pawson and Tilley (1997).

Realist researchers say that finding extensive evidence of social structures is difficult, so a positivist approach is not helpful. We rely more on human judgements about how much information is accumulating. Houston (2001) points out that all human activity takes place in open systems, which are constantly changing and depend on human beings' decisions, which are not fully determined by their own psychology or social circumstances. Expecting to use evidence to predict human activity is therefore impossible. We should refer more to events containing tendencies and being influenced by psychological and social mechanisms. By examining these tendencies and influences, we can see the underlying mechanisms at work.

This concept of *emergence* is important in understanding the realist critique of EBP, which often ignores emergent properties. EBP assumes either that we can observe everything that exists, or that what actually happens is all that might happen. However, we cannot empirically observe every aspect of a social work agency and the other social structures that affect our work. Archer (2000) proposes, moreover, that although language and interaction are important, it is our practical experience of the world that allows our humanity to emerge and become our personal identity. So what we do in relation to other people is what mainly gives us an identity. In turn, this emphasizes that practice, rather than what we think or theorize about, is what produces reality.

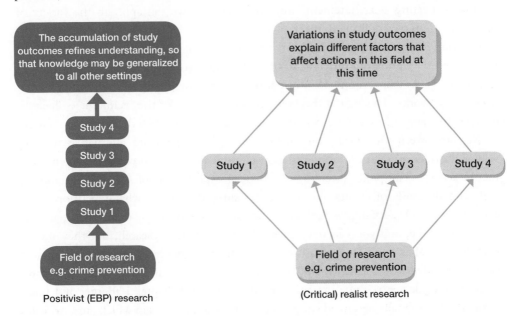

Figure 2.5 Positivist (EBP) and realist research compared

Figure 2.5 compares the assumptions of realist and positivist research. Pawson and Tilley (1997) describe research on and the evaluation of projects to prevent and reduce crime. Each project is in a different geographical area and social context, so the initial social structures and the outcomes of similar project activities vary. However, by examining a number of projects, researchers can identify the different factors that affect how projects work. The more studies you have, the better you can understand the range of factors explaining the variations that these different social factors cause, and the more social factors you can identify that are relevant to this field of study. In positivist research, on the other hand, the assumption is that the outcomes of the different studies can be combined. The more studies you have, the closer you can get to saying what the outcomes might be in all similar circumstances. To the critical realist, there is no right answer, but you can understand better the factors you have to take into account. If you carry out studies over time, the critical realist would expect to identify trends as social circumstances change, while the positivist would expect to get closer to a full understanding of what will happen, whatever the social circumstances. Therefore, for the realist, it is impossible to identify particular interventions that will always have the same effects as EBP assumes. Moreover, as society changes, what will be needed will tend to move towards a different pattern. But, for a limited period, relevant factors that might be helpful in setting up, as in this case, a crime prevention project would be identifiable.

Many people argue that this is a reasonable approach to take to the knowledge requirements of social work. We have some knowledge and information to guide us, but we have to apply it with an awareness of the change that is going on all around us. Therefore, flexibility and following the principles and guidelines of practice theories are more practical than expecting clear statements from research that we can apply to the variety of human situations we are likely to meet.

Following this principle, a social work researcher could see how a social work technique works in a number of different settings. It might work well in some circumstances but not others. As you accumulate information, you can identify those circumstances that affect how it works. This would then tell you how the use of the technique is likely to change with changes in social factors affecting the context in which the technique is used.

EBP, empowerment, social construction and realist ideas are alternative ways of looking at evidence, each exploring different cultural and social forces that influence our practice actions. The political, cultural and social expectations of social work, and the needs and demands of clients, contribute pressures that affect what practitioners are required to do. Pre-existing social constructions also affect us. Social constructions change over time, and you can trace these changes through research, but they show a good deal of stability and are the basis on which many people carry out their social interactions. Provided it is constantly updated to respond to social changes, social research can provide evidence to guide practitioners. As we saw in Chapter 1, Berger and Luckmann (1971) originally described social construction as a process in which current reality is determined, for the participants in any social environment, by their own social constructions. Research can provide evidence about that reality, but we must recognize that it is determined in social relationships and forms a constantly changing reality.

Conclusion: how social workers can evaluate social work theory

Chapter 1 set out the arguments for using practice theories to guide our practice and as a way to incorporate different views about the objectives of social work. I argued at the outset of this chapter that practitioners need to be aware of the range of social work practice theories available and what they might contribute to our social work practice. Practitioners may be able to select a practice theory to use that is appropriate to their setting, or they may develop an eclectic practice drawing on a combination of theories in the context of their agency, team and personal requirements.

The significant debate about the role of empirical research evidence in evaluating practice theory remains unresolved. Strong contending groups in the politics of EBP are ranged against each other. While most people would agree that the available evidence should influence how services and agencies develop and manage their services through guidance, research dissemination and professional debate, there are serious questions about whether social research can ever be adequate or appropriate to guide practitioners' decision-making and actions in every situation that they deal with. It is unrealistic to review the evidence relevant to every case every time a practice decision must be made. Not enough research is yet available to help in many areas of practice. Many factors affect whether a practitioner's actions are effective in achieving their desired outcomes, and many of those factors are based on the social context and the personality, skills and interactions of the people involved, both practitioners and clients, rather than on researched intervention techniques or services.

Therefore, it is unlikely that we can make generalized deductions from research about what to do in particular situations. Politicians and policy-makers make demands on social work practice to help manage crime and community problems that research does not or perhaps cannot help us with. The centuries-long debate between the interpretivist and positivist views of knowledge suggests that these questions raise fundamental issues about the nature and possibilities of human knowledge that may never be resolved.

Social workers must still provide services and take action. Research evidence will contribute to their service, and must influence social workers' thinking, but it is not the final answer in evaluating practice theory. It is the process by which practitioners interact with their evidence and knowledge, in cooperation with their colleagues in teams and agencies, that will enable them to use the framework of practice theory to make practice decisions. The next chapter examines the current understanding of the process of applying practice theory, using knowledge and evidence to make practice decisions and interventions.

Additional resources

Further reading

Mathews, I. and Crawford, K. (eds) (2011) *Evidence-based Practice in Social Work* (Exeter: Learning Matters).

An introduction to some of the issues about supporting practice with evidence.

Gray, M., Plath, D. and Webb, S. A. (2009) *Evidence-based Social Work: A Critical Stance* (London: Routledge.)

The most comprehensive review from a critical stance of the EBP movement.

Journals

To explore current debates, you should look at journals concerned with social work education or research. Extensive collections of papers were published in 2007 in the Fall edition of the *American Journal of Social Work Education* (volume 43, issue 3), and the September edition of *Research on Social Work Practice*, which give a good picture of issues debated at conferences during that period.

Most social work journals contain empirical social work research and debate about theory: the following emphasize empirical research in social work:

Journal of Research on Social Work Practice – Sage Journals

Nordic Social Work Research – Taylor & Francis for the (Nordic) National Associations for Social Work Research (FORSA)

Qualitative Social Work: Research and Practice – Sage Journals

Social Work Research – Oxford Journals for the (American) National Association of Social Workers (not an international journal, since its board only has US members)

Websites

http://www.campbellcollaboration.org/

The Campbell Collaboration is a website that collects evidence about successful interventions in a range of social science disciplines, including a social welfare group. To find this, go to the website, click on 'coordinating groups', then 'social welfare', then 'social welfare reviews' to access a list of topics covered.

http://www.cochrane.org/

The related healthcare site, the Cochrane Collaboration, has a much more extensive range of studies, but most of its content is not relevant to social work. If you work in healthcare, you might find useful material.

Other useful sources of research summaries are:

http://www.scie.org.uk/; http://www.iriss.org.uk/

SCIE (the Social Care Institute for Excellence) and IRISS (the Institute for Research and Innovation in Social Services) are the two main UK bodies disseminating knowledge and information about social work and its practice. Both websites contain extensive resources, including videos.

SCIE provides Social Care Online, an extensive searchable database of publications on social care and social work: http://www.scie-socialcareonline.org.uk/default.asp. You can register to receive listings of new publications in areas you are interested in.

http://www.rip.org.uk/

Research in practice (RIP) (on work with children and families).

http://www.ripfa.org.uk/

Research in Practice for Adults (RIPFA).

Connecting theory and practice

3

Main contribution

This chapter aims to help practitioners with building connections between theory and practice so that they can feel confident in enabling the interaction between theoretical ideas and practice.

Main points

- Generalizing about our practice by building theory helps practitioners to achieve consistency and accountability.
- Connections between theory and practice are not linear processes of deduction and induction, but complex responses to current ideas and social needs: even stimulating ideas may be difficult to use as guidelines for practice.
- We often need to adapt and transfer theories between different settings, cultures and specialisms.
- Critical reflection and its components offer structured ways of working on theory–practice connections.

Practice ideas

- *Learning transfer* needs to occur between practice cultures, settings, specialisms and theories.
- *Process knowledge* about how practitioners make decisions and judgements, working through various stages of practice, helps when making theoretical decisions in practice.
- *Use of self* and *emotional intelligence* help turn theory into action
- Reflection, reflexivity, critical thinking and *critical reflection* are ways of making connections between theory and practice.

Major statements

Connecting theory and practice is an arena that sees perennial conflicts between the interests of agencies, education and practitioners in social work (Smid and van Krieken, 1984). From the 1970s onwards, after the end of the post-Second-World-War period of increasing prosperity in the West, agencies began to assert greater managerial control over using knowledge in practice, an issue that had, until then, mainly remained in the academic sphere (Payne, 1991). You could see the debate about evidence-based practice (EBP) (see Chapter 2) as an attempt to reassert academic knowledge as the main source of knowledge for practice.

Education and ideas in social science had escalated the theoretical debate from the 1960s onwards, leading to the proliferation of social work theories examined in Chapter 2. This plurality of theories led to attempts to distinguish between them, focusing on competing political belief systems in the 'theory wars' between 1970 and 1990. Historical tensions in social work between a focus on 'clinical' and 'social' ideas mirrored the conflict between the Western and communist political systems that was playing out at that time. But many practitioners sought a more eclectic practice that incorporated both perspectives in theoretical developments, often using systems theory.

During the same period, Schön's work (1983) developed techniques emphasizing reflection when responding to complexity and variability in interpersonal practice in many professions. Fook and Gardner (2007) built up a major model using these and related ideas in their handbook on critical reflection, which represents the most significant current stream of thinking.

Why do we use theory in a practical activity?

Picking up the argument I made in Chapter 1 about how theory is useful, this chapter focuses on how we make it useful. We saw in Chapter 1 that many practitioners see social work as a practical activity, something that we do, and theory as different, something that we think and talk about. But many writers, recently for example Gray and Webb (2013: 4), assert that we cannot separate theory and practice in everyday life or in social work.

Smith (2007) argues that having a body of theory offers normative generalization; normative means that the generalizations include or assume the values that we aim for in our practice. He suggests that because the generalizations that theory offers include values, it is easier to make fine distinctions than crude political judgements, to connect personal identities with policy debate and to avoid quick fixes just aiming for the obvious positive results. Generalization also allows us a broad strategy into which we can fit more detailed everyday practices. Most of the time, we take the everyday prescriptions of a theory for granted.

Example *The theory of making tea*

If you want to make a cup of tea, you pour boiling water onto tea leaves. You may remember school lessons that only water at around 100°C works. You cannot make tea on a mountain or on an aeroplane because physics tells us that water boils at a lower temperature if the air pressure is reduced. But, for most general purposes, all you need to know is how to do it. The theory is there but you don't need it to live your everyday life, although professional tea graders or tasters need a detailed awareness of the theory to do their job.

But to practise social work you need to have a good understanding of how it works; we saw in Chapter 1 that this is what practice theory tries to offer. For everyday purposes, automatic pilot will do, but we and the human beings we are working with are complicated beings in complex social relationships. To make social work's difficult decisions, therefore, theory gives us an organized system for deciding on actions to take.

Pause and reflect *How might generalizations help us?*

Make a few notes about how generalizations might help with understanding complex human lives.

Some suggestions

Complex people – ourselves and our clients – and complex situations in a complex society lead to many variations in how things work. Consequently, we will need to respond with a variety of different kinds of interventions. Generalizations help us to classify situations and interventions.

Generalizing through theory helps us to:

- be consistent and well-organized in what we are doing;
- align our work with the best-informed systematic guidance – in Chapter 2, we discussed the debate about how far this should be based on empirical research;
- explain what we are doing to clients and get their informed consent to interventions;
- explain what we are doing to our managers, our colleagues in other professions, the public, policy-makers and politicians. All have an interest in the value and quality of our practice.

Spong (2007) focuses on the importance of scepticism and belief as part of the relationship between theory and practice. Scepticism is important because it reduces tendencies to:

- use authoritarian forms of practice;
- use expert knowledge to assert authority over clients.

Thus, scepticism is a crucial part of the shared value principles of practice. Social construction theory is sceptical that there is any one 'true' representation of reality. It proposes that, rather than being a 'true believer' in one theory, we acknowledge the uncertainty inherent in the range of ideas that are available (Spong, 2007). This view suggests that theory instead helps to provide metaphors for what is happening in people's lives and pictures of the possibilities that are open to them. It provides an explanatory system for clients to believe in.

We saw in Chapter 1 that many people have difficulty with using ideas to influence how they do things. As adults, we have a good deal of experience of human interaction, so we do not come completely new to social work. We know how we meet other people; we have worked out practical ways of understanding what other people are thinking and feeling, the 'informal theories' of Chapter 1. Once we start doing social work, we find ways of working, often adapting to the specific work patterns we see around us. How are you supposed to fit a formal theory into that?

People sometimes talk about the application of theory to practice. In Chapter 1, I argued this does not, however, happen in that way in social work. Clients and practitioners meet together in agencies and have an impact on each other. Other arenas of political and social life also have an influence, often through what social workers, clients and agencies bring to the interaction. Therefore it is more accurate to see theory and practice as acting in a mutual process in which each has an influence on the other.

If using theory is important for these reasons, we have to have ways of working with it. This chapter reviews some of the ideas about working with theory and connecting theory and practice that have been used in social work to help with this.

> **Pause and reflect** *How are theory and practice different?*
>
> Make some notes on your thoughts on and typical reactions to both theory and practice, on the connection between doing and thinking. Is thinking something you like to do? Or do you prefer to get on with what needs to be done? In what ways do you think about what you do? When you do things, how does this affect your thinking? What makes something a practice and something a theory? What connections and disconnections do you experience between theory and practice? Do you find yourself using theory when you are doing something? Is theory relevant to a practice at all? Try sharing your views with others and finding out how much people agree or have a different take on the connection between theory and practice.

Some suggestions

Here are some thoughts I have. I find some ideas really attractive. Concepts like empowerment, flexibility and resilience stimulate and interest me and might be relevant to how I do social work. But when I look at them, I see that the words need filling out and that complications need exploring. I often find it hard to follow detailed discussions about philosophies and ideas; I want to see them put into practice. This is for two reasons. One is that I want to see whether the people who are using these ideas can connect them with the real world in a way that helps me to understand them. The other is that if I am going to use them, I need to turn them into practical actions.

Thinking beyond our own feelings, research shows that many people come into social work with aspirations to 'make a difference', 'change the world' or 'help people'. Hindmarsh (1992), who studied twenty-two new graduates of social work in New Zealand and summarized much of the world literature, argued that a sense of opposition to the status quo motivated a large number of people's decisions to enter social work; we should try to help things 'get better'. Through helping others and supporting social change, these people aimed to act on this feeling of opposition.

With such aspirations, the motivation and fascination that we sometimes get from theoretical concepts can lose their enchantment. Talking about ideas might lead to time-wasting, difficult-to-understand theoretical debates. Secker's (1993) study found that most students using social work theory had great difficulty in connecting it to practice. They kept finding conflicts between different theories and were unable to make connections between the academic theory they were taught and informal sources of theory. Can we limit all of this theoretical detail?

One possible answer, which we met in Chapter 2, is that social work agencies give guidance, instruction and supervision to their practitioners based on their policies, their social role and a systematic review of the evidence that is relevant to their work. This makes it clear what practitioners' aims and role should be. Practitioners receive training in refining and using interpersonal skills from their professional education. Agency mandate and policy plus your own skills guide you in how to carry out the tasks for which you are employed. Why bother with theory, then? In reality, practitioners may sometimes find that agencies, through their formal management systems, create barriers that restrict social workers' confidence in putting their professional identity into practice. As a result, social workers become alienated and isolated. In this sense, how we experience agencies can play out the oppositions we see in the world, the very ones that social workers are setting out to resolve. In such situations, Hindmarsh (1992) suggests that social work education, including theory, gives practitioners confidence, self-awareness and a framework of practice and identity as a practitioner. Theory, then, can help us to stay on course and achieve some of our aspirations to change the world.

Beckett (2006: 189) identifies four important ways to liberate the idea of social work from that of purely a sort of technical activity that you can learn from guidelines:

- It deals with inherently uncertain situations …
- which are also unique …
- to which each practitioner brings different skills and orientations …
- and which generate value questions as well as knowledge questions.

These are very similar points to the criticism of using research through EBP that we met in Chapter 2.

Plurality (Borden, 2010a) is another difficulty. It may seem good to have the large range of theories we found in Chapter 2 available to use, but the variety competes, conflicts and confuses. There seems to be endless circular criticism and debate about the minor elements of one theory or another. How do you, and indeed why should you have to, choose between them or work with your team and agency at combining them?

I started this section by asserting that theory and practice are inseparable. But achieving this is easier said than done, and it can be hard to turn an idea into practice. A concept such as empowerment, for example, can set a general direction for actions that you might choose to take. To create a generalizable practice theory from this concept, however, a practitioner would have to use different views of what empowerment might mean in many different situations. It is not surprising that books about practice theories are so general as to be of no practical use, or so detailed that practitioners cannot remember all the elements they have to consider.

This chapter suggests three possible ways in which social workers can deal with these complexities:

- by understanding theory–practice connections, to see how theory and practice influence each other;
- by selecting from, combining and adapting aspects of different theories – the eclecticism referred to in Chapter 2 – to help practitioners deal with plurality;
- by using critical reflection techniques to help them apply ideas creatively to practice situations.

The next section deals in turn with each of these approaches to using theory and practice together.

Practice approaches to using theory

The development of connections between theory and practice

We may see the connections between theory and practice in different ways. Figure 3.1 presents some ideas as diagrams; I have adapted and developed the main points from Carr (1986). I ask, in each case: 'does this happen?'

Figure 3.1 looks at deductive and inductive processes of theory development. We met these ideas in Chapter 1, and they suggest that generalized theory connects to a practice theory, which then connects to practice itself.

Deductive processes suggest that practice theory comes from general social ideas, that is, from the 'top', the political–social–ideological arena (see Figure 1.8). Suitable ideas are turned into practice theories, which are tested out in practice. Research through EBP or accumulated practice experience tell us 'what works'. Ideas that have worked in practice gain support; failed theories are rejected.

Inductive processes propose the opposite – that ideas for practice theory come out of practitioners' daily experience, from the 'bottom', the client–social-worker–agency arena, and are then transferred 'up'. Research and professional debate test these out, confirming what works, and help to formulate them into theories. These might then in turn influence general social ideas. Not every practice idea makes it all the way to general social influence, although if a social work practice becomes widely used, it is likely to become known about and influential when services are designed. In addition, not every general social idea extends to being useful and effective in practice, even though some practitioners might find them interesting.

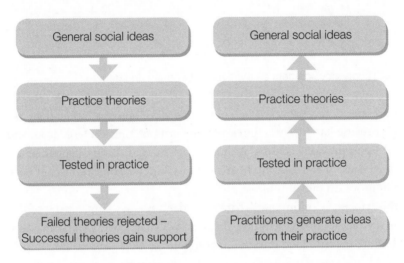

Figure 3.1a Top-down (deductive) and bottom-up (inductive) theory development

Does this happen? The accounts of social work theories in Part 2 suggest that the main approach is deductive: theories in psychology, sociology and broad political and social philosophies inform most practice theories, and their originators draw on social work experience to interpret these ideas for practice use. The problem with this top-down approach is that theories are not designed with social work in mind. General ideas are interpreted and turned into guidelines in the agency–professional arena but these often fail to produce a useable approach. As a result, practice theories are often just aspirations or ideals, rather than offering concrete guidance. Another problem is that their guidance for practice and the research testing of their effectiveness may have been done in an academic or psychotherapy setting, which may not transfer to a social work agency.

Figure 3.1b sees theory and practice as being involved in a continuing process of enquiry and debate. Concerns emerge about social problems, what they are and why it is important to respond to them. These concerns may come from experience or research. As concerns emerge, people make proposals about action – what we should do about these concerns. The discourse here may take place in all the arenas, each having some influence. A debate takes place and refines understanding of the problems and the proposals, and people devise interventions that might help us to take action. These are then taken up and tried out in practice experience and research. The outcomes of this experience and research are articulated and then debated. These further debates identify useful outcomes, problems and then further interventions, which then also go through the testing and experience process.

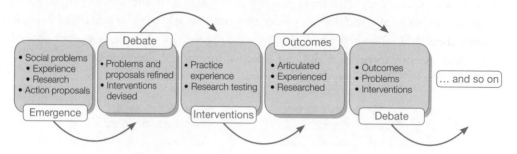

Figure 3.1b Theory development as a process of enquiry and debate

I have presented this process as a continuing development rather than as a circular one. This is because later debates, interventions and outcomes emerge from and progressively build upon previous actions. Although debate and testing happen at every stage, we do not go back to the drawing board with each new problem; instead we constantly build and improve on previous ideas.

Does this happen? Continuing debate and adaptation is characteristic of the development of many of the longer standing theories, which we will look at in more detail in Part 2. Ideas are incorporated into the mainstream, or they seem to lose importance and are replaced by renewed ideas. For example, the emphasis in psychodynamic theory started from a debate between diagnostic and functional ideas, formed a psychosocial model and then shifted towards attachment and relational ideas. Behavioural practice has incorporated cognitive elements. Radical theory shifted away from Marxism; there was a period of doubt and then a move towards critical ideas.

Among the concerns about seeing theory–practice connections in this way are that theory, instead of providing secure guidance, is an always-shifting progression of changes. Nothing about theory is ever decided, and the use of theory seems to be about constantly renewing fads and enthusiasms, rather than about clear systematic professional guidance for practice (Howe, 2009). On the other hand, this model realistically sees social work responding and constantly renewing as social life and ideas change.

Figure 3.1c takes up this idea that theoretical development progresses. It sees theory and practice as interacting in a 'bottom-up' process. In this model, as practice experience accumulates, it is articulated and refined using theoretical ideas and tested through research. The theory is refined by further tested experience and may incorporate further theoretical ideas; these are then in their turn further tested and refined. And so the process continues.

Does this happen? This model recognizes a reality of social work development since the 1960s – that experience and theories interact with each other, and useful ideas are borrowed from other lines of development. What may have been a practice theory with a clear ideological or research base becomes adapted to include elements of other theories. Eventually, the theory as people practise it becomes an amorphous collection of ideas whose origins are hard to disentangle. This enables practitioners to use a wide variety of theoretical ideas, but theories used in this way seem to offer no clear direction.

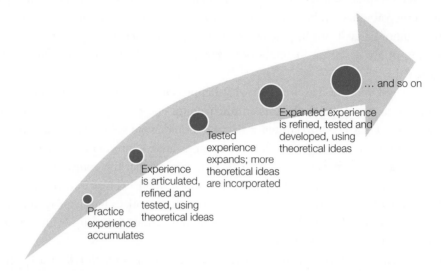

Figure 3.1c Theory development as a process of accumulation

Taking the above point further, Figure 3.1d presents a model which accepts that practice ideas come from a variety of sources: research, practice experience and theoretical ideas. Because most social work is practised in agencies, these ideas need to be incorporated into a practice that is sanctioned by agencies. Agency practice often limits or adapts how theory is implemented, and this constrains how we can use practice theory. Once agencies recognize constraints on the ideas, experience and research that formed a theory, developments may occur in the theory to make it more relevant. These constraints sometimes mean that the theory cannot be used in the reality of agency practice, and the theory loses influence.

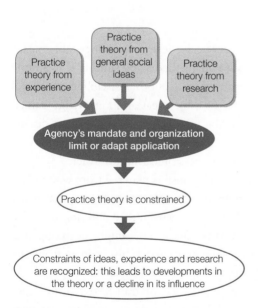

Figure 3.1d Practice constraints as a degradation or limitation of theoretical development

Does this happen? This model recognizes another reality of social work development: that people like the ideas of a particular theory, but find their agency a hostile environment in which to practise these ideas. They feel constrained, rather than enabled, by the agency's responsibilities, and come to reject an apparently attractive theory because they find they cannot carry it out in practice, or they feel that agency constraints are part of their feeling of always being in opposition; Hindmarsh's (1992) research showed that this happened.

Induction and deduction aspire to fit what happens in social work theory and practice into a logical model in which there is an unchanging end-point: a theory or a practice that is accepted. Hearn (1982) contends that we should avoid seeing theory and practice as two ends of a dumb-bell, but rather see them as always intertwined and relating to each other in a variety of ways. The other models suggest that the connections between theory and practice are complex and continuing. Harrison (1991), an American studying British social workers, found that they did not experience work as highly programmed or ordered but as a 'seamless integration of thought and action' following from their own typical way of thinking things through.

Any approach to theory–practice connections needs, therefore, to reflect a variety of interests: research, practice, agency management and social work education. These interests interact all the time and are constantly adapting theory and practice in relation to each other.

Rather than seeking connections between theory and practice, it may, however, be more helpful to practitioners to examine how they use ideas to think about the situations they face in practice and who influences that thinking.

Adapting and transferring theory

We saw in Chapter 2 that most social workers practise eclectically, which inevitably means adapting theory. There are other ways in which we adapt theory: by shifting it from one setting or client group to another, or by transferring it from another discipline into social work. Transfer of learning is about the possibility of using ideas and knowledge gained from one area of practice in another (Cree and Macaulay, 2000). People often discuss transferring ideas from one country or culture to another, which all needs adaptations and changes to organizational requirements in the process of learning transfer.

One situation in which social work theory adapts or transfers material from wider ideas arises when ideas become incorporated into a general approach to social work that many practitioners use. For example, most social work is fairly open-minded and non-directive towards clients. There are practical reasons for this because clients might not cooperate with someone who was too directive. But this general approach also comes from the long-standing influence of psychodynamic theory (Chapter 4) on social work.

A second common situation in which theory is adapted or transferred from wider ideas arises when a theory is relevant to and applied in specialized settings. The particular perspective and its wider theory then become more important in what the worker does in that setting than it is in general social work. We saw in a case study in Chapter 2 how influential attachment theory (discussed in Chapter 4) was on work with children.

Social work occasionally develops its own theories independently; task-centred work is an example of this. More commonly, however, social work theories select from, embroider and develop ideas from other academic and professional fields. Accreting theory in this way means that social work ideas connect to and originally came from wider bodies of knowledge and theory, and may, in turn, contribute to those wider bodies. For example, feminist theory has been significant in social work, and studies in social welfare and policy have influenced the wider feminist debate. Social work adaptations may, however, become decoupled from developments in the main body of the original theory. Thus, social work's distinctive view of a theory has the same view of the world and may share some of the same original literature with the external body of literature. Some influence may continue in either direction, but the connections are usually relatively sparse for workers in everyday practice.

A practitioner in a women's refuge, for example, might be closely in touch with and committed to feminist theory. A practitioner in a therapeutic community for mentally ill people might be in touch with aspects of psychoanalytic theory on groups and institutions. Practitioners in an acute psychiatric unit might be actively involved in cognitive-behavioural treatment. These specialist settings may then have an influence on social work more directly than the wider bodies of ideas do. Social work theory is therefore often at some distance in time and interpretation from ideas in wider theoretical debate.

One way of adapting theory is to shift between different theories as your work moves through different phases. Pružinská (2011) studied 461 Slovakian social workers working in a general government agency. They emphasized different theoretical models at different stages in the social work process. For example, they used a humanistic, open, non-directive approach at the assessment stage, but more structured cognitive-behavioural approaches when attempting behaviour change. Another important adaptation was to truncate the full use of procedures or stages of intervention because agency pressures meant that they did not have enough time to work through every stage. Pružinská also found that the social workers' overall view of social work influenced and adapted how they used particular models. The following case example shows this at work.

Case example: Maintaining coherence while using different theoretical models at different stages

A social worker helping families care for their children saw practice humanistically and presented her social work task to a female client and her family as a shared developmental process. However, later on, when introducing cognitive-behavioural work to improve skills in communication and organization in the family, the practitioner discussed this as a separate stage in the sharing process rather than as a social learning or behaviour change technique. She felt this maintained a coherence throughout the process of her work with the client, while allowing her to draw on different techniques when they were most appropriate.

This book focuses on social work theory used in non-specialist social work. Wider bodies of theory may have no direct or influential relationship with the usual use of the related social work theory. Workers in specialist agencies that have particular theoretical directions develop a greater knowledge of and commitment to that theory than the average worker in general social work. Details of theories used in depth in a specialist setting cannot always be entwined with opposing distinctions or concepts in a more general social work practice, but we can often learn from them. Dual process theory (Stroebe and Schut, 1999), for example, does not have an equivalent in general social work, being concerned with ambivalent reactions after the death of a loved one. The idea that distressed people shift between alternative and incompatible reactions to a life event is a generalization of the idea, and this may help us to understand ambivalent reactions in other settings.

Wider bodies of understanding affect general social work theories by their direct use, without being adapted into full-scale social work practice theories. For example, Gray and Webb's (2013) edited collection examines a range of social theories that have not been adapted into social work practice theories. Ideas from wider bodies of thought may contribute to adapting practice theory by helping to explore a situation or find a useful perspective.

Debates and conflicts, for example mutual criticism between clinical and social change theories, also exist within social work. Understanding the points made in criticizing a theory can help us decide what aspects of it to include or exclude from an eclectic general theory that we use in practice.

Process knowledge about the way in which practitioners make decisions and judgements helps when making theoretical decisions in practice. Dealing with a problem in our lives usually involves working through a series of stages. This sees social work as a process – a series of actions and the factors affecting them that go towards making or achieving something (Payne, 2009b: 161). Instead of seeing ourselves as dealing with a succession of one-off events, we connect interactions over a period of time with clients, identifying a structure and organization in what we are doing together. This is how we come to see the different events as part of a whole that leads to an outcome. One of the helpful things about many social work theories is that they help us to identify stages in what can otherwise seem to be a confusing progression of events.

Sheppard et al. (2000; Sheppard and Ryan, 2003) report empirical studies in which practitioners pursued two processes: critical appraisal of the situation and then hypothesis generation, which allowed them to work out ways of intervening. Figure 3.2 illustrates the processes that Sheppard et al. identify.

Critical appraisal included focusing attention on particular issues that clients faced, querying information that the practitioner received, not taking it for granted and following this up by making causal inferences about what was going on in a case. All this enabled practitioners to make sense of clients' situations. The hypotheses that the practitioners used were of three kinds. Partial hypotheses were limited to particular aspects of the case. Whole-case hypotheses tried to analyse the total situation that the client and practitioner faced. Speculative hypotheses involved practitioners in thinking out which interventions and legal or administrative procedures might be required. They then created rules of action based on their assessment of the problem and their legal and professional mandate, which gave them guidelines to follow as they worked with clients and other agencies. Social work theories offer generalized forms of such guidelines to act on.

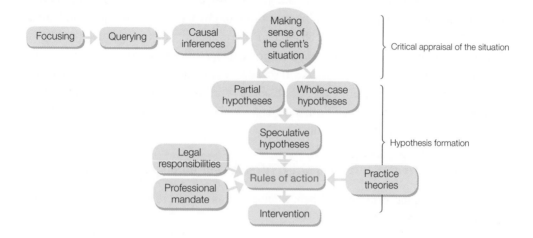

Figure 3.2 Sheppard et al.'s process knowledge
Source: Sheppard et al.(2000) and Sheppard and Ryan (2003).

Many practitioners, however, find it hard to make a generalized theory personal enough for them to be able to carry it out. Howe (2009: 170) points up the 'use of self' as an important skill that helps to turn guidelines into action. Your own life experience can contribute to the process of working with your client. For this to happen, you have to be self-aware – to be able to think about both the best and weak aspects of how you deal with problems.

Case example: Carrie's fear of crying focuses her use of self

Carrie works with children; she had to visit a couple she was working with whose three-month-old baby had died in an accident. They were very upset and, as a person who experienced strong emotions herself, she feared that she would break down and cry when listening to them talking about what had happened. Her supervisor said that expressing emotion like this was unprofessional; she had to be strong to support the parents.

A colleague talked through with Carrie how she would handle it. Together they looked at her beliefs about social work practice and her personality. She realized that, to her, being genuine in how she reacted to clients' experiences was an important social work value.

Many social workers would agree, and it is a major feature of humanistic practice (see Chapter 10). She also questioned whether expressing emotion would weaken the support she could give to the parents. Sharing their emotions would, she thought, strengthen their relationship and allow her to offer greater support because they would all feel closer in their relationship. After this discussion, Carrie resolved to meet the parents and express her emotions as they affected her at the time. In fact, she did not cry, because she was concentrating so hard on listening and discussing the parents' reactions that she did not need to express her own feelings. That happened later, talking it through with her husband.

There are several important points about this case example. First, it shows how an awareness of self, that is, knowing how you might react to a situation, enables you to anticipate potential problems and manage them appropriately. Second, Carrie did not take for granted simply one way of thinking about the process of this planned interview. Instead, she looked at how expressing emotions might have both strengths and weaknesses. As we will see later in this chapter in more detail, 'not taking for granted' and 'looking at different possibilities' is an important part of being critical when you are reflecting about the right action to take in social work practice. I identified this in Chapter 1 as an important 'shared principle' of all social work practice theory. Third, this is an example of supervision in which both a manager and her peers contributed to help Carrie practise effectively and think critically.

Pause and reflect *Repressing or expressing your emotions in practice*

Do you think good professional behaviour requires you to repress or express your emotions when working with clients?

Some suggestions

To show clients your sincerity in your relationship with them, you often need to express the powerful emotions you feel when working with them. It may sometimes be indulgent, however, to express your emotions. Ask yourself whether you might be showing off what a 'feeling person' you are, perhaps overreacting rather than reacting genuinely. In addition, some people find emotional expression embarrassing, or it makes them feel that you are weak or unhelpful. Sometimes, therefore, we have to manage our emotional expression to behave in ways that best help people feel comfortable working with us.

So, social workers can usefully both experience and express their emotions in ways that allow them to manage their emotional reactions and also allow their clients to experience their emotional reactions as helpful. Howe (2008) connects the use of self with the idea of 'emotional intelligence', which he suggests is an important characteristic of good social workers. Goleman (1996) identified the importance of emotional intelligence in parenting and many other social situations. This comprises an interaction between:

- self-awareness and self-management (intrapersonal intelligence);
- awareness of others and the capacity to manage relationships with others (interpersonal intelligence) (Morrison 2007: 251).

People with emotional intelligence have developed skills in perceiving and identifying feelings in others. They integrate emotions with thinking to improve their capacity to access and manage their own and other people's feelings. Social workers who have developed emotional intelligence are likely to be better able to engage with others, carry out social work assessments, make decisions and collaborate with others. As professionals, they are likely to be better able to deal with stress, build resilience to adversity and cope better with difficulties in their practice (Morrison, 2007). Howe (2008) argues that emotional intelligence permits practitioners to move from observing and monitoring their own and their clients' behaviour towards managing the environment around them.

This section explored a number of different ways in which practitioners adapt theory as they use it:

- transfer of learning about a theory between disciplines, cultures and specialisms;
- adapting theories as you work through different phases of work in a case;
- using specialist theories that align with those of colleagues from other professions;
- using ideas from wider bodies of theory;
- understanding critiques by looking at the debates among theories;
- using process knowledge to make better adaptations between theory and practice;
- understanding the use of self and emotional intelligence in using practice theory.

Reflection, reflexivity and critical thinking

Contemporary thinking about the best ways to use our self as part of the social work process, incorporating and contributing to theory as we do so, focuses on a set of related ideas:

- reflection
- reflexivity
- critical thinking
- critical reflection.

In this section, I separate out these ideas to explain the differences and connections between them and how they are used in social work.

Reflection – what is it?

Reflection describes what a mirror does. When you look in a mirror, it 'turns back' (re-flects) an image, giving a picture of things, people and events that are happening within the scope of its surface. That image usually includes you, the observer who is looking, unless you stand to the side so that you are out of sight, and it is always an image, not the reality, of the scene. For example, reflected images are always inverted, so we never see a completely accurate picture. Perhaps you have had the experience of picking up a hairbrush while looking in a mirror, and starting to brush on the wrong side, because you have not compensated for the inversion. So, although it is not without its difficulties, the image nevertheless helps us to see, evaluate and react to ourselves and our surroundings. It helps us with the use of self.

The idea of reflection has been used in a stream of writing to help professional practitioners plan and conduct their work with a greater understanding of the situations they are facing. Some of that writing also claims that reflection helps to develop practice theories for professionals: they use the ideas inspired by reflecting on particular incidents to adapt existing theories or create new ones. Beckett (2006: 190) suggests that reflective practice is helpful to:

■ test out theoretical ideas and research findings against your own experience;
■ clarify the theoretical ideas behind your actions;
■ challenge your assumptions;
■ challenge your agency's assumptions;
■ generate feedback between you, your colleagues and your clients.

Most writers see reflection as a more or less complicated circular process. Jasper's easy to remember 'ERA' – experience–reflection–action – summarizes the main points (Figure 3.3): you have an experience, you reflect upon it and this changes the way you act in the future.

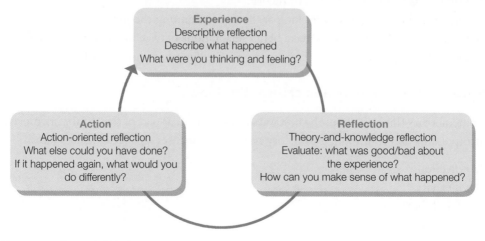

Figure 3.3 The reflection process
Source: Jasper (2003) with additions.

I have also added some points from other writers to Figure 3.3. Borton's (1970) reflective framework suggests that you reflect upon different aspects of the situation at each stage: description, theory-and-knowledge and action reflection. This makes it clear that reflection is more than the thinking-about-it phase – you should pay attention to the whole process. Gibbs's (1988) reflective cycle details the actions associated with each stage. When you are experiencing the events, your reflection is descriptive: you describe what happened and unearth how your thoughts and feelings reacted at the time. Moving on to the reflection stage, you bring your theory and knowledge to bear. This allows you to evaluate the experience and decide what was good or bad about it, what went well and what led to problems. At this stage, you are trying to make sense of what happened. At the third stage, your reflection shifts towards action. Does your 'making-sense' reflection suggest others ways in which you could have acted? In turn, does this help you to plan to do something different next time something like this happens?

Most agree that active use of the idea of reflection in social work originated from the work of Argyris and Schön (1974; Schön, 1983, 1987). Schön was an educationalist, Argyris an organizational sociologist, so they focused on different ways of using reflection. Schön was mainly interested in training professionals to develop and use knowledge by being more thoughtful about their practice, while Argyris was more concerned about how people adjusted to the pressures of working in complex organizations. Both of these issues are important to social workers.

However, Redmond (2006) shows that reflection has a longer history, in particular citing Dewey (1933), the American philosopher of education, who also influenced social work through his impact on pragmatic philosophy, problem-solving and task-centred practice. Dewey distinguished trial and error experiments from reflection. Experiments, in his view, simply told you what worked, while reflection was a creative process that produced new ideas (Redmond, 2006: 10). The reflection is crucial to learning from experience or from research, because it enables you to reconstruct or reorganize the experience in a useful manner.

Reflection approaches have been widely used and systematically developed in teaching education and have subsequently influenced nursing and social work. The argument for reflection as a practice in these professions is that it:

- recognizes and values human relations as a special feature of practice in those professions;
- proposes a way of developing generalized theory from practice.

Gardner (2003) developed a mode of critical reflection in community work situations, which helps us do the same thing when we are working with collectives as well as when we are working with individuals:

- seeking subjective histories and narratives from the people involved;
- making sure that those least likely to be heard are included;
- enabling participants to make connections between broader structural issues and their personal experience, which is a feminist approach;
- paying attention to processes as well as outcomes.

Reflection: debates

Debates about reflection connect with the literature that we met in Chapters 1 and 2 which contrasts interpretivist and social construction views with positivist views of knowledge. Proponents of reflection try to describe realistically how professionals use knowledge in working with people. They argue that 'people-work' has a different character from work with natural substances, such as engineering, so it requires a different kind of knowledge used in different ways. Professions such as engineering use 'technical rationality'. Natural substances, as opposed to human beings, always perform in the same way, provided there are similar conditions. For example, water always runs down to find the lowest point, although in cold conditions it freezes and loses this characteristic. But given the same conditions, you can always predict what water will do. Working with human beings is not predictable in the same way. Even so, some professionals who work with human beings can operate in technical-rational ways. This is because some aspects of their practice also use natural substances. For example, doctors use medication, which has predictable effects on the human body. These ways of using knowledge are technical-rational applications of knowledge.

However, the communication aspect of medicine – interacting with people, a characteristic also found in other caring professions such as social work, nursing, teaching and similar professions – uses knowledge in a more flexible way. Argyris and Schön suggest that workers using this kind of knowledge have guidelines for good practice and use these to carry out their work in a practical way. When they come across a new situation, they try 'practical experiments', new ways of working, which then adapt the guidelines. Education for such professions involves helping people to identify when a new situation has arisen and how to develop new guidelines using practical experimentation. Reflective practice involves more than carefully thinking things through and taking all aspects of the situation into account (Payne, 2009c). It implies doing this in a structured system, like that described in Figure 3.3, either while we are taking part in the situation (Schön calls this 'reflection-in-action') or as a learning or review technique to improve future practice after the event ('reflection-on-action').

Writers on reflection call upon a range of ideas. Mezirow (1981) draws on the work of the German philosopher Habermas (1986 [1971]), who identified three different ways of understanding the world around us: technical, practical and emancipatory. Each of these has a different approach to research and education that influences different cultures and ways of thinking within a society; these ideas extend the discussion of knowledge, theory and EBP that we explored in Chapters 1 and 2.

Habermas (1986 [1971]) says that technical knowledge is based on empirical research into observable events, governed by technical rules that tell us whether or not something was correct; Chapter 1 referred to these as 'accepted scientific processes'. Research in such fields is an 'instrumental action': when we have identified what is true, this allows us to plan our actions so that we can achieve our aims. So knowledge becomes an instrument in our planning towards achieving our objectives. EBP sees knowledge in this way. Practical knowledge is based on a systematic investigation into different points of view about the meaning and importance what is happening around us. Research in practical knowledge involves 'communicative action', in which different points of view are argued out to a conclusion, which in turn allows us to interpret the world around us. Emancipatory knowledge allows us to take both technical and practical knowledge further. By examining the different points of view that emerge through exploring practical knowledge, we can free ourselves, through self-reflection, from the limitations of the assumptions about any particular point of view. If we can achieve this transformation in ideas, we can understand and avoid or reduce the effect of forces that create barriers in achieving what we want to do. I discuss other aspects of Habermas's contribution to social work in Chapters 11 and 12.

Mezirow (1991) goes on to argue that adult education has a role in 'perspective transformation', so that people may become more conscious of barriers to achieving their personal aims. This, in turn, connects with the work of Freire (1972), who argues for conscientization (consciousness-raising in feminist theory) as an important objective in adult education and community work because people cannot develop themselves until they become aware of social barriers to change; I look at his work more fully in Chapters 11 and 12. Brookfield (1990) picks up something of the organizational perspective introduced by Argyris in emphasizing the need to create a learning environment in which reflection can take place successfully.

Example *Knowledge and prevention in child welfare services*

An example of these different forms of knowledge can be found in Murphy's (2009) study of preventive child welfare in Ireland. Her analysis of the history of ideas about prevention connects with the history of social work in several Western countries. The idea of prevention as an objective in social work grew out of the success of public health interventions in preventing disease. Family support services in social work were seen as a way of preventing children from coming into state care. This is an instrumental use of knowledge: services plan to use social work as an instrument to improve family functioning and achieve the pragmatic objective of reducing the number of children cared for by the state.

At the same time, radical social work raised the possibility of stimulating employment, reducing poverty, improving education, healthcare and housing and providing community development. If you did this, families and children would have fewer pressures on their lives and more resources to respond to difficulties in their communities. This is an example of practical knowledge. Different ways of dealing with the families' and children's problems in deprived communities were set against each other, debated and to some extent brought together. This was done by providing professional family support services in community settings with considerable local participation in community development. US experience of similar debates and developments leading to Head Start, the 1960s' poverty programme for deprived children that is the source of later developments, such as the Sure Start programme of the early twenty-first century in the UK and other local initiatives to support children's early development in urban communities, followed a similar track.

However, political differences about the value of these approaches, research evidence about their effectiveness and economic change from the 1980s in many advanced countries reduced the resources available for public services. This led to a tightening of focus, so that prevention became focused on preventing child neglect and abuse. These aims displaced broader positive objectives seeking children's, community and family support and empowerment. Emancipatory knowledge identifies different interpretations of prevention that exist in debates about preventive services. Without resolving these different interpretations, we cannot use any technical research knowledge to achieve preventive objectives, so we have to decide on our aims first. Murphy points to the importance of cultural ideas about families. 'Familism' policies, for example, marginalize children because they emphasize adult relationships within the family role to support employment, housing and economic policies.

It is not easy to develop reflective practice. Goodman (1984, cited by Jasper, 2003) suggests that people's reflective skills develop through three stages:

- reflection to achieve specific objectives, such as fitting in with the practices and policies of the agency;
- reflection on the relationship between principles and practice: theory–practice connections;
- reflection to incorporate ethical and political concerns, which might be particularly relevant to critical and feminist practice but includes concerns for the underlying politics of all theories.

Cultural ideas sometimes reflect the views of different minority ethnic groups. The following case example shows how different cultural interpretations of the nature of the problem presented problems in providing appropriate help.

Case example: Chinese and Western views of mental illness

Mr and Mrs Ho were a Chinese couple living with their daughter in a large Western town. Their daughter developed anorexia because of stresses and bullying at school. Her parents were most upset when this was referred to a mental health service by the school. They said that their culture regarded mental illness as a matter of shame for the family and refused to participate in their daughter's treatment. Their doctor therefore referred the daughter to a young person's advisory service, whose social worker focused on developing family support for improving the daughter's relationships at school. Removing the focus on psychological problems was satisfactory for the family.

There are, however, criticisms of reflection approaches. First, they may assume that we can respond effectively to every variation in the situations that we deal with by simply changing the existing guidelines for action. Second, even if we could do that, reflection assumes that others will accept the changes that practitioners identify in the social order and social relationships. In both cases, more may be required. Existing agency mandates constrain practice that seeks to change the present social order, and practical experiments that conflict with existing guidelines, as we saw in discussing Figure 3.1d. Third, reflection assumes that professionals have enough discretion to carry out practical experiments, and the power to achieve the necessary changes, whereas many professional jobs are constrained by agency policies or government regulators. Fourth, reflection assumes that all problems are within the capacity of some rethinking by a professional, whereas many require additional resources.

To deal with these points, our practice has to include ways of working on situations for which wider change and additional or different resources are needed. Critical reflection (see later in the chapter) and critical theory (see Chapter 12) take up reflection and use it to seek additional human and economic resources.

Reflexivity

Reflexivity derives from qualitative research methods, particularly as applied in feminist research. It means a cyclical process in which we study how the things that we observe affect our thinking and how that then affects what we do.

Traditional research methods, as we saw in Chapter 2, assume a neutral observer looking at social situations from the outside. Critics have pointed out biases arising from the social assumptions and constructions of researchers that make neutrality impossible. Feminists, followed by researchers in disability and more generally in health and welfare and the social sciences, moved towards research methods that involved the people who were being researched more actively in the process. Ethnographic methods, in which the researcher is a participant observer in the events and situations being researched, included specific attention to how researchers were affected by their observations and how this then affected their behaviour. Feminists and disability researchers sought to develop collaborative methods in developing research objectives, carrying out research, analysing data and disseminating the results. These approaches included building interpersonal relationships with the people being researched rather than maintaining a stance as a neutral observer. Research was sometimes managed or influenced by representative groups of the people being researched. In addition, there were also developments in working as collaborators with people affected by the research (Finlay and Gough, 2003).

Fook (2012: 49) distinguishes reflexive thinking from reflective thinking, although she acknowledges that they are connected ideas. Reflexive thinking tries to understand different perspectives on a situation. Reflective thinking, however, is a process of working things through. Parton and O'Byrne (2000) describe reflexivity as a way of responding to the uniqueness of each individual. It involves thinking about both our response and the uniqueness. So, we are not being reflexive unless we try to find the uniqueness of the individuals we deal with and also respond to it. While theory enables us to generalize about issues, reflexivity picks up how individuals are affected by the issue. If we look at that individuality, we inevitably see that the theory may help us but it is not quite right in their particular case, so we adapt it.

Finlay (2003) identifies the following ways of being reflexive:

- Introspection, looking into our own mind and working out how we are thinking and why.
- Intersubjective reflection, that is, joint introspection involving the participants.
- Setting up systems for mutual collaboration, so that processes for influencing each other's thoughts are established and agreed.
- Using reflexivity as a social critique. If we say we have been working reflexively, we are implying a criticism of people who have not taken the trouble to do so.
- Using reflexivity as ironic deconstruction. Here, the process of thinking together identifies where the use of power and authority by the people involved has affected the neutrality. In this process, we begin to question taken-for-granted patterns of sharing thinking, for example a husband and wife's normal power relations.

Taylor and White (2000) discuss studies in health and social welfare that use such methods to uncover systematic behaviour that is not prescribed by practice theory. For example, they show how, in interviews, clients established their credibility, entitlement to services and 'moral adequacy' and gave their story authenticity by describing details of their actions. Such findings have implications for how to practise according to theory.

Case example: Hayley's 'crisis' questions led Soumen to defend his family's 'moral adequacy'

Hayley was working with Soumen, his wife and two pre-school children because of allegations of poor standards of care. She found that the family seemed chaotic, experiencing constant emergencies when plans for caring for the children went wrong. Crisis intervention theory suggested to Hayley that she should find out how the family coped with previous crises, to see if they had learned unhelpful coping practices. However, although she had a good relationship with Soumen, she found that he talked about how well they had managed particular situations, while his wife became silent and did not seem to connect with these past events. Soumen had interpreted Hayley's questioning as critical and wanted to assert their family's 'moral adequacy' by showing the worker how well they had managed in the past. After discussing this with her supervisor, Hayley shifted to a more narrative, strengths-based approach, emphasizing the past strengths and weaknesses of family care in a more balanced way.

Redmond's (2006) research on an educational project to develop reflective thinking with social workers and other professionals is an example of using reflexivity.

Example Reflexivity may be seen as rotating practitioners' models of the situation they are working with

Redmond's idea was that practitioners had a model in their head that evaluated clients. This model changed as the practitioners' understanding of different views in the situation were rotated by the process of the project (Figure 3.4 is my diagram showing Redmond's idea).

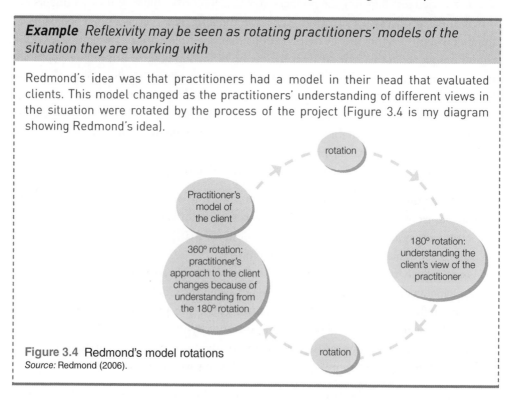

Figure 3.4 Redmond's model rotations
Source: Redmond (2006).

Working with the parents of disabled young people, for example, a practitioner's evaluation might be that a parent was 'confused' about the practitioner's role. The first stage would be to 'rotate' the practitioner's model (a 180° rotation), so that the practitioner would use the clients' words to describe practitioners; this is an example of using description as a method in the first stage of a reflection. A parent might use the words 'pushy friend' to describe the practitioner, expressing the thought that practitioners presented an impression of being friendly, but had a hidden, professional agenda. When the practitioner used this phrase, he or she could see that the apparent confusion was not just a failing in the client's perception, but had emerged from the ambiguous aims and behaviour of the practitioner. The next stage would be to rotate the practitioner's model again (a 360° rotation in total) so that the practitioner could use the understanding gained from the 180° rotation to change their behaviour. In this example, the practitioner would be open about their agenda for change alongside their supportive style. This would in turn help to remove the clients' confused behaviour.

Critical thinking

Ideas of reflexivity have been particularly applied in critical thinking on practice. The term 'critical thinking' has two meanings. One refers to the study of the logical use of language to guide thought processes, using ideas from rhetoric and logic (Bowell and Kemp, 2002). Thinking about how language is used by clients or colleagues helps us in practice by identifying the important points of clients' and colleagues' thinking.

The second meaning of 'critical thinking' refers to using reasoned thinking, questioning existing assumptions and testing them against evidence and observation. Gambrill's (2006) *Social Work Practice: A Critical Thinker's Guide* uses the term in this sense. Glaister (2008: 8) refers to 'open-minded, reflective approaches that take account of different perspectives and assumptions'. She argues that critical thinking improves our capacity to handle uncertainty and change. She presents two guiding principles: respecting others as equals and having an open approach, not taking things for granted. Her approach identifies reflexive principles as basic: forming effective relationships so that workers can incorporate multiple perspectives in their thinking, seeking to empower people by increasing their opportunities and making a difference so that the client's experience of life is better. This might involve thinking about the quality of the client's life in the round, instead of focusing on concrete tasks and objectives.

Payne et al. describe critical thinking techniques as follows:

- Examine the language used to identify hidden and untested assumptions.
- Consider different sides to any judgements or evaluations you make by reflexively putting yourself in the position of others involved.
- Question ideologies that have been used or implied; ideologies are systems of thought, often derived from political or moral principles, that have an impact on how we behave.
- Look for contradictions implied in the thinking.
- Value openness as a way of maintaining equality between participants, and including all participants in the work.

Payne et al. argue that this leads on to practical techniques:

- Examine evidence about the situation through different perspectives, thus avoiding risk and opening up opportunities.

■ Contextualize your exploration of the evidence by making explicit the value positions implied by the evidence you have chosen to use.

■ Develop an overview of the implications of the whole situation.

■ Test out your judgements and decisions with colleagues, clients and others involved before acting.

The next case example illustrates how reflexivity can help with critical thinking about your own and other people's values.

Seeing the application of the theory from a potential client's point of view helps us understand how to present our approach in a balanced or positive way. It also draws attention to possible failings in the theory. For example, one of the potential criticisms of crisis theory is that it concentrates on things that have gone wrong rather than on strengths.

Ideas such as using diaries and journals or structured questionnaires or discussion techniques to guide reflection can help people to see the events from the points of view of different participants. Critical incident analysis – selecting 'critical' or particularly significant incidents from a case or area of practice – can help to focus reflection (Fook et al., 2000; White et al., 2006: 15–16).

Case example: Henry's death and his marriage

I worked with Henry, a dying man whose relationship with his wife had become more conflictual. He blamed her behaviour for difficulties in their marriage. Reflecting, I considered possible reasons why this might be and talked over explanations with both partners. His wife thought that he was projecting some of his behaviour onto her (to use a psychoanalytic term; see Chapter 4). This means that he complained about her alleged unfaithfulness and criticized her for this because he knew she criticized his (also alleged) unfaithfulness. Their two children thought different things about their parents' behaviour and relationships. Being reflexive also meant putting these ideas into the discussions with Henry.

Thinking critically, I was aware that some of the conflict reflected changes in attitudes to what is acceptable in gender relations. Henry took it for granted that unfaithfulness is natural in a man, but not in a woman, but this double standard is no longer acceptable in contemporary attitudes. One of my aims was to get him to acknowledge changes in the social order of gender relations, so that both he and his wife could agree about the good and bad things in their marriage, and he could say 'sorry' before he died. Practice knowledge (Earnshaw Smith, 1990) tells us that dying people often think about the past and try to set things right in their relationships. For Henry, this meant looking at changing social values and thinking about setting things right with his wife according to new rather than old values, reflexively including alternative ways of looking at things.

Secker's (1993) study of social work students using theory shows how a reflexive approach may benefit practice. She found that some students were fluent in using theory because they had particular social skills. They listened well and tried to tie ideas to what clients told them. They could develop ideas, drawing on a range of different courses and making connections, rather than seeing pieces of knowledge as separate. They also discussed their ideas well with the clients concerned, so that they could test out the validity of their application. A successful use of theory requires social and interpersonal skills, and the self-confidence to discuss ideas reflexively, rather than a detailed understanding of or discussion of theory, so that clients are participating in the construction of practice. Crawford et al. (2002) used student reflection in groups with practice educators (field supervisors) to help interweave theory, practice and reflection.

All this work draws attention to the importance of involving clients, service users and members of the community as well as multiprofessional colleagues in reflection. It need not only be a professional or only a social work activity; indeed, it cannot be if it is also to be reflexive. Clients may also transfer learning from one experience to another.

Case example: Josie discusses theory openly with her clients

Josie was helping Jane, a mother whose husband's family had accused her of going out with 'other men' and leaving the children alone when he was working on a night shift. Jane denied this and counterclaimed that her husband went out drinking and did not contribute to child care responsibilities. Josie suggested to Jane that it often helped in relationships that people should not make accusations, but should instead focus on times when people did help each other and discuss together the factors that had led to that helpful time. Doing this, Josie avoided using jargon from strengths-based practice, but explained something practical that Jane and her husband could do. She agreed to come back for a joint session using this way of looking at a problem and, in later meetings with Jane and her husband, got them to try out this approach at least once each week and then discuss it with Josie afterwards. This gave them positive actions to focus on, which reflected existing successes in their relationship. The promise of later discussion meant that they knew there would be a review of whether they had completed their 'homework', and this put pressure on them to keep to the plan.

Critical reflection

Critical reflection is a recent development that seeks to put facets of these ideas together. In critical reflection, reflection ideas and critical thinking are expanded using critical social theory, which in various ways does not take existing patterns of thinking and social organization for granted. This offers practitioners helpful alternative ideas when shifting their own perceptions and those of their clients and colleagues.

Gould and Baldwin (2004) connect critical reflection with how well organizations in general and social work agencies in particular develop good practice. They argue that social work agencies need to become 'learning organizations', facilitating a flexible response to new situations. Otherwise, they cannot identify new social trends that are having an impact on clients. In addition, they cannot capture and develop new practices as they emerge out of experience. I noted earlier in the chapter that achieving learning organizations was an important aim of the work of Argyris, one of the founders of reflective practice. If, as McDonald (2006) suggests, practitioners and clients are always responding to change as it affects economics, politics and ideas, social work organizations need to be able to learn about change and ways to deal with it. Critical reflection joins effective supervision and an evaluation of services as techniques that can develop learning organizations. Howe (2009) sees reflection as important because it helps in dealing with uncertainty and enables practitioners to become emotionally available, that is, so that clients feel they are available, rather than being preoccupied or authoritarian.

Baldwin (2004) identifies four organizational threats to critical reflection:

- Managerialism is a problem because it insists on the right of managers to control practice so that it furthers organizational rather than professional aims. In addition, it relies on rationalist techniques, such as eligibility criteria for services, targets and performance indicators, to evade the uncertainties that may arise when organizations emphasize professional management.
- EBP favours evidence that is at odds with reflective practice using cooperative, inclusive relationships between practitioners and clients.
- Rational implementation of policy reduces the flexibility of organizations to deal with change.
- Failures in critical analysis may exist, for example taboos on discussing issues that are too difficult for the organization to deal with.

Baldwin also proposes that critical reflection offers clear opportunities for social work agencies because it offers methods for:

- exploring situations and difficulties;
- the management of professional discretion;
- the management of innovation, particularly where practice is complex;
- replicating cooperative inquiry within organizations;
- strengthening teamwork;
- facilitating participation.

Fook and Gardner's (2007) important text sets out (in Chapter 4 of that book) a *critical reflection process* as a training model concerned with introducing critical reflection into an organization. This draws attention to the importance of how the organization works as a starting point; for example, a large, formal, bureaucratic organization operates differently from a small, informal organization without much of a hierarchy. The preferred model is as follows:

- Establish small facilitated groups, with voluntary membership, enabling dialogue and a focus on the communicative process, space for individual reflection and enough time for members to present and reflect on a critical incident.
- Use examples of specific and concrete practice experience.
- Each individual is directly involved so that they can work on their own experience in a participatory climate: the facilitator starts by modelling a reflection on their own experience.
- Use critical reflective questioning in a trusting and collegiate environment.
- Unsettle assumptions that are not explicit, leaving outcomes open-ended so that creative options are enabled (stage 1). Sue White (2006) talks about the reflexive practitioner as a 'trickster', acting perhaps mischievously, ironically, humorously to create lively talk, and crossing troubling boundaries to combat occupational liturgies. Here,

for example, the idea of 'liturgy' describes professional language as being like the conventions of a religious service, running along repetitive themes rather than developing creative and innovative rational thoughtfulness.

■ Devise new practices and approaches separately from the 'unsettling' stage; otherwise, people often move towards solutions or outcomes rather than analysing the situation adequately (stage 2).

Conclusion: using theory–practice ideas

Chapter 2 looked mainly at how theory and knowledge should influence practice, while in this chapter we have explored how practice and theory interact in complex ways. These concepts are not 'either-or' but 'both-together'. You cannot deduce logically from theoretical ideas what to do in practice. You can, however, use practice experience to build up practical ways of testing out and incorporating ideas into your thinking to help you plan effective interventions:

■ Adapting and transferring theory from one setting, culture or specialism to another can be achieved by using different theories in different phases or aspects of your work.

■ Process knowledge helps you to understand your thinking as you move from making sense of a situation and deciding on the appropriate interventions.

■ Emotional intelligence enables practitioners to manage the emotions they experience in their work.

■ Critical reflection has developed as an important way of using theory. It involves:
  - reflection-in-action during interactions with service users;
  - reflection-on-action, individually, and with supervisors and with peers, both to look back and to plan for the future;
  - ERA, moving from an experience, reflecting on it and then taking action on the reflection;
  - reflexivity, understanding the full range of perspectives of people and agencies involved;
  - critical thinking, questioning existing assumptions about situations;
  - critical reflection, using critical social theory, which continually questions the exiting social order.

Additional resources

Further reading

Schön, D. A. (1983) *The Reflective Practitioner: How Professionals Think in Action* (New York: Basic Books).
  The classic book on reflective practice. Although readable and valid, it needs to be updated with more recent texts.

Taylor, C. and White, S. (2000) *Practising Reflexivity in Health and Welfare: Making Knowledge* (Buckingham: Open University Press).

A good research-based account of reflexivity applied to practice, using recordings from practice.

Fook, J. and Gardner, F. (2007) *Practising Critical Reflection: A Resource Handbook* (Maidenhead: Open University Press).

White, S., Fook, J. and Gardner, F. (eds) (2006) *Critical Reflection in Health and Social Care* (Maidenhead: Open University Press).

These two books document the most important recent developments in reflection in social work. The *Handbook* sets out the theory and describes an educational programme that trains you to use it, while the edited collection contains a wide range of conceptual and practical papers.

Journals

Reflective Practice – Taylor & Francis.

A journal covering a wide range of professions.

Websites

http://socialworkpodcast.blogspot.com/2009/08/theories-for-clinical-social-work.html

The Social Work Podcast offers an interview with Joe Walsh, the American author of a book on clinical social work theories. The interview explores why theory is helpful to practitioners in settings where social work is, as often the case in the USA, seen as 'clinical' or 'treatment', and focuses on psychological interventions.

http://plqss.learningnetworks.org.uk/LO8-Introduction.html

The Scottish website IRISS, for example with this webpage 'Integrating Practice with Theory', introduces a way in which you can draw on theories in understanding practice situations. It builds particularly on Lishman's (2007) book for practice educators, although it oversimplifies the complexity of the interactions between theory and practice discussed in this chapter.

http://www.wilderdom.com/experiential/elc/ExperientialLearningCycle.htm#isa3stagemodelmorepractical

To follow up information about ideas about learning cycles, a range of them are reviewed, with diagrams and citations, on a useful website, Wilderdom, about 'natural living and transformation', which covers informal education using outdoor activities. This webpage deals with 'Experiential Learning Cycles: Overview of 9 Experiential Learning Cycle Models'.

http://mcgraw-hill.co.uk/openup/fook&gardner

A useful website containing practical materials for working with Fook and Gardner's critical reflection ideas, discussed above, is available from their publisher, McGraw-Hill.

REVIEWING SOCIAL WORK THEORIES

2

Psychodynamic practice 4

Main contribution

Psychodynamic ideas are distinctive in social work because they emphasize the importance of people's feelings and internal conflicts in creating and resolving the problems
that they face. They are valued as a rich fund of ideas for practice. In the history of social
work, they have had a strong impact on how social work is practised and have helped
shape its focus on people's psychological reactions to their social environment as the
source of personal and social problems. Psychodynamic practice, therefore, demonstrates
how the problem-solving objective of social work supports the existing social order by
helping people to adjust to the society around them.

Main points

A wide range of psychodynamic ideas is available, drawing on psychotherapy using ego,
object relations, self and relational psychologies (see Figure 4.1 later in the chapter and
its associated commentary to understand these terms).

- Psychodynamic theory is an important source of cultural ideas and social work practice
  conventions.
- Criticism focuses on the limited empirical support for psychodynamic practice, its
  focus on an insight into individuals' psychological functioning as the basis for understanding and intervention, its limited applicability in practice, its cultural and social
  assumptions and its assumption that early experience underlies current behaviour.
- Value issues arise from individualism and determinism in psychodynamic theory; that
  is, it explains behaviour as being decided by individuals' psychology.
- Psychodynamic theory offers ideas about structures in people's minds, that is, the id,
  ego and superego, how these develop and how to intervene.
- The main use of psychodynamic theory in social work is psychosocial practice in which
  the person-in-environment is the focus of attention; applications in groupwork and
  residential care have also been influential.

- Recent developments in attachment theory are relevant to child and adolescent mental health practice, child protection and loss and bereavement.
- Psychodynamic ideas are a rich source of complex ideas for interpreting behaviour.

Practice ideas

☐ *Anxiety* and *ambivalence* are derived from the inadequate resolution of problems in an earlier period of life. In turn, they lead to powerful feelings of aggression, anger and love.

☐ *Attachment* refers to the behaviour and emotional reactions of children seeking proximity to a person whom they perceive offers security in an environment in which they fear danger.

☐ *Attunement* is the process of appreciating and responding to emotions and attitudes that lie underneath the surface behaviour.

☐ *Coping* is the ability to manage present problems without anxiety.

☐ *Defences* and *resistance* are two common psychological barriers to working on life issues. They derive from a poor resolution of past problems.

☐ *Transference* and *countertransference* are technical terms in psychoanalysis, interpreted for social work to mean the effect of past experience that is transferred into present behaviour patterns. Practitioners can reflect on how clients react to them and how this makes them feel, so that they can directly experience how clients behave with others and how others might feel.

☐ *Relationships* with people may be used to model effective thinking and self-control, and as a vehicle to gain influence and confidence to explore psychological issues; this is 'relational practice'.

☐ *Working-through* is a process of repeatedly remembering crucial examples of problem behaviour as they occurred, exploring what happened and thinking about ways in which events and their emotional consequences might have been different.

(*Sources*: Partly from John and Trevithick (2012) and Froggett (2002).)

Major statements

It is not easy for anyone to convey in one book the full range of psychodynamic practice. Brandell's (2004) account is fairly broad but uses much technical psychoanalytic jargon and focuses on a clinical, psychotherapeutic approach to social work that is rarely seen outside (and possibly also inside) the USA. However, it provides a picture of psychodynamic social work that remains true to its Freudian origins.

There are various streams of current social work practice that draw on psychodynamic ideas, and these are set out in Figure 4.1 later in the chapter. Goldstein (1995, 2002) and her associates (Goldstein and Noonan, 1999; Goldstein et al., 2009) have written extensively about how the psychodynamic ideas of ego, object relations, self and relational psychology (see Figure 4.1) are used in psychotherapeutic social work, that is, a practice that aims primarily to change people's behaviour and the impact of feelings and thinking on it. This work represents a renewal and development of ideas over a fifteen-year period, and demonstrates the detailed practice prescriptions available in these perspectives.

Ruch et al.'s (2010) approachable collection of papers offers a comprehensive view of relational practice from British sources. Freedberg's (2008) thoughtful feminist perspective on social work relational practice also usefully illustrates how critical and other perspectives make connections with, and in the process shed new light on, psychodynamic theory in social work. Attachment theory, is, however, the most significant recent application of psychodynamic theory in social work, and practical and research-based texts have recently appeared from Howe (2011) and Shemmings and Shemmings (2011).

As with many psychological approaches, these social work texts overlap with books from psychological and other mental health professionals pursuing the same perspective; I refer to some of these in this chapter. There is no one particular text, therefore, that represents a 'preferred' account of psychodynamic ideas in social work practice: they are all useful in different ways. In the application section of this chapter, therefore, I have summarized a selected aspect of Brandell as the general text, giving an impression, using a recent text by Shemmings and Shemmings (2011), of how social work practice draws on the ideas of attachment.

The debate summary

The main areas of debate about psychodynamic practice in social work are:

- its scientific status and the lack of empirical support for its use;
- its focus on internal psychological functioning, which fails to incorporate the social issues that affect practice;
- its limitations as a basis for practice;
- the cultural assumptions it makes;
- its assumption that earlier experience strongly influences current behaviour.

The scientific status of and empirical support for psychodynamic practice

Sigmund Freud, the great psychoanalyst and the original source of psychodynamic ideas, was trained as a doctor and aimed to create a science of the mind. Psychodynamic theory therefore, much like a science, tries to analyse aspects of mind based on careful observation and subsequently engages in critical analysis and philosophical debate about its observations and findings. Much of what is written about psychodynamic theory involves detailed analyses of case studies, but although these are often fascinating to read, they do not provide any confirmation of how exactly it is that behaviour is influenced by mental processes and social work interventions (Walsh, 2010). For positivist critics, psychody-namic theory is flawed because it is based on metaphorical ideas about structures and movements in the mind that cannot be directly observed but are rather inferred from interpretations of behaviour and people's own descriptions of their thoughts. However carefully you test these interpretations and descriptions of the self, it is impossible confirm their accuracy. Many psychologists and others therefore reject psychodynamic theory as an evidence base for practice with human beings.

Against this, as we saw in Chapter 2, there is an increasing body of evidence that most forms of psychotherapy and counselling in which practitioners rigorously apply a model of practice are effective in helping many people. There is also growing research supporting the use of particular practices related to attachment theory and some of the practice techniques that have developed using relational and attachment ideas. Moreover, the basic principles of psychological social work practice can be seen to be influencing each other to produce broadly similar eclectic types of practice. Goldstein and Noonan's (1999) book demonstrates this by linking short-term ego psychology in psychodynamic practice with some elements of cognitive-behavioural practice (see Chapter 6) and other models of service delivery in current agencies. This demonstrates the usefulness of psychodynamic theory, in that it provides a rich set of interpretive ideas to help practi-tioners explore what is happening in their clients' minds in their day-to-day work.

The exclusion of the social in psychodynamic practice

The second major area of debate about psychodynamic theory is that it overemphasizes psychological factors and psychological interventions, to the exclusion of social and soci-ological explanations and social interventions. That is, environmental factors are given less prominence than internal psychological ones. This limits the possible range of inter-ventions that can be undertaken by social workers and means that they start from a narrower set of assumptions (Strean, 1979). Psychodynamic ideas have limited concern for social reform, which excludes a major element of social work (Strean, 1979).

Other theoretical problems follow from this psychological emphasis, such as the tendency to blame people for what has happened to them, 'victim-blaming' in social construction theory. Psychological theory makes individuals responsible for particular events and their causes, whereas many problems that an individual faces stem from social factors. For example, psychological approaches might lead you to believe that unem-ployed people are lazy and have not tried to get a job, that an offender is innately amoral, or that a neglectful parent is disorganized or evil. The expectation is that these people can reform by making more effort to educate themselves or change their attitudes, with perhaps a little help. Alternatively, the psychological model can lead to a more medical model of thinking, that is, that the individual's problem arises from poor or inadequate mental functioning. In this way, alcoholism or drug misuse are seen as diseases that need to be cured rather than as an individual's reaction to social experiences. These are over-simplified accounts of these problems since economic downturns create unemployment, and social conditions such as poverty and poor education contribute to addiction, crime and family problems. Clearly, not every individual affected by these problems is solely responsible for what happens to them, and their psychological functioning is unlikely to be the only source of the problem on which we should focus our interventions.

Having said this, not everybody reacts in the same way to social pressures, so individual psychological factors may also be important alongside social factors. In addition, psychodynamic theory is social in the sense that it understands people's life issues as stemming from how the psychological and the social interact, as in attachment, relational and object relations theories. The problem is that practitioners and specific theories often overemphasize the individual and psychological because that is the main function of social work practitioners in many services, particularly when dealing with individuals who have mental illnesses and are psychologically distressed. These theories give us ideas that help us work on these important matters.

The limitations of psychodynamic theory in practice

Psychodynamic intervention focuses on changing behaviour through insight. This means that practitioners aim to influence people over a period of time by getting them to understand themselves better through building a relationship with them and trying to influence them over a period of time. As a 'talking' therapy, psychodynamic intervention prefers clients with psychological problems who can express themselves well and who can take part in discussion and self-examination. This approach is more appropriate to mental health services and long-term engagements with clients, and less appropriate for short-term help or situations where the agency's focus is mainly on delivering social care services. It also plays down the importance of less articulate clients, working-class people and people with more practical problems (Strean, 1979). The use of insight as a major therapeutic technique may lead practitioners using a psychodynamic approach to stop at the point where clients have understood what is happening to them emotionally. But this does not help them to take practical action to do make a positive change. Since psychoanalysis is non-directive, refusing to give advice or organize practical moves towards change, this tends to make workers' help insubstantial.

Case example: Julia's social work career

Julia' first job in social work was a temporary job in an adult services team, mainly working with older people who were becoming increasingly frail. She used a set of forms and procedures that were agreed between her agency, social care providers and healthcare organizations in the area, and her main task was to assess people to identify which package of care services they should receive. Increasingly, 'cash for care' personalization meant that Julia started from a budget set by an agreed 'resource allocation system', and after assessment her clients' family members managed the budget for the services. After that was arranged, she did not maintain continuous contact with the clients or their families. ▶

Her next job was with a community mental health service, where she provided crisis services as part of a team consisting of a psychologist, a psychiatrist and several community psychiatric nurses. Much of this work involved sorting out practical living problems and social security difficulties, and arranging services. Julia was also involved in supporting people with longer term mental illness, but this mainly involved performing routine checks and ensuring that they were still using their medication and services such as day centres.

After some years, Julia obtained a post in a secure unit for mentally disordered offenders, where each member of the social work team built up relationships with a small number of patients in the unit, all of whom had committed serious offences such as arson, murder or rape. Where appropriate, the team planned and arranged the patients' discharge, under the long-term supervision of a psychiatrist and the social worker.

It was only in this post that Julia found relationship-based psychodynamic theory useful in working with nearly all her clients. Previously, she had only occasionally used some of these ideas, when clients needed to think more than usual about their direction and plans for the future. It is this kind of experience that makes many practitioners doubtful about the relevance of psychodynamic theory to their work, even though they find its ideas interesting and stimulating.

Originating in middle-class Jewish Vienna, psychodynamic theory is limited by the cultural assumptions of its time. It takes a white, middle-class perspective as the 'norm', and there is a danger that deviations from this are seen as abnormal behaviour that should be 'cured'. For example, there can be significant variations in how children are treated or expected to behave across cultures and ethnicities, and if this deviates from the 'norm' set by psychodynamic theory, it could lead a practitioner to believe that treatment is needed, whereas it may be better to work towards society's acceptance of a wider range of child care practices. Similarly, the historic attitude of psychodynamic theory to homosexuality sees it as a deviation, related to maternal relationships, that requires treatment. Current thinking sees this as objectionable (Strean, 1979: 56) in both its attitude to women and the assumptions that it makes about gay and lesbian relationships. Finally, psychodynamic theory's account of the 'innate' qualities of women reinforces stereotypes of them as primarily domestic and child-bearing, and also as socially, intellectually and perhaps morally inferior to men.

Many current social ideas about ethnic, cultural and gender issues could be used to enrich psychodynamic theory, but since, in spite of interest in relational and attachment ideas, it does not now form a central basis for social work, these ideas have not been incorporated into it, but develop separately from what is now a minority, specialized interest. For example, Clarke (2003) argues that insights from psychodynamic theory may help us to understand the complex emotional responses involved in how racist behaviour develops. Bonner (2002) argues that this and ideas about intersubjectivity, ethnocultural transference and racial enactments could contribute to the use of psychodynamic theory in dealing with minority ethnic groups. In addition, psychoanalytic ideas have contributed to feminist perspectives on psychology, for example in Mitchell's (1975) work on psychoanalysis as a useful means of understanding how men achieve and maintain supremacy in a patriarchal society. This may help practitioners to understand and work with some of the social processes by which women's lives are dominated by men's assumptions.

Psychodynamic theory, therefore, has less influence in social work than it might, for two main reasons. First, the historic cultural assumptions of psychodynamic theory limit its applicability in contemporary society since it establishes 'normal' ways of relating to others (for example, it views successful personal development as being contingent on traditional relationships with parents). Second, while psychodynamic theory might adopt a wider range of ideas and approaches to add to its interpretive richness, and we can see this happening particularly in feminist thinking, its isolation as a complex and separate stream of thought means that this happens only rarely.

The central assumption of psychodynamic theory is that present behaviour arises from past experience and, in particular, relationships. This raises the problem that, to achieve change in present behaviour, clients and social workers have to engage in a long-term process whereby they examine events, issues, emotions and relationships in their clients' past. In this way, psychodynamic theory does not fit with current practice, in which clients' current concerns are important priorities, or with the shared value principles of social work agencies (set out in Figure 1.7), which are positive and look to the future. Psychodynamic theory's 'deterministic' assumption is that past experience dictates present behaviour and makes it difficult for people to change their own behaviour. Other theories see behaviour as emerging from a wide range of social and psychological factors and therefore much more open to change.

Nevertheless, there are advantages to the backward-looking, problem-based, causation-focused approach of psychodynamic theory. For example, it can help and motivate the family members of clients who suffer from poor mental health to manage often difficult and frightening behaviour if they understand some of the possible causes behind it. Psycho-dynamic practice helps them to 'make sense' of seemingly incomprehensible reactions.

Despite criticism of practical problems in using psychodynamic theory in social work, there are some advantages to understanding its ideas. Psychodynamic perspectives help us to understand the origins of the source of many important ideas that we take for granted. 'Conflict', 'aggression', 'mother–child relationships', 'ego', 'sublimation', 'repression' and 'resistance' are all terms we use, often without a thought for their technical meanings or the theories from which they originated. These ideas are all valued because, even with their limitations, they offer a sense of the complexity of human life and development, and how our minds and bodies interact with each other and the social environment.

Wider theoretical perspectives

Psychoanalysis

Psychodynamic perspectives come from psychoanalysis, which is based on the ideas of Freud and his followers and later developments of their work. The term 'psychodynamic' is, however, broader than 'psychoanalysis'. It emphasizes that the mind (the 'psycho' element of the term) is our dynamo: our minds both motivate and direct or manage our behaviour. Since the 1960s, practice theory emerging from this idea has been called 'psychosocial' because it looks at how the mind and the behaviour it produces influence and are influenced by people's social environment.

Psychodynamic ideas were influential during the period 1930–60, when social work was becoming established; they therefore underlie the 'traditional social work' that many other theories have developed from or reacted against. Because of this, elements of these ideas still influence everyday practice. Another reason for this pervasive influence is that psychoanalysis is well known in Western culture and most people have some awareness of its basic concepts, so it forms a culturally shared language about problems of the mind. However, psychoanalysis (as opposed to psychodynamic theory) is mainly used in specialist, psychiatric settings and is very used rarely by social workers.

Pause and reflect *Psychoanalytic ideas with cultural influence on social work*

Think about and note down some terms and ideas that you think most people will have heard of that originate from psychoanalysis. What do people generally understand by these? Try asking some people who have not studied it before.

Some suggestions

- People often refer to mistakes made in speech that apparently reveal hidden thought processes, sometimes of a sexual nature, as 'Freudian slips' (Urban Dictionary, 2012). An example of this is in a speech by President Bush (the father) in which he states, 'For seven and a half years I've worked alongside President Reagan … We've had triumphs. Made some mistakes. We've had some sex … uh … setbacks' (from a speech in 1988; http://www.liveleak.com/view?i=bb3_1189010008).
- A common image from psychoanalysis is that of a patient undergoing psychiatry, lying on a couch talking, with the psychiatrist sitting out of sight listening. This is a picture of traditional psychoanalytic treatment.
- The description of someone as 'defensive' or 'well defended' when they deny something about themselves that is obvious to others from their behaviour demonstrates the widespread use of psychoanalytic jargon. It comes from the psychoanalytic idea of defence mechanisms.

Common-sense understanding of psychoanalytic jargon does not always fully represent the complexity of psychodynamic ideas. Yelloly (1980: 8–9) gives the example of the meaning of 'unconscious' to show how rich psychodynamic ideas are. When some thoughts and feelings arise that are not compatible with other beliefs that we hold strongly, psychodynamic theory talks about 'resistance'. Here, the mind does not allow the contested ideas into the conscious, preventing this by a process called 'repression'. But this is not about people refusing to admit something; repression covers up the ideas so successfully that people are not even aware of them and their mind is not even aware of the reality that 'I don't go there.' Distinctive ideas like this influence popular culture because they offer striking and creative metaphors of behaviour and how thinking influences it.

Figure 4.1 shows the three main aspects of psychoanalytic theory. First, it describes metaphorical structures in the mind such as the id, ego and superego. Second, it demonstrates how people build up these structures by going through psychological stages, and how their behaviour may be affected in the long term by disruptions to this development. Finally, there is a treatment theory on how to deal with behavioural problems that come from the disrupted development. In the USA, some different forms of psychoanalysis still influence social workers if they specialize in a counselling-style treatment of people with psychological problems. US social work texts therefore deal more fully with these.

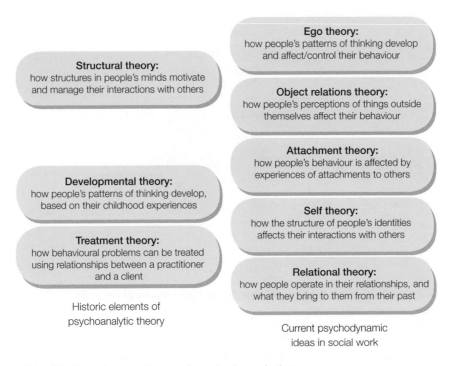

Figure 4.1 Historic and current types of psychodynamic theory
Source: Yelloly (1980) and Perlman and Brandell (2011).

Borden (2009) shows how different ideas and approaches within psychoanalysis are associated with key thinkers, and how discourse swung between these over the course of the twentieth century. These approaches, which affected social work, psychotherapy and counselling, include:

- a focus on a child's early experience of relationships as a source of behavioural tendencies and personal and social problems;
- the importance of taking into account both psychology and social understanding;
- the importance of relationships as a basis for helping people.

The right-hand column of Figure 4.1 sets out current thinking derived from this discourse and how it applies to psychodynamic theory in social work. Ego, object relations, attachment, self and relational theory are not completely distinct ideas but are emphases. As the figure implies, the earlier ideas in the list draw more strongly on structural theory, the later ones lean on developmental theory, and the last two listed call on treatment theory.

Psychoanalytic *structural* theories start from metaphors for the structure of the mind, and I show in Figure 4.2 how they are understood from a social work point of view, with the main focus on psychodynamic ideas, on the mind, having the most prominence.

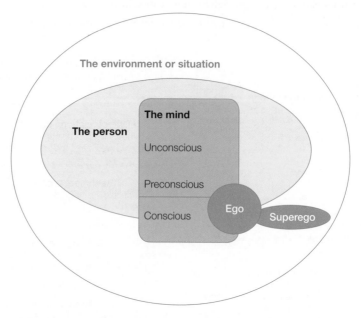

Figure 4.2 Psychodynamic social work ideas about the structure of the mind
Source: Inspired by Walsh (2010: Ch. 3).

Figure 4.2 shows that, in psychodynamic theory, the mind consists of a small area of conscious awareness and a much larger area of unconscious mental activity. We are mostly unaware of thoughts in the unconscious mind, but some of them are preconscious so are accessible to us at times with effort and help. The ego manages relationships between the conscious and the unconscious, and is informed by principles created within a superego, which is developed through interactions with other people in our environment. The mind forms part of our person and we exist in our social environment (referred to as our 'situation' in earlier social work thought). It is the person-in-environment that social workers focus on, rather than the person's mind in isolation, which clinical psychologists or counsellors emphasize.

> ## Case example: David's unconscious feelings about his mother
>
> David was a teenager who was a 'young carer' for his mother. She was socially isolated because her physical disability kept her mainly in the home, and depressed because of its impact on her life. There were two younger children in the family. David was very strongly attached to his mother and worked to keep the household going. People in the wider family, at his school and in social agencies admired his commitment to helping her. However, his mother reported to her social worker that he sometimes got angry, shouted at her and hit her, but she begged the social worker not to take this up because she did not want David's support withdrawn. The social worker thought that as people often report abuse when they want a practitioner to take some protective action, she also wanted to support and protect David and make sure that the younger children were safe. When the social worker talked the situation over with David, he denied that any of these events had happened and got angry with her for questioning his commitment to his mother.

Our starting point in understanding what happened with David comes from the basic idea of psychoanalysis, that we have to look at people's feelings and attitudes to understand how they are driving their behaviour. When we see inconsistent or unexpected behaviour, thinking about what is going on in people's minds helps us to understand how the psychodynamic process in people's minds might be affecting their external behaviour. The important psychodynamic idea of the *unconscious* suggests what might be going on in David's mind. We often have many conflicting feelings about situations that are important to us, and some things are so important to our stability that feelings which conflict with them become unacceptable to us. We therefore use *defence mechanisms* to protect ourselves against them, so that we can avoid facing up to the conflicts. Perhaps David has committed himself so completely to helping and supporting his mother that all of his feelings reflect this dedication to her. However, it is more likely that he is frustrated that his commitment to her means he is, for example, not able to join his friends in shared leisure activities. He may also feel that his mother should work harder to improve, for example that she should snap out of her depression in response to his love and kindness. Helping her is so important to him that his mind does not allow these conflicting resentful thoughts into his conscious. Instead, he *represses* them, pushing unacceptable feelings into a box and keeping the lid on them.

The psychodynamic unconscious consists of these forcibly hidden ideas, which are there whether or not we think about or are even aware of them; they are often deeply concealed. Many repressed thoughts are dynamic, in the sense that they cause us to act even if we are unaware of them. *Aggression*, in which deeply concealed feelings often turn into destructive impulses against others, is another important idea in psychoanalysis. Thinking about all this, it is possible that David is repressing his frustration as a defence against any bad feelings towards his mother, which would make it hard to carry on being the calm and supportive young carer. This frustration leaks out in the aggression he demonstrates towards his mother.

In the unconscious, *drives* (or 'instincts' in early translations of Freud's writing) are mental pressures to relieve physical needs such as hunger or thirst. Drives create tension, which generates energy or *libido*, pushing us to act in order to meet the need. There are a number of different types of physical needs, and sexual tension, even among young children, is very important in creating drives.

Psychoanalytic theory proposes that our minds contain three main structures: the id, ego and superego. The id, or literally, 'it' – an undifferentiated pressure from an unknown source (Wood, 1971) – is generated by drives. It pushes us to act to resolve our needs, but our actions do not always bring the desired results. The ego is a set of pragmatic ideas about how to understand and manage the environment that develop when the id finds that simple behaviour does not resolve needs. For example, when they are very young, infants cry when they are uncomfortable; whatever the reason for the discomfort, parents react to the crying. Later, babies learn to control the excretion of faeces as the ego learns that parents and others disapprove of excretion in the wrong place or time. They learn when muscular tension means they should go to the toilet, and as this learning becomes successful, they are rewarded by parental approval. The ego is thus said to manage 'object relations': this term refers to all relationships outside ourselves, with both people and things. The superego develops general moral principles that guide the ego in doing this and that come from our parents and from observing how other people behave.

An important feature of the personality is how the ego manages tensions. The need of the ego and superego to exert control over the id to achieve social acceptability creates further conflicts, and this produces anxiety. The ego uses defence mechanisms to manage anxiety, and one of these mechanisms is repression, which affected David in the case example. Other important defence mechanisms are:

- *projection* – unwanted ideas that the ego wants to protect us from become attached in our minds to another person or thing;
- *splitting* – contradictory ideas and feelings are kept in separate mental compartments and applied to different people or situations, leading to inconsistent behaviour;
- *sublimation* – energy (from the id) that is directed towards unwanted activities (often sexual) is redirected towards more acceptable activities;
- *rationalization* – people believe in acceptable reasons for particular activities and the repression of emotionally unacceptable reasons for behaviour.

Freud's later work and that of many of his most important followers moved from an early emphasis on drives to concentrate on ego and object relations, which is linked to the idea discussed earlier in the chapter of the ego managing our environment. These theories propose that children have the capacity to deal with the outside world from an early age and that development of the ego is the growth of our capacity to learn from experience. This involves the use of rational parts of our minds in thinking (cognition), perception and memory. Building on these ideas in the USA, Harry Stack Sullivan's theories of the 'self', later developed by Kohut, have been important in social work (Perlman and Brandell, 2011).

Psychoanalytic *developmental* theory proposes that the interaction between these mental structures leads children to develop through a series of stages. At each stage, particular behaviours are more prominent than others, but as children progress they build on the behaviours associated with previous stages. So, at a very early stage, babies gain satisfaction from sucking, such as at a mother's breast or a bottle, to satisfy the need for food. Sucking is still satisfying in later stages, for example in eating candies or sweets or in sexual activities, even if other behaviours have become more important. Sometimes, even though adults have a wide range of satisfying behaviours and activities to choose from, they become unconsciously attached to behaviour associated with particular stages (*fixation*). They are driven to seek that form of satisfaction to an unreasonable degree and consequently cannot use the full repertoire of behaviour available to them.

Children start in a stage of *primary narcissism*, seeking only a gratification of their own needs. They then learn through social interaction, at first with parents, that they must compromise and also consider the needs of others. In each stage proposed by Freud, the focus of attention is on a particular need. The first stage is oral (hunger as children learn to wait for their next meal), the next is anal (as they learn to manage excretion), then phallic (identification with same-sex parent as they learn to manage appropriate relationships in the family) and then Oedipal (attraction to the opposite-sex parent). In a latency period, sexual tensions are quiescent because drives are managed through a resolution of Oedipal conflicts, and after this, during puberty, social learning channels sexual development towards external partners rather than parents.

Associated with the stages of development is the idea of *regression*. This occurs when people who have progressed through the later stages fall back on behaviour associated with earlier stages under some present stress. Regression is contrasted with fixation, in which individuals have never progressed and are stuck in the behaviour of the early stage.

Erikson (1965) expanded on these stages of development. He suggested that, at each stage, the rational mind deals with a maturational crisis presented by the social circumstances of our life. His work, which has influenced social work and crisis intervention in particular, emphasizes cultural and social pressures rather than inner drives (Yelloly, 1980: 12) but is not well supported by research (Gibson, 2007). Other psychodynamic theorists and practitioners who have had an impact on social work include Melanie Klein (1959), Salzberger-Wittenberg (1970), Winnicott (1964) and Bowlby (1951, 1969, 1973, 1980, 1988). They have primarily influenced practice with children, important because of social work's role in many countries in investigating and caring for neglected or abused children and supporting deprived families in managing child care.

Psychoanalysis gained its early influence on social work because its accounts of how early relationships influenced later behaviour helped practitioners to understand and work on children's relationships with their mothers. One of the still-used key concepts of Winnicott's work is 'good-enough parenting', in which parents provide a home environment that is helpful to a child's development. Bowlby directed the psychoanalytic interest in early mother–child relationships towards research and theory about maternal deprivation. This is the idea that if we deprive children of contact with their mothers, their personal development is impeded. More recently, this has developed into more extensive theory about the importance of attachment (Howe, 1995, 2005, 2011; Howe et al., 1999; Aldgate, 2007; Shemmings and Shemmings, 2011).

Attachment primarily relates to the child's relationship with the mother but can also include other carers, and a child's experience of attachment affects the development of other relationships that they have with other people in later life. The effects of loss of attachment are especially important, for example after the death or other loss of a parent, such as by divorce (Garber, 1992). The idea of loss has a wider importance in psycho-analysis, and there are several different approaches to bereavement and grief (Berzoff, 2003). Mourning is a response to all kinds of loss, not just the death of someone close (Salzberger-Wittenberg, 1970). Parkes and Prigerson (2010) interpret bereavement in many situations as regression to childhood experiences of stress due to loss. However, a large variety of other factors apart from maternal deprivation, including the social environment, can affect a child's personal development, and many social and psychological factors help to protect against its damaging effects (Rutter, 1981).

Treatment in psychoanalysis and its influence on social work intervention

Classic psychoanalysis required therapists to be 'blank screens', making themselves as anonymous as possible so that patients could project their fantasies onto the therapists. This idea survives in social work in that practitioners should aim to be non-directive in their relationships with clients, allowing the client to lead the direction of the intervention. A more modern interpretation of this arises in relational theory, which emphasizes creating a therapeutic alliance through a relationship with the client and securing commitment to objectives and interventions. This is an interpretation in psychodynamic theory of the 'shared value principles' (Figure 1.7) of many social work theories.

Another influential psychoanalytic treatment concept is *transference*. Psychoanalysis argues that patients often transfer unconscious feelings about their parents onto the therapist, behaving as though the therapist were that parent. By stimulating transference, therapists can get patients to act out conflicts arising from their early relationship difficulties with their parents, thereby revealing the source of the present behavioural difficulties. Social work adapts this idea, referring more generally to how the emotional remains of past relationships and experiences affect our present behaviour and relationships (Irvine, 1956). *Countertransference* occurs when therapists irrationally react to their patients by bringing in their own past experiences to the relationship between the client and practitioner. Again social work adapts this idea, proposing that practitioners should be aware of their reactions to clients. Being made to feel protective or angry, for example, by a client often mimics how the client makes other people who are important to them feel and helps the practitioner to identify and work on the client's relationship problems.

We have seen that psychoanalytic treatments are strongly concerned with *insight*, that is, revealing hidden thoughts and feelings. Undesirable behaviour may be caused by repressed conflicts leaking out in various ways, requiring more than ordinary attempts to disclose its origins. Once revealed and properly understood, the conflicts no longer cause difficulties in behaviour.

Case example: Dealing with David's anger

Looking back at the previous case example of David, a practitioner might try to open up a discussion of David's hidden feelings or conflict by saying that it would not be surprising if he became frustrated and angry with the demands of his situation. The practitioner could demonstrate acceptance of these feelings by saying, for example, that many people in David's situation would feel frustration and anger, and in this way might help David to express them verbally. By doing this, David might be helped to understand how these feelings are affecting him so that he no longer needs to lash out at his mother. In practice, a simple comment will usually not be enough to make a difference, and the practitioner would repeatedly have to demonstrate acceptance as situations arose in which David expressed his hidden feelings.

Ideas about insight are also used in ego psychology practice, although they have been reworked. Ego psychology practice emphasizes ego support over trying to change behaviour by revealing its causes. Ego support concentrates on helping people manage their relationships with the outside world through extending rational control of their lives. Using this approach to practice, the social worker might focus on helping David identify times or situations when he is likely to become angry and think about how to manage and control this behaviour. Alternatively, the practitioner might organize opportunities for respite from caring for his mother and encourage him to take part in leisure activities with people of his own age, thus helping to reduce the stress of responsibility.

Connections

Psychosocial practice

Prior to the 1960s, most social work theory was based on psychodynamic ideas, and this is now called psychosocial theory. Distinct streams of thought within psychosocial theory are usually now taken together as basic ideas about practice, for example by Teater (2010):

- *Psychosocial*, formerly diagnostic, theory (Woods and Hollis, 1999) focused on the diagnosis, assessment and classification of treatment as a basis for exploring the 'person-in-situation'. Some writers, following ecological theory, now refer to the 'person-in-environment' (Karls and Wandrei, 1994).
- *Functional* theory (Smalley, 1967) emphasized the function of social work agencies in giving practice its form and direction. Its lasting influences on social work include the idea of self-determination, the importance of structuring practice around time and the emphasis on process and growth (Dore, 1990).
- *Problem-solving* casework (Perlman, 1957a) focused on exploring problems that clients presented and on improving their capacity for coping with them. A forerunner of task-centred casework that emphasized problem analysis (see Chapter 5), it is still used as the conceptual basis of important texts, such as that of Compton et al. (2005),

who connect it with ecosystems theory (see Chapter 7). Problem-solving is an intuitively obvious description of what social workers do with many clients (Shier, 2011) and appears in the International Federation of Social Workers' (2000) international definition of social work as a social work objective, as we saw in Chapter 1.

Psychodynamic groupwork and residential care

Psychodynamic theory has been applied to residential care work through three main theoretical developments (Righton, 1975):

- *Planned environment therapy* (Franklin, 1968; Wills, 1973) was originally based on work with maladjusted adolescents during the Second World War. It has its roots in psychoanalytic theory and radical education and is used by some schools for young people with emotional and behavioural disorders.
- *Milieu therapy* is a mainly American concept seen in the work of writers such as Polsky (1968) that is based on psychodynamic groupwork with maladjusted young people.
- *Therapeutic communities* (Kennard, 1998) derive from the work of Jones (1968) and Clark (1974) in psychiatric hospitals, and are used in community mental health settings, including day hospitals, hostels and housing schemes.

The psychodynamic groupwork of Bion (1961) generated the idea of 'group dynamics', which is also widely used in social work. He theorized that, in groups, people behave according to 'basic assumptions' about power and leadership within the groups. Basic assumption behaviour often gets in the way of the group's formal task. Furthermore, Foulkes (1964) introduced the idea of the 'group matrix', the totality of communications and relationships in a group that enables group members to develop a shared meaning of group events. It is associated with the idea of 'group spirit' and Bowlby's concept of a 'secure base' in attachment theory (Rawlinson, 1999). Froggett (2002) discusses how psychodynamic group approaches assist in containing problems in secure bases within the matrix. Other well-known contributions include Menzies-Lyth's (1988) research showing how staff facing difficult emotional situations in hospital settings used psychological defences to maintain their emotional equilibrium, and Bettelheim's (1950) atmospheric accounts of psychoanalytic residential care practice with disturbed children, which called on his wartime concentration camp experience.

Perhaps the most widely influential model of residential care practice is the therapeutic community. Kennard's (1998) account of its main attributes is as follows:

- It takes place in an informal and communal atmosphere.
- Group meetings are a central aspect of therapy, for information-sharing, building a sense of cohesion, making decision-making open, offering a forum for personal feedback and allowing the community to influence its members.
- All participants share in the work of running the community.
- Residents have a therapeutic role with each other.
- Authority is shared between staff and residents.

■ Common values include the belief that individual problems are mostly about relationships with others, that therapy is a learning process (referred to as 'insightful
learning'; Hinshelwood, 1999) and that members share a basic psychological
equality as human beings.

The politics of psychodynamic theory

Psychoanalytic theory has influenced social work theory in three phases (Payne, 1992).
At first, before the 1920s in the USA and the late 1930s in Britain, it had little impact.
After this, there was a period in which it became dominant in social work thought, and
this lasted until the end of the 1960s, culminating in psychosocial practice. Since then, it
has been one of many contested theories, used largely only by specialists, and retaining a
more general background influence because of its impact on 'traditional' social work
practice. Meyer (2000) sees its influence as a 'legacy', and Danto (2011) describes social
work and psychoanalytic ideas as a 'partnership'.

The influence of psychodynamic therapy on social work can be seen in social work's
emphasis on relationships (Perlman, 1957b) and its permissive, open, listening style of
practice (Wallen, 1982). It also encouraged seeking an explanation and understanding of
personality rather than action, and emphasized feelings and unconscious factors (Yelloly,
1980) rather than events and conscious thought. Many ideas, such as the unconscious,
insight, aggression, conflict, anxiety, maternal relationships and transference, come from
psychodynamic theory. These are terms that are often used in watered-down strength as
a common language in social work and everyday life. Psychodynamic theory gains some
of its importance by their continued availability to practitioners.

The important focus in social work on childhood and early relationships and maternal
deprivation comes from psychodynamic theory, and this has led to the current importance of attachment theory. The emphasis on mental illness and disturbed behaviour as a
focus of much social work comes from the importance in the 1920s and 30s of social
work's association in the USA with psychiatry and psychodynamic treatment. Insight as
an important part of social work understanding and treatment originally comes from
psychodynamic theory. We give less emphasis to social factors in social work than to
psychological and emotional ones because of the influence of psychodynamic theory
(Weick, 1981). That influence continues partly because, in the USA, social work has a
very strong role in mental health services, and psychological therapies have a greater
importance there than in European welfare states and the less developed services of many
resource-poor countries.

Much of the critique of the use of psychodynamic theory in social work discussed in
the debate section above comes from an unrelenting attack from cognitive-behavioural
perspectives and evidence-based practice on the interpretive and metaphorical style of
psychodynamic practice. Similarly, critical theorists attack psychodynamic theory's failure

to incorporate a critical analysis of the current social order. From these two perspectives, psychodynamic practice is not sufficiently supported by positivist research and fails to incorporate a critical social analysis.

Values issues

The main values issue with psychodynamic practice arises from its psychologistic individualism, which can be seen as a strength or a weakness depending on your point of view. Psychodynamic perspectives in social work assert the individuality of each human being and the unique way in which internal emotions and drives create each individual's behaviour. This view respects human beings by helping them to make sense of their experiences and their present strains and stresses, and has led social work to give prominence to the self-determination and individualization of clients and their problems.

On the other hand, we have seen that focusing on the psychological can result in victim-blaming and can affirm cultural, racial and gender stereotypes. By assuming that past experience is responsible for present behaviour, and by emphasizing the difficulty of internal psychological change, psychodynamic practice may create more barriers to change than practice theories focused on the present and future. Furthermore, psychodynamic ideas do not address social change or excluded or oppressed groups since they presume an existing social order to which individuals adapt, although they encourage concern for changing individuals' immediate situation. Their psychological focus means that they may neglect social explanations for clients' problems, and this contributes to negative stereotyping by assuming that people's problems come from their psychological make-up rather than from external factors that they can have little control over. This, again, can result in victim-blaming.

Another key values issue within psychodynamic theory is that it is deterministic, assuming that present behaviour is strongly influenced, some would say determined, by earlier experience and in particular by relationships in childhood. This raises the question of whether it is realistic to expect that it is possible to change such ingrained patterns of behaviour, and furthermore whether this change can be brought about merely by gaining insight into a person's development. Because the theory proposes that psychological defences are very entrenched, simply understanding why they have arisen might not be enough to allow individuals to make changes in their lives. If that is so, psychodynamic theory in some ways rejects the possibility that human beings can ever change themselves, and in emphasizing the power of the mind suggests that social interventions might not be able to achieve change. Social work's value base, on the other hand, strongly emphasizes that people can make changes in their lives and acknowledges the importance of social relationships and institutions in facilitating this.

Applications

Psychodynamic theory is currently applied in a variety of ways, as we saw in Figure 4.1. Maroda (2010), a psychiatrist, helpfully summarizes the main elements of psychodynamic practice techniques, as shown in Figure 4.3. You can trace these back to some of the historic ideas of psychoanalysis, but she updates them and makes them relevant to everyday experiences. For example, looking back to psychoanalytic treatment in which patients projected their personality through transference onto the 'blank screen' of a neutral psychoanalyst, she talks about difficulties in practitioners' self-disclosure in their professional relationships. This refers to working out how much you should disclose about your personal life to clients. An example of the relevance of this issue to social work is a practitioner talking to clients about their own children. A client with her own child care problems may not want to hear about the practitioner's difficulties. On the other hand, clients may value knowing that practitioners have personal experience of the situation they are going through. A good general rule that I follow is to ensure that anything I disclose about myself has to have a clear benefit for the client. This guidance about how to act in difficult interactions with clients is one of the reasons that many practitioners value psychodynamic theory.

> **Pause and reflect**   *Looking at underlying factors in behaviour*
>
> Look at the examples in the third column of Figure 4.3, which are adapted from Maroda's examples or my own experience, and in each case think about how looking at the client's feelings about an issue reveals what might be happening in the client's relationships.

Some suggestions

As a social work practitioner, I have often had to 'manage emotion', that is, I have helped people who cannot express their true feelings about their relationships. This is sometimes a matter of working on their social skills and explaining to them how to raise any issues they might have in ways that facilitate a discussion but are not critical or result in conflict. Most of the time, however, it is a matter of understanding what may have caused the client to feel and behave a certain way towards someone. For example, a client's parents may have been unable to accept their angry behaviour when they were children, so the client never learned how to calm down from anger and focus on repairing their relationships. Another example I often come across is when a client is frustrated by their husband, even though other people who know him see him as loving and supportive, because the support is too controlling and does not allow the client the freedom to make mistakes or strike out in her own direction.

Figure 4.3 Maroda's psychodynamic techniques

Technique	Role in practice	Example
Emotional engagement	You need to share the client's concerns, feeling empathy with them	An unconfident person may become overreliant on relationships with practitioners, rather than learning how to build effective social relationships
Mutual influence	You need to immerse yourself in the client's view of the world, and demonstrate you are understanding it	Clients need to feel your empathy but may make demands for excessive reassurance of it, or expect an alliance that colludes with their biased perception of important relationships when these need to be challenged or goals for change set, for example in adequate care for children or the questioning of oppressive marital relationships
Regression	You can understand clients' vulnerabilities better by enabling them to go back to important emotional experiences and act out what happened	Help the client to experience the emotions and reactions to important events, both negative and positive, in their life experience, for example how they felt about relationships with their parents or bullying at school. However, a repeated return to negative experiences can get in the way of progress
Evaluating interventions	You need to track how clients are responding to your interventions as you go along and not only at the end of the intervention	Clients may be challenging or difficult to engage through anger or depression. You need to think whether expressing these emotions is confirming present behaviour or whether they are expressing something that helps them move forward
Self-disclosure	Disclose information about yourself and react immediately when this will help and not hinder develop the relationship and emotional exchange	Clients often express important emotions, such as sadness and anger. You should react with your genuine emotional reactions if this will be positive for the client, for example enabling them to see how people react to how they are. You should be cautious about reacting when you are revealing material about yourself with no therapeutic purpose
Managing emotion	Emotion is integral to cognition and brain functioning; identifying sources of emotional reaction helps manage it	Adults may fear to express anger because angry responses were rejected by parents who expected calmness, but may find this frustrating because they cannot express relationship difficulties in their marriage or in work teams
Confrontation and anger	Identify and practise how to express difficulty or conflict in emotionally important relationships	Questioning, confronting, expressing frustration and anger, and setting limits to behaviours can all be rehearsed with practitioners
Erotic feelings	Sexual feelings – attraction or disgust – are often ways of seeking control of others	A loving male partner who is always sensitive and supportive to enable women to achieve more in their work may be valued and enhance the relationship because of his support, but also control the woman's self-expression and self-development

Source: Maroda (2010).

Example text: Brandell (2004) on psychodynamic social work

The Preface explains that I summarize in each chapter one or two 'example texts' used by social workers, which show how the theory being considered is used in comprehensive accounts of social work in the tradition of that theory. I explain the criteria I use to select these texts in the Preface and in the 'major statements' sections of each chapter.

Figure 4.4 Brandell's four elements of psychodynamic social work

Element	Important ideas	Practice implications
Assessment	*Multideterminism*: any mental event or aspect of behaviour may have multiple causes and serve several psychological purposes for the individual	Practitioners must explore a range of aspects of psychosocial functioning before developing a treatment plan
Beginning treatment	Creating *an effective treatment relationship within a holding environment* helps to form a *therapeutic alliance* between practitioner and client	In the early stages, a focus on creating a secure environment for working with the client and developing a relationship has priority
Middle-phase treatment	Practitioners use various interventions to help clients *work through* important psychological problems to remove the client's *resistance* to gaining insight	In this phase, practitioners use techniques that confront clients' avoidance of dealing with their psychological problems
Termination	Practitioners prevent the *reversal* of the client's progress in the future by allowing *separation* from the therapeutic alliance and facilitating future independent development of the client's individuality	Practitioners focus on helping clients to maintain psychological strengths independently in the future, and arrange follow-up to reinforce and check further progress

Source: Brandell (2004: 133–254).

Calling on the importance of process from functional social work, Brandell (2004) identifies four elements of 'dynamic therapy', set out in Figure 4.4. The starting point, dynamic assessment, makes clear that most problems faced by clients are caused by several different factors. Therefore practitioners should not assume that there is only one source, and should realize that the different factors probably interact. The main factors to look for are:

- understanding precisely the presenting problems that clients bring to the practitioner and the range of antecedent factors that led to clients deciding to get, or being referred for, help;
- understanding how clients characteristically deal with the world outside themselves, in particular psychological defences and strategies for adapting to, alleviating or overcoming anxiety and other emotional responses to difficulties in their lives;
- examining ego functioning, that is how clients deal with external threats and difficulties;

■ examining self-cohesiveness, that is, clients' views of themselves as a person, and the extent to which this is consistent and organized;

■ strengths and weaknesses in clients' present psychological functioning – their 'mental state';

■ areas of life that clients find they are dealing with effectively and feel that they are competent to deal with – competence and efficacy;

■ how the practitioner responds to and feels about the client;

■ constructing a picture of how the psychological factors are interacting with the innate characteristics of the client (a 'dynamic–genetic formulation');

■ making a plan for treatment.

Brandell (2004: 137) makes the point that agencies often require practitioners to come up with a statement too early, often mainly describing problems and needs that fit a pre-formulated guideline. Describing American clinical settings, he discusses the need to make assessments that fit the American Psychiatric Association's *Diagnostic and Statistical Manual* (DSM), and this point equally applies to assessment documents such as the UK's single assessment process and the common assessment framework. Psychodynamic assessment looks not only at apparently problem behaviour, difficulties in childhood development and social dysfunctions, but also at clients' strengths and assets, their family, community and social environments and the resources available to help clients. In this way, it is much broader than many clinical psychology, psychiatry or counselling assessments. This requires a longer assessment process, including interviews with family members, and some broader investigation of involvements with other services. This often runs alongside the initial responses to problems that require immediate action.

Assessment outcomes start from a summary of information about the client, together with a mental status examination of current behaviour and psychological issues, the client's cognition, that is, their thinking abilities and their capacity for insight into their situation, and their behaviour. The next element of the assessment is ego and superego functions: can clients manage their drives and impulses, tolerate guilt and frustration and be flexible in how they defend themselves psychologically against threats? What is their potential to work in relationships, as demonstrated by their relationships with family and community members and the practitioner? How far can they integrate contradictions in their lives and manage the pressures of daily living? Clients' self structure and self–object relations should then be reviewed: do clients have a realistic view of themselves and have sensible, well-organized aims in life? Competence and efficacy come next: what have they achieved, in school or work, in their family relationships and leisure, and what does this show about their self-confidence and their ability to use their strengths and overcome weaknesses? Finally, the dynamic–genetic formulation looks at how their experience and strengths have combined with and made use of their innate capacity to result in the person that the practitioner will work with. The treatment plan follows on from this.

Although I have presented this in everyday language and generalized the material that Brandell discusses, his account, full of polysyllabic jargon, focuses on individuals presenting mental health problems, and this indicates the important role of this form of practice in US social work.

Brandell's account of beginning treatment contains ideas drawn from psychoanalytic history. It starts from creating a 'holding environment', based on Winnicott's ideas about 'good-enough parenting' in working with children; it also connects with the 'secure base' of attachment theory. The practitioner takes a genuine interest and concern for the client, creates a safe place for clients to express emotions such as anger, fear and frustration that it is difficult for them to express elsewhere, and allows them to build a relationship with the practitioner.

Case example: Should Diana get her children back?

Daisy was a child protection social worker working with Diana and her partner, Sean. Their two children were being looked after by the local authority and were placed with foster parents after they had been found neglected because of Diana and Sean's heavy drinking. During several visits to the children at the foster carer's home, Diana had been very obviously drunk, and this led to a withdrawal of the arrangements for the children to have regular contact with Diana. When Daisy next visited, Diana and Sean, both drinking, were very angry and aggressive towards her, expressing the fear and anger they felt about the decision, as well as their frustration about their inability to control their drinking behaviour. Diana later visited Daisy at her office; they made plans for Diana to separate from Sean and for him to move to a local hostel. Then Diana would work to change her alcoholic behaviour and see the children at a contact centre. Over several more months, Diana, with ups and downs, improved steadily and resumed contact at the foster carer's home, at the same time making plans for a better home environment.

In this case example, Daisy provided a 'holding environment' by not overreacting to the emotional turmoil of her visit, although for her own safety she and Diana together worked out some ground rules for behaviour for future visits. She also helped Diana to make and carry out positive but realistic plans for the future when Diana had expected to be given no further chances.

This case example also illustrates the three important features of relationship in psychodynamic social work:

- *Transference–countertransference* – the anger and fear expressed by Diana in reaction to Daisy's authority, as though she were Diana's violent parents, shows how she was transferring and demonstrating in this present authority relationship her fears about her past relationship. This led Daisy to feel she had to react to control Diana and Sean's behaviour.
- *Real relationship* – the relationship has to reflect the realities of how the participants in it take on their responsibilities and roles in relation to one another. In a real relationship, Daisy made it clear what was unacceptable in Diana and Sean's behaviour, but by working positively on plans for the future that respected their parental roles, she did not react to the countertransference by becoming overcontrolling like Diana's parents.

■ *Therapeutic alliance* – by managing future behaviour on visits, establishing a new programme for contact with the children and helping Sean and Diana work on their alcohol problems and parenting responsibilities, Daisy created an alliance in which they both took on responsibilities to move forward again, in spite of a difficult event. Again, this is one of the 'shared value principles' of social work practice theories.

As clients and practitioners move into the middle phase of treatment, they 'work through' resistance using various dynamic techniques, detailed below. Earlier in the chapter, we looked at some general information about resistance: this happens when clients avoid engaging with their problems by either becoming silent, talking about unimportant issues, being late or missing appointments, or on the other hand are unduly emotional, keep finding practical difficulties with plans or are overcompliant, almost 'working to rule' instead of being flexible. Another form of resistance may arise because the emotional problems provide some benefit in relationships, as we will see in the next case example.

Case example: Gillian's use of emotion in managing the relationship with her family

Gillian was a woman with a history of depressive illness. Her husband and teenage sons complained that this made her very dependent on them, prevented her from working and required long-term medication for agoraphobia, a fear of open spaces that confined her to the house. Attempts to help her live a more normal life led to outbursts of severe depression, crying and emotional behaviour. After this, her family told her social worker that this was so distressing they accepted that nothing could be done and they would continue to support her at home. It seemed to the social worker that Gillian was using her extremely emotional behaviour to gain her family's compliance with her dependence on them.

Working-through is a repeated process (one of the shared value principles of social work practice theories, an 'action sequence' used in psychodynamic practice) of remembering crucial examples of problem behaviour as they occurred, exploring what happened and thinking about ways in which events and their emotional consequences might have been different. If practitioners are not careful, this can become repetitive, merely allowing people to express hopelessness. Therefore, it is important to help clients see how alternatives might have been possible and plan for different ways of handling them in the future. Brandell (2004: 192) points out the connections with narrative and social construction ideas.

Another important way of working is through *interpretation*. The practitioner works with the client and observes their behaviour. This allows practitioners to build up a picture of resistances, conflicts and their origins in past experiences or innate tendencies. Interpretations are explanations of these observations that enable clients to use this new knowledge to rethink their behaviour and plan to behave in alternative ways. Practitioners need to make interpretations work by helping clients to think again or plan anew. Change is not achieved just by explaining something, but by working with clients to react to the interpretation.

Other important dynamic techniques include the following:

- *Exploration* is a description of behaviour and events that enables clients to understand them better.
- *Ventilation* by expressing emotions such as anger, anxiety or fear allows clients to move on from their feelings and act rationally again. Practitioners connect the ventilated feelings with events and relationships so that clients understand where their strong feelings come from and can manage them better.
- *Clarification* involves reflecting on how the individual's environment has affected them, exploring patterns in behaviour and how these have developed so that, by understanding them better, clients can adapt their behaviour.
- *Sustainment* aims to improve clients' self-esteem or self-confidence by the social worker being understanding and interested, expressing a wish to help them and having confidence that they can make progress as they are adapting their behaviour.

The following case example shows many of the dynamic techniques we have described in action.

Case example: A single parent makes a new start

Catarina had two children by two different male partners, neither of whom had remained in touch with her. She had enjoyed the experience of having the children at home as babies but disliked their moves to become independent of her and make contacts outside the home. Her mixture of anxiety and depression meant that they stayed at home to support her. Their resulting poor school attendance led to referral for social work help to avoid legal action being taken.

Catarina knew she needed to change, but she found it hard to find work and support the children in being more independent. The practitioner helped her to explore how she had come to have the children without a continuing relationship with a male partner. This, she felt, came from her own mother being more interested in her relationships with men than in Catarina, leading to a lack of confidence that she would be loved. Catarina expressed her anger and hurt about this and connected it with her fear that her children would also reject and move away from her. Catarina and her social worker also looked at ways in which she could plan to support the children in school and build up her work skills, so that she could create a different kind of relationship with them while also establishing a new direction for herself. The practitioner talked over Catarina's plans regularly with her and pointed out when her activities had been successful.

The final stage is *termination*. The practitioner and client go through a process of identifying what has been achieved and making plans for further progress. Some kind of ritual of leave-making may also be useful. More recent developments include planning a follow-up session to reinforce progress and future plans, and to evaluate the treatment.

Brandell's (2004) discussion of practice with different client groups provides a more detailed explanation of a wide range of dynamic techniques.

Example text: Shemmings and Shemmings (2011) on attachment theory

Shemmings and Shemmings (2011) provide an up-to-date account of theory and research on attachment, mainly in work with children, although there is some coverage of work with adults. Concerns about child care are so important in social work that this focus is relevant for many practitioners. We have seen that Bowlby's ideas centre on how infants become attached to a person at a very early age; this attachment is expressed in behaviour because the infant tries to be in close physical proximity to that person. Through their interactions with this attachment figure, infants build up a picture in their minds, an 'internal working model' of how relationships usually work. This is eventually extended to other people, and the model becomes less of a working model, being a more fixed expectation of how people behave towards the child and how the child should behave in reaction to that.

The four main components of attachment are as follows:

- The attachment figure becomes a *secure base* for us.
- We *seek proximity* to our secure base when we are afraid, hungry or ill.
- We use the secure base as a *safe haven* when we explore new experiences.
- We experience distress as a *separation protest* when the attachment figure becomes unavailable to us. This might happen to children when parents who are a secure base are absent and to adults when they are cut off from a spouse or partner who is their secure base. This might happen to adults when they are away from home or when they are bereaved.

These ideas were explored in a classic experiment, the 'strange situation procedure', which is usually carried out with children aged between one and three years. There are seven stages to this, set out in Figure 4.5.

Figure 4.5 mentions three types of reaction in which children seek proximity to a carer:

- *Secure* children have learned that they can safely express their need for proximity in the carer's presence, and the carer will try to understand the need and help to manage the distress. They will go to the carer on their return, and the carer will react supportively and lovingly.
- *Insecure avoidant* children have learned that they should not display their feelings so they repress and suppress their anxiety. Although upset when the carer leaves, they appear unmoved when the parent returns because the carer clearly expresses that they expect the child to manage their emotions.
- *Insecure ambivalent* children have learned that the carer does not react consistently, and the children also react randomly and unpredictably. When the carer returns, they switch in a haphazard way between wanting proximity and continuing to play. The carer's efforts to calm the child's distress is *misattuned* because of a failure to pick up what reaction the child finds helpful.

Figure 4.5 The strange situation procedure

Stage	Event	Reactions
Preparation	The child plays; the parent is present and uninvolved	Independent play is the starting point for the procedure
First appearance of the stranger	The stranger enters, chats to the parent and offers a toy to the infant	The child looks to the carer for reassurance but does not respond directly to the stranger
First separation	The parent leaves the room, and the stranger leaves the child to play. If the child stops playing, the stranger tries to interest the child in the toys	Even when the carer leaves, most children do not go to the stranger
First reunion	The parent returns and waits for the child to respond; the stranger leaves	Three alternative reactions depend on whether child is securely or insecurely attached (see text), all representing an organized way to *seek proximity*
Second separation	Once the child settles, the parent leaves the room	The child cries and goes to the door *(separation protest)*
Second appearance of the stranger	The stranger re-renters the room and tries to interest the child in a toy	Most children do not go to the stranger
Second reunion	The parent re-renters, waits for the child to respond and then picks up the child; the stranger leaves	Three alternative reactions recur

Source: Shemmings and Shemmings (2011: 23–8), derived from Ainsworth et al. (1978).

Across many different cultures, about 60% of children fall into the secure category, about 25% are insecurely avoidant and about 11% are insecurely ambivalent. All of these forms of attachment behaviour are *organized* in that the child is making a contribution to his or her survival in the relationship with the carer, having learned what works best in maintaining this particular carer's proximity.

The remaining small group of around 4% of children exhibit *disorganized attachment*. Contradictory behaviour is the main characteristic of this form of attachment. For example, the child approaches the carer, but fearfully or looking away, or the child freezes, that is, stops moving, when the parent enters. Children who show disorganized attachment behaviour are overwhelmed by fear because they do not know what to do to maintain safety and proximity. As infants, this disorganized behaviour resolves itself quickly into an organized pattern. Adolescents with disorganized attachment behaviour are punitive towards the carer, being aggressive or threatening, or more apparently caring by being excessively polite and helpful. Each of these reactions is an attempt to control or manage the carer's behaviour. Disorganized attachment behaviour results from unpredictable or malevolent behaviour by the carer. It is strongly associated with the child going on to experience mental health problems in adolescence and adult life and to repeat this kind of parenting with their own children.

Many factors affect whether a person's attachment behaviour is disorganized: there is no simple connection between the events in the child's life and their attachment behaviour. Shemmings and Shemmings (2011) review this as a series of pathways. There are several main factors that can generate disorganized attachment behaviour, and as children follow their pathway through life, the extent to which these factors are important increases or reduces. Moderator variables in the child's life reduce the effect of a factor, and mediator variables change how disorganized attachment occurs when the factor arises.

Disorganized attachment mainly arises from the quality of the protective behaviour that carers exhibit. More children who are ill-treated by their carers exhibit disorganized attachment than children who have little experience of family violence. This is because the child experiences ill-treatment and danger from a person who would be expected to provide protection in their relationship.

Carers who behave in this way may have experiences in their lives that leave them unable to be appropriately protective. Unresolved trauma, abuse or loss in the parent's life means that the parent experienced fear, helplessness and anger that prevented them from being able to comfort or sooth the child when this was required. Other relevant factors may include parental insensitivity, an inability to react due to depression or drug or alcohol abuse or to marital disharmony, and frightening parental behaviour such as dissociative behaviour (behaving as though disconnected from the present situation and feeling shut out from current events), rough handling or withdrawn behaviour. In these instances, the carer is unable to provide care and support because their behaviour is the source of the need for care and support.

These factors in the carer's behaviour do not, however, always lead, either on their own or together, to disorganized attachment. The relevant mediator is likely to be the carer's capacity for mentalization and reflective function. This is the carer's capacity to explore his or her own mind and experience and to be prepared and able to see the child as an independent being who is similarly capable of reaching understanding and thoughtful progress in their lives. An inability to value the child's independent life in this way may mean that the various combinations of factors in the parent's life are pulled together along a pathway of experiences leading to ill-treatment and onwards to disorganized attachment.

Neurological, biochemical and genetic factors also affect how children and parents relate to one another. The neurotransmitter oxytocin is associated, for example, with social recognition, trust, love and care-giving behaviours, and there is evidence that mothers with a poor regulation of oxytocin display less sensitive parental behaviour. Another neurotransmitter, dopamine, is connected with how people regulate stress and cope with difficulties in their lives.

Practitioners use a number of these ideas in working with children who have disorganized attachment. Assessment scales and tools have been devised for exploring attachment behaviour and measuring the experience of frightening or insensitive carer behaviour (Prior and Glaser, 2006: 96–155; Shemmings and Shemmings, 2011: 65–83). They focus on identifying children who need help and on identifying the behaviours of carers.

Howe (1995) suggests that assessment practice using attachment theory involves looking at:

- *present relationships*, especially their content and quality, function and structure;
- *relationship history*, and how it displays various types of attachment behaviour;
- *context*, such as particular stresses of the environment on present relationships;
- *content and quality*, looking at the affective tone of relationships, whether there is an emotional bond between people, and their operational style, that is, how they regulate the relationship.

Case example: Two single mothers' approaches to their daughters

A single mother developed a close relationship with her only daughter and controlled her behaviour by trying to explain rationally why her daughter should behave or react in desired ways. In childhood, this often led to lengthy conflict or impasse, but in adulthood the daughter found it easy to ask for support and help from others and developed effective relationships. In another similar relationship, the mother was absent a great deal and relied on a series of instructions and the daughter's 'duty' to behave appropriately and not embarrass her mother. This also used rational means, but was not allied to the loving relationship and constant interaction of explanation, and in adulthood this daughter avoided intimate relationships and had very little contact with her mother.

This case example demonstrates how two different approaches to developing attachment relationships with a child have long-term consequences. Although each mother might disagree with the other's approach, the important thing for the long term is the children's security in knowing that the mother's style of attachment will be consistently pursued.

A range of interventions have also been developed; those that are best supported by evidence focus on improving carers' sensitivity to children and changing carers through foster and adoptive care (Prior and Glaser, 2006: 233–60; Shemmings and Shemmings, 2011: 173–219). Mentalizing and reflective function approaches focus on increasing the carer's capacity to mentalize about other people. A good way of working on this is to get them to mentalize about the practitioner; to do this, the practitioner provides mentalized experiences as an example. The next case example provides an illustration of this, which shows how the process of providing mentalized experiences is not the same as being empathic in the way that humanistic counselling proposes (see Chapter 10).

Case example: Mentalizing about removing a child from the mother's care

Caitlin feared that the children's social care services were considering removing her daughter from her care. She came to the office to see her social worker, Hannah, to discuss her daughter's progress at nursery and to ask for help with social security allowances. They had a good relationship, but on this occasion Caitlin expressed a lot of anger about Hannah's attitude: 'looking down your nose at me, when I don't have any money or strength to do all the

▶

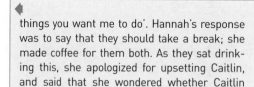

things you want me to do'. Hannah's response was to say that they should take a break; she made coffee for them both. As they sat drinking this, she apologized for upsetting Caitlin, and said that she wondered whether Caitlin was thinking of Hannah as mainly someone who was criticizing and judging her. Doing this, she was drawing attention to an aspect of Caitlin's mentalization. There was some truth in this because she did continually have to make assessments about how Caitlin's daughter was doing. Then Hannah moved the discussion on to the main things that Hannah had think about when she was doing her assessment.

The practitioner's approach here is tentative, because mentalizing is difficult, but it helped the carer to consider a range of things that might be on Hannah's mind so she could be seen by Caitlin both as helpful and as assessing the situation. Techniques are also available using video-taping and have been found effective. For example, Phillips (2011: 181) describes filming a parent–child interaction and getting the parent to speak for the child and mentalize the child's experience by writing subtitles describing the child's behaviour to put on the screen. He suggests that watching and exploring their interaction with their own child can increase their sensitivity in dealing directly with their children. Other studies involve instructing a carer to play on the floor with the child, with the child leading the activity. The carer then reflects on the experience and on how they think the child was thinking about what they were doing. Such an approach encourages a reflective capacity in the carer (Prior and Glaser, 2006: 239–41). Many agencies use parent education or parent and child play informed by practitioners' interventions, as we saw in the extended case study in Chapter 2 on the organization of a child and adolescent mental health service.

Shemmings and Shemmings (2011: 203–19) describe a project that builds on this approach in child safeguarding work. The practitioner observed the carer with the child and gave them increasingly difficult tasks to see how sensitively the parent introduced them and gained the child's compliance. In another project, work with children to identify abuse used story stems. Here, the practitioner starts a story of an event in family life that the child completes, indicating their expectations of how they are treated within their own family or in other social situations.

The connections with psychodynamic theory are clear from this summary of attachment theory and social work. The focus on emotions, early childhood development as the basis for later relationship and emotional problems, and practice based on understanding and insight are typical of many psychodynamic theories. Attachment theory may be important for work with children, where it is well supported by research in child development, but its application to adults is less well evidenced. Moreover, its social work application produces only a sketchy set of ideas for practice, although it gives a good basis for a confident explanation of childhood problems. It takes up some ideas from cognitive and learning theory, particularly in its emphasis on therapy as learning. This is a point at which practice ideas from cognitive-behavioural therapy might be included in the general approach set out for practice in attachment theory.

Conclusion: using psychodynamic theory

Psychodynamic theories have provided a rich source of ideas and metaphors for practice in more therapeutic or clinical settings; we all use psychodynamic metaphors to express common ideas about how people are influenced by their past in their thinking. Being aware of the historic importance of psychodynamic ideas as the source of many practices in social work allows practitioners to think critically when they use what appear to be perfectly natural techniques that in fact derive from psychoanalytic ideas. Contrary to psychodynamic ideas, however, social work practitioners are usually cautious about whether in many situations it is useful to delve into our clients' pasts to understand how problems have developed, rather than focusing on their present predicament.

Attachment theory and relational theories using self ideas have developed a modernized practice that has moved away from traditional psychoanalytic ideas and from the historic psychosocial practice presented in Brandell's (2004) text. Attachment theory is well supported by research and has been informative for practitioners working with children and young people, in child protection practice and in loss and bereavement work. As we saw in the extended case study in Chapter 2, it has also been used in child and adolescent mental health services.

While psychodynamic ideas can be applied in many different situations, they focus on mental health and emotional problems, and are probably of most use in mental health services. They are sometimes used in specialist settings in mental health and having a good knowledge of them enables connections with other professionals to be made if you practise in such agencies. Brearley (2007) argues that psychodynamic theory is helpful in the type of practice that requires an understanding of communications and the way in which people's feelings and drives can distort how they understand what others communicate to them.

Additional resources

Further reading

Brandell, J. R. (2004) *Psychodynamic Social Work* (New York: Columbia University Press).
  The most extensive broad account of psychodynamic social work.
Cassidy, J and Shaver, P. R. (eds) (2008) *Handbook of Attachment: Theory, Research and Clinical Applications* (2nd edn) (New York: Guilford).
  A very extensive edited collection, a reference work drawing mainly on clinical psychology and psychiatry, covering attachment ideas relevant to all age groups.
Ruch, G., Turney, D. and Ward, A. (2010) *Relationship-based Social Work: Getting to the Heart of Practice* (London: Jessica Kingsley).
  This thoughtful collection of papers comprehensively describes relational practice.
Goldstein, E., Miehls, D. and Ringel, S. (2009) *Advanced Clinical Social Work Practice: Relational Principles and Techniques* (New York: Columbia University Press).

This is a very comprehensive and detailed account of relational theory, which allows an advanced practitioner to build on the relational ideas briefly covered in this chapter.

Freedberg, S. (2008) *Relational Theory for Social Work Practice: A Feminist Perspective* (New York: Routledge).

This useful and practical text marries psychodynamic relational theory with feminist ideas.

Howe, D. (2011) *Attachment Across the Lifecourse: A Brief Introduction* (Basingstoke: Palgrave Macmillan).

Howe, D., Brandon, M., Hinings, D. and Schofield, G. (1999) *Attachment Theory, Child Maltreatment and Family Support* (Basingstoke: Macmillan – now Palgrave Macmillan).

These two books provide a good review of attachment theory applied to social work: the first and most recent extensively reviews current theory, balancing evidence about attachment in adulthood, with the better established work on attachment in childhood strongly reflected in the second book.

Parkes, C. M., Stevenson-Hinde, J. and Marris, P. (eds) (1993) *Attachment Across the Life Cycle* (London: Routledge).

A good account of practice applications of attachment theory at various life stages; it is not specifically about, but is applicable to, social work.

Journals

Journal of Social Work Practice – Group for the Advancement of Psychodynamics and Psychotherapy in Social Work; Taylor & Francis.

Psychoanalytic Social Work – Taylor & Francis.

Smith College Studies in Social Work – Smith College School of Social Work; Taylor & Francis

Therapeutic Communities – Consortium for Therapeutic Communities, and Nottingham Institute for Mental Health, UK.

Websites

http://socialworkpodcast.blogspot.co.uk/2009/12/psychoanalytic-treatment-in.html

The Social Work Podcast has in interesting interview with Dr Carol Tosone about current psychodynamic social work practice.

http://www.aapcsw.org/

The main asset of the American Association for Psychoanalysis in Clinical Social Work website is its online journal.

http://www.gaps.org.uk/

The website of the Group for the Advancement of Psychodynamics and Psychotherapy in Social Work also has a useful trove of articles and publications.

http://www.therapeuticcommunities.org/

The Consortium for Therapeutic Communities has a useful website, covering residential work using this psychodynamic model of practice.

Crisis and task-centred practice 5

Main contribution

Crisis intervention and task-centred practice continue to be important in social work because they offer brief, structured models of intervention which address clearly definable problems that will respond to active efforts to resolve them. This focus on the shared principles of defined positive aims and action sequences makes them easy to grasp and apply. By giving priority to the main issues that clients have identified for themselves, these models of practice respect clients and engage their commitment, which is important for the professional working alliance and the shared value principles of human rights discussed in Chapter 1 (see Figure 1.7). There is an evidence base for their efficacy, especially in task-centred practice, and overall both models are practical and easy to justify in busy social agencies.

Main points

- Both crisis intervention and task-centred practice are brief, structured theories that deal with immediate problems; they may be less helpful when dealing with long-term individual care and social issues.
- Both models have research support, and task-centred practice has been widely validated in many different countries and settings.
- Contracts made between clients and practitioners have been criticized for making the relationship too formal. Less formal but still explicit agreements are instead increasingly being used in task-centred practice.
- The focus of crisis intervention and task-centred practice on practical responses and their consequent success in achieving political support may lead to an uncritical acceptance of their failure to tackle social oppression or other social causes of clients' problems.
- Both models enhance accountability to clients by focusing on their priorities and experiences.

- Crises are a turning point in people's lives when their usual ways of resolving a problem fail. People experience feelings of tension and disorganization when crises affect their lives.
- Crises occur when 'hazardous' events disturb an existing steady state in which people can manage the events that affect them; a precipitating factor then generates a state of active crisis.
- Crisis intervention focuses on people's emotional reactions to events in their lives that are perceived as significant. People can be shown how to build on their existing strengths by identifying new support systems and learning new coping skills.
- Task-centred practice is built on a sequence of identifying and prioritizing the problems chosen by the client and then undertaking tasks to deal with those problems.

Practice ideas

☐ *Crisis* is used in two ways: to refer to a process of events in people's lives that provides a focus for practitioners to work with clients, and to refer to commonly occurring elements in life that present a series of maturational tasks for us to complete.

☐ Both theories use *brief* interventions.

☐ Both theories use *structured*, *planned* and *directive programmes* of intervention.

☐ *Tasks* are structured elements of intervention in task-centred practice, but are also important challenges in life that have to be overcome in order to achieve emotional satisfaction and to maintain positive social relationships within crisis intervention.

☐ *Contracts* or *agreements* with clients help them to participate in and structure treatment plans.

Major statements

Crisis intervention

American texts present a multiprofessional perspective, bringing together psychology, psychiatry and social work; this reflects the historical source of the theory within the mental health professions. They also reflect the fact that, in the USA, crisis theory is used in emergency practice settings, such as crisis mental health and rape crisis teams. The most authoritative and comprehensive statement from a social work source is Roberts's (2005a) *Crisis Intervention Handbook*. However, this is an extensive edited collection covering a multitude of topics in great detail and is less concerned with exploring the underlying theory. James's *Crisis Intervention Strategies* (2008) offers a respected single-authored work from a psychiatric perspective and, as with Roberts, detailed material on specialized areas. Kanel, a psychologist (2012), offers a long-standing practical guide that is firmly underpinned by theory.

Other texts that extract a distinctively social work perspective from this broader perspective are those by Loughran (2011), which helpfully reviews different theoretical approaches to crisis intervention, and Thompson (2011a), which briefly summarizes the main social work approach. Because of its concision, I refer mainly to Thompson as the example text in this chapter, with additional material from the other sources.

Task-centred practice

You can find the classic statements in Reid and Epstein (1972a, 1972b) and Reid (1978, 1985); later texts that involved the creators of this approach are those by Tolson et al. (2003) and Epstein and Brown (2002). A UK text that provides an approachable overview is Marsh and Doel's (2005), used as the example text in this chapter along with additional material from the other sources.

The debate summary

The main areas of debate about these models take place around their short-term focus and their structured programmes of intervention. Criticisms arise because the general success of both of these practice models in agencies may detract from other ways in which they are not so effective. The structured nature of the interventions of these models, and their short-term focus, means that they are not the first choice where constant debilitating crises and long-term psychological problems are the main issue, or where long-term care services are being provided. They may be used in child protection work or when working with long-term conditions or increasing frailty in old age to achieve results when a specific problem or a particular crisis occurs. In such cases, however, supportive work, the provision of services, longer term efforts to bring about change or longer term supervision to prevent deterioration or risk will often also be required. Moreover, neither model works well with people who do not accept the right of the worker or agency to be involved in helping them.

Many social workers find the clarity of the processes involved in these models very attractive, but they may oversimplify the complexity of the issues in people's lives. In particular, the models' structured nature and their focus on the concepts of 'crisis' and 'task' mean that they may define social problems in behavioural terms and according to the practitioner's assumptions. Practitioners may, as a result, fail to identify the broader social issues and structural failings that have led to the problems. However, their structure and clarity may help practitioners to find a 'way in' to a complex situation. The short timescale may also be useful where people are have limited capacity to focus on important issues, such as clients with learning disabilities, or where they have limited commitment to the intervention, because for example they are offenders or they abuse drugs.

Crisis intervention and task-centred practice both represent a trend in social work, reflecting the second shared value principle (see Figure 1.7), towards clearer, more focused activity than is seen with the long-term, non-directive, insight-giving methods of psychodynamic work. This trend, however, has been criticized; see in particular Thompson (2011a: 13), who argues that there is an overemphasis in crisis theory on internal emotional reactions. You could argue that this emphasis is actually an advantage, since the theory provides guidance for dealing with emotional reactions. Kadushin (1998) proposed that adaptations to conventional interviewing and practice techniques from psychodynamic theory are required to implement brief, focused therapies. For example, the need to establish a relationship rapidly means presenting a warm, intelligent impression from the outset. Focusing on the present and on solutions, rather than exploring problems and their history in detail, are also important. Practitioners are not attempting an overall 'cure' but the resolution of specific issues 'for now'.

Both theories, however, aim to achieve the social work objective of problem-solving, using a (conventional social work) individualizing relationship with clients who are treated using a medical model: problems are treated much like illnesses, and it is the social worker's job to solve them, just as it is the doctor's job to cure physical ailments. Crisis intervention, with its more pronounced psychodynamic roots, places more emphasis on emotional responses and irrational or unconscious behaviour than does task-centred work, which assumes that clients exhibit greater rationality. However, cognitive-behavioural practice has had an impact on both models, leading to a shift in brief practice using either model towards more cognitive practice. For example, Dattilio and Freeman (2007) offer an account of crisis intervention that is strongly focused on cognitive-behavioural strategies, and Roberts (2005a, 2005b) also emphasizes this.

In addition, Thompson (2011a: 13) suggests that crisis intervention theory would be better balanced if it emphasized the development of support systems to prevent or resolve crises. Caplan and his research team did move into this field, which I cover in Chapter 7 because of its theoretical connection with systems theory. One of the problems with Thompson's point is that there is not enough time in many agencies to develop a support system around a client within the period of a crisis before practitioners have to move on to the next case without a longer term plan being in place. Crisis theory also recognizes that clients may not be ready to work on long-term issues once the immediate problem has been dealt with. Thompson (2011a: 14) also reports criticisms of a failure to recognize cultural and family contexts and social divisions. These points might equally be made about task-centred practice. In both cases, this reflects the liberal or neo-liberal political philosophy and social order perspective behind problem-solving as a social work objective.

It is possible, however, to adapt the theories, particularly task-centred practice, in which there is some research on these possibilities, to a focus on the family or community. However, because their aim is to be brief and focused, it does not seem unreasonable to limit their perspective to a particular issue in someone's life. Clients can of course plan to handle such issues by building family and community supports as part of crisis resolution, or by tasks working on such support. These criticisms also need to recognize the reality that most social work is concerned with individual problem-solving, and these techniques are well-designed for that.

Furthermore, the idea of using 'contracts' in classic task-centred practice has been criticized. Rojek and Collins (1987, 1988) argued that it offers a false sense of equality between practitioners and clients. If you talk about a 'contract' with your client, it implies an equality that conceals your hidden power in the relationship, which comes from your official role and professional status. Power imbalances between clients and practitioners with official roles prevent the mutual cooperation implied by the model. In response to this, Corden and Preston-Shoot (1987, 1988) argue that contracts can benefit client–practitioner relationships by making them more specific so that each person has a clearer sense of where they stand. In fact, contract work does achieve results in allowing people to attain the desired ends, again a shared value principle (see Figure 1.7). Some writers emphasize written contracts for this reason, but others have moved towards the concept of less formal, more fluid agreements. This does not, however, address the issue that clients may feel pressed or even pressurized into an agreement by the power of the practitioner or agency, or by the urgency of their need for the agency's resources.

In addition to these areas of debate, there is also a political critique around agencies' potential misuse of these models of practice, to the disadvantage of clients who may need more extensive provision. The success of these two approaches to social work comes from the attractiveness of their clear and simple approaches and the practical usability of the basic ideas of 'crisis' and 'task'. Their effectiveness in dealing with the presenting problems may result in society avoiding longer term and more deeply seated responses to social oppression. Gambrill (1994) argues that task-centred work – and by extension many forms of brief therapy – provides a minimal response to severe social problems. It thus conceals resource inadequacy and the failure of political will to respond realistically to deep-seated problems of poverty and social inequality.

This debate arose at the time these theoretical models were gaining influence, as social work was becoming a much larger scale profession within extensive welfare states. The focus and brevity of these treatments offered an economic approach during this expansion compared with longer term methods that would have increased costs to an impossible extent and required a greatly expanded workforce. Moreover, involvement in the front line of public services put social workers in touch with the crises in people's lives in a way that did not happen as much when they were trying to deal with longer term problems or offering care over the long term. Task-centred work offered clearer accountability and a focus on outcomes for the influx of less experienced, less well qualified and more infrequently supervised workers employed in settings requiring public scrutiny. It is also generic and can be applied in any setting with any person (Doel and Marsh, 1992: 6).

The research-demonstrated effectiveness of task-centred work also made it much more politically acceptable to agency managers and funders, and supported a profession that was at times embattled by criticism of its effectiveness. Some research support for crisis intervention also exists (see Parad and Parad, 1990: 16–18). In addition, task-centred work has been popular with clients because of its clarity and sense of direction, and because it actively involves people in a sense of partnership (Gibbons et al., 1979).

However, its simple concepts belie its complexity, and it is hard to train people to use it well (Marsh, 2007: 192, 196). Ford and Postle (2012) suggest that its structured approach permits it to incorporate a variety of social work practices within the restrictions of current agencies.

Wider theoretical perspectives

Crisis intervention

The classic formulation of crisis intervention as a technique is in Caplan's (1965) book on preventive psychiatry. This source indicates the method's origins in mental health work and its focus on the prevention, rather than the treatment, of illness. A famous paper by Lindemann (1944) described the grief reactions of various groups of people as they coped with the death of family members in a major fire disaster. They managed their bereavement crisis better if they had coped with previous crises in their lives, but less well if they had not resolved past problems. A group of mental health workers around Lindemann and Caplan constructed the ideas of crisis intervention over two decades while working with several community mental health problems. Their work influenced social support and networking ideas (see Chapter 7).

Traditional crisis intervention uses elements of ego psychology from a psychodynamic perspective (see Chapter 4), and recent developments have incorporated a wide range of theoretical perspectives (Loughran, 2011). The main focus is on emotional responses to external events and how people can be helped to control them so that they can then move on to resolve the difficulties they are facing. Young (1983) draws parallels between the concepts of crisis intervention and ideas from Chinese philosophy, and Kanel's work (2012) also discusses this. Young points to the 'doctrine of the mean', that is, keeping our system in balance leading to a state of harmony, which reflects the Chinese philosophical assumption that people naturally gravitate towards fulfilment. The idea of *wu wei* proposes that life is constant change; people should study the changes that are affecting them and try to harmonize themselves with them. You could use this Chinese emphasis on harmony in practice that typically draws on Western theory. This idea is discussed further in Chapter 10 on humanistic practice.

Task-centred practice

Task-centred work originated wholly within social work, although it is influenced by cognitive-behavioural clinical psychology. It grew from a famous series of studies by Reid and Shyne (1969) and Reid and Epstein (1972a, 1972b); you can refer to Marsh and Doel (2005) or Fortune (2012) for an account of these. The starting point for these studies was the assumption in prestigious family social work agencies that people required long-term psychotherapeutic help. They discovered, first, contrary to expectations, that cut-down long-term treatment was as effective as long-term treatment that ran the full course. Second, 'planned short-term treatment' was also effective. Task-centred practice was based on this experience and also found to be effective.

The task-centred focus on specific problems has links with Perlman's problem-solving approach to casework (see Chapter 4). Reid and Epstein, the original creators of the theory, later developed their shared ideas in different directions. Epstein (Epstein and Brown, 2002) maintained an emphasis on using brief methods, using task-centred work eclectically in a wide range of practice. Reid, however, loyal to the more behavioural theoretical stance of his early years, merged his task-centred practice ideas into a wide range of structured interventions. An example is his book *The Task Planner* (2000), which formulates standardized plans for a wide range of human issues that affect clients. The books published towards the end of these authors' lives reflected these different directions. Both are examples of the shared value principles (see Figure 1.7) of formulating clear aims and action sequences.

The current use of task-centred practice is less distinct from other brief approaches than it was in the 1980s, when it was the main form of brief social work practice. However, it continues to be influential because its particular procedures are well defined and worked out to apply within social work roles. In addition, research has shown them to be effective in a variety of countries and situations (Tolson et al., 2003; Marsh and Doel, 2005). The 'effectiveness and replicability' sections of the 'Pre-treatment considerations' chapters in Tolson et al. (2003) contain good summaries of and citations to the research base. Marsh and Doel (2005) provide a more extended research review.

The main reason for this effectiveness is that the basic elements of the approach help to gain clients' commitment through a clear focus on the specified outcomes they are concerned about and a limited time commitment, an example of the shared value principle of 'alliance' (see Figure 1.7). Compared with more therapeutic approaches that focus on exploring emotional and interpersonal issues, task-centred practice is a practical, advice-giving style of work that is valued by clients who prefer more direction rather than an exploratory style. Other brief, structured programmes of intervention relying on empirical psychological research (for example, cognitive-behavioural and solution-focused practice) are worthwhile for similar reasons. Therefore, these models, and the cognitive-behavioural methods that they are similar to, are the most widely used examples of a range of 'brief treatment' approaches in social work.

Connections

The crisis intervention and task-centred practice models of social work have some common features, forming connections with each other. Both stress brief interventions, although we can string these together in a series if we are providing long-term care and support. Reid (1992: 12) acknowledged the influence of crisis intervention on the development of task-centred work. Golan (1986: 309), viewing the relationship in the opposite direction, claimed that research on task-centred work supports the sort of practice interventions proposed by crisis intervention theories, although this research did not set out to show this: she was interpreting the results. Stewart and MacNeil (2005: 532) suggest that task-centred practice can help to formulate plans for action in crisis work, and Behrman and Reid (2005) propose an integration of both models for post-trauma intervention. Both crisis and task-centred work are structured, so action is planned and fits a preordained pattern. 'Contracts' or other explicit agreements between social worker and client are used in both models. Reid and Epstein (1972a: 26), however, specifically distinguish the task-centred approach from crisis intervention. They say that task-centred work deals with a wider range of problems and emphasizes clear definitions of target problems, tasks and time limits. They stress links with functional casework, with an emphasis on time limits, client self-direction and having a clear structure and focus in the process of work.

Crisis intervention and task-centred theory also have other differences. While both try to improve people's capacity to deal with their problems, the circumstances in which they should be used and the focus of the work differ. Crisis intervention is, classically, action to interrupt a series of events that are disrupting people's normal functioning. It deals only with the consequences of the *one major issue* (the series of events), as defined by the situation; this is an example of the shared value principle (see Figure 1.7) of disrupting existing or taken-for-granted patterns of behaviour in a psychotherapeutic theory. Task-centred work and other therapies do not necessarily focus on an immediate situation; rather, they seek to identify and respond to major *priorities* in people's continuing problems. Crisis intervention uses practical tasks to help people readjust, but an important focus is individuals' emotional response to crises and long-term changes in their capacity to manage everyday problems. Task-centred work focuses on performance in practical tasks that will resolve particular problems, and success in achieving tasks helps emotional problems. Finally, crisis intervention theory is based on the origin of life difficulties, whereas task-centred work takes the problems as given, to be resolved pragmatically.

Not only are there many connections between crisis intervention and task-centred practice, but there are also connections between these models and other theoretical traditions in social work. Task-centred work has links with behavioural approaches (see Chapter 6), and its history is part of the movement to develop evidence of successful practice and a more eclectic and integrative practice drawing on research evidence (Rzepnicki et al., 2012). Neither approach is formally connected with behavioural approaches. When task-centred casework was formulated, it rejected any specific psychological or sociological base for its methods and sought to be 'eclectic and integrative' (Reid, 1992: 13). Many behavioural ideas, such as conditioning, play no part in task-centred work, and it deals with broader classes of behaviour than behavioural work normally covers. However, Gambrill (1994) argued that, as it has developed, it has increasingly used behavioural methods. She thinks that, because it reformulates and simplifies these, task-centred practice confuses the development of cognitive-behavioural theory by denying its origins. This may be so, but this is now widespread in social work thinking. I think she was protesting about the adoption of the practice of formulating clear outcomes as a shared value objective (see Figure 1.7), and I do not think this trend can now be reversed, even if it detracts from the purity of cognitive-behavioural methods.

The politics of crisis intervention and task-centred practice

Parad and Parad (1990: 4–5) reject 'theory' as a description of crisis intervention, reserving this term for 'scientific' theory. Neither practice focuses on social change, and they may be criticized as being mainly technical responses to immediate problems. This makes them attractive to public agencies and supporters of problem-solving views of social work, compared with those favouring the explicit political focus of critical theories, which also had a currency as these models were rising to prominence. Crisis intervention and task-centred theory have had greater staying power. The partnership approach and clarity of task-centred work and the emphasis on looking at environmental pressures have led to claims that they are both effective in use with anti-discriminatory work, offering empowerment and dealing with structural oppression (Ahmad, 1990: 51; O'Hagan, 1994). Although crisis intervention seems specific in focus, it is a general technique for dealing with people's problems when it deals with 'situational' crises that are affecting someone at the present time.

Case example: Peter's father's divorce

Peter, a young man in his twenties, had difficulty in going to visit his father in hospital when he was seriously ill, possibly dying, because it reminded him of how angry he had been when his father had left the family during his divorce. During his everyday interactions with his father, Peter kept these feelings hidden, but his increasing awareness of his father's possible death made him want to talk to his father about his anger. A conflict emerged between the father and son on the ward, and a social worker was asked to help.

Major social transitions such as birth, marriage, divorce and death tend to bring previous conflicts within families to the front of people's minds, providing an opportunity to deal with feelings left over from the past or to cement existing conflicts. One issue is that children are sometimes not involved in decisions at the time, so their feelings are not fully understood and talked through, being left to be dealt with at the time of a later crisis.

Parad (1965) argues that people approaching agencies do so when they experience crises in their capacity to manage their lives. The crisis is what motivates them to come, or leads other agencies to refer them or require them, to seek help. Thus, everyone coming to an agency for help can be seen as being 'in crisis', so that crisis intervention is relevant to all social work. The use of Erikson's (1965) analysis of developmental crises through which we achieve a resolution of basic psychosocial life tasks (see Chapter 4) makes clear the concept's relevance to many personal difficulties.

Values issues

Both these approaches focus strongly on the shared value principles of transparency and accountability to clients, being strongly focused on clearly specified, positive outcomes and specified action sequences (see Figure 1.7). The focus on clients' experiences and priorities, and their own objectives and the use of agreements, also demonstrates that the respect for clients' rights is important in both models. While the practitioner defines and manages the process to be followed, the concepts of crisis and task are intuitive to many clients and the people around them, so it is easy to engage them and the work seems appropriate. Accountability to and self-determination by clients are therefore strongly enhanced. Their intuitive and practice-based approach also commends them to many agencies and politicians who might question more esoteric therapeutic methods and objectives, and they therefore enhance political and social accountability for the profession.

Applications

The most important applications of crisis intervention are in the field of suicide prevention, rape, domestic violence and other emergencies of this kind. In the USA, local services in each of these areas are documented in Roberts (2005a), James (2008) and Kanel (2012), which also cover applications in services dealing with trauma, children and youth, victims of violence and health and mental health crises (such as grief and bereavement, post-traumatic stress disorder, addiction and people affected by HIV/AIDS). The use of crisis intervention in these services reflects the current inclusion of psychological and mental health responses to serious events, where concern about psychological difficulties after life events such as accidents was previously less well provided for.

Crisis intervention started from, and continues to be used in, mental health services. An important current use is in home treatment for crisis resolution, in which multidisciplinary teams visit people experiencing a mental health emergency and try to resolve any problems, reducing the need for emergency admission to psychiatric care (McGlynn, 2006). The ideas are also used in managing stress through debriefing people after major disasters (Flannery and Everly, 2000).

Applications of task-centred practice focus on a wide range of situations in a variety of social work agencies, such as resolving financial or employment problems or organizing family care arrangements.

Example text: Thompson (2011a) on crisis intervention

Thompson (2011a) sees a crisis as a turning point in people's lives, at which time their usual ways of coping with a problem fail and they are pushed to find a new strategy. He distinguishes between the meaning of crisis in crisis intervention theory and the everyday meaning of crisis as a 'disastrous event' or a time when people experience a lot of stress.

Crisis intervention theory focuses on people's perceptions of events, rather than the events themselves. Something that objectively seems quite minor may tip a particular person into a crisis. However, crisis intervention theory is extensively used in services dealing with overtly disastrous events, such as violent crimes, natural disasters and accidents, and traumatic situations such as divorce, unemployment and sudden serious illness. It is also used in services dealing with important life transitions, such as moving from school to work (Roberts, 2005b: 4). James (2008: 3–4) reviews a range of definitions and points to important aspects of crisis situations. These include feelings of tension and disorganization in life that immobilize people from taking action to overcome obstacles to important life goals.

James (2008: 14–16) identifies three historic models of crisis intervention and sees contemporary 'expanded' (2008: 14) theoretical developments as eclectically combining elements of all three:

- The *equilibrium model* was Caplan's (1965) original approach. It sees people as being in a state of psychological disequilibrium. They need to return to a steady state in which they can deal with issues in their life effectively.
- The *cognitive model* is associated with work by Roberts (2005a, 2005b). People are seen as thinking in a faulty way about events that surround the crisis.
- The *psychosocial transition model* is associated with developments of Erikson's (1965) model of developmental crises arising as people move through the life stages. People are seen as going through a particularly important psychological or social change as part of their development.

Thompson starts with two aspects of a crisis. The objective aspect is the external factors that make up the crisis situation: the personal, social and economic circumstances of the people involved. The subjective element is made up of the perceptions and personal reactions of the people involved and how these affect the crisis situation.

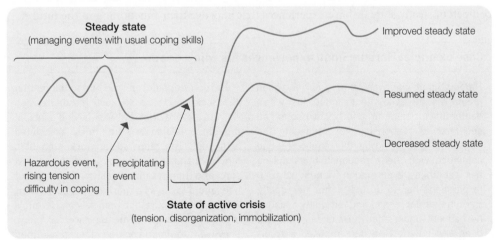

Figure 5.1 The concept of crisis
Source: Adapted from Hill (1965) and Thompson (2011a).

Figure 5.1 shows how a crisis process continues for a period. The starting point is that people normally function in a steady state (Rapoport, 1970: 276). This does not mean that things are unchanging for them. Rather, it means that, as things happen to them, they can 'cope'; that is, they can respond to events changing and developing in their lives. 'Steady state' implies that people can manage new events in their lives and deal with social change. Earlier concepts of crisis used the idea of equilibrium or homeostasis, which saw people's lives as being in balance, with the crisis knocking them off balance; the idea of steady state is more respectful of clients' normal coping skills.

A *hazardous event* is an event or series of events that people find it hard to cope with. It leads to increasing tension as they cast around to find ways of dealing with the new disturbing situation. It is not a crisis, but it puts people at risk if further events upset their already disturbed steady state.

The next element of the process occurs when people react badly to a *precipitating event*. This is something that happens to them that represents both danger and opportunity (James, 2008), and thus becomes meaningful, important and sometimes threatening. As people try to manage both the events and their own reaction, they use coping mechanisms that have worked before. However, if the usual methods seem not to work on this occasion, fear, tension or confusion rises. Picking up Caplan's (1965) terminology, Thompson calls this the 'impact stage'.

At this point, people begin to experience a high level of discomfort, a *state of active crisis*, as their normal 'steady state' feels completely disrupted. Thompson calls this the 'recoil stage'. They experience confusing and powerful emotions, physical complaints such as sleeplessness and stomach upsets, and erratic behaviour as they increasingly desperately try to find ways of dealing with the problem. The state of active crisis, or period of recoil and disorganization, resolves for better or worse over about six weeks. If resolution is unsuccessful, a person will function less well in the future and be more liable to bad reactions to later hazardous events. If they resolve the crisis well, they may resume their previous competent steady state or have experiences that improve their functioning in the future.

Case example: Haroun Singh experiences his wife's death

Haroun Singh, who worked hard earning good money as an accountant, found his wife's death difficult since he and his two sons had seen her as responsible for managing the household and caring for the family. She had continued with these responsibilities during her last illness, even though friends had tried to persuade her to do less. After her death, Haroun was depressed and felt guilty because he had not understood how ill his wife had been and now felt he had imposed a traditional view of her role in the family upon her, even though they were trying to construct a new life with more 'modern' Western values.

Haroun's doctor referred him to the mental health crisis centre because his depression was so severe that he was having suicidal thoughts; suicide is sometimes associated with guilt. The team social worker enabled him to discuss his feelings with his eldest son, and they planned jointly to carry out household tasks as a mark of respect to their wife and mother, rather than rely on Haroun's mother to provide domestic care for them. They went to Asian cooking classes together, building a relationship with each other, developing new interests together and developing new community links.

In this case example, the period during which Haroun's wife was ill and Haroun's lack of sensitivity in his marital relationship meant that their family life was being managed inappropriately. This represents the hazardous event that Haroun and his sons coped with but began to find more and more difficult. The mother's death was a precipitating event and, when combined with the family's failure to deal with the hazardous event appropriately, led to immobilization and chaos. When Haroun and his sons became aware of and expressed their emotions, and made plans to respond in a new way, they demonstrated an improved steady state. Family relationships improved and it is likely that any later crises in the family would be better managed through the acquisition of new skills. It is also likely that Haroun and his sons would not demonstrate such a lack of awareness of their family responsibilities in the future.

Pause and reflect *Jeanne debates whether to report a rape*

The following case example presents a more complex set of issues around understanding the different factors creating crises in people's lives. After reading it, think through different scenarios that might arise from Jeanne's experience. Should she see what happened as a rape? Should she make a complaint to the police?

Case example: Jeanne's dilemma

Jeanne was a young woman earning her way through university by working as a cleaner. She felt under a lot of financial pressure as a single parent with two children. While working in one particular house, she met the student son of the person who owned the house and, one evening after she had finished work, they went out for a coffee and talked about their university experiences. When she went to clean the house the following week, he was in bed, having come home late from a party, and was still drunk. He became amorous and, although she tried to resist, they had sex. She was upset about this chain of events and so, on finishing work, she talked over her experience with a friend. Her friend felt strongly that this was rape, whereas Jeanne was more ambivalent, feeling that she had consented at the time, and also being aware of her loneliness and sense of responsibility for her children. She did not want to get the young man into trouble, or to upset his parents and possibly find it more difficult to get cleaning work in the area as a result. On the other hand, she did not want anything like this to happen again. She became very miserable and indecisive, with her friend suggesting that she should be angry and go to the police.

Some suggestions

The rape may have been a precipitating event, but there are also other factors creating the state of active crisis for Jeanne. These include her own emotional reaction to the event, her relationship with her employers – the boy's parents – her feelings about the shared life experience she has with the boy, and the anger and emotional pressure put on her by her friend whose emotional reaction to the situation is different.

At the moment, the event has led to a state of personal crisis, but reporting the event to the police may apply further emotional pressures to Jeanne. It may, for example, lead to public conflict involving her employers, the boy's parents, having to give evidence in court and having some of her emotional ambivalence revealed and tested. Does she feel strongly enough about the event as rape to report it? There may also be public consequences that she cannot know about. For example, other women may have been raped by the same man. There may also be public policy consequences; for example, the police may fail to protect women from rape if they do not have sensitive ways of dealing with it or if the courts humiliate women during the process of the trial. These factors often lead women to fail to report rape. Similarly, if there is a high level of HIV/AIDS in the community, Jeanne may face the personal crisis of deciding whether to have a test for infection. Her decisions may be affected by or lead to public debate on some of these issues.

Thompson (2011a: 20–3) proposes three main strategies and a range of therapeutic activities for dealing with crises, which I have set out in Figure 5.2. It is important to keep the structure of the three strategies clearly in mind since the situation may at first appear chaotic to the practitioner. These strategies are central in building a relationship between the social worker and the client that offers calming support (a shared value principle of alliance), identifying other support systems and introducing the client to new coping mechanisms.

Figure 5.2 Crisis intervention strategies and interventions
Source: Thompson (2011a: 20–3).

The helping process then proceeds according to the usual social work model, starting with assessment. Thompson again divides these into two elements, principles and skills, as set out in Figure 5.3. Throughout these formulations, the balance between emotional responses and more rational coping and planning is a distinctive element of crisis intervention. Practitioners need to enable the client's expression of an emotional response to hazardous and precipitating events and situations in the state of active crisis. At the same time, it is important to ensure that this does not impair any work on developing support and coping. Thus, early assessment avoids getting into detail, and it is important to manage time and strategy effectively so that poor coping mechanisms do not become ingrained and lead to a reduced steady state.

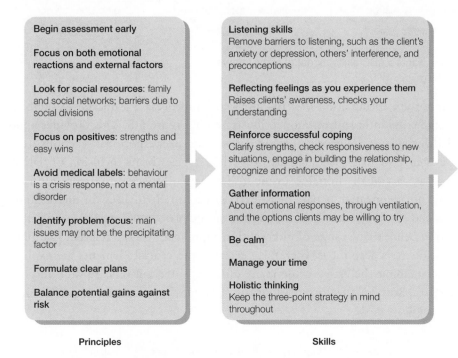

Principles

Begin assessment early

Focus on both emotional reactions and external factors

Look for social resources: family and social networks; barriers due to social divisions

Focus on positives: strengths and easy wins

Avoid medical labels: behaviour is a crisis response, not a mental disorder

Identify problem focus: main issues may not be the precipitating factor

Formulate clear plans

Balance potential gains against risk

Skills

Listening skills
Remove barriers to listening, such as the client's anxiety or depression, others' interference, and preconceptions

Reflecting feelings as you experience them
Raises clients' awareness, checks your understanding

Reinforce successful coping
Clarify strengths, check responsiveness to new situations, engage in building the relationship, recognize and reinforce the positives

Gather information
About emotional responses, through ventilation, and the options clients may be willing to try

Be calm

Manage your time

Holistic thinking
Keep the three-point strategy in mind throughout

Figure 5.3 Crisis intervention assessment principles and skills
Source: Thompson (2011a: 26–43).

For the same reason, Thompson's (2011a: 46–62) intervention methods focus on avoiding delay, working intensively in the short term rather than aiming to develop a long-term strategy. However, listening is key to all this, because failure to pick up important emotional and practical issues in the client's life may mean that you develop an unhelpful strategy. You might use several treatment methods, but the direction of practice is future-oriented and time-limited and should come to a clear conclusion, so that the client feels the state of crisis has been worked through and they are resuming their steady state. Again, this represents a shared value principle (see Figure 1.7) applied in this theory. Thompson also emphasizes being proactive in reducing distress and in planning and implementing future coping strategies straight away. Practice focused on emotional reactions to events and also on social responses that will support clients and develop their coping ability are equally important. You can see many of these points in Haroun Singh's case above.

Kanel (2012), while using a similar process model, emphasizes the practice skills involved at each of her three stages, particularly in the final stage (the client's skill development). This is summarized in Figure 5.4.

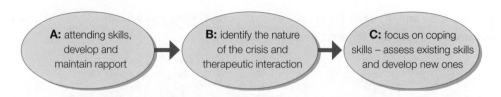

Figure 5.4 Kanel's ABC skills model of crisis intervention
Source: Kanel (2012).

An important formulation of crisis intervention process is Roberts's (2005b: 20) seven-stage crisis intervention model, illustrated in Figure 5.5. This provides a more extended account of the process but similarly emphasizes emotional reactions. It also shows evidence of Roberts's emphasis on crisis services in its inclusion of 'lethality measures' as part of the initial assessment. The actual process of crisis resolution is, strikingly, not delineated as part of Roberts's account. It focuses on understanding the crisis and planning intervention, but not on the process of intervention itself, the assumption being that a range of intervention approaches will be relevant in different models. Roberts's account is, therefore, eclectic: the crucial elements are exploring and understanding the crisis, while many different interventions are valid responses to the crisis. Both of the formulations are examples of an action sequence shared value principle.

Figure 5.5 Roberts's seven-stage crisis intervention model
Source: Roberts (2005a: 20).

Example text: Marsh and Doel (2005) on task-centred practice

Task-centred practice is a striking example of the repeated use of the shared value principle (see Figure 1.7) of using action sequences in practice; this is set out in Figure 5.6 below.

There are several components of the initial sequence, as the client is taken into the agency and the task-centred process is set up:

- The mandate comes from clients' informed consent and the legal and agency responsibilities imposed on practitioners.
- Clients present their issues, all of which have two elements: things that are wrong and things that they want to achieve.
- The aim of practice is to achieve the goals.
- The first stage of practice explores clients' problem stories to enable both clients and practitioners to move beyond the immediate worries or issues presented in the referral. This ensures the identification of issues that might otherwise not immediately have come out. For example, issues may not be presented because clients feel anxious about discussing them, or both clients and practitioners may think that particular problems are not the province of social workers.
- Clients' problems are often complex and interrelated, so they are disentangled in order to identify priorities and so that each issue can be assessed separately in relation to agency or legal requirements on practitioners.
- General aims are refined so that they become separate, specific, clearly defined goals.
- Time limits are introduced to increase motivation and enable people to assess their priorities and progress.
- Recorded agreements are drawn up that identify and clarify the mandate, problems, goals and time limits.

Case example: Multiple definition of problems – Joan's job

Joan, a young woman with a history of depression, was referred to a mental health service. The practitioner discovered that her inability to find a job was worrying her most, and began to work out a plan in which they would share undertaking a series of tasks to find one. Before completing this, however, the practitioner visited Joan's home to find that her mother preferred her to remain in the house to help domestically with the elderly grandparent who was also living there. Also, Joan's father felt that working in a shop, which Joan preferred, was not socially acceptable. He wanted her to learn office skills at college. The practitioner first had to resolve the different perceptions of Joan's family duties before being able to continue with the job hunt.

This case example illustrates the reality that people share some problems with others who may not acknowledge and define the problem in the same way. As a result, their priorities may be different from those of the practitioner's main client.

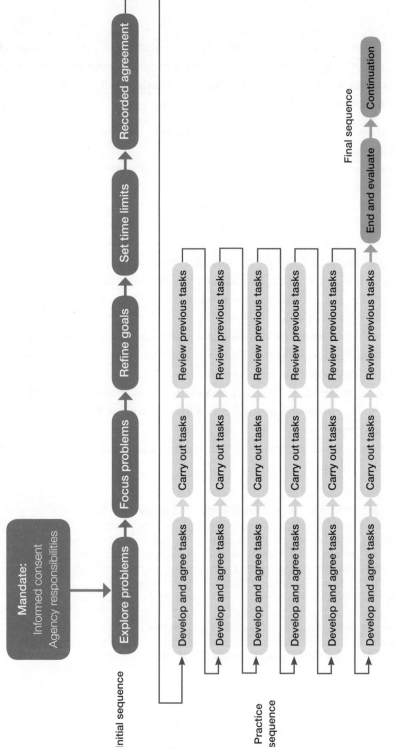

Figure 5.6 Sequence of actions in task-centred practice

After the problem has been prioritized, the practitioner and client agree tasks that move towards the goal, and carry these out together. At their next meeting, they review any progress made towards completing the tasks and then develop new ones. This process is repeated within the time limit, and so the sequence will continue:

- Tasks represent incremental changes on the path from priority problems to priority goals. They involve joint, coordinated actions, and not intentions.
- Task development involves defining the task so that those involved understand it and any barriers to achieving the goal, and are aware of the support and rehearsal required. Rehearsal might involve clients practising, with practitioners, skills that they need to carry out the agreed tasks.
- Review involves regular reflection on problems, goals and tasks in order to guide any subsequent action.

As they reach the time limit, practitioner and client go into the final sequence:

- Planned ending involves evaluating the work done, any new skills acquired and the success that has been achieved in moving towards the goals.
- Continuation means exploring the need to work on continuing problems, goals and tasks with new agreements and within new time limits.

We can now look in more detail at how to carry out the stages of this process.

Marsh and Doel (2005) identify the phases of exploring problems as set out in Figure 5.7; I have divided up the final phase of selection in this account. The additions stage is important because clients may not be aware of, or give adequate consideration to, problems identified by others. Marsh and Doel (2005: 70) identify three important requirements for the selected problem to be dealt with effectively that confirm the need for consent to be an important factor:

- The client acknowledges the problem and is willing to work on it.
- The client is in a position to alleviate the problem, given help.
- The problem is specific and relatively limited in scope.

Figure 5.7 Exploring problems

Action	Practitioner's role
Scan	*Elicit* the problems as expressed by the client in broad outline
Additions	*Disclose* problems identified by others or mandated by a court or by agency requirements
Details	The practitioner and client jointly *investigate* each problem
Quotations	*Summarize* each problem in one simple statement in the client's words
Prioritize	The client takes the lead in *prioritizing* the problems ...
Select	... identifying with the practitioner the *lead* problem selected for them both to work on

Source: Marsh and Doel (2005: 16, 34–5, 70).

> ### Case example: Exploring Ethan's drug problems
>
> Ethan was referred by the court to a drug treatment centre for help with controlling his drug habit because he had been arrested several times for theft offences associated with the need to buy drugs illegally. He wanted to concentrate on housing difficulties and relationship problems with his girlfriend, but the practitioner pointed out the need to demonstrate to the court that progress had been made with Ethan's drug addiction as well. However, they agreed that Ethan could not promise not to commit any more thefts, since this problem was too wide in scope and not sufficiently specific. The selected problems that he was prepared to work on were, in order of priority, his housing, his relationship and his drug use problems. Ethan had some doubts about whether he could resolve the drug use problem, but, with the practitioner's help, he was prepared to try.

In defining goals, Marsh and Doel (2005: 36) recommend the well-known SMART formula, which states that problems should be:

- specific
- measurable
- achievable
- realistic
- timely.

Motivation on the part of both the client and the carer is important to achieve the goals, so that they genuinely see them as alleviating the problem. The goals also need to be feasible, so that the client can complete them without too much support or involvement from others, and desirable, so that they seem ethical and reasonable to those involved.

The agreement can be recorded in a formal way, occasionally in a legal document, such as a supervision order for children in need, which often has conditions; alternatively, agency guidelines may provide a formula that practitioner and client can start from. Where the process is more voluntary, some practitioners use flipcharts and come up with a list of bullet points. Where literacy or understanding is a problem, for example, if clients cannot read a written document, or if learning-disabled clients require constant reminders and clear simplified explanations, symbols or simple diagrams may help. Computer clip art or stickers may also be useful in such situations, provided it is culturally and ethnically appropriate.

Task development involves creating actions that are a step towards the agreed goal and should be part of an overall plan, so that practitioners and clients can see where each task will lead and how it will contribute to the final goal. Some tasks occur within sessions between the practitioner and the client; some are in the form of homework, to be done between sessions. They should not be too trivial, or so large as to be overwhelming: big tasks should be divided up. Tasks may be set just for an individual, to be done either by the client, balanced against tasks performed by others, or by the practitioner or another person by agreement. Tasks may also be reciprocal: the client acts on one aspect of a task, and the practitioner or another person on a balancing task. Some tasks may be jointly undertaken, in that the client and practitioner carry out the task together. Some are one-offs; others are repeated.

Following the task planning and implementation sequence, set out in Figure 5.8 and devised by Reid (1978, 2000), has been shown to improve success rates in devising and carrying out tasks.

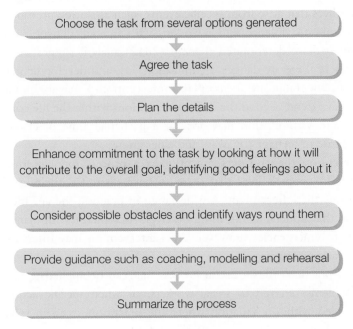

Choose the task from several options generated

Agree the task

Plan the details

Enhance commitment to the task by looking at how it will contribute to the overall goal, identifying good feelings about it

Consider possible obstacles and identify ways round them

Provide guidance such as coaching, modelling and rehearsal

Summarize the process

Figure 5.8 Task planning and implementation sequence

Reviewing tasks that have been agreed involves reporting back on what has been done and what the outcomes were, and rating their success. Reporting back involves looking at the experience of working on the task: how long did it take, what skills were learned, was confidence enhanced? Success should be celebrated; goals not achieved should be reviewed to see if there are lessons to be learned about the obstacles to completion and other alternatives. The outcomes can be rated from 1 to 5, ranging from no success to complete success. These results can then inform the development of the next task. After the task has been reviewed, it should be put back into context to evaluate how much it has contributed to the overall goal.

The final evaluation looks backwards over the whole task-centred process. It covers five points:

- The beginning – what was the situation when we started?
- The written agreement – what did we agree to do?
- The goal – what was our aim, did we achieve it?
- General points – what was most useful, what got in the way?
- The future – will we be able to do this again, what more is needed?

Conclusion: using crisis and task-centred theory

Many practitioners and agencies use the concepts of crisis intervention and task-centred practice to formulate practical, short-term responses to people who come to them with troubles in their lives. Crisis intervention is widely used in services dealing with emergencies in people's lives that arise from specific events, such as suicide prevention, in dealing with rape and domestic violence, and in working with mentally ill people whose ability to function seems to have deteriorated. Kanel's (2012) analysis suggests crisis services as being useful where there are danger, victimization, loss and developmental crises. While these last two are the traditional focus of crisis intervention, Kanel also points to developmental crises that extend beyond the difficult transitions within the life course. These are where danger and victimization may arise at a particular time of change in life, for example in the case of teenage runaways and elder abuse.

Crisis intervention theory offers practitioners a process for exploring and understanding events in people's lives that seem to have disrupted their usual capacity to manage situations that affect them. A wide range of practical therapeutic interventions can be built on that understanding using other practice theories. In many agencies that do not deal with emergencies, however, crisis intervention may offer a helpful set of concepts at the assessment stage.

Task-centred practice offers a useful process that can be applied to a wide range of short-term problems referred to social workers, or when specific action to tackle a problem is needed within a situation where the practitioner's main role is providing ongoing care and support. It is particularly helpful because it respects clients' priorities and can be clearly explained and justified to clients and their families and communities, as well as to agency managers and their political masters.

Additional resources

Further reading

James, R. K. (2008) *Crisis Intervention Strategies* (6th edn) (Belmont, CA: Thomson Brooks/Cole).

Kanel, K. (2012) *A Guide to Crisis Intervention* (5th edn) (Belmont, CA: Brooks/Cole Cengage Learning).

Roberts, A. R. (ed.) (2005) *Crisis Intervention Handbook: Assessment, Treatment, and research* (3rd edn) (New York: Oxford University Press).

These three books are up-to-date and comprehensive alternative resources on American crisis intervention practice.

McGlynn, P. (ed.) (2006) *Crisis Resolution and Home Treatment: A Practical Guide* (London: Sainsbury Centre for Mental Health).

A useful practical guide drawing on current UK mental health practice, and available on the internet from http://www.centreformentalhealth.org.uk/pdfs/Crisis_resolution_and_home_treatment_guide.pdf

Loughran, H. (2011) *Understanding Crisis Therapies: An Integrative Approach to Crisis Intervention and Post-traumatic Stress* (London: Jessica Kingsley).

A good account of crisis work using a range of theoretical concepts.

Thompson, N. (2011) *Crisis Intervention* (Lyme Regis: Russell House).

A brief account of crisis intervention ideas.

Marsh, P. and Doel, M. (2005) *The Task-centred Book* (London: Routledge).

Tolson, E. R., Reid, W. and Garvin, C. D. (2003) *Generalist Practice: A Task-centered Approach* (2nd edn). (New York: Columbia University Press).

Good accounts of task-centred practice from, respectively, Britain and America.

Payne, M. (1998) 'Task-centred practice within the politics of social work theory', *Issues in Social Work Education* 17(2): 48–65.

An analysis of the development of the debate about task-centred practice.

Websites

http://www.patient.co.uk/doctor/Crisis-Intervention.htm

This website offers a brief summary of the use of the theory, aimed at UK National Health Service patients who might find themselves referred to a crisis intervention service.

The widely cited http://www.crisisinterventionnetwork.com/ now appears not to be functioning. Instead, an internet search for 'crisis intervention service' will produce a listing of services across the world using crisis intervention ideas.

http://www.crisisprevention.com/

This is the website of the Crisis Prevention Institute, a training organization focusing on enabling education, health and social care organizations dealing non-violently with challenging behaviour. Its website contains useful information and resources, for dealing with aggression in residential and education settings while working with young people, people with mental illness and people suffering from dementia. There is also a UK branch (although this offers fewer resources): http://www.crisisprevention.co.uk/

http://www.undp.org/content/undp/en/home/ourwork/crisispreventionan-drecovery/overview.html

Disaster relief also uses ideas about crisis, and the UN Development Program has a useful site, again with many helpful resources.

http://www.oocities.org/taskcentered/index.html

The Task-centered Social Work Practice and the Family website provides a brief account of task-centred work, references and a useful case study.

The widely cited http://www.task-centered.com/ appears now to be mainly concerned with education and links to social work issues do not work.

Cognitive-behavioural practice

6

Main contribution

The main contribution of cognitive-behavioural therapy (CBT) theories to social work is that they emphasize the importance of developing people's rational management of their behaviour so that we can better understand the source of their problems. The practice that arises from theories of CBT focuses on how to manage and change people's behaviour to resolve social problems that affect them. Although it is now seen as a single form of practice, CBT was built up from two main theoretical strands: behaviourism, supported by learning and social learning theory, and cognitive theory.

Main points

■ The 'behavioural' part of CBT practice focuses on defining and addressing people's problem behaviours, particularly social phobias, anxiety and depression.

■ The 'cognitive' element of CBT practice focuses on addressing problems in how people's thinking affects their behaviour.

■ Measurement is important in CBT, so careful assessment and monitoring of the individual's progress is an important aspect of practice.

■ Research evidence for the effectiveness of CBT is strong and is important for both theory and practice.

■ The main techniques of CBT are well defined and technicist. They include respondent and operant conditioning, social learning (including skills training) and cognitive restructuring of people's beliefs.

■ Social learning techniques such as assertiveness and skills training are used more widely than in CBT, as part of groupwork and in feminist practice.

■ More specific techniques are used in clinical settings where supervision and training in their use are available.

■ The use of CBT practice has been controversial because of its association with the debate surrounding evidence-based practice (EBP).

- CBT is used in criminal justice settings, and motivational interviewing is used with challenging, hard-to-engage clients.
- Mindfulness techniques focusing on clients' paying attention to important issues in their lives can be combined with CBT interventions.
- Neuroscience research examines how brains process perceptions about the world, thus providing evidence about how people's thinking interacts with their behaviour. The subject matter and science base of neuroscience connect with the concerns of CBT and are an increasing influence on social work knowledge.

Practice ideas

- ☐ *Behaviour* therapies focus on changing specific behaviours.
- ☐ *Cognitive* therapies focus on changing inappropriate thinking processes.
- ☐ *Cognitive-behavioural* therapies focus on how thinking processes generate behaviour patterns.
- ☐ *Social learning* focuses on the learning that results from people's perceptions of social experiences.
- ☐ *Assertiveness training* enables people to practise behaviours so that they can gain confidence in these behaviours, thus improving their overall social confidence.
- ☐ *Reinforcement* of useful behaviours is used.
- ☐ *Modelling* is a form of social learning in which people understand and copy useful behaviours from a valued role model.
- ☐ *Motivational interviewing* may be used to engage challenging clients.
- ☐ *Mindfulness* techniques focus on paying attention to important issues in our lives.

Major statements

Early influential writers on behavioural practice were Thomas (1968, 1971) and Fischer and Gochros (1975) in the USA, and Jehu (1967, 1972) in the UK.

It is difficult to identify a recently published text from a social work source that specifically theorizes CBT social work practice, for three reasons. One is that CBT practice is now such an important element of EBP that general introductory texts from this perspective, such as those by Gambrill (2006) and Sheldon and Macdonald (2009), often include significant elements of CBT without specifically theorizing CBT practice. The second is that CBT is part of the range of counselling and clinical psychology theory that is used in mental health and other clinical social work. A text specifically focused on social work is therefore less important than it once would have been as social workers can draw on general CBT texts if they work in these fields. Moreover, many techniques are specialized in their application to particular client groups. For example, the well-regarded social work text of Ronen and Freeman (2007) is an edited collection covering different mental health problems, rather than a comprehensive theorization. The third point follows from this: many texts apply to specific health and social care fields and can be used by all the professionals who work in those fields, including social workers. Examples are Sage et al.'s (2008) text on CBT in chronic illness and cancer, and Clarke and Wilson's (2009) text on CBT in acute inpatient mental healthcare.

I have therefore selected as an example a clinical psychology text (Dobson and Dobson, 2009), which accurately reflects the current strong shift towards cognitive rather than behavioural interventions in current practice. Another asset is how it defines the research base of interventions for different conditions.

The debate summary

Controversy surrounds CBT because it lies at the centre of the debate about EBP (see Chapter 2). Among the most important claims for CBT are that it has the best and longest developed evidence base for its effectiveness, but among its most important critiques are the limitations of this claim, particularly in relation to taking a broad view of social work practice. The main area of contention is whether its focus on defining and modifying specific problems in the client's behaviour achieves success only with a limited range of mainly mental health problems. While strong evidence for its effectiveness in this area is welcome, it comes at the cost of focusing on and perhaps amplifying problems, rather than looking positively at strengths and objectives, as strengths and solution-focused practice proposes (see Chapter 9). Because of its focus on problems, CBT thus runs contrary to the shared value principle of seeking positive objectives. Against this, CBT has a strong focus on outcomes, which contains the forward-looking element of the shared value principles.

In addition, such practice is not relevant to the broad range of services that most social services deliver to their clients. You can see the evidence by examining Dobson and Dobson's (2009) list of well-conducted review articles that demonstrate the effectiveness of CBT for psychological conditions, mainly various forms of anxiety, phobias, depression and post-traumatic stress disorders. Thomlison and Thomlison (2011: 83) cite a wide range of reviews of empirical support for CBT that covers mainly psychological problems. Broader, but less rigorously analysed, accounts of CBT that focus on social work responsibilities may be found in Sheldon (1998, 2012) and Thyer and Kazi (2004).

The controversy surrounding the evidence for CBT's effectiveness began historically in the 1960s with the behaviourists' trenchant attacks on psychodynamic models of social work, which were the first criticisms of the influence of psychodynamic practice. The behaviourists criticized the ill-defined outcomes of psychodynamic practice, which were based on assumptions about psychological structures within the mind that we cannot examine empirically. The strong argument for CBT, continually emphasized by enthusiasts, is its empirically tested success in attaining results. This does not mean, however, that CBT is always applicable – it must be appropriately deployed (Dobson and Dobson, 2009: 262–4).

Many of the arguments on behalf of CBT are put forward with a messianic zeal, which can sometimes lead to intemperate attacks on its opponents, and this element of academic point-scoring turns many practitioners off. Accepting the arguments put forward by CBT requires acceptance of the relevance of positivist research methods in social work, modernist ideas about knowledge and linear models of explanation. Chapter 2 reviews how quantitative and experimental research methods, like those used in CBT, emphasize the modernist idea that there is a universal knowledge which is relevant in every culture. Such methods seek simple cause and effect explanations of behaviour. All this is connected with a 'positivist' research tradition, disputed by interpretivist writers, who argue that human beings are constantly interpreting the world around them and do not operate by fixed researchable rules. Writers from each of these perspectives often seem to talk past each other, pressing their point of view rather than addressing the points being debated. For these reasons, many people feel that debates about CBT are a good example of sterile conflict over theoretical ideas, which contribute little that can help practitioners.

One advantage of accepting the positivist argument is that such methods are acceptable when working with other professions, particularly medicine and psychology, whose knowledge bases emphasize positivist research techniques. In this way, CBT connects with arguments that the professional standing of social work would be enhanced by this form of academic validation. Accepting this argument, however, means choosing a theory of practice simply to appear 'professional' according to the values of a different profession.

Research (Cort et al., 2009; Moorey et al., 2009) has shown that it is possible to teach selected CBT techniques that experienced practitioners from several professions can use, without using CBT fully. Findings like these do not mean that anyone can simply deploy tricks learned from CBT (Dobson and Dobson, 2009: 262–4). Using CBT comprehensively with a range of clients requires extensive training and supervision, but borrowing techniques in clearly defined situations can be helpful as part of a wider service.

Critical and feminist theory criticizes CBT for its individualist focus, seeing all problems as coming from an individual's mind, and ignoring the impact of social oppression. The positivist research methods used to test practice techniques are also claimed to be unsympathetic to the needs of women as clients and practitioners. These points are sometimes misrepresented in the CBT literature. For example, Dobson and Dobson (2009: 247) present the issue as CBT being antifeminist 'because it encourages logical thinking, and makes women believe that they are irrational', and as resting on 'a rational and intellectual theory that ignores the social context of problems'. Dobson and Dobson's argument suggests that the critical and feminist critique is of CBT's emphasis on rational thinking and research. Their argument here diminishes the much more important element of the critique, which says that CBT and similar individualized therapies fail to see that individual problems are mainly manifestations of oppressive social structures. It is better to see these structures as an important source of both the problem and the social perception that this is a problem that requires individuals to change.

The claimed evidence base of CBT is destroyed if you reject the idea that the problem behaviour of individuals ought to be the main focus of social work interventions. Building on these ideas, the feminist critique goes further, to question CBT's way of thinking and researching; this way of thinking, being pragmatically focused only on identifiable behaviours, fails to understand the way in which behaviours originate from social interactions with powerful individuals, and in the case of feminist thinking, with powerful men, in a paternalistic social structure.

The critical and feminist claim is that this failure of understanding in CBT negates the value of behavioural and cognitive change. Such change will be ineffective in the long term if it does not tackle the social structures of oppression that are manifested in individuals' problems. It is also contrary to the values of social work, which incorporate knowledge from social as well as psychological sciences, and attempt to change both social and individual factors involved in the issues the profession seeks to tackle.

> **Pause and reflect** Fabia's life objectives
>
> Review this case example to identify alternative explanations and approaches that might be used.
>
> **Case example: CBT to help Fabia**
>
> Fabia was referred for help with depression and feelings of personal inadequacy in caring for her two young children. It appeared to the doctor who referred her that these feelings were an extension of postnatal depression, and that her care of her children was not a matter of concern. After carrying out an assessment prior to proposing CBT, the practitioner focused on her anxiety about not being able to help her children develop as she would wish, alongside her feelings of depression associated with the feeling that her life had no purpose. Fabia had previously been a successful lawyer, but had agreed with her husband to make a commitment to focus on child care for this period of her life; she very much wanted to be a successful mother, putting this alongside her long-term career objectives. Since many of her fears were irrational, the practitioner judged that a programme of CBT could fairly quickly remove many of her difficulties.

Some suggestions

Rather than attempting to remove Fabia's problem anxiety and depression, for which CBT might well be effective, it might be better to use humanistic, solution-focused or feminist approaches that would concentrate on thinking through Fabia's life objectives and perhaps renegotiating a reorganization of family responsibilities with her husband. Their decision that she would concentrate on child care for a while might reflect a tension between her needs or wishes to achieve a successful career and to achieve being a successful mother. However, it might also reflect social assumptions about the role of women in marriage and child care, which the couple have not thought through in the context of the tension in Fabia's feelings and mind. Moreover, because CBT focuses on identifiable behaviours, which are seen as problematic, it would not explore positive development of her life objectives.

Wider theoretical perspectives

Overview: sources of CBT

Cognitive and behavioural ideas come from four main streams of psychological writing, as shown in Figure 6.1. These are: first, learning theory leading to behaviour therapy; second, a number of cognitive therapies including reality and rational emotive behaviour therapy; third, social learning theory and social skills training; and fourth, mindfulness thinking.

Historically, learning theory came first and developed into clinical psychology using behaviour therapy based on psychological research. The psychodynamic and perhaps conventional view is that behaviour comes from a process that goes on in our minds. This has connections with philosophical ideas about what the mind is and whether it is the seat of our humanity, what Christians call a 'soul'. A related question is whether environmental influences limit people's freedom or whether they are free to act according to their will, that is, with what their mind wishes. Learning theory does not deny that this may be so, but it argues that we cannot know what is happening in someone else's mind. Therefore, we can only study and influence the behaviour we can see. Except for some inborn reflexes, we learn most behaviour, that is, it originates from influences outside ourselves. It follows that we ought to be able to learn new behaviour to meet our needs, and that new behaviour could be learned to replace existing behaviour if it were causing us problems. Psychological therapy based on learning theory, therefore, focuses on various ways of 'conditioning' behaviour, that is, doing things in a consistent way that will train people to adopt a changed behaviour. This contrasts with some psychotherapeutic ideas such as psychodynamic theory, which aims to understand behaviour, where it originally came from and what changes may take place in our mind as we make changes in our behaviour.

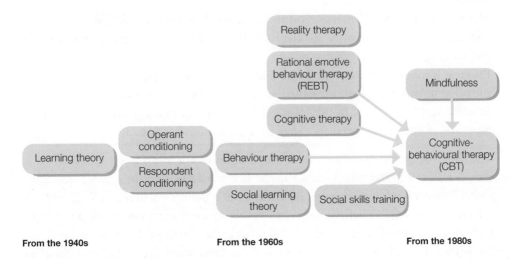

Figure 6.1 Sources of current CBT

Source: Selected and simplified from Mansell (2008: 20).

Many practitioners, however, felt that behavioural practice aiming to condition or train people in specific behaviours seemed to be effective for a few psychological problems but was limited in dealing with the more complex social issues found in social work. *Social learning theory* (Bandura, 1977) extends these ideas. It proposes that most learning is gained by people seeing behaviour going on around them and thinking about what they see. They can therefore learn by copying the example of others around them; this is called modelling. Helping people to develop social skills in this way increases the treatment options available in basic behaviour therapy.

Cognitive theory is in part a development of behaviour theory and therapy, its emergence having been made easier by the availability of social learning theory. It also grew out of therapeutic developments of a pragmatic kind, devised by writers like Beck (1989; Beck and Beck, 2011) and Ellis (1962; Ellis and MacLaren, 2005), who were concerned with psychiatric conditions such as anxiety neurosis and depression. Another cognitive approach, Glasser's (1965) *reality therapy*, was also important for social work because it originated from residential work with young women. Cognitive theory argues that our perceptions or interpretations of the world around us affect our behaviour as we learn. Apparently inappropriate behaviour may therefore arise from misperception and misinterpretation, rather than from disorders of conditioning. Therapy tries to correct the misunderstanding, so that our behaviour reacts appropriately to the environment.

Gambrill (1995) has identified the main positive contributions of *behavioural practice* as being that:

- It focuses on specific behaviours that worry clients and others around them; if we change the behaviour, we remove the concern.
- It relies on behavioural principles and learning theory.
- Practitioners make a clear analysis and description of problems, based on direct observation.
- Methods of assessment, intervention and evaluation are explicitly defined.
- Factors influencing behaviour are identified by changing some factors in the situation and looking for the changes that result.
- Progress is monitored using subjective and objective measures, comparing data about the present with data about the situation before the intervention took place.
- Practitioners help clients to use changed behaviours in many situations (generalization) and maintain improvements after the intervention has ceased.

The positivist approach of behavioural work means that it uses a linear model of explanation: A leads to B and then C in a straight line of explanation. In practice, the linear model of explanation is implemented in 'single-case' experimental designs (Kazi, 1998) in which practitioners define behaviours to be worked on, carry out an intervention and then test whether there has been a change. A careful definition of target behaviours is followed by measuring in a planned way how often these behaviours occur during a 'baseline' period. The intervention then follows, and occurrences of the behaviour during and after the intervention are also measured. After one period of intervention, there is sometimes a 'reversal period' in which the practitioner returns to their own baseline behaviour and the target behaviour is again measured. Intervention then starts again. In this way, we can test whether the intervention or something else is creating the behaviour change. This approach has, however, been criticized from the critical realist and social construction perspectives (see Chapter 2) because it may reduce the complexity of our understanding of mutually interacting social factors to an oversimplified model of behaviour.

In learning theory, behaviour is caused by antecedents, that is, things that have already happened; when we behave in particular ways, this has consequences for us, which then form antecedents for later behaviours. Figure 6.2 illustrates this in the left hand-column; the other columns show some of the different approaches to changing the contingencies that might affect behaviour. *Behavioural practice* is mainly concerned with changing contingencies that affect antecedents and behaviours (Gambrill, 1995). *Social learning theory* focuses on how we learn from social situations when we see how others who model the appropriate behaviour act successfully (vicarious learning). *CBT* methods are therapeutic procedures that focus on changing thoughts and feelings alongside, instead of or as a precursor to changing behaviours.

The behavioural and cognitive elements of CBT sit uncomfortably together. A good example of this is Macdonald's (2007) brief account, which goes into some detail about behavioural theory and techniques, and the research that supports them, while skipping over cognitive ideas and being more critical of its research base. Thomlison and Thomlison's (2011) account, on the other hand, focuses more strongly on the cognitive element, reducing the emphasis on behavioural conditioning. These authors emphasize (p. 94) the eclectic theoretical sources of CBT and the fact that behavioural assessment is required to identify the precise techniques that will be appropriate for particular issues. Thyer and Myers (2011) deal with this issue by seeing cognitive theory mainly as a development of social learning theory; as a consequence, they treat cognition as a behaviour susceptible to behavioural treatments, rather than as a separate type of mental process.

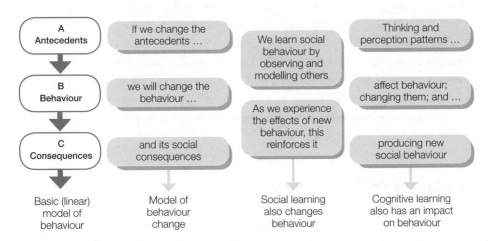

Figure 6.2 Cognitive-behavioural models of practice

Connections

The main aims of behavioural social work are to increase the desired behaviours and reduce the undesired ones, so that people respond appropriately to social events. CBT theorists argue that this increases people's capacity for leading a full and happy life. An insight into people's problems often helps because it speeds learning, but there is no evidence that it is necessary or that it is enough to get people to change. Writers on CBT practice claim that warm, trusting personal relationships between workers and clients help in behavioural work, as they do in other forms of social work. Behavioural social work can be used in many social work situations. The authors in Cigno and Bourn's (1998) edited collection describe direct work with children and child protection, people with severe learning disabilities, offenders, carers, individuals with addictions, people with mental health problems, and those in residential and group care for elders. Behavioural and CBT practice is also widely used in clinical psychology and in some specialized forms of counselling.

Cognitive theories established a position in social work theory during the 1980s primarily through the work of Goldstein (1981, 1984), who sought to incorporate into them more humanistic ideas, such as a focus on people's feelings and attitudes, alongside rational thinking processes. This development was suggested by the fact that behavioural ideas concern the nature of the mind (Chatterjee and Brown, 2012) and how perceptions and understanding are processed. Social construction and humanistic ideas (see Chapters 9 and 10) claim that perceptions and their processing vary legitimately, and that people's reality is what they perceive and understand. Allied to cognitive ideas, this allows us to accept that clients' understanding of the world is relevant to their rational thinking. There is, therefore, no need to see clients' perceptions as wrong and attack them. This element of acceptance frames CBT in ways that seem more natural to the conventions of social work. The crucial aspect of Goldstein's work is, then, the inclusion of the humanistic element.

Theories of CBT are primarily a Western model of practice since they emphasize the psychological change of individuals, rather than the broader social groupings that might be more relevant in developing countries; they also use a Western model of scientific method, which is less influential in many Eastern countries. This group of theories is, for example, not covered in Kumar's (1995) Indian review of social work theories. A non-Western interest in EBP is put forward in Thyer and Kazi's (2004) edited text on EBP, which includes chapters from Hong Kong and South Africa. However, these chapters are primarily about the evaluation of social projects and social development, rather than about the practice of CBT itself.

The politics of CBT theory

CBT has a limited use in specialized settings with particular client groups. It is often used for school phobia, for childhood problems and in psychiatric settings, particularly, in the case of cognitive methods, with mild anxiety and depression. The extended case study on child and adolescent mental health services in Chapter 2 shows how it may contribute in this setting. Criminal justice settings have also used specific formulations of CBT practices, which I discuss more fully later in the chapter. One reason for the success of CBT social work in such settings is that clinical psychologists, and to a lesser extent other medical and nursing staff, can offer supervision and provide a sympathetic environment and a patient-centred setting for these therapeutic methods. Such advantages are less easily available in conventional social work agencies, with their wider social mandate.

A major difficulty with CBT is its technical character, with much jargon and many formal procedures, apparently worked out in set systems. When these procedures have been applied to particular service responsibilities, they have often been 'manualized', that is, set out in a manual of procedures for practitioners to follow. Such an approach may suit some clients or workers who like to see an ordered, explicit approach to problems that can be clearly explained and justified. Manualization gives useful guidance and support to less experienced practitioners, but it may seem dehumanizing and inflexible. Where practitioners have a good level of training, support and experience in CBT, they are able to use the methods more flexibly than this, but of course the risk is that less experienced practitioners with fewer qualifications and little or no supervision will be pressed to follow manuals rather than build up the skills they need to use CBT flexibly.

Behavioural social work has had considerable theoretical influence, but it has not succeeded in gaining widespread usage, except in specialist settings or for particularly relevant problems.

Values issues

Values are a major concern that many practitioners have with CBT. Since practitioners use CBT to manipulate behaviour, clients may be unable to consent. This could lead to these techniques imposing social expectations on unwilling clients and pursuing social or political policies that could, at the extreme, be used for authoritarian political control. Supporters of CBT argue that clients' consent is ethically required and practically necessary if the approach is to be successful. In addition, the most ethical treatment is one that works best, and CBT has been well validated within the limitations of its model of research.

All techniques can, of course, be abused in the wrong hands. Watson (1980: 105–15) argues that the fact that this may occur is not a sufficient answer to the ethical problem. Behaviourism, the basic theory underlying CBT practice, inherently assumes that all behaviour is caused by something. If people decide that they want changes that might be achieved by CBT methods, they are acting using their own reasoning freely, in the sense of deciding without any constraints on their decisions. However, what happens if behaviour is considered socially undesirable, for example by a court or by people able to put social or other pressures on a client? Clients might then be persuaded that changing their behaviour is right, good or adaptive to social conditions. In such cases, we are moving from unconstrained reasoning to decisions being made in pursuit of social goals. The only ethical position that maintains clients' rights to self-determination is to use the technique only where the client's own purpose is to free themselves from a particular behaviour, for example where it is compulsive and clients wish to but cannot control themselves.

Behavioural models have sometimes been misused. Residential care homes, for example, have used the reward and punishment aspect of behavioural methods in oppressive or abusive ways. One instance is the 'pin-down' scandal that occurred in residential homes for children in Britain (Levy and Kahan, 1991). Here, certain behaviourist ideas justified locking children up for long periods without day clothes. Sheldon (1995: 237–41) argues that, in this sort of situation, some methods are used where the people concerned are already motivated to oppress clients. Any method could then be misused to do so. However, Watson's (1980) objection to claims of misuse being discounted because they are bad uses of the theory still applies; it is the particular methods proposed by this theory that lead to the potential for misuse.

Sheldon (1995: 232–4) argues that no social work methods, including CBT, are so powerful that they can overcome resistance, and that other kinds of work also involve a control and limitation of freedom. However, this seems a weak protestation when CBT in particular claims to be more successful than other social work or therapeutic techniques. Moreover, we should not put people in the position of having to resist an oppression, but should protect them from this. Sheldon further argues that we should measure any disadvantages of the CBT model alongside its advantages. While we should take a balanced view of arguments, however, evidence of effectiveness cannot balance moral objections of oppression or the risk of it, because this would mean saying that the ends (an effective treatment) should justify the means of achieving that effectiveness (which would seem to justify repugnant oppression).

Applications

Overview of CBT approaches

Some basic ideas from learning theory and behavioural treatment are necessary to understand the approach. Sheldon (1998) has identified several important ideas underlying behaviour therapy:

- respondent or classical conditioning;
- operant or instrumental conditioning;
- learned helplessness (a complex theory which I do not discuss here);
- social learning and modelling;
- cognitive factors such as disorders of perception or attribution (the meaning attached to events and experiences) and catastrophic thinking.

All these ideas are directly applicable to social work. The following account relies on the writing of Sheldon (1998), Macdonald (2007) and Walsh (2010).

Respondent conditioning is concerned with behaviour (anything we do) that responds to (is produced by) a stimulus (a person, situation, event or thing, usually in the environment). *Conditioning* is the process by which a behaviour is learned, that is, connected more or less permanently with the stimulus. When we have learned a response to a stimulus, we have modified our behaviour.

Many behaviours are *unconditioned* – they happen naturally. An unconditioned stimulus produces an unconditioned response; for example, people's eyes water in a high wind, they salivate when given food, they withdraw their hands sharply when burned, and they are sick when they eat a noxious substance.

Case example: Getting muddy at the park

Feliks was a young child who regularly got into trouble with his mother for getting muddy at the park. This led him to learn to associate going to the park, rather than being muddy, with his mother's disapproval.

Behaviours are *conditioned* when responses become *associated* with a stimulus that does not naturally produce the response. An example is if our eyes were trained to water when we were given food. We call these *conditioned stimuli* and *conditioned responses*. Conditioned responses become *generalized*, that is, the person applies them to similar situations.

Case example: Feliks and the park again

Feliks avoided going to the park because of his mother's disapproval, but eventually he found it difficult to go out at all, generalizing his reaction because of her disapproval. This meant that he played in the house rather than going to the park. In his teenage years, he became involved with a local gang at school because he had few active pursuits.

Such responses are the mechanism that underlies many social phobias and post-traumatic stress disorders. People develop a response to one stimulus and it begins to affect them in other situations.

Extinction occurs if the association between the conditioned response and the stimulus is not kept up. The conditioned response fades away and loses its connection with the stimulus. This provides an important basis for treatment, since both the connection between the stimulus and the response and the ensuing generalization can be extinguished.

Case example: Extinction process

When Feliks was referred to the child and adolescent mental health service, a programme was developed in which he was taken by his mother to the park in easy stages to learn by experience appropriate things to do there, thus learning that their visits did not have to lead to his mother's disapproval.

Some kinds of behaviour are incompatible with other behaviours. For example, a completely relaxed person cannot be anxious or violent. *Counterconditioning* seeks to associate desirable responses with particular stimuli, so that they act in competition with the undesirable responses.

The most commonly used counterconditioning technique is *systematic desensitization*. Clients are taught practical techniques of relaxation or are offered other means of personal support. They are then slowly reintroduced to the unwanted stimulus and use the relaxation or support to fight against their anxiety. This approach is often used for school phobia or agoraphobia (a fear of open spaces or going outside the home).

Counterconditioning is also used in sexual therapy. Pleasant sexual responses are learned in supportive surroundings and gradually introduced into more ordinary sexual situations that have previously caused anxiety. For example, a man who ejaculates prematurely learns to control ejaculation while stimulated by his partner when full sexual intercourse is not permitted, until he feels confident of control. Transfer to sexual intercourse follows later.

Case example: Counterconditioning in enuresis

One example of these techniques is in conditioning children who are enuretic, that is, they wet the bed at an age when they should have learned not to do this. A loud buzzer or bell is connected to an electrical contact placed within a soft mat under the child. The buzzer sounds when some urine reaches the mat, and the child wakes and can complete urination in a toilet. This process has two effects.

First, the child is conditioned to wake when the bladder is full, so avoiding bed-wetting. Second, the tone of the bladder muscle is improved, strengthening the capacity to get through the night without wetting. These responses are set up as a form of counterconditioning to the natural process of reflex urination when the bladder is full (Morgan and Young, 1972).

Most behaviour does not develop from unconditioned stimuli, and *operant conditioning* deals with a wider range of behaviours. It is concerned with behaviour that operates on the environment, and can be used with complex and thought-out behaviour. In contrast, respondent conditioning is mainly concerned with learned automatic responses.

Operant conditioning was the original form of behavioural practice that focused on changing the contingencies that were affecting behaviours, leading to new consequences (see the first sequence in Figure 6.2). Something happens, an *antecedent* event – A – which produces a behaviour – B – which tries to deal with the event, and because of that behaviour, consequences – C – arise. Social workers manage *contingencies*, which affect the relationships between behaviour and consequences that strengthen or weaken behaviour, by *reinforcement* and *punishment*. Reinforcement, whether positive or negative, strengthens behaviour. *Punishment*, whether positive or negative, reduces behaviour. Positive always means doing something; negative always means taking something away. Both approaches can be used together.

Extinction is also an operant learning technique. It differs in principle from extinction in respondent conditioning. In operant conditioning, it means removing the relationship between a behaviour and its consequence. With negative punishment, we may remove a consequence that has nothing to do with the behaviour. Extinction might be used where an avoidance of homework is leading to arguments between a child and her parents. The arguments positively reinforce not doing homework because they take up time and emotional energy that can then not be applied to the homework. Instead of arguing, the parents put the child and the homework in another room, thus withdrawing the reinforcing behaviour. Unlike extinction in respondent conditioning, this is not solely avoiding making a response. Instead, it is about positively removing the relationship between a consequence and the behaviour that led to it.

Positive reinforcement is usually preferable to or should be used with other techniques. For example, extinction gives no control over the behaviour that might replace the undesirable behaviour – it might be equally undesirable. Positive reinforcement allows the favoured behaviour to be encouraged alongside the extinction of the unwanted behaviour. In addition, the unwanted behaviour may increase temporarily to test out the new response and this is hard to cope with, so encouraging useful behaviour makes the process easier.

The main process in *social learning* is *modelling*. Hudson and Macdonald (1986) describe this as follows:

■ A person sees someone else performing an action and pays attention to it.
■ The observer 'forms an idea' or code in their mind for how the behaviour is done, including some rehearsals in practice or in their mind.
■ The observer identifies circumstances in which the behaviour occurs and has consequences.
■ When an appropriate situation arises, the observer repeats the behaviour according to the 'idea' of it which has been formed.

Seeing a feared behaviour performed by a role model helps many people to appreciate that there will be no adverse consequences. Most people learn practical skills or behaviour by watching a demonstration of what to do and experimenting while in a supportive environment; receiving feedback and encouragement are an important part of this. This work has led to skills training programmes, anger management classes and similar ways of helping people to learn new behaviours.

Sheldon (1998: 23) summarizes the important factors in *social skills training* programmes as follows:

■ Specify problems where there are gaps in a client's behavioural repertoire and the ways in which new behaviours would help to fill the gaps.
■ Divide the problems into small components or stages.
■ Help clients to identify mistaken thinking (cognitions) that may hinder them.
■ Demonstrate the desired behaviour, and then get the client to rehearse it.
■ Connect chains of small behaviours together to make more complex behaviours.

■ Help clients to understand how to discriminate between situations where it is useful and not useful to use the behaviour.
■ Introduce real-life difficulties.
■ Set real-life practical assignments and get clients to report back.

Assertiveness training is a technique derived from social learning theory used for people who lack confidence. Workers help them to practise appropriate forms of behaviour in a supportive environment, so that they are enabled to use these in, ideally, increasingly difficult real-life situations.

Among *cognitive-behavioural therapies* are the following:

■ *Coping skills* contain two elements: a 'self-verbalization', that is, an instruction to ourselves, and the behaviour that results. Difficulty in coping with situations may arise from an inability to work out what to do in order to self-verbalize, or from an inability to act on our instructions. Meichenbaum's (1985) stress inoculation training aims to reduce or prevent stress by teaching clients what to say or do in difficult situations. Ronen (1998) suggests that focusing on skills related to self-control may be helpful in direct work with children. In addition, practitioners make changes to reduce any stress in the client's environment.

■ *Cognitive restructuring* is perhaps the best-known form of cognitive therapy and includes Beck's cognitive therapy and Ellis's rational emotive behaviour therapy (REBT, formerly RET). In Beck's cognitive therapy approach, clients collect information about how they interpret situations, and the social worker questions and tests out how these work. In REBT, irrational beliefs dominate clients' thinking, which leads to three things: first, 'awfulizing', that is, seeing things as unreasonably negative; second, a low tolerance for frustration, that is, feeling that it is impossible to bear uncomfortable situations; and third, 'damnation', that is, feeling that you are in essence bad because you have failed at something. Social workers question and attack the irrational beliefs that underlie these reactions. Sheldon (1998, 2012) emphasizes the need to attend to disorders of perception and attribution. Perception affects how someone sees what has happened to them; attribution is the judgements they make about the meaning of their experiences.

Case example: The threat of unemployment

A lorry driver was threatened with dismissal because he was seen driving unsafely. He perceived this as unfair, which might have been a misperception, and also thought that the manager was determined to dismiss him to save money. This is an attribution of an explana- tion of behaviour that may have been unstated or may not even have occurred to the manager. Cognitive therapies might concentrate on giving the driver the skills to interact with the manager and reduce the driver's inappropriate negative thoughts about the manager's attitude.

■ *Structural cognitive therapy* is concerned with three 'structures' of belief in clients' minds. Core beliefs are assumptions about ourselves; intermediate beliefs are explicit descriptions people make of the world; and peripheral beliefs are the plans of action and problem-solving strategies that we use daily. Workers focus on beliefs at the periphery that cause problems but use the process of change to explore the origins of these beliefs in deeper ideas.

Criminal justice

CBT is widely used in criminal justice settings, in community settings to prevent progression to more serious offending and in prisons to reduce recidivism. These provide a good example of the practical use of CBT techniques in agency programmes. Elements that are often included are social skills training, anger or aggression management and efforts to change faulty reasoning, often with a moral element. A US government study refers to six commonly used programmes:

- aggression replacement training, which includes all three of these elements;
- strategies for self-improvement and change, focusing on substance abuse;
- moral reconation therapy, concentrating on moral reasoning and the individual's acceptance of responsibility for their criminal behaviour, reasoning and rehabilitation; devised by Ross and colleagues (Ross et al., 1988, 1989) in Canada, this approach was applied in the Welsh STOP (Straight Thinking on Probation) programme (Raynor and Vanstone, 1994, 1998; Raynor et al., 1994) and elsewhere in the UK;
- relapse prevention therapy, also focusing on substance abuse;
- the skills and education programme Thinking for a Change (T4C) (Milkman and Wanberg, 2007).

A critique of reasoning and rehabilitation in the UK applies to many of these programmes, and helps us to see some of the potential criticisms of applying CBT techniques in wide-scale agency programmes. CBT here was seen as prescriptive, as following a detailed manual of action and as using an explicit teaching programme; it was an example of the problems of manualization, discussed above. The aim was to move offenders away from stereotyped thinking about their own needs and position, and allow them to see situations more broadly and from different perspectives. They would then also be able to think through their problems more rationally and find alternative ways to deal with them.

The reasoning and rehabilitation programme was criticized for its racism and lack of flexibility, for the way it forced practitioners to comply with interventions, for negating the importance of self-determination as a principle underlying effective CBT practice, for using strict procedures that treated people as machines and for not responding to the social and economic causes of much offending (Neary, 1992; Pitts, 1992). The way in which the programme gave priority to managing its general objectives, rather than individuals' needs and wishes, was also criticized (Oldfield, 2002; Raynor, 2003). This CBT approach, however, fitted well with an increasing emphasis on 'offence-focused' work with offenders, driven by political and policy trends as well as theoretical developments in professional practice. This changed emphasis concentrates on offenders reviewing their offences and the patterns of behaviour that led to them, and may be presented politically as a focus on the offence, rather than on the welfare of the offender.

Motivational interviewing

Motivational interviewing is an example of new practice ideas drawing on the concepts of CBT (Miller and Rollnick, 2002); it has also been used in criminal justice settings, and particularly with people with substance abuse problems. Its main use is to engage clients who are not motivated to change their behaviour, and there is research evidence of its helpfulness with such clients (Teater, 2010: 136–7). Figure 6.3 draws together important principles of practice for motivational interviewing, derived from the original ideas and interpretations of the model for social work.

Figure 6.3 Principles of motivational interviewing

Principle	Practitioner's actions
Express empathy to understand the client's ambivalence	Reflective listening helps in understanding and accepting the client's starting point of view and drives towards change
Develop the discrepancy between the client's values and current behaviour	Motivate clients by helping them see the discrepancy between their goals and where they are now
Handle, 'roll with', side-step resistance	Avoid counterproductive arguments, clarify free choices, identify and work with ambivalence, avoid impasses
Support self-efficacy	Build the client's belief that they can change (an important motivator) and are responsible for change

Source: Miller and Rollnick (2002), Marshall (2009), Teater (2010: 120–1) and Walsh and Corcoran (2010).

The main focus of motivational interviewing is to identify and harness motivations for progress or change that may be hidden in a destructive lifestyle; this is done by helping clients to understand the gap between their unhelpful thinking and the possibility of implementing a change in their lives. Practitioners bear in mind a series of stages through pre-contemplation, contemplating the possibility of change, preparing to change, taking action and then working on maintaining the change. I say 'bear in mind' because this in fact rarely happens, and reluctant and challenging clients often slip back (Teater, 2010). Maintaining a picture of the process, however, helps practitioners to sustain progress through any difficulties.

This approach has connections with humanistic practice in its person-centred approach and its emphasis on empathic relationships with challenging clients, illustrating the importance of the shared value principle of alliance. Without alliance, it is impossible to help destructive, disengaged or hostile clients. Other aspects of the shared value principles demonstrated in this model of practice are using the positive objectives from clients' identified motivators, and making sure there are clear sequences of actions and processes.

The development of motivational interviewing and other CBT practices in criminal justice points up social workers' need to find ways of tackling clients who are very hard to help.

Mindfulness

Mindfulness is a fairly new set of ideas that derive from two main sources:

■ Buddhist thought, and the psychology developed from it, which includes studies of meditation, including transcendental meditation, and its consequences for the way our brains work;

■ social learning and other ideas in CBT, which stress the importance of focusing attention on defined behaviours (Hick, 2009).

These concepts also have connections with everyday ideas, research on interviewing and communication, and ideas about reflective practice (see Chapter 3), all of which emphasize paying attention to the people you are interacting with and being receptive to their communication. They also connect with the shared value principles of alliance and rights.

In Buddhist thinking, mindfulness is 'bare attention', unconditioned by social expectations and external demands, and is a preparation for and precondition of liberating yourself from current demands, so that you can cultivate your mental capacity to experience and understand the world (Mace, 2008). You pay attention in a disciplined way to your body and its breathing, your mental patterns, your reactions to stimuli outside yourself and your fears about external realities affecting you, as part of a process of ridding yourself of these limitations. All this generates the capacity to clear your mind and develop positive abilities in thinking and 'clear comprehension' (Mace, 2008: 23).

There are four main forms of mindfulness-based psychotherapy that may be helpful to social workers, especially where they are dealing with people suffering anxiety and depression:

■ *MBSR – mindfulness-based stress reduction* is used to help people who are affected by major or chronic illness become more mindful about their attitudes to the condition. They receive training in self-monitoring and managing stresses, in using formal stress-reducing techniques such as yoga and in more generally being aware of stressors in everyday activity. Group discussion is used to promote individual learning.

■ *MBCT – mindfulness-based cognitive therapy* is similar to MBSR, aiming at 'decentring', that is, shifting people's emphasis in thinking and priorities in life away from stressful cognitions. There is less focus on bodily sensations and mood and more on identifying negative cognitions. There are various derivatives of MBCT for specific conditions connected with cognitive functioning, for example eating disorders.

■ *DBT – dialectical behaviour therapy* originally focused on helping people with self-harming behaviour and 'borderline personality disorder' who have experiences that they think invalidate them as people, with the result that conventional psychological treatments focused on behavioural problems make them feel even further rejected. After initial agreements between practitioners and clients about the emotions and reactions leading to the out-of-control behaviour to be tackled, a mix of individual support and skill training is used to manage clients' emotions and help them feel more effective in dealing with the situations they are facing.

▨ *act – acceptance and commitment therapy* (usually not ACT, which implies assertive community treatment, a case management approach employed with mentally ill people) uses many similar ideas, but its main focus is on developing the self as a context for making behavioural changes. Clients work on identifying and rejecting aspects of their current self, such as overdependent relationships, that seem substantial and continuing, but can be altered so that they are less important and can be changed. The approach involves a menu of specific procedures.

Developments in neuroscience

Social work thinking is increasingly taking into account recent developments in neuroscience (Applegate and Shapiro, 2005; Farmer, 2009). This has particular relevance to CBT for two reasons. One is that neuroscience draws on an explicit knowledge base in the physical and medical sciences that connects with CBT's emphasis on scientific knowledge as an important foundation for practice. The second reason is that neuroscience can offer insights that increase our understanding of how psychological and social relationships are processed in our brains. We know that the physical state of our bodies affects how our brains work: this is why relaxation is effective in dealing with anxiety. We also know that our state of mind and our beliefs can have important consequences for our bodily functions.

Example *The neuroscientific basis of drug abuse*

Social workers often deal with people who abuse drugs of addiction, such as cocaine or heroin, or become addicted to medication such as tranquillizers. Recent research has demonstrated how these drugs work to change the transmission system in people's brains and nervous systems, making them more amenable to the pleasure of using drugs and less able to respond to other psychological rewards such as sex, food and humour (Farmer, 2009: 142).

Miehls (2011: 81–8) summarizes the key areas of neurobiology in social work as:

▨ plasticity – the capacity of the brain to reshape itself by improving connections between neurons; for example, forging attachment in childhood generates new neural connections;
▨ the different development of the right and left hemispheres of the brain, giving rise to different impacts of behaviour;
▨ information-processing and memory;
▨ the impact of physical and psychological trauma on brain development.

Applegate and Shapiro (2005) and Farmer (2009) focus on the structure of the brain, how messages are transmitted in the brain and across the nervous system, and how these process may go wrong. Farmer (2009) examines evidence that particular areas of the brain are linked to certain important areas of human behaviour, including remembering, learning and mirroring, which allows us to learn physical and social skills by watching others, and leads finally to the human ability to use the brain to understand itself.

Much current neuroscience research explores the functioning of areas of the brain itself and how chemicals improve or inhibit neurological connections between the body and the brain. Information that affects how people interpret their perceptions of other people are transmitted through the nervous system. A stimulation (such as observing a piece of behaviour in another person) passes along the nerves via a series of impulses that are fired off from the observation. A part of the nerve, the axon, sends out a chemical, a neurotransmitter, which affects a receptor on the other side of the gap between this and the next nerve, allowing information on the observation to be passed between the nerves. The neurotransmitter is then taken up in the first axon, to be used again. If this chemical is taken up too rapidly, it leads to changes in people's mood because the transmission of perceptions and feelings about the outside world is altered. People who work in mental health will be familiar with the use of medications known as SSRIs to treat depression; the well-known anti-depressant Prozac is an example of these. SSRI is an abbreviation for 'selective serotonin reuptake inhibitor', the neurotransmitter involved being serotonin; when the SSRI reduces (inhibits) the reuptake of serotonin, it improves the person's mood (Applegate and Shapiro (2005: 3–7).

In children, it is well-established that a lack of experience and stimulation hinders the development of neural connections in the brain. This may come about through neglect by the parents or extreme financial poverty, and then makes the children less responsive to further social experiences.

Brain and personal development continues throughout life. For example, neurons continue to be generated in the brain, although the plasticity of our brains – their capacity to change flexibly – reduces after childhood. It is this plasticity that helps people repair the damage of early attachment problems, which we met in Chapter 4. Evidence that there are chemical 'rewards' for good bonding experiences helps us understand why later good parenting can compensate for some of the damage caused by poor attachment in early childhood. It also reinforces the physical and emotional benefits of practitioners' work on improving children's social relationships and experiences. Farmer (2009) identified four areas where neuroscience knowledge may be helpful to social workers. These are set out in Figure 6.4 and identify what knowledge may have implications for social workers and consequences for how we should practise.

You may resist placing too much emphasis on neuroscience knowledge because its focus on physical changes in the brain and body seems to negate the humanity of social work's emphasis on the psychological base of human freewill, and because of the importance of social relationships for our development and way of life. However, neuroscience offers a better understanding of the physical factors that affect psychological reactions and social relations, although it does not say that physical factors override the psychological and social. It is obvious that physical pleasure and pain affect how we behave and how we relate to other people.

Figure 6.4 Farmer's important areas of neuroscience knowledge

Area of practice	Important knowledge	Practice implications
Attachment and bonding	Evidence that bonding may generate brain chemicals (oxytocin, vasopressin) that produce feelings of reward and pleasure	Experiences of bonding may be rewarding and compensate for an earlier lack of attachment
Trauma	Evidence that physical and chemical changes in the brain are connected to unhelpful reactions to stress (serotonin, corticotrophins)	Importance of preventing and responding to stress reactions after crises and in long-term caring
Psychotherapy	Evidence of chemical and brain changes resulting from mental illness and from psychological interventions	Linking medical and psychological interventions may improve the effectiveness of both
Medication and drugs of abuse	Evidence of the diverse and complex impact of various combinations of drugs used for medication and in abuse	Exploring the detailed psychological and social consequences of both medical and abusive drug use

Source: Farmer (2009).

The following case example illustrates how understanding that an increasing disability may affect a client's behaviour allows us to deal with people helpfully. Using neuroscience knowledge enables us to incorporate the social into wider interventions.

Case example: Mrs Folwell's arthritis

A care assistant visiting Mrs Folwell, an older woman with severe arthritis, talked to her social worker about how difficult both the family and the assistant herself were finding it to maintain build relationships with Mrs Folwell because of her tetchy manner, constantly complaining and criticizing others. The social worker asked the assistant to remember a time when her back had been playing her up and she had constantly found it difficult to bend down or get into her car. 'Now think how it must be to find it painful to move every joint in your body every minute of the day. Wouldn't you get irritated with everything around you?' This insight helped the assistant to be more sympathetic with Mrs Folwell's crotchety manner.

Example text: Dobson and Dobson (2009) on CBT

Dobson and Dobson (2009) start from three important principles of CBT, which make clear its ideological position that it is critical of psychodynamic perspectives:

- The access hypothesis claims that all of our thinking is knowable to us; nothing is hidden in an 'unconscious'.
- The mediation hypothesis claims that our rational minds manage our emotional responses; we do not have solely emotional responses to experiences in our lives.

▪ The change hypothesis, following from these two points, is that since our thoughts are knowable and control our reactions to events, we must be able to modify our reactions to what happens to us. We become more able to deal with and adapt to the world by understanding our reactions and using cognitive strategies to manage them.

The context in which we work, in particular to a demand from agencies for structured, well-evidenced interventions, supports the value of CBT in practice. The emphasis on CBT reflects the importance of individualism and independence in Western society. The fact that Dobson and Dobson make this point illustrates the analysis of CBT made by the critical perspective in social work (see Chapter 12) that writers in this tradition simply accept the reality of current social assumptions, rather than devising an approach that contests them.

The first stage of CBT intervention is *assessment*. A range of assessment instruments are available for use by psychologists, the main purpose of which is to arrive at an assessment of a formal 'diagnosis'. CBT practice, however, particularly as social workers use it, requires a focus on understanding the problems to be tackled. The reason for Dobson and Dobson's (2009: 17–18) distinction is the requirement in some countries, in particular the USA, to confirm a diagnosis in accordance with manuals of diagnostic criteria so that clients may claim insurance cover for the cost of their treatment. This is, however, not an issue for social workers in most countries, and it is important to distinguish the need for this in some jurisdictions from the requirements of CBT practice.

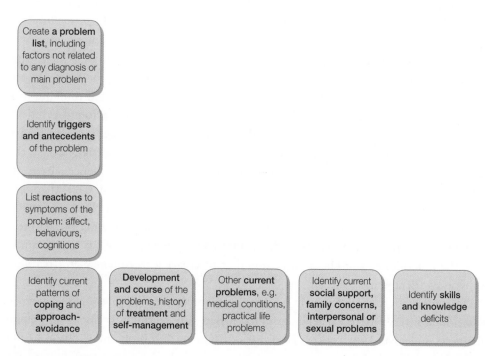

Figure 6.5 CBT assessment
Source: Dobson and Dobson (2009).

I have summarized social workers' formulation of a CBT assessment in Figure 6.5. The main distinguishing feature in the first three assessment tasks listed is the strong focus on specifying the problem and the thinking patterns related to it. Nevertheless, it is useful to explore a range of other issues that may support or obstruct interventions, or that are not relevant to the behaviour problem but may also need sorting out.

Case example: Fred's anxiety

Fred was referred for CBT to deal with extreme anxiety about his work after changes in his responsibilities and pressure from a new manager. Among the additional factors identified were his elderly mother's care because of her increasing disability due to arthritis, and financial problems because his wife had recently been moved to a part-time job. Practical help was also needed with these factors, although they were not strong contributors to his level of anxiety.

Assessment is not a once and for ever action, since CBT assumes that clients will need to do homework in between treatment sessions; therefore, various questionnaires, self-report measures and ways of observing and monitoring specific behaviour changes will be needed. Some information may come from family members or other services involved with clients.

The next stage is devising a *case formulation* and discussing this with the client. I have set out this process in Figure 6.6, drawing on Dobson and Dobson's (2009: 44) diagram of the CBT model of emotional distress. This uses cognitive theory to propose that people have certain core beliefs, assumptions and schemas, which, when triggered by life events, lead to distorted thinking. This is often in the form of automatic thoughts, because a trigger automatically generates the distorted thinking from the (irrational) core belief. This then leads to emotional and behavioural reactions, which feed back into the core beliefs and confirm them. The reactions also lead to avoidance and withdrawal from situations where the core beliefs are triggered, so that new learning is less possible. The case formulation draws on evidence about the particular problem and how it may be tackled, as well as general CBT theory. It proposes a model of what is happening to the client and enables a client and practitioner to have a discussion about the important processes that are going on, and start a discussion on how these may be tackled. Out of the discussion of the case formulation, the practitioner and client work together to create a treatment plan, treatment goals and a therapeutic contract.

Different models of CBT vary in how they present the next stage: should we start on behavioural interventions to generate initial progress in learning, or focus on helping clients to understand the process of distorted thinking? Dobson and Dobson (2009: 75), acknowledging the issue, suggest starting with behavioural strategies on a principle of 'let's get on with it'; this will then provide further information to adjust the

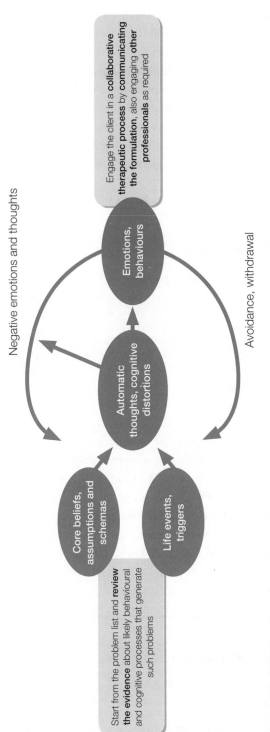

Negative emotions and thoughts

Engage the client in a **collaborative therapeutic process** by **communicating the formulation,** also engaging **other professionals** as required

Emotions, behaviours

Automatic thoughts, cognitive distortions

Avoidance, withdrawal

Core beliefs, assumptions and schemas

Life events, triggers

Start from the problem list and **review the evidence** about likely behavioural and cognitive processes that generate such problems

Figure 6.6 CBT case formulation

case formulation and plans. They then interweave 'psychoeducation' into this process, so that the experience of change helps the client to understand the problems and the process of treatment. Practitioners may well want to switch between interventions and helping people understand cognitive factors.

The treatment process then moves through the sequence, an example of a shared value principle of specifying the sequences of action applied in this theory (Figure 6.7). While practitioners usually tackle each of the requirements in this sequence, a good deal of flexibility in exploring issues as they are presented by clients is required; the sequence does not therefore form an inviolable order of proceedings, but indicates the important areas to be covered, more or less in this sequence.

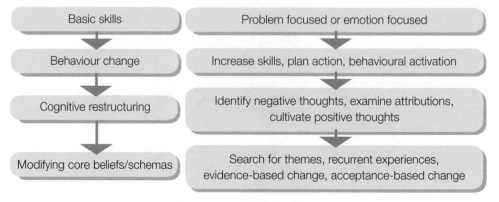

Figure 6.7 The CBT treatment sequence

The starting point lies in developing skills to manage the problems and the emotions associated with them. For example, parental management programmes, work training or communication skills may help people to deal with practical problems in their lives. We saw an example of this using CBT in the case study of child and adolescent mental health services in Chapter 2. Emotions-focused work might include relaxation techniques, helping people to create a structured routine that avoids problems, sleeping well and remaining fit.

Behavioural interventions involve activating clients with a planned series of progressive tasks, getting them to maintain a schedule to monitor their progress. For example, where there are communication difficulties, clients may be provided with some training in how to deal with situations, and they might try this out in practice. Assertiveness training and social skills training in dealing with common situations may also be helpful.

Case example: Faisal's social activities

Faisal was a young man with learning disabilities who was living away from his parents in supported accommodation for the first time. His care workers rehearsed with him skills in greeting and having practical conversations with shopkeepers, cashiers and other people he met in his daily round. He practised a new one every week between the training sessions and scaled the increase in confidence he felt with each successful communication.

Another common behavioural approach involves a series of exposure treatments in which people are progressively exposed to situations that they find difficult. For people who are agoraphobic, for example, this may be going to the front door, then outside, then to the road, then to the corner of the street and so on. Clients learn relaxation and breathing techniques and have support from familiar people to help manage their anxiety levels as they develop their experience. We have seen that the theoretical source of these is more behavioural.

Three elements of CBT are effective when intervening in emotional disorders:

- Change people's thinking (cognitive appraisals) about the situation they are facing that is leading to the emotional disorder.
- Prevent people from trying to avoid negative emotional experiences; instead, try to support them to face up to and get through bad experiences.
- Encourage actions and activities not associated with the negative emotions (Barlow, Allen and Choate, 2004, cited by Dobson and Dobson, 2009).

Pause and reflect *Freda's school-related anxiety*

(The case study and associated text have been written especially for this book by Emma Reith-Hall)

Look at the following case summary and make a note of the issues you would identify that a social worker might need to tackle. Compare your thoughts with the ideas the social worker used in the following account. Track the interventions that the practitioner used in Dobson and Dobson's (2009) account of CBT, or through the other forms of practice discussed above.

Case example: Freda's story

Freda, aged 13, lived with her mother (a part-time care assistant), her father (a plumber) and her brother, aged 16, in a medium-sized city. The family environment was secure and stable with no particular stressors. A paediatrician referred Freda to the child and adolescent mental health service, describing Freda as an 'anxious school refuser'. This problem had been ongoing for two years since Freda had been bullied when she was aged 11. Freda had returned to school briefly on a part-time timetable, but had stopped attending again after being bullied by a different group of peers. When referred, she had not yet returned to school, but she wanted to go back to the same school. Her parents wanted to support her but did not want to make matters worse by pressurizing her. Freda had lost contact with most of her friends and rarely went out, although she contacted one school friend via texts and social networking. The referral explained that Freda was concerned about her weight and had a poor self-image. She sometimes reported feeling low, being tearful and wishing that she did not exist.

When I received the referral, I considered some issues that might have been relevant, and Figure 6.8 indicates what went through my mind. The figure illustrates that CBT practice requires you to take into account a broad range of considerations, including social and attachment issues, even though the starting point of the referral was 'anxiety', which led the team leader to think that a CBT intervention might be used. Before making the decision to use a particular model of practice, it is important to rule out other things that may be more important than the presenting issue of 'anxiety'; some of these issues might need to be addressed using alternative interventions.

Figure 6.8 Issues in Freda's family

Potential issues	Questions arising from the referral applied to Freda's family
School	Is the current educational provision appropriate for her? What is her academic performance? Has she any learning difficulties?
Risk	Assess possible links between bullying and teenage suicide
Physical health	Freda is worried about her weight
Emotional health	She has a poor self-image and experiences bullying. Is there any social phobia?
Anxiety	Assess the level of and reasons for anxiety about school. Referral shows that Freda wants to return to school
Depression	Low mood is mentioned in the referral. Is this connected with low self-esteem, negative thoughts or poor sleep? Is there evidence of self-harm or suicidal ideation?
Family issues	Are there signs of parental illness, domestic violence or parental substance misuse? Are there signs of worries about a parent or family member that mean Freda wants to stay at home? Is anxiety a family theme? A learned behaviour? A child protection issue?
Relationships	Assess family and social networks
Attachment, early years	Assess attachment behaviour, in the past and now
Hopes and goals	General life aims and specific aims around school: the referral says she wants to return, but school refusers often do not share their parent's goal of returning to school

The assessment involved working with Freda and her family to clarify goals, and also factors in their lives that would influence decisions about intervention with Freda. I did this by looking at the 'Four Ps' (Carr, 2006). These are set out in Figure 6.9, dividing the factors that might be affecting Freda into four groups, to be talked through with Freda and her parents. When making an assessment using this formulation, there is a predominant focus on social factors, particularly family issues that might affect the person in particular. In this case, an important reason for this was the way in which family factors may have been an important source of stressors potentially perpetuating Freda's problem behaviour. For example, Carr (2006: 497) talks about: 'An anxiety-oriented family culture, which privileges the interpretation of many environmental events as potentially hazardous' as a factor that makes it seem almost natural for a child to be anxious about difficult situations because the members of the family often behave that way too.

The Four Ps formulation is typical of current social work in that it does not neglect biological and genetic factors and balances personal and contextual factors, so that any psychological and social issues affecting the problem are carefully examined. First, there may be some features of Freda's background that predispose her to anxiety. Second, there may be factors in her life that build up and perpetuate anxiety once she experiences it.

Next, there may be factors that protect her from feeling anxious – people who suffer anxiety can often find useful resources within themselves or in their environment to help them. Finally, I pulled out precipitants for the school's concern about her, which had in turn led to the paediatrician's diagnosis of 'anxious school refuser' and to the referral.

The list of perpetuating factors was very much as the referral had led me to expect, so there were no hidden concerns that might have led me to broader work with the family or school. On the other hand, it was a relief that there were many protective factors, which meant that there would be strong support from Freda's family and social network for a direct intervention working on the thinking patterns that had led to her anxiety.

Assessment also needed to engage Freda in developing a detailed understanding of what was happening to her. I built this up by working through a formulation of the onset of problems, explaining that antecedent or preceding events lead to a process of thinking that raises anxieties and feelings about the anxiety, and then leads to the behaviour that is seen as difficult (Stallard, 2005). I talked through this sequence with Freda, so that she confirmed and began to see the importance of the process of her thinking. The original important events and experiences for Freda were of being bullied for the first time, some years previously. This had led to the development of core beliefs, that is, ideas about herself that became part of her personal identity; there were beliefs that 'I'm a failure; I'm worthless.' These led on to assumptions predicting that 'I am always going to be bullied' and 'I will always be unattractive.' These are irrational because, while a fear of being bullied or a perception that you have some unattractive features may be reasonable, it is not rational to believe that you will be bullied or unattractive all the time and in all situations, and that you cannot do anything about this. Challenging these irrational beliefs would give Freda the opportunity to deal with events that might affect her in the future.

These assumptions are triggered, that is, brought to the forefront of Freda's mind, by events that happen to her. So when, in her next school, where the second previous incident of bullying took place, she had a period of sickness and was again bullied, these confirmed the core beliefs and assumptions and caused automatic thoughts to rush through her head: 'I'm fat and ugly, people will laugh at me, I might cry.' This produced an emotional reaction of worry and sadness, which led Freda to think 'I have to stay off school.'

CBT interventions focus strongly on the current situation. Freda and I explored this by picking up a recent event that had been difficult, in that it had caused Freda to become very anxious. This was 'thinking about going to school again.' She completed a simple formulation of her thinking:

1 *What did you think?* – I will be bullied. What if I can't cope?
2 *How did you feel?* – Anxious, worried and scared.
3 *How did your body change?* – Feel sick, can't breathe, feel sweaty and shaky.
4 *What did you do?* – Stayed at home.

There were four main aims of the first intervention session. The first was to use these *two assessment activities* as part of 'introducing CBT', since engaging in assessment is an

Figure 6.9 Assessing the Four Ps

Predisposing factors		
Biological factors • Genetic vulnerability to anxiety or depression	Psychological factors • Low self-esteem • Shy temperament • External locus of control – feeling unable to exert control over anxiety-provoking events	Attachment and early life • Anxious attachment

Perpetuating factors		
Personal		*Contextual*

Biological factors
• Dysregulation of:
  – GABA (the neurotransmitter gamma aminobutyric acid)
  – adrenaline
  – noradrenaline
  – serotonin
	Psychological factors
	• Avoiding school
	• Threat- and danger-oriented cognitive set
	• Hypervigilance
	• Misinterpreting somatic symptoms as ill health
		Treatment factors
		• Denial, low motivation, non-engagement
		• Poor communication/liaison between family and agencies
		• Unhelpful school placement
		• Lack of knowledge among school staff

Protective factors		
Personal		*Contextual*
Biological factors • Good physical health	Psychological factors • High self-esteem • Easy temperament • Optimistic attributional style • High IQ • Good coping strategies • Internal locus of control	Treatment factors • Acknowledge problem, shared goal, commitment and motivation • Coordinated, joined-up approach from agencies • Freda has been reintegrated to school before

Precipitating factors

• Bullying – 'Bullying by peers and victimisation by teachers may precipitate anxiety problems' (Carr, 2006: 504)

• School transition	• Abuse
• Life stressors	• Bereavement, loss or separation
• Illness/injury	• Moving house

Family influences
• An anxious parent
• A theme of anxiety or threat within the family

Family factors
• Modelling, reinforcement of avoidant behaviour
• Poor knowledge of anxiety
• Overinvolved parent–child interaction
• Insecure parent–child attachment
• Neglectful parenting
• Low parental self-esteem, poor coping strategies
• Triangulation
• Parents seeking repeated medical examination for somatic symptoms
• Parental issues, e.g. substance misuse, domestic violence or physical/mental
  illness, which may compound the child's anxiety
• Family stress, social isolation and disadvantage

Family factors
• Secure attachment
• Authoritative parenting
• Good communication
• High marital satisfaction
• Good understanding of anxiety
• Parents' internal locus of control
• Good parental self-esteem/coping strategies
• Optimistic attributional style of the parents
• Absence of domestic violence, parental substance misuse or parental illness
• Low family stress
• Good family support network
• High socioeconomic status

important part of beginning the intervention. This built an experience of a working relationship, clarified the issues that we were to work on and established a focus for our action. The second aim was to define the problem, set goals and timescales and think about the resources that we needed to use. We defined on a scale from 1 to 10 how serious the problem was at referral and now, and what point on the scale would be reached when the work had been completed. This technique is drawn from solution-focused practice. Many interventions call on activities drawn from a wide range of theories with separate origins. The third aim was to explain how CBT worked, through the experience of the assessment process and through explaining the principles of managing anxiety. The fourth aim was to coordinate the expectations of Freda's family, school and other agencies through completing the 'common assessment framework' process, which establishes regular feedback to any other agencies involved.

The work then proceeded through a typical pattern for CBT interventions: a series of working sessions with Freda, interspersed with 'homework' in which she established and reinforced changes in behaviour, as shown in Figure 6.10. The beginning homework was to keep an 'anxiety diary' of any events that led to anxiety, and of the thinking, bodily symptoms and behaviour that resulted. These were reviewed in the first part of each subsequent session. The second session focused on *physiological factors*. The aim was to increase Freda's awareness of the physiological changes that affected her when she became anxious, and help her to learn relaxation techniques to manage these changes. The techniques included practising a deep breathing exercise, a panic breathing exercise and muscle tension and release exercises, listening to a relaxation CD, and visualization techniques. The aim of visualization is to help people shift their picture of how they behave in a stressful situation by visualizing different ways of reacting in a place and at a time when they feel safe. This helps them to practise safely various alternative ways of dealing with something they find difficult, and practise managing the anxiety as they visualize the problematic situation. The homework after this session was for Freda to try out the various relaxation techniques and record in her anxiety diary how effective she felt they had been.

In the third session, we looked first at the diary, discussed which relaxation techniques appeared to be effective and considered how Freda could adapt her behaviour in response to this learning. The main aim of the session was to explore *environmental factors*. We looked at what had and had not helped her in the past when she had tried to manage a difficult situation. To build on this, we used a 'brick wall and ladder' worksheet. This created a picture of the steps on a ladder that would enable Freda to get over a brick wall in her way. The homework for this session involved Freda identifying ways in which she could address the blocks standing in her way, for example calling on a school friend to accompany her.

The fourth session addressed Freda's thoughts and *thinking patterns*. The aim was to look at negative automatic thoughts and begin cognitive restructuring. This involved helping Freda to identify dysfunctional or negative views of herself, or how the world, in the shape of her school and potential bullies, operated, and then to learn how to challenge these thoughts rationally and develop alternatives or arguments against them in an organized way. As homework, Freda was to attend a school evening meeting looking at curriculum options for the following year; as well as using her anxiety diary, she prepared for this by rehearsing her responses to possible questions and situations, and the relaxation techniques she could use in this situation. Building on our work on cognitive restructuring, Freda's homework consisted of identifying thinking errors and listing adaptive thoughts.

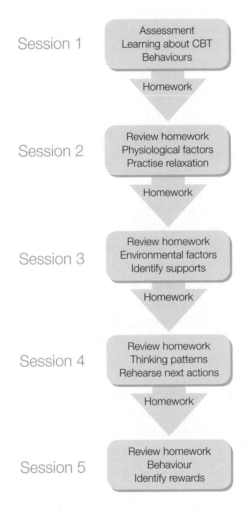

Figure 6.10 CBT intervention programme

The fifth session worked on Freda's *behaviour*, building on her homework and her experience of the options evening. Homework reviews focused on how her belief in her thoughts had been affected by the behavioural experiment of attending the options review. This enabled her to look again at a simple formulation of her cognition, affect, physiology and behaviours using this new experience of the real world. She identified and rated her previous and current experience, and identified the rewards she felt as a result of success with her new experience. Her homework was to attend the first day back at school, on a part-time timetable that had been agreed through the coordination arrangements set up at the beginning.

The sixth session *reviewed* the whole experience. The main focus was on how Freda could manage situations in which she felt stuck, using the techniques she had learned. For example, she could restart her anxiety diary, practise relaxation and work on cognitive restructuring. It was important for her to realize that she could manage any difficulties on her own but that I was available for her to return to if she needed it. This proved not to be necessary, and Freda's progress at school became satisfactory.

Conclusion: using CBT

The main uses of CBT are in mental health services, particularly where depression and anxiety are an issue. It is also used where behavioural change is needed to tackle a learned psychological disorder, that is, where an adverse reaction to life experiences has been built up into a pattern of behaviour. These situations often occur where someone is avoiding something that they recognize they need to do, or where they accept people around them such as their spouse, parents or peers telling them that they have to change their behaviour. Social learning can also enhance people's skills to deal with things they find difficult in their lives, and is often used with people with learning disabilities to improve their interpersonal and practical skills. Some very structured forms of CBT have been used with challenging clients, such as substance abusers, who are very hard to engage, as well as in criminal justice settings. While these have been enthusiastically taken up by some agencies, controversy about the values inherent in CBT theory and about the emphasis on positivist EBP research as the basis for CBT has limited its impact on general social work practice in many settings and in many countries.

Important characteristics, particularly of behavioural theory, are its highly structured approach (Teater, 2010: 157), careful assessment to identify precisely the behaviours that are being targeted, and development of a programme of behaviour change considering only that behaviour. This means that offering the approach to a wider range of clients would require extensive and in reality advanced training in the techniques and experienced supervision that would support their appropriate use. This is inappropriate and unavailable in the average social work agency, but it is relevant in specialized mental health services, and the research most strongly supports CBT in these areas. Some practical ways of working on patterns of unhelpful thinking that get in the way of wider helping services can be useful as a specific intervention when practitioners are involved with a broader range of help.

Additional resources

Further reading

Dobson, D. and Dobson, K. S. (2009) *Evidence-based Practice of Cognitive-Behavioral Therapy* (New York: Guilford).

A good example of a clinical text on CBT.

Ronen, T. and Freeman, A. (eds) (2007) *Cognitive Behavior Therapy in Clinical Social Work Practice* (New York: Springer).

A comprehensive edited collection, with detailed accounts of practice with different client groups, that authoritatively presents the arguments in support of CBT.

Cigno, K. and Bourn, D. (eds) (1998) *Cognitive Behavioural Social Work in Practice* (Aldershot: Ashgate).

A useful collection of theoretical and practice articles.

Crane, R. (2009) *Mindfulness-based Cognitive Therapy* (London: Routledge).

A good summary of some basic techniques in mindfulness-based CBT.

Hick, S. F. (ed.) (2009) *Mindfulness and Social Work* (Chicago: Lyceum).

A good range of articles showing how mindfulness is applied in social work.

Journals

Journals in this field such as *Behavioural and Cognitive Psychotherapy* or *Cognitive and Behavioral Practice* are multiprofessional and mainly written for and by psychologists and psychiatrists.

Websites

http://www.rcpsych.ac.uk/mentalhealthinfo/treatments/cbt.aspx

A good account of CBT for public information, provided by the British Royal College of Psychiatrists.

http://www.nhs.uk/conditions/cognitive-behavioural-therapy/Pages/Introduction.aspx

A similar public information website for the British National Health Service that contains a video of a CBT therapist discussing the technique.

Systems and ecological practice

7

Main contribution

The main contribution of systems and ecological ideas to social work is to integrate interpersonal interventions involving individuals with interventions that also engage with families, communities and other social agencies. This is done through a focus on how social and personal factors interact, helping people to adapt their social environment and their reactions to it so that they can live more harmoniously. A recent emphasis on 'green' policy issues such as sustainability in the natural environment is a new contribution to social work and care services and connects with ecological ideas. Ecological systems theory, while it sometimes refers to green issues, is mainly concerned with the social rather than the natural environment.

Main points

- Systems theory integrates social intervention with individual help. Although it seeks to provide for both social reform and psychological models of practice, it focuses on maintaining the status quo rather than achieving more radical social change.
- Systems theory allows for multifactorial explanation, but this creates complexity, making it difficult to give clear practice guidance, especially on choosing the level of intervention.
- Ecological systems theory focuses on psychological and individualistic equilibrium rather than on important environmental or 'green' issues.
- Macrosystems incorporate meso (middle-sized) systems, which in turn incorporate microsystems. Some writers refer to mezzosystems: this means the same as mesosystems. A focal system, the one that you are focusing on, is part of bigger suprasystems and includes smaller subsystems.
- Holistic, empowerment and anti-oppressive aspects of systems are valued, but holism may lead to a loss of focus and a failure to gain genuine consent, which in turn leads to hidden oppression.

- Systems interact with each other through complex processes in which information and action form flows of energy within and across the systems' boundaries. If we explore these interactions, we can understand how people in families, communities and wider social environments affect each other.
- In the USA, ecological systems theory became a predominant practice model because it incorporated elements of traditional psychodynamic practice. This meant that traditional therapeutic processes could be integrated into social and empowerment aims.
- Ecological 'life' models of social work seek to incorporate an awareness of social concepts such as fit, adaptedness, life stressors and the life course, which have been drawn from ecological ideas into practice.
- Social networking is an important application of systems ideas.
- Sustainable social development, and therefore concern for the natural environment, has become increasingly important in developing countries.

Practice ideas

- *Systems* focus on the connections between, and the resources of, families and groups, and on helping those connections to work well.
- *Life stressors* apply energy in the form of stresses to a system; this system may be a person or a family or community.
- *Fit* and *adaptedness* between individuals and their social environments are important concepts incorporated from ecological thinking.
- Work to initiate, maintain and improve social *networks* and mutual support is a development of systems ideas.
- *Resilience*, the capacity to bounce back from adversity, has emerged from ecological thinking as a practice objective.

Major statements

Because the use of general or ecological systems theory is virtually universal in the USA, most introductory and generalist textbooks from northern America assume this perspective. Consequently, many American texts on systems or ecological systems theory have become broad introductory texts. Gitterman and Germain's (2008) account re-engineers their pioneering 'life model' for the twenty-first century and is still the most significant theoretical formulation of an ecological model. I will therefore use it as the main example text in this chapter.

Texts from European countries use some systems concepts, but this is not a significant model of practice. Nash et al. (2005b) use ecological systems theory as a framework for a range of theories relevant to Aeroteroa/New Zealand. They propose a holistic theory base in which people are seen as part of the ecosystem of their environment. Within that ecosystem, practices are needed that develop communities, work with strengths and, using attachment ideas, rework relationships. This is an example of how different levels of systems allow us to incorporate a range of theories with different focuses.

The debate summary

Social work debates about systems theory cover four main points.

▶ **Systems ideas include the social in problem-solving social work, but without including the full implications of social change and systems theory**
Systems theory benefits social work because it incorporates social factors as well as psychological functioning into people's lives, balancing the two most important elements of social work aims. Compared with practitioners in healthcare, clinical psychology or counselling, social workers look at individuals in the context of their whole family and social environment. Other professions emphasize a focal individual; everything else is background, in which families, communities or other agencies help or hinder the health or well-being of individual patients. Social work emphasizes individuals' interconnections with other individuals and groups in their environment.

However, critical theory complains of the limited usage of systems and ecological ideas in social work. Systems ideas in social work focus on how systems maintain, reproduce and adapt themselves, rather than on the possibility, desirability or inevitability of a significant wider change in these systems. Part of the reason is that extensive development in cybernetics, biology and the social sciences is only weakly reflected in the social work literature. The idea of *complex adaptive systems*, for example, refers to large systems with many small component parts. While their complexity makes them seem chaotic, that complexity contains patterns that enable us to understand how they work. The same ideas may be used to explore artificial intelligence in computers and ecological systems in nature, and extensive scientific work has had limited impact in social work.

Greene (2008) draws on this terminology to identify some implications for social work, for example the importance of how the energy created by interventions in stable systems allows the 'emergence' of new behaviours and opportunities for change. For example, when a practitioner intervenes in a stable family, they may liberate opportunities for changes in family relationships. Becvar et al. (1997) propose that these ideas are important for groupwork. Has social work become stuck in an outdated, perhaps oversimplified reflection of systems theory? Some people would argue the opposite – that this is a complex area of study and social work practice, and has focused on those aspects that particularly fit its approach.

▶ **Systems ideas, in particular adaptation, assume the status quo rather than seek appropriate social change**

The idea of adaptation, which is particularly used in ecological systems ideas, is an extension of the problem of a limited use of systems ideas in social work. There are three main issues here. One is that, by stressing adaptation, we may fall into the 'get real' trap. This trap is an oversimplified ecological idea that clients need to adapt to the realities of the pressures upon them. But broader systems ideas suggest that we should also look at whether the realities are appropriate and just, and think about changing *them* as well as, or instead of, the client. The second issue is that we may think that total adaptation is possible and desirable. Against this, we have to realize that there are conflicts and inconsistencies in life, and people may need to be helped to accept and live with those inconsistencies. The third issue is that people may adapt too readily to the expectations around them. There may be better balances in their lives than the one they have come to, or the one that other people expect them to conform to. They may prefer a different way to adapt to the same pressures, or a different approach might be better for them or the people around them. So in social work practice, many practitioners are cautious about assuming that their task is to get people to adapt to others' expectations.

▶ **Systems ideas allow for multifactorial explanations, but the complexity of this is a barrier to clear prescriptions for action**

Social work uses systems ideas to include the variety of factors, interacting in different ways, in the system they are working with, but it is difficult see how the theory helps to identify and achieve outcomes. Systems theory says that everything is connected, so you could intervene in the system, but, like pushing on one ball in a net bag full of balls, all the elements could readjust so that everything looked the same afterwards. On the other hand, you might make a change in one member of a system, perhaps a family, and ripples of influence could spread out, achieving significant movement. It is hard to predict how all the interactions in the system will work to achieve the outcomes that you and members of the system are aiming for. The theory does not tell you which is going to happen. It feels like giving the system a nudge and hoping that something will be dislodged, or turning the computer off and on when it hangs, but not really knowing what went wrong.

On the other hand, systems ideas avoid the theoretical problems of cognitive-behavioural therapy and other theories that use linear cause and effect explanations. There may be a long line between what caused a problem and the present situation, but it may equally well be a short hop to a way of resolving it, based on the present circumstances. It may be more efficient to look at resolution rather than trying to explain or understand the situation (Greene and Lee, 2011: 69). On the other hand, we noted in relation to psychodynamic theory that many people value being able to 'make sense' of what has happened to them.

Case example: Pete, a hyperactive child in the Marsalis family

Joanie Marsalis found her hyperactive child, Pete, very stressful to deal with, and she forced herself to be ever-reasonable and responsive to his demands so that she became a calming influence. This put further pressure on her, because she always had to be present to maintain a calm environment. Her husband, Sevvy, got into conflicts with Pete, in which Joanie tried to mediate. Her constant involvement with Pete meant that she did not give herself enough space and time to relax and share personal activities with Sevvy on their own.

What are the options for dealing with these feelings? Joanie could take on extra stress for a time to change their family's behaviour patterns, and in the long term the pressure would be less. For example, she could get Pete to accept that she and Sevvy should have time out from dealing with Pete all the time. She could explore alternative support systems for set periods, so that Pete could learn to respond to others and so that she and Sevvy would not be at loggerheads over Pete's behaviour all the time. She could reward them all by having some special time with Pete and Sevvy together. She could work with Sevvy to agree a shared approach to dealing with Pete's behavioural problems.

Figure 7.1 is a diagram of some of the systems we can identify in this case example. There are three microsystems – the three individuals; and three mesosystems – the three pairings of the individuals, Joanie and Pete, Sevvy and Pete, and Joanie and Sevvy. There is a macrosystem, the nuclear family. Pointing these out, though, presents us with one of the problems of systems theory, because we could equally well talk about microsystems as being parts of each of these individuals and identify wider macrosystems such as their extended family or community.

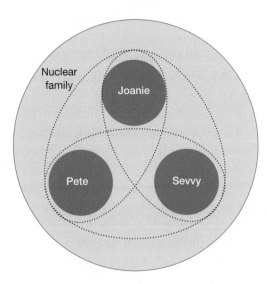

Figure 7.1 Some systems in the Marsalis family

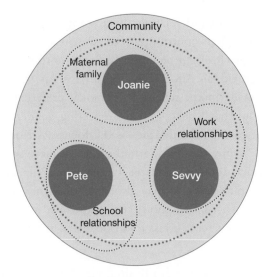

Figure 7.2 Some more systems connecting with the Marsalis family

Figure 7.2 illustrates some further systems connected with the Marsalis family, which at the same time highlights some of the criticisms of systems theory. Here, the microsystems have remained the same – the individuals – but there are two types of mesosystem. One is another system outside the family that each individual is part of: Joanie's maternal family, Sevvy's work relationships and Pete's school relationships. The family now becomes a mesosystem, but a different kind of mesosystem, shown with a blue dotted instead of a grey dotted line round it. This is because the macrosystem is the community. I have chosen to set out Joanie's mesosystem as her (the maternal) family, but you might ask whether Pete is not also a part of that system. I have selected Pete's school relationships, but Joanie and Sevvy might have different relationships at Pete's school, for example being more focused on the staff than the other students. Instead of including the paternal (Sevvy's) family, I have focused on his work relationships; feminists would argue that this may also reflect a gender bias in my assumptions about what is important in a man's life.

Pause and reflect *Selecting levels and focuses*

Looking at my comments on the case study and at Figures 7.1 and 7.2, can you identify some criticisms you would make of systems theory as a basis for analysing relationships and practice?

Some suggestions

One of the problems with systems theory is that it gives you no clue to the level at which you should tackle the issues, or which elements of them you should work on. A children's service might be presented with Pete as a problem child, with the family at the meso level. On the other hand, a family therapy approach tells us that relationships between all the family members contribute to the way in which Pete has become problematic to other people, so it might be better to focus on the network of relationships rather than any one individual. Another important issue is that the choices of focus and level that I have made might reflect my personal preferences or assumptions. A feminist might point out that I have, perhaps reflecting gender bias, selected Sevvy's work relationships but Joanie's family roles as the focus. A critical practitioner might focus on the choice of 'family' as an important macro or meso system. Doing this may reflect a social assumption about the greater importance of the family rather than, say, an ethnic group in people's lives. It may also reflect another social assumption that socially accepted formal social structures, such as family and community, are more important than other less evident or less traditional structures, such as ethnic, gender or national identity.

▶ Ecological systems theory has a very limited view of ecological issues, applying them mainly to psychological and individual equilibrium rather than broad ecological issues

A fourth area of debate is around the limited use of ecological ideas in much ecological theory in social work. It does not reflect the increasing importance of 'green' issues, such as environmentally sustainable living, because it accepts an individualistic approach to ecology; this approach argues that ecology is about conserving the existing environment rather than looking at social change to respond to ecological problems, and concerns social rather than individual adaptation as an aspect of ecology.

The eco-social approach uses ecological ideas politically to combat social exclusion, including such ideas as environmental impact statements (Matthies et al., 2000a, 2000b, 2001; Närhi, 2002). Eco-feminism (Besthorn and McMillen, 2002) argues that political and social systems, including ideas such as ecological systems theory in social work, oppress women's concern for sustainable and sustaining environments. These ideas have not yet, however, had a big impact in social work practice. Mary (2008) explores some of the issues, and Coates (2003) offers a well-worked out ecological approach to social work focused on sustainable development in all societies, not only those that are resource-poor. In addition, Dominelli (2012) has recently tried to develop a 'green' social work.

We need to understand the complexity of interdependence and value the diversity of both human and natural forms. Coates (2003) uses the systems idea of boundaries to emphasize that the earth is a closed system, with limited resources, and that our lives should be sustainable. By concentrating on social and cultural objectives, systems ideas in social work treat the physical environment in which we all live as a 'lifeless backdrop' (Zapf, 2010) to the traditional concerns of our services. Because social work is based on interpersonal practice, it fails to take into account how those relationships are constructed by the physical environment around us and how human behaviour affects the environment (Hawkins, 2010).

Wider theoretical perspectives

Overview of systems ideas and terminology

Concepts about the structure of systems are illustrated in the diagrams in Figure 7.3. The main ones are as follows:

- *Systems* are entities with boundaries within which physical and mental energy are exchanged internally more than they are across the boundary.
- *Energy* (in this context) is actions, resources (such as effort, money and time) and information. If you provide help and information or get extra social security for a family, you are putting energy into the family system.
- *Levels* of systems refer to the fact that large macrosystems contain smaller mesosystems, which in turn contain microsystems. The system level selected as the focus of concern may vary. For example, individuals are part of suprasystems such as families and organizations, which are bigger than the individuals but encompass them. The focal system is also made up of subsystems; for an individual, this includes their body and its elements, and their mind.
- *Closed systems* have no interchange across the boundary; a closed vacuum flask is an example.
- *Open systems* occur where energy crosses the boundary, which is permeable. For example, a teabag in a cup of hot water lets water in and tea out but keeps the tea leaves inside.

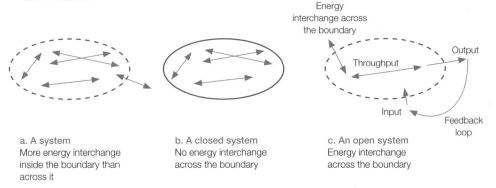

a. A system
More energy interchange
inside the boundary than
across it

b. A closed system
No energy interchange
across the boundary

c. An open system
Energy interchange
across the boundary

Figure 7.3 Systems concepts

Systems operate by processing energy. We can understand the way in which systems work by looking at Figure 7.3c, which shows how an open system may be changed by using energy:

- *Input* is energy being fed into the system across the boundary. We intervene by giving information or arranging resources, and the system changes because of this input.
- *Throughput* is about how energy is used within the system. The information or resources change what is going on in the system.

- *Output* is the effect on people or things outside the boundary of energy that has passed out into the environment. The system changes, and this affects how others perceive it or act as a result of what people in the system do.
- *Feedback loops* occur when the outputs affecting the environment lead to further inputs into the system.

A simple example of the processes shown in Figure 7.3c is if you tell me something (input into my system). This affects how I behave (throughput in my system), my behaviour then changes (output) and you observe this change. So you receive feedback that I have heard and understood what you said (a feedback loop).

Systems have a number of characteristics:

- *Entropy* – systems use their own energy to keep going, which means that unless they receive inputs from outside the boundary, they run down and die.
- The system's *steady state* is how it maintains itself by receiving input and using it. This idea suggests that systems, such as human beings, families or social groups, can incorporate change without changing their fundamental identity. You maintain your steady state if you are resilient in the face of change. Resilience is an increasingly important concept in social work. We met steady state ideas in crisis theory (see Chapter 5).
- The system possesses *homeostasis* or *equilibrium*. As the previous point describes, an element of a system's steady state is its ability to maintain its fundamental nature, even though input changes it. So I may eat cabbage, but I do not become cabbage-like. I remain me, while the cabbage is digested and gives me energy and nourishment. Part of it becomes output, through heat, activity and defecation.
- *Differentiation* is the idea that systems grow more complex, with more different kinds of components over time.
- *Non-summativity* is the idea that the whole is more than the sum of its parts.
- *Reciprocity* is the idea that if one part of a system changes, that change affects all the other parts. They therefore also change.

As a result of reciprocity, systems exhibit both *equifinality* (reaching the same result in several different ways) and *multifinality* (similar circumstances leading to different results) because the parts of the system interact in different ways. These ideas help to understand the complexity of human relationships and why the outcomes of similar actions vary.

Social systems may possess *synergy*, which means that they can create their own energy to maintain themselves. For example, human beings interacting in a marriage or in a work team often stimulate each other to maintain or strengthen those relationships. This builds up bonds within the marriage or the group and makes it stronger. This is an example of *non-summativity*, because these bonds could not be achieved without the interaction within the system. Without creating synergy, the group or marriage would have to be fed by outside energy, or entropy would occur.

Connections

Systems theory had a major impact on social work in the 1970s. Two forms of systems theory are distinguished in social work:

- general systems theory;
- ecological systems theory.

Hearn (1958, 1969) made early contributions, applying systems theory to social work. The greatest impact came with two simultaneously published interpretations applying systems ideas to practice: those of Goldstein (1973) and Pincus and Minahan (1973). These had considerable international influence. The later development by Siporin (1975) and Gitterman and Germain (2008; Germain, 1979) of ecological systems theory had a considerable impact in the USA. This draws on the ecological systems theory of Bronfenbrenner (1979), an American child psychologist who described child development using ecological terminology.

These ideas have been developed in the USA and Canada over several decades and been expressed in ecosystems and ecological systems theory texts that, as I mentioned when discussing major statements, have become widely accepted general formulations of social work, influencing many other texts on practice. While the UK and other countries are aware of systems ideas, particularly in family therapy, the literature related to ecological systems has not had anything like the same influence, and systems theory is little used in practice texts. Therefore, there are few connections between systems and ecological ideas and other social work theory in the non-US theoretical literature, whereas in the US literature these ideas are central to most forms of practice. This is one of the major distinctions between US and non-US accounts of social work practice. Systems ideas are, however, present in the non-US literature in the assumption that a distinctive feature of social work, as compared with the cognate professions, for example medicine, nursing, teaching, psychology and counselling, is the way in which social work practitioners work with family and community relationships as well as with the focal patient in healthcare and the focal pupil or student in education.

The politics of systems theory

Systems theory was an aspect of the reaction against psychodynamic theory in the 1970s. Its sociological focus seemed to counter psychodynamic failures in dealing with the 'social' in social work. In addition, its wide applicability incorporating social ideas seemed to be a new view of social work as a single professional entity rather than a series of specialist services. In the USA and the UK, separate professional organizations within social work had been merged (in the 1950s and 60s, respectively). In the UK, separate local government agencies had been merged in the Seebohm reorganization, and many European countries followed a similar trend. The systems theory focus on 'wholes' (Hanson, 1995) and integration (Roberts, 1990) was thus an attractive contribution to social work. Another source of influence was its importance in family therapy, which infiltrated social work in the mid-1970s. Here, systems theory is a major perspective, since it provides a way of understanding how all the members of a family can affect and influence one another. This capacity to deal with the analysis of relations among people in groups was also important in systems theory, being useful in residential care (C. Payne, 1977; Atherton, 1989).

Compared with radical theory, the other sociological critique of traditional social work theory that was influential in this period, systems theory did not propose critical ideas that attacked social organization and social policy. One reason for its success has been that it accepts and analyses existing social orders rather than, as with radical and critical theory, analysing and attacking them. It was incorporated into existing accounts of traditional psychodynamic social work, such as Woods and Hollis's (1999) account of psychosocial practice. Systems theories offer a context for understanding how the public and private interact and how various change agents might be involved, and also raised for the first time as a central aspect of the theory the possibility that practitioners and their agencies might themselves be targets for change.

The acceptance of present social orders therefore allows the ideas of systems theory to fit well with a profession and agency structure that is part of the state and has authority and power. Systems theory gained influence when social work was expanding and taking up roles in state agencies in many countries. Unlike critical theory, it relates successfully to psychological theories, since it does not reject theories at this level of human behaviour but permits their incorporation into its wider framework.

General systems theory has declined in influence within social work, being replaced by ecological systems ideas. The new perspective of complex adaptive systems, discussed briefly above, emphasizes complexity and chaos theory.

Values issues

Teater (2010: 32–4) identifies empowerment, holism and the anti-oppressive aspects of systems ideas as important values advantages of systems theories. She points to the issue, however, that looking holistically at a wide range of systems in the client's life may mean overassessing by taking too wide-ranging and detailed a view of matters beyond the client's understanding and genuine consent. An example is Howe's (1989) study of family therapy using systems ideas. He found that clients often did not understand or accept the practitioners' focus on family interactions rather than on a child's individual responsibility for difficult behaviour. In addition, looking broadly at systems in the client's life may come up against limited access to information for taking a broader perspective. Practitioners might identify wide-ranging problems that lie outside the role or resources of the agency and social worker, and might look at people who are part of a client's systems but who do not give consent for involvement with the practitioner or services.

Two substantial critiques of social work's use of systems and (particularly) ecological ideas suggests that this usage has not kept up with the shared value principles identified in

Chapter 1 as developing in current social work practice. One issue is the focus on problems and poor adaptation, rather than the positives and strengths in people's environments. Another is the limited incorporation of critical social analysis. The discussion of Gitterman and Germain's ecological systems theory as an example text later in the chapter gives a good example of how this critique points to weaknesses in the links between ecological and systems theory and currently theorized social work values.

One of the most important arguments for including social factors in environmental concern and environmental sustainability within social work practice is that of social justice (Dominelli, 2012), an integral value in all social work practice (International Federation of Social Workers, 2000). If social workers are to act justly, they must connect the help they give their clients to achieve a secure, healthy and satisfying life with the need of all human beings to achieve the same life objectives. In addition, it would be environmentally unjust to support people now to the detriment of the resources available for people in the future (Muldoon, 2006), so social workers must also consider how the resources used in their present helping might damage future generations, and must moderate their actions accordingly. Consequently, the International Federation of Social Workers (2012) is developing a 'global agenda' to incorporate these ideas into social work thinking (Hall, 2012). Zapf (2010) suggests that there are three common themes in this literature about social work and the environment:

- Seeing people in their physical place, such as their homes or communities, integrates human activity and well-being with the physical environment.
- Sustainability is achieved through processes such as stewardship (looking after the world around us) and living well in our place (for example, by being concerned about our neighbours).
- Multidisciplinary processes that include practitioners at every level of services are needed to respond to environmental crises; social work cannot leave it all to environmental interventions at the political level. For example, most people need to be persuaded to concern themselves with the environment in order to defend it. Therefore, to engage everyone in working for a sustainable environment, 'green' social work cannot ignore poor people because, if their needs are not met so that they have the resources in their families and communities to engage with environmental sustainability, broader society will not be able to meet environmental objectives either.

Mary (2008) suggests that social workers focus on social units such as a family or the community, rather than the world as a whole. The systems of knowledge in social work have been reductionist, concentrating on evidence that a particular intervention will achieve a change with a particular individual. Social work assessments also look for information about individuals and their surrounding social contexts. But this approach to people and their social context neglects the wide world in which they live, although major social changes such as globalization are changing the society in which these clients live. This requires a sustainable social work, with four main themes:

- long-term sustainability in all that we do – social work must abandon 'quick fixes' that use a large volume of resources in favour of a way of life that lives in harmony with the planet;
- seeing the world as an interactive, interconnected web of life – everyone is reliant on everyone else;
- the link between science and spirituality – this makes a connection between the knowledge that people have and use and all the aspects of the world that have meaning or are important for them;
- creating a partnership model of human relationships and society that says 'we are not the most important thing; what is important is how we live with other people'.

Applications

Systems practice

The starting point of systems practice is to avoid focusing only on the individual. In a classic analysis, Pincus and Minahan (1973) identified four main systems relevant to social work practice, set out in Figure 7.4, with an addition by Compton et al. (2005), which draws attention to the way in which the social constructions of the political, legal and professional environment of social work affect its practice, as we saw in Chapter 1. In some ways, this account merely transposes ideas such as practitioner, agency and client into systems terminology. To treat this as a simple renaming, however, misses the point of seeing these ideas as people and organizations linked in complex relationships with each other, whereas psychosocial practice is individualistic, concentrating on the client and seeing all the other factors as secondary or indirect work.

Figure 7.4 The main social work systems

System	Description	Further information
Change agent system	Social work practitioners and the organizations that they work in	
Client system	People, groups, families and communities who seek help and engage in working with the change agent system	*Actual* clients have agreed to receive help and have engaged themselves *Potential* clients are those whom the worker is trying to engage (e.g. people being investigated for child abuse)
Target system	People whom the change agent system is trying to change to achieve its aims	Client and target systems may or may not be the same
Action system	People with whom the change agent system is working to achieve its aims	The client, target and action systems may or may not be the same
Professional system	People within the agency, legal, professional and research communities influencing the change agent and action systems	Professional systems construct the practice undertaken in relation to other systems through the processes discussed in Chapter 1

Source: Pincus and Minahan (1973) and Compton et al. (2005).

Pincus and Minahan (1973) have also identified three kinds of helping system in which social work practitioners operate:

- informal or natural systems (such as family, friends, postal workers and fellow workers);
- formal systems (like community groups and trade unions);
- societal systems (for example, hospitals and schools).

Case example: Seeing practice in systems terms

Gahan was a mental health practitioner working with Jareb, who had a diagnosis of schizophrenia and lived in supported living accommodation near his parents; they also provided him with a lot of help. In addition, Jareb was regularly visited by a carer employed by a local mental health association that was contracted to provide this support.

One aspect of Gahan's work was building a personal supportive relationship with Jareb. Most of what he did, however, was maintaining a liaison with Jareb's carer (a formal system), dealing with the commissioning and review of the contract with the mental health association (a societal system) and encouraging and advising Jareb's parents (a natural system). Thus, although Gahan as an individual was the change agent, his agency (that is, the impact he was able to have on

the situation) came about because he was part of a change agent system, the community mental health team with its connections with two societal systems: the local community healthcare trust and the local authority. Although Jareb was an individual client, Gahan and Jareb together worked with a client system that included other residents in the supported living accommodation who strongly affected Jareb's life, and Jareb's parents. Although Gahan's target system could be any of these elements of Jareb's life, his action system might well vary from the target system. For example, to influence the housing trust (target system) that provided the accommodation, he supported Jareb (action system) in making applications, and his doctor (formal system) in providing additional support.

This account shows the different focus of systems theory, compared with individualistic, psychotherapeutic practices such as psychodynamic or cognitive-behavioural therapy practice. Those theories offer no basis for including work with anyone except the client themselves. This is particularly relevant for social workers and for social work as a profession, because most other similar practitioners, for example clinical psychologists or counsellors, work only through their relationship with the client. Social work, on the other hand, naturally includes engagement with all these other social elements. Johnson (1999) argues that this is a major, and uncelebrated, characteristic of social work; it distinguishes social work from similar professions and enables practitioners to explain to their colleagues how they are different.

Building on this key advantage of systems ideas, Evans and Kearney (1996) show how you can look within the social networks and systems for possible targets for action and for power relationships, and involve each in a social work process. In their view, systems ideas help us to maintain consistency in practice with all these different elements, because it makes us analyse all the elements of the system that practitioners need to engage with. Systems theory suggests that you should start from the context in which you operate, its opportunities and constraints, with the aim of being involved and thinking about your powers and responsibilities and the likely or intended effects or outcomes. The following case examples illustrate these points.

Case example: Involvement with different aspects of a family's needs

A practitioner became involved with a family because of concerns about the neglect of their children, so the initial context of the intervention was the agency's responsibility for child safeguarding. The same family was referred to a colleague for help with family relationships, and another agency was asked to assess how to care for an older relative. Each practitioner thus had a different set of aims and responsibilities, which came from their agency contexts. However, the work each did might have been similar. Each would look at how pressures on the family created different aspects of their problem, and each would respond to the protection, relationship and service provision concerns. So they would have been able to coordinate their practice so that each supported the aims of the others while working to achieve their own objectives. There would be no point in trying to promote family relationships and neglecting the needs of the older relative or child safeguarding.

Recognizing the importance of context in defining what we are doing extends from the importance of consistency. Context defines what your aims and responses should be.

Case example: Context defines responsibilities with a disabled person

Gareth, a disabled person in specialist housing, was referred for mainly practical services from an adult social care agency. In carrying out the assessment, Helen, the practitioner, identified family relationship problems in Gareth's sister's family, which meant that she would soon have to move away and be unable to support Gareth. This potential change in carer support might have destabilized Gareth's situation and meant that more services would have been needed. Helen therefore spent some time helping the sister resolve her marital conflicts, and this again stabilized Gareth's support. Although Helen's manager criticized her for spending this time on someone who was not one of the agency's clients, she argued that this support for a carer who was part of Gareth's support system was relevant to their agency mandate.

The adoption of a positive approach partly emerges from the importance of consistency and context: the context makes clear the responsibilities that come from the agency's role, and allows the practitioner to deal with complex systems of relationships in the family or community while maintaining a consistent focus on their agency's main objectives. Practitioners may feel that, in many situations, there is no progress to be made: for example, how can you help a mentally ill man who is incarcerated for life in a secure unit for serious offences? However, activities such as improvements in his education, encouraging him to maintain relationships with others and renewing connections with estranged family members may all make a significant difference to the client's life experience in the unit, even if it does not eventually lead to discharge and the resumption of family and community life.

Identifying patterns of behaviour helps to see positive possibilities, where behaviour in one social system has created learning for use in another. It also helps to identify where changes are needed. For example, a person having relationship difficulties with their neighbours may reveal similar patterns of behaviour in a day-care setting or a social setting, which may help practitioners to identify a possible target area for work on relationship or behaviour problems. Success in learning how to manage relationships in one setting might then be transferred to relationship difficulties with neighbours.

Systems theory, therefore, emphasizes process, that is, how relationships and interactions occur, as well as content and outcomes. Practitioners may be able to identify positive skills and relationships in one part of someone's life that can be transferred to other situations where there are difficulties. It may also be helpful to identify how systems are interacting together to create problems in an unexpected area of life. For example, poor relationships within a family may reduce the influence of the family in helping a child to overcome difficulties at school.

Working with others is an important bonus of systems theory. It emphasizes how working indirectly with other agencies or with families and networks can have an influence on clients. Joint working is also a product of systems thinking; practitioners interact with networks associated with clients and with colleagues and agencies.

The next subsections on family therapy, residential care, ecological practice and social networking all pick up elements of practice that use or develop from systems ideas.

Family therapy

Family therapy is a multiprofessional field of practice engaging psychiatry, clinical psychology and social work. The three main theoretical bases for it all draw on systems theories, because practice examines interactions between people as part of their family group:

- *Structural family therapy* seeks to change the structure of family relationships by observing patterns in relationships among family members and helping people to alter structures that are not working properly. An example is helping a parent to set boundaries for a child whose behaviour is having an adverse effect on other family members.
- *Strategic family therapy* focuses on people's day-to-day strategies for influencing other family members and maintaining their own identity. An example is looking at repetitive behaviours that lead to conflict.
- *Systemic family therapy* explores possibly hidden social rules within the family that are adversely affecting relationships. An example is where there is conflict about roles based on unspoken gender assumptions about a husband not being actively involved in child care (Walker, 2007).

Solution-focused and narrative practice (see Chapter 8) is increasingly used in family work, and this is extending and to some extent providing a critical perspective on systems-based ideas in family therapy and broader family practice. Both these perspectives have, for example, an emphasis on positives in the family and forward-looking perspectives on family life, rather than concentrating on analysing problems in the family's life.

Systems in residential care practice

Atherton (1989), applying systems theory to residential care, focuses on its concern with how people relate to one another within social situations, rather than as individuals. It is difficult to deal with the complex understanding needed to work effectively in the residential care setting because people are part of a group of staff and residents and all have contacts with an outside world as well as interrelationships within the residential unit. The systems idea of boundaries helps to limit the complexity to particular issues or relationships within the residence or within the client's network. Similarly, the idea of feedback loops helps to identify the interaction between different factors in creating situations that practitioners must deal with. Systems theory also helps to create a focus on present communication among the individuals in residence, both as a way of explaining how problems are maintained in the situation and as a way of intervening. This avoids the complexity of trying to work on complex past causes of problems.

Residential care settings are bounded by the fact that everyone lives together. This means that they are self-regulating systems that are to some degree closed, and practitioners can explore the ways in which they are open and closed and the consequences of this for clients' lives and the life of the residential community. The relatively closed and self-regulating aspect of residential institutions has the advantages of offering security to residents; however, rather than exploring and trying to understand what is going on so that people can develop their skills and capacities to live their lives more effectively, practitioners and residents often focus on controlling events. They do this by establishing norms for how things ought to be done, and attempt to minimize risk by reducing the unexpected events adversely affecting the smooth running of the residence. In this way, residential units try to establish homeostasis or a balance, which enables them to manage external events and any other factors that may upset their smooth running, rather than create a steady state that allows them to incorporate change (Brown et al., 1998).

The problem with this approach in residential care is that people learn how to manage difficulties in the care home, but then have difficulty in transferring this knowledge to more complex situations once they leave the boundaried environment of the residential setting. Atherton seeks to develop practice to help residents and the residential unit become more open and flexible in dealing with the outside world as a way of dealing with this problem. This is a useful example of how you can apply systems theory to understanding complex interactions and provide guidance on worthwhile directions for social work intervention.

Eco-social and eco-critical practice

Coates (2003) suggests basic ecological ideas of social work, set out in Figure 7.5. The idea of 'the importance of becoming' means seeing possibilities in situations that we are dealing with – what realist theory (see Chapter 2) calls emergent properties – rather than only what exists now. Looking at this analysis points up the ways in which ecological theory focuses on social connections and positive engagements between individuals and the communities they are involved in; this sense of the positive aspects of connectedness is also important to feminist theory (see Chapter 12).

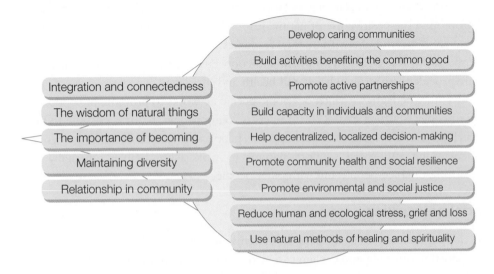

Figure 7.5 Basic ecological concepts and social work practice implications
Source: Coates (2003).

Närhi and Matthies (2001) call on a German discussion of the American literature to suggest that the relationship between the person and the environment should not be seen as a dichotomy but as an integrated whole. People's entire life context, and not merely their social relationships, should be the focus of attention. Practical environmental and green projects, shared living and workshop projects for young people all enhance people's self-understanding of political and social relationships and develop social self-consciousness and concern for the environment. Current thinking encouraged non-sustainable lifestyles based on employment that increasingly did not exist because of globalizing social forces benefiting capital- and pollution-intensive industries. Moreover, sedentary lifestyles have been unhealthy, using highly manufactured foods and encouraging smoking. People should be helped to develop more inspiring, diverse and stimulating environments than the gloomy and excluding housing living conditions they are often given.

This is a particular challenge for workers in day and residential care, and where the practitioner's job is establishing packages for home care provision. Cultural and ethnic diversity provides opportunities for creating a richer social environment, but it is often treated in a divisive and excluding way. Promoting social inclusion by proactively encouraging people to become engaged in mutual help and community involvement makes the best use of human and cultural resources in any community. Boeck et al. (2001) propose that any eco-social approach to social inclusion should incorporate both the British emphasis on the redistribution of resources and the French tradition of focusing on social capital, including the ways in which relationships can exclude social groups.

The main approaches to eco-social work are:

- holistic analysis, drawing on the needs of the global environment and including environmental impact analysis of the social area in which the social workers are operating; this will also involve citizens in planning and social action relevant to their interests and needs;
- promoting the positive use of natural resources and self-consciousness about lifestyles that are respectful of environmental resources;
- concern for the social environment and cooperative networks through which services are provided, especially schools and health and social care agencies;
- 'adventure pedagogy', which develops specific networks to promote life opportunities for people; Matthies et al. (2001) refer to young people, but it is possible to imagine such practice extended to disabled people, people with mental illness and older people.
- networking and social support systems to work with disabled, mentally ill and learning-disabled people and with older people.

Social networking

Developing networks in social support systems emerged in mental health work as a way of supporting isolated people when psychiatric hospitals were being deinstitutionalized in the 1970s (Caplan, 1974; Caplan and Killilea, 1976; Maguire, 1991; Cohen et al., 2000). Where isolation from social support is short term, there is evidence that re-establishing previous links is effective, while long-term isolation requires group- and community-based work (Eyrich et al., 2003). This work also connects with macro practice (see Chapter 8).

According to Seed (1990: 19), a network 'is a system or pattern of links between points ... which have particular meanings' for those involved. Practitioners focus on clients' networks and agency links that form a pattern in the clients' daily lives. The aim is to identify formal and informal social networks, extend them and make them usable in helping the client. Networks may be more or less dense or of varying quality, depending on, respectively, the amount of contact between particular parts of the network and the value placed upon it. They may also have a variety of features, such as being concerned with home, work, leisure or care.

Network analysis is an important area of sociological theory. Like family therapy ideas, it proposes that structured social relationships located in systems of social relationships are a more important determinant of life than are individuals' personal attributes, particularly in dyadic relationships such as marriage. The assumption is that the world is composed of networks rather than groups, and that acting on these relationships is a more important social intervention than individual methods can be. The main uses of network analysis in social work practice have been in examining, understanding and working with caring networks among members of a community and in situations where informal care is provided to people needing support (Kirke, 2009).

Networking tries to connect interpersonal work developing people's relationships with community work or macro practice. It may be a basis for practice in developing partnerships with service users and the community (Trevillion, 1999) and in multiprofessional teamwork (Payne, 2000). Trevillion sees social workers as potential community brokers, able to link users with a variety of community resources; this has links with empowerment practice. Gilchrist (2004) combines networking with chaos and complexity theory, suggesting that community development often seeks to recreate close interpersonal connections within communities that probably exist only in romantic notions of what communities used to be like. Meta-networking connects human-scale interpersonal networks together to create a pattern of links. This is better than trying to integrate complexity so actively that it makes the world seem chaotic and hard to grasp and understand.

Example text: Gitterman and Germain's (2008) life model of social work

The life model draws on a number of ecological concepts, set out in Figure 7.6, with a summary of their explanation and value in practice. We have noted one criticism of ecological theory –it takes for granted that its main aim is individuals' adaptation to the environment. Gitterman and Germain attempt to deal with this by defining fit and adaptation as being undertaken by both people and their environment. Nevertheless, the authors' focus is still on *improving* fit through adaptation, making the assumption that improving fit is a desirable and achievable objective. Critical theory suggests that this is not always possible and that, even if it can be achieved, it might not benefit individuals or oppressed people; conflict and a rejection of fit and adaptation might be a better value position for social work to take. This position can, however, be criticized for being unrealistic, bearing in mind that most social work practitioners are employed by government agencies or other representatives of powerful interests in society.

In the context of the issue about fit and adaptation, Gitterman and Germain's (2008: 56–7) account of power is extremely limited. They refer only to the abuse of power and see it as something held by abusive special interests such as private corporations, political interests or the financial system. Power is analysed only as creating damaging exchanges between people and environments. Gitterman and Germain's analysis of power does, however, explain how these broad social factors can be understood to damage the reciprocity of exchanges, and presents the role of social work as restoring that reciprocity or at least acting upon those damaging exchanges. Gitterman and Germain refer to reciprocality; I use the term reciprocity here since it accurately implies their emphasis on the exchanges being seen as valid or appropriate by the people involved. Critical and empowerment perspectives focus more strongly on the wide availability of power in society and the possibility of enhancing the power of oppressed groups. Moreover, the emphasis on the negative aspects of the power of special interests ignores the potential misuse of power by people in oppressed groups if they become offenders and or otherwise abusive, for example of children. Power may be used to promote social order and stability.

Figure 7.6 Ecological concepts in the life model

Ecological concept	Meaning	Implications for practice
Reciprocity	Continuous exchanges occur between people and their environment	Exchanges in both directions continuously affect people and their environments
Adaptation, adaptedness, fit	People's needs, capacities and goals may or may not fit well to their environment, and adaptive exchanges release and support adaptedness	Adaptation is change by the person or environment that improves fit. Adaptedness supports or hinders human growth and well-being, and enriches or degrades the environment
Habitat, niche	Habitat is the physical and social context within which people live. Niche is people's place within the community that is living in that habitat	Habitat includes physical environments and social institutions. Niche includes roles, statuses and cultural expectations such as rights
Power, powerlessness, pollution	Abuse of power in support of sectional interests creates social and environmental pollution	Abuse of power creates destructive exchanges which in turn create environmental stressors that impose enormous adaptive tasks on oppressed people
Life course	The non-uniform pathways of biopsychosocial human and environmental development, involving historical, individual and social time	People and environments can develop in diverse ways through their self-regulating nature. This can generate new forms and structures, and produce shifts in the values and norms affected by global, local and personal factors that create historical contexts, life experiences and social transitions
Life stressors, stress, coping	Life stressors are transitions and events that disturb the fit and adaptedness between person and environment, leading to stress that is beyond our coping ability	People can cope, using behaviours and thinking to change themselves, the environment or the exchange between them. In this way, they can manage their negative feelings about life stressors and reduce the negative physical and emotional impacts of stresses on them
Resilience, protective factors	Resilience is the capacity to bounce back from adverse events, assisted by protective factors in the person or their environment and exchanges between these	Biopsychosocial and environmental factors may offer protection to people and their adaptedness. This can include the temperament of the people involved, family patterns, external supports, wider social factors in the environment, critical turning points and decision planning to respond to them, good fortune, use of humour and helping others

Source: Gitterman and Germain (2008: 51–70).

Gitterman and Germain (2008: 57–9) use the ideas of the life course to emphasize the diversity of possible paths that people might take through life. This transcends the assumption of life cycle models to understand human development; these may include Erikson's stages of human development, which we met when considering psychodynamic and crisis theory in Chapters 4 and 5, and similar ideas that assume a fixed progression through a sequence of life events. The life course idea allows for different family patterns, shifts of values and norms and different experiences of time, for example experiencing change as rapid and therefore a pressure, or as slow and therefore more easy to cope with.

The life model is presented in Figure 7.7. People follow their life course, a unique pathway that incorporates both their identity as an individual and their environment. They experience life stressors – the transitions, events and pressures that disturb the stability of people's fit and adaptedness to their environment. The weight given to uniqueness and diversity gives an impression of openness and flexibility and claims to be in line with the aims of cultural awareness. It is not clear, however, why this emphasis should lead to anti-discriminatory practice as the acknowledgement of diversity does not necessarily achieve equality or respect for others.

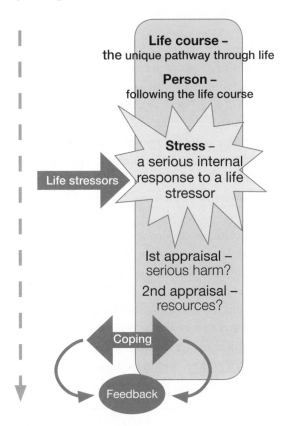

Figure 7.7 The life model of social work practice

Stress, the physical and behavioural response to stressors, arises from a disturbance of fit and adaptedness. People appraise situations that they face, first to see whether harm or loss may affect them, and then to identify the resources and actions they could use to cope with what is happening, and to work out how far these resources could help. Coping implies using behaviours and thinking that allow us to manage ourselves, the environment or the exchanges between these to manage 'the negative feelings aroused' (Gitterman and Germain, 2008: 63). The emphasis on stress and coping with feelings here is a limited conceptualization of responding to stressors, implying that what is required is simply psychological adaptation; however, it may be that life stressors are avoidable, or that changeable environmental events may require wider coping with practical matters. Feedback on individuals' actions from their personal responses and the environment helps them to evaluate how successful they are in coping.

Ecological systems theory is an important source of ideas about resilience – the capacity to bounce back from or retrieve gains from adverse events or situations. Gitterman and Germain (2008: 63–6) refer to identifying and making use of factors in the individual or their environment that may help them to cope with stresses. These authors' view of this concept is again limiting, since they refer, for example, to the capacity to help others being 'protective' towards an individual, and to the relationships involved in this, whereas feminist ethics of care theories (see Chapter 13) propose that this is a positive feature of relationships that is integral to people caring for each other. This adds to the sense that Gitterman and Germain's ecological systems theory is concerned with dealing with failings in people or their lives, rather than with natural exchanges. It may be a characteristic of the problem-solving aspect of social work practice that gives us this sense of dealing with something that has gone wrong, rather than being engaged with a natural life process.

Gitterman and Germain's (2008) approach recognizes this by adding some commentary on deep ecology and eco-feminism, the concept of eco-feminism incorporating some of the ideas dealt with in Chapter 12. Deep ecology refers to the natural interdependence of all living beings and their environments, what Coates (2003) referred to as the wisdom of natural things.

In the life model, practice is divided into three main stages (Figure 7.8). In the initial phase, the model emphasizes preparation, which is often not a strong element of practice theory. This phase incorporates reflection as part of preparation, with reflection on both the situation and the clients' perceptions of their reality. Emphasizing clients' choices is similarly a salient feature of the initial phase. Are they involuntary clients, forced by circumstances or legal and administrative procedures to become involved with the practitioner? How far are their choices restricted by their situation or powerlessness? The delineation of an ongoing phase emphasizes how you can use the life model for short or long interventions and caring processes as it is concerned with engaging with life issues. Working on agreed goals is a crucial aspect of this phase.

The life model is practised in eight modalities, a common social work term in the USA, referring to work with individuals, families, groups, social networks, communities, physical environments, organizations and politics. Thus, the model is intended to be applied in all these forms of practice, and Gitterman and Germain's account deals with them all in some detail.

Gitterman and Germain's model assumes that assessment, monitoring of progress and evaluation of the success of the interventions continue throughout the process. This involves client participation, systematic planning to manage large amounts of data and

Figure 7.8 Main areas of life model practice intervention

Phases	Stressors	Main issues	Examples
Initial phase: preparations and beginnings			
Ongoing phase	Stressful life transitions and traumatic events	Life transitions	From school to work or single life to marriage, retirement, thwarted ambition
		Losses or threats	The death of a loved one, natural disasters, chronic illness, disability or pain
	Environmental stressors	Social environment	Neighbourhood conflict, discrimination against minority groups
		Social networks	Inability to make friends or support others
		Physical environment	Poverty of the environment
	Dysfunctional family processes	Poverty	Inability to provide housing, food or support
		Neglect, abuse	Domestic or child abuse, neglect, inability to nurture children or relationships
		Family structures	Conflict in the wider family or between generations
		Family processes	Secrets or lies between family members
		Family transformation	Divorce, children leaving home, death of family members
	Dysfunctional group processes	Factions, scapegoating	Client or others in groups behave badly toward others
	Interpersonal processes between practitioner and client	Agency's and practitioner's authority, responsibilities and sanctions	Admission to care, refusal of service, charges for service
		Professional role and socialization	Clients' racism and the difficulties raised by the practitioner's duty to challenge it
		Difference	Age, class, ethnicity, gender, sexuality
		Attempts to control	Behaviour in community or residential care
		Content that is (to the client or family) taboo	Sexual issues or drug abuse
		Client defences	Hope
Ending phase			

Source: Gitterman and Germain (2008: 191–413).

emphasizing needs and achievements in improving 'fit'. In assessing an individual, you look at four factors: the nature of the life issues to be worked on, clients' expectations, and strengths and limitations, together with support and gaps in the environment. Family assessment looks at possibilities for changing the exchanges between the individual, the family and the environment. Similarly, in group living or where peer groups or work groups are important in the client's life, it can also be important to assess the exchanges with those groups. For example, if family or group members are making demands on the client, support for the family or group might be better provided by helping other members of the family or community to manage a problem, rather than putting pressure on a client to change unreasonably.

Case example: Tyler's drug abuse and Mrs Garrod's housing

Mrs Garrod was a woman in her seventies receiving an extensive package of social care services to help her manage increasing frailty due to serious arthritis. She found her pain very difficult to cope with. Her grandson, Tyler, was a drug abuser who had periods of disturbed life, including homelessness. When homeless, he often crashed out in Mrs Garrod's single-person retirement apartment, although this was not permitted by the tenancy agreement with the housing provider. Tyler's mother had given up trying to manage his behaviour or help him. A care worker discovered him sleeping in Mrs Garrod's living room. Reacting to this, the social worker convened a strategy meeting with the housing provider, the care worker, Tyler's mother, Mrs Garrod and herself. It was agreed that supported housing would be provided for Tyler in a hostel, to enable a very strong line to be taken with him about not making demands on Mrs Garrod. This helped her to accept that he would be supported even when she refused to accommodate him.

In this example, individuals, the family and the environment, which included the housing and drug support agencies, were all participants in the reassessment that had arisen from an awareness of how Tyler was exploiting his grandmother's concern for him, contrary to her healthcare needs. Here, the environment was altered to help both Tyler and Mrs Garrod.

The preparation phase requires reflecting on the information that the assessment has produced. This is important so that there can be empathy with the people involved, because conveying empathy requires getting 'inside' another person's life course and their environment.

The initial stage similarly involves engaging with the extent of the choices available to clients in their life course. This is important in developing a shared focus on what services are being sought and how this connects to the practitioner's understanding of what the agency can offer in view of its assessment of the clients' needs. Clients' choices need to be available to them, and one aspect of this is the extent to which they accept their own part in the difficulties, both in creating life stressors and in their reactions to them. Using their shared focus, practitioners and clients also need to explore the nature of life stressors: do they arise from stressful life transitions or traumatic events? Similar issues also arise in crisis intervention assessment, since, as we saw in Chapter 5, it can be hard in that model to distinguish hazardous events that create a vulnerability to crises and precipitating events that generate the downward spiral into a crisis. The concept of life stressors found in the life model bears many resemblances to the concept of crisis.

The main skills used in the beginning phase are thus enabling people to explore and clarify the situations, the environment in which they has arisen and the personal consequences for them, guiding them to create an understanding or what may be a complex sequence of events. During the initial stage, practitioners work with clients and others involved to define the goals, according to the main areas of social work help, which I discuss next.

The ongoing stage of life model practice involves using a wide range of social work skills. Figure 7.8 lists, with some examples, five main areas in which social work may provide help.

The ending phase may occur when clients and their families complete a planned programme of help or cease to receive services for some other reason, such as when the practitioner leaves the service, when the agency service or policy changes or when the modality of the service changes; for example, someone who has been cared for at home might enter residential care. Practice around ending includes:

- working on relationship issues;
- moving through a process of separation or change, during which there may be negative and positive feelings;
- dealing with sadness;
- responding to a sense of release;
- evaluating the service.

These may affect the practitioner as well as the client and other people around the client.

Gitterman and Germain (2008) go on to explore skills in influencing community and neighbourhood life, organizations and agencies (both the practitioner's and others that are involved in exchanges with clients) and political and legislative movements. This may be an aspect of working with a particular person-in-environment or a more general feature of practice that seek social improvements for whole communities and groups in need.

Conclusion: using systems and ecological theory

Social workers use systems and ecological theory in the following ways.

▶ **Explaining and justifying the aims of social work to clients and colleagues from other professions**
You can make clear how social work does not focus just on individuals, but also on the family, carers and community around them. This is helpful to healthcare and education professionals because they have a perspective that emphasizes work with individual patients and students. Social work complements this; colleagues can understand better how changing the dynamics and resilience of the family or community can help individuals.

▶ **Clarifying options for indirect intervention**

You can use systems ideas to identify systems other than your client that you should intervene with. Use this to explain to clients or colleagues how it will help to influence another agency or professional or a distant member of the family.

▶ **Explore intervention with part of a system as a way of influencing the whole**

You can think through how changing someone's behaviour can affect other members of their family and communities. In addition, you can see how encouraging development in one aspect of someone's life can strengthen them elsewhere. For example, if you can strengthen their spirituality, they may be better able to cope with the stresses of an illness.

▶ **Explore clients' adaptations to their environment alongside adaptations within their environment to meet their needs**

You can avoid making the mistake of expecting clients always to adapt their behaviour to others in their family, or to the situation they find themselves in. The opposite is also true: sometimes we think that organizations or policies are so unfair that clients should not be expected to accept what is happening to them. But very often, when clients make some changes, the organizations and people around them are helped to adapt too. Ecosystems ideas say that you should find ways of adapting families, communities and organizations so that they meet clients' needs better. You will usually have to work on both the client and ecosystems together as if you are not doing this, you might be missing something.

▶ **Thinking about the sustainability of interventions**

Do clients, carers, families and the community have the resources to sustain the change you are proposing? It is no use changing clients' behaviours if, in turn, the family or some other community, such as their workplace, needs help to support them to accept the new identity of the person you are working directly with.

▶ **Reading and critiquing American textbooks**

Most social work texts in the USA take systems terminology and ideas for granted. People from other countries making use of American ideas and research need, therefore, to understand the theory's main points and be aware of questions about it. American readers need an awareness of the critiques of systems social work that arise from the majority of other countries in the world that do not take this approach for granted.

Additional resources

Further reading

Gitterman, A. and Germain, C. B. (2008) *The Life Model of Social Work Practice: Advances in Theory and Practice* (3rd edn) (New York: Columbia University Press).

Mattaini, M. A. and Lowery, C. T. (eds) (2007) *Foundations of Social Work Practice: A Graduate Text* (4th edn) (Washington, DC: NASW Press).

Two important American presentations of systems-related theory, the second being an edited collection with contributions by well-known authors.

Nash, M., Munford, R. and O'Donoghue, K. (eds) (2005) *Social Work Theories in Action* (London: Jessica Kingsley).

An Australian perspective on systems theory.

Matthies, A.-L., Närhi, K and Ward, D. (eds) (2001) *The Eco-social Approach in Social Work* (Jyväskylä: SoPhi).

A useful account of theoretical and practice aspects of the eco-social approach.

Payne, M. (2002) 'The politics of systems theory within social work', *Journal of Social Work* 2(3): 269–92.

An analysis of the development of the debate about systems theory.

Wakefield, J. C. (1996) 'Does social work need the eco-systems perspective? Part 1: Is the perspective clinically useful?', *Social Service Review* 70(1): 1–31; 'Does social work need the eco-systems perspective? Part 2: Does the perspective save social work from incoherence?', *Social Services Review* 70(2): 183–213.

A helpful evaluation of American ecological systems theory in practice.

Websites

http://en.wikipedia.org/wiki/Systems_theory

Wikipedia on systems theory (although not always accurate in all its implications) gives you a picture of the huge range of uses of systems theory that is available, in particular 'complex adaptive systems'. This leads you into some ideas about chaos and complexity theory, which you can find being increasingly covered in social work writing.

http://www.uwindsor.ca/criticalsocialwork/

The work of Coates and his colleagues on ecological sustainability has been developed in others papers, particularly this special edition of the internet journal *Critical Social Work* (2010: volume 11: 3).

Macro practice, social development and social pedagogy

8

Main contribution

The main contribution of these ideas to social work is the priority they give to the social and educational, rather than the psychological, as a focus for intervention. Their practice emphasizes engaging people with similar interests in a particular locality or a particular social issue, or individuals with particular social needs, so that they will come together, identify shared concerns and work jointly to overcome them. This chapter brings together these traditions. The focus of these ideas on social and educational development means that they form a bridge between problem-solving and empowerment objectives in social work.

Main points

- Macro practice (the American term, with an emphasis on policy change) and community work (the international term, with an emphasis on social change) are practices that help people to come together to identify issues of concern and take action to resolve them. Both practices have been influenced by social development (until the 1980s often known as community development) in resource-poor countries.

- Social development is the main form of social work in resource-poor countries. It seeks to incorporate social progress with economic development in areas where economic development often takes political priority. Social development has been influenced by community work methods.

- Social pedagogy is a European practice used particularly with children in residential and day care. In some countries, it emphasizes community work in which there is an interaction between individual and collective self-development and education.

- Community social work is a largely British practice, strong in the 1970s and 80s, in which social work in large general public agencies organized its services to focus on the needs of small communities. It sought to link social work with a range of practical social care services to provide locally responsive services meeting identified needs, while engaging those communities in volunteering and mutual support.

- Poverty and social exclusion are important targets of social development in resource-poor and rich countries.
- Social entrepreneurship, a development of the early twenty-first century, aims to build business-like professional attitudes and organizational structures among the social professions.

Practice ideas

- *Activation* aims to engage people who are immobilized from making progress in their lives so that they can undertake useful personal development, motivating them and giving them experience to take up the positive opportunities they encounter. A common example is activating unemployed people to improve their education and engage in volunteering and community activity to improve their employability.
- *Capacity-building* seeks to build the understanding and skills needed to enable excluded individuals, groups and communities to participate more effectively in their communities.
- The development of *social capital* increases the community and social infrastructure as an important resource for communities and individuals in societies.
- *Social inclusion* and *exclusion* focus on the ways in which stigmatized and disadvantaged communities should be helped to play a stronger role in society by being provided with opportunities and resources for participation.

Major statements

Modern texts on macro social work, community work and social development set out the principles and methods of practice that have been applied to practice in their countries of origin. They are adaptable to other societies, but none has a wide international reach.

Many important discussions of social development are texts that focus primarily on practice in resource-poor countries, with more general features that can be applied in industrialized countries. For example, Singh (1999) provides an extensive account of Indian rural development, summarizing various perspectives on social development, identifying approaches to rural development and providing many case studies. However, these are primarily about social development as an adjunct to economic development, rather than as a practice. Several American texts (for example, Midgley, 1997; van Wormer, 1999) mainly focus on comparative welfare systems and policies, rather than on practice in its own right. Midgley's *Social Development* (1995), however, focuses primarily on social development practice, so I present this later in the chapter as the exemplar of theory in this field.

An expanding area of study focuses on the particular needs and shared interests of rural areas (Pugh and Cheers, 2010). Lohmann and Lohmann (2005) emphasize that research has not found any major differences between the needs of rural and urban communities. They argue that an important issue for workers in rural areas is the romanticism about living a traditional lifestyle in a beautiful natural environment, while the social isolation of, for example, mentally ill individuals, older people and people with learning and physical disabilities is ignored. Moreover, the lack of surveillance of social behaviour in rural areas may lead to inadequate protection for vulnerable adults and children. Rural social work therefore has no distinctive practice theory beyond considering these implications when working in rural settings.

No comprehensive text on social pedagogy exists in the English language. Lorenz's (1994) study of European social work contains a theoretically informed summary. Kornbeck and Jensen's (2009) collection gives an overview of the role of social pedagogy in several European countries, indicating how it varies according to the country in which it is practised. There is also research and commentary on efforts to implement Danish methods of social pedagogy in British residential care (Cameron et al., 2011; Petrie, 2011), but this does not offer a comprehensive theoretically informed account of practice. I have therefore brought together a practice account of social pedagogy theory from these sources using my experience in the Central, Eastern and Nordic areas of Europe.

Because this chapter emphasizes social development as an element of the international understanding of social work, Midgley's (1995) text is given priority as an example text. Burghardt's (2011) text on macro practice is used as an example text on the main points of community work as an aspect of Western social provision.

The debate summary

The debate about macro, social development and social pedagogy theories turns on three issues:

▶ **Are these theories part of, separate from or in opposition to social work?**
Community work has traditionally been seen as a basic social work method, alongside casework with individuals and families and groupwork. If you accept this, macro and social development theory is integral to social work, and every practitioner will need to use it sometimes, even though their main focus may be elsewhere. For example, child protection usually involves investigation, assessment and help for individuals and families, but family support work in day centres calls on groupwork and community work techniques. Adding groupwork and macro practice to work with individuals and families is often called 'integrated practice' in the USA.

The problem with integrated practice is that the personal inclination of many practitioners to do therapeutic work with individuals and in families is distant from the practice methods of social development. This is because the need to focus on tight timetables and clear interpersonal objectives in interpersonal therapeutic work clashes with the longer timescales and broader social objectives of macro and community work. Therapeutic practice, using the shared value principles discussed in Chapter 1, therefore becomes separated from macro and community practice into different agencies, or at least different departments of agencies. In addition, practitioners working mainly with individuals and families do not feel that they have the expertise or mandate to work at the macro level, and vice versa.

Many practitioners of community work, macro practice and social pedagogy see the ideals of their work as being in opposition to the individualistic problem-solving objectives of much individual, family and group social work. Community work is to them partly about transforming the present way of organizing society and includes resistance to authority; individual practice, however, aims to help individuals and families to adjust to potentially harmful social pressures or to mitigate the pressures on individuals, rather than seeking a change that will affect wider society. To its practitioners, social pedagogy is about personal and social development objectives rather than reinforcing present social priorities.

None of these methods is clearly associated only with social work. They are sometimes regarded as separate professional activities, as part of wider development work, as part of other professional responsibilities or, as with social development, as a separate professional career for Western workers in international non-governmental organizations.

Another aspect of this debate is that these ideas emerged in different geographical locations and thus seem less universally relevant than other forms of social work. Social development originated and is most used in resource-poor countries alongside economic development. Social pedagogy is, in many countries, a separate practice focused on the education and personal and social development of individuals and social groups. This distinguishes it, in those countries, from a more pragmatic and problem-focused social work or social assistance. Therefore, theorization, professional development and agency organization are separated from social work in the approaches of social development, community work and social pedagogy. There are separate national and international organizations for social development and social pedagogy. A good example of the consequences of this separation is the claim that introducing social pedagogy into UK residential work with children was the transfer of a new discipline from Denmark rather than an implementation of an existing social work practice.

▶ **Although there are similarities between them, are these theoretically related practices or were they constructed to respond to particular national or regional social issues?**

These practices come from different theoretical sources. Community and macro work originated to improve the social participation of excluded peoples in developed countries. Social development arose to engage social capital – the power we gain by having wide and supportive networks of relationships – in economic development in resource-poor countries, and social pedagogy started as an educational development process in mainland European countries. Community work and social development have shared origins and have seen many exchanges in knowledge. Macro work is an American formulation of community work ideas, often also incorporating advocacy for progressive social causes. While social pedagogy developed from primarily German and Polish social philosophy, so is theoretically separate from Anglo-American practice, it has clear overlaps with the social work professions and community work practice. For example, in some central European countries, virtually all social care services are provided by pedagogues, and practitioners trained in social work and social pedagogy are interchangeable. Since all these practices call on similar skills, values and theoretical ideas, it is unreasonable to make too much of their separate theoretical sources.

▶ **Are they social change or social order theories?**

The ideas of macro practice, social development and social pedagogy overlap with those of critical, empowerment and advocacy practice. The main source of this connection is a shared emphasis on the social rather than the individual and psychological. However, critical theories focus strongly on social change as an ultimate objective. Macro, social development and social pedagogy theories are, however, generally used within state services, where therapeutic and problem-solving practices are the main form of practice; this practice accepts the existing social order and seeks reform and social improvement rather than the more extensive social change that critical theories aim for.

Midgley and Conley (2010b), in concluding a set of case studies that extended Midgley's theory, defend social development theory as a form of activism, while claiming that anti-oppressive, critical and empowerment theories are idealistic and have not achieved social change. Midgley and Conley see social development as a form of progressive social change incorporating human rights, peace and social justice (2010b: 198). It is unclear whether they mean 'progressive' as a way of referring to progression as movement through a series of stages towards an objective, or in the alternative sense of movement towards more enlightened social conditions. Midgley's (1995) text, summarized as the main example text in this chapter, uses both ideas. He emphasizes that his approach to social development (as opposed to ideas of economic development) is distinctive because it aims for more enlightened social conditions. However, both these senses of the word imply evolutionary social change, whereas critical theory seeks 'transformation', which implies a change in the underlying social structures. It is clear from Midgley and Conley's comment that they do not think that social workers can achieve transformation in most situations. While they may be right, this defines their theory as a problem-solving theory accepting the present social order, rather than as a critical social change theory.

As theories focused on the social, all these groups of theories have a broader perspective than individual change or therapeutic and clinical theories. However, macro and community work practice, social development and social pedagogy lean more towards an acceptance and maintenance of the existing social orders, and, as the discussion in Chapters 11 and 12 shows, critical and empowerment theories lean more towards social change in those orders.

Wider theoretical perspectives

Introduction to the perspectives

Macro practice is the term used in the USA for an aspect of social work that focuses on building new organizations and influencing existing social institutions for the benefit of people who are excluded from, or neglected by, powerful interests in society. Other countries mainly use the term 'community work', or a variation of it, to describe this aspect of practice. Macro practice in the USA emphasizes cause advocacy that aims to include policy change as an important component. Case advocacy, in which practitioners argue for services on behalf of individuals, families and communities, is sometimes used as an element of community work practice both in the USA and elsewhere. Because advocacy has developed its own theoretical literature, I treat it as a separate body of theory connected to empowerment practice in Chapter 11.

Social development theory organizes ideas about macro work into a system of practice for developing the strength and resilience of social institutions, mainly in local communities in resource-poor countries and regions. Economic development often mainly benefits the interests of the rich, and social development seeks to enable poorer and more oppressed groups of people in a society to share in the benefits of economic development. Social development is the major form of social work in many resource-poor countries.

Social pedagogy is a significant tradition of social work in mainland Europe, contributing a conception of social work as a positive educational process for individuals and groups with shared interests. It is largely absent from social work in English-speaking countries, although there are occasional attempts to transfer it, and its practice has resonances with some residential child care and community work practices. It avoids the negative connotations of Anglo-American social work traditions that see social work as a process for resolving problems; in this way, it represents the positive objectives of the shared value principles (see Figure 1.7). Chapter 9 shows that strengths, narrative and solution perspectives seek similarly to reduce social work's focus on problems in many countries.

Social pedagogy provides a holistic conception of practice that brings personal identity and social group membership together. This avoids the priority given in social work in English-speaking countries to individual behaviour and psychology, replacing it with a focus on personal psychological development through education, without the implication that we do the work because of people's personal problems. In this way, it also has connections with humanistic perspectives on social work, which are dealt with in Chapter 10. The individualistic priority of practice in English-speaking countries mainly relegates the social aspects of the situation to being a context for the main, individualistic, intervention. Ecological systems theory, as we have seen in Chapter 7, is an example of this tendency. In some countries, social pedagogy is mainly practised in community facilities, such as pre-school or after-school groups for children and young people; hence the use of the term 'pedagogy', because it refers to teaching methods and the teaching profession, is often taken to focus on children. Other countries refer to a more extended meaning of pedagogy as an educational process, for example, in 'guardian pedagogy' (child safeguarding and similar processes) or 'gerontopedagogy' (positive practice with older people).

Because many of the techniques are similar, community and macro practice and social development have influenced each other, particularly in the administration of British, and to some extent French, colonies until the 1960s, and through the social development work of the United Nations, which has often called upon community work expertise. Social pedagogy connects with youth and community work, and also with day and residential care for children. Although these methods focus on the social, they mainly seek the personal development of relatively small groups within the present social order, rather than seeing such development as forming steps towards achieving broader social change. Thus, all these theories mainly formulate problem-solving and therapeutic practices rather than being social change theories.

Social development ideas and economic development

Social and community development is an aspect of the wider development of localities, areas, regions and countries, and is related to economic and industrial development. Ideas about development have a long history. The economies of European countries developed from the eighteenth century onwards, and those of many other countries in the nineteenth and twentieth centuries. Weber (1930) famously argued that non-European countries developed slowly because their cultural inheritance did not include the Protestant work ethic of northern European countries. Sinha and Kao (1988b), however, criticize this as an ethnocentric view, and argue that other Western concepts, such as individualism and achievement motivation, are connected with Western economic development. We have to be careful of assuming that Western individualism and go-getting are better than the philosophies of many African and Asian cultures, which emphasize achieving interdependence and accepting traditional values.

Economic and social development is now associated in many people's minds with resource-poor former colonial countries, particularly in the southern hemisphere. Their economic and social development is often contrasted with that of Canada, European countries and the USA, which are often described as 'Western', 'industrialized' or 'developed' nations. These terms, if we use them to refer to regions of the world, present problems. For example, Australia and New Zealand are in the southern hemisphere but are usually described as 'Western' countries because their economic and political systems are similar to those of Canada, European countries and the USA. Another example is Japan, which has a developed economy and a democratic political system similar to those of Western countries, but is located geographically and culturally in the Far East. Western industrialized countries are often described as 'developed', and historically many countries in Asia and Africa have been described as 'developing' (the politically correct term) or 'underdeveloped' (a more judgemental term). Both these terms, however, imply that it is desirable or necessary to have economic development following along the lines of Western countries, when many people would question that assumption.

Responding to these concerns, I use the term 'resource-poor' to refer to countries, primarily in the Southern hemisphere, that pursue a policy of economic development to improve the economic and social capital available to their peoples. All governments seek to increase the amount of economic activity in a region or country to combat poverty, and this has other economic, social and political consequences. Competing theories take different views of the relationship between the market and economic development, as well as of the role of the state in intervening to build markets or reduce social problems resulting from market capitalism. Modernization views argued that improved efficiencies in the economic markets of resource-poor countries would allow them to achieve Western standards of living. Neo-Marxist 'dependency' views argued that multinational corporations have sought to maintain the dependence of resource-poor countries on developed Western economic systems (Hulme and Turner, 1990: 34–43). Recently, there has been concern about the impact of globalization, in which a whirlwind of political, economic and cultural changes have led to increased interdependence, with increased cultural and economic dominance by Western countries replacing the political control through conquest that occurred in the colonial era (Payne and Askeland, 2008). Much of this debate is not relevant to the mainly social elements of development, although ideas from these theories have influenced social development theory.

Economic and social development may also be used in less developed areas or regions of countries that are economically successful, for example northern Britain, southern Italy and Greece in the European Union. Economic development in such regions aims mainly to combat widespread poverty among populations (Jones, 1990). Such poverty is often associated with social issues that are also of concern to social workers. Examples include health and disability, education, women's roles, industrialization and urbanization, with its related problems such as crime and family break-up. Social or community development is a strategy for dealing with those consequences. Governments may also seek to reduce the economic and social demands on the wealth and income of a region or country. They might do this by, for example, trying to control increases in the population or in social and health costs. In countries that are economically well developed, social and economic development is also concerned with inner city deprivation, declining industrial regions and environmental planning. Dealing with these social issues or the development process has sometimes led to a call for community work.

By the 1980s, *neo-populism* (Hulme and Turner, 1990) aimed to generate small-scale development created by cooperatives working as rural villages, using labour-intensive appropriate technologies, rather than seeking the urban development that is typical of Western countries. Related to these ideas are the theories of *eco-development* and *ethno-development* (Hettne, 1990). *Eco-development* seeks 'sustainable' development that does not encroach upon natural resources (Estes, 1993). Development should, in this view, be more people-centred and concerned with local issues. We have seen in Chapter 7, on systems theory, that sustainability has become an increasingly important element of the critique of the mainly therapeutic ideas of ecological social work. *Ethno-development* acknowledges that the focus of development cannot be the nation state or small groups. Ethnic groups within nation states often conflict over the use of resources and power in the nation, and such factors must be acknowledged and worked with. These ideas connect with some of the concern to acknowledge black or African-centred perspectives that is discussed in Chapter 14.

An important related concept is the Latin-American Catholic idea of *liberation theology*, which has influenced south American social work (Gutiérrez, 1973, 1992; Evans, 1992; Skeith, 1992). Traditional Christian ideas were considered as accepting oppression as the preparation for a happier afterlife. Liberation theory contests this by seeking a movement from oppression to liberation within the concrete issues of daily life. In this view, both personal and 'social' sin, that is, structural oppression by social institutions, must be overcome by non-violent social change through personal empathy with others and their social situation, in the same way that Jesus Christ acted. This has provided a religious basis for seeking social change. Liberation theology has therefore encouraged the church to use community work techniques in the predominantly Catholic Latin-American countries. However, its explicit rejection of the existing social order has been controversial in the Church, partly because in areas where it is vigorously adopted, it has sometimes set the Church against the state.

Many development theories focus on women, partly because of their importance in local and family economies in many developing countries. This focus has also occurred in response to worldwide feminist social movements that aim to achieve greater justice, independence and self-control for women and publicize issues of concern to them, especially child care (Yasas and Mehta, 1990; Mokate, 2004; World Bank, 2012). Disability and rehabilitation have also become an increasingly important issue for international social development, and working on all these issues makes the best use of human resources in every country (World Health Organization/World Bank, 2011).

Finally, important social movements responding to local ethnic and cultural needs in different countries also contest the significance of the centralized state and globalization (Guidry et al., 2003) and the role of social work as a force for social regulation (Thompson, 2002). Fisher and Kling (1994) argued that social movement theory connects community development ideas with wider forms of resistance among communities by shifting the focus of socialist action from class to community. Martin (2001) argues that feminist and other new social movements have achieved changes in social policy by symbolic challenges to cultural assumptions. An example is the recognition that women's self-help movements are the only way to make a substantial difference with postnatal depression as interpersonal help from people with shared experiences makes a major difference. Thus, Western social policy becomes more responsive to a role for social work that is about organizing self-help rather than providing direct care.

Social development ideas

Social development has been variously defined, and these definitions are controversial. An important, often-quoted definition by Paiva (1977: 332) is 'the development of the capacity of people to work continuously for their own and society's welfare'. This focuses on improving individual capacity within the context of wider social development. Hence, Paiva (1993) argues that this does not exclude four other important aspects of social development: structural change, socioeconomic integration, institutional development and renewal. Jones and Pandey (1981) focused on the element of institutional develop-ment, that is, making social institutions meet the needs of people more appropriately; their definition (p. v) is that 'Social development refers to the process of planned institu-tional change to bring about a better fit between human needs and aspirations on the one hand and social policies and programs on the other.'

An early official view is contained in the Preamble of the International Development Strategy for the Second United Nations Development Decade, quoted by Jones (1981: 2):

> As the ultimate purpose of development is to provide increasing opportunities to all people for a better life, it is essential to bring about a more equitable distribution of income and wealth for promoting both social justice and efficiency of production ... Thus qualitative and structural changes in society must go hand-in-hand with rapid economic growth and existing disparities ... should be substantially reduced.

This shift in thinking from an official concentration on economic planning led to an emphasis on social planning. As a result, institutions could be organized to support economic progress (Hardiman and Midgley, 1989). Asian writers (for example, Khand-walla, 1988; Sinha and Kao, 1988a) focus on understanding and aligning the values represented in a society and the values of the development process. More recent literature emphasizes the important of achieving social equality alongside economic growth.

Wilkinson and Pickett's book *The Spirit Level* (2010) explored socioeconomic inequalities in relation to a wide range of social and healthcare issues both between and within countries; it covered social issues of concern to social workers such as mental health and drug use, physical health and life expectancy, obesity, education, teenage births, violence, imprisonment and social mobility. Wilkinson and Pickett came to the conclusion that the important health and social problems of the rich world are more common in more unequal societies. The differences are large, with these problems being from three to ten times as common in the most unequal societies compared with the least unequal. Moreover, countries consistently experience high levels of social problems; if they have one area of difficulty, they are likely to have others. Wilkinson and Pickett conclude that everyone in a particular society benefits from equality. Exploring the pattern of rises and falls in inequality in particular societies, they also conclude that the political will to reduce inequality has consistently been shown to improve both equality and the significant social problems that arise from it. Ideas about social capital argue that groups and communities can increase the resources available to resource-poor popula-tions by increasing the number and range of social networks that they are part of.

Pandey (1981) identifies three basic strategies in social development, defined according to their purposes:

■ *Distributive* strategies aim for improved social equity between groups nationally.

- *Participative* strategies aim to make structural and institutional reforms to involve people in development and social change.
- *Human development* strategies aim to increase the skills and capacity for people to act on their own behalf in improving the economy and institutional development of their area.

Potter and Brough (2004: 340), reviewing research into capacity-building, argue that it is more than just education or personal development for individuals, although it may include these elements. Capacity-building programmes for community development include four elements:

- the structures, systems and roles in the organizations involved;
- staff and training, and the personal development infrastructure;
- the skills of the personnel involved, including volunteers and community members;
- tools, including facilities and techniques.

Each element is required to make effective use of each of the others, so they build on each other in a complex matrix.

Midgley (1993) divides social development ideologies into three types of activity, rather than concentrating on objectives, as Pandey does:

- *Individualist* strategies focus on self-actualization, self-determination and self-improvement.
- *Collectivist* strategies emphasize building organizations as the basis for developing new approaches to action – these are institutional approaches.
- *Populist* strategies focus on small-scale activities based in local communities.

Midgley's book *Social Development* expands on these types of activity, and I discuss them more fully when I consider this as the example text later in the chapter.

Hujo and McClanahan (2011) suggest that development policies have to be developmental, democratic and socially inclusive if they are to achieve both economic and social development.

Social enterprise

Social enterprise is an important new element in social development theory and is used in Western developed countries as well as resource-poor countries. Instead of developing new services by creating public sector, non-profit or mutual-aid services, social enterprise creates profit-seeking businesses, with three main characteristics:

- The business aims incorporate social objectives as an important priority.
- Profits are recycled to support the social objectives rather than being paid as dividends to the entrepreneurs.
- By establishing a business, rather than a charity or public service, the entrepreneur repudiates authority and sets the direction of individual or social change in favour of the service users (Ashton, 2010).

One of the advantages of social enterprise over other structures for social development is that the potential profits can provide independence from control by government or external financiers of charities, who often represent the interests of social elites. It makes social provision financially sustainable by providing independent sources of finance, and focuses on seeking innovation rather than welfare services aimed at maintaining social support (Mawson, 2008). Particularly with minority and excluded groups, social enterprise permits a focus on economic development through creating small and medium-sized enterprises within minority ethnic communities, achieving social development alongside financial independence. An example is Delgado's (2011) analysis of social enterprise with Latino minorities in the USA as a form of community social work.

Clark (2009) proposes the particular capabilities of the social entrepreneur, as set out in Figure 8.1. This is a useful formulation because it clarifies that entrepreneurial behaviour is a social concern, without too much of a business or money-making focus.

Figure 8.1 The capabilities of the social entrepreneur

Capability	Explanation: you are...
Dedication	Committed to a social goal or purpose
*Focus	Discriminating between potential activities, according to the extent to which they contribute to the purpose
*Advantages, profit orientation	Identifying clearly the gains for different potential participants, as part of finding the right targets
*Ego drive	Wanting to make a difference that others recognize, through knowing your own strengths and others' views of you
Urgency	Against wasting time, wanting instead to take action now
Courage	Determined when faced with problems
Activator	Wanting to make things happen, especially where progress is slow or has stopped
Opportunity	Seeing possibilities rather than barriers
*Creativity	Buzzing with ideas, opportunities and solutions
Expertise orientation	Aware of your own limits and the need to find others with expertise to contribute
*Team	Getting the right people together
Seeing individuals' contributions	Seeing and using others' strengths

*These are the most important themes.

Source: Clark (2009).

Social enterprise uses the microfinance approach to alleviate poverty. Microfinance provides loans to enable small businesses to take off. Other important areas are: healthcare, education and training, particularly to improve the participation of people with learning disabilities and their relatives in society; environmental projects; community and housing regeneration; welfare projects to combat unemployment; alcoholism and drug abuse projects; and advocacy and campaigning, for example through Fairtrade and Traidcraft, which provide a good economic return for businesses in resource-poor countries that export to richer countries (Nicholls, 2006: 14).

Social entrepreneurship can address the market failings of conventional business and social institutions. Examples are the failure of business to operate in poor areas, the withdrawal of governments from social provision, the withdrawal of churches from areas where they have marginal support, and social provision where there is not enough tax revenue or other finance to support the development of local community-based organizations (Nicholls, 2006: 16). A variety of models of management are possible. For example, the enterprise can be completely integrated into social provision, separated from it or partly incorporated (Alter, 2006).

Social pedagogy

Social pedagogy developed from the work of German philosophers Diesterweg and Mager (Hämäläinen, 1989, 2003; Lorenz, 1994: 91–7), aiming at those social aspects of education that particularly focus on poor people in societies. The theory emphasizes that education can make a major difference to the lives of poor people; it can be used to combat social exclusion and develop social identity, aiming at personal and social growth through problem-solving rather than simply the resolution of personal problems (Hämäläinen, 2003).

Case example: The social pedagogy pilot programme in UK children's residential care

From 2008 to 2010, a UK project experimented with using social pedagogy in children's residential care (Cameron et al., 2011). This led to useful resources being available in English for the first time, many of them on the internet (see the Additional resources at the end of this chapter). The project recruited social pedagogues to work in UK children's homes according to three models: homes where pedagogues already worked, but had no mandate for change; homes where pedagogues were introduced with a mandate to change the practice in the home; and homes where the main responsibilities of the pedagogues were in training. There was a comparison group with no input from a pedagogue. The project found that structural issues in the management of children's homes, which in turn reflected value differences about holistic working, made it difficult to introduce social pedagogy in the British setting. The following account extracts the main theoretical points about social pedagogy practice that the project demonstrated.

This project identified four main elements of social pedagogy in the context of children's residential care (Cameron et al., 2011: 13):

- a broad understanding of care as being holistic and multidimensional;
- helping children to learn in an enriching way by facilitating their capacity to think for themselves;
- developing authentic and trusting relationships between children and adults that included authority and affection and a reasonable degree of privacy for the child;

▨ empowerment in the sense of encouraging active engagement in the children's own lives and in society generally.

The relationships established between pedagogues and children enable practitioners to model this approach to learning and developing themselves, so that children can learn from pedagogues how to handle themselves.

This paragraph identifies in *italics* the main practice principles explored in the project described in the case example. Social pedagogy practice was *holistic*, seeing children as thinking and feeling, and as having a physical, spiritual, social and creative existence that was expressed in their interactions with the adults as they shared the same *living space*. The task was to create interactions that allowed the children to express that full existence. The *heart* aspect of social pedagogy gave importance to both adults and children expressing emotional and ethical reactions as they interacted. The *hands* aspect of social pedagogy meant using everyday activities of care and life to express the relationships between the adults and children through interactions. The *head* aspect of social pedagogy gave importance to reflection, not just to produce reports and records, but also as a shared activity of making sense of what was going on in the home together. The *three Ps* meant that the pedagogues saw the professional, personal and private aspects of their lives as linked, using their professional skills as part of a shared life with the children, while preserving privacy for what should remain private in the children's and adults' lives. The *common third* was the creative, everyday tasks and leisure time that the children and adults shared and was the medium of working with the children. *Teamwork* with a range of colleagues and acting as role models of appropriate behaviour and relationships were also important.

This theoretical framework was found to be important to guide pedagogues in using experiences of living to work with and help children. Its use was, however, inconsistent with homes where everyday activities were seen as a non-professional routine rather than an opportunity to be with the children, and where working with the children was seen as a series of identified and programmed tasks.

The value of this theoretical approach is consistent with the broader ideas of the therapeutic community movement, discussed in Chapter 4, and connects with research into residential care practice in the UK. Brown et al. (1998) found that homes worked well if the social, formal and belief goals were all in concordance, and worked less well where there was dissonance. Where there was concordance, the staff culture was supportive of the children, and the children then also developed a positive culture of mutual support, leading to good outcomes. Whitaker et al. (1998) found that staff worked with individual residents to define goals that identified the desired improvements and took opportunities to work towards those goals, being flexible about how to achieve them but persevering with them. Reparative experiences meant understanding what needed repair, disconfirming unhelpful fixed beliefs (for example, that all adults are untrustworthy), finding daily experiences that confirmed progress, being ready to listen while being sensitive to readiness to talk, combining non-verbal symbols and explicit acts of caring, and valuing successes through occasional celebrations. With groups, the work provided opportunities for activities that helped residents to learn to work together, successfully handle their relationships with others, gain self-respect and be valued by others. Social pedagogy provides a theoretical framework for such practice that has been found to be effective.

In some countries in mainland Europe, social pedagogy practitioners form a separate professional group whose focus varies in different countries. The Netherlands introduced a policy of social renewal, using community development to integrate action on employment, the environment, welfare and education in deprived localities (Winkels, 1994). *Animation* in France also has an informal education role through artistic work that is concerned with social development and education through leisure activities (Lorenz, 1994: 99–103).

Case example: Kevin, a hyperactive child

Kevin, aged 9, was referred for assessment in a child and adolescent mental health service as being extremely hyperactive; his situation illustrates how the social pedagogy approach thinks differently from conventional social work. The concern about hyperactivity is a judgement made by his teachers and parents. It presents their idea about his relationship with the world and the other people in it. The starting point of the assessment was how this happened, how the behaviour developed and how others reacted to it.

The social pedagogy approach is to arrive at an overall view of the hyperactivity in relation to the personality of both the child and the family, and to the social environment around Kevin. The next question is 'what should I do?' Social pedagogy argues that you should use the balance between the child and the collective around him: the child may only gain the will to develop his behaviour and grow in different ways by the surrounding collective world responding to and joining in that development. Individual variation in the collective is a sign of its quality, because it contains the resources that allow and help its participants to develop. Kevin may gain ideas about how it is possible to, or how he would like to, behave, and the collective of his family and school can give him the will to behave; they can also control how he behaves so that he may perceive other ways of acting. Kevin makes the choices, but he learns about the options and how to implement them from his parents, his school and his peers. People educate themselves in interaction with others and in the interchange of perceptions about the world. Liberation, in social pedagogy, is found in the mediation of one's views and behaviour through the collective; language plays an important part in this, since self-understanding comes through discussion and debate in the collective.

These ideas are an attractive basis for developmental work with children in residential and day care and in informal education and community work. These concepts have many connections with the self-realization and personal growth of humanist ideas, and with G. H. Mead's ideas about the interaction with the self and the other (see Chapter 9). They also have connections with critical and feminist thinking in the dialogical process and in the use of language and collective experience as the basis of both shared and personal experience.

Connections

Social development, macro and community work and social pedagogy relate to participatory approaches in all kinds of social provision; they all require skills in interpersonal and group communication that relate closely to social work skills and connect to empowerment practice (see Chapter 11). Self-help organizations can also be important mechanisms for these practices by generating increased interpersonal skills. In participating in a variety of ways, individuals can be involved through local grassroots organizations. This helps in their personal education and development. It also helps to give priority to local wishes, avoiding situations in which external political influences or social assumptions such as gender oppression override the community's interests.

However, there is a critique of participation as an ideal of social development. Midgley (1987) argues that views of participation as being all-important do not deal adequately with the role of the state in modern life, instead relying on individualist, populist and anarchist views of the world. Seeking participation as an ideal of service provision has been described as a new 'orthodoxy' (Stirrat, 1997) and as 'tyranny' (Cooke and Kothari, 2001). The reasons for these concerns about participation are that the user or carer's internal knowledge and understanding may be limited so that external input and analysis may be needed to achieve successful outcomes. In addition, participative exercises may throw up apparently strong views when a wider range of opinion has not been revealed through adequate consultation. Weaknesses in representation may therefore weaken the value of participation. In addition, people living in a particular locality or who appear to have related interests may be assumed to have a community of interest when there are hidden divisions between different groups. A plurality of views among participants may make it difficult to make decisions or resolve disagreement. Participants may also be manipulated. Agencies or official interests may in addition set the parameters of participation inappropriately to meet their own objectives and not those of the people involved.

These points are an argument for a careful implementation of participation and a careful consideration of the opinions that result. Nkunika (1987) argues that appropriate organizational bases for facilitating participation are needed.

Current approaches to development increasingly focus on issues of poverty, employment and enterprise, particularly social enterprise, issues of diversity, ethnicity and colonialism, and issues of technology, sustainability, gender and urbanization (Allen and Thomas, 2000). Many of the issues in social development concern poverty, gender and ethnicity and their consequences for identity, either gender, ethnic or national identity. Thus, social development increasingly connects to ideas from social construction, feminism and multicultural sensitivity (see Chapters 9, 13 and 14, respectively).

The politics of social and community development

Social and community development is often peripheral to the main areas of social work practice in Western countries. In non-Western countries, however, if we exclude health and social security provision, it is often the main form of social intervention, although welfare provision is also sometimes needed and provided, especially in urban areas (Hardiman and Midgley, 1989: 237–57). *Social development* grew out of *community development* work in the later colonial period. The experience was reimported to Britain and the USA in the 1950s and 60s and influenced an explosion of radical community action in the 1960s and 70s. Attempts were made to develop Western social work throughout the world, which led to welfare services and social work education in casework and groupwork in many countries (Brigham, 1977. Walton and el Nasr (1988) call this the 'transmission' phase of interaction between social work in Western and resource-poor countries. This spread was, however, widely seen as inappropriate for indigenous cultures and social needs (Midgley, 1981).

During the 1980s, social development therefore became the model of work that was considered most appropriate for most resource-poor countries (see, for example, Midgley, 1989; Hall, 1993a) and it has been most strongly extended there. Schools of social work shifted from teaching Western social work models to a stronger focus on social development; they also saw the human focus of social work as valuable for counteracting economic approaches to development (Osei-Hwedie, 1990). This change took place at least partly to maintain the schools' credibility in a period when ethnic and cultural interests were achieving importance in many countries. However, a good deal of theoretical development has come from Western writers, also in schools of social work, who have had experience of developing countries and call on work from within them. Sustainability in social development proposes forms of economic and physical development that nurture human welfare through decentralization and democratization (Lusk and Hoff, 1994).

Elliott (1993), among others, argues that the experience of social development in developing countries is relevant for Western countries. This is because Western countries face wide disparities in poverty and economic development within their borders, making a social development approach relevant to them too. Because of its emphasis on participation and people constructing their own approach to problems and issues, the approach may also be helpful where countries seek to deal with the needs of isolated or marginalized communities, for example where native populations have been oppressed by incomers (O'Brien and Pace, 1988). Social development theory is also a useful counterbalance to a Western influence on global social work ideas, enabling a primarily non-Western model to gain wide relevance for practice.

Values issues

The central value issue in macro practice is to manage the intrusion of the agency's and practitioner's objectives into the objectives of the collective or community that the practice is designed to help. There may also be differences among objectives espoused by various members of the community or collective. In individual practice, clients have the right to determine either the priorities, the problems to be dealt with or the solutions and aims of the work. These are often negotiated with them through creating a practice alliance, which also respects their rights to determine what happens as the work proceeds, as we see in the shared value objectives (see Figure 1.7). Alternatively, there are clear responsibilities for the practitioner to intervene, for example to prevent child abuse or personal and social risks from mental illness, disability or ageing.

In macro practice, practitioners have to manage what Banks (2003: 106) calls 'paren-talism', the tendency on the part of the agency to want to control or even set the aims and methods that members of the community or collective will follow. We can often see this tendency in government policy. For example, social entrepreneurship sometimes seeks to get local communities to organize themselves to create effective businesses, or to generate employment, when this would not be the desired method or priority of members of the community. Ideas such as 'capacity-building' may seem insulting to members of the commu-nity (Banks, 2003) and impose professional or political ideas about what the community or its members should achieve, rather than members identifying what they should achieve. If you are concerned with community or social development, what are the boundaries of the community that you are developing? Do that community's interests overlap or conflict with the interests of other communities that you are not concerned with? Are you sure that all interests within it are represented? And what constitutes development? Some people would see having projects to provide work or additional housing as valuable, while others with a green perspective might see these as damaging to the environment.

One of the dangers for social work agencies involved in community or social develop-ment is a focus on social welfare issues, when the community may have other priorities, as the following case example shows.

Case example: A volunteering scheme for a housing project

A settlement received government fund-ing to promote volunteering in a housing project, recruiting unemployed young people as volunteers to visit a growing number of older people. This met government priori-ties in helping unemployed young people and the needs of older people that could not be met by employing social care staff. Local community representatives on the settle-ment's management committee objected to this project for two reasons. First, they did not see volunteering as helping young people into work. Second, they thought it was more important to find volunteers to help in the local school, which, because of poor standards, was threatened with merger with another school; they feared this would take local services out of the community.

Connected with the issue of conflicting priorities is the question of leadership. When does raising community members' consciousness about the problems that they face and the causes of those problems become setting the direction and focus of the community's objectives? Government agencies have in the past criticized community work practitioners for encouraging local communities to protest about official services or policies, rather than do positive practical work (Loney, 1983). Burghardt (2011) discusses 'chutzpah', the enthusiasm and self-confidence to motivate a group of people to believe that they can take action about problems they share and do something about them. When does having chutzpah as a source of encouragement become taking over the community's rights to participative self-management? On the other hand, when does encouraging participation become the practitioner avoiding professional responsibility?

Banks (2003) suggests that dealing with such issues involves interprofessional and multiprofessional working that recognizes multiple accountabilities to many different groups in the community and among agencies involved with the community or collective. Working in this way allows practitioners to test out a variety of alternative perspectives on the role they and their agency are taking. Gilchrist (2004), pursuing her networking approach to macro practice, argues that practitioners have a responsibility to build links and reciprocity among community members. She argues that macro practice also has a responsibility to focus on reducing inequalities in a community and between communities, promote diversity and reduce conflict.

Applications

Macro/community work practice

Macro practice aims to achieve lasting change that alters the economic, political and social environment so that people excluded by powerful interests in society from participating in the major decisions that affect their lives achieve an increasing influence and capacity to achieve their individual and collective life goals. Most macro practice works with communities, that is, groups of people who have shared interests in a particular social issue. Their shared interest sometimes derives from the fact that they live in the same locality.

> **Pause and reflect** *Communities and shared interests*
>
> Note down some communities that you are involved with: both locality-based communities and those that are a community with a shared interest for other reasons. What shared macro aims do they want to achieve, and how does that fit the definition of macro practice?

Some suggestions

I thought about the network for refugees and migrants that covers my area. It involves a number of people who work providing services and support to refugees and migrants who are newly arrived in the country. Both newly arrived migrants and migrants who are already in the process of becoming established are entitled to membership. The network provides practical and personal help to individual migrants and their families. It also provides personal support to people who are appealing against immigration, housing and social security decisions, but it does not always advocate on their behalf. These services are not, however, macro services.

The network selects a limited number of cases to advocate for, where taking up the particular case might make a point of principle that would benefit other migrants. It also uses its experience as the basis of public education to persuade other local people and organizations to be more accepting of migrants in the area and to persuade other public services to be more responsive to migrants' needs. These aspects of the network are macro services: they aim to change, mostly in small ways, the way in which our society deals with migrants, so that new migrants can more easily settle and begin to develop a new life in the area. In addition, good experiences of understanding why people migrate and their many difficult experiences might help the general public to develop attitudes that are more accepting of social changes in their area.

At times and in places when community work and macro practice have been valued by people in political power, social services agencies with a broad focus have often employed professional community workers and included elements of macro practice in their service. More recently, this has often been confined to specialist agencies working in areas where there is political support for considerable social development, for example in inner cities or where the closure of a major employer has led to economic difficulties for people in a city. Major social issues are often targeted through techniques such as activation practice with unemployed people, with the aim of helping them to adapt their skills and behaviour so that they are better fitted to current employment markets. This use of specialized community work is similar to the use of social development practice in developing countries, and can call on some social development techniques in the same way that social development theory interchanges with community work. Non-specialist practitioners occasionally include an element of community work in their practice as a special project, developing support groups, participation initiatives or community organizations that benefit particular groups of their clients. After initial positive experiences, however, such approaches have become entwined with the reform of unemployment benefits systems and have lost much of their community work emphasis, becoming primarily concerned with the compulsion, particularly of young people, to take up employment on potentially unfavourable terms (Lindsay and Mailand, 2004; Clasen and Clegg, 2006; Graversen and van Ours, 2009).

The main social focuses of macro social work are:

- small groups, which can bring together people who are experiencing shared problems in a particular locality, for example teenage offenders;
- families, parents or mothers who can be brought together to deal with pressures arising from care or community responsibilities, for example mothers with behaviourally disturbed children, or parents in an area where there is extensive teenage violence or drug-taking;
- areas where there are cultural issues, such as clashes between different ethnic groups, or where social cohesion is lacking because the culture has been lost after the closure of a local industry;

- areas where new communities are being formed, for example in renewed housing;
- issues that arise for particular work communities, such as health and safety issues, or particular jobs leading to social isolation, for example through shift work or isolated minority ethnic groups working in specialist restaurants;
- areas where there is concern about the environment, for example campaigning against new road, rail or airport infrastructure projects or the loss of local leisure environments through housing or industrial development;
- issues concerned with shared spiritual concerns, for example where there are isolated faith groups whose interests are excluded from schools, workplaces or community provision (van Wormer et al., 2007).

Example text: Burghardt's (2011) macro practice

This text is an American account of macro practice based on a strong political perspective. It is based round three basic theoretical assumptions:

- Each historical period reflects the political and social status quo of its time and also the particular degree of struggle between the contending interests in the society of that time.
- Every method of practice contains elements that create relationships between the participants of social work so that there is a pattern of dominance and subordination or of self-determination between practitioners, clients and the groups around them in society.
- To foster voice, participation and self-determination among their clients, practitioners must maintain a strategic view of their practice that transcends the political and social environment of the present historical period.

The aim is to make interventions that are progressive in two senses. The first sense is that the interventions lead people to feel that they have made progress in their lives; this is progressive in the everyday sense of achieving steps forward. The second sense is that this progress also leads to a greater participation and self-determination in matters that are important to them; this is progressive in the political sense that it allows whole population groups to achieve greater power over their lives.

Burghardt proposes two types of assessment as the basis of macro practice. First, it is important to assess the political and economic environment, so that you can judge the barriers and limitations to what may be possible for a particular group in the population you are working with. This incorporates into your assessment the political and social environment of the particular historical period. While there is no point in going up against insuperable historical and political odds, Burghardt cautions against being too pessimistic. The second element of assessment is of the community you are working with. There are two parts to this. First is to look at the issues the community is facing and what the groups you are working with want to achieve in responding to those issues. The second part is to look at your own personal goals and strengths in working with the group to achieve their aims. It is important not to mix up what *you* want to do with the *community's* aims, which should be the deciding factor. I have set out this assessment process in Figure 8.2.

Figure 8.2 Burghardt's macro assessment
Source: Burghardt (2011).

Figure 8.2 shows how these two assessments are linked. Looking at the issues that the community is facing and its objectives, you identify things that the community wants to try to do and bring these together to make meaningful goals. You can often identify goals, that is, the end results that people want to achieve. If so, you may need to develop steps moving towards that goal. The people involved should also debate their values. Three kinds of issues often arise. First, is it more important to meet identified needs or mainly to build skill and confidence? Second, is it more important to overcome oppressions that people are experiencing or to seize opportunities that are waiting to be taken up? Third, is it more important to rely on the professional advice you receive or follow the preferences of the people involved? You need 'tactical self-awareness', that is, a balance between working on something that feels comfortable for you and working on things that go beyond your skills but which you know are needed and wanted by the people you are working with.

Moving on from your own personal goals and strengths, Burghardt emphasizes the importance of being aware of the community's strengths and development. In most community work, there is a balance between doing things and working on building up the strengths of the people involved. There may be a pressure to get things done; however, this should not altogether dominate helping people and groups in the community you are working with to develop the skills and relationships that will help them achieve additional successes in the future.

An important part of assessment in community work is a concrete process of engaging people in identifying the needs that significant groups in the community want and feel able to achieve, as well as the resources that are potentially available to achieve them.

The next important stage is building trust among the people involved so that they can make progress towards their objectives. Here, Burghardt identifies one of the most important personal and social conflicts for the practitioner in community practice. He talks about the combination of chutzpah and humility that is required to achieve community work objectives. On the one hand, the chutzpah, a self-confidence to express and push forward towards objectives, needs to be balanced by a humility that accepts the role and engagement of others. How can a practitioner provide the energy and commitment that will move things forward towards a bigger vision without becoming dominant in a way that excludes people from the community in setting the direction of their action and actively participating? Burghardt's answer to this common tension is to foster relationships that allow people to achieve small steps towards a broader vision. It may also be important to allow the small steps that are being achieved to shift the strategic direction and timing of innovations that are moving towards the wider objectives and also sometimes redefining them.

Case example: Saving the settlement

A long-standing settlement (a social agency committed to community work) in a very poor area of the city experienced a funding crisis as its long-time director, a social worker, moved towards retirement. The chair, a woman who had become part of the settlement's management through her participation in pre-school activities, was advised by the community liaison officer for the local government council and the treasurer that the accumulated reserves would soon run out, having been used to cover a deficit in the running costs for some years. The local council gave a grant to employ a social enterprise consultant in part-time work to prepare a business plan for developing the settlement's strategy and programme, while a senior project leader acted as director. A six-month period of local consultation under the consultant's leadership produced a plan in which urban regeneration and community crime prevention grants were used to develop new activities for young people using information technology. For the families, the focus was housing problems, and these approaches were grafted on to existing youth clubs and the advice service.

In the longer term, it was clear that major construction work would be needed to update the building, and that this would be best achieved by taking on contracts for health and social care work because there were no other sufficient sources of capital for building development within the settlement's range of activities, even though health and social care work would be new to the settlement. During this period of consultation, difficulties arose with the management of the pre-school and holiday projects for the children, and it was clear that the acting director was unable to manage conflicts and poor professional practice among staff in this area, in which he had no previous experience. Part of the reason for the difficulties was that several staff in pre-school work feared, from the direction of the consultation, that their work would be closed down in favour of new directions. However, their projects had considerable local community support.

In answer to these problems, the consultant took over the directorship as a full-time post, to the relief of the acting director, and became involved in the detail of managing the settlement's services. As a result, he began to see ways of building on the pre-school work as part of the health and social care developments, integrating them into the future strategy. The daily involvement enabled him to build more solid relationships with a range of staff in the settlement, even though this detailed work was not a comfortable fit for his skills as he currently saw them.

This case example, which I return to below, illustrates the importance of connecting the chutzpah involved in getting external support to buy in to a new strategic direction and provide extensive funding with the humility of working on the 'little things' needed to maintain participation in continuing streams of work. Making these connections eventually achieved an integration of aspects of the agency and its community that had felt excluded from the excitement of the new developments. For the enterprise consultant, his self-awareness about being uncomfortable with the micro-management role that he was taking on enabled him to see this as a tactic for moving towards the wider strategy while also improving his practice skills – an example of Burghardt's 'tactical self-awareness' in a practitioner.

The next stage of Burghardt's analysis focuses on framing the issues in the community. This is done through the social construction of a holistic perspective on the issues that are of concern to the community; these issues are then connected with the skills and personal development required by the members of the community involved in the work. The case example shows how it is important to maintain a focus on the issues identified by the collective decision-making of the community within the structures that have researched need and options for development; in this way, collective concerns can be connected with objective decision-making based on management and resource demands. This should, in turn, be added to the personal development required from the participating community members. The issues need to be considered in tandem with how community members can develop the skills to meet and overcome them.

Community issues need to be framed in a concrete way, along with the specific aims and the actions to achieve those aims, as in task-centred practice. The practitioner also needs to examine how well people are working together and how they can improve their capacity to achieve these aims. Practitioners need to observe how community members carry out innovations and develop their thinking and relationship skills, just as in social work practice with individuals. They do this, however, with a focus on achieving community aims rather than individual empowerment. One of the important strategies for observation and individual development in framing tasks and objectives is looking for changes, contradictions, paradoxes and tensions in relationships and shared actions.

Following on from this, practitioners need to use their own chutzpah to develop from leadership towards co-leadership in which community members increasingly take important roles in responding to community issues. This means focusing not only on the problems and issues in the community, but also moving towards a holistic focus on developing leadership skills in the organization. This is an important middle step towards developing people's intellectual and political skills so that they can achieve a critical consciousness about the social processes that are affecting their community. Figure 8.3 shows these three important steps.

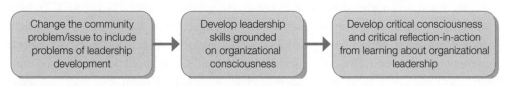

Figure 8.3 Burghardt's grassroots leadership development
Source: Burghardt (2011: 144).

The point of this analysis is to understand that people in the community usually start from an awareness of the issues within their community. They then need to move on to thinking about how the organization can provide leadership to respond to these issues. In developing an understanding of how they can lead organizational change, they learn how to develop their own individual needs and strengths to meet the challenge that the issue will give to the organization. As a result, they can develop an understanding of how to analyse and respond to issues in a more critical way.

As part of this work, the next stage of macro practice is to develop coalitions with other organizations and social networks involving people who can provide resources and experience to support the objective. An important aspect of this is to identify where social divisions such as race, gender, class, sexuality and age are barriers to achieving the objective. Are obstructions being caused by interests in other organizations or resistance to progress that would instead benefit the interests of people in the organization that the practitioners are working with? Historically, social class has been an important factor in the social exclusion of populations in poverty from being able to obtain resources for their community. To work on these issues, people may have to explore their own personal life experience of oppression, identify barriers to progress and patiently identify ways of gaining trust and support.

Case example: Reviving the settlement

In framing the issues, one of the important difficulties facing the settlement was the interests of staff providing different services to maintain their aspect of the organization, so that the staff and parents involved in pre-school provision feared the loss of their work in favour of work with older age groups. However, by engaging in the development of the organization's plan, their contacts with the education sector were helpful. It became possible to plan for development of their work to provide a family centre that would assist local social workers in safeguarding children. This in turn meant that they could offer resources, organizational coalitions with local government departments and social networks with practitioners in the area.

A factor in their re-engagement in the change plan was a developing personal trust in the consultant as the settlement's new director. He was a young father and sometimes placed his children in day care with their service, and they came to see him more as an ally than a male 'superprofessional' with interests in male-oriented services using computers with young people at risk of offending. This loss of trust arose partly from a gender and class division and partly from the way in which he had been appointed to his new post in a top-down way in a financial crisis, rather than through procedures that involved staff in building support for him.

Important aspects of Burghardt's analysis are the importance of the critical analysis and the respect for rights that is one of the shared value principles (see Figure 1.7). Later aspects of Burghardt's analysis focus on developing community practitioners' skills in strategic planning, and on how practitioners can develop skills as front-line supervisors of community members. These skills include critical reflection about actions that community members are taking, and understanding the roles of politicians and the senior managers who are responsible for ensuring the compliance of community organizations with legal requirements and political directions.

Example text: Midgley's (1995, 2010a) social development

Midgley's (1995) book *Social Development* offers a coherent account of social development ideas. Midgley and Conley (2010a) updates this account and includes recent case studies; I have woven some of these updated points into the main theoretical presentation of the 1995 book.

The book sees social development as 'a process of planned social change designed to promote the well-being of the population as a whole in conjunction with a dynamic process of economic development' (p. 25). The aim is to create resources for the community by linking social with economic development, and it rejects the idea that welfare depends on economic growth. Instead, it is important that they go together in concert; social development must be compatible with society's economic objectives. Midgley argues that it transcends both residualist approaches that target welfare on the most needy groups in a society, and also institutional approaches that seek wide state involvement in welfare; there must be a balance between these views in policies on social development. Midgley claims that development is distorted when social progress is not aligned with economic development. This may happen where one group, often a white or colonialist minority, achieves wealth at the expense of an impoverished majority, or where military expenditure diverts money away from the promotion of welfare towards other objectives.

Social development aims to promote people's well-being through creating social changes so that social problems are managed, needs are met and opportunities for advancement are provided. In setting these objectives, Midgley sidesteps potential debates about how and by whom well-being, problems, needs and opportunities are defined. In this way, he accepts the present social order. Social philanthropy, whereby individuals take social responsibility for helping other individuals through ideals of charity in Christianity, or zakat in Islam, is one organized form of welfare. Midgley makes a distinction and draws a connection between social development and social work in the same society. Social development promotes social work, in which educated professionals provide personal help, as well as the provision of social welfare services as institutional structures that improve social well-being.

Social development is unlike these forms of welfare in that it does not deal with individuals by treating them or rehabilitating them to existing structures. Rather, it aims to affect wider groups, such as communities or societies, and the social relations that take place in those societies. It is universalistic rather than selective and seeks growth rather than simply returning people to an existing level of well-being. It seeks also to follow a process of social change through deliberate human action. A long history of idealist social theory suggests that such social interventions can achieve a change in the various directions that a society prefers. An important context for such ideas in the twentieth century was the creation of the welfare state and the development of social planning. These provided, respectively, for extensive social intervention for the general benefit of populations in industrialized societies, and for organizing the environment and social provision to support those interventions. Latterly, attempts have been made to achieve such developments in underdeveloped countries, especially through the agency of the United Nations and similar international organizations.

Social development is a process. The meaning of process is not the same as in psychodynamic theory, where it concerns the interaction between communications, actions, perceptions of these and responses to them. In social development, process is more concerned with the idea that interventions are required in a connected and coherently planned series. The preconditions for achieving social development mean removing obstacles to this progression. Modernization views suggest that cultural and social ideas need to change to facilitate economic and social development, and claim that education and literacy work would overcome traditional attitudes, for example where men's views or tribal interests dominate family decision-making. In addition, population control would reduce the pressures on the family and the community resources of large families. Migration from rural to urban areas should be reduced so as to prevent pressure on urban infrastructures leading to squalid conditions. However, these controls on freedom of action are oppressive, and efforts to impose them have often not been successful. An alternative view about obstacles to social development suggests that government interventions and unrestrained capitalism (for example, land or housing tenure and the control of financial resources) have been just as significant as obstacles to development as have modernizers' social factors.

Other writers, particularly Marxists, have suggested the importance of apocalyptic events to get development moving. For example, Lavalette and Ioakimidis (2011) collected studies of social welfare responses to natural disasters and civil wars; they call this 'social work *in extremis*'. They suggest that indigenous organizations create social structures that provide welfare support for affected populations. These actions are often separate from government responses or may oppose government provision tainted by involvement in conflicts. This can create alternative and sometimes original forms of social work.

According to Midgley (1995), several elements are required for an adequate social development theory:

- An *ideological commitment to progress is an important prerequisite for social development*. However, this concept implies accepting modernist ideas that knowledge and social institutions move forward to a social ideal. Critics of such ideas see the economically developed countries of the West as being part of a process of social, economic and moral decline. Midgley argues that social development theorists do not adequately respond to critics of the idea of progress.
- Development is also taken to require *intervention*. This concept, however, may also be criticized. Intervention can lead to distortions that harm social relations. New Right perspectives oppose intervention because it interferes with the market and freedom of choice. Marxist, neo-populist perspectives argue that planners cannot know and be all things. Small-scale developments responding to local wishes are likely to be more responsive and to concern the real issues faced by disadvantaged groups.
- *Economic factors* must also be considered. Social intervention in the cause of well-being has a value in its own right and not merely as a promoter of economic efficiency. It

should not be subsumed in economic objectives, or made dependent on their achievement. It is difficult to see how to promote economic and social development as part of the same activity, but this is needed. Many individuals, families and small communities that social workers and social development workers deal with need to find effective ways of promoting their economic well-being while also dealing with personal problems.

- *Ideological strategies* that inform social development need to be considered. These are the individualist, collectivist and populist strategies listed in the section on 'Social development ideas', earlier in this chapter.

- The *goals* of social development may be to seek a complete reorganization of society according to some overall plan, or to seek more modest steady improvements through smaller scale changes. Some goals also focus on material improvements, while others focus on personal and group self-fulfilment.

The strategies for social development categorized by Midgley under the three headings mentioned above operate at three levels in societies:

- *Individualistic* strategies focus on helping people to become self-reliant and independent, although not necessarily self-interested. At the national and regional levels, a creative enterprise culture does not put obstacles in people's way. Education and training, personal, financial and advisory support and transitional help away from a dependence on social security or relatives may all help people to achieve economic self-reliance. This may lead to greater personal independence and emotional security. We might take similar approaches with mentally ill people or people with learning disabilities to achieve independence from institutional care. The approach might also be used for young people leaving care. Social workers have often been too concerned with traditional welfare concerns, such as child care, and have failed to ensure that needs for education and opportunities for work and housing have been met. Helping groups of young people to share skills and work together can also benefit them. In small communities, cooperative work or small enterprises using available skills, unpaid work exchange schemes with their own currency or credit unions can be participative ways of encouraging social development.

- *Collectivist* strategies are communitarian in focus. They assume that people in existing social groups can organize themselves to meet their needs and gain control over resources and the issues that face them. This is the basis of community work and community development. The number of links between individuals in a locality are increased, and opportunities for coming together around issues of concern are created. For those who share a problem, such as mental illness, or a human condition, such as being a woman and suffering gender oppression, this can lead to personal support, but more importantly it may also lead to individuals' efforts to gain control of their situation. In other cases, shared responsibility for caring for elderly mentally frail relatives or a shared wish for improvements to local facilities may lead to cooperative work. This kind of work has a long history in community work. Work with community groups may focus on education by studying local or industrial history, literature or writing skills, and artistic work such as music, community photography, painting murals or graffiti, or drama.

■ Government also undertakes development work. *Statist approaches,* that is, those that see the main responsibility for well-being in any society as lying with the government, argue that this should be so because the state embodies the interests and social aspirations of its people. Only the state can develop through large-scale social planning and mobilize considerable resources. At a more individual or group level, the statist approach would be to campaign for service improvements and effective and coherent plans. Movements for equality, social justice and the countering of oppression often rely on achieving legislative change. For example, attempts have been made to change the law to avoid discrimination against disabled people or to promote the availability of services or protection for particular groups.

Midgley proposes an institutional perspective on social development that pluralistically includes elements of all three levels of work. This seeks to mobilize social institutions, including the market, the state and community organizations, to promote people's well-being. Social workers should accept and facilitate the involvement of diverse organizations in social development through managed pluralism, working within the state, in local organizations and in commercial and market enterprises. A degree of training and clearly identified professional roles are required to distinguish social workers with different interests from activists and community members. Social development effort should be located at every level of social organization, not merely locally, but also regionally and nationally, so that these efforts may be mutually supportive.

These approaches are needed to align economic and social development. Formal organizations and social structures are needed to coordinate economic with social development efforts. This might be done by social planning forums. We should plan to ensure that economic development has a direct benefit for social well-being. This might include encouraging landscaping around new industrial developments to benefit householders, social facilities such as day nurseries associated with new factories, and mutual activities such as charitable donations and programmes. In addition, social development activities should be devised that have a benefit for economic development. The community centre should encourage work training in an area with high unemployment, for example. Efforts to reduce crime on housing estates or encourage community businesses with social and economic objectives are another possibility. This also serves to avoid those concerned with unemployment or dereliction in their area seeing social help as irrelevant or of a low priority.

Midgley and Conley (2010a) extend these ideas by incorporating concepts of social investment and the role of social enterprise as ways of developing child welfare, mental health services and work with homeless people.

Conclusion: using macro, social development and social pedagogy ideas

Most social workers will use macro practice from time to time in their work, setting up support groups or local organizations where they have identified important social issues affecting their work. Others may take this up as a specialization. Ideas of social entrepreneurship identify the importance of having a focus on innovation and sustainable financing through developing business alongside social objectives. Social activation emphasizes the importance of stimulating the energies of people who have been excluded from existing social opportunities, and social capital emphasizes how increasing the number and extent of people's social networks can increase the human resources available to everyone in the community.

- Social and community development provide a wide social focus for social workers' interventions to help oppressed people, much more so than systems theory, which focuses on the interpersonal.
- Social development and social pedagogy have developed outside the conventional Western social work literature and offer insights drawn from alternative theoretical and practice perspectives.
- They confirm and promote the existing social order.
- These theories raise questions about how we should see 'progress' and 'development', which we often talk about unthinkingly as positives rather than recognizing the potential losses associated with them. Modernization theories also often assume that the social change they promote is always beneficial, whereas groups with differing interests may have various points of view or be in conflict.
- The detail of community work methods provides a useful codification of experience when dealing with community and social development.

The perspectives considered in the next four chapters incorporate these theories into a more critical perspective of whether the present social order is adequate to meet the needs of oppressed groups within society.

Additional resources

Further reading

Midgley, J. (1995) *Social Development: The Developmental Perspective in Social Welfare* (London: Sage).

Midgley, M. and Conley, A. (eds) (2010) *Social Work and Social Development: Theories and Skills for Developmental Social Work* (New York: Oxford University Press).

A good account of social development theory and practice, mainly in resource-poor countries, and a recent update with case studies.

Nicholls, A. (ed.) (2006) *Social Entrepreneurship: New Models of Sustainable Social Change* (Oxford: Oxford University Press).

A good general text on social entrepreneurship in resource-poor and developed economies, including important contributions by ground-breaking contributors to this field.

Mawson, A. (2008) *The Social Entrepreneur: Making Communities Work* (London: Atlantic).

This account of social entrepreneurship focuses on innovation through community interventions, with many practical examples based on work in London neighbourhood.

Journals

Community Development Journal – Oxford University Press.

Indian Journal of Social Work – Tata Institute of Social Sciences, Mumbai.

Journal of Social Development in Africa – associated with the School of Social Work, Harare, Zimbabwe, this journal is now published online at http://www.ajol.info/index.php/jsda/index. You can gain access to many African journals from AJOL (African Journals Online).

Social Development Issues – International Consortium for Social Development/Lyceum Books, Chicago.

Websites

http://www.un.org/womenwatch/

The WomenWatch website of the United Nations Inter-Agency Network on Women and Gender Equality provides useful links to a wide range of social development issues concerning women.

http://www.infed.org/index.htm, http://www.infed.org/biblio/b-socped.htm

An informal education website, with useful resources on the history and nature of community work. The second page given here offers a well-informed account of social pedagogy.

http://eprints.ioe.ac.uk/view/subjects/Y.html

The government-funded and government-supported project to develop social pedagogy in UK children's residential care provides for the first time good resources in English on this particular form of social pedagogy. The Thomas Coram Research Unit of the University of London Institute of Education provides a database of publications, which include several on social pedagogy and cover the findings and life of the project.

This project also led to the setting up of a group of enthusiasts who operate a website at http://www.socialpedagogyuk.com/, and separately another group who support this work with an informative website at http://social-pedagogy.co.uk/index.htm.

http://www.thewhocarestrust.org.uk/pages/social-pedagogy-what-is-it.html

The good Who Cares? Trust briefing website aimed at young people and professionals who might come across this innovation.

Strengths, narrative and solution practice

9

Main contribution

The main contribution of these perspectives is a forward-looking approach, rejecting 'problem-solving' as a focus for individual help. They help clients and their families to recast apparent problems by looking for strengths in their present lives, allowing them to build positively for the future. A focus on building resilience is an important feature, and increasingly many of the ideas are being picked up in empowerment and critical theories.

Main points

- Strengths, narrative and solution perspectives share a positive forward-looking practice approach based on amplifying the strengths in clients' lives.
- These perspectives share theoretical sources in social psychology and are all influenced by the impact on psychology of postmodernist, social construction ideas (see Chapter 3).
- The origins of these ideas in social psychological and postmodern social construction theories link the narrative, solution and strengths perspectives.
- Postmodernist thinking offers ideas about how power relations are expressed in the way in which people use language. Although it allows for ambiguity and disagreement in how people interpret the world, it may also seem bewilderingly circular in its ways of thinking.
- Concerns that postmodern perspectives lead to moral relativism (see Chapter 1) are countered by their emphasis on the alternatives that are open to people, given practitioners' assistance.
- Clients face difficult realities, and agencies' social order roles require practitioners to manage difficult behaviour and tackle serious social problems. Whether the focus on being positive allows for that is debated.
- In practice, sessions between clients and practitioners focus on positive planning for motivating 'homework' between the sessions.
- Some evidence that a strengths perspective is effective in care (case) management and interpersonal practice with women subjected to domestic violence demonstrates the wide applicability of the approach, but research support for it is as yet weak.

Practice ideas

☐ *Deconstruction* (drawn from the arts and literature) involves taking apart a situation through analysing its elements, and then exploring whose power has made those elements important in the situation.

☐ *Discourse* (drawn from sociological research) explores situations through examining the language used by the people involved. This enables practitioners to understand the different positions that people express or demonstrate about the situation. In turn, this process exposes the tensions and systems of mutual support that exist in responding to the situation.

☐ *Exceptions* are successful behaviours in people's repertoires that practitioners amplify to overcome perceived problems in people's lives.

☐ The *miracle question* helps clients to identify their objectives clearly.

☐ *Narrative* is more than the story that someone tells about their life or an event in it. It includes the way in which the narrative selects aspects of that life or event, as well as the language used to present the narrative. Moreover, an awareness and analysis of how the story is constructed makes it possible to identify alternative constructions that provide the potential for change.

☐ *Scaling* helps clients and practitioners to be specific about their aims and achievements.

Major statements

This chapter brings together interpretations for social work of three perspectives drawn from psychological therapies. Because these developed in the late twentieth and early twenty-first centuries, many social workers still draw on the major statements made by the founders of these perspectives in psychology: White and Epston (1990) in narrative practice, de Shazer (1985) in solution-focused work and the positive psychology of Seligman (1998).

Saleebey's (2009a) strengths-based practice is an important social work foundation for these psychological ideas, but his main work is an edited collection of practice accounts rather than a theoretical text. Connected with strengths-based work is the idea of resilience, applied extensively by Walsh (2011) in family social work and by Greene (2012) in an edited work. In addition, Rapp and Goscha's (2006) important statement of strengths-based ideas, which is supported by research, contains influential strengths-based research as an aspect of case management in mental health. Myers's (2008) concise general interpretation of solution-focused social work is a useful introduction. Similarly, Parton and O'Byrne's (2000) constructive social work (their term, implying that their approach is useful and positive, and also that it uses construction ideas) brings together a sophisticated interpretation of social construction ideas combined with solution-focused practice. However, Greene and Lee's (2011) interpretation of solution-oriented social work is a ground-breaking text, incorporating connections with strengths and narrative ideas. It is used as the example text in this chapter because of the way it brings together many of these ideas based in social psychology, postmodernism and social construction.

The debate summary

The strong argument in favour of these perspectives is their emphasis on building non-judgementally on the positives and achievements in people's lives. Instead of concentrating on the deficits in clients' social relationships or behaviour, you extend their advantages, offer alternative perspectives and in doing so reduce the importance of the deficit in people's lives. A person with physical disabilities, for example, does not want to look at problems in their life that come from the disability; instead they want to find ways of making their life a positive experience. These theories are a powerful source of the shared value principle (see Figure 1.7) of working towards positive objectives.

These practices are also significant implementations of the shared value principles of alliance and rights. All of them focus strongly on involving clients in exploring their own worlds, understanding and participating in decisions and planning interventions. Narrative practice, in particular, emphasizes open-minded listening to the clients' interpretations of important turning points in their lives; the clients and practitioners then work together to co-construct alternative and potentially more satisfactory narratives that will form the basis of new directions in life. Their working together on construction means that this term 'co-construction' becomes an important, often-used concept.

Three connected difficulties arise in critiques of these perspectives; I deal with two first here and then add the third later in the chapter. The first two difficulties are as follows:

■ Being positive does not sufficiently recognize the reality that clients and the people around them experience damaging problems.
■ The social control role of many social work agencies and the social mandate for social work interventions comes from demands for people to manage their behaviour appropriately.

Many people come to practitioners because of the negatives in their lives rather than the positives. Clients may find the unrelentingly positive focus of solution and strengths perspectives unrealistic because they refuse to acknowledge worries about the impact of serious problems in clients' lives. Alternatively, clients may find these approaches disrespectful because they are always shifting the focus onto positives rather than accepting clients' own perceptions of what is important. Clients may want the opportunity to explore and work on their problems (as in cognitive-behavioural therapy [CBT]), or on making sense of their family background or life experience (as in psychodynamic practice) (Walsh, 2010: 248). The answer to this point is that the ethical requirement to secure clients' informed consent to the way you want to work also means exploring alternative possibilities and gaining clients' acceptance of your approach (Payne, 2011a: 50–6). Narrative practice permits a fuller exploration of clients' experiences and the development of alternative perspectives, identifying the ambiguities in life experiences. However, it offers fewer structured guidelines for practice – indeed, this is one of its attractions for practitioners working with complex interpersonal difficulties.

The second point extends the same issue to social expectations of professional practitioners: social work agencies are mandated through policy and law to deal with social problems and difficult or disapproved-of behaviour. Focusing on positive possibilities may raise questions about whether social workers can achieve this social expectation using ideas with a positive focus.

Case example: Solution-focused questioning in child safeguarding

This is an excerpt from a press comment on the 'Baby P' case in the UK, in which a partner of Baby P's mother and his friend who was living with them violently killed an eighteen-month-old infant:

It was this philosophy — Solution Focused Brief Therapy — which ... [the] social services used in their dealings with the benighted mother of poor Baby P. The fact that she was a shockingly bad mother, neglectful and prone to shacking up with violent maniacs, was thus largely ignored, and instead the people charged with the care of Baby P concentrated on what her mother sort of hoped for, in a rather vague sense, in the future. What a fantastically stupid form of 'therapy'. (Liddle, 2009)

A television report about the same case included a more positive balancing comment:

Andrew Turnell, an international expert in solution focused work in child protection, said ... 'Solution focused therapy provides tools that are like scalpels for a doctor, but they have to be used in the context of a risk assessment framework where everybody knows we're talking about the safety of children.' (BBC, 2010)

I juxtapose these comments to show the gap that may arise between common-sense public expectations and competent professional uses of a theoretical idea in social work. Liddle is expressing the not-unreasonable public expectation that, in an important area such as protecting children from violent adults, practitioners should give priority to the social order expectation that parents are not violent to their children, or should focus on the need for the child's living arrangements to change. Turnell, in contrast, makes the point that appropriate and specific training and professional support underlie competent practice, which also has to take account of the social responsibilities and issues of risk and security in the lives of vulnerable people. The professional perspective is that solution work would build or amplify the capacity of Baby P's mother to care for her children and the men's ability to moderate their behaviour, and would not harp on about their difficulties. This approach, however, needs to take place within a safe, protective environment. Liddle's account also illustrates how easy it is to caricature a theoretical concept without fully appreciating all its practice implications, which demonstrates how careful practitioners need to be in presenting their work to outside observers and how assiduous they need to be in implementing all the requirements of the theoretical models they use.

The answer to such complaints about this and other social work theories is also contained in these comments. Liddle complains of the vagueness, the 'sort of' character of the positives that the practitioner was working on. Turnell wants practice to have 'scalpel-like precision'; the weakness in the services' response comes from failing to achieve that. Where necessary, I cover later in the chapter the prescriptions contained in all these forms of practice for challenging present behaviour and assumptions. Turnell's related point is that the service context in which the theory was being used means that its helpful aspects could only benefit clients when they had first been secured from the risks that led to the service's involvement.

This exchange reminds us of the general point about using theory, raised in Chapter 2, that we must use theory with an understanding of what the theory requires us to do, and within the social context and the mandate that our society and agency has been given. You start from the responsibility for safeguarding children and adults, and then use the theory accurately insofar as it furthers those aims.

The third difficulty that arises in critiques of these perspectives is as follows:

■ The reliance on linguistic interventions and changing people's perspectives on their problems makes these approaches inappropriate for persistent and serious social problems and for busy agencies dealing with people with difficult, multiple problems.

This third point connects to the previous critical points: social work deals with serious matters in people's lives, and these cannot be turned round by linguistic gymnastics. To think that would imply a lack of respect for the real problems that clients face. Ideas such as narrative theory emerge from psychotherapy, which does not focus on the service-providing responsibilities of most social workers. Many agencies have to make plans according to legal, management and policy requirements, such as the requirement to create packages of care for people with long-term conditions so that they can live safely at home. Busy practitioners have many service responsibilities, have to juggle insufficient resources in short timescales and do not have the time to use a therapeutic narrative approach.

Practitioners argue three points against these criticisms. First, simply pursuing management or service priorities is a false economy because you do not then explore how clients and their families see the issues, which is one of the assets of narrative theory; this then leads to dissatisfaction and complaints. Second, you fail to focus on clients' priorities. Ethically, this is wrong: the service is for them and is not a rationing system for the agency. Practically, by ignoring clients' priorities, you may fail to engage their participation. Third, your assessment may prove unsatisfactory because you have failed to get a complete picture of the situation. Again, narrative theory points to the possibility of many alternative ways of interpreting and constructing any situation, the events that led to it and the opportunities that might spring from it.

Case example: Putting the forms aside to get the story and find the strengths

Gail was a social worker in a hospital. One of her main roles was arranging for the discharge of older people who had completed their treatment. She was often under pressure to free hospital facilities for other patients and meet clients' wishes – they mostly wanted to go home as soon as possible. In addition, she had to comply with complicated application processes and funding arrangements to get packages of services together.

►

Like many practitioners, however, Gail found it more effective to start from asking about clients' priorities. She brought the forms to the bedside and said, 'I'm going to fill in these forms so that I can make applications for you, but I'm just going to put them aside for a while, so that I can get the whole picture from you. Would you start us off by just telling me, what is the main thing on your mind at the moment?' Gail often found that the client's main priority was a matter of family or home responsibilities rather than the treatment or care options. She would then ask the client to give her a picture of the whole situation and explain how the client came to be in the hospital. This led to a story that explained how the client saw the issues in the home situation. Finally, Gail asked what the client thought was most important about going home. This enabled Gail and the client to focus on the positives in the move and the client's objectives.

As well as there being these difficulties connected with the mandate for social work, Gray (2011) summarizes a range of criticisms stating that the focus on strengths in all of these theories is poorly defined and empirically supported only by anecdotes and case studies rather than rigorous research. Presentations of narrative and solution practice overestimate the practical effect you can have in very deprived and excluded communities. Gray argues that this practice comes close to accepting the individualistic neo-liberal perspective that self-help and mutual support will be sufficient to overcome even major social adversity. Research on solution-focused therapy is 'equivocal' in its outcomes (Corcoran and Pillai, 2009: 240), and the impact of these criticisms is heightened in situations where there are insufficient resources, professional supervision or skill in precisely implementing these theories.

Wider theoretical perspectives

An important social work source of these ideas lies in Saleebey's strengths perspective, with its four main principles:

- Every individual, family, group and community has strengths.
- Troubles may be injurious, but they are an opportunity to grow (a principle we met in crisis work – see Chapter 5).
- Assume that you do not know the limits of people's ability to grow, and take their aspirations seriously.
- People are best served by collaboration (Saleebey, 2009b).

The broader source of these perspectives is social psychological therapies, in contrast to the alternative structured brief psychotherapies that we explored in Chapters 5 and 6. Historic writing in sociology and social psychology, such as the work of Mead (1934), connects how people construct their personal identity into a 'self' through interactions between their mind, with its rational thinking and emotional reactions, and the external social world that they experience. Strengths, narrative and solution practice all rely on and combine social construction and postmodernist thinking with social psychology.

Before we look at the practice, therefore, how have these broad sources influenced this practice? Social work has been aware of social psychology, social construction and post-modernism, but these had little practical impact until strengths, narrative and solution theory interpreted them in a new way.

Social psychology in social work

Social psychology studies how individuals constantly interact within the social groups they play a part in, as well as how relations within and between groups help to create and maintain people's social identities. This includes ideas about how people behave in relation to, and therefore influence, others, and the effects of social factors such as stigma, stereotyping and ideology on behaviour in groups.

Consequently, social psychology considers the effects of communication, and therefore language and speech, on social interactions. 'Communication studies' researches the use of language and other symbols in communication between human beings as individuals, within groups and more widely in organizations and social collectivities (Adler et al., 2011). Social workers use language to influence clients, which means that the communication processes through which they do so gives them power over clients; in addition, research and study on communication assists practitioners' understanding of how they can use patterns of communication effectively. Thompson (2011b) emphasizes the importance of language as an aspect of culture. He shows how people's use of language in communications contains symbols of their culture, as well as how poor communication across cultural boundaries may make social work practice difficult. He also includes a focus on written communication, for example in letters and mobile phone texting. Neurolinguistic programming (Angell, 2011) is a therapeutic practice that originated from the detailed study of the language interactions of therapists, and it offers an understanding of how information received from the environment is processed through language and then organized by an individual during helping activities such as social work.

Role theory explores the creation of roles as a process of constructing ourselves a place in social relations (Lyon, 1993). *Structural-functional role theory* assumes that people occupy positions in social structures. Each position has a role associated with it, and roles are the sets of expectations or behaviours associated with these positions in social structures. How we see our roles affects how well we manage change. *Dramaturgical role theory* (Goffman, 1968) sees roles as 'enactments' of the social expectations attached to a social status. People pick up signs about others in social interactions, and we influence others' views of us by managing the information they receive from us, through *performances*. Our performance is usually idealized so that it includes common social expectations. We emphasize in this way some aspects of our role and conceal others. Some behaviour also reflects role conflicts and ambiguities. Role theory is easy for clients to understand; it also does not criticize them in a personal way, so it contributes easily to intervention. Moreover, role theory takes in a social perspective on behaviour, making it a useful link between behavioural problems and the social environment.

> ### *Pause and reflect* Criticizing social psychology's contribution to social work
>
> Consider criticisms from other theoretical perspectives that may be made of this role analysis, and of the explanations that social psychology provides for Grace and her mother's situation.
>
> #### Case example: Grace caring for her mother
>
> Grace, a middle-aged woman, worked as a secretary, having been divorced by her husband. She had brought up her children successfully alone, and her daughter had stayed at home with her. Her elderly mother, also alone, was blind and later had a fall in her home. The doctor to both families suggested that they should live together, so Grace could provide greater security for her mother. This arrangement became difficult and a social worker was asked to help.
>
> Using ideas from role theory helped to explain that there was *role conflict* here between Grace's working role and her role as a caring daughter; both roles were important to her. This was both *inter*-role conflict, because the work and daughter roles conflicted, and *intra*-role conflict, because it appeared that the mother's expectations about the role of a caring daughter conflicted with Grace's and, indeed, those of the doctor and Grace's daughter, who was still living at home. Looking more deeply into the situation, Grace was suffering from *role ambiguity* – she understood and appreciated all these views of her role as daughter, so she was herself uncertain about how she should behave.

Some suggestions

The focus here is on role theory as an explanation; one weakness, however, is that, unlike other theories, it does not help us to intervene. Psychodynamic theory is a structural-functional theory and therefore resonates with role ideas. Psychodynamic practice would focus on the history of relations between the mother and daughter, and psychodynamic practitioners would use this to explore their changing roles. Crisis theory could be used to explore how the fall was a precipitating event that brought a sequence of life events to a head in the crisis; at this point, the conflict over Grace's caring role could allow the strong differences in social attitudes to the caring role to be brought out and dealt with. Feminist theory would criticize the mother's and the doctor's assumptions about the role of women as carers. Social psychology focuses on social identity, so while it identifies the issue of women's identities in this situation, it does so with a neutral stance, while feminism makes a more critical analysis of sexist assumptions about the role of women.

This brief summary of alternative theoretical frameworks that might be applied to the same case shows how social psychological theories produce interesting analyses but fail to offer useful practice prescriptions or directions for practice. As a result, practice theory has not directly emerged from social psychology a separate theory in its own right.

Social construction ideas

The impact of social construction and postmodernist ideas in the 1990s was crucial in extending social work's use of ideas from social psychology. In earlier chapters, we saw how these ideas propose that people learn to understand the world around them as they experience the culture and history of their society through developing shared understandings and interpretations of the world as it affects them. Therefore, patterns of social relationships create shared social expectations about how people should behave in different social settings. Many practitioners find this theory attractive since it offers the possibility of achieving changes in behaviour by changing social structures around clients and, more importantly, by changing perceptions of and interactions about social expectations.

It is important to understand the difference between social construction and individual constructions of the world. Kelly's (1955) *personal construct theory* proposed that each individual manages their behaviour according to 'constructs' or pictures of the situation in their mind. Everyone constructs events differently from each other. Therefore, looking at and changing people's constructs may help to change their behaviour. Figure 9.1a illustrates how personal constructs are the internal pictures of the world that people build up through their own perceptions, and shows how each personal construct differs from other people's constructs. Looking at the diagram, you can see that the picture of the interview is reversed; each person sees it differently because they have processed the information about what is going on in the interview from their own point of view.

The study and therapeutic use of perceptions and interpretations of the world is often called 'constructivist' and relates to cognitive therapies. Constructivist practice focuses on misperceptions and inappropriate thinking, which means that accurate perceptions are not well processed. This has recently extended into the use of neuroscience in therapy, as we saw in Chapter 6.

(a) Personal constructs are individual perspectives

(b) Social constructs correspond with shared social realities

Figure 9.1 Personal and social constructs compared

As we saw in Chapter 1, social construction differs from these ideas about personal constructs. Figure 9.1b illustrates social constructions. It shows that people build up shared pictures of the world. They do this through social interactions with each other, using language and creating shared ideas expressed in language. This social and linguistic process takes place in social and historical contexts. Through these interactions, they come to have the same sense of what is real in the social and cultural context that they share. Practice based on these ideas is often called 'constructionist'. Practice focuses on how the shared picture has been built up and how the impact of such shared conceptions or the context in which they have their effects may be changed.

Strictly, then, constructivist theory is about how we process the reality around us through perceptions, through the way our brains work and through our rational thinking. Social psychological construction theory, on the other hand, is strictly about how we use language in our interactions with other people to create a shared understanding of reality. However, not all writers make this firm distinction between constructivist and constructionist ideas. This is because many people see these practices as interrelated because they are all concerned with constructions and how they may be changed.

Three areas of social construction theory are important for social work (Payne, 1999a):

- the social construction of reality;
- claims-making in the formation of social problems;
- sociological work in social categories and social differences.

The *social construction of reality* that we met in Chapter 1 shows how shared social constructions contribute to socializing individuals into social groups and society. In this way, social ideas are so widely shared that they become a reality for the participants in that society. *Social problems* arise when a social group successfully makes a claim about a social issue, particularly using mass media, that it is problematic and requires social and political action. The argument is that social problems are not themselves inherently problematic: rather, their problematic status is created by 'claims-making'.

Pause and reflect Underlying claims of constructions about social problems

Examine these two statements and consider what constructions of marriage and social stability underlie the claims about divorce.

Case example: Claims about divorce

Here are two views taken from two groups campaigning on the internet about divorce:

[The] availability of no-fault divorce has served to increase family dissolution at a rate greater than ever before in history; furthermore, it undermines the institution of marriage itself. (Craven, 2009)

We owe all the wonderful aspects of modern marriage to one thing: divorce. Divorce means choice ..., that two people do not have to remain bound to each other until the grave ... Divorce means that human beings can determine the path their life will take ... divorce is also the great equalizer, and the hallmark of a truly advanced society in terms of women's rights. No woman can ever claim to feel 'like property' or 'subjugated by men' where are there are equitable divorce laws in place. (Bell, 2011)

Some suggestions

The first view presented in the case example claims that divorce is a social problem, while the second claims it as a social benefit. Underlying the first claim are assumptions that marriage creates social stability and is desirable, and that effective divorce leads to instability and is undesirable. The second claim suggests that, on the contrary, the availability of divorce brings social benefits that enhance social stability. Claims-making in the formation of social problems is a special case of the social construction of reality. It shows how groups create social constructions about particular aspects of our social life.

Work on *human categories* points out that many apparently physically determined human categories, such as men and women, become overlaid by social assumptions and behaviour. So, because only women can be mothers, people assume that being caring is a 'natural' female characteristic, when some women are socialized and perhaps pressed into accepting caring roles contrary to their individual preferences. Research through detailed conversation analysis demonstrates that the assumptions of the people involved, or organizations and social structures, often create human categories (Jokinen et al., 1999; Karvinen et al., 1999; Hall et al., 2003). For example, Juhila (2003) points out that, in a social work relationship, it appears that only two roles are available – social worker and client – and that these are asymmetrical in power. The social worker has institutional power drawn from professional knowledge and authority from being part of the agency, while the client controls access to personal information and family relationships. More complex relationships than this are possible, and different kinds of social work relationships might be imagined. Feminists, for example, seek greater equality (see Chapter 13).

All this work draws attention to how analysing human interactions carefully gives access to a complex understanding of how identity and behaviour is created in social relations. Understanding this, practitioners can use similar interactions to change people's perceptions and social constructions, and thus change their behaviour and social relationships. This possibility is the source of constructionist social work.

We saw in Chapter 1 that critical social psychology studies how groups and individuals construct their identity. Conventional psychology assumes a fundamental personal identity, the 'self'; we saw in Chapter 4 that this is also important in psychodynamic psychology. Critical psychology says that consciousness and the self emerge from the meanings constructed by participants in social relations and their practices within those relations (Wetherell and Maybin, 1996). This happens through a reflexive cycle in which how we see the outside world is interpreted through our understandings, language and power relations. These interpretations then lead us to behave in ways that may reinforce or contest such social practices. Thus, social construction in psychology emphasizes the possibility of change in response to social relationships, such as those that a social worker or therapist might create, rather than there being an unchangeable basic personality.

The French philosopher Foucault has been an important influence on the development of these ideas (Chambon et al., 1999). Irving (2009) identified three phases of the development of Foucault's theory. The first examined how the social and human sciences, including social work, created 'epistemes' – conceptual frameworks that were used to create moral and legal norms and establish regulatory practices in society. Social work practice is one of these, regulating people's behaviour so that they live according to accepted moral and legal assumptions. In the second phase of development, Foucault's analysis looked at how knowledge is managed by powerful social structures to prevent hidden or subjugated knowledge from emerging into people's awareness. The third phase concerned how people used experiences in their lives to transform their 'self'.

Witkin and Saleebey (2007) propose a social work that achieves transformations through such methods as 'en-voicing' and 're-enchantment', using different forms of talk, writing and the use of art to explore ambiguity and uncertainty in knowledge. Similarly, Borden (2010b) brings together a range of practice approaches that seek to express and work on less obvious aspects of life. These include psychobiography, in which people are enabled to explore valuable aspects of their life experience so that they may connect internal emotional reactions to external realities that have affected their lives (Clark, 2010). Another possibility explored in Borden's book is the use of reminiscence and life story work to help people secure their personal identity as their life changes; this will help in enriching personal relationships between older or disabled people and their family carers (Gibson, 2011). Kemp's (2010) research proposes that a better understanding of how people experience different geographical places and physical spaces in their lives may also be an important factor in practice.

In all these examples, helping people to think in alternative ways about their experience of their lives and their environment makes it possible for practitioners to renew or redirect clients' understanding of their lives and the opportunities that may be open to them in the future. Narrative theory particularly picks up these ideas and seeks to open up such alternatives and new directions.

Modernism and postmodernism in social work

Many people argue, however, that traditional approaches to social work disparage the flexibility of thinking and practice implied by this focus on the availability of alternative interpretations, which is implied by postmodern and social construction ideas. This is because social work has often been regarded as *modernist* because it represents universal and timeless humanistic ideas that people in an ordered society are responsible for others. Its methods have always assumed, again humanistically, that human beings can and should manage their lives using their rational minds, and that helping can and should use evidence-based practice, drawing on knowledge gained through positivist scientific methods (Payne, 2011a). These in turn assume that the world can be known through observation and experiment. In addition, social work contends that human beings can be understood through research relying on rational analysis based on external observation (Brechin and Sidell, 2000). Because of its modernism, many of social work's theories seek 'grand narratives', that is, overall perspectives that offer a strategy for collecting evidence that will eventually explain human life and the development of society in a general way.

Postmodernism contests this view that the world and human beings may be understood rationally through evidence built up into one overall perspective of human society. It therefore disturbs the stability of some of the assumptions that have been held to underlie social work practice. Postmodernism and modernism are not, however, mutually exclusive alternative ways of thinking, because they coexist and interact, and both can benefit practitioners in undertaking social work. Moreover, the approach of postmodernism to social issues reflects the reality of a more complex and nuanced human society in a better way than a single, perhaps oversimplified, perspective can ever do.

Postmodernism contains two elements: a set of ideas and a set of social trends emphasizing those ideas within social relations. Postmodernism does not cancel out modernism. Instead, the importance of postmodernism is that it sets up an opposition or discourse about modernist ideas. Its ideas say, 'Modernist ideas are not the only way of looking at things; consider alternatives.' Postmodernist social trends say, 'A characteristic of present-day societies is that they are open to engaging with alternatives, rather than being a single set of social assumptions' (Chambon and Irving, 1994).

The main implication of postmodernist thinking for social work practice is an assumption that practitioners can always find alternatives to any system of social thinking. Therefore, any social order, anything that says this is how the world is, or how it should be, cannot be taken for granted. Postmodernism is interpretivist (Brechin and Sidell, 2000); it points to how knowledge is biased by the decisions of researchers and practitioners to choose natural and social events to observe and investigate, and also biased by the way they choose to investigate and work on the issues that they identify. We met these ideas in Chapter 1.

Practice ideas from postmodernism: deconstruction and discourse

Deconstruction and discourse are important practice ideas derived from postmodernism; they connect with the importance in all social work of understanding and interpreting communication of many different kinds.

Deconstruction originates in the arts and literature (Bertens, 1995: Ch. 5). It starts from understanding a situation by taking it apart to see its elements more clearly. More than this, it implies 'self-reflexivity'. What this means is that any communication contains a message relevant to a particular situation, *and also* a message or analysis about how communication and analysis are carried out in this setting, *and also* a message about the nature of the setting or social institutions within which the communication is occurring. Understanding the ways in which communications are carried out and their institutional context allows you to identify important aspects of social relationships, in particular of the use of power between different social groups. Communication is important because deconstruction works by looking at how the people involved use language.

Case example: Talking to children about death

I work in a hospice, a social institution that cares for people who are dying in the advanced stages of serious illnesses and people who are bereaved; this service is called palliative care. Many younger and middle-aged dying people have children, but they often do not talk to their children about their illness and impending death. Among the reasons for this is that intense efforts are made by healthcare professionals to cure their illness, and patients often maintain hope in the possibility of cure. It is also a social convention that parents protect their children from unpleasantness. As a result, they avoid telling their children about their illness until they are close to death, do not plan how their children will be cared for after their death and may refuse to allow children to go to the funeral of the parent who has died.

Palliative care social workers often advise parents in this position quite strongly to be open about their illness and death, but family members often resist this advice. In promoting openness in this way, the social workers are communicating an analysis of the situation that parents are often not familiar with in their ordinary social setting, because parents usually try to protect their children from the unpleasant aspects of life. This is also an unfamiliar view in healthcare organizations, such as hospitals, where the focus is on cure rather than planning for death. Moreover, practitioners are demonstrating that the hospice is a different kind of healthcare institution. Other patients at the hospice also communicate outside the social convention, demonstrating different kinds of communication and showing that this is a place where communication is different from what is conventional. For example, one patient told me that he watched and listened to how other people in the day centre explained their illness to other people. He said this helped him learn alternative ways of talking to members of his family about his own illness and approaching death.

Such a failure to be open with children about their parents' serious illness enables us to identify a power imbalance in relationships. Parents do not accord children the same rights to knowledge as adults; this identifies children's limited power in their social relationships with adults (Reith and Payne, 2009). This important personal and interpersonal decision is guided by social relationships and expectations. Views revealed in discussion with dying people and their families express attitudes about parental responsibility and childhood that are held within the culture of the people involved. Uncertainty in the public mind about these issues is often dramatized in radio and television programmes and discussions.

Moreover, there is a clear discourse here. Discourses are social interactions, that is, interactions between people and sometimes among groups of people (Fairclough, 1992). These interactions are expressed in language; they enable people in social groups and societies to build up a shared understanding of the meaning of pieces of behaviour. So people understand what dying may mean because other people explain it to them, or because they see coverage on television programmes, or because in discussing the world they gain an impression of what it is, or because they actually experience it happening to someone else.

The language used in any discourse is important, but discourses may also include actions, discussion and writing because meaning is demonstrated by what people do as well as what they say and write. For example, parents talking about a relative's death often go quiet when their children enter the room; the children get a picture of what is going on from this behaviour, but they may interpret their parents incorrectly. The child may come to think that they are to blame for a relative's death, for example through being too noisy when the relative was ill at home.

The idea of discourse allows us to rise above any particular interaction and ask about the social constructions and power relations represented within it. When I talk openly about the dying process with a client who is dying, I demonstrate a position in the cultural discourse about openness. The client may later talk with a relative who does not like to express emotions about dying. If the client then talks to a third person unconnected with their family, they might choose either position – openness or discretion – or indeed some compromise. By looking at a succession of behaviours like this, the discourse and some of the power relations within it become clearer. How culturally free, for example, is the client to adopt my open position with someone who believes that it is socially wrong to talk about death? Having a spouse who prefers discretion may prevent both from adopting a more open position with another relative.

By helping people to deconstruct discourses in their lives, social workers can give people greater power in their relationships with others. This is because giving people a broader experience of alternatives in social relationships offers them 'social capital'; we met this concept in Chapter 8. Bourdieu (1977) emphasizes the importance of the capital held by individuals and groups within their fields (Smith, 2001: 137–9). This gives them power – the capacity to influence the fields they are involved in. *Economic capital* is the accumulation of resources that gives people and groups the financial power to achieve influence. *Cultural capital* is the capacity to understand and interpret the world around us in complex ways. People gain influence if they have secure and well-understood ideas about how to interpret the world, such as those offered by integration within a profession such as social work. *Social capital* is the power that we gain by having wide and supportive networks of relationships.

Social science often focuses on economic capital, but postmodernism suggests that cultural and social capital can be just as important in giving people opportunities to gain power over their environment. An example of this is the man, described above, who learned from other patients in the hospice day centre how to discuss his death with his family members. He gained greater cultural and social capital because, through experiencing the hospice, he gained alternative ways of interpreting how to manage the reality that a person is dying (cultural capital) and how to gain support without alienating family members who did not want to talk with him about his death (social capital).

Connections

We have seen that strengths, narrative and solution perspectives on social work make important links between therapeutic psychological models of practice and postmodernist social construction theories, which in turn link to and have influenced critical and feminist ideas. They maintain the trend in present-day psychology and psychotherapy, as well in the shared value principles of social work (see Figure 1.7), to define and work on specific behaviours; however, they shift the focus in CBT and task-centred practice from looking for problematic behaviours towards looking for specific behavioural objectives in the future. As a result, people who like the specificity of CBT often remain comfortable with narrative, solution and strengths practice even though it incorporates more flexible and interpretive techniques. Part of the reason is that research on solution-focused practice has come from a psychological mode of research, looking at the success of the model in achieving individual behavioural change. Another reason is that more interpretive ideas that nevertheless respect cognitive-behavioural thinking make a useful addition to the practice options available in CBT.

Similarly, by incorporating social construction ideas, strengths, narrative and solution ideas offer an important practice dimension for critical and feminist theory because they offer specific practice techniques that can be used in the more equal dialogue methods used in these forms of practice.

An example of the interconnections is Milner's (2001) work with women subjected to domestic violence. Milner links narrative and solution-focused approaches with feminist thinking in discussing her work with young women who have been abused as children or in violent domestic relationships with men. Part of her approach in working with women is 'serious gossip'; in this, she shares with other women who are clients important emotions about the clients' experiences, as well as laughter and tears about events in their lives. She argues that women who have been abused in their lives often need a feeling of safety and control in their lives. They may blame themselves unrealistically for what has happened to them (and may have been led to that self-blame by the way in which their abusers blame them for provocative or difficult behaviour); they may also accept a diagnosis of depression from the mental health services. This leads to a discourse between practitioners and clients that focuses on a reflexive discussion concerned with valuing yourself, and 'your self', for example as a carer or emotional support in the family. It involves helping women to set realistic personal responsibility for, and in, their relationships, and to explore the uncertainties. This helps women to create resistance to oppression by subverting the problem, setting boundaries and relationship styles that resist oppressive or violent behaviour in their relationships.

Narrative discussion with abusing men is different (Milner, 2001: Ch. 4). They are rarely voluntary users of social work services, often resisting involvement in personal discussion until they become involuntary clients, for example as offenders or drug users. Male service users often have an internal dialectic (an unspoken tension reflecting competing responsibilities and social roles) about being dominant and controlling in their relationships and in their work settings. They need to find alternative ways of valuing themselves as men and in their relationships with women.

The politics of narrative, solution and strengths practice

Thus, the claims made by solution-focused practice differentiate it from other psychotherapies, while drawing on some aspects of psychotherapeutic practice in other traditions. In Figure 9.2, I summarize Myers's (2008: Ch. 3) useful analysis of the contrasts between solution-focused and traditional social work theories. Solution-focused practitioners reject the focus on emotions and how problems have arisen from past experiences that is typical of psychodynamic practice. Solution-focused practice draws its emphasis on looking at specific behaviours and competences from CBT, the currently dominant therapeutic approach in clinical psychology. However, it does not look backwards at 'antecedents' as a way of changing behaviour, but concentrates on planning for objectives. From the humanistic psychologies, solution-focused practice derives an emphasis on exploring how people interpret their experiences, and on engaging clients' participation. However, the solution-focused approach differs from psychodynamic and humanistic therapies because it rejects practitioners' expertise in understanding and interpreting behaviours according to some existing therapeutic model of humanity. It also avoids looking at the broader emotional and holistic explorations that psychodynamic and humanistic psychologies propose.

Figure 9.2 Myers's differences between solution-focused and traditional social work

Solution-focused practice	Traditional practice
Accept people's experiences	Investigate 'truth'
Search for solutions	Understand the causes or sources of problems
Focus on competences	Focus on the problems that people experience
Focus on what people want to talk about	Focus on past issues that are theorized as relevant
Focus on behaviour rather than emotions	Focus on emotions linked to past events
Avoid diagnosis, categorization and pathology	Analyse problems that are theorized as important
Be respectfully uncertain	Draw inferences based on theorized explanations
Avoid blame and focus on good attributes	Make normative assumptions about appropriate behaviour
The practitioner is the expert on techniques and processes	The practitioner makes sense of and 'solves' the problem

Source: Myers (2008).

Values issues

I have suggested that these theories present two value issues to practitioners. First, in its social order role, the social work profession is expected to enforce the accepted moral expectations of the people it works with (Payne, 1999b). The second issue is that the moral response to this may be refusing to blame people when they have no responsibility and working to improve the situation.

Some writers suggest that postmodernist thinking therefore requires a moral and political relativism, which argues that nothing can be known or finally agreed. Not so: postmodernism instead asks us to seek out and examine alternative ways of seeing what we think we know and what we expect. Looking at possible alternatives allows us to test out how complete our present understanding is. Moreover, where we do find alternative explanations, it invites us to seek more complete understandings that allow us to see how several alternatives may be true (Fawcett, 2009).

Case example: A disabled man's allowance is withdrawn

The mother of a disabled man in his twenties was angry at the withdrawal of a financial allowance that paid his expenses to visit her regularly in her home. His social worker's practice focused on her concerns and on the psychological aspects of social work, thinking that the mother had made her son overdependent on her and was behaving irrationally because his dependence met her emotional needs. From this point of view, the son would benefit from greater independence. Ideas from the independent living movement for disabled people support this interpretation.

However, from a family resilience point of view, both the man and his mother were strengthened by maintaining the contact between them. A feminist theorist might suggest that the practitioner was viewing the mother's strong emotional response negatively. Perhaps this was a paternalistic, rationalistic assumption that calmer rational thinking should dominate a relationship between a parent and a man in his twenties. Critical social work theory might emphasize the importance of public financial support for vulnerable and deprived groups such as disabled or bereaved people in the community. In this view, withdrawing the allowance created appropriate anger. A community activist might well value the continuing relationship between mother and adult son as evidence of good community and interpersonal links.

This example draws attention to two things. First, different people can look at the same situation in many different ways. Second, we should explore the evidence for the different interpretations of situations if we are to understand them in a more complex way. Social events and relationships, particularly in the view of narrative practice, are always complex, shaded by the social histories of the event and the relationships that are part of it. Understanding complex situations requires social workers to see them from alternative interpretations, as viewed by different actors in the situation. Moreover, far from rejecting concrete evidence, a complex, in-the-round understanding of the situation requires a greater attention to evidence and careful research; this is because it allows us to separate the different strands and varying points of view within the complexity and decide which are relevant and which are not. Otherwise, we work on a limited caricature of the situation.

Rather than rejecting social order and social structure, postmodernism accepts that social order is valuable and necessary, but it asks us to understand the complexity and implications of the present social orders and structures and of possible alternatives to them. Social workers need to examine different positions about the social order and how it is changing if they are to help their clients deal with a complex situation in which there may be many different competing attitudes to be resolved. Thus, it is important for social workers to explore debates and discourses about important issues in society, so that they can follow trends on issues of concern in social work, such as the role of the family. Examining these debates enables practitioners to understand who has power and influence in that discourse, both widely in society and between the individuals and family members they may be working with.

Applications

Many accounts of the application of strengths, narrative and solution perspectives treat these as separate practice theories, deriving, as we have seen, from separate psychological therapies. However, as this chapter shows, they have a shared theoretical source in social construction theory in social psychology, and in related ideas such as postmodernism. Greene and Lee's (2011) book shifts from the terminology of 'solution-focused' as part of a move away from separate theoretical traditions, incorporating strengths, solution and narrative ideas together. Hence, they rename their approach 'solution-oriented', for the same reason that Parton and O'Byrne (2000) referred to 'constructive' social work. They explicitly connect the development of their ideas with constructivist and social construction ideas, and with ideas about resilience and positive psychology.

Example text: Greene and Lee (2011) on solution-oriented practice

Figure 9.3 sets out Greene and Lee's (2011) framework for solution-oriented practice.

Figure 9.3 Solution-oriented practice framework

Action	Aim
Engage the client	Co-constructing a collaborative therapeutic framework
Listen to the client's story	Defining and deconstructing the client's view of the main presenting problems
Define the client's view of the outcome goals	Making the client's perspective concrete, specific and focused on behaviour
Identify and amplify the client's view of successful solution patterns	Identifying what happens when things are better or the problem is less frequent, less intense or non-existent
Intervene to disrupt patterns maintaining the situation	Changing first-order patterns to achieve second-order change
Termination and follow-up	Enabling clients to accomplish personally meaningful goals that will lead to completion of the intervention and engage processes of self-evaluation for both practitioner and client

Source: Greene and Lee (2011).

The first phase is engagement, and in this and subsequent formulations of practice, we see the current shared value principles fully in use (see Figure 1.7). Practitioners should emphasize collaboration by their use of language: what do you want work on today?, what can we work on together today? They assume that clients have strengths to bring to the work, and when clients mention problems, practitioners redirect their thinking towards strengths. Practitioners also avoid getting involved in using service jargon or psychological or medical diagnoses as the basis of their work. Instead, they start from being curious about what clients want to achieve, using that curiosity to help clients define the aims of their joint work. They work with the client's language, values and ideas about how to change. An important aim is to externalize the problem: clients are people with problems; they are not themselves problems. Practitioners should aim to be empathic in responding to clients' experiences and to demonstrate an unconditional positive regard, not judging clients but accepting what some might see as their failings, so that they can move forward to work positively.

Case example: Approaching a child safeguarding visit with a mother

Gillian was a child protection social worker visiting Hazel, a mother with two children who was considered to be in need of help and support. She started off by asking what Hazel she would like to work on today. Hazel, however, was still angry about what she saw as criticism of her child care skills from a recent child safeguarding conference she had attended. She said that since Gillian was checking up on whether her children needed protection, perhaps she should examine them. Gillian suggested that they should both watch the children playing for a while and talk over the particular ways in which they had developed since the last time she visited. She asked Hazel to talk about the things she could see had improved in the children's play. This initial response concentrated on specific behaviours rather than broad labels about 'poor parenting' and on positive improvements that could be reinforced. Gillian also got Hazel to work with her, rather than taking responsibility for deciding what to do, although she proposed a shared action plan as a practical basis for making further decisions.

The second stage of Greene and Lee's (2011) framework involves defining and deconstructing problems from clients' perspectives. Two important points to start with are that diagnostic labels, such as 'depressed' or 'drug user', are full of assumptions that we should focus on identifiable problems. Using problem labels leads us to treat the client as 'a' or 'the' problem and to think of the problem as an unchanging state that defines the client, rather than as something that affects them in an aspect of their personality or a part of their life. Talking about problems also sustains clients, families and other agencies in the assumption that the main role of the practitioner lies in resolving a problem. Gillian and the agencies involved in safeguarding children in her area see Hazel as a poor parent instead of seeing her range of parental behaviours, some helpful, some not, and the variety of other social pressures placed on her.

Solution-oriented practice uses clients themselves as assessors, starting with a narrative approach and asking them to tell their story. As they do so, they define different elements of the situation that they are trying to deal with. In particular, the client should be the assessor of what is important in the narrative for contributing to plans for intervention, in the same way that task-centred practice (see Chapter 5) works with clients' priorities. As the process of talking through the narrative in solution-oriented practice goes on, practitioners should maintain a focus on what clients can do and on their strengths. In uncovering clients' stories, 'staying on the surface' is important, so that you focus on what clients are concerned about now rather than elaborating on what led up to this point. As you listen, you try to get clients to focus on and define the precise issue they are trying to deal with, what they have done to work on it and what they did that was successful. In addition, you extract possible resources in the client, family or community that they might have used but did not. You then try to identify the client's main goal, using scales: 'On a scale of one to ten, how much do you want to deal with your worries about your daughter?'

The next stage of defining outcomes goals is particularly crucial and marks a shift in Greene and Lee's (2011) presentation from an emphasis on narrative to a process that is particularly characteristic of the solution practice. Research on goals and the experience of defining them more generally in clinical psychology and social learning, summarized in Figure 9.4, supports the approach.

Figure 9.4 Research and experience supporting goal definition

Theoretical assumptions about having goals	• This directs attention and effort towards relevant aims and away from irrelevant aims
	• It energizes participation
	• It supports persistence
	• It leads to a search for relevant knowledge and strategies
People can use goals better if ...	• They are adjusted to clients' present capacities
	• Clients' capacity is improved by training
	• You show clients you have confidence in their capacity
	• You model how to achieve the goal
Goals should be ...	• Personally meaningful and important to clients, leading to improvements in their lives
	• Small enough to be achieved
	• Concrete, specific and behavioural so that you can measure success
	• Defined positively as achievement, rather than negatively as stopping the process
	• Realistic, bearing in mind other aspects of clients' lives

Source: Greene and Lee (2011).

Greene and Lee (2011) borrow from solution-focused practice some useful standard questions that you can use as part of goal-setting, which I summarize in Figure 9.5. Some of these are famous formulations, strongly associated with particular styles of therapy; others are sensible strategies to include important issues. Scaling can also be taken forward in more detail. For example, you can ask clients to scale from one to ten how clients would rank themselves when they decided to approach or were referred to the agency, their rank now, what their rank would be when the problem was less serious, and the rank that they are aiming at.

In the next stage, you find out possible solutions from within the client's present pattern of behaviour and amplify them. You do this within a session and then set a task for clients to do as homework.

The important point here is that research shows that clients do better if they have positive expectations of success, so you are asking questions not only to find things out, but also to provide a 'scaffolding' to build up clients' confidence and motivation. We saw this in the questions that helped to set goals, presented in Figure 9.5. Scaffolding is a collection of external supports that allow learning to take place and can later be discarded, so that you do not have to go through this procedure for ever. The practitioner introduces these supports, mainly by the way they use language: you focus on things that can change, and whose change will create a new situation. You do this by identifying positives in events that have already taken place:

▪ between deciding to come or being referred for help and the present time;
▪ when something that is usually or often a problem worked without problems – forming exceptions to the usual pattern of events;
▪ when the client had past successes but does not achieve these now;
▪ when the client has recently been successful but there are still worries that a past pattern of failure may recur;
▪ where the client or family have very severe problems but are coping – what has enabled them to cope?

Figure 9.5 Useful goal-setting questions

Questions	Illustration	Comment
The miracle question	This might seem a strange question: if there were a miracle and this problem was solved overnight, how would you know the miracle had happened when you woke up in the morning?	Enables you to be precise about the change you are looking for – helps to clarify your goal
The time machine question	If you could travel in a time machine into the future, to a point when this problem had been solved, what would be better for you? What would people say about you that would tell you this problem had been solved?	Enables you to be precise about what the gains would be, individually and in relationships – a motivating factor
Outcome questions	If I met you in the street three months after our final session together – If I were a fly on the wall at your home or office for a day – If I made a video of you now and another one the day before our last session – • What would I notice that would be different about you or your situation? What would you tell me that showed that you no longer had this problem?	Clarifies the precise behaviours and situations you are aiming at
Follow-up questions	• What would have to happen to show that the miracle had started? • If a small part of the miracle had happened, what would you notice that was different? • When are the times that the miracle begins to happen? • What would need to happen for those times to occur more often?	Clarifies possible steps toward the goal
Relationship questions	• Who would be the first person to notice that something was different? • What would they notice? • What would it mean to them?	Connects the goals to improved relationships – a motivating factor

Source: Green and Lee (2011): 82–90.

You follow these points up by asking if these are changes or exceptions that the client would like to continue, and clarifying what happened to lead to the change, exception, success or coping behaviour. The aim will be to repeat these behaviours or situations more frequently.

Using language means getting clients to be specific in their descriptions of behaviour and events. For example, if a client says, 'I get anxious about going to school/work/ the shops', you ask: 'How do you know when you're getting anxious?' or 'What precisely do you get anxious about?' Look for nouns and verbs that are vague. Comparisons, judgements or 'nominalizations' – in which a word is used to describe the client's state – can all be challenged. You ask: 'Badly behaved compared with who or what standard?', or 'Tell me about when you were successful with that.' You should also challenge clients' language of 'lost agency' – when how they speak suggests that they do not think they have any options or control over what happens. Avoid asking 'What are your problems?' or 'Why have you been referred?' but 'What do you want to work on today?' The idea of reframing clients' understanding of behaviour comes from family therapy; you present, as a possibility, alternative interpretations of clients' negative judgements about situations.

Narrative therapy also introduces the idea of 're-storying' the client's narrative. As they tell you their story, you identify exceptions that provide 'sparkling moments' or unique outcomes when things went well, and then you build upon those. By finding out in more detail what went right, you can create a new story and 'thicken' its plot. Some possibilities are set out in White's (2007) formulation of narrative strategies, summarized in Figure 9.6, to which I have added some practice examples. This is part of continuing development in narrative theory.

What stands out from White's moving and detailed case studies is the care with which he gets even very disturbed people to participate in working things out for themselves. 'Highlighting unique outcomes', for example, is similar to the 'exceptions' we find in solution-focused practice; that is, they are descriptions of occasions when the people involved did not experience the problem that they are worried about. White does not point up the exceptions himself. Rather he gets the participants to work through the 'scaffolding' of expressing their surprise and appreciation of how things went well, and then to build up to some explanations of why that might be by looking at the event in more detail. Only then does he encourage them to take the logical step of making generalizations about what works for them, and finally to think about plans for the future. Doing this work for them, he says, can be an imposition 'and risks alienating people who seek consultation' (White, 2007: 217). The important point is the detail of how to use participants' own stories and thinking about them to build up to plans, rather than relying on therapeutic assumptions of what works, which is what a structured theory, such as cognitive-behavioural methods, would propose.

Figure 9.6 White's mapping of narrative practice

Practice	Explanation	Examples
Externalizing conversations – treat the problem as something outside the client; it does not define them and come from how they are	Many people believe that problems in life come from their identity, others' identities or the relationships between our identities. When we act in line with these beliefs, we reinforce them as 'truths' about these identities	Parents believe that their child's behaviour comes from a psychological disorder. White asks the child to paint a picture of the disorder's twin and gets the parents to cooperate in reminding him to do so. They can then talk about the features of the disorder
Re-authoring conversations – ask people to develop their narrative to include 'missing' or neglected aspects of it	Many people can tell a story of their problems, its history and the predicament in which it places them. Re-authoring allows them to focus on other, less problematic aspects of it	A mother fears her teenage son is considering suicide because of a pointless existence. She knew he was concerned more about her than himself when her estranged abusive husband was violent. White asks her to tell him stories about other things that show that she was precious to him. This produces evidence of much positive behaviour, which shows that he had not 'messed up' in life; White asks her to keep telling these stories to her son to remind him of what he can achieve
Re-membering conversations – ask people to revise significant people and identities in their life story, making some more important and others less so	People can re-engage positively with relationships in their past and value them, consequently valuing themselves in those relationships	A woman feels worthless because of childhood abuse, but she tells a story about a neighbour who took her in, fed her and taught her new skills. White asks questions about the aspects of her personality and skills that the neighbour valued
Definitional ceremonies – engage witnesses external to the story to explain what aspects of the story they were drawn to or interested in. The observer then retells the story, offering how it resonates with them and then how the story has moved them on in their understanding	People can hear external observers' perceptions of what is important in their stories. The observers are new to the participants and present new metaphors and understandings that can stimulate rethinking	An external observer describes an incident between a mother and daughter as a storm they are travelling through together. Exploring this metaphor with White enables the family to see their relationships in a different way
Highlighting unique outcomes – 'exceptions' to the problems usually experienced are highlighted by getting people to identify what aspects of them made them different	People can explore why the exceptionally positive event worked out so well and can identify how to transfer what they did to other experiences	A mother describes how a normally aggressive son avoided conflict over a housing problem. By getting them to look at how this came about and see what they both did differently, White engages the mother and son in learning how to achieve such a result again
Scaffolding conversations – identifying possible steps in the 'proximal zone for development', building up confidence to plan for the future	Many people leap from present problems to trying to do too much. By exploring what worked in particular events, they can build up their confidence in steps towards taking the next significant action	White moves in careful exploration and confidence-building stages before encouraging people to make concrete plans

Source: White (2007).

Greene and Lee's (2011) formulation of solution-oriented practice shifts towards the end of sessions with clients. Practitioners work with clients to create tasks to carry out between sessions. Doing this collaboratively creates a commitment to the goal of the task. The emphasis on the shared value of alliance (see Figure 1.7) connects with the importance in narrative practice of the practitioner and client 'co-creating' new narratives to test out new directions in life and move towards taking them up. Greene and Lee (2011) adjust tasks to fit the client's readiness to change:

- Customer clients realize the problem and want to take action.
- Complainant clients can define the problem but cannot see what actions they might take.
- Visitor clients do not agree about the problem and do not want to take action; involuntary clients subjected to a court order or unwillingly referred by other agencies often fall into this category.

This leads to a hierarchy of tasks that are set between sessions with the practitioner, as in Figure 9.7. If the client has so far made no engagement, a minimal task might be set. If they have decided they want to work on something, but have not yet decided what this might be, observational tasks might be appropriate. If they understand and can look for exceptions, more complex tasks might be set.

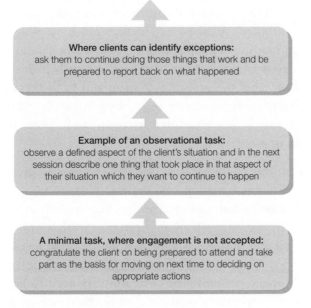

Where clients can identify exceptions:
ask them to continue doing those things that work and be prepared to report back on what happened

Example of an observational task:
observe a defined aspect of the client's situation and in the next session describe one thing that took place in that aspect of their situation which they want to continue to happen

A minimal task, where engagement is not accepted:
congratulate the client on being prepared to attend and take part as the basis for moving on next time to deciding on appropriate actions

Figure 9.7 Levels of tasks in solution-oriented practice

Other possibilities are the observational task of keeping a record of things that clients are doing that create exceptions or overcome problems, and the prediction task of predicting how often an exception behaviour will occur in a specified period (for example, the next morning or the next day). These tasks related to exceptions increase clients' awareness of what is working and alert them to occasions when they can make exceptions happen. Finally, you can ask clients to behave as though the miracle has happened and record what occurs.

In later sessions, practitioners follow up on the tasks and may be able to record changes in the scaling of problems and the frequency of exceptions. However, clients often maintain existing patterns of behaviour, and the people around them often support this by giving advice and guidance, which clients sometimes take as continuing criticism that they are deficient in the skills to improve. It may therefore be important to disrupt existing patterns of behaviour that have become part of the normal life of clients and their families; note again the shared value principle of disrupting existing patterns of behaviour (see Figure 1.7). Among the approaches to this are the following:

- Set practical tasks, as in task-centred practice (see Chapter 5).
- Disrupt the pattern by using indirect tasks. These might include suggesting that clients voluntarily try to do more of the tasks that 'just seem to happen'. An example is agreeing that the client will argue with their wife for one hour each night. This, first of all, limits the occasions on which it is acceptable to argue, and thus allows other more positive behaviour to emerge. Second, because it enforces arguing every night, it helps people become aware of how they start arguments and what they argue about. Such agreements often lead to the couple finding it difficult to argue because all the common linguistic cues in their relationship that lead to arguments are disrupted. All these experiences can be explored. 'Restraint from change' interventions involve suggesting that the client should not try to do too much. This can be helpful for clients who have unusually high or low expectations of themselves as it takes the pressure off them and helps them participate in the process by making the practitioner seem supportive. As clients start to make improvements, it may be important to warn them not to worry if they do not keep up the same rate of progress.

As the helping process continues, practitioners continue to use scaling to provide feedback about how things are going, and evaluate progress using a single-subject or single-system evaluation design: this involves looking regularly at the changes in each of the main goals. In this way, evaluation of progress, with a view to terminating the helping process or closing the case, is built in from the beginning of the engagement with the practitioner. Clients can be encouraged to use self-evaluation of their progress, although undue pessimism or optimism may need to be challenged. They need to recognize the importance of the contributions they have made to achieving their goals – it has not been done *to* them – and to see themselves as having achieved the success. The changes can be consolidated by clarifying the details of the changes in behaviour or situation achieved, helping clients learn how to track progress for the future, and helping them identify markers for any recurrence of their difficulties.

Conclusion: using strengths, narrative and solution ideas

Strengths, narrative and solution ideas form a distinctive perspective on practice, as well as proposing some specific techniques. They have all been used with the full range of clients that social work practitioners work with; in addition, there is research validation of solution-focused practice and strengths work in care management. However, there have been criticisms that it is overoptimistic to expect these psychological models to have an impact where severe adversity and social exclusion are affecting the surrounding community.

These perspectives require a forward-looking focus on the positive outcomes that clients desire. They therefore connect with both the shared value principles in Figure 1.7 and also research and aspirations in social work that emphasize enabling clients to be in control of the outcomes that they want to achieve. The practitioner is required to maintain a positive, forward-looking approach rather than focusing on clients' problems or deficits. In this way, the perspective connects with the social model of disability and citizenship models of practice, rather than focusing on problem-solving.

Because all of these perspectives draw on postmodern social construction theory, they accept that people can change if their understanding of their social experience changes. There is criticism that this perspective does not recognize the responsibility of social work to maintain the social order and achieve mandated social objectives such as changing criminal or disordered behaviour or getting people out of expensive hospitals and into more economical community facilities. However, social work aims to achieve these social objectives through a practice that is respectful of clients' own objectives and acknowledges the need to engage people in making their own changes and incorporating their own objectives into wider social outcomes. Taking more time to manage work with clients appropriately and respectfully is more likely to engage them in using their strengths than jollying them along to meet the service's targets.

Important features of practice within this perspective, therefore, include:

- drawing out people's own narratives that incorporate their understanding of their lives and their objectives in working with the practitioner;
- maintaining a positive focus on the desired outcomes;
- using techniques that maintain clients' forward-looking and positive objectives;
- working to identify personal strengths and enabling social niches in clients' lives;
- identifying positive exceptions to patterns of life that people can amplify to develop their strengths;
- looking for clients' own solutions by getting them to observe the successes in their lives;
- maintaining a forward impetus by working actively with clients in sessions to identify solutions and strengths, and setting forward-moving tasks that aim towards useful desired objectives.

Additional resources

Further reading

Rapp, C. A. and Goscha, R. J. (2006) *The Strengths Model: Case Management with People with Psychiatric Disabilities* (2nd edn) (New York: Oxford University Press).

Saleebey, D. (ed.) (2009) *The Strengths Perspective in Social Work Practice* (5th edn) (Boston: Pearson).

These two books provide different but complementary perspectives on strengths-based practice. Saleebey's edited book is an important source of the original ideas used in this model of practice.

Parton, N. and O'Byrne, P. (2000) *Constructive Social Work: Towards a New Practice* (Basingstoke: Macmillan – now Palgrave Macmillan).

This important book makes clear the social construction sources of strengths and solution perspectives.

Journals

You can find articles on many of these perspectives in mainstream social work journals.

Websites

http://www.dulwichcentre.com.au/

The Dulwich Centre, Australia, is the workbase of White and Epston, important original thinkers in narrative therapy, and offers useful resources; it includes free access to downloadable videos.

http://www.narrativetherapycentre.com/index_files/Page378.htm

This useful introductory website is provided by the Narrative Therapy Centre, Toronto, Canada.

Important bases for solution-focused therapy are:

- The UK Association for Solution-Focused Practice – http://www.ukasfp.co.uk/
- The Institute for Solution-Focused Therapy, Chicago, which is one among many internet promoters of the ideas of solution-focused therapy in the USA – http://www.solutionfocused.net/home.html
- The original source of solution-focused therapy, the Brief Family Therapy Center, Milwaukee, which has closed since the deaths of de Shazer and Berg; however, a legacy website provides some useful resources – http://www.sfbta.org/BFTC/Steve_de_Shazer_Insoo_Kim_Burg.html
- The Kansas University School of Social Welfare (Saleebey's original base), which has an extensive website with links to other sites that focus on his approach – http://www.socwel.ku.edu/strengths/index.shtml
- The Brisbane Institute of Strengths Based Practice, which takes in a number of forms of research and practice connected with strengths-based work – http://www.strengthsbasedpractice.com.au/index.htm

Humanistic practice, existentialism and spirituality

10

Main contribution

The main contribution of humanistic and related practice to social work is its focus on the aim of enhancing individual personal development. The aim is to understand our personal identity in relation to others, not just to their identities but to the totality of who they are and the relationships they are part of. This becomes a way of empowering all aspects of our human creativity in support of human rights in human society.

Main points

- Humanism, existentialism and spirituality are different interpretations of important elements that are found in the human experience and social work.
- Many cultural views see spiritual concerns as universal, and therefore as a significant factor in all helping activity, such as social work.
- Western societies often favour secularism, particularly in public services, as being a neutral position between religious and spiritual beliefs, but this implies a rejection of spirituality that may be seen as hostile to people with a commitment to a particular faith or belief. Understanding the spirituality of many minority ethnic groups in Western countries is important for an adequate understanding of their social and personal needs.
- Symbolic interaction, phenomenological sociology, Laing's view of mental illness, Rogers' client- or person-centred practice, gestalt therapy, Gandhian social work and transactional analysis (TA) are all relevant ideas focusing in different ways on the human experience, social justice, and social and ecological sustainability.

Practice ideas

- ☐ *Self-actualization* and *self-fulfilment* are social work objectives that are drawn from humanistic psychologies.

☐ *Empathy, congruence, genuineness* and *unconditional positive regard* are the attributes of a practitioner in successful practice.

☐ *Scripts* and *games* are patterns of behaviour drawn from TA.

☐ Spiritual ideas of *wholeness* and *connectedness* contribute important human aims and values to social work.

☐ The interaction of *body, mind* and *spirit* is an organizing concept in spiritual care.

☐ *Decentralization, sustainability* and *interdependence* are important social objectives drawn from Eastern thinking.

☐ *Democracy* and *participation* as elements of practice are influenced by humanistic psychologies.

☐ *Dread* and *alienation* in people's lives, drawn from existential theory, have resonance for many social workers.

☐ The TA metaphor of people having a *parent, adult* and *child* interacting internally and externally has also influenced social work.

Major statements

Humanism and existentialism are systems of secular (non-religious) philosophical beliefs: I describe some important aspects of their principles that have influenced social work in the 'Wider theoretical perspectives' section. Unlike purely secular views, which reject religion, humanism is regarded as a spiritual system of beliefs. Its contribution mirrors the role of spiritual thinking in social work, which is therefore also included in this chapter. Humanistic social work draws on humanistic psychologies and psychotherapies, which incorporate some humanist ideas; again, I describe some of the important points later in the chapter.

My own humanistic social work (Payne, 2011a), influenced by sociology, and Lee et al.'s (2009) integrative body–mind–spirit social work, based on Eastern philosophies, offer examples of practice interpretations of the spiritual elements contained in these ideas in systematic accounts of secular social work practice; I discuss these briefly below in the 'Applications' section of this chapter. Glassman's (2009) humanistic groupwork represents in particular the contribution of ideas of democracy and human rights, demonstrating that humanistic practice is more than a secular spirituality, and I present it as an example text for this reason. Because of its theoretically informed account of spirituality in practice, I have included a brief account of Holloway and Moss (2010), supplementing material on humanistic practice with theory that is concerned with these issues.

The debate summary

There are two reasons why humanism is widely accepted as a central value of social work. First, the origins of social work are associated with the shift of welfare provision from the Christian churches to become part of the secular role of the state. The second is that practising social work requires a belief that social problems may be understood and overcome by the application of human reason and understanding; this high valuation of rational knowledge gained through research and scholarship is a fundamental tenet of humanism.

The primary critique of humanistic practice is the way in which it draws on the openness of the humanistic psychotherapies to a broad range of ideas, including the arts and spirituality as important elements of human experience. In treating these as valid ways of understanding and interpreting human experience and social problems, humanistic practice goes against the shift towards secularism that is seen in public services in Western societies; it also goes against the contemporary emphasis, discussed in Chapters 2 and 6, on evidence-based practice (EBP), of rational, positivist knowledge as an important knowledge base in social work. Humanism is often seen as supporting secular science as the major basis of successful human development; this is because of its assertion that a distinctive feature of humanity is the human capacity to manage the natural and social environments through observation, experimentation and rational analysis. It might, therefore, be seen as a supporter of a technical social work or EBP. However, it values all human knowledge and creativity, and not just knowledge created by the limited research methods of EBP. It also values shared human experience as the basis for human understanding, contrary to the emphasis of EBP on neutral external observation.

Humanistic social work sees perspectives such as cognitive-behavioural therapy (CBT) as being too technical and agency practice as often too bureaucratic. This critique reasserts the importance of believing in the capacity of human beings to improve themselves, which many see as central to social work. So emphasizing the humanity of the objectives and ideals of social work is a counterposition that rejects overtechnical practice. It seeks to re-establish the focus of social work as empowering and liberating rather than problem-solving in character. Humanistic practice also questions critical, social change views of social work by its focus on exploring, understanding and coming to terms with human experience, rather than resisting adverse social forces. Nevertheless, existentialism particularly relates to critical theory in its concern about alienation. Humanistic ideas, however, explain and approach alienation differently by exploring and understanding the experiences that connect alienation with wider life experiences, while critical theory interprets alienation as a social failure.

The explicit use of humanistic psychotherapies has not developed strongly in social work. The one consistent element over several decades has been Rogers's person-centred practice, with its thoughtful focus on personal empowerment with individual clients (Rogers, 1977). Person-centred practice was originally called 'client-centred' practice, the terminology changing to emphasize the importance of the free individual rather than the client role. Current writing on client-centred, person-centred, personalized or service user-centred practice often refers to the need to focus on clients' needs and wishes rather than agency priorities, and it is not connected with Rogers's theory. Rogers's influence has primarily been on the cognate field of counselling, where his approach is the source of a major stream of practice, equal in impact to that of CBT and solution-focused practices.

TA is a good example of the reasons why humanistic theory is a fringe interest in social work. Influential in the 1980s, with its terminology of scripts and games, it is now regarded as a fringe psychotherapy. Its vogueishness means that many see it as giving superficial accounts of behaviour in a semi-humorous language, perhaps making people feel that they are not being treated with respect, rather than permitting a thoughtful analysis of behaviour. For some practitioners, on the other hand, its entertaining and unportentous terms can help them to look at behaviour in a new, easily grasped way.

Existential ideas have also had periods of importance, but their source in a 1950s philosophical trend, occasionally revived, disconnects them from mainstream social work. Powerful ideas about 'being' and 'dread' speak to some practitioners, but for many it seems a quirky interest rather than a solid basis for practice. Similarly, some work on spirituality focuses on writers' own Christian or Islamic faith, or draws on inspiration from less well-known religions that interest people because they seem exotic or out of the ordinary. This makes issues of spirituality seem to be a personal preference or an area of personal development rather than a professional responsibility in work with clients. Such attitudes are reinforced because public agencies are required by many legal and administrative systems to have a secular stance. Cnaan et al. (2002) and Dunham et al. (2009) explore the influence of religion on social work agencies and practice. In addition, the development of transpersonal psychotherapies emphasized the presence of spiritual and transcendent aspects of human life in much human experience and has been applied to social work (Canda and Smith, 2001). Transcendence is concerned with areas of life where we relate as humans to forces outside ourselves that we cannot readily perceive by rational means.

Some of these trends are criticized because they seem to be rejecting rational, evidence-based practice with definable and quantifiable outcomes. Moreover, interest in Eastern religions, such as Daoism and Buddhism, suggests an exploration of the out-of-the-ordinary from personal interest, rather than it being a rational or thoughtful evaluation of ideas that are particularly relevant to practice in contemporary societies.

Humanistic ideas, therefore, seem interesting but insubstantial. They concern aspects of human experience that are important to many people; however, their lack of clarity and the difficulty of forming clear targets and agreed explanations make these ideas hard to turn into an operational language of practice in a public profession – and this means that they do not adopt those shared value principles discussed in Chapter 1 that require specified aims and actions sequences in practice theories. Humanistic and related views of social work are therefore often a source of public criticism of social work for being vague and idealistic. Although these ideas have potential explanatory power in helping practitioners to understand clients, they may not be widely accepted among the powerful groups in society that social workers seek to influence on behalf of their clients.

Answering this, some of the important research on the effectiveness of therapeutic relationships comes from this tradition. It shows the importance of the skills and person of practitioners in their relationships with clients. It is the source of the research support for empathic and genuine relationships with clients, and attempts have been made to measure these elements. Although such relationships are not sufficient for therapy to be effective, they are necessary to therapeutic success. So, while they must be present for these techniques to be useful, they have to be part of other activities that intervene effectively in clients' behaviour or social circumstances.

Wider theoretical perspectives

Humanism and existentialism are ways of looking at life that are based on well-established philosophies. *Humanism* believes in the capacity of conscious human beings to reason, make choices and act freely, uninfluenced by higher beings such as gods and religion or superstition. Humanism is different from humanitarianism, which is a philosophy of being humane and a practice of treating people with kindness because we value their humanity. Humanism, however, values human caring in social relationships as an essential aspect of humanity. It is also associated with democracy, because it believes in the capacity of human beings to value and help one another, thus restraining damaging pressures from our social environment and the natural world.

Existentialism is concerned with the meaning for human beings of the fact that they exist, that we are human *beings*. It focuses on the capacity of people to gain the personal power to control their lives and change ideas governing how they live. Major streams of thought are based around the work of Büber, Kierkegaard and Sartre. Sartre's work has had most impact on social work theory (Blom, 1994), particularly through Thompson's (1992) book. Existentialism accepts that people are both 'subjects' and 'objects', that is, they both act on and are affected by the environment. The environment often seems to contain absurd and alienating experiences and suffering, and existentialism speaks to us of their impact on people's lives.

Although social work is associated with secularization in some Western societies, welfare often remains connected to religious faith. This is because many individuals take up social work as a way of putting their faith into practice, and many social work agencies continue to be associated with or developed by churches and faith groups. In addition, social work with individuals often raises or deals with spiritual issues in people's lives. *Spirituality* is a human search for meaning and purpose in life, seeing being human as integrating a wide variety of experiences into a whole personality. Many Eastern philosophies, including Zen Buddhism, Hinduism and Islam, have relationships with spirituality and some of the elements of humanism and existentialism. This is because they emphasize the process whereby human beings realize their capacity to enhance their own well-being through spiritual self-development.

Similarly, African and Caribbean spiritual perspectives have had a considerable influence on what Martin and Martin (2002) call the 'black helping tradition' in social work in the USA and elsewhere. In this tradition, the spiritual self interacts with a racial self and a communal self. Similarly, Maori and aboriginal spiritual beliefs have influenced practice ideas in New Zealand and Australia, and this has filtered into international practice, for example in the adoption of family group conferencing as a form of family and child participation in decision-making across the world (Marsh and Crow, 1997). Traditional care-giving in African tribes connected with black spirituality, which created a sense of the sacred and divine that gave African-American people a sense of dignity and self-worth as slaves in the nineteenth century; it has therefore been valued as a cultural tradition in Caribbean and north American communities who are of African origin. In particular, family relationships and child care were important sources of solidarity and maintained connections across the generations (Graham, 2002).

Humanist and existential ideas also connect with 'green' environmental political and social philosophies (George and Wilding, 1994). These emphasize the importance of human beings controlling their destructive capacities and living in harmony with their environments. These views are increasingly influential on younger people through the impact of eco-critical ideas (see Chapter 7).

Similarly, we can see relationships with feminist theories. This is because they focus on women's shared experience in developing a consciousness of their oppressed social position (see Chapter 13). Both humanistic and feminist ideas favour participative self-development while recognizing the need to control the destruction that is implicit in existing social relationships.

Connections

Humanistic social work developed from two groups of ideas, presented in Figure 10.1. The first group was interconnecting traditions of humanistic, transpersonal, constructivist and existential psychologies, all influencing each other; these led in turn to the second group of humanistic and existentialist psychotherapies. Broader sociological and social work thinking contributed to the interpretation of these as a humanistic social work.

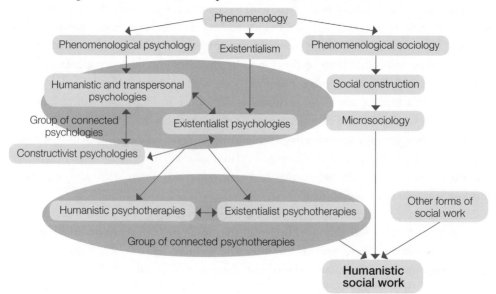

Figure 10.1 Ideas contributing to humanistic social work
Source: Adapted from Payne (2011a: 9). Reprinted with permission from Lyceum Books.

Much of this thinking was originally influenced by phenomenology, a philosophical and sociological system of thought that emphasizes how our understanding of the world comes from the appearance of phenomena, such as objects or events, how we perceive them and how we process our perceptions in our thinking. This is affected by the phenomena themselves, of course, but how we see them can be just as or more important than reality in influencing how we act. Phenomenology is connected with the interpretivist and social construction views of knowledge that we met in Chapters 1 and 9, which say that what we know of the external world is interpreted through our perceptions and thoughts.

Humanistic models of practice are based on the common idea that human beings are trying to make sense of the world they experience; we met this as an important idea in psychodynamic theory in Chapter 4. In addition, social workers are trying to help people gain the skills they need to explore themselves and the personal meanings they attach to the world they perceive, which in turn affect them.

Humanistic models propose that people's interpretations of their own selves are valid and worthwhile. The importance of spirituality in many cultures means that it is an important issue in understanding social work approaches in African and Eastern countries and in working with black and minority ethnic groups. Many ideas from spiritual perspectives in such cultures are consequently beginning to influence Western social work. Graham (2002), for example, presents aspects of African-centred world views as both a critique of Western social work theories and a way of understanding African-Caribbean people. We saw in Chapter 6 how mindfulness has been adapted in CBT as a form of self-control, having been taken from Eastern meditation as a form of control of the self. Such practice is becoming increasingly mainstream in Western social work and counselling. However, it is questioned for similar reasons to why the impact of Western social work in Eastern and African practice is criticized – that is, it does not connect well with the role of social work in Western welfare regimes. The potential interaction with ecological ideas is an example of this. Ecological systems theory (see Chapter 7) has been mainly concerned with intervening in social relations rather than, as humanistic and spirituality practices would suggest, harmonizing human relationships with the natural environment.

Well-known systems of practice and writers in social work and related fields implement these principles that are common to humanistic approaches, and their ideas have filtered into more general use. Examples are Laing's (1965, 1971) views of mental health, Frankl's (1964 [1946]) logotherapy, Rogers's (1961) person-centred therapy, Gandhian theory from India and Berne's (1961) TA. Different conceptions of spirituality and the arts are part of the connections of humanistic practice with wider systems of thought in social work.

Laing explicitly used existential ideas as well as psychoanalysis in his early work on theories of mental illness. He argued that we can understand schizophrenia as a person's reaction to a bewildering or possibly damaging social environment. Disturbances in family communications lead to one family member being caught between conflicting demands from others, and the disturbed reactions are diagnosed as schizophrenia. Particularly in psychiatric settings, Laing's work taught social workers to be cautious about medical diagnoses that fail to consider social and family factors as possible elements in the cause of problems.

Frankl's work (1964 [1946], 2011 [1948]) focuses on introspection about our life experience (1964 [1946]: 98) and people's drive to find meaning even in the most painful and difficult circumstances. It thus expresses many of two basic points of humanistic practice. The first is looking inside ourselves through serious and organized reflection to understand others by comparison with our own experience. Introspection connects with the use of meditation (Keefe, 2011) and other Eastern philosophies in practice (Brandon, 1976; Lee et al., 2009). The second basic point is the importance of achieving security with ourselves, others in relationship to ourselves and our lives, through searching for meaning in our life experiences. This has in turn influenced current conceptions of spirituality in therapeutic work.

In social work, Krill (1978) and Thompson (1992) use existential ideas explicitly to inform approaches emphasizing emotional reactions to human experience as the basis of practice. Goldstein (1984) tried to bring together cognitive and humanistic psychologies in an important forerunner of current interest in humanistic practice. In addition, humanistic groupwork developed in encounter groups and similar opportunities for self-expression.

Rogers's (1951, 1961) person-centered practice, and its three conditions of effective therapeutic relationships discussed earlier in the chapter, was also a decisive influence on humanistic practice in both psychology and social work. Rogers's conditions are that *clients should perceive* that practitioners act as follows:

■ They are *genuine and congruent* in their therapeutic relationship (that is, what they say and do reflects their personality and real attitudes and is not put on to influence clients).
■ They have *unconditional positive regard* for their clients.
■ They *empathize* with clients' views of the world.

Carkhuff and his associates (Truax and Carkhuff, 1967; Carkhuff and Berenson, 1977) have adapted these ideas into a more general concept. Rogers's ideas then become, first, honesty and genuineness; second, (non-possessive) warmth, respect and acceptance; and third, empathic understanding. Empirical work has confirmed that these are the effective elements in therapeutic relationships. Rogers's work and many other ideas in humanistic psychology derive from Maslow's concern for 'self-actualization' and the attainment of 'human potential' (Maslow, 1970).

Another important thinker to influence social work was Gandhi, an Indian leader who formulated a philosophy of social development. His approach was committed to the welfare of untouchables (people of the lowest social caste), women and those living in rural areas (Muzumdar, 1964; Howard, 1971). Kumar (1995) summarizes the main points of Gandhi's philosophy as follows:

■ There is a reliance on Vedic philosophy, an important basis of Hinduism.
■ People are both interdependent and self-reliant.
■ The spiritual is important in all worldly affairs.
■ Faith in purity of means rather than achieving ends is important.
■ Totality and holistic ideas are important, especially in relation to political independence. Social development, self-reliance and education should go with political independence as such ideas are important in social development (see Chapter 8).

■ Formal legal authority is disapproved; interdependence and self-reliance are, as the previous point suggests, more important.

Gandhi proposed rural development based on cottage industries, physical labour rather than the use of machinery, a decentralization of power and social justice and the equitable distribution of wealth. Kumar (1995) argues that these romantic philosophies nevertheless connect with the social work values of promoting self-reliance, mutual help and personal and social development that rely on small, local groups rather than top-down direction. The process and means by which activities are carried out and the high value attached to collaboration and an avoidance of compulsion are also shared philosophies.

Transactional analysis derives from the work of Eric Berne (1961, 1964). It is a humanistic therapy since its basic principles rely on the assumption that people are responsible, autonomous agents who have the energy and capacity to control their own lives and solve their own problems, being prevented from doing so only by left-over failings from early childhood behaviour patterns (Pitman, 1982).

There are four elements of TA: structural, transactional, games and script analyses. *Structural* analysis proposes that our personality has three 'ego states', or ways of thinking about the world. These are associated with typical behaviour patterns. The parent state is a collection of attitudes typical of the sort of injunctions that a parent figure might give to a child and the sort of perceptions that a child might have of such a figure. The child state contains feelings and attitudes left over from childhood, typically rather self-centred, but also uncontrolled and potentially creative. The adult state manages, mostly rationally, the relationships between the ego states, and between them and the outside world. These concepts are like the psychoanalytic structures of the superego, id and ego, but TA is less concerned with internal interactions among parts of the mind, drives and irrational responses.

Transactional analysis is about how the ego states in one person interact with those in another. Transactions are exchanges between people's ego states, which may be open or hidden, and problems arise when open and hidden messages involve different ego states or transactions.

Games analysis is concerned with patterns of interaction and behaviour. People have three groups of emotional needs:

■ stimulation, which they fulfil by artistic, leisure and work activities;
■ recognition, which is met by receiving 'strokes', either non-verbal or verbal, positive or negative, from others (for example, a smile and a thank you or a scowl and a criticism, respectively);
■ structure in life, particularly of time.

The pattern of strokes and life experiences that we get used to in childhood sets up our life position, which is about how we feel about ourselves and others, and our general attitude to the world. There are four life positions (Harris, 1973):

■ I'm OK – you're OK, when you feel good about yourself and others.
■ I'm OK – you're not OK, when you feel good about yourself but not about others.

- I'm not OK – you're OK, when you feel bad about yourself and see others as more powerful and capable than yourself.
- I'm not OK – you're not OK, when you are critical of both yourself and others.

Games are typical patterns of ulterior transactions that recur, reflect and promote damaging life positions. Social workers analyse games with clients, who can then understand and avoid them in favour of more satisfying interactions.

Script analysis is concerned with seeing how transactions in the past have led to present life positions and games.

The politics of humanistic and related ideas

We have seen that the debate about humanistic practice centres on the importance it gives to personal experience, including experience drawn from the arts and spirituality, as an important sources of ideas. Brandon (1976, 2000), for example, offered Zen ideas and Daoism as useful contributions to social work. His was an intense and personal vision in which social workers should use all the elements of their personality to arrive at an authentic interrelationship with people in distress. Unlike many humanistic approaches to therapy, which have been criticized as therapies only for those who are mildly disturbed, seeking greater personal fulfilment, Brandon sought to approach people in extreme difficulties. Work was directed towards self-understanding, enlightenment (the Zen concept is *satori*, a leap towards intuitive understanding) and self-growth for both the social worker and the client. An important idea was 'hindering', which is connected with critical anti-oppressive ideas about social barriers getting in the way of people achieving social objectives in their lives. Hindering was focused less on social barriers and more on obstructions to people's movement towards self-development, and enabling them to avoid the many features of their environments that were obstructing them. Brandon's approach relied on personal charisma and sharing between clients and workers.

Several writers, for example England (1986), argue that we should see social work as an artistic endeavour rather than an application of social science. Walter (2003), using theatrical ideas, argues for a sense of improvisation and for seeing interactions with clients as provisional rather than contractual. This means that practitioners should not start out by tying down in plans everything that they are going to do with clients, but rather should set out on a process and let it lead them into new aspects of the client's needs as these emerge.

Spirituality as an element of practice has experienced a resurgence in the twenty-first century (Nash and Stewart, 2002; Canda and Furman, 2009) because of the following factors:

- Religion and spirituality are integral parts of living in any society and are therefore relevant wherever social work is practised.
- There is a need to respond to ethnic and cultural minorities in Western societies.
- Political interest lies in the possibility of faith communities and churches making a stronger contribution to organized care and community services, thus contributing to social stability (Cnaan et al., 2002; Dunham et al., 2009).

■ There exists a criticism of materialism and consumerist tendencies towards commodification in Western societies, that is, treating everything as though it was a good to be purchased in the economic system. In addition, there is a perceived need to rebalance these tendencies with different ways of finding meaning in life.

Although spirituality is relevant to everyone, there remains the question of whether religion should be included in social work theory. A range of social work writing seeks to document religious or spiritual beliefs in particular cultures and ethnic groups so that practitioners not familiar with those cultures can understand them better. This approach to including religion in theoretical writing does not prescribe these religious beliefs as the basis of a practice theory: it suggests rather that practitioners need a knowledge of the religions they will come across. Other writing seeks to extract useful ideas for practice from particular ethnic and cultural beliefs. Examples include Lee et al.'s (2009) body–mind–spirit practice, which uses ideas from Eastern philosophies, and is discussed in the 'Applications' section. Books on Christianity and Islam and their relation to social work, for example those listed at the end of this chapter, do not offer a generalizable practice theory; instead they seek to make practitioners aware of issues of importance in those religions and their place in contemporary societies.

I therefore see the awareness that issues of spirituality are important for many clients as an important contribution of the ideas presented in this chapter to practice theory in general. Focusing on spirituality in general allows practitioners to include in their practice the reality that a commitment to faith and a belief in particular religions are important to many people they work with. Practitioners with a particular faith commitment may also wish to demonstrate that commitment in their practice, but social work theory in general requires openness to work with clients' own religions. A theory constructed around any particular religious commitment, such as a practice theory of Christian or Islamic social work, is ethically impossible, since it would involve imposing practitioners' views on their clients. I discuss this issue in the section on 'Values issues'.

The way in which a particular spiritual tradition in its ethnic context may be helpful to social work can be seen in Graham's (2002) work on African-centred world views. This is a particularly well-worked out example of the applicability of non-Western spiritual ideas to social work. Graham's approach draws on classical African intellectual traditions. It is also influenced by the civil rights and Pan-African movements, which seek a unification of African world views following the social fragmentation caused by the experience of slavery and colonialism. The approach used in relation to African intellectual and faith traditions is also applicable to systems of faith and belief in other ethnic groups.

The emphasis is on identifying, analysing and celebrating what is special about being African through cultural symbols, rituals, art, music and literature, so as to revise the commonplace disparagement of Africa and its peoples. This would identify and affirm a distinctive African place within wider social theories and practices. The principles of an *African-centred world view* are as follows:

■ All things, for example people, animals and inanimate objects, are interconnected.

▨ Human beings are spiritual; that is, they are connected to others and to their creator.

▨ Individuals cannot be understood separately from their collective identity, particularly their twinlineal (that is, taking account of both their father's and mother's parentage) family trees. People's lives and experiences are integral to their family and community histories and connections, and commonalities are more important than individuality.

▨ Mind, body and spirit are one, equal and interrelated; each should be equally developed towards *maat*, a balanced sense of truth, right, harmony and order.

Thompson's (1992) comprehensive assessment of the value of existentialist thought for social work practice is based on the ideas of Jean-Paul Sartre. A central notion here is *'being'*. 'Being-in-itself' is mere existence. 'Being-for-itself' is existence in which we are conscious and can therefore have potential, for example by making plans and decisions about how we want to be. Blom (2002) argues that, in this perspective, neither practitioner nor client can know each other in advance from the perspective of the other or from the basis of formal knowledge because there can be no prior expectations of how a human being might be. Practice relationships are a struggle between the experiences of two others outside themselves. Through this struggle between the different views of each other, we can take part with another person in social and personal transformation. But we cannot understand what is 'inside' them or how they would typically act, as psychological theories would propose. They have the free will to act, and our two conceptions of each other interact freely, allowing us to begin to gain external views of the other.

Values issues

Humanistic ideals of treating people as wholes, and as being in interaction with their environment, of respecting their understanding and interpretation of their experience, and of seeing clients at the centre of what workers are doing all fit well with many of the shared value principles of social work (see Figure 1.7). We see them in a wide range of social work theories discussed in this book, except for cognitive-behavioural theories.

Two important values objectives are central to humanistic practice approaches. The first is the idea that practitioners have a responsibility for being genuinely concerned about and connecting with their clients, treating them with warmth and acceptance. The second is the importance of human rights as being integral to the humanity of every person; this leads to a consequent emphasis on human equality between practitioners and clients. The special importance of this value position is that many psychological approaches to practice emphasize individuality because it allows a clear ethical focus on particular clients and on clients' consent to and, through self-determination, control of what takes place in practice. Individuality in psychological theories is instrumental: it is emphasized because it helps practice to be more effective. Humanistic practice, on the other hand, values individuality because this is fundamental to humanity.

Spirituality raises a concern that workers might import their own values into practice. This requires looking for connections with other relevant views, an awareness of the social worker's own spiritual beliefs and their commitment to avoid imposing it and to promote inclusiveness in practice (Hodge, 2003a, 2003b; Osmo and Landau, 2003). Research and the development of assessment tools may also be helpful. An example is spiritual eco-maps (Hodge and Williams, 2002) and spiritual life maps (Hodge and Limb, 2007); these provide visual ways of stimulating an exploration of, respectively, the client's present faith and belief commitments and their religious life history.

Applications

I draw the main practice elements of humanistic practice from my analysis of humanistic social work (Payne, 2011a). This starts from the principle of two accountabilities. One is responsibility to the social mandate for our work, derived from policy and law and enforced in our employment and professional responsibilities. This is balanced by an interpersonal accountability to clients, their families and communities, enforced through our compassion and our professional responsibility to achieve their informed consent to our shared activity. We also need to balance interpersonal work with clients and efforts at change in their social environments. Interpersonal work helps clients to be effective in achieving personal change and to believe that they can be effective in influencing themselves and the environments in which they live and work. We balance this aspect of practice with the recognition that those environments are also engaged in continuing change, and we have to bring together that change with the personal changes that clients are making, so that the two reinforce each other.

Humanistic practice must operate through interpersonal and social equality. This is because, as this practice sees the humanity of all human beings as equal, human rights are integral to humanism. Humanistic practice is therefore strongly committed to the shared value principle of equality and respect (see Figure 1.7). This is implemented in humanistic practice because practitioners treat clients, in terms of their personal identity, as being human in the same way as they do themselves. In addition, they seek to achieve equality of treatment between different social groups and between people within social groups by, for example, avoiding bullying and oppression in families, schools and workplaces.

The commitment to equality also connects with Rogers's (1961) emphasis on the practitioner being non-directive, non-judgemental and an active listener, using 'accurate empathy' and 'authentic friendship'. Rogers also concentrated on the importance of the 'self' seeking personal growth. There is an emphasis on the 'here-and-now' rather than on the history of clients' problems. Because of the belief in clients' uniqueness, Rogers gave less emphasis than most problem-solving social work theories to the diagnosis and classification of conditions. Everyone is an individual in this view.

Humanistic practice must also be flexible in the way in which it responds to human beings, and it must be prepared to engage with the complexity of everyone's personal identity. We do not expect human beings and their relationships to operate in just one way; instead, we expect that all sorts of responses to situations are acceptable and workable. We do not explain behaviour in a linear way, but accept that many different factors interact in all sorts of ways that we cannot fully understand.

Caring and creativity are essential in humanistic practice. The term 'caring' is preferred to 'helping' because helping implies that one person has both expertise and good intent, which reduces the freedom of the person being helped. Caring involves creating a caring environment that enables caring to take place; in this, there is a care-giver who is predisposed to caring and who performs acts with the client that have the behavioural qualities of care-giving. All this enables a caring relationship to unfold in which connections can develop between the cared-for person and the care-giver. This allows practitioners and clients to use creativity as part of the work that they do together, stretching the practice and generating additional connections between the participants, as well as empowering clients and the people around them to be creative in resolving the issues that they are facing. England (1986) extended views of social work as art into a humanistic theory based around the ideas of 'coping' and 'meaning'.

Self and spirituality are linked in their importance in humanistic practice. Personal development is an important human right, enabling people to move towards self-actualization. An important aspect of this is the opportunity for everyone to build their personal identity, understanding the characteristics they share with others and the diversity of human beings, which strengthens their differences from others. Our identities are both internal and personal because they emerge from our nature and experience, and external and social, because they emerge from our interactions with others and the world around us. Our identity is a dialectic, an internal debate, between our experience of ourselves and our experiences of the world around us. Our spirituality develops from this dialectic: it is how we give meaning to our own existence and the existence of others in relationship to us. This idea of internal dialectic is secular and connects with spiritual ideas such as prayer and meditation.

The importance of human rights and the value placed on the balance between our internal and external experiences make security and resilience important objectives in social work. This contrasts with a conventional view which suggests that social work is often about assessing and managing risk. Humanistic practice aims to help people find ways of living that help them to be secure in the decisions they have made and social situations they are part of, and which help them to bounce back from adversity. Thus, humanistic practice rejects problem-solving as a social work objective because it sees problems as a natural part of the human condition. We should enhance people's emotional and physical security and resilience, so that they can respond to the situations that life throws at them. In this way, humanistic practice offers a positive view of humanity and the human situations that people are part of, rather than focusing on the deficits in individuals and their social environment.

Ideas about mindfulness, which we met in Chapter 6 and which draw on Buddhist thinking, are increasingly influencing a wide range of therapeutic practice. Lee et al.'s (2009) body–mind–spirit social work draws on three perspectives from Eastern thought: yin–yang, Daoist and Buddhist teachings. Its integrative view of change rejects the linear conception of change that is common in Western practice. The linear view proposes that you start from people's problems, use knowledge to understand the causes of the problems, and then use theoretical understanding to suggest a technique for change that removes the problems and achieves well-being. As part of this, clients' active participation enables them to achieve greater control over their lives and problems.

Eastern thought has a view of change that is different from Western thinking; reality is constantly changing and life is always in a state of becoming. No final state of well-being is therefore possible. Life and reality are in constant movement and exist in patterns that we can understand through a direct experience of their meaning rather than through rational analysis. Breaking things down into parts of concepts reduces our understanding of the balance and interdependence of the events in our lives. Balance, or the Buddhist 'middle path', implies not a compromise but an incorporation of different elements into a unified whole. In this context, we should, rather than trying to attain rational control, try to let go of our concern for transient socially based standards and desires, which limit us; instead, we should connect with what would bring us inner harmony, which in turn incorporates the 'wisdom and intelligence of nature' (Lee et al., 2009, p. 25). We should transcend our focus on the development of our self and our family and lose our attachment to worldly desires. The two important features of this approach to change that should not replace the Western view, but should complement it, are:

- seeing balance as central;
- including spirituality in the conception of healthy change.

Case example: Jabari's unemployment

Jabari was referred to a mental health service with depression resulting from unemployment. He had lost his job some months previously and had since made many unsuccessful applications for similar jobs. In his family, it was regarded as an important responsibility for men to be employed, and Jabari's father was particularly critical of his failure to work. Although Jabari did voluntary work for a local charity teaching new migrants English, and had started to take information technology classes at the local college, encouraged to do by his employment adviser as a useful contribution to his skills, his father did not feel that this was making a contribution to the family. Jabari found that he enjoyed the voluntary work and considered that he might train as a teacher; however, his father and brothers felt that this was not 'man's work', and it would mean a long period before he could earn a good income again.

A conventional Western approach to this situation would be to concentrate on improving Jabari's mood, and working with the family to reduce the conflicts that might be contributing to his depression. The body–mind–spirit approach is to reject a single definition of men's work and the role of employment in defining their personal contribution to the family. These views are keeping Jabari in a system of thought that prevents him from making progress. Working with Jabari and the family therefore has a focus on how family members are balancing different aspects of human contribution, rather than on trying to get them to adapt their behaviour. It recognizes that Jabari's 'failure to contribute' through working is not 'wrong' or 'inadequate' but something they all need to take into account in thinking about how their family functions. His changing his mind is not the only thing that is important here, because all elements of his own and external states need to change. Rather than wanting to get back to the previous balance of Jabari working and making his contribution to the family as it was functioning, they all need to accept the present situation. Being mindful of the present in this way, the family can transcend or rise above the difficulties within it, to recognize ways in which they can work effectively, including Jabari in a new way.

In this way, people and our practice accept that 'change is the rule, rather than the exception' (p. 39), and that movement as change takes place when the forces affecting us allow us to develop and change. If we are mindful of what exists in the present, we can find ways of using this, accepting and going with the flow of change, using whatever strengths we have and being compassionate with others who are sharing the situation with us.

Body–mind–spirit practice emphasizes the importance of interventions that use the body. Lee et al. (2009: 127–70) describe a number of techniques that involve touch; well-known examples are the use of massage and acupressure points. They also recommend using rituals, such as taking time out of difficult periods of the day to drink tea or coffee. In this case, they emphasize the importance of setting aside time and going through a ritual of preparation and savouring the drink. This helps to create balance in a complex life and therefore greater tranquillity.

Using physical processes in this way makes it possible to connect the body with the mind and spiritual growth: I deal with spiritual care in greater detail when discussing Holloway and Moss (2010) later in the chapter. It is also important to create a good balance between focusing on and actualizing our self and focusing on and actualizing others for whom we have responsibilities. This can often be important where we are helping those who are caring for older people or people with disabilities. Carers may concentrate so much on the quality of life of the person they are caring for that they fail to ensure they themselves remain healthy, develop their education or maintain their work skills, which will secure their quality of life in the long term after their period of caring responsibilities has ended.

Example text: Glassman's (2009) humanistic groupwork

Groups are places where individuals are valued and take mutual responsibility for each other, which creates a 'pocket of humanistic egalitarian life' (Glassman, 2009: 3) that enhances social and mental health. This account of groupwork derives from democratic and humanistic values, stating that differences among group members enrich everyone. It describes people's:

- inherent worth and equal right to opportunity;
- responsibility for and to one another, and the fact that they are socially interdependent;
- right to belong to and be included in emotionally and socially supportive systems;
- right to voice, to participation and to being heard;

- right to freedom of speech and self-expression;
- enrichment by others who are different from them;
- right to freedom of choice;
- right to question and challenge professionals.

Groups develop in a series of stages, and people's behaviour and the themes of group interaction are consistent within the stages. Humanistic theory allows members to use groups' development actively in pursuing their personal development. The *stages* are as follows:

- *We're not in charge.* Group members approach each other and the group with caution, uncertain about the group's norms. The practitioner helps to identify common needs, interests and links between members, inviting mutual trust and support – a 'partner-ship in mutual aid' (p. 64).
- *We are in charge.* Some members attempt to impose their agenda or direction on the group, which produces resistance and conflict. The practitioner helps them under-stand that they are in the process of agreeing shared norms.
- *We're taking you on.* Group members challenge the practitioner's role and struggle with how to engage with or reject the practitioner's help. The social worker helps them to explore their feelings about the practitioner and to remove barriers to using their potential contribution.
- *Sanctuary.* Members feel achievement and inclusiveness through working on power and authority, and feel a new caring, effectiveness and closeness. The social worker shares this feeling of engagement and helps the group to use the security they have created to work on real problems.
- *This isn't good any more.* Group members do not want to take the risk of struggling with their problems, and feel disenchanted and angry with the group. The social worker demonstrates confidence in their capacity to work on problems and encour-ages them to explore rather than reject their negative feelings.
- *We're okay and able.* By working through their ambivalence about whether the group can help them, the group's members gain confidence that they can work out difficult problems. They choose from the various options that are available to them from the skills in the group. The practitioner helps them to enhance their capacity to clarify, focus, resolve conflicts and act.
- *Just a little longer.* Group members want to keep on with the security of the group, since it has been successful in helping them with their problems. However, they can now use their experience to manage more effectively on their own. The social worker helps them to separate from the group, valuing and confirming the helpful progress that has been made.

The objective of groupwork is to develop the 'democratic mutual aid system'; processes for achieving this are set out in Figure 10.2. Practitioners help group members to express and simultaneously carry out ('actualize') their purpose. This function is achieved by a range of practical techniques for getting the group to establish its goals, and for dealing with the conflicts and difficulties that arise in working on the goals. These are set out in Figure 10.3.

Figure 10.2 Developing the democratic mutual aid system

Aims	Technique	Actions
Develop cohesion and emotional bonds between members	Facilitate collective participation	Foster valuing and accepting each other Scan the mood of all the group members Engage the group as a whole Establish group identity and cohesion
Modulate expression of feeling	Express feelings appropriately and respect differences	Prevent premature or overwhelming emotional disclosure Identify and universalize people's stories
Facilitate processes of decision-making	Develop rules, leadership and followership, and goals	Check feelings and opinions Reweave a range of views as collective perceptions Help compromise and consensus to be developed
Process the here-and-now	Foster expression of feeling and democratic norms	Open up awareness and ownership of the group and its process Foster feelings of belonging, inclusion of others and being heard
Express feelings about the practitioner	Enable an understanding of and demystify the practitioner's role	Ask the group to share their feelings about the practitioner Identify and respond to indirect expressions Own up to mistakes
Set goals	Enhance conscious ownership of the group, and crystallize cohesion and identity	When goals are questioned, reweave individual needs into common goals
Promote good and well-being	Identify and summarize individual feelings so that you can prevent dissatisfaction from being hidden and festering	Ask for and take part in rounds of reactions to the group's experience, without comment or assessment

Source: Glassman (2009: 103–27).

In addition, social workers use several interpersonal skills in their practice to achieve these two purposes. These skills are as follows:

■ *Demanding work, directing, lending vision and support* occurs where workers use their own commitment to move members forward when they are stuck; they do this by focusing their attention on acting and helping them to do so. All these techniques require workers to be active and positive, rather than reflective and neutral.
■ *Staying with feelings* involves social workers acting as a model for expressing feelings positively, but also helping members to express their feelings when they are uncomfortable.
■ *Silence* conveys respect and support for members who are struggling with difficulties.
■ *Exploration* helps to involve members in free-flowing activity. Open-ended questions, curiosity and interest stimulate involvement.
■ *Identification* involves pointing to repetitive patterns of behaviour and thinking in the group.

Figure 10.3 Helping groups establish and work on group goals

Aims	Technique	Actions
Role rehearsal	Experiment with new experiences	Imagine and play out alternative behaviours in new situations
Programming	Learn how to plan future change	The experience is one of generating, exploring and evaluating ideas for the group programme
Group reflective consideration	Clear up distortions in thinking	Recall events and how they affected people
Interpretation	Expand awareness of meaning	Identify alternative ideas about events
Feedback	Enhance feelings in relationships	Discuss 'I perceive' and 'I feel' about group events
Conflict resolution	Prevent conflict escalating	Identify when you feel there is conflict, fostering and modelling how to explore issues
Mending the group	Help the group rebuild after failures	Start a discussion of hurt feelings, exploring group members' strengths and achievements
Confrontation	Face painful and divisive events	Stop the group, pointing out patterns of unhelpful behaviour and assisting in planning the change that is required
Data and facts	Increase knowledge and skills in finding it	Collect and share information, giving people experience of finding useful materials
Self-disclosure	Display your commitment to accepting group and human fallibility	Share feelings, limitations and vulnerabilities
Dealing with the unknown	Enable the group to overcome their inhibitions in handling an issue	Encourage the discussion of feelings and risks, helping members to explore them and supporting members if moving forward
Taking stock	Enable passage to new agendas	Help the group discuss salient themes and learning, and plan future ventures

Source: Glassman (2009: 129–74).

Example text: Holloway and Moss (2010) on spirituality and social work

Holloway and Moss (2010) describe the historical relationship between religion, spirituality and social work as being tentative and at times hostile. In Figure 10.4, I have adapted their diagrams of these relationships to show some of the interactions with social work.

All societies are simultaneously both secular (that is, people in that society do not believe in the existence of a god or higher being) and religious (that is, people in that society do believe in a higher being). Most people, however, regard spirituality as an element of being human. This comprises a sense of mystery and awe as they experience the world around them: 'Wow: it's amazing!' Responding to that sense, people wish to see the meaning and purpose of those mysterious and awesome aspects of their world, their life and their place within that world and life: 'Why and how is it amazing?' These two elements form the main basis of spirituality, which is at the centre of Figure 10.4. Religions such as Buddhism, Christianity, Hinduism, Islam, Judaism and many more provide organized systems of thought about that mystery and meaning, as well as rituals that involve the worship of a higher being or beings who give that meaning and purpose to the world. Religion may be a part of some people's spirituality: hence it is denoted by the dashed line in Figure 10.4 as an area within spirituality. The arrows show religion and spirituality extending people's engagement with aspects of life that they perceive as the good and the dark side of life. Social work similarly interacts with the good and dark aspects of life, through its caring and helping roles that help towards empowerment and enlightenment, and its engagement with abuse, discrimination, exclusion and despair.

Everyone experiences spiritual needs and distress, and various attempts and systems have been developed to asses and measure this (Hodge, 2001). These involve systematic ways of looking at how people decide on the meaning and purpose of their life and their actions within it. Spiritual assessment also explores whether people are able to transcend suffering and despair, building self-esteem and hope. It seeks to identify the beliefs that help individuals deal with problems in their lives, sometimes in particular focusing on religious beliefs.

Figure 10.4 Religion, spirituality and social work
Source: Holloway and Moss (2010: 40–4).

Evidence suggests that health and quality of life are enhanced by happiness, hope and positive feelings about our lives and experiences. Spiritual care seeks to achieve this by achieving:

- *transcendence*, a sense of purpose, hope, meaning and affirmation in life, sometimes in the face of oppression or difficulty;
- *transformation*, by enabling people to change their identity, enabling them to become self-affirming and able to deal with and prevent the difficulties in their lives;

- *wholeness*, by shaping people's identity as a whole, integrating a focus on social structures as well as personal well-being;
- *hope*, by helping people to think about the opportunities available to them for improving the quality of their life in the future;
- *resilience* in the face of negative events, by developing skills in bouncing back from things that go wrong.

This is done through meaning-making, by searching for, expressing and sharing with others the meaning that people give to events in their lives, bringing together the past, the present and potential futures. Helping people to develop spiritual narratives enables them to see how the meaning of events has changed over time for them, and to reinforce beneficial changes.

Spiritual care may be undertaken by individual practitioners, according to their commitment and expertise, or as part of a team that sometimes includes spiritual care specialists such as chaplains. Many aspects of spirituality involve developing or enabling people to participate in spiritual and faith communities.

As in personal construct theory (see Chapter 9), how social workers, clients and others around them attach meaning to events crucially affects how practitioners deal with them. The idea of making sense is a way of humanizing and interpreting clients as being worthwhile contributors to society.

Conclusion: using humanistic social work

Social work practitioners use humanistic social work because it provides a principled approach to understanding human beings as wholes, which is more flexible, less deterministic and less judgemental than many psychological ideas used by social work. The interaction between clients' perceptions and interpretations of the world and the reaction of the world to clients shows how situations arise in which clients' apparently bizarre or bad behaviour is established or amplified by social processes. These ideas can be a useful way of explaining clients' behaviour and problems without blaming clients who are the victims of these social processes.

Theories of humanistic social work emphasize that respect for whole persons and the common good are an essential part of effective practice and the value base of social work. Artistic and cultural understanding through metaphor, experience, revelation and faith are important parts of the lives of many people in all cultures and of all social workers themselves. Valuing spirituality and human fulfilment has always engaged a commitment among clients and social work practice ideas. Understanding and accepting the role of spirituality and the way in which people interpret social experience is essential to understanding many clients and to understanding the particular cultural experiences of minorities who may be oppressed or excluded in many societies. The technical, rational and secular elements of social work have, however, often downplayed the importance of these elements of practice. Many practitioners therefore find that the humanistic and spiritual elements of practice provide a useful balance to the main rationalist thrust of social work practice.

Additional resources

Further reading

Canda, E. R. and Furman, L. (2009) *Spiritual Diversity in Social Work Practice: The Heart of Helping* (2nd edn) (New York: Oxford University Press).

A leading American text on spirituality in social work.

Glassman, U. (2009) *Group Work: A Humanistic and Skills Building Approach* (2nd edn) (Los Angeles: Sage).

An excellent account of humanistic groupwork incorporating humanist ideas.

Cnaan, R. A., Boddie, S. C., Handy, F., Yancey, G. and Schneider, R. (2002) *The Invisible Caring Hand: American Congregations and the Provision of Welfare* (New York: New York University Press).

Dunham, A., Furbey, R. and Lownes, V. (eds) *Faith in the Public Realm: Controversies, Policies and Practices* (Bristol: Policy Press).

Two important texts from the USA and UK that demonstrate the role of religion in social policy and social work agencies.

Holloway, M. and Moss, B. (2010) *Spirituality and Social Work* (Basingstoke: Palgrave Macmillan).

Hugen, B. and Scales, T. L. (eds) (2008) *Christianity and Social Work: Readings on the Integration of Christian Faith and Social Work Practice* (3rd edn) (Botsford, CT: North American Association of Christians in Social Work).

Ashencaen Crabtree, S., Husain, F. and Spalek, B. (2008) *Islam and Social Work: Debating Values, Transforming Practice* (Bristol: Policy Press).

Three important texts covering spirituality and two important world religions, and their role in social work practice.

Payne, M. (2011) *Humanistic Social Work: Core Principles in Practice* (Basingstoke: Palgrave Macmillan).

A general account of humanistic social work practice.

Graham, M. (2002) *Social Work and African-centred Worldviews* (Birmingham: Venture).

An outstanding account of African spirituality and its relevance to social work.

Martin, E. P. and Martin, J. M. (2002) *Spirituality and the Black Helping Tradition in Social Work* (Washington DC: NASW Press).

An interesting text covering the history of black contributions to social work and its relationships with spirituality.

Nash, M. and Stewart, B. (eds) (2002) *Spirituality and Social Care: Contributing to Personal and Community Well-being* (London: Jessica Kingsley).

A variable edited collection, with some useful introductory material.

Pitman, E. (1983) *Transactional Analysis for Social Workers* (London: Routledge & Kegan Paul).

The only extended analysis of the application of TA to social work, but its age reflects the way in which TA has remained a separate therapy.

Thompson, N. (1992) *Existentialism and Social Work* (Aldershot: Avebury).

An outstanding discussion of the theoretical and practical application of existentialist ideas to social work.

Journals

Journal of Religion and Spirituality in Social Work (formerly *Social Thought*) – Taylor & Francis.

Social Work and Christianity – North American Association of Christians in Social Work.

Journal of Humanistic Psychology – Sage.

Although not a social work journal, this is the major international journal on humanistic practice.

There are a variety of magazines on humanism. In the USA, *The New Humanism* is important; in the UK, the main source of information is *New Humanist*.

Websites

http://www.youtube.com/watch?v=nd282Et6hy4

A short informative video on existentialism and social work.

http://www.nacsw.org/

The website of the North American Association of Christians in Social Work, which contains useful information and bibliographies.

http://thenewhumanism.wordpress.com/about/

The blog of the *New Humanism* magazine.

Empowerment and advocacy

11

Main contribution

Empowerment and advocacy enable social workers to construct help and alliances that give people chances to achieve a greater understanding of, and a change in, their lives. Empowerment seeks to help clients gain powers of decision and action over their own lives by reducing the effect of social or personal blocks to exercising their existing power, increasing their capacity and self-confidence to use their power, and transferring power to people who lack it. Advocacy seeks to represent the interests of powerless clients to powerful individuals and social structures.

Main points

- Empowerment and advocacy are social democratic practices enabling people to overcome barriers in achieving their life objectives, to gain access to services and to improve services, contributing to practice a focus on social injustice.
- This practice is also used by critical, feminist and anti-discrimination theories.
- Advocacy originates in legal skills and is a role for many caring professions.
- Advocacy represents people in two different ways: speaking for them, and interpreting and presenting them to those with power.
- Cause, or policy, advocacy promotes social change that benefits groups and their interests, whereas case advocacy seeks to establish individuals' and families' welfare rights.
- Advocacy on behalf of people with disabilities, particularly learning and physical disabilities and mental illness, was an impetus for the advocacy movement.
- Advocacy and empowerment are connected with self-help and individuals and communities participating in decisions that affect them.
- Empowerment aims to achieve the social justice objectives of social work, both in the way it is practised and in its aims; this is increasingly being implemented through advocacy practice.
- Normalization and social role valorization, which originate in and are related to advocacy movements for people with learning disabilities, seek positive environments for people living in residential settings.

■ Empowerment theory is closely related to the history of the struggle for equality by black people in America.
■ Power cannot be given to people; practitioners must help them take it for themselves.
■ There is evidence that group empowerment work with people from deprived communities can increase later citizen participation.

Practice ideas

☐ *Barriers* or *blocks* may prevent people from achieving their social objectives.
☐ *Normalization* aims to create environments for people in residential and other care institutions that would be widely valued.
☐ *Validation* of people's feelings and experiences is important.

Major statements

Empowerment ideas, of which Lee's (2001) monumental account is still the most comprehensive presentation, are steadily being displaced in their importance by the concept of advocacy, an area in which theoretical work has recently flowered. Jansson's (2011a, 2011b) important US texts on policy influence build on his (1994) idea of 'policy practice' as an aspect of social work. Like other similar books, for example Cummins et al. (2011), the main focus is, however, on policy change and social reform; these texts are often compendia of lobbying and policy change information in the USA, which limits their usefulness elsewhere. Hoefer's (2012) model is applicable to more local and case-based attempts to influence policy, and to practitioners who only occasionally use advocacy as part of more generalist practice. I have therefore used this as an example text in this chapter. Wilks's (2012) comprehensive theory-informed text using British examples usefully brings together political and cause advocacy and interpersonal case advocacy.

In the UK, advocacy has been a significant practice in work on children's rights and work in the mental health field, particularly with people with learning disabilities. Recent specialist texts include Boylan and Dalrymple (2009) and Donnison (2009), while the Brandons' work (for example, Brandon 2000) was influential longer ago. There is also a specialist field of welfare rights advocacy in the social security and related systems, which many now regard as a specialist non-social work field even though social workers still work in this area (Bateman, 2005).

The debate summary

Debate about advocacy and empowerment centres on whether these are critical theories of practice whose main objective is social change. Alternatively, do they mainly represent a more social democratic objective that aims to improve the position of particular clients, families and communities? Their emphasis on increasing people's power and control in their own lives (Beckett, 2006: 126), and on influencing service provision for the benefit of clients and service user groups (Braye, 2000), suggests they give a lower priority to social change than critical practice theory demands. Many accounts aim primarily to achieve well-being for individuals, families and communities within oppressive social circumstances, rather than bringing about social justice and social change. Leonardsen (2007), for example, argues that the crucial element of empowerment in individualistic practice is to help people develop a capacity to interpret the meaning of their situation and act upon it. Again, Eamon's (2008) account of empowerment focuses on the effectiveness of cognitive-behavioural therapy in empowering 'vulnerable populations', justifying this psychological intervention as empowerment because such populations are the main focus of social work.

Critical theorists argue, therefore, that empowerment and advocacy are not structural in their explanations of social and psychological issues and fail to seek social change outcomes (Rojek, 1986; Humphries, 1996). For example, critical views would say that offending among social groups of young offenders from ethnic minorities in poor areas is produced by structures of inequality in society that have led to poor education services for them in areas of poor housing with few positive leisure facilities for young people and a background of endemic drug abuse. Empowering young black people in such areas to appreciate education or to realize the health and social disadvantages of drug misuse, and advocating for better work opportunities in such areas, are insufficient to overcome the way in which social attitudes and services are organized to the disadvantage of young people in this position.

Such views say that empowerment and advocacy ideas are inconsistent in helping clients because they raise understanding but do not enable them to act on the structural explanations of oppression that logically follow from this. Therefore, they do not empower but only demystify the effects and sources of oppression on people's lives. Pease (2002) argues that empowerment theories are based on modernist ideas that power is held by dominant social groups, rather than postmodernist conceptions that it is spread throughout social systems and often available to be developed by vulnerable or excluded social groups.

Empowerment practice, however, helps practitioners to think about social barriers to achieving their clients' objectives and motivates them to deal with the injustice affecting their clients. It also encourages them to enable their clients to participate in the decisions affecting them and build their capacity to achieve what they want in life. Empowerment practice reflects a commitment to self-determination, client participation and the openness of practitioners and services to being influenced by their clients, what Beckett (2006: 126–7) calls 'power-sensitive' practice. Because practitioners are usually not in a position to achieve social change in their agencies or in social policy, they can, by being power-sensitive, avoid oppressive actions in their practice and in how they implement their agency's requirements. Ezell's (1994) study found that most American social workers undertook some advocacy, mainly case-based and internal to their own agencies. Cause advocacy was carried out on a voluntary basis. Cnaan (1996) argues that American society is multilayered and incorporates both ruthless capitalism and complex systems for promoting welfare and independence through voluntary and community endeavour; this is true of many Western societies. Advocacy and empowerment might therefore be seen as a social work contribution to this complex social picture.

Moreover, not all clients can achieve a high degree of empowerment. Empowerment and advocacy fail to deal adequately with clients who are incapable of achieving power and control over their lives and those who need protection, since practitioners may disappoint or mislead them about the possibility of their own empowerment. Boehm and Staples (2002) found, in focus groups with clients, that different kinds of clients expected different forms of empowerment; they argue that one generalized theory of empowerment for all clients is insufficient. Very damaged, oppressed and institutionalized clients can achieve greater self-control and power through empowerment and advocacy, but this should not exclude therapeutic work for their benefit as well. Freddolino et al. (2004) make a similar argument about advocacy – that it should be used differently in different situations.

If we accept that empowerment and advocacy do not aim for social change, they and the multicultural theories discussed in Chapter 14 lie between 'liberation for well-being' theories and social change theories. In the same way that macro, social development and pedagogy practice bridges the problem-solving and empowerment views of social work, so empowerment and advocacy incorporate objectives of both empowerment and social change social work, not fully adopting either view.

Another issue where social workers deal with individuals is that the empowerment of individuals may not extend to their wider community or networks. So empowered individuals may be taking power and resources from others in their oppressed environment, to the community's disadvantage, rather than taking it from wider society. Where social and political resources are limited, empowerment may set oppressed or deprived groups against others rather than uniting them.

Wider theoretical perspectives

Advocacy has its origins particularly in the legal field. There, 'advocacy' is the term applied to lawyers' practice in the courts and elsewhere in representing their clients. In addition, advocacy is an explicit group of skills, with a literature base that forms an important element in legal training. Social workers might gain useful skills by pursuing similar skills training, but this is rarely actively done in social work education. Advocacy is also used as a skill and value objective in other professions, so is not unique to social workers. For example, the UK professional code for nurses enjoins: 'You must act as an advocate for those in your care, helping them to access relevant health and social care, information and support' (Nursing and Midwifery Council, 2008: 3).

The term 'empowerment' has a very broad use in several disciplines. An important source is political science and political sociology, where the study of power is concerned with which political and social groups can achieve their outcomes against the wishes of other groups. The important sociologist Weber (Gerth and Mills, 1948) identified economic power and ideology as ways in which dominance is gained over some people or groups in society by others; these can include people with access to political power, people with access to opportunities in the economic market who gain socioeconomic power, and groups with a status deriving from honour and prestige. Marxist thinking proposes that socioeconomic power, which leads to the division of people into social classes, is the most important of these.

More recent sociological thinking has emphasized that elites in society gain dominance over others by a variety of means (Mills, 1999 [1956]; Bottomore, 1993) and have established patterns of power that maintained their power, even though they could not always enforce their wishes. Gramsci's 'ideological hegemony' (Ledwith, 2011) proposed that power could be sustained through dominant ideologies, or systems of belief, in societies that became so established in the society's culture that most people assumed it was right to comply with them. The Frankfurt School of sociologists, including Habermas, explored how power in societies was exercised by elites through social and ideological assumptions and forms of communication (Houston, 2013). The political philosopher Lukes (2005 [1974]), in an influential analysis, identified three dimensions of power. The first two are direct influence over decisions, and influence over which issues are seen as important, which may lead to decisions not being taken. The third dimension is indirect influence, which shapes people's preferences, for example through the media or advertising; this prevents issues even arising.

Because these developments in thinking suggest that dominance over people is often achieved through people's lack of knowledge and understanding of their situation, they suggest that people may overcome social barriers in their lives by a better understanding of the limitations on their opportunities to take action. In this way, they may be empowered to take action to overcome the barriers. This idea gained traction through movements concerned with civil and consumer rights during the 1960s and 70s. It became important in movements against discrimination on grounds of race, gender, disability and sexuality, which I discuss more extensively in Chapter 14. Used more widely, it has come to mean techniques for encouraging employee participation in businesses (Clutterbuck and Oates, 1995), campaigns to enable communities to participate in local issues (Craig and Mayo, 1995), and encouraging communities to become engaged in 'green' issues (Blewitt, 2008).

Connections

Empowerment and advocacy ideas within social work

The main role of empowerment and advocacy theory within the range of practice theories has been to incorporate into social work practice aspects of critical theories, without drawing on the Marxist roots of critical theory (see Chapter 12) and ideas about anti-discrimination (see Chapter 14). Because empowerment is an attractive, intuitive and positive idea, it has come to influence social work practice very broadly and is used independently of its theoretical underpinning. Used in this way, empowerment ideas offer practice techniques that rely on self-help, mutual assistance and participation in planning and managing services, as well as on the participation of clients and their carers in making decisions that affect them (Adams, 2008).

Ramcharan et al. (1997) distinguish empowerment and advocacy:

- in informal settings, such as family relationships;
- in formal settings such as agency decision-making processes;
- in legal settings such as courts or tribunals that give clients access to influence decisions, seek redress for injustice or have negative decisions reassessed.

Seen in this way, empowerment and advocacy are not primarily aimed at social change, but many practitioners feel that empowerment and advocacy methods achieve social progress through individual and group learning and encourage participation in broader social movements, for example organizations to support the informal carers of older or disabled people. Therefore, empowerment and advocacy practice is included in community and social development and macro-social work (see Chapter 8), as well as critical, feminist and anti-oppressive practice (see Chapters 12–14); in this way, it contributes to their objectives without necessarily adopting their theoretical position. For example, a group of women from a minority ethnic group might be helped in getting better resources for their families through a women's group – a classic piece of empowerment practice. This may give some of them the confidence to play a more active part in organizations campaigning for women's rights – an emancipatory outcome. The work may also give the agency information to seek changes in the policy or welfare systems that disadvantage the women – a social change outcome. To carry out empowerment and advocacy work without planning for these further outcomes fails to extend the possibilities towards critical social work, although it may be more acceptable to agencies that have been established to help individuals rather than wider groups.

Policy, welfare rights and non-instructed advocacy

From the 1970s onwards, advocacy has been incorporated into general social work practice in two ways. *Case advocacy* is provided by professionals to enhance people's access to the provisions designed to benefit them. *Cause advocacy* has sought to promote social change for the benefit of the social groups from which the clients come.

In the USA, advocacy mainly refers to cause advocacy to change legislation or policy on particular issues that affect social work client groups. This kind of 'policy practice' (Jansson, 2011a) is an identifiable stream of professional practice there. Early in its development, case advocacy was seen as a supplementary service for clients with whom practitioners were working on behavioural or social issues. Freddolino et al. (2004) distinguish four types of advocacy service to clients:

- protecting vulnerable people;
- creating support that enhances functioning;
- fostering identity and control;
- protecting and advancing claims or appeals.

The first three of these are objectives within interpersonal practice. The last may be an aspect of practitioners' administrative roles, for example completing applications for a service within the agency or with other agencies. Going further, case advocacy of this kind might involve acting on clients' instructions in appeal processes or pressing their case with another agency in other ways. An important strand of practice lies in *welfare rights*, which is concerned with ensuring that clients benefiting from other welfare services receive their entitlements to that provision. This term initially focused on social security benefits but now has wider application. It is concerned with rights because, unlike many welfare services, such benefits are often founded on legal entitlements.

The boundaries between welfare rights, with its legal implications, and helping practice in social work are blurred, since practitioners need relationship skills to work with people to understand their rights and help them to take up opportunities. Poverty and economic welfare are important aspects of many clients' problems, and are the product of inequalities and social barriers in society. An effective response to these issues is integral to helping practice in social work, although specialized social security assessment and advocacy may require non-specialist social workers to refer clients elsewhere. Bateman (2005) develops an account of the welfare rights advocacy skills that are needed for such work in ways that can be widely applied in social work. This includes a focus on particular kinds of interviewing and value principles similar to those of social work, except that advocates only work following clients' wishes and instructions. Skills such as assertiveness and negotiation are crucial here.

A more critical perspective describes 'systemic advocacy' in two ways: first, as practice that develops a social movement involving and acting on behalf of the needs of a particular group of people (Boylan and Dalrymple, 2009: 120–5), and second, as the provision of a service to protect the rights and interests of a vulnerable client group such as children (pp. 126–8) or disabled or older people. Although this kind of work is often seen by many practitioners as their personal responsibility, policy development and influence is a significant part of the work of many third-sector agencies and government agencies, both local and central. Social workers are ideal candidates for these roles because of their broad social science background. Practitioners can then identify colleagues in these roles; feeding clients' experiences and needs to them is a form of policy practice that is available to people in ordinary social work roles.

Advocacy of this kind, in which practitioners act only on clients' instructions, following a legal model of distinguishing advocacy and the helping role, is the main characteristic distinguishing advocacy from other help. Boylan and Dalrymple (2009: 108–18) also identify a range of 'non-instructed advocacy' to implement empowerment and advocacy approaches where the helping role predominates or agency constraints make it impossible to take up a full advocacy role. Practitioners often use these approaches alongside instructed advocacy, where this is possible. This requires giving priority to instructed advocacy, identifying clearly when only non-instructed advocacy is viable. Many of these ideas build on the experience of citizen and self-advocacy discussed in the next subsection, with approaches of:

- *person-centred advocacy*, in which practitioners develop a trusting relationship with their clients, enabling them to act and speak on their clients' behalf;

- *human rights advocacy*, in which practitioners make decisions based on clients' rights according to various charters of rights or other principles;
- *watching brief advocacy*, in which regular contact enables practitioners to pick up and respond to difficulties where clients are unable to communicate for themselves;
- *best interests advocacy* (a legal requirement for some mental capacity decisions in healthcare settings), in which the practitioner defines the client's best interests and acts only on these.

A difficult aspect of advocacy is the dual but related meanings of 'representation'. Advocates 'represent', in the sense of acting and arguing for the interests of their clients. However, Philp (1979) uses the term 'advocacy' to imply the aspect of social work that 'represents', in the sense of interpreting or displaying clients' value as human beings who are part of society to powerful groups in society. So advocacy can mean a service that argues clients' views and needs, a set of skills or techniques for doing this and the interpretation of powerless people to powerful groups. Used in this sense, all social work is advocacy, because many social work actions are about interpreting misunderstood and undervalued social groups to wider society.

Citizen, self and peer advocacy as empowerment

A different form of advocacy work, incorporating the other elements of advocacy services, grew up during the 1980s. It started as a process of increasing the capacity of people with mental illness or learning disabilities to manage their own lives. A movement then grew up to give them assistance in achieving their civil rights within institutions, and in leaving institutions where they may have been held by compulsion (Brandon et al., 1995). This movement has been particularly important in promoting the independence of people with all kinds of disabilities. One area of work lies in helping the families of people with disabilities to present the difficulties of both disabled people and the families caring for them.

Empowerment here is not just about arguing for particular services to be provided or needs met. Bayley (1997) discussed, for example, how many people with learning disabilities suffer from a relationship 'vacuum' and need help in developing relationships in the main settings in which they live – their home, work and leisure settings. Self-advocacy, mainly for people with learning disabilities, involves helping people to speak for themselves. This takes place particularly in official planning processes, such as case conferences or individual programme planning meetings. It is a group activity, where people meet together to discuss their situation and use this support to present their personal difficulties and wishes within this context. Similarly, citizen advocacy involves volunteers in developing relationships with potentially isolated clients, understanding and representing their needs. Peer advocacy derived from self-help organizations in which people recovering from difficulties in their lives work together to represent individual needs. It is a short step from all these approaches to more general campaigning in the interests of the group represented.

These originally separate forms of advocacy have become linked and have developed as 'cash for care' or 'self-directed care', policy terms that refer to services in which, instead of professionals organizing packages of services, people are given 'direct payments' (the UK term) to buy their own care. Personalization policies have encouraged representative organizations for people with disabilities to take part in service planning and case management. 'User-led organizations' are thus a recent outgrowth of practice that have emerged from advocacy ideas. Bowes and Sim (2006) show, in research on black and minority ethnic groups, that the success of involving oppressed groups depends on a responsive attitude among public authorities and on effective professional support.

Self-help and participation

An important area of empowerment practice has been to assist the development of self-help and mutual aid groups (Gitterman and Schulman, 2005; Adams, 2008). Here, practitioners support groups of people sharing the same problems to come together to support one another. Many mutual aid groups form around particular health conditions or in the fields of mental health and addictions. During the twenty-first century, work with informal carers ('care-givers' in healthcare jargon) has been an important focus for this work. Mondros and Wilson (1994: 2–5) classify the theoretical work on these activities into four groups:

- theoretical debate about the origins of social discontent;
- classifications of community organizations;
- descriptions of poor people's campaigns for power;
- practice wisdom about organizing to help such groups.

Practice may be concerned with community development approaches or may be more therapeutic, encouraging people from vulnerable populations to support one another. Community development approaches connect with consumerism, which aims to promote opportunities for service consumers to criticize and complain about the services that do not suit their needs. Croft and Beresford (1994) argue that a participative approach is valuable because people want and have a right to be involved in decisions and actions taken in relation to them. Their involvement reflects the democratic value base of social work; it increases accountability, makes for more efficient services and helps to achieve social work goals. It also helps to challenge institutionalized discrimination. Croft and Beresford's view of participatory practice has four elements:

- *empowerment*, which involves challenging oppression and making it possible for people to take charge of matters that affect them;
- *control* for people in defining their own needs and having a say in decision-making and planning;
- *equipping people with the personal resources* to take power, by developing their confidence, self-esteem, assertiveness, expectations, knowledge and skills;
- organizing the agency to be open to *participation*.

> **Pause and reflect** *Celia's care decisions*
>
> Consider a case example. What barriers exist for Celia, Joan and Joan's husband to achieve what they want? What approaches might the social worker use to be effective and appropriate as Celia's advocate and to empower other members of the family?
>
> ### Case example: Should Celia's social worker advocate on her behalf?
>
> Celia is a fifteen-year-old girl who has been looked after in a children's home since her alcoholic mother separated from her father, a violent and abusive man who is mainly employed on sea-based oil platforms around the world. Celia would like to live with her elder sister, Joan, who is married; Joan's husband has convictions for dealing in drugs some time ago. However, their home appears stable and warm, and Celia enjoys visiting them. At a case review, the practitioner's managers refuse to accept the risk of criticism if Celia lives with Joan and her husband. Celia asks her social worker to advocate on her behalf at the meeting; the social worker is aware that this request for advocacy would be seen by her managers as being unable to act in Celia's best interests, which may be contrary to her wishes. However, there is no alternative advocate.

Some suggestions

In this case example, we can see many of the issues that practitioners face in trying to represent and advocate for the interests of their clients in agencies, particularly when the agency has legal responsibilities for managing the client's life beyond the general 'duty of care' that any agency owes to someone for whom they provide a service. The practitioner's agency responsibility for acting in the child's 'best interests' limits the possibility of being an instructed advocate. An empowerment approach suggests, however, that it might be possible to help Celia and Joan to work together, supporting each other to represent their position; the practitioner would be in a position to move in and out of the 'best interests' and 'human rights advocacy' roles.

User- and carer-led practice

An important development of self-help and participation is the growth of user- and carer-led organizations. This has been a characteristic of organizations concerned with disabilities (Barnes and Mercer, 2006) and mental health problems. During the latter part of the twentieth century, organizations set up to help people with disabilities or health problems increasingly shifted from being the providers of services to being membership organizations led by people directly affected by the disability. Service-providing, and official, organizations often develop partnerships with user- or carer-led agencies. The concept of user-led innovation has also influenced design and technology, drawing on the experience of making computer technology 'user-friendly'. The idea of the 'expert patient' has developed in healthcare, particularly in the management of chronic conditions, where patients and care-givers often know more than professionals about the process of managing a disease as part of daily life (Tattersall, 2002). Official terminology refers to this a 'user-led self-management'.

Advocacy and empowerment theory provide a basis for practice in policy developments such as cash for care, direct payments and personalization, where user- and carer-led organizations have become important partners in professional practice. Thus, the idea of *co-production*, in which service users and people in their social networks create appropriate services together with professionals, has become an important development (Hunter and Ritchie, 2007).

The politics of empowerment and advocacy

Empowerment and advocacy have been available in social work for some time but did not come to the centre of thinking until the 1980s. Simon (1995) argues that empowerment is a long-standing ideal of American social work, and Ezell (1994) claims this for advocacy. However, this history is mainly in the arena of personal helping, rather than political and social change. There are few recent developments of empowerment ideas, and the emphasis in theory development is increasingly on advocacy. Wilks's (2012) text links theory and practice in a range of settings, building skills and strategies for use in many client situations.

Rees's (1991) important analysis of the political role of empowerment in social work identifies five essential practice ideas within empowerment:

- *Biography* analyses clients' experience and understanding of the world, allowing us to draw in a wide range of ideas. It places the present struggle in context, allows us to understand the continuity and coherence in people's experience and helps to identify what prevents people from acting. Exploring a biography raises the potential of changing the way someone participates in future events.
- *Power* needs to be understood as potentially liberating as well as oppressive. Empowerment ideas view power as something that might be used positively; it is not, as in radical theory, always oppressive. Rees values understanding power as it affects those who are subject to it. He focuses on politics as a process of obtaining resources and settling conflicts by using influence through power struggles. He also emphasizes how the use of language expresses power relations.
- *Political understanding* needs to inform practice, observing both constraints and opportunities. Social work acts always involve either accepting or seeking to change an existing way of organizing power relations. Belief in economic and political liberalism (see Figure 12.2) as the best way of understanding human life is allied to the managerial control of agencies and social systems in the cause of 'efficiency and effectiveness'. Setting this against the ideal of social justice shows how managerial purposes express different and more oppressive goals than the justice purposes of social work.
- *Skills* can empower. Gaining and using skills can be an important way of experiencing liberation.

▨ *Interdependence of policy and practice* must be established. This is contrary to convention, which regards the development of policy as lying outside the role of practitioners and their work with clients.

Gutiérrez et al. (1995) studied social workers' views of empowerment in the USA. Their concepts included control over people's lives, confidence in our ability to act over issues that are important to us, the ability to recognize or develop our own power to act, being aware of and having access to choices, and independence from others to make our own decisions and act on them. In another study, Gutiérrez (1995) found that consciousness-raising groups increased the ethnic awareness of people from a minority group; this led them to change their way of understanding their problems and the way they might change their situation. This would be more likely to make them more politically active in ethnic minority issues. This research gives some support to the assumption that raising consciousness can lead to empowerment.

Speer and Peterson (2000) created a scale to measure how individuals analysed changes in their empowerment, covering cognitive factors such as beliefs about how power was exercised, emotional factors such as whether they felt they had influence in various situations, and behavioural factors such as whether they had taken part in various forms of political influence. All this research demonstrates a movement towards providing empirical support for empowerment practice and raising its professional rather than ideological stance.

Normalization or *social role valorization* (Wolfensberger, 1972, 1984; Race, 2003) is related to empowerment (Brown and Smith, 1992) and provides a theory focused on a particular client group – people with learning disabilities – although it may be more widely applied. It seeks to change healthcare and social work practice to encourage greater equality and participation for people with learning disabilities. Its approach is to offer people in residential settings valued social roles, such as helping others and participating in decision-making about their own lives, as well as a lifestyle as close as possible to those valued by people outside institutions. Normalization was an influential development in the residential care field (Sinclair, 1988). It is also used as a philosophy for people being reintegrated into the community from hospital or residential care. Ramon (1989) argues that it involves attempts to change attitudes among the general public and those professionals who are providing services, as well as those of people with disabilities and the organizations involved with them. Recent policy moves to focus on dignity as a human right in care services (Social Care Institute for Excellence, 2011) are an example of current developments in this area.

Values issues

The main values issues that arise with empowerment and advocacy are concerns about people's capacity to participate in social institutions and act and speak for themselves, and the problem of conflicting interests. Central to empowerment and advocacy theory is the recognition that disabilities and an experience of long-term oppression generate social barriers; this may mean that people do not have and cannot develop the personal skills, emotional strength or resources of money and time to advocate for their own interests, even if this would ideally be the most empowering course of action.

A further issue is the possibility that services and the personal and professional experience of practitioners may be so distant from the requirements of some minority groups, for example people from minority ethnic groups, that practitioners are unable to identify with and represent their interests.

In making the link between empowerment and social change objectives in social work, empowerment and advocacy theories demonstrate how the shared value principles of critical practice and rights concerns may be incorporated into practice that is not fully critical in its objectives. If practitioners are, because of their work roles, unable to fully engage in critical practice, this provides them with theory that can facilitate some social change objectives within a practice that is more focused on problem-solving and empowerment objectives.

Applications

Three main aspects of empowerment are important in applying a quite complex range of theory to practice:

- participation in decision-making, including the right and opportunity to choose alternatives, including the possibility of exit and the capacity not to use particular services or elements of them;
- voice – the capacity to influence what services are provided and how this is done;
- rights, which are entitlements to services or standards of provision based on enforceable legal and policy decisions (Boylan and Dalrymple, 2009; developing Hirschman, 1970).

Soares et al.'s (2011: 424–5) discussion of practice with older adults illustrates how needs for empowerment and advocacy arise in all these areas with this client group. They stress, for example, the importance of focusing on clients' loss of control in their lives, and on finding ways of increasing their control over the decisions and actions affecting them. Practitioners should also reinforce people's rights and ability to speak for themselves in decisions about their medication or location of care. Garvin (2011: 324–5), discussing groupwork with adults, usefully identifies important additional features of empowerment practice, which I have restated more broadly:

- Consider the extent to which issues or problems are related to forms of oppression.
- Give clients significant influence over the process of your practice.
- Work on changing oppressive circumstances alongside any behavioural change efforts.
- Help people to achieve a critical consciousness to understand the forces that maintain oppressive social circumstances and whether these are at work in their own situations.

Rose and Black's (1985) work, in which they describe a project promoting independent living for mentally ill people in the community, is a cornerstone of the theoretical development of empowerment and advocacy from a critical theory perspective. They based their approach explicitly on the work of Freire (1972), whose radical theory of education I discuss further in Chapter 12. Following Freire's ideas, Rose and Black sought to empower people to become subjects (active in planning and developing their role and position) rather than objects (allowing others to dominate) in their lives, by involving them in the process of advocacy. *Critical debate* with clients entered the clients' present subjective reality and explored objective reality with them. As a result, clients saw various situations in which their subjective reality limited their control over their environment. Clients are engaged in a *transformation* from dependence to interdependence, with collective networks of social support. Total autonomy was not considered desirable (or attainable for many people) – we are all to some extent interdependent with others.

Rose and Black's work was educational, using Freire's ideas. All social exchanges were seen as having a political content in that they either accepted or denied the present social order. By *dialogue* in a situation of trust, with people who behave authentically (in humanist terms), clients engage in a *praxis*, acting and experiencing the reality that results from their actions; this in turn affects later actions. Praxis is not a synonym for practice experience; it involves recasting a practitioner's perspective on social explanations because of an improved understanding of the social causation of what appear to be personal problems (see Chapter 12 for a more extensive discussion).

In Rose and Black's study, practitioners tried to get inside and understand clients' reality. Clients' history in the mental hospitals oppressed them through institutionalization, poverty and material deprivation, and they took these experiences into their own view of the world. Self-expression was encouraged, helping clients to gain vitality and an acceptance of their own capacity and worth. The main treatment process was validation, which aimed to reconnect clients to their capacity for self-expression. This was done by trying to understand the reality of the clients' own life history, and rejecting their internalized judgements that they were incompetent. Clients became 'producer–participants' in their lives rather than the passive consumers of services.

In a later formulation, Rose (1990) identified three principles of advocacy and empowerment practice:

- *Contextualization* involves focusing on clients' own understanding of their 'social being' rather than on social workers' assumptions or policies. This allows a dialogue to develop based on clients' reality. In the dialogue, clients are enabled to express, elaborate and reflect upon their feelings and understandings about life.
- *Empowerment* is a process through which social workers support clients to identify the full range of possibilities that might meet clients' needs. The work centres on helping clients to make decisions that will affect their lives.
- *Collectivity* focuses on reducing feelings of isolation and connecting clients to relationships. Experiencing this form of socialization produces stronger feelings of self-worth among clients. Similarly, an important principle of Moreau's (1990) structural approach to social work, as well as of feminist social work, is to collectivize rather than personalize experience.

The assumption of empowerment practice is that practitioners lend their power to clients for a period to help them attain control over their lives and therefore permanently take power. To do this, practitioners need resources. Moreover, we should not mistake empowerment for enablement. Unlike enablement, empowerment is not limited to allowing or assisting people to take actions, but is aimed at relinquishing power and transferring it to others so that they can permanently control their lives.

The role of empowerment is unclear where protection for clients or the security of the public is at issue. Ideas such as normalization and self-advocacy have often become associated with civil liberties perspectives that focus on the need to free people oppressed by assumptions about their dependence on care. However, it is not empowerment if you fail to provide the services that clients need.

Case example: Moving into a mental health hostel

Kevin was discharged from a mental hospital to hostel accommodation. This transfer was set up to offer a great deal of freedom of action for Kevin, but security was present via a system in which a social worker was 'on call'. Jo, Kevin's social worker, explained this, but Kevin did not understand what 'on call' meant. Then Jo arranged to show him how to use local shops, but failed to check that Kevin's social security allowance had arrived or that he had some provisions until it did. Kevin did not feel that he could raise these problems because the social worker had already been so helpful, so a later visitor found him unable to make a hot drink. In supervision, Jo said she felt she had been giving him increased freedom in a 'normalized' environment; however, he did not yet have the resources, skills and self-confidence to use that freedom.

This case example illustrates the importance of not using the idea of empowerment to avoid responsibility for assessing and providing appropriate care and support. Gray and Bernstein (1994), describing a South African project to help 'pavement people' (that is, homeless people, who in hot climates are able to live on the streets), argue that practical help is an essential part of responding to serious difficulties and that it becomes part of empowerment strategies where this is recognized; however, this is not the case where it just takes over clients' responsibilities without making provision for the development of their self-confidence and life skills.

Example text: Lee's (2001) empowerment approach

Lee's (2001) starting point is social work's aspiration for social justice and caring communities, engendering hope and power, particularly among black peoples. Although it emerged from work with ethnic minorities, empowerment practice listens to the voices and dreams of powerless groups such as children and women. Lee focuses particularly on the international economic system as a contributor to poverty. Despite its being a clinical practice dealing with individuals and families, empowerment also seeks to be community-oriented. Three concepts are central to this:

- developing a more positive and potent sense of self;
- constructing the knowledge and capacity that is needed to achieve a critical perspective on social and political realities;
- cultivating resources, strategies and competences to attain personal and collective goals.

Practitioners should try to create a sense of community with clients so that they may jointly challenge the contradictions arising from the vulnerability and oppression that is found within a society of the affluent and powerful. Individuals gain power from having a critical consciousness, in the Freirean sense, and a knowledge of structural inequalities and oppression. Transformation occurs when people can see alternatives to their present predicament as a result of consciousness-raising. This allows people to avoid self-blame for their problems, accept personal responsibility for trying to achieve change, and work to enhance their effectiveness in making changes. The central practice method is working to achieve a sense of community within a group.

Aspects of empowerment that connect with other perspectives on social work are as follows:

- Empowerment is a biopsychosocial theory, employing ideas such as ego functioning from psychodynamic practice (see Chapter 4), and adaptation and coping from ecological practice (see Chapter 7).
- Construction and narrative approaches (see Chapter 9) make it clear that how people construe their situation is important. They also promote the idea that people can be co-constructors of their environment.
- Cognitive theory focuses on helping people to remove false perceptions and beliefs (see Chapter 6).
- Feminist, interactionist and integrated approaches emphasize how workers may mediate between different social groups (see Chapter 13).
- Groupwork and community work approaches are central to Lee's empowerment practice (see Chapter 8).
- Social work has a dual emphasis on individuals and their environments, removing both direct and indirect blocks to power. Its ethical basis requires action to respond to discrimination and a special focus on people suffering from oppression. Therefore a mere understanding of oppression and treating all people the same are not sufficient; oppression must be acted upon, and oppressed peoples should identified for action.

Lee's vision of the empowerment that underlies practice is outlined in Figure 11.1. An essential requirement is to maintain a *multifocal vision* of the world, which provides a 'lens' that informs practice principles; these in turn guide the selection of practice methods. This multiple focus is considered important as it means that an understanding of the complexity of the factors affecting oppression can be incorporated into practice.

Figure 11.1 Lee's empowerment vision

Multifocal vision	Description
Historical view of oppression	An understanding of the history and policy affecting oppressed groups
Ecological view	An understanding of individual adaptation/coping, ego functioning, cognitive-behavioural learning and power
'Ethclass' perspective	An appreciation of the relationships between class, poverty, power and oppression
Cultural/multicultural perspective	Attention to the norms, nuances and expectations of the client's culture, and to potential diversity
Feminist perspective	Identification and conceptualization of women's different 'voice' and limitless power
Global perspective	An awareness of global interdependence and social exclusion
Critical perspective	A critique of oppression and a linking of individual and social change

Source: Lee (2001).

Empowerment principles

All oppression destroys life and should be challenged
Maintain a holistic vision of situations of oppression
Assist people to empower themselves
People who share commonalities need each other to attain empowerment
Establish reciprocal relationships with clients
Encourage clients to use their own words
Focus on the person as victor, not victim
Focus on social change

Empowerment practice

Prepare to enter the client's world:
• 'tune in' to the client's world
• think what it might feel like

Enter and join forces:
• ask for the client's story
• show the social worker's commitment
• mutual role definition

Mutual assessment:
• share knowledge of community resources/issues
• assess family, ego and narrative
• assess empowerment: basic information, life transitions, physical/mental health, interpersonal patterns, the socioeconomic and physical environment, oppression, power and powerlessness, strengths

Problem definition and contracting, including:
• client *and* worker tasks
• multiple oppression in the contract

Work jointly on problems:
• client takes responsibility for empowerment
• social worker empathy assists working jointly on problems
• show awareness of threats of oppression
• share reflection/consciousness of problem interactions and socioeconomic stresses
• critical praxis on problems of oppression
• identify personal/communal strengths

Leaving:
• deal with feelings about ending
• consider/consolidate gains
• reunification with community
• identify power gains

Evaluation:
• ethno- and gender-sensitive, evaluation
• research impact of oppression, strengths, language styles and concerns of minority experience
• include data from reflection and participation
• do not overvalue simple and measurable aims

Figure 11.2 Lee's principles and practice of empowerment
Source: Lee (2001).

Lee's (2001) account of practice is set out in Figure 11.2. While Lee's account specifically rejects the structural perspective of critical practice, she usefully emphasizes the importance of understanding the effect of global economic and social developments as an important element in people's oppression; this represents a wider perspective than that of many social work practice theories. This is an example of how empowerment links, but does not fully incorporate, empowerment and social change objectives in social work. Lee's account of working jointly provides a helpful analysis of the skills and approaches of social workers. In addition, her 'leaving' task of *reunification* with the community, to which might be added family and other social networks, is a useful reminder of the need to connect the personal gains that have been made with the experience of the people who surround the client. Lee's suggestions about focusing on measures of oppression in evaluation are also creative.

The book then goes on to discuss group and community empowerment, using similar techniques.

Example text: Hoefer's (2012) advocacy for social justice

Hoefer's starting point is a unified model of advocacy practice that is structured by keeping in mind the objective of achieving social justice, either for individual clients or for social groups. There are six stages, set out in Figure 11.3. This figure overemphasizes the stages of understanding the issue and planning, when of course the action stage of educating, negotiating, persuading and presenting information is where the job gets done: I summarize some of the content of these stages below. Preparation is, however, important in any successful social work practice, and understanding and planning are an important part of ensuring a structure and purpose for actions of advocacy. Another important feature of Hoefer's approach is that it is relevant both to responding to a client, group, family or community who want or need something achieved on their behalf, and also to a planned assault on an issue by a group of professionals or a lobbying or pressure group.

Hoefer also identifies a number of factors that affect current advocacy practice:

- Information technology and the internet provide resources and opportunities for influence that were not available in the twentieth century.
- Political behaviour is changing, and formal democratic involvement waxes and wanes. In the USA, there have been increases in the proportion of people who vote in major elections, while in other countries there have been decreases. As well as this, engagement in specific issues and campaigning outside general political parties is widespread.
- To justify the resources spent on it, advocacy as part of practice needs evaluation and outcome measurement just as much as therapeutic practice does. Political and social commitment is no substitute for this focus on effectiveness.

■ Maintaining and advancing social justice seems to be increasingly important, because social divisions are making it more difficult for people to climb the social ladder and obtain information that will help them meet their needs. In addition, I would add in consumerist societies where the media do not focus on social equality or need, where a practice concern for social justice compensates for a lack of public awareness.

Figure 11.3 Hoefer's unified model of advocacy practice

Stage	Explanation	Example
Getting involved	Psychological readiness to expend energy, time and other resources to pursue social justice	Identify motivations, e.g. anger at unfairness, or limitations in policy
Understanding the issue	Agree a mutually acceptable definition of the issue	Review alternative beliefs about the issue, and bridge different viewpoints
	Agree who is positively and negatively affected by the issue	Which social groups gain and lose by the issue?
	Agree the causes of the issue to be tackled	Review evidence of the effect of different causes and agree which can and should be tackled
	Review the proposed solutions to identify how they will lead to social justice	Rank the proposed solutions according to the extent to which they achieve social justice
Planning	Identify the aims	Identify alternative options and select one or more that will lead to greater social justice
	Identify the targets, that is, who you want to influence	Explore who may have influence
	Assess when you can act	Timing may affect success; e.g. influence may be more successful at particular stages in the budget round
	Identify possible ways of acting	Assess whether education, negotiation or persuasion will be effective, and target preferences for contact
	Gather information and incentives for affecting the target	Collect statistical information and personal stories, and provide pressure through demonstrations
Advocating	Carry out planned actions	Speak to people, organize lobbying, write letters and influence the media
Evaluating	Keep track of attempts to influence and their apparent success	Check whether events and communications have occurred
Ongoing monitoring	Check on the extent to which changes have taken place, and identify additional related issues and opportunities for influence	Work out criteria for success, e.g. changes in attitudes, policy, practice or timing

Source: Hoefer (2012).

Social workers engage in advocacy because it is integral to their ethical codes and to practitioners' core beliefs in human rights, social responsibility, individual freedom and self-determination; this is an expression of the shared value principle of rights (see Figure 1.7). The commitment to individual practice may, however, reduce the position of advocacy in practitioners' priorities. Ezell (1993) found that practitioners became engaged in advocacy because of their perceptions of their personal values, their professional responsibility and their wish to achieve social change.

At the 'getting involved' stage of advocacy practice, practitioners have to consider recruiting colleagues who are able to make a contribution to taking part in advocacy, either in their team, to increase the commitment to advocacy in the team's practice, or as part of a specific advocacy project. Hoefer (2012: 47) notes that the education and values of practitioners and others may affect their sense of professional responsibility, personal interest and skills. People may also be identified for participation because they have a record of participating in other organizations concerned with advocacy; this will already have increased their skills and their commitment of time to this area of practice.

Case example: Choosing a new team leader

A new team leader was being selected for a social work agency to supervise and manage a group of six practitioners working with different groups of clients. This team covered a large area of social housing with many social problems and some signs of active engagement from religious organizations trying to develop social change.

The applicants were surprised to find that they were being questioned about their involvement in organizations outside their professional work. One had been on the committee of a welfare rights advocacy organization and was active in a local mental health association. In his interview, he was tested about whether he saw his welfare rights involvement as being relevant to the mainly individual work of the team. He felt this was critical questioning fuelled by a concern that he would be a trouble-maker if hired as an employee. He argued, defensively, that experience of advocacy was an important skill that he could bring to the team. He was surprised to be offered the job and immediately afterwards to become the agency's representative on a community study project in the area, liaising with a variety of local community groups. The agency gained a great deal of credit in the community for his engagement.

The 'understanding the issue' stage requires an attempt to define the problem that should be tackled. The aim should be to describe the gap between the present situation and an appropriate situation, as established by principles of social justice. In addition, some parameters should be set around the definition, for example the area to be covered, so that practitioners do not unrealistically set themselves to change the world. The next step is to decide who is affected, remembering that some people are advantaged by this situation while some experience losses because of it.

> **Pause and reflect** *Think about who loses and gains by examining an 'understanding the issue' statement*
>
> An example of an 'understanding the issue' statement that might be relevant in many social work agencies is: 'Families with children of minority ethnicity in our area are more likely than families from the majority population to have their children investigated for child neglect and abuse'.
>
> Thinking about this example statement, who might be gainers and losers in this situation?

Some suggestions

The groups who lose may be obvious: these are the children and families who are unnecessarily investigated and who have their families disrupted by investigations and legal proceedings. There are others who may lose too, for example colleagues in the children's social care teams who have an added workload of investigation and the added pressure of feeling that they may be involved in a racist policy. Resources for other children who might need investigation and help will also be tighter. In addition, pursuing the present situation might raise social tension in the area and lead to allegations of discrimination in children's social work. The point about this account is that it is not only those individual families who are directly treated in an unjust manner who experience losses: there are often more general social losses as well, and identifying these may help you to devise useful advocacy interventions.

Turning to the other side of this issue, it may be hard to see who gains from the situation in this example. Among those who might gain are groups in society who see the particular minorities in this community as inferior, incompetent, neglectful or lazy, or who have other racial stereotypes in their minds. Another group of gainers might be politicians or managers who are risk-averse. They might fear that it will cause trouble for the agency if it investigates why more child abuse investigations are arising among minority ethnic groups. For example, they might fear accusations of racism in decision-making or, on the other hand, criticism for being 'politically correct' because, instead of letting child care decisions go forward as they arise, they are planning to investigate the outcomes of an apparently racially motivated policy. So they gain from avoiding the issue, because they avoid the problems associated with it. It is easy to think that nobody gains from an unfair situation; however, being clear that there will always be those who gain from injustice often helps to identify useful interventions or suitable targets for intervention using advocacy.

The next step is to identify the immediate and long-term causes of the problem, and to explore the values underlying the causes that people are aware of. Finally, possible solutions need to be identified and explored. Various ways of thinking creatively can help to achieve this. One example is generating ideas among people working in a group. An important skill in doing this is to suspend judgement for a period while extracting ideas – even silly or joke ideas are noted. The ideas are then evaluated and prioritized separately. Other ways of generating ideas are:

- identifying present practice and asking what would happen if you did the complete opposite; how could you do this?
- superoptimization: running through a list of 'what would happen if we ...?' ... expanded resources, set different goals, minimized the perceived causes, found a new technology; again, how would you do this?
- feasibility approaches: 'what can be done?' Here you look at all aspects of the situation that could be changed and then examine which of these should be tried. In addition, look at which is easy to do and which is difficult.

Finally, in understanding the issue, you examine what the impact of the various solutions would be on social justice. You can create a scorecard for the alternative strategies. Figure 11.4 sets out a scorecard for the issue I used in the previous Pause and Reflect example.

Figure 11.4 Social justice scorecard for policy alternatives: minority families

Attributes of social justice	Alternative strategies		
	Do nothing	Change referral and assessment procedures	Develop education in local community centres
Respect for basic human rights	Low	Medium	Medium
Promotion of social responsibility	Low	Medium	High
Commitment to individual freedom	Low	Low	High
Support for self-determination	Low	Low	High

The next stage is planning – the process of creating a map of how to move from the present situation to the future situation of improved social justice for one or more people. Figure 11.5 sets out an advocacy map that can be used to establish your agenda for practice. It is necessary to prioritize the outcomes you identify. For example, are a client's desired outcomes more important than wider outcomes for other groups? Is it important to achieve short-term outcomes to gain support, or can the focus be on longer term outcomes that may better achieve a shift in social justice?

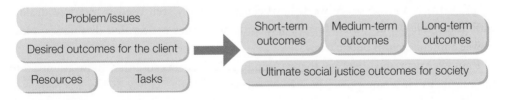

Figure 11.5 Advocacy mapping to set the advocacy practice agenda
Source: Hoefer (2012: 85–97).

The main approaches to advocacy are:

- education, including consciousness-raising;

■ negotiation, which is an attempt to use communication to achieve approval, acquiescence or action from another person or body;

■ persuasion: an attempt to achieve gains for all parties in a situation by sending messages that influence the receiver of the message so they will agree to your proposals.

Most of these approaches involve the skilled presentation of information – in person, by written communication or using the media.

Pause and reflect *Potential advocacy approaches*

Looking back at the previous Pause and Reflect box on the families of children from minority ethnic groups, identify the potential techniques which could be used in that situation for each of the approaches to advocacy.

Some suggestions

An approach using education might involve undertaking research and writing a report. Negotiation might involve using statistics to influence decision-making processes in the agency. Persuasion might involve supporting people in making complaints about how they were treated by the processes.

Following the advocacy process, the evaluation stage contains an observation phase, in which the advocacy map is used to understand the resources used, tasks undertaken and outcomes that have been achieved, adapted or not achieved. A judgement phase follows, in which we examine alternative views of the success that the outcomes have had in achieving the objectives of the clients and the people around them, as well as wider social justice objectives. These are very often only partially achieved; if this is the case, practitioners need to continue to monitor the situation to identify further possible changes.

Conclusion: using empowerment and advocacy theory

Empowerment and advocacy work has been particularly well used in practice dealing with vulnerable groups, including people with disabilities or learning disabilities, older people and children in public care.

Empowerment and advocacy theory help practitioners because they draw attention to the possibility of seeing power positively as being available within society for people to use. If you keep the possibility of empowerment in your mind, and try to incorporate it into your objectives, you can often help clients develop greater control over their lives, at the same time increasing their skills in doing this for themselves in the future. Practices such as crisis intervention, task-centred practice, social pedagogy and social development, and humanistic, strengths, solution and constructionist practice all provide a theoretical basis for including this approach.

Empowerment ideas also offer practitioners useful and practical ideas for including in their practice issues of oppression, critical thinking and joint working with clients. Some evidence supports the effectiveness of group methods that promote solidarity and consciousness-raising. This is why empowerment has been seen as a valid conceptualization of the social work role in achieving 'liberation for well-being'.

Advocacy, both as a policy or systemic practice and on behalf of clients and vulnerable groups, is integral to many social work roles, and the development of advocacy skills and actions is a crucial element of helping many clients. Assessing your client for an appropriate package of care may be seen as an administrative function, but advocacy within the agency's decision-making systems is also important. Many long-term care arrangements for children and adult client groups hold advocacy as being essential for practitioners representing their clients' interests. Advocacy also requires skills in developing self- and citizen advocacy, and practitioners act as instructed advocates in advocacy services for vulnerable population groups. Advocacy is often the main focus of the practitioner's tasks in task-centred practice, and is a supplementary role in therapeutic practice according to many models.

Although it often draws on critical practice ideas and ideals, we cannot see empowerment theory as a critical practice; however, it offers a useful way for many practitioners to think about all their work. Advocacy is an increasingly important role for social workers in all that they do and is, in these less deferential times, an increasingly important form of practice within social work agencies.

Additional resources

Further reading

Adams, R. (2008) *Empowerment, Participation and Social Work* (4th edn) (Basingstoke: Palgrave Macmillan).

A good conceptual text on empowerment as a way of developing clients' participation in the services and decisions that affect them.

Bateman, N. (2005) *Practising Welfare Rights* (London: Routledge).

A very extensive detailed practical guide to welfare rights advocacy.

Boylan, J. and Dalrymple, J. (2009) *Understanding Advocacy for Children and Young People* (Maidenhead: Open University Press).

A theoretically informed and detailed account of skills and services responding to the right of children and young people.

Wilks, T. (2012) *Advocacy and Social Work Practice* (Maidenhead: Open University Press).

An outstanding broad and theoretically informed account of advocacy practice.

Gutiérrez, L. M., Parsons, R. J. and Cox, E. O. (2003) *Empowerment in Social Work Practice: A Sourcebook* (2nd edn) (Pacific Grove, CA: Brooks/Cole).

Lee, J. A. B. (2001) *The Empowerment Approach to Social Work Practice: Building the Beloved Community* (2nd edn) (New York: Columbia University Press).

These are well-established American texts.

Jansson, B. S. (2011a) *Becoming an Effective Policy Advocate: From Policy Practice to Social Justice* (6th edn) (Belmont, CA: Brooks/Cole).

Hoefer, R. (2012) *Advocacy Practice for Social Justice* (2nd edn) (Chicago: Lyceum).

Two useful American texts on policy practice.

Mullender, A. and Ward, D. (1991) *Self-directed Groupwork: Users Take Action for Empowerment* (London: Whiting & Birch).

A ground-breaking practical text on empowering groupwork, which is being updated at the time of writing.

Race, D. G. (ed.) (2003) *Leadership and Change in Human Services: Selected Readings from Wolf Wolfensberger* (London: Routledge).

A useful selection of writings from an important contributor to ideas about normalization.

Websites

http://www.scie.org.uk/index.aspx

The Social Care Institute for Excellence (SCIE) website has a number of resources about advocacy in social work; search the website for information.

http://www.actionforadvocacy.org.uk/index.jsp , http://www.siaa.org.uk/

The UK organization Action for Advocacy and the Scottish Independent Advocacy Alliance both have useful reports and documents covering several different client groups.

http://www.justice.gov.uk/downloads/protecting-the-vulnerable/mca/making-decisions-opg606-1207.pdf/

A useful guidance booklet for independent mental capacity advocates, a legally mandated advocacy role often undertaken by social workers, is available from the UK Department of Justice. This contains useful information about advocacy roles.

You can find useful information and link on children's advocacy on the websites of:

- Voices for America's Children – http://www.voices.org/about
- and the UK organization Voice – http://www.voiceyp.org/

Critical practice

12

Main contribution

Critical perspectives help social workers to avoid assuming that the way things are is the way they have to be. They offer critiques and alternatives to the present social order – how society is arranged around us. From these, practitioners can analyse and deal with the social factors that underlie the present problems they are grappling with, or with social barriers to the positive aims they are trying to achieve.

Main points

- Critical theory argues that social problems are created more by the structure of society and the cultural assumptions generated by dominant groups that oppress subordinate groups. Individual, psychological factors in people's make-up are a less important source of people's problems.
- It aims to free clients from the limitations imposed by the existing social order by using interventions that acknowledge the social source of people's problems and avoid blaming and oppressing clients.
- Critical practice emerged in the late 1990s, reviving radical theory from the 1970s that had been strongly influenced by the Marxist emphasis on socioeconomic class as an explanation for the inequality of oppression. By incorporating feminist, anti-discrimination, empowerment, postmodernism and social construction ideas, contemporary critical practice incorporates a broader range of points of social criticism into its explanations than radical theory does.
- Critical practice draws on a transformational political philosophy and rejects social work practice that accepts conservative, liberal, neo-liberal or social democratic political philosophies based on social policy. See Chapter 1 to review how these political philosophies link with the three views of social work objectives.
- Critical theory focuses on structural rather than personal or interpersonal explanations of social problems, and on inequality and oppression.

■ Critical practice promotes consciousness-raising about social inequalities, political action and social change to combat cultural hegemony, through which powerful people maintain a social order that benefits them by influencing the media and education.

Practice ideas

☐ *Praxis* builds on people's experience of oppression, injustice and inequality to inform an ideological understanding of how society works. It also strengthens our capacity to pursue social transformation.

☐ *Dialogic* practice, that is, working with people in dialogues, involves equal relationships in which views of social situations are exchanged and discussed.

☐ *'Conscientization'* – Freire's term (see also Chapter 11) – is working to help people to understand and be able to criticize how social structures are implicated in their oppression. It also involves them in identifying and taking action over the practical consequences.

Major statements

Critical theory is actively debated, and there are several streams of thought.

In Chapter 2, I noted texts on social work practice that focus on practitioners developing critical thinking (Jones-Devitt and Smith, 2007) that avoids taking for granted social or intellectual assumptions that may not be made explicit in accounts of theory; Gambrill's (2006) text and Fraser and Matthews's (2008) collection of papers are examples of this approach to critical thinking. Glaister (2008) refers to critical analysis being concerned with the reality that multiple perspectives on social situations demand constantly renewed inquiry into the ideas we are using. She connects this with reflection and reflexivity, concepts and practices that we met in Chapter 3.

In a practice activity like social work, critical thinking and analysis must lead to critical action. So what is critical action? Critical practice theory goes beyond critical thinking to incorporate social ideas that dispute commonplace assumptions about how societies, social relations and social institutions are currently ordered. Such a practice questions the current social order and seeks to replace it with alternatives. If your analysis of problems in life focuses on weaknesses in the present social order, rather than on clients' personal failings, you would inevitably focus on changing that order, rather than on changing your clients' behaviour.

The three main current streams of work on critical practice theory are as follows:

■ One is eclectic, seeking to include a range of theoretical sources including Marxist, feminist, anti-oppressive and empowerment ideas. The most extensive recent accounts of these ideas are contained in Allan et al. (2009) and in Fook's (2012) book, which I use as an example text in this chapter.

- Mullaly's (2007) structural social work is the major statement of Marxist social work (see later in the chapter) based in a Canadian theoretical tradition of which Moreau (1979, 1990) was a founder; I also present this as an example text.
- The third influential group, based in the north-west of England, represents the current iteration of 'radical' social work, also with a Marxist base. Alongside collective volumes, the major text is by Ferguson and Woodward (2009). This is, however, primarily concerned with a political positioning of social work, rather than being a practice model, and therefore does not meet my criteria for being an example text.

The debate summary

The central debate about critical social work lies around its argument that many or most social problems come from the structure and organization of society rather than from individuals' behaviour. It follows that the appropriate response is social change to eliminate the source of the difficulties. While many practitioners might accept this analysis, most social work practice is with individuals distressed by the behavioural and interpersonal effects of these social problems. In addition, many social work agencies focus on providing social care services to individuals and help people to deal with problems that affect them and their families; critical action does not always fit with this service priority. Since most social work practitioners are employed by government agencies, their roles are limited by the legal and policy mandate given to their agencies. Opponents of critical theory claim that achieving broad social change is therefore difficult, and they give priority to helping people meet immediate social needs and deal with distress, using social analysis to understand the position of these clients more fully.

The following theoretical debates stem from this discourse about whether social change can be central to social work practice, so the seven points I have identified here overlap.

▶ The ideological and political aims of critical theory

Some aspects of critical theory overtly use Marxist and neo-Marxist theory to proclaim that all social work incorporates an ideological and political objective for social work practice. Marxist theory proclaims that some elite groups or social classes in capitalist societies maintain dominance over other social groups through controlling the economic system in ways that maintain their political and social ascendancy; I explain Marxist views on capitalism later in the chapter in 'Wider theoretical perspectives'. Neo-Marxist theories are developments of these ideas, written after the death of Marx himself. Important neo-Marxist writers who have influenced social work include Gramsci (Ledwith, 2011) and the Frankfurt School of sociologists (see the next section for details).

Critical theory says that if you reject this Marxist theory as an important contribution to social work analysis, you have not understood the full picture of how present social arrangements disadvantage and oppress people. That oppression causes or worsens the problems that practitioners work with because clients start from an economically and politically disadvantaged position in society. Other motivations for social work, such as religious commitment and problem-solving to help with personal and family change, need also to incorporate a recognition of this oppression within their practice.

▶ Critical theory's social analysis

Some writers on critical social work theory claim that critical social theory derived from the Frankfurt School of writers, in particular Habermas (1986 [1971]; Houston, 2013), is essential to any theory that we designate as critical. The ideas of the Frankfurt School are derived from Marxist theory but are significantly different. In particular, these ideas say that the dominant groups in society maintain their control through gaining social acceptance for cultural and social ideas, and that the way in which these ideas are communicated in society, for example through the popular media, maintains the ascendancy of these dominating groups.

Some critical social work theory also incorporates postmodern social theory and hermeneutics. Hermeneutics is the study of interpretation; it claims that you can understand society and social relations by seeing how different groups of people put into words and then interpret others' behaviour and actions. Such theory contradicts Marxist and Frankfurt School critical theory.

We saw in Chapters 1, 2 and 9 that postmodern ideas claim that how people interpret reality in the context of their cultural and social history influences how they react to the circumstances and events that affect them. Therefore, when cultural and historical change takes place, people respond by adjusting their interpretations of reality. Marxist and Frankfurt School critical theory is determinist: it says that the realities of cultural, economic, political and social experiences form people's perceptions. The inherent flexibility of postmodernism is inconsistent with the determinism of Marxist theory. Postmodernism objects to 'grand narratives' – social explanations based on generalizations about social trends influencing how society is organized. Radical theory, on the other hand, is based on 'historical materialism', an analysis of the history of how the economic system creates class structures in contemporary society. Since this offers a 'grand narrative' of how society is structured, it cannot include postmodernist ideas. Other examples of grand narratives that postmodernism would question are Marxist explanations that social problems are caused by class conflict or, alternatively, by individuals' psychodynamic conflicts. Both are equally unacceptable generalizations to postmodernists, who would argue that they provide only partial explanations of complex social processes. On the other hand, Marxists see poverty and inequality as self-evidently important in creating social problems, and criticize the postmodern concern with language and identity (Ferguson and Lavalette, 1999). Both sets of ideas, however, have a shared focus on not taking the present social order for granted. This allows many critical practitioners to accept elements of both ways of thinking.

▶ Critical theory's analysis that social work is a significant form of social control, allied to political and social elites in supporting the existing cultural, economic and social order

Critical theory is significantly different from psychotherapeutic, problem-solving and empowerment views of social work because of its position that social work has, as part of its everyday practice, a social control function to promote conformity with what Pearson (1975: 129) calls 'the binding obligations of civil society'. It is to everyone's benefit that children are socialized into good behaviour, that offenders cannot run riot and that mentally ill people are not distressed. Social work potentially contributes a positive and helping element of social control; this can be added to interpersonal pressures from family and friends, created by the social order, towards reasonable behaviour, moral guidance by religion and belief, and authorized action by the police and other official bodies. But where and when should we be controlling? Critical social workers argue that we should challenge control by social workers, particularly those employed by the state, when it is exerted on behalf of the dominant interests of capitalist society.

There are several problems with this position. First, it equates power with the social control of the individuals and small groups that practitioners work with. In addition, it fails to focus on important issues such as religious oppression and human rights abuses, for example child and domestic abuse and, more broadly, torture and lack of political freedom to express views and vote accordingly. This may be because the texts come from Western countries where such rights are well accepted. However, this cannot be assumed in many countries. In addition, individuals in many Western countries suffer from some abuses of this kind, and social workers provide valid and useful help in matters such as domestic violence. Critical theory thus seems to lack a sense of appropriate priorities: personal help is more urgent than changing the world. In one way, however, traditional radical theory has the advantage over contemporary critical concern for inequalities in that it focuses on structural inequalities, particularly of class and wealth. Concern with gender, race and other 'isms' can be criticized for focusing on what are, in the radical perspective, secondary issues.

Second, even if you accept that social work does contain significant elements of social control, it is a fairly benign activity compared with the sorts of control that human rights charters are concerned with. Social workers are not usually imprisoning or torturing people, for example, and the control exerted by social work is balanced by positive help.

Third, power cannot just be equated with social control, and it is not exercised just by elites or people who can use dominating physical power. Potentially, many sources of power exist and many people can access at least some of these. Empowerment ideas, as we saw in Chapter 11, say that people can resist others applying power to them, and that they can gain power through cooperation with people who share their interests. Critical practice that includes postmodernist and construction ideas recognizes these other forms of power because it is partly about helping people to use them.

▶ **Empirical support for practice**
The ideological and political focus of critical theory means that it does not offer prescriptions for practice that can be tested empirically; its prescriptions derive from its belief and perspective. Against this, critical research identifies useful ways of understanding social factors that are only weakly represented in more psychological theories. Marxists would say that their method of investigation by historical analysis and debate is a legitimate

form of study. More broadly, critical theory argues that positivist science (see Chapters 2 and 6 to review other issues about positivism) maintains the ruling hegemony. (Hegemony is maintaining social control by using indirect means such as ideas, philosophy and culture rather than direct means such as torture and violence; we met this idea looking at empowerment in Chapter 11.) It does this by accepting and promoting the present social order, and is therefore biased in its methods of investigation in dealing with critical ideas. In this view, all theory represents ideological positions, often in support of an oppressive ruling class.

Like many ideologies, critical theories define objections in their own terms and explain them away. Objections to critical theory are often taken to be representations of oppressive ideologies, and the same is said of other theories that have ideological elements. An example is psychodynamic theory: if you dispute psychodynamic ideas, your objections may be claimed to come from your unconscious fears or conflicts in looking at areas of thinking that are emotionally or psychologically difficult for you. So some people argue that, as with psychodynamic theory, critical theory requires you to be a believer, rather than relying on evidence to support its position.

▶ **The tension between the broad social objectives of critical theory and the need to offer prescriptions and support for interpersonal and clinical practice**
Many social work roles involve providing help for individuals and families with clear social needs. Critical theory leans towards collective action, and this tends to neglect clients' immediate personal needs. It therefore creates a tension between helping and respecting people as individuals with personal and family needs, while also seeking collective social justice (Scourfield, 2002). This sometimes seems unethical, uncaring or impractical because it is not what the social services are set up to do, or because it provides only a partial explanation for the behaviour and events that social workers meet. Against this point, making analyses and using broad social ideas can be useful in interpersonal practice because these give you tools for thinking issues through in a way that does not take conventional thinking for granted. They also allow you to look at the broader issues that influence what happens to individuals.

However, to critics of the humanistic and psychodynamic approaches, the concentration on material and social issues and the promotion of services such as welfare rights advice ignores clients' humanity and their emotional and personal problems. Instead, critical prescriptions come by deduction from the theory rather than being an inductive response to the problems that many clients present. So the theory risks failing by working from its own assumptions rather than those of the people served. It is one of the criticisms of evidence-based practice (EBP) commentators that critical theories arise from social workers' assumptions about people's positions, rather than from what clients themselves think. The critical response to this point is that when people's consciousness is raised, they often become aware of alternatives to existing assumptions about society.

▶ Critical theory's weakness in providing explanations of emotional and other
psychological issues and prescribing in detail what you can do about them

Leonard's (1984) thoughtful development of a Marxist individual psychology tried to
connect broad general explanations from social theory with an understanding of individual responses, and repays careful study. Critical theory often uses techniques from
social construction that allow clients' voices, especially marginalized and excluded voices,
to be heard and responded to. Empowerment theory connects with participative and
user-led approaches. In addition, a perspective that offers a coherent and engaging view
of the world is useful in itself even if it does not provide detailed help for practice. The
incorporation of feminism into critical theory has also led to important practice ideas of
dialogue and consciousness-raising gaining influence.

▶ Conscientization or consciousness-raising relies on insight

We saw in Chapter 4 that gaining insight does not necessarily lead to a change in people's
thinking and behaviour, because someone who gains insight into a problem may not
have the skills or strength to change their thinking or behaviour. This is even more true
with insight into how social pressures prevent change, because we have less influence on
social oppression than on our own thoughts and skills.

Critical theory, in answer to this, argues that insight in psychological models of practice is concerned with changing attitudes and behaviour to align clients' behaviour with
the expectations that are present in the accepted social order. Improved self-awareness in
psychodynamic and humanistic theories only aims to make people feel better and not to
achieve the social change that critical theory seeks.

Critical theory claims that conscientization avoids the problems of psychological
insight therapies because the aim is not just understanding, but an interaction of action
and understanding other through praxis. Against this point, however, the critical theory
argument here seems to want to replace bad practice in psychological therapies with good
practice in critical practice. But there is good practice in psychological therapies, which
involves helping people to use their insight effectively; the critical theory point bypasses
this possibility in psychological therapies. It is equally possible to imagine a poor critical
practitioner who might not be able to link insight and action in critical practice.

▶ Critical theory accumulates problems and criticisms in social organization but
can seem negative and demotivating because it does not offer a clear positive
(Rojek et al., 1989)

If you find that many things in the organization of society wrong, you can appear very
negative to your colleagues and to the people that you are seeking to influence. This
conflicts with the shared value principle of aiming for positive outcomes (see Figure 1.7),
even though critical theory is the major source of the influence of the critical practice
principle. Critical theory can also seem like a conspiracy theory: it often seems that every
proposal from people with the power and resources to make it work is treated with suspi-
cion, and that only oppressed people can make a valid contribution to social innovation.

Critical practitioners can see the downsides of every social innovation, rather than trying to make the good things work.

▶ **The interests of the social groups involved in any issue often conflict, making it difficult to organize alliances between them**

Some critical theories emphasize inadequate and oppressive environments and services as a better basis than individual psychology for explaining clients' problems. At its worst, this can substitute blame for local environments and their occupants in general, rather than blame for the individual victim, as an explanation. This might lead social workers' support for clients to be seen as being in opposition to the needs and interests of others in the same environment, since the needs and wishes of the poorest cannot always be aligned with those of all oppressed groups.

Case example: The housing project for mentally ill people

Kevin was a social worker on a project team to set up a scheme for supportive housing for recovering mentally ill people. The team worked closely with their clients in the area and their relatives, who supported setting up the scheme. However, many other residents in the area combined together in a campaign to stop the project because they said it would bring more difficult people into the area, which was already deprived.

Mentally ill people and local residents in this case example were both oppressed groups, but their interests were opposed. While this was so at least initially, effective social development or community work with all groups in the area achieved rapprochement.

Wider theoretical perspectives

Overview of critical practice theory

Critical practice uses ideas from several different sources, set out in Figure 12.1. Four main groups of social theory are relevant: Marxism and structural social theory; Frankfurt School critical social theory; feminism and the social model of disability, with their contribution to anti-oppressive ideas; and postmodernism.

Critical theory emerged from radical views of social work, which, after a period of influence in the depression of the 1930s, regained significance in the 1970s. Radical practice lost influence as Marxism became discredited after two political changes: the collapse of communist regimes in Eastern Europe and Asia in the early 1990s, and the success of neo-liberal and economic rationalist regimes such as those led by Margaret Thatcher and Ronald Reagan in Western countries (de Maria, 1993).

Although radical practice theory waned, social criticism deriving from radical thought is now more essential to social work than it was before its period of influence. Radical theory was criticized for not providing adequate accounts of interpersonal

practice and migrated towards social democratic practice theories, such as empowerment and advocacy (see Chapter 11). This created a theoretical environment in which
these ideas and also consciousness-raising in feminist practice re-established their influence. Lavalette's (2011) contributors, reviewing early texts, point to the continuing
importance of ideas about class and the use of community work as a technique
promoting cooperative endeavour.

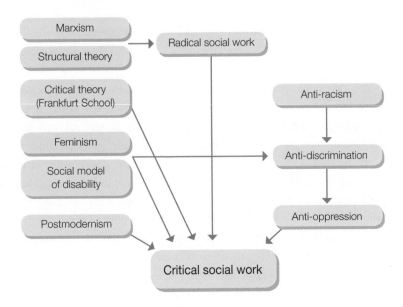

Figure 12.1 Sources of critical practice theory

  Feminism and the social model of disability had both a direct and an indirect influence on critical social work through their impact on ideas on anti-oppression; I
explore these ideas more in Chapters 13 and 14. The critical theory considered in
this chapter thus forms an overarching framework with important connections to
feminist and anti-oppressive practice. Critical theory also informs some aspects of
empowerment and advocacy theory (see Chapter 11) and calls upon postmodernism
(see Chapters 2 and 9).
  All these ideas have led to the development of theory that takes mainly a social change
view of social work. In Chapter 1, I briefly mentioned that such theories are strongly
associated with a socialist political philosophy, and that their questioning of liberal or
neo-liberal political philosophies is crucial to understanding the aims and emphases of
critical theories. Stark's (2010) account of the main neo-liberal ideas in Figure 12.2 helps
us to understand their opposition to critical theory. Because they give absolute priority to
economic welfare, they devalue collective or mutual provision as a limitation on people's
economic freedoms.

Figure 12.2 Neo-liberal principles

Priority for the economy and markets	People's freedom to pursue their own economic interests is fundamental to all other freedoms
The least possible activity of the state	The state interferes with our freedom to pursue our economic interests
Greater globalization	This maximizes efficient provision for people's needs
Deregulation	Deregulation maximizes freedom in pursuing our own interests
Social policies and values are irrelevant	Provided we can pursue our own interests, we can achieve the maximum welfare for ourselves and therefore for all

Source: Stark (2010).

Socialist ideas originate from the social theory of Marx and his followers. Marxist theory is, as we have seen, materialist, that is, it claims that the social organization of society arises from the economic system through which natural raw materials are converted to human use. As societies become more complicated, economies have to accumulate capital, that is, the resources needed to create goods on a large scale, for increasing numbers of people to consume. Some people – capitalists – are able to generate capital: they use it to set up industries that employ people as labour. Most people are working class; they do not have capital and can only take part in the economy by selling their labour to the capitalists. They thus become beholden to the capitalists, who gain control of the economy and society to support their financial interests. Society becomes organized in the interests of the capitalists rather than people in the working class.

Inequality is built into a capitalist system for two reasons: first, because their financial power means that capitalists gain more from the economy than working people; and second, because working people's dependence on capitalists for their livelihood means that they cannot assert their own interests. The state and government depend on capitalist finance so also fall in with the interests of the capitalists' financial power. A middle class develops, which consists of people who have jobs requiring education and advanced skills; these enable them to manage the economy and social structures in the interests of capitalists.

Social workers are part of this middle class. Like healthcare or education workers, their role in a capitalist economic system is to facilitate a healthy and well-educated workforce and make the social system work smoothly, again ultimately in the interests of capital. Among other things, they help to support families, protect children and care for disabled and older people so that the economy continues to produce effective workers who are not troubled by difficulties in their lives. Divorce, chaotic families with poor child care and distress because disabled and older people are not well cared for would disturb the economically productive flow of life.

Contemporary structural and critical theory is mainly a development of what Rojek (1986) calls the 'contradictory' view of social work. This is expressed most clearly in Corrigan and Leonard's (1978) social work text. This sees social workers as agents of control on behalf of ruling elites who, at the same time, have some potential to undermine a society based on class and inequality. Social workers can achieve this by increasing the capacity of oppressed people to live their lives more satisfactorily, thus reducing control on behalf of capital and inequality, and they offer some of the knowledge and power of the state to support this process. So although the state and social workers ultimately operate on behalf of capital and to the detriment of the working class, the contradiction in their role is that it helps to mitigate the ill-effects of the dominance of the interests of capital and to awaken working people to the oppression and inequality that is still affecting them.

Because the contradiction in their social workers' role between being both controlling and helping leads to other contradictions, people become more aware of inadequacies in the way in which society is organized. For example, through being helped to use play and education as a positive influence within their family life, people become aware that the broadcast and computer media use entertainment to direct their interests away from the education and self-development that may lead them to question political and social assumptions. This awareness eventually contributes to wider social change.

These ideas suggest that what determines the social problems and issues that arise is the social structure of any society, which derives from the economic system, rather than the cause being individual problems or inadequacies. Structural explanations are determinist, that is, they emphasize that the social order has such a strong influence on our social relations that we have little influence on social arrangements. Inequality and injustice affecting particular groups in society come from their positions in the social structure. Removing inequality and injustice is a major aim for social action, and analysing injustices affecting various groups is a significant part of socialist concern. This has led to perspectives that broaden the range of factors leading to inequality and injustice beyond the significance given to social class in traditional Marxist thought. Important among these perspectives have been feminist thought (Chapter 13) and anti-oppressive theory (Chapter 14), which focus on the oppression affecting particular social groups.

An important principle of socialist ideas is that the best way of organizing society is through cooperation and sharing in social structures that encourage equality rather than inequality. This influences the kind of help that practitioners should offer: for example, it encourages groupwork and community action that stimulates mutual help and cooperation.

Contemporary critical theories, in particular those of the Frankfurt School of social thought, Habermas (Houston, 2013), Beck (Adam et al., 2000) and Gramsci (Ledwith, 2011), go beyond Marxism. An important contribution of these writers is to emphasize how cultural and moral beliefs and structures are essential aspects of the way in which social orders are maintained through hegemony. Because social work is concerned with trying to influence people's beliefs and perceptions about society, it is important to integrate these cultural aspects of society into practice. Allan's (2003) analysis of the relationship between modernist and postmodern critical theories in particular emphasizes the importance to contemporary critical theory of analysing discourses through cultural and social relations; it sees power as being available to be used, rather than just oppressive, and as open to self-reflection and the reflexive creation of theory with clients. We saw in Chapter 11 that, although they contribute to and use empowerment and advocacy techniques, critical theorists attack these practice methods unless they are used within a structural and critical perspective.

Connections

One of the most important uses of critical theory is as a broad theoretical framework within which empowerment, feminist and anti-discriminatory theory can be positioned. Accounts of feminist and anti-discriminatory theory particularly rely upon critical theory as a generalized starting point for their particular focus, and assume a critical practice as the basis for using their ideas.

Critical theory mounts a significant critique of 'traditional' social work, that is, practice relying on psychological explanations of social problems and taking for granted the present social order. The main issues, which we have come across in considering practice theories with mainly problem-solving objectives, are as follows:

- Explanations in traditional social work reduce complex social problems to individual psychological ones. They 'blame the victim', making clients responsible for problems that have social origins. In doing so, they deflect attention away from social circumstances. We saw in Chapter 4 that psychodynamic theory, the main source of traditional social work, has been criticized for this.
- Related to this, ideas such as adaptation and 'fit' in ecological theory (see Chapter 7) assume that it is desirable for people to adjust to the present social order rather than question and fight against the undesirable features of contemporary society.
- Traditional theory 'privatizes' people with social problems, for example by seeing the problems as confidential. This cuts clients off from others who would share that experience and possibly deal jointly with it.
- Traditional theory strengthens and follows the oppressive social order of capitalist societies (partly from McIntyre, 1982).

In spite of this critique, there are links between many critical theories and traditional social work. Webb (1981), writing originally about radical practice, identified four main ones:

- Both accept that society contributes to generating personal problems.
- In both, the relationship between people and society is transactional, reflexive or interactive, so that we can affect our social circumstances as they affect us.
- Both seek autonomy for clients. Traditional social work criticized critical practice for ignoring it in pursuit of general social objectives, which may conflict with individual needs and wishes. Radicalism criticized traditional social work for ignoring oppressive social constraints to conform.
- Both value insight, as we have seen, so that clients can understand their circumstances in order to act on them. However, the purposes and means of action are different, and each perspective would deny the value of each other's forms of action.

Critical practice also raises concerns about social work's system of service provision. Because agencies are part of social systems that support the present social order, which benefits the ruling elites, they have inherent failings as vehicles for helping oppressed people (Ryant, 1969). There are several major issues:

■ *Social control* and the extent to which social work exercises it through the state on behalf of the ruling class. Critical theory is cautious of controlling activities.

■ *Professionalization* and social work education that promotes the interests of the profession to the disadvantage of the interests of oppressed communities and individuals. Critical workers seek alliances with working-class and community organizations rather than professional groups; this contrasts with the emphasis on engaging with professional lobbying groups as a tactic that we met in some work on systems theory and empowerment (Chapters 7 and 11).

■ Whether *critical practice is possible* in view of social and agency constraints on social workers and the individual focus of much social work. The focus on collective and political work has led to the suggestion that critical practice is not possible in state agencies and charities, which are controlled on behalf of the ruling elites through the political system or the management bodies that socially represent the ruling elites.

Critical practice is concerned with how the professionalization of social work disadvantages clients' interests and leads social workers to become part of the state and social interests that oppress clients. It also seeks the profession's development even where this is contrary to clients' interests. Moreover, professionalization encourages an emphasis on the technical rather than the moral and political aspects of helping, separates social work from other related professions by emphasizing qualification and promotes professional hierarchies, thus incorporating inequalities (Mullaly and Keating, 1991). The work of Illich et al. (1977) showed how professions are often established to act in their own interests rather than in the interests of those they serve. The role of social work education is an example of this process. Radicals argued that it trains students for 'traditional' social work, reinforcing social control, individual explanations of clients' problems and conventional rather than critical interpretations of society (Cannan, 1972).

Critical social work argues that practitioners should limit their professional status and education, which emphasize their social distance from, and cut them off from alliance with, clients. It is, however, concerned about deprofessionalization because of managerialism, which seeks to exert control over practitioners' discretion to act on behalf of and engage with clients' social and political interests. Carried to extremes, managerialism makes critical practice impossible.

An important source of critical practice is the work of the radical South American educationalist, Paolo Freire (Leonard, 1993); we met his work in Chapter 3 on reflection and reflexivity and in Chapter 11 on empowerment and advocacy. Freire's (1972) approach focuses on education with people whose communities are oppressed by poverty and powerlessness, so has many connections with social pedagogy. Such people are 'objects' who are acted upon, rather than having the freedom to act that people who are 'subjects' have. However, there is a 'fear of freedom', which must be disposed of. This is done by education through involvement in a critical dialogue in which pure activism (trying to act without reflection and analysis) and pure verbalism (constantly talking about what to do without action) are merged together in praxis. This involves acting on analyses of social situations and influencing the analysis by the experience and by the effects of the action.

The politics of critical theory

The resurgence of critical practice in the 1990s reflects, I have suggested, both the climate in the political–social–ideological arena of discourse about social work (see Figure 1.8) and the recasting of radical ideas within social work, influenced by feminism, by concern about racism and wider oppressions, and finally by critical theory. Pease (2009), tracing the transformation of radical into critical social work, also notes the importance of concern about the technicist implications of EBP and managerialism.

Bailey and Brake (1975, 1980) saw radical practice as 'essentially understanding the position of the oppressed in the context of the social and economic structure they live in' (Bailey and Brake, 1975: 9). Practice focused on helping individuals and families is not rejected, only that which supports 'ruling-class hegemony', in which the ruling classes use ideology to maintain control of the working classes. Lavalette (2011) also points to the relevance of racism, women's issues, LGTB (lesbian, gay, transgender and bisexual) rights and the concern to enable service users' voices to influence practice and service development. Lavalette and Ferguson (2007) and Lavalette and Ioakimidis (2011) also show that conceptualizations of social work emerge from experiences of disasters and political conflict that are different from practice in stable and developed economies; these conceptualizations often reflect significant attempts to change social structures. Lavalette and Ioakimidis's argument is that extreme situations make clear the need for a radical transformation of social systems that is concealed by the stability of developed economies.

A particularly important radical perspective, based on Freire's work (1972; Brigham, 1977), developed in Latin America during the 1960s and 70s. Liberation from the struggle to subsist is not a form of social action that stems from reform maintaining society in a steady state; instead, it requires revolutionary change (Lusk, 1981) involving a substantial change to political and cultural systems of thought. For example, a stronger focus on 'green' environmental policies rather than economic growth as a political priority might remove many aspects of oppression that come from giving priority to success in economic markets. A related set of ideas came from 'liberation theology' (see Chapter 10); this Latin-American interpretation of Christianity focused on supporting poor and oppressed populations rather than on the interests of rich capitalist elites. These views led to a 'reconceptualization' of social work in Latin America (Costa, 1987) away from individual problem-solving and towards user-led mutual help projects.

Conscientization is a crucial contribution to social work that has come from Friere's ideas. It requires helping oppressed people to gain a critical consciousness of the social structures that are implicated in their oppression, including the impact of cultural hegemony. By this process, they become aware of their oppression rather than accepting it as inevitable. Through participation in dialogue and praxis, they can then take action to lose their fear of freedom and some of their powerlessness.

Values issues

Values debates about critical practice focus on claims that it sees social change as being more important than individual help and the relief of individual distress. This sets long-term objectives against short-term help. Another aspect of this is the unrealistic tendency to blame social factors for personal misbehaviour, which encourages offenders or people behaving badly to evade personal responsibility for their actions. This in turn leads to criticism of social workers as being 'soft' on crime and antisocial behaviour of all kinds by excusing it.

The emphasis on long-term social change rather than immediate personal help was particularly characteristic of early presentations of radical social work, and is denied by current-day critical practitioners. Mullaly (2007), for example, points out that dealing with the personal and psychological consequences of oppression for clients is a crucial element of critical practice. He also argues that people must accept personal responsibility for their bad behaviour, even though practitioners refuse to denigrate or blame them for the structural causes of it.

Applications

De Maria (1992) sets out radical practice methods that have been largely adopted by critical practice. These are as follows:

- Social work action should be sensitive to the relevant social causes.
- Practice must be constantly tailored to the oppressive social situations that practitioners deal with.
- Practitioners should be alert to resisting claims that low-level gains, such as client empowerment, are problematic for powerful interests. For example, they may experience pressure to limit client empowerment because it makes the job of running the agency more difficult.
- Social work is concerned with inherent humanity, and no single political or theoretical position has a monopoly of the values that support such objectives.
- Critical thinking should lead to action, not merely hand-wringing about social concerns.
- It is important to preserve narratives about real life that explain and point up injustices.
- We should focus on things that are marginalized by conventional thinking.

The idea of praxis is an important aspect of all critical practice. It means that we must implement theories in practice, so that practice reflects on and alters the theory behind it. As we act, the ideas we use in acting find meaning in, and are therefore expressed by, what we do; they also change our view of ourselves as we experience the ideas in practice (Ronnby, 1992). This conception has many links with reflexivity and reflective practice, discussed in Chapter 3. Praxis argues that theory must come partly from ideas outside daily practice, otherwise it would be only a simple reflection of that practice, but it must not lie totally outside recognizable practice.

Case example: How praxis works

After qualifying as a social worker, Kevin's first long-term job was working in a service for children with emotional and behavioural difficulties and their parents, mostly using cognitive-behavioural and solution techniques. To broaden his experience, he then took a job with a family agency, working with children's problems in a very deprived part of a major city. He worked with several families whose problems had their roots in poverty arising from the closure of several big industrial employers in the city. For many of the parents who had worked in these factories, their family problems arose from the sudden drop in their incomes and consequent family problems, the parents' psychological reactions to unemployment and poverty, and difficulty in providing for their children in the way they had expected. Kevin found that they resisted work on behaviour change with the children.

The agency decided to approach this by working with the parents using groupwork, and Kevin used narrative ideas to allow groups of parents to describe and record their experiences in group writings and videos, and eventually in creating websites for them to express their experiences. Their joint exploration of what had happened made him aware of their anger at the bankers and the owners and managers of the industrial companies, many of whom were still doing financially well out of their investments. Some of the parents shared literature about the economic and social reasons for changes in industry, including ideas about globalization reducing the power of local economies to resist international financial trends. Kevin also had the experience of being with some of the families who, inspired by the international 'Occupy' movement that had led demonstrations and the occupation of important financial centres, occupied the head offices of a local company.

Eventually, Kevin moved on again to work as a manager in child safeguarding and these experiences led him to emphasize narrative techniques exploring families' experiences of life. He also used the techniques to seek to distinguish clients for whom poverty and adverse life experiences had led to chaotic family lives from those in which behavioural difficulties were the main focus of work. He was then able to work with these groups in different ways, including sharing experience through groupwork to develop mutual support.

The importance of this case example is how listening, involvement in and acceptance of the experience of the families affected by industrial closures led Kevin to change his methods of work with them, and in turn his values and ideology of practice. He did not reject his previous practice experience or his responsibilities in child safeguarding work, but rebalanced his whole philosophy of practice.

Example text: Mullaly's (2007) 'new' structural social work

The main focus of structural social work is oppression. Structural social work is so called because social problems are inherent in our present capitalist social order, and therefore the focus of change should be mainly on social structures and not individuals. Social inequalities come mainly from social structures and not from individual differences. Practitioners should therefore be aware (Mullaly, 2007: 288) that present society is limited as a satisfactory social system, as social work is always either reinforcing or opposing the status quo in that society. Individual, family or subcultural solutions do not resolve social problems; critical social analysis is an important social work skill, and structural social work is a way of life and not just a practice method. You have to live structural practice – it is not a technique.

Structural social work is inclusive because it is concerned with all forms of oppression: one is not more important than another. The state's institutions, such as the legal, education, healthcare and social welfare systems, are part of oppression on behalf of ruling elites. Similarly, knowledge and culture are not neutral but also operate in the interests of ruling elites. Social structures, ideology and personal consciousness are connected, each affecting how the others develop.

In addition, structural social work uses a dialectical analysis, seeing both sides of social problems, the personal and the political. As we saw in Chapter 11, a dialectic is an internal discourse between two different and often opposing aspects of a situation. Structural practice sees individuals as having 'agency', that is, the capacity to take successful action for social change, working together with structural forces that also have the capacity to affect change.

Mullaly (2007) starts from the position that the welfare state and social work are in crisis because capitalism is in crisis. This supposition of critical writers has been so consistent over the decades that, as an analysis, it loses credibility. Marxist thought often seeks for the 'crisis' that will cause the downfall of capitalism. Radical social work sees the demise of welfare states in Western societies and globalization as part of this crisis. It connects with concerns about the deprofessionalization of social work in conservative welfare systems that are focused more on efficient management than professional practice.

Debate about and prescriptions for practice should be rooted in an understanding of the political paradigms that are dominant in a society: Mullaly explores neo-conservative, liberal or neo-liberal, social democratic, Marxist, feminist, anti-racist and postmodern critiques and the 'third way'. The third way is a development of social democratic ideas associated with the sociologist Giddens (1998, 2000) and the former British Prime Minister Tony Blair. It accepts the important role of the economic markets as the foundation of social progress, but seeks to manage and regulate the oppressive social consequences of market capitalism such as low wages and high unemployment. Despite this broad analysis, the main focus of Mullaly's (2007: 204–51) reconstruction of his structural social work remains on a socialist approach rejecting the neo-conservative and liberal ideas summarized in Figure 12.2 earlier in the chapter.

Another important aspect of structural social work is a rejection of social order perspectives of society, which see society as 'orderly, stable and persistent, unified by shared culture and values and a consensus on the desired form of society and its institutions' (Mullaly, 2007: 227); such perspectives are typical of social work that primarily has problem-solving objectives. Having such a perspective is inconsistent with a social change perspective, which identifies significant conflicts of interest in societies, which a social order perspective ignores. Social groups and institutions that are committed to the value of social order cannot represent the interests of those whose interests conflict with that order. It is important to understand this point: structural social work does not claim that conflict is desirable and that practitioners should promote conflict. Instead, it claims that because conflicts of interest exist between oppressed people and the social order, conflict over ideas and practices is inevitable. Structural social work, as with all critical practice, asks: 'What side are you on?' If you are going to support the interests of people suffering oppression, you are inevitably part of that conflict of interests.

As with all Marxist theory, structural social work is dialectic, that is, it always participates in actions that form part of the debate between the different interests in society. Thus, everything in societies is connected, and change is constant as different interests interact with each other. Events and actions accumulate from small beginnings until they lead to evident changes in the quality of the relationships between different groups in society. That major change comes about through a unity between people who struggle with interests that are opposite to theirs. Oppressed people must inevitably be struggling against the groups and actions that oppress them. To achieve change, it is necessary also for practitioners to participate in those struggles, by whatever interpersonal and inter-group actions are possible. That united struggle accumulates changes, which inevitably lead to qualitative changes in society (Payne, 2009e).

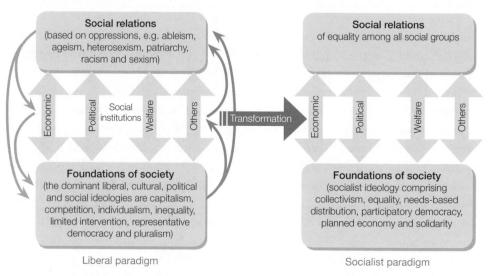

Figure 12.3 Structural analysis of society

Mullaly (2007: 246) thus presents a structural analysis of society, as set out in Figure 12.3, which redraws, amalgamates and to some degree simplifies two of Mullaly's diagrams. Society is seen as a system of social relations among a variety of social institutions. In the liberal paradigm, both the institutions and the relationships are determined by the dominant ideologies of the ruling elites; hence the arrows representing that influence are strong. The social relations, operating both through the institutions and also directly, reinforce, but do not determine, the ideologies that provide the foundation for the structure; so in the diagram these are represented by paler arrows. You can to some degree influence the ideological foundation through building social relations and social institutions, for example effective welfare and mutual support. Unless you change the ideology, however, you cannot achieve a major change in the social structure. Therefore, it is crucial for effective social change that there should be a change in the dominant ideological paradigm through enabling people to have experiences that enable them to develop a praxis. As we saw above, praxis implies a change in ideology that arises from an insight into and understanding of the experience of oppression.

Such a change in ideology leads to a transformation from a liberal to a socialist paradigm, in which social relations are based on equality between all social groupings, and the foundations of society are based on socialist ideologies. A dialectic between social relations and the ideological foundations of society becomes possible through participatory democratic institutions.

Oppression is therefore the main focus of structural social work; this will enable practitioners to identify when oppression is taking place and to participate with other groups in combating it. Mullaly's (2010) book focusing on practice on this issue is an important extension to his structural practice theory. Oppression is always group-based and relational. It is not just a restriction of our freedom or violence towards us. It is carried out in the interests of social groups and affects other groups. There are always oppressing groups enjoying the power and other advantages that result from the oppression they are exerting, and subordinate groups who are affected by the use of that power and advantage.

For example, mental illness does not oppress mentally ill people, but they may be oppressed by healthcare professionals who gain status and power by their rights to manage and control the behaviour of mentally ill people as part of their role in treating them for their illness. Again, it is not that the professionals oppress mentally ill people. Rather, it is the assumption that their behaviour needs control that creates oppressive mechanisms and a cultural assumption that mentally ill people need control. For example, there is a widespread assumption that many mentally ill people are aggressive and violent, whereas this is exceptional. The creation of controls appropriate for the few creates a social assumption that then stigmatizes all mentally ill people and engages professionals unwillingly in an oppressive position.

A number of myths about the dangers that oppressed groups present to wider society thus set off oppression and perpetuate it. If we can see these being used as arguments for restrictive or controlling processes, this helps us to identify oppression. I have set Mullaly's list of myths out in Figure 12.4, with examples offering a fuller explanation and some suggested alternative perspectives.

Figure 12.4 Myths of oppression

Myth	Example	Alternative view
Scarcity	There are not enough jobs or services for everyone	A minority owns most of the resources, which could be better distributed
Majority	The majority view should prevail	Minority alternatives should be respected
Objectivity	One group's observations, knowledge and understanding about people and social relations are true	A range of different perspectives may have validity
Stereotyping	All members of a group are the same	Many different aspects of a personal identity exist and contribute to group identities
Victim-blaming	People are the architects of their own misfortunes	Many problems have multiple sources and causation is neutral, while blame is a moral judgement
Competition and hierarchy	Competition and aspiration are natural and naturally lead to classifying people	Cooperation is an equally important human characteristic; people do not need to be graded
Supremacy	Western education and science is a better base for understanding	A range of learning and research methods contribute to human understanding
Class	Most people belong to a middle class that lives in harmony with others	A range of social groupings exist whose interests may be in conflict or in harmony

Source: Adapted from Mullaly (2007).

Pause and reflect *Your examples of oppression myths*

Think of an example in your experience of each of these myths and consider whether an alternative view of the situation is more appropriate.

Some suggestions

Here are some examples I thought of. Consider a scarcity myth: people sometimes say that immigrants come from poorer economies to improve their income and are prepared to accept jobs for lower wages than the indigenous population will agree to. The alternative view is that people migrate for a variety of other reasons, such as moving from a rural to an urban economy, improving their family life or providing opportunities for their children's education, and often take jobs that indigenous populations do not wish to do. And a stereotyping myth: Muslims need time off from work to pray several times a day. The alternative view is that, in Western societies, there is a wide range of religious commitment among Muslims, as with many other religions, and we have taken for granted the holidays that go with Christian observance.

Oppression is an issue of social justice because these myths lead people to evade the fair social processes and practices that would normally operate to create just outcomes between people from different groups. It also leads people to misunderstand the fairness of outcomes because they think of the advantages that oppressed groups gain as being losses for themselves. Many areas of oppression, however, concern non-material goods such as rights and responsibilities, and in this situations nobody incurs a loss if another group gains. Current-day political decisions are often based around social identities, and this reinforces oppression because it leads to stereotyping.

Case example: The disability and youth groups in a community centre

A community centre had started as a youth centre and the committee now wanted to broaden its work; it was suggested that a group for local disabled people would be helpful. The organizers of the youth group argued against this, saying that it would inhibit the young people from boisterous activity, from 'letting off steam', because they would have to be careful of noise and restrict their activities so that disabled people would not be injured by sports activity. The organizers of the disability group suggested an experiment for the two groups to meet. It was found that the members of the disability group enjoyed meeting the other young people socially. In addition, two disability group members, including one in a wheelchair, volunteered to work with the youth groups, which led to the setting up of a youth group for physically handicapped and able-bodied young people together.

This example highlights some scarcity and stereotyping myths: the inability to adapt the centre's facilities for the use of both groups, and stereotypes of the social identities of both young people and their behaviour and disabled people's attitudes and preferences. The protesters had not realized that both groups might gain from the change.

The main forms of oppression are:

- *exploitation* – the use of the energy and resources of the oppressed group for the benefit of the dominant group;
- *marginalization* – failure to consider the interests of the oppressed group and value their contribution;
- *powerlessness* – inhibiting development of the capacity to influence decisions affecting the oppressed group;
- *cultural imperialism* – assuming that there is a universal experience of the world which creates norms that oppressed groups should accept;
- *violence* – physical attack, harassment, ridicule and intimidation, and the fear of these, which inhibits oppressed groups in achieving their goals or living as they wish.

Pause and reflect Examples of oppression

Look at each of these forms of oppression and identify examples from your experience.

Some suggestions

My thoughts about these forms of oppression started from considering exploitation arising from the assumption that women will care for dependent people in their families without wages and without considering the effect on their career or personal aspirations. I have also experienced the marginalization of young people in residential care when they have not been involved in decisions about the activities that were available in the residence. I wondered too about cultural imperialism found in the common assumption that social development perspectives are not relevant to Western social work because in the West most social workers provide individual help and assessment to people at risk of abuse and neglect, with behavioural problems or needing social care services.

Practitioners in social work will be constantly working with situations in which 'structural violence' occurs, that is, damage to people and their lives that arises from structural inequalities. As a result, their clients will be affected by the oppressive myths found in the housing, retail, employment, education, healthcare and criminal justice systems. One example many practitioners accept is that people from working-class families, offenders and mentally ill people smoke heavily as a response to the stresses in their lives. Accepting this fails to acknowledge that advertising and media representations of smoking, acting on behalf of elites that make profits from tobacco, emphasize its benefits in managing stress, rather than making clear the health problems that smoking gives rise to.

There are two different forms of reaction to oppression. First, people accommodate to or comply with the oppression that they experience, accepting their inferior status. You often hear people say things like: 'I don't really understand what's happening; I'm not so well-educated as you, but my children have gone to university, so they will be in a better place.' The second reaction is resistance by developing a politics of difference; that is, individuals build up and value the differences between their group and others.

Policies of assimilation and multiculturalism assume that oppressed groups will come to accept and take part in the dominant group's assumptions, or will participate in mutually respectful relationships that ignore the history and reality of oppression. Establishing a politics of difference, however, acknowledges and tries to do something about oppression by dominant groups. For example, valuing the experience and social contribution of older people and having geographical communities where older people live that provide for their cultural interests accepts their marginalization from wider relationships in society.

So far, we have been examining the structural analysis of oppression that informs structural social work practice. Around 80 pages of Mullaly's (2007) 398-page book – about 20% of the total – covers structural practice, which makes me wonder about his claim that it is a myth that structural social work is strong on critique but short on practice (2007: 290). I have summarized the main points of his account of practice in Figure 12.5. Mullaly divides practice into two elements: working within and against the system, and working outside and against the system, the latter focusing on political action.

An important aspect of practice is the analysis that 'the personal is political', a concept often claimed by feminist theory and practice. This idea proposes that practitioners

Figure 12.5 Structural social work practice

Practice	Elements	Actions
Intrapsychic and interpersonal work	• Counteract the damaging effects of oppression • Build strengths for individual and collective action against oppression	• Counsel on psychological effects • Enable people to be agents of their own change • Engage critical reflection on the effects of existing social arrangements • Set up groups with people in similar situations to develop political awareness, self-define a new identity and develop confidence to assert a more authentic identity
Empowerment	• Reduce alienation and sense of powerlessness • Help people gain greater control in their lives	• Remember that practitioners cannot empower others, only assist in self-empowerment • Engage in mutual problem-solving with the client • Avoid exploiting the helping process for your own benefit (e.g. being seen as a kind or supportive person) • Facilitate the voices of clients being heard
Consciousness-raising (conscientization)	• Understand dehumanizing social structures • Aim to alter social conditions • Base this on the client's situation and experiences • This is part of, and not a substitution for, support, services, advocacy, referrals and improving immediate lives	• Help people gain insight into their circumstances with a view to changing them • Increase self-confidence and assertiveness • Provide information and education about structural issues • Use dialogue, mutual learning and critical questioning • Show personal and social empathy; reflect back the personal experience and link it to social factors • Engage structural empathy … and ask where these factors come from • Open a dialogue on the social functions of oppressive actions
Normalization	• Clients' experiences are not unique… • … and are a logical outcome of oppression	• Provide information that others are similarly affected • Link client with others in the same situation
Collectivism	• People are social beings, dependent on others	• Form groups of people with similar experiences • Refer to groups or helping organizations in the community
Redefining	• Redefine assumptions that problems come from individual, family or subcultural defects	• Employ critical questioning, dialectical humour, metaphors, storytelling, checking inferences, mental imagery, persuasion and use of silence to identify alternative explanations
Dialogical relationships	• Participants in social work are equal participants • Practitioners are not experts, professionals or therapists	• Share case-recording so that clients contribute to the records of their lives • Involve clients in decisions affecting them • Get clients' feedback on services • Provide information on agency roles and clients' rights • Reduce social distance by self-disclosure, casual dress and explaining your actions

Source: Mullaly (2007: 288–320).

should understand that every practice action contains implied political objectives, and that it is helpful to clients to understand how their present apparently personal troubles connect with political and structural forces. The aim is to reduce feelings of guilt and blame. Structural social work does not, however, negate personal responsibility: it is not acceptable to say 'society made me do it' or 'it's all a capitalist plot'. Irresponsible or bad behaviour is not acceptable, but we do not blame people or say that everything about them is bad because they are affected by oppressive factors in society.

In addition to the interpersonal practice guidance offered in Figure 12.5, Mullaly points to the practice implications of taking structural approaches to practice in mainstream agencies. Various approaches facilitate continuing practice in this situation:

- Be clear about the 'control and pacification features' of mainstream agencies.
- Find structural ways of challenging oppression by the agency.
- Protect yourself and your colleagues from reprisals.

> **Pause and reflect** *Structural challenge in your agency*
>
> Identify ways in which you could achieve each of these means of facilitating structural practice in your agency, ideally sharing these in discussion with others.

Some suggestions

Among the techniques I have seen practitioners use are seeking solutions that reflect people's realities and do not blame individuals. Practitioners have included these alternative views in case recordings, have developed information leaflets describing clients' rights and entitlements to services, have formed groups with colleagues with similar views and have been tactful and constructive rather than attacking. They have sought to be practitioners who provide solutions, not problems.

Working outside the organization includes:

- an awareness of the alternative services and organizations that can help clients in different ways, and making referrals to them;
- being involved in and involving clients in social movements and coalition-building that aim for social change;
- participation in trade unions and professional associations that work on achieving beneficial social change, rather than merely supporting self-interest;
- encouraging an awareness among practitioners, clients and carers of debates in electoral politics and opportunities to be engaged in politics; this includes encouraging mutual support groups to be aware of and involved in policy development, sometimes using social media and other informal means of communication;
- supporting the revitalization and development of the public sector as a socially progressive force;

- developing discourses that are critical of the dominant social order;
- emphasizing human rights to recognize that everyone has a shared interest in having their needs for health, autonomy and well-being met.

Example text: Fook's (2012) critical practice

Fook argues that a critical tradition in social work connects with a concern with the social rather than the personal, which the structural critique builds on. There is, however, no complete divide between structural and 'traditional' thinking, and individual psychological and interpersonal experiences are valid. Postmodern and poststructural ideas offer the possibility of incorporating multiple perspectives into our practice. Critical theory allows us to incorporate reflective and interactive ways of knowing, and to recognize connections between structural oppression and our personal self-limitations and the possibilities for both personal and social change.

Fook's approach to social work concentrates on rethinking our ideas about practice in four different ways.

Knowing

Critical practice questions both what we know and how we know it. Modernist ideas see knowledge as having achieved the status of objective understanding, that is, as being widely regarded as validated. Professions maintain their social position by their generation and disseminated of such accepted knowledge. Critical reflection allows us to apply knowledge from a wide range of sources, including clients and their communities. We should use a variety of ways of knowing and sources of knowledge, being inclusive in the range of people we involve in developing our knowledge.

Power: who has power and how they use it

This is important because power is often seen as a commodity, something that someone or some group has, instead of something that can be shared. Following from this, we tend to see groups as opposed to one another: if we think one thing, then someone who thinks something different is an enemy. However, we should accept that differences exist, and try to account for contradictions in our thinking and get other people to see the contradictions in the way they are behaving. There can be no assumptions about what is empowering to individuals: their reactions may vary.

Discourse, language and narrative

The Marxist concept of ideology sees it as a system of beliefs that has been institutionalized as part of the way in which a society or part of a society operates. This system interacts with the theories, explanations, behaviour and practical consequences related to the beliefs. In turn, the beliefs, behaviour and theories all affect and support one another.

However, this way of seeing ideology leads to a number of problems. Different explanations are, according to a person's ideology, seen as true or false. Your behaviour is similarly seen as directional, that is, it always works in favour of one point of view rather than another. There is also a rational superstructure of ideas (an assumption that all ideas have to fit into an entirely consistent and rational pattern) and a lack of plurality (an assumption that multiple perspectives can coexist, or that ideas may be ambiguous) or contradiction (an assumption that ideas may have elements within them that contradict each other) in thinking; in this way, inconsistencies are ironed out.

Postmodern discourse views about understanding, however, run counter to these views. They suggest, calling particularly on Foucault's work, that understanding is constructed by social practices, particular forms of subjectivity and the power relations inherent in knowledge. Language is not seen as neutral but as colouring how we think and what we know. The narrative that we tell about something chooses between possible alternatives so that our communications convince others that what we say is true. If we can rethink it, a different interpretation may become true.

Identity and difference

Critical theories question the traditional idea of a set, continuous self and identity. Part of this has to do with language. For example, we tend to think of things as dichotomies: what we are and what we are not. If I say that I am a quiet, studious person, it excludes the possibility of being a lively, socially active person. However, critical ideas suggest that we can change and be contradictory and multiple – many things at once. We should see ourselves as whole people who can develop more complexity and diversity.

Figure 12.6 is my representation of the important elements of Fook's critical practice. Each element converts one of 'new ways of thinking' into a practice, and has connections with solution practice, discussed in Chapter 9. Contextual practice (that it, working on the family, community and social environment rather than directly on the client's behaviour) draws on the empowerment and advocacy approaches discussed in Chapter 11. By emphasizing 'unsettling' dominant discourses, Fook emphasizes how critical theory is an important source of the shared value principle of disrupting current social assumptions through critical practice (see Figure 1.7).

An overarching practice approach relevant to much critical practice is the poststructuralist idea of deconstruction, which we met in Chapter 10; Fook's book provides a critical theory analysis of this idea that shows how you can use deconstruction in work with clients. This is particularly important in disrupting current assumptions throughout, but especially in understanding clients' situations and empowering them. The main sequence of practice action is as follows:

■ *Deconstruction* may, for example, tease out the range of individual and social factors that influence what is happening to the client.
■ *Resistance* involves thinking out ways in which events are pushing clients to go against their own beliefs. For example, changes in social security or employment policy may give priority to a single parent getting a job rather than caring for a young child.
■ *Challenge* involves finding positive ways of disagreeing with unhelpful pressure, for example identifying positive progress in the social relationships made by a mentally ill person to contest demands that their behaviour be managed by increased medication.
■ *Reconstruction* may, for example, involve planning a new pattern of life that combines the preferred aims of the client with demands for compliance with external demands.

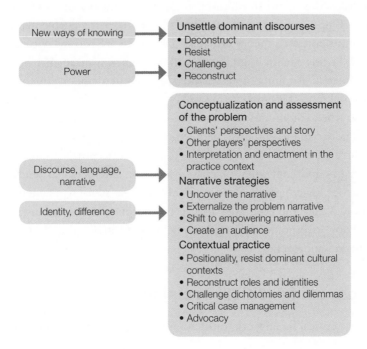

Figure 12.6 Fook's critical practice
Source: Adapted from Fook (2012).

The ideas of resistance and challenge derive from radical theory. Critical practice also has similarities with cognitive practice (Chapter 6) because it suggests that we should not be misled by irrational ways of thinking. Critical practice differs, however, because it emphasizes particular areas of irrational thinking (misunderstanding about discourses of dominance) and flexibility, and focuses on change in a particular direction (towards reconstructing relationships that enhance clients' understanding and use of power). These again connect more closely to radical thinking.

Critical practice also rejects the authoritative 'therapist' practitioner that is implied by cognitive theories in favour of a more complex relationship between social worker and client that reflects the ambiguities of their relationships, both between themselves and in the networks of relationships in the practitioner's agency and in the client's social environment. For example, feminist ideas have been criticized for assuming that women always have shared interests, whereas women in good jobs have few shared interests with new migrants living in poverty. We may, however, seek equality and shared experience with clients while realizing that this is not always possible or helpful (White, 1995). I take this point further when I discuss V. White's (2006) work in Chapter 13. In these ways, critical practice directly picks up and uses empowerment and feminist theory (see Chapters 11 and 13), but it has a different view of them.

Fook (2012) takes up Adams' (2008) critique of empowerment theory, discussed in Chapter 11, that it is not possible to empower people – they must empower themselves. Mullaly also makes this point. In addition, empowering one person or group may disempower others. Empowerment may also be diluted to mere enablement, particularly where, as in anti-oppressive theory (Chapter 14), there are too many target groups for empowerment; in this situation, addressing all of them will mean that none of them is addressed adequately. An ambiguous relationship between empowerment and self-help illustrates this problem. It is empowering to help yourself, but it is not empowering to be forced to do so when you do not have the resources. Consequently, Fook emphasizes the importance of not trying to empower people unrealistically.

The final three aspects of critical practice – problem conceptualization and assessment, narrative strategies and contextual practice – focus on interpersonal practice and, with contextual practice, macro practice and an involvement in social work agencies and social work education. While she continues to use the deconstruction–reconstruction model throughout, Fook incorporates a range of practices through using narrative and other social construction approaches.

Conclusion: using critical social work

Practitioners use critical social work to offer a framework of practice that enables them:

- to practise in ways that emphasize social change rather than, or as well as, problem-solving and empowerment;
- to become aware of and avoid oppressive systems in society where they blame and victimize clients, particularly in their own agencies and their own practice;
- to provide a theoretical framework emphasizing social justice and equality in their practice in interpersonal work as well as in advocacy;
- to keep in mind alternative ways of exploring, assessing and acting in social situations that do not take for granted the current social order, particularly where this is oppressive to their clients and the communities they are working with;
- to have a critique of individualistic, psychological practice techniques, which assist them to think critically;
- to provide a broad framework in which they can incorporate the ideas of feminist and anti-discriminatory practice.

In these and similar ways, the availability of critical practice avoids social work staying with the status quo. In addition, as with social construction, humanist and empowerment theories, critical practice remains positive about the possibilities for change, in spite of barriers and social resistances that make both personal and social change difficult. The difficulty for many practitioners is that the strong analysis of barriers and social oppression in these theories can seem too negative to maintain their positive motivation in practice.

Additional resources

Further reading

Allan, J., Briskman, L. and Pease, B. (2009) *Critical Social Work: Theories and Practice for a Socially Just World* (2nd edn) (Crows Nest, NSW: Allen & Unwin).

Fook, J. (2012) *Social Work: A Critical Approach to Practice* (2nd edn) (Los Angeles: Sage).

Healy, K. (2000) *Social Work Practices: Contemporary Perspectives on Change* (London: Sage).

Mullaly, B. (R. P.) (2007) *The New Structural Social Work* (4th edn) (Ontario: Oxford University Press).

Important critical practice texts and collections, all deriving from Australia.

Ferguson, I. and Woodward, R. (2009) *Radical Social Work in Practice: Making a Difference* (Bristol: Policy Press).

Lavalette, M. (ed.) (2011) *Radical Social Work Today: Social Work at the Crossroads* (Bristol: Policy Press).

Recent accounts drawing on radical social work.

Journal

Journal of Progressive Human Services – Taylor and Francis; see
http://www.tandfonline.com/toc/wphs20/current

Websites

http://www.uwindsor.ca/criticalsocialwork
The internet journal *Critical Social Work*.
http://www.radical.org.uk/barefoot/
The Barefoot Social Work website has useful information, although it is not always regularly updated.

Feminist practice

13

Main contribution

Feminist perspectives contribute to social work a focus on explaining and responding to the oppressed position of women in many societies. This is important because, in most societies, women are the main clients of social work, and most social workers and social care workers are women. Feminist perspectives, therefore, help everyone – not only women – to understand how their social role and position is worked out in society; in particular, they allow the female majority of social workers and their clients to practise in solidarity with each others' worldviews. Feminist practice contributes practice methods and skills in collaborative dialogue and groupwork that can be used to achieve a consciousness of issues that affect women in their social relations within societies. These can also be applied more widely.

Main points

- Feminist thinking has a long history, dating from the nineteenth century, with several differentiated perspectives. It concerns how, in many aspects of life, women and their social relations are dominated by social relations based on men's assumptions.
- Critiques of feminism in social work question whether using it excludes men and risks placing women's issues into a ghetto. These critiques also suggest that limiting feminist practice to issues of concern to women has made feminism invisible by failing to develop generalist theories of practice using feminist ideas.
- Alternative feminist perspectives of liberal, radical, socialist, black and postmodern feminism focus on the different ways in which oppression may affect women.
- In social work, feminist thinking raised concern for women's conditions, developed a women-centred practice, focused on women's distinctive voice and identity and celebrated women's diversity.
- Specifically, feminist practice focuses concern on women's experiences and roles in child care, their role in the reproduction or development of social and economic systems, and the importance of reconstructing private relationships on a more equal footing.

■ Feminist practice seeks commonalities between female practitioners and the women they work with and takes place in a dialogic, egalitarian relationship. This has been an important contribution to critical theory.

■ The ethics of care position emphasizes the feminist view that caring derives from interpersonal connections within relationships, rather than from rational, planned service provision.

Practice ideas

☐ *Consciousness-raising* (connected to the critical practice of conscientization) is a strategy for stimulating awareness and change.

☐ *Reflexivity* was first used as a research tool and subsequently adapted as an element of practice.

☐ *Dialogue* is a process through which different perceptions are described and opposed against each other in an example of egalitarian relationships. It acts as the vehicle of a practice that values and empowers women and all clients.

☐ Social and personal *identity* and the social processes by which it is formed and by which it changes are an important aspect of creating and intervening in diverse relationships.

☐ The *ethics of care* position argues that women's caring arises from relatedness.

Major statements

Dominelli's (2002a) *Feminist Social Work Theory and Practice* is a rare contribution in that it provides a coherent account of a structural perspective on feminist theory that has application to practice. Earlier statements have been provided by Dominelli and McCleod (1989), Hanmer and Statham's *Women and Social Work* (1999) and the edited text by Bricker-Jenkins et al. (1991). These give extended theoretical analyses, useful explanations of issues of concern to women in social work and very useful accounts of practice, respectively, but they do not incorporate more recent developments in postmodern feminist thinking. The edited collection of van den Bergh (1995) reflects a range of perspectives on practice issues.

V. White's (2006) account of feminist social work is based on evidence collected from interviews with feminist women, this approach representing feminist styles of research and analysis. It gives a sense of collective endeavour to create theory by two means: first, inclusively through dialogue, the external process in which women debate issues in relationships of equality, and secondly through dialectic, the internal process through which people argue out in their minds opposing and different ideas to form the basis of their decisions, thoughts or actions. Because White exemplifies feminist thinking in this way, and presents an up-to-date and practical account of what it is like to practise using feminist ideas, I use it as the example text in this chapter.

The debate summary

Debates about feminist theory reflect attitudes towards women and feminism, in particular existing gender inequalities. Feminism asserts that women are oppressed by social structures and relationships in society that privilege men and male views of social priorities, excluding and devaluing women and women's views of society. This leads to the oppression of women, particularly those with little social or economic power. Since that oppression derives from inequalities arising from gender divisions, it is important to understand how the experience of this oppression makes it difficult for women to achieve their aspirations and attain well-being. It also makes it difficult to intervene to challenge and change that oppression.

One criticism of explicitly using feminist theory is that focusing on women's issues excludes equally important concerns that mainly affect men, including violence and exploitation in employment that is different in nature from women's oppression in these situations. It might also fail to examine the effect of gender divisions on men's problems. In addition, the focus on women's issues may exclude men's participation. While a feminist criticism of many societies is that women are assumed to take on caring roles and the management of social relationships in families and more widely, there has been no concerted attempt in social work to engage men in family and social care. But there is evidence that if a caring role is required of them, particularly in intimate relationships, they do perform it; this has been shown, for example, in Parker's (1993) study of men's care for wives affected by severe disability and Fisher's (1994) discussion of men's caring role in community care services generally. By concentrating on women, the critics say, feminist ideas fail to pick up important opportunities to change gender relations and roles for the benefit of both sexes.

Against this point of view, feminist theory points to evidence of widespread gender inequality and the consequences of the exploitation of and violence towards women, as well as the neglect of their needs. Recognizing this, some men support women's movements and engage in 'pro-feminist' theorization.

Using feminist theory is useful because most social work involves women working with other women; feminist ideas inform this majority practice. In addition, in most societies, women are significantly more affected by poverty and many other social disadvantages than men. Against these points, women may be the main clients of social work only in particular welfare systems. Some of the Nordic welfare systems, where social work is associated with the social security system, generate social work with men more easily, since men are referred for social work when seeking financial benefits. The focus on women might also be a product of preference or comfort among practitioners for working with the female members of families rather than the male. The organization of social services in the daytime, involving domestic visiting, family care issues such as child care and care for frail older people, generates a focus on women, given current social assumptions.

Another problem with the explicit use of feminist ideas is that it places women's issues into a ghetto as an area of special interest, rather than gaining credence for feminist analysis more widely. Orme (2003) argues that feminist caution about pursing the path of creating extensive feminist models of general practice renders feminism invisible and its critique of how social agencies operate ineffective. The priorities of feminist social work may be justified, however, because the history of social work and its role in surveillance on behalf of a patriarchal welfare state means that women remain socially oppressed and social work does little to alter that.

Resistance to feminism lies in the refusal of male institutions, including marriage, employment and social work agencies and education, to give up their power. This is the other side of seeing feminist ideas as a matter of special interest rather than a general critique of social ideas and practice. The social relationships that are critically analysed by feminists do not change, even though feminist ideas are not directly contested in social work. For example, there have been continuing criticisms of the lack of women in senior positions in social work organizations in proportion to the number of women in the organization, and, in universities, of women's lack of influence over and leadership in academic work. Reactions have often been defensive, and no theoretical analysis justifying these inequalities is presented by the opponents of feminism. Discrimination against women continues to be commonplace in the workplace and in welfare provision, and women are disadvantaged economically and socially everywhere, especially in resource-poor countries. There is thus clearly an issue to be addressed by a profession that tries to help people in this position.

Wider theoretical perspectives

Feminism has a history stretching back for more than a hundred years. The first wave of feminist activism, which ended in the 1930s, was concerned with gaining political and legal property rights. From the 1960s onwards, the second wave of feminism was concerned with how the continued inequality of opportunity in work, political influence and the public sphere generally connected with attitudes towards women in the private sphere, in interpersonal relationships.

Some people also talk about a 'third wave', a backlash against the influence of feminist thinking, that requires continued campaigning to sustain improvements in the equality of women with men. You can analyse this backlash as a post-feminist era in which assumptions that equality is an unachievable false goal replace social movements aiming to free women from social domination by men and male assumptions. This view proposes that feminism has spoiled many female advantages and preferences, for example, being free to use female attractiveness to men to gain social advantages, or being able to prefer being a full-time mother rather than working.

Alternative feminist perspectives

Since the 1960s, feminism has developed alternative perspectives to explain the inequalities between men and women:

▪ *Liberal feminism* (Reynolds, 1993; Dominelli, 2002a) seeks regular improvements in equality between men and women, particularly in workplaces and in caring and family responsibilities. This view argues that sex differences (the physical differences) between women and men have been translated by cultural assumptions into gender differences (social assumptions about the differences between men and women's behaviour and interests). Gender assumptions affect social relations even though sex differences are often unimportant. The answer to inequalities is to change gender assumptions by promoting equal opportunities by legislation, by changing social conventions so that gender assumptions lose their powerful effect and by altering the socialization process so that children do not grow up accepting gender inequalities.

- *Radical feminism* (Reynolds, 1993; Dominelli, 2002a) attacks patriarchy, the aspects of social systems that give men power and privilege. This view values and celebrates the differences between men and women. It seeks to promote separate women's structures within existing organizations and women's own social structures.

- *Socialist feminism* (Reynolds, 1993; Dominelli, 2002a) points out that women's oppression comes from the inequality inherent in the social structure of a class-based social system. Marxist theory (see Chapter 12) says that women's role in capitalism is to reproduce the workforce for capitalism's benefit. They do this by carrying out domestic tasks and child care, and socialist feminism focuses on this. Socialist feminism also emphasizes how women's oppression interacts with other forms of oppression, such as race or disability. This approach to feminist thinking proposes that the oppressive characteristics of social relations should be analysed and understood, so that diverse interests can be met in alternative ways.

- *Black feminism* (Collins, 2000; Dominelli, 2002a) starts from racism and points to the diversity of women and the different kinds and combinations of oppression by which they are affected. Collins (2000) suggests that, because black women are oppressed in many areas of social and domestic life, their experience of oppression is heightened compared with white women. There are diverse responses to such oppression depending on the particular experience, and connections are made with other campaigns for social justice because of the connection with different areas of oppression. Important connections are made to family experience in slavery, and to historic family and social patterns derived from African and other originating countries.

- *Postmodern feminism* (Sands and Nuccio, 1992; Dominelli, 2002a) identifies the complexity and sophistication of social relations that involve women by examining how discourse in society creates social assumptions about how women are and should be treated. One of the important features of postmodern feminism is its concern to question categories rather than accepting them. Deriving from Foucault's (1972) work, postmodern feminism also looks at social relations in which powerful groups, in this case particularly groups dominated by men and men's interests, surveil (consistently and oppressively watch) and discipline others, in this case particularly social groups within which women have influence. The aims of surveillance and discipline are to maintain a social order that sustains male power. Social work intervention often forms part of surveillance and discipline, for example in managing child development or youth offending in poor families, or in restricting access to life-expanding opportunities for disabled and older people.

While there are overlaps between different forms of feminist theory, they also criticize each other. Liberal feminism is criticized for ignoring real differences in the interests and experiences of men and women. In addition, promoting equal opportunities – the main prescription of liberal feminist theories – is sometimes ineffective in furthering women's equality since opportunities do not always lead to fair outcomes if other aspects of inequality do not allow women to make use of the opportunities. Radical feminism is criticized for focusing on gender differences and the common experiences of women, ignoring the diversity of interests among women. Emphasizing gender difference may play down women's capacity to achieve social change and may trap them in a 'victimized' role. Socialist feminism is criticized by radical feminists because it mainly limits its analysis of power relations between men and women to economic power and misses, for example, male violence. Others say that the socialist focus on class and economic oppression offers inadequate explanations of patriarchy.

As with all postmodern perspectives, postmodern feminism may be criticized for emphasizing relativity of social understanding, in the same way as postmodernism is criticized more generally for moral relativity (see Chapter 9). This is integral to feminist thought, since it sees gender as socially constructed assumptions, rather than depending on the sexual identity of women. However, postmodern ideas emphasize how language creates different social perspectives and categories. It thus implies that 'woman' is not a single category, and diffuses the focus on women's exploitation and oppression (Forcey and Nash, 1998). Some feminists, therefore, have been concerned that the influence of postmodernism has damagingly reduced the feminist focus on men's oppressive power (Fawcett and Featherstone, 2000); others, however, argue that it enables practitioners to understand complex gender and other relations.

Connections

A well-developed feminist social work analysis does exist. In a paper that was influential in initiating a feminist debate in social work, Sands and Nuccio (1992) emphasize the importance of 'problematizing' social and gender categories; this means avoiding taking for granted assumptions about social categories and the characteristics of people who are categorized in various ways. For example, we should not assume that women are natural carers for children and men are not natural carers merely because women have the biological role of having babies. Why should there be a simple either/or distinction? Taylor and Daly's (1995) collection considers the historical development of women's role as being subservient to men in general social conventions, the law, medical practice and religion, which have had a considerable influence on the development of social work. This identifies many areas in which gender categories are taken for granted. Van den Bergh's (1995) collection examines issues of importance to women that have influenced feminist practice, including peace, social justice and violence against women.

Domestic violence is a good example here. Conventional attitudes often assume that women who ask for police help later change their minds about prosecuting a violent male partner and thereby waste police time. Feminist thinking recognizes the many social pressures that lead women to accept even a violent relationship. Examples of these pressures are the views of other family members, conventional assumptions about the importance of sustaining a marriage for the children's sake, the sense of failure in an important relationship and the financial power that men sometimes have in a marriage. However, an important way of moving towards a position of justice for women in violent relationships is to help them make decisions that take dealing with these factors into account.

Feminist and critical practice theory

Feminism has been an important contributor to critical practice, as we saw in Chapter 12. This is because it is an important critique of taken-for-granted social attitudes because it questions how gendered social assumptions affect relationships and social institutions. It is impossible to conceive of current-day critical practice without incorporating a feminist perspective.

Feminism is also a significant contributor to critical practice *theory*. We saw in Chapter 12, for example, that Fook (2012), a major contributor to the development of critical theory, states that feminism has been a major influence on her. However, feminist ideas are woven within her work rather than being explicitly identified. Healy (2000) sees feminism as going beyond critical practice. This is because it is open to a wider range of explanations of oppression than class and racial divisions are.

In addition, it gives priority to interpersonal and personal experience as an expression of oppression and a contributor to social change. For example, a Marxist explanation of racial oppression claims that it arises from the need of capitalist societies to maintain an impoverished population available to take low-grade jobs; feminism, however, would look additionally at how economic pressures on poor families make it difficult for women to facilitate their children's education and interpersonal skills. Thus, the feminist view does not exclude the issues of socioeconomic class, but looks at more complex explanations of interpersonal and social relationships. Feminism is prepared to look at the interactions between different forms of oppression, rather than giving priority to one system of social oppression. On the other hand, Fook (2012) also sees feminism as part of critical practice because it refuses to take the present social order for granted.

Much of Fook's material on feminist social work particularly emphasizes the way in which gender difference and power are linked. Social and physical difference may become associated with the use of power in complex ways. For example, people may too readily give up making choices that might be open to them because they do not go far enough to deal with difficult relationships or issues. They might happily accept and value professional expertise or the help they receive, when they might also enter into a dialogue in which they may question particular things that do not suit them.

Case example: Money and power in a family relationship

An elderly woman in a residential care home valued the care given her and appreciated her sister's frequent visits to take her out. However, the sister also managed the resident's money and was very careful with it. In one incident among many, the sister was slow to replace expensive batteries in the resident's hearing aid, thus isolating her socially. The resident would not question this, because she did not want to upset her main support. When the care home manager raised concern about this at a review, the social worker got the sisters to discuss this on the basis that small things are important when life is restricted by being in residential care. More broadly, having this particular incident questioned might mean that the sister would be more thoughtful about their different attitudes to money in the future.

The social worker also thought about whether this behaviour might have been financial abuse of a vulnerable person. She judged that action might have been needed to protect the resident from misuse of her money if the sister had not shifted her stance.

One of the important aspects of postmodern feminism, to which we now turn, is an awareness of the diversity of behaviour – the view that 'women are always oppressed, never the oppressor' is not always true.

Feminism and postmodernism

Sands and Nuccio (1992) and Healy (2000: 46–55) discuss some of the ideas that postmodern feminism contributes to social work, both of them focusing on poststructural theory. Poststructuralism, a set of theories of French origin, contests 'logocentrism' – the idea that there is a single, fixed, logical social order that can be identified as reality. This connects with other postmodern ideas that question the possibility of understanding the world according to linear explanations of cause and effect. Consequently, there will be a wide diversity of social forms and behaviours.

One of the important areas of postmodern feminism is that it addresses complexities and ambiguities in women's lives (Healy, 2000: 42; Orme, 2009b: 200). Orme's (2003) criticism of some social work for people with long-term conditions is that it sets up a 'male' system for assessing need and allocating care services that relies on routinization and checklists. Generally, feminist thinking sees managerialist and rational systems as characteristic of male thinking and relationships, attributing less structured approaches to setting up systems as being more characteristic of female experience and thinking. First, this only partly represents the possibilities in the situation. Formalizing decision-making helps to permit greater equity and social justice in the provision of services, although it may dehumanize the way in which services are provided (Payne, 2009d; Orme, 2003). Second, formalized decision-making may also mean that people in more senior roles in care agencies, more often men than women, manage these 'male' decision-making processes to allocate inadequate resources, leaving female relatives or less powerful practitioners and carers to manage the human consequences of this lack of resources.

Caring continues to be needed even if resources are inadequate, and there is evidence of both men and women accepting and negotiating caring roles in a complex interplay of relationships. Postmodern feminist theory acknowledges and seeks to understand this diversity and the multiple discourses that exist. However, it is criticized by structuralist writers such as Dominelli because this emphasis on diversity makes it less easy to gain solidarity for political and social action to improve resources. Sands and Nuccio (1992) identify feminist thought that emphasizes 'positionality' or 'both/and'; we met this in Fook's analysis of critical practice, which relies strongly on feminist thinking. Here, while engaging in social action for better resources, practitioners would emphasize and document the universal experience of women in providing caring, and promote men's support for the need for social change, while in other situations practitioners would value and recognize diversity.

Feminist thinking also gives an important role to identity and its sources in people's social experience. People's sense of themselves derives from myriad social relationships and the institutional and personal influences upon them (Jenkins, 2008). It is thus constructed in the social and historical period that they experience. Exploring the factors that create someone's identity and how this relates to group membership is an essential part of postmodern feminism (Sands, 1996). It is also relevant to ethnic and cultural sensitivity (Chapter 14) because an important aspect of social identity is national identity and the factors that create it or may be assumed because of it.

Postmodern feminism particularly focuses on the deconstruction of these sorts of discourses about women in society. The approach tries to destabilize conventional behaviour and assumptions, and to provide openings for alternative and diverse interpretations. So, looking at issues of identity, it questions whether people have a single, stable and perhaps developing identity throughout life; instead, adopting alternative understandings of social experiences might enable people to reconsider and change the main identity that they assume. An example is women who fall in with conventional assumptions about women's roles in marriage and playing a major role in raising a family but then, on divorce, find a strong lesbian identity. This change does not reject a woman's identity as the 'mother of a family' but is not a development of heterosexual identity; it is a complete change of conception of the woman's self. Another example is that postmodern feminist thinking contests language that, by moderating and managing the impression of behaviour, denies domestic and sexual violence against women and children (Healy, 2000: 40).

Case example: The man who 'tapped' his wife

A practitioner interviewed a man to question his violence towards his wife. He started by describing the event as 'I tapped her one' (hit or slapped her lightly once), whereas the police account that had led him to be imprisoned was of a public argument in the front garden of their house. Getting the man to describe what happened in detail, the practitioner eventually got him to describe injuries such as grazes, cuts and bleeding, aggression such as shouting, and how he had knocked her down and pushed her over a fence.

Here, by challenging a vague moderating presentation of the event, the practitioner highlighted the reality of gender violence. Another example of language use in particular discourses that needs to be questioned to achieve destabilization is describing the sexual abuse of children as expressions of affection.

Another important area is reassessing the cultural characteristics of the 'feminine body' (Healy, 2000: 49–51); the French writer Cixous has been influential on social work writing in this area (Sands and Nuccio, 1992; Healy 2000). Women's bodies are not simply physical objects; instead, their physical character and their differences from male bodies are interwoven with cultural assumptions and expectations. Social assumptions about what is a good or attractive in a woman's body vary between cultures, and different presentations of a body incur social assumptions. For example, a rounded, fleshy female body might be regarded as maternal, warm and comforting, or as representing overindulgence or lack of control in eating. In another culture or class, however, the rounded fleshy body might be regarded as an ideal of sexuality.

Postmodern feminism attaches a high value to diversity and women's individual choice. Social workers might be concerned about obesity leading to ill-health or early death in clients, for example, without recognizing the emotional needs met by eating. They may also fail to recognize the consequences of poverty and assumptions about the role of women in families, which may cause a woman to eat poor food, which may lead to obesity, while giving the better quality food to her children and male partner. For similar reasons, feminism is also important in anti-oppressive perspectives, because gender divisions are important sources of social oppression. In addition, oppression arising from gender divisions may magnify the experiences of oppression felt by black and ethnic minority women.

Other interactions with theory

There has been concern about the way in which women's socialization is inconsistent with male definitions of management. For example, a female manager might give importance to mutual trust and support in her relationships with team members, and accept flexibility in their working hours to facilitate child care. A male manager, on the other hand, might emphasize clarity of instructions and reporting in his relationships and encourage long working hours to complete tasks, seeing family commitments as antagonistic to meeting work objectives. Patriarchy means that male assumptions about what is good management practice prevail in organizations. This means that women do not attain senior roles in agencies consistent with their representation among social workers generally; they are also sometimes unhappy about the way in which authority and power are exercised within social work. Some writers (Coulshed et al., 2013) have developed distinctively feminist approaches to social work management as a consequence.

Feminists seek to understand the lives and experience of women from their own perspectives and values, which are different from men's, and thus avoid looking at them from the point of view of men. An important method is consciousness-raising by forming groups to share experiences and provide mutual support. Longres and McCleod (1980) relate consciousness-raising to the conscientization of Freire (1972), which connects directly to critical theory. We saw in Chapter 12 that feminist thinking has had a strong influence on critical theory and is a relevant perspective in many of the theories presented in this book.

Similarly, in social work, it is argued that goal- and task-oriented practice, as well as positivist demands for scientific or evidence-based practice, are male-defined priorities that use male language and a male way of thinking (Collins, 1986; Fawcett et al., 2000). Walker (1994), however, points to the gains achieved by the scientific method and argues that the criticism should be of the uses to which it has been put. Moreover, the 'ethics of care' position argues that caring is devalued by patriarchal societies because it is associated with women. Parton (2003) argues that the focus of social construction theory on plurality of knowledge and voice connects to this view by accepting alternative narratives and possibilities in practice.

Many complexities are presented by work with men, since gender relationships are unlike many other forms of oppression and discrimination (Christie, 2006). This is because men and women are in close relationships, while many oppressed groups, such as gay and lesbian people and people in ethnic minorities, often live much of their social life in separated social groups (Milner, 2004). Thus, feminist practice may give low priority to working with men, for example by working with the victims of domestic violence rather than the male perpetrators. People concerned with anti-discrimination will, however, find it easier to identify the benefits of adjusting oppressive relationships and actions for all parties involved; I explore this more fully in Chapter 14.

Pro-feminist ideas have therefore been generated to help in working to make sexual stereotypes more explicit. This may be helpful in practice aimed at reducing violence and sexual exploitation, as well as in social work education to see clearly where oppressive assumptions about male–female relationships require different ways of working (Cavanagh and Cree, 1996). Work with men and boys seeks to remove any damaging effects of their socialization into conventional male behaviour. In addition, it aims to reduce their tendency to become isolated because of the expectation that men do not need help or support, as well as their tendency towards aggression and violence (van Elst, 1994). Social conflict that adversely affects women justifies special attention to working with men so as to resolve issues of masculinity that cause problems for the men involved – or more widely.

Working to change men may, however, be criticized if it leads to working with men as an instrument to achieve improvements for women, unless it is clear that it also benefits the men involved. Otherwise, our practice may subject men to change for general social benefit rather than their own. Pro-feminist work with men, therefore, needs to understand the benefits both for the men involved as well as for women and wider society; as part of this, it needs to generate informed consent by the men for interventions in their lives.

The politics of feminist social work

Feminist social work theory emerged out of the commitment of women social workers to wider feminist movements in Western societies in the 1970s. It became associated with the radical social work movements of the 1960s and early 70s, but its earliest writings came from a broader, more liberal tradition in response to general movements to improve civil and human rights. During the 1970s, academic work and radical theory on women's caring roles influenced professional thinking. Conversely, feminist movements affected counselling approaches to women's well-being and health. There was also campaigning around issues affecting women, particularly violence, rape and prostitution. Orme (2009a) identifies four main areas of feminist social work:

- *women's conditions* – with women sharing the experience of oppression and discrimination in many areas of life, and professionals being disadvantaged in pursuing their work and professional advancement;
- *women-centred practice* – where the focus is on identifying women's particular needs and responding to them;
- *women's different voice* – women experience the world differently, and have views that are different from those of men, particularly in matters of social and moral concern;
- *working with diversity* – because of their shared experience of oppression, women were able to identify, value and respond to many different sorts of social diversity. This is an important source of the feminist contribution to anti-oppressive and critical practice.

The focus of feminist theory is often on situations where women have suffered domestic violence or sexual assault. Alternatively, domestic and sexual violence may arise where women are strongly involved because of social assumptions about their gender roles. Violence against women and sexual problems, for example, are part of wider social and health issues that women play an important role in resolving within families. For example, mental health, substance abuse, homelessness, poverty and child welfare often fall to be dealt with by women (Valentich, 2011). Scourfield (2006), exploring child welfare practice, notes that since social work operates individualistically, and child care is, in a patriarchal society, carried out by women, child protection work will inevitably involve a scrutiny of mothering, rather than of issues of child poverty and poor nutrition. Feminists propose a rebalancing of the way in which we think about such issues. Callahan (1996), for example, suggests concentrating on:

- women's experience of child care as a central aspect of understanding work with children;
- families and the female role within them as crucial elements of child care;
- reproduction as an element of society that is as important as economic production;
- relationships that need to be reconstructed to see the connection between private relationships, between spouses and between women and children, so that they interact with public definitions of what is considered to be appropriate and are then enforced in family relationships.

Values issues

Commonalities

An important value position in feminist practice is that women share important commonalities; that is, they have shared experiences as victims of oppression by a patriarchal society that privileges men's ways of thinking and living. This is a source of identity for women and a basis for building relationships between practitioners and clients, enabling women to support each other (Orme, 2009b).

Teater (2010) suggests that there are four important shared commonalities in feminist social work practice:

- ending patriarchy;
- empowering women;
- understanding people, particularly women, in their environment or social context, making the personal political and the political personal;
- raising consciousness among women and men of the way in which social structures establish gender inequalities.

This may, however, be another situation in which women's diversity is a factor. For example, many social workers do not share the same experience of poverty and difficult experiences in the labour market as many of the women they work with, but they may share the experience of sexual bullying (Penketh, 2011).

Dialogic practice

We have seen that an important tenet of feminist social work theory is having a dialogic relationship between practitioners and clients. What would dialogue consist of? An aspect of dialogic practice is to see dialogue between participants in a social situation as always being open-ended (Healy, 2005: 51–5). It is important to avoid defining the required outcomes in advance, or allowing people with institutionalized power, often men, to close off the debate before the participants in the situation have been able to engage adequately with different points of view. The following case example illustrates how a practitioner refused to let the husband's assumptions limit the range of family issues explored in an assessment, while not completely excluding the male perspective that he represented.

Case example: Dealing with all the issues in an assessment

Jackie was carrying out an assessment of a family referred because the daughter Nichole was presenting behaviour problems at school; there had previously been concern about the physical abuse of younger children in the family. Naomi, the mother of two of Jacob's children, was talking with Jackie about the difficulty of integrating two of Jacob's older children from his previous relationships into the family; Jacob, however, wanted the conversation to focus on Nichole and her difficult behaviour at home, as well as at school. Jackie managed to maintain a more complete dialogue that included Naomi's thinking by stopping the conversation and getting them to agree to look at each child in turn and list both the positives and negatives about each one.

Feminism and the ethics of care view

McLaughlin (2003) identifies debates between social theories and feminist thinking. An important example is standpoint theory, a feminist extension of a Marxist perspective. This argues that different social groups each represent particular perspectives (standpoints) on society, each standpoint incorporating a group's economic and social interests. The theory proposes that women constitute such a group with a coherent standpoint, which reflects their economic and social oppression by men. According to standpoint theory, all oppression stems from economic oppression. Postmodern perspectives, on the other hand, emphasize the complexities of the cultural and linguistic aspects of power relations between women and men in what may be a post-feminist era. In this view, women's ways of thinking and talking about relationships represent a specific cultural position; they are not subsidiary to a more general explanation, such as the economic emphasis of standpoint theory.

The idea of the 'ethics of care' is an important example of the alternative cultural expression that women's thinking and actions represents. It argues that women have a distinctive approach to care relationships in society that comes from their relationships and social experience. That experience and the consequent understanding of care in a different way from men's understanding does not, therefore, emerge from economic oppression, as standpoint theory would suggest, but from the differences between women's and men's experience.

Gilligan's work (1982) contributing to the 'ethics of care' position has been influential in social work and related professions (Koggel and Orme, 2010, 2011). Gilligan showed that women and men have different modes of reasoning about moral questions, including the nature of caring (Rhodes, 1985). The conception of caring contained in the ethics of care proposes that women experience caring attitudes and caring behaviour as coming from the connections between people. Men, on the other hand, provide caring because of a commitment to duty, responsibility and social expectations.

Davis (1985) applies this to social work, arguing that female 'voices', both generally and in social work, have been suppressed in favour of a male positivist perspective; this is therefore about both gender and the approach to understanding knowledge. Such a perspective argues for alternative ways of defining social work and its knowledge base, and for ensuring that agencies are not managed to exclude women and their perspectives.

Pause and reflect   *Mr Jones's attitudes*

This example of Hilda, an informal carer for Mr Jones, offers a picture of how feminist thinking offers a new perspective on these traditional social work debates. It uses an ethics of care analysis of gratitude that has been proposed by Mullin (2011).

Looking at the situation presented to the social worker in this case example, how do you evaluate the different points of view? What actions would you take?

> ### Case example: Hilda, Mr Jones, gratitude and caring labour
>
> Mr Jones was a disabled man, aged 86. Hilda, aged 62, his major carer, was his daughter-in-law, whose husband, Mr Jones's son, had died. Hilda began to experience heart failure and had to reduce the amount of activity in her busy life. Mr Jones had been a miner and had strong socialist beliefs, having been involved through his trade union in important strikes and working-class campaigns during his working lifetime. A social worker was asked to carry out an assessment to decide on an appropriate package of care to meet his increasing needs.
>
> The social worker came upon a hidden tension between Hilda and Mr Jones. Mr Jones felt that, as his deceased son's wife, Hilda had a duty to the family to care for her father-in-law, and he took everything she did for granted. Hilda, on the other hand, had formed a new relationship and wanted to get on with her life, feeling tied by her responsibility for Mr Jones. She was willing to be to some degree supportive, but felt he should show how much he appreciated her help in his relationships with her. Mr Jones felt that asking for social services help was an abandonment of her duty.

Some suggestions

The practitioner thought that the tensions stemmed partly from a generational difference in attitudes to the role of women; she thought that Mr Jones seemed to feel that caring in families should be natural and had not seen that it was usually an imposition by men on women's aspirations. By listening carefully to Hilda, the social worker was able to empathize with and respect her sense of frustration at not being able to move on in her life, which had arisen from social restrictions because of the gendered expectations that came from her former marriage. Hilda found the social worker's empathy respectful and supportive. However, it seemed to Mr Jones that these two women were 'ganging up' on him.

Mullin (2011), in her thoughtful ethics of care analysis of gratitude in caring relationships, contributes to our thinking here. She points out that women are usually more able and willing to express gratitude than men. This, she suggests, arises partly from what research has identified as a traditional male identity that conflates gratitude with indebtedness and dependency on others, which men are often brought up to avoid. Women, on the other hand, equate gratitude with a process of building connections between the cared-for person and the carer. The tension between Hilda and Mr Jones partly expresses his fear or rejection of a feeling of being dependent. However, it also expresses Hilda's lessening respect for him. For example, because she is focusing on her current life priorities, she is neglecting to respect his contribution to his family through a hard and difficult work life, and his political and social contribution to his community and more widely through his socialist commitment. The practitioner is allied with this, because she is focusing on Mr Jones's current care needs, rather than viewing his life holistically and incorporating a rounded view of his personal identity.

In a later intervention between them, the practitioner presented the argument that Mr Jones's socialist views should lead him to accept social services care because it was his right to receive it, both as a citizen and as someone who had contributed through taxes to providing services. This statement did try to use a recognition of and respect for his whole identity to balance his fear of dependency. Mr Jones replied that, if so, Hilda's expectation (and by implication the social worker's view, too) that he 'should grovel to be cared for in his old age' was wrong. Mullin (2011: 118) argues that gratitude is justified by good quality care provision and respect for the cared-for person; I have suggested that the tension found by the practitioner reveals what Mr Jones experiences as a lack of respect. Consequently, the quality of care was inappropriate for Mr Jones's psychological needs, because it rejected an important part of his feelings – his belief in the duty of women in his family to provide care – and this meant he was unable to feel and express gratitude.

There is a further point too. Mr Jones also felt that his socialist worldview and contributions to society through his work and campaigning life had been largely dismissed by the society and the state, as socialist ideas and trade unionism had recently lost their influence in society. Mullin (2011) argues that an essential element of working with caring relationships is to understand and work with the personal responses, attitudes and needs of both the cared-for person and the carer in a connected relationship, recognizing how these have been shaped by social hierarchies and public debate. The ethics of care view takes a feminist view that caring is about the connections between people, and feminist social work requires a thoughtful analysis of the connection itself and both sides of it. The practitioner needed to spend more time exploring feelings in this relationship before she could successfully interweave formal caring services with Hilda's caring help.

Applications

Feminist practice

In Figure 13.1, I set out some general ideas about appropriate feminist practice strategies, which I then go on to discuss more fully.

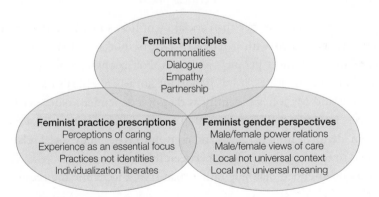

Figure 13.1 Feminist practice strategies

Source: Orme (2009b), Healy (2000) and van den Bergh (1995).

Orme (2009b) identifies three main strands of feminist practice:

- feminist principles, which form commonalities between feminism and social work based on the values shared by all women because of their shared experience;
- prescriptions for practice in working with women and men that derive from feminist thought;
- using feminist perspectives to understand the gender dimensions of practice.

Orme's (2009b: 71) assessment of the main contributions of feminist theory to practice are that it highlights, and therefore allows responses to:

- the use or misuse of power between men and women;
- ethics of care issues about privileging (male) rational, logical ways of responding to people, as against focusing on (female) ways of promoting the connectedness and relationships between people, including between practitioners and clients;
- the ways in which caring is positive, or may be demeaning, unhelpful and oppressive in relationships;
- the ways in which identity is connected with oppression, because identifying people with particular groups may make it easy to ignore or devalue their experience and contribution to social solidarity;
- the need to shift individualization from constraining us, by failing to connect with the diversity in people's lives, towards liberating us, by offering opportunities to respond to people's specific needs;
- people's personal, individual and private experiences as being important in thinking about and taking action, including political action, on the social issues that those experiences reveal;
- the way in which empathy allows people to express their needs and wishes.

Healy's (2000: 51–5) principles of postmodern feminist practice include similar points, while also supporting many elements of critical practice:

- Focus on social practices rather than social identities, so that we do not assume one single identity associated with a range of factors, but seek the complexities of the different factors that affect people's identities. For example, looking back at the case study on Hilda and Mr Jones, it was important not to see Hilda's identity as that of an informal carer and Mr Jones's identity as that of a dependent older person in need of care services. Looking at their relationship and social expectations in a more rounded way, we can identify caring practices and conventions in family social relationships that contributed to forming the conflicts between them.
- Promote an open-ended dialogue rather than trying to define the required outcomes too closely.

Van den Bergh (1995) also identifies similar principles of postmodern practice that are allied to some points from standpoint theory:

- promoting partnerships rather than domination;
- focusing on local contexts and truths, rather than seeking universal claims;
- establishing meanings that are relevant to particular communities and stakeholders.

Van den Bergh argues that feminist social workers achieve objectives by developing knowledge and understanding, emphasizing connectivity, caring, mutuality and a multiplicity of perspectives. Knowledge should be used for helping to respond to social issues and inequalities, rather than for its own sake.

Many of these points are expressed in a coherent account of feminist practice in White's (2006) text, which also makes clear how they may be implemented in the face of the pressures of current agency and social constraints.

Example text: V. White's (2006) 'the state of feminist social work'

V. White started from a sense of unease that current theory and practice were not incorporating feminist ideas and activism. She experienced four tensions between feminist social work theory and the experience of being a feminist social worker:

- Theory assumed that a feminist identity was an unproblematic base from which to launch a feminist practice, whereas experience suggested that feminist identities were fluid, fragile or, for some people some of the time, non-existent.
- Theory assumed that the commonality of experience between women practitioners and clients was the basis for a non-hierarchical, non-oppressive, egalitarian practice, whereas experience suggested that gender might not be a basis for egalitarian relationships – relationships that might not even be possible at all. I looked at this issue in discussing values issues above.
- Theory assumed that the goal of egalitarian relationships was empowerment, whereas in practice it was unclear what empowerment was.
- Theory played down or avoided the statutory basis or legal mandate for social work, whereas statutory and legal responsibilities and powers in practice constrained feminist practice.

Creating a feminist social work identity for the practitioner is the basis of feminist practice, and early writing assumed that a feminist social work identity is rooted in an eclectic approach, accepting that diverse perspectives should be included in an open-ended practice. Most views of feminism share a questioning of assumptions that women's social roles are mainly domestic and concerned with child-rearing, and that it is acceptable for women to take low-paid, low-status roles in the workplace. Thus, a feminist social work practice identity might build on that agreement. However, the diversity in the positions of women across the world suggests that although this may be a reasonable position for middle-class women in developed Western countries, the standpoint of a working-class woman or a woman in extreme poverty in sub-Saharan Africa means that a shared identity might be impossible.

Therefore, some feminist theory has argued for the importance of hearing and valuing alternative and suppressed voices, showing how black, disabled or lesbian women experience the world differently from many other women. This might be used to challenge and refine mainstream feminist understanding, so that a united feminist identity includes valuing difference while also sharing some common experience and goals as women.

In contrast to attempts to broaden a unified but eclectic feminist social work identity in this way, some have argued, calling on postmodern ideas, that it is important to emphasize how power, diversity and difference are diffused throughout society and among women; a non-oppressive feminist approach would value and acknowledge a kaleidoscope of experience and perspective. Nevertheless, women characteristically think of 'women', feminism' and 'gender' as an important aspect of any analysis of a social situation and perspective, in spite of a diverse range of splintered identities that derive from different experiences. Is this eclectic feminist identity enough to form the basis of a feminist social work practice that advocates egalitarian relationships and empowerment?

Seeking egalitarian working relationships between practitioners and clients is a fundamental practice objective of feminist social work. The aim is to minimize power differentials and develop a woman-centred practice that respects and values women and affirms their particular experiences. Building woman-to-woman relationships, rooted in shared experience, is more important than competing specific tasks or agency objectives.

Case example: Feminist woman-centred practice with an older man and woman

Alice was the care manager for an older man, Joel, who was in need of social care services because of his increasing frailty. His main carer, Karina, was his wife of forty years, and as he had become more frail, their relationship had deteriorated. She felt that he had become hectoring and demanding of her time for his care, rather than giving her the freedom to pursue her own interests, as she had done when they were both at work.

Because Alice's assessment at the outset was mainly of Joel's needs, she focused on his problems. The agency's policy was that services should not be organized on the assumption that a wife would take on a caring role. However, Alice found that it was in practice hard not to build the routine services round the main role of a spouse who was able and willing to take on many caring responsibilities as a normal extension of married life. For example, meals services were not required because Karina cooked for her husband, but this was also a burden on her when Joel could make little contribution to buying and preparing food.

In thinking this, Alice was identifying the reality that the attempt to make the position of men and women equal through this agency policy did not fully work, because everyday assumptions about husband–wife relationships hindered full equality. Indeed, many clients and their spouses wanted to continue in that caring relationship. Because Alice saw that Karina was getting very tired and that there were tensions in the relationship, she suggested that she should undertake the separate assessment of carers' needs that law and agency procedure said should go alongside Joel's assessment, and offered to do this over a cup of coffee in a local cafe.

Alice and Karina met in the cafe a few days later; this took their relationship outside the formal interview setting (implementing a feminist practice), even though it was clear that Alice was fulfilling an official task. It also allowed Karina to talk over some of the tensions in the way Joel's changing behaviour was affecting her. They spent some time together teasing out the feeling of responsibility and duty that Karina experienced, alongside her feelings that she did not want her marriage to develop in this way, although at the same time she recognized that her husband's frailty made this necessary. Although Alice did not have similar responsibilities in her life, she demonstrated a shared analysis of what was going on by recognizing and expressing the tension that lay behind some of Karina's concerns.

Their plans included Alice accepting the responsibility for pushing Joel to accept an involvement in creative activities at a local day centre, with Karina supporting this suggestion rather than having to take the lead in persuading Joel. This would give Karina some time free from the constraints of Joel's dependence. Alice also wrote into the carers' assessment the need for a regular monthly meeting between Karina and herself to think through Karina's feelings and possibly plan other activities for Karina. Over a period, additional support services were required for Joel, and these were planned first between Alice and Karina so that Karina was strongly engaged in the planning, rather than having to resist or just accept if plans were made directly with Joel first.

Pause and reflect Is Alice and Karina's work a 'feminist conspiracy'?

In planning together and focusing on Karina's needs as a carer, Alice and Karina were creating a more egalitarian relationship, which gave Karina more power in the situation and met some of her needs. This joint planning process also used a task-centred technique of sharing the tasks, rather than the practitioner working out tasks that would help the client. It accepted Karina's neglected needs as being just as important in the social work role as the task of carrying out Joel's assessment and service provision; a less feminist approach might not give the priority that Alice did to Karina's needs. However, Joel is the client. Is his world view being neglected through this feminist focus?

Some suggestions

Answering this question, it is important not to see an opposition between meeting Karina's needs more fully and meeting Joel's needs (in feminist terms this is not an 'either/or' but an 'and also' situation). Enabling Karina to express and explore the tensions in her attitudes, and helping to meet her needs as a full-time carer, allowed her to take on the caring role successfully, while understanding and responding to some of her ambivalence about it. An effective relationship grew up between practitioner and carer, which would benefit Joel. It also permitted a strategy for starting his day care which reduced the risk that his tense relationship with Karina would be worsened – also a benefit for him. The practitioner therefore did not damage the outcomes she achieved for him, but she achieved them in ways that benefited Karina, and permitted Alice to engage in an egalitarian approach to her work. She also complied with the legal requirement to assess and respond to carers' needs.

Returning to White's account, the empowerment of women is a major objective of practice in the eclectic feminist position, and is intended to transform the position and capacity of women to achieve equality in their social roles and positions. However, empowerment has a range of meanings. In many state agencies, and elsewhere, it is a synonym for enabling clients to participate in decisions that affect them rather than gaining significant influence over their own lives. It may also be taken, in agencies, to mean clients gaining control over services rather than over their own life experience. Neo-liberal theory sees empowerment in almost the opposite way, as freeing people from interference by the state or from a dependence on the state and its services.

Feminist theory sees empowerment as an outcome of egalitarian services and practice, since it validates women's life experience and enables women to seek their own objectives instead of or alongside agency objectives; they thus gain greater control over their lives and the services that are provided. One of the problems is that this conception of power is individualistic: it may lead to women having greater influence in their interpersonal relationship, but does not change the way in which society routinely excludes women from power. This is particularly an issue where feminist practice takes place in agencies, particularly state agencies, where hierarchical power structures accept men's dominance of decisions and social relations. Significant empowerment for women may be obstructed by such structures, even if empowerment is possible in organizations such as women's organizations providing refuge from domestic violence.

In state agencies, or in agencies where men's perspectives are dominant, conceptions of empowerment may privilege male hierarchical understandings of power relations and ideas of empowerment that do not seek to transform women's positions. In addition, feminist writing about social work is often based on experience in student placements and specialized agencies rather than mainstream state agencies; it is doubtful, then, that feminist practice is transferable to such agencies. Feminist writing also often conflates ends and means when considering social work. Feminist literature assumes that practitioners are sufficiently autonomous to be able to adopt a feminist identity and use feminist methods in practice, whereas a common experience is that state agents shape the means by which feminist practitioners can operate, because it sets ends that exclude feminist objectives. Possible practice options are to:

- transcend agency limits by finding spaces within agencies to practise using feminist ideas and your feminist identity;
- transform social work by shifting it outside the state apparatus, allowing feminist practice to develop without restriction;
- accept that feminist practice is antithetical to state social work and not to seek to practise feminist ideas outside state agencies.

One possibility is to focus on anti-discriminatory practice (see Chapter 14), which may be more easily assimilated in state practice than a practice that seeks liberation for women.

A significant question is whether the regimes in social work agencies can be adapted or developed to form an appropriate environment for feminist practice. Practice is not just an individualized atomistic function directly connected to social work's legal and social policy mandate; that mandate is carried out through agencies. Similarly, agencies are not just organizations within which social work is carried out, as, by fulfilling their legal and social responsibilities, they contribute to creating the social work that practitioners do. We saw, when discussing Figure 1.5, that the interactions between managers and practitioners within agencies form an important arena in which social work is created. Two important conceptions of the relationship between social work and agency exist:

- *Bureau-professional regimes* are regimes in which practitioners' professional roles provide flexibility and discretion within a bureaucratic organizational structure. These assume that there is a constantly changing balance in our practice between the agency's requirements of us, political power, and our professional skills and values, used with judgement and flexibility. While political power creates the policy that generates those requirements, it is balanced by creative responses in situations that are too complex to be dealt with through rules-based practice. In the latter part of the twentieth century, agencies became larger (for example, through the creation of large generic agencies with wide service responsibilities) and more politically important (for example, as concern grew about child safeguarding and serving a growing population of older people); as a result, the impact of agency controls became more important.
- *Managerialist regimes,* also called 'new public management' (Clarke and Newman, 1997), were initially a political response to the perception, particularly among neo-liberal thinkers, that comprehensive welfare states were unaffordable. To manage the expenditure, managerialist regimes set objectives, using numerical measures and financial controls to assert control over local services. They also aimed to decentralize management so that each unit of the organization was, like a small business, required to meet its objectives. Concern for equal provision across decentralized units, however, reduces the possibility of flexibility to respond to local circumstances and needs. All these factors reduce the professional discretion of practitioners in the bureau-professional balance. Legalism enhances the detailed use of law and regulation as a way of specifying practice on behalf of powerful state interests, using detailed policy and practice guidance. Controlling procedures and, with the greater availability of computer technology, the documentation and surveillance of professional actions tends to deprofessionalize practice and reduce opportunities to practise creatively using feminist ideas.

Managerialism reshapes bureau-professionalism by subordinating professional concerns to budgetary and management efficiency, and by colonizing professional concerns. Being a good professional, then, requires loyalty to the quality of service aims, which seems professional and reasonable but excludes the kind of interpersonal objectives that feminist theory would propose.

These managerial changes reshape what practitioners seek to do in their interpersonal relationships with clients. This is not a simple process in which feminist practices are dominated by management, but it does reshape the negotiation between politicians, managers and practitioners. An important way in which feminists have sought to influence this negotiation is by getting more women into management jobs. This can have two effects: it incorporates women's ideas into the agency and political debate, but it may also lead to a form of management that is more respectful and enabling of practice that achieves feminist objectives. Social work education has also been affected by these changes in organization because, internationally, higher education has become a more managed regime concerned with costs and economic development, rather than being a site for developing individualized academic concerns. In addition, agency managements have achieved a greater control of curricula and teaching methods as part of the process of inculcating political, managerial and legalistic control into professional practice.

Examining the different identities that women might adopt, and the theoretical concepts that they might identify with, White explores three areas:

- *Identification with issues about social division* – practitioners inconsistently identified with terms such as equal opportunities, anti-discriminatory practice and anti-oppressive practice. However, none used terms referring to gender, feminism or women, suggesting that general terms were more widely used in day-to-day work.
- *Women's interests* – practitioners identified with terms that focused on including women's interests in their practice concerns. However, they mainly applied general anti-discriminatory or anti-oppressive practice to work with women, rather than putting this into a specific form of practice.
- *Feminism* – women saw identification with feminism as potentially problematic; four stances were taken here. A small group identified themselves as feminist and valued their identification with a specific school of thought. Some saw themselves as feminist with reservations, seeing feminism as validating the importance of valuing women's perspectives in their practice, while not associating themselves with the radical connotations of the term. Others saw themselves as not being feminist but drew on feminist principles in their practice. Another group saw themselves as not being feminist at all, either because their life experience had not made this a major priority for them or because they thought that feminism did not adequately address the different position of working-class women.

White's (2006) research also looked at women practitioners' experiences of important issues in feminist thinking. On the possibility of egalitarian relationships and empowerment with clients, they recognized that there was some shared experience that could enhance practice, particularly in groupwork; however, most felt that equal relationships were not possible because of power differences associated with their professional role or the agency's function. Similarly, in relationships with students, practitioners recognized shared experiences and often found it easier to build good working relationships with women and men students, but felt that students had to find their own way in dealing with inequality and oppression. Most saw empowering women clients as a crucial aspect of their professional role, mainly seeing empowerment as facilitating participation and partnership.

Many women valued managerialism because of the clarity it injected into clients' rights and their responsibilities, making their work more organized. However, they disliked the focus on financial assessment and the shortage of resources that led to rationing rather than an open-minded offering of service. Another difficulty was the way in which a focus on a 'core business' (treating the social work agency as a business organization, focused on financial efficiency rather than caring priorities) meant several things: that related helping was less easy to offer; that possibilities of taking up collective work using group-work, preventive work and counselling roles were closed down; and that the approach led to a loss of discretion. Finally, computerization took up time and limited creative possibilities in practice.

Practitioners accommodated in various ways and raised various challenges to these difficulties. It was to some extent possible, particularly in local teams, to negotiate over discretion and flexibility, and to change attitudes to oppression and the position of women; it was, however, more difficult to influence wider departments. It was also difficult to influence sexist attitudes in other work settings, for example those that involved the police or senior doctors. Voluntary, non-profit organizations were valued because they could be more radical than official agencies, could accept a referral of work outside the agency's 'core business' and were more flexible and friendly towards women's issues. Engagement in wider campaigns was difficult for many because of lack of energy outside their main work and family roles. They were ambivalent about taking on management roles because of a commitment to practice and because they were unable to accommodate to or change management attitudes based on male conceptions of the role.

Conclusion: using feminist theory in practice

It is clear from White's (2006) research that using feminist ideas in practice is problematic for women, and is probably also for men. Feminist theory has been criticized as a perspective because its limited focus and priority for women's issues, its marginalized position in specialized agencies and its limited research base mean that it is hard to apply generally. However, feminist theory has changed thinking about gender roles and relationships in relation to social policy and welfare services. It has raised awareness of the importance of women's shared experiences in working with other women, particularly those in oppressed situations.

The main features of feminist practice are as follows:

- Feminist practice creates dialogical, egalitarian relations. This requires an open approach to creating a debate about possibilities with clients, rather than a questioning style of interpersonal practice. So, instead of constantly asking questions from a checklist, opening a discussion allows clients and their carers to raise issues and express their opinions, rather than sticking to the agency's agenda. This does not mean that feminist practitioners are unchallenging: they constantly seek to unsettle conventional gender-based assumptions, implementing the shared value principle of 'critical practice' (see Figure 1.7).
- It focuses on personal identity, particularly women's identities. This requires helping clients to clarify and pursue important personal objectives that strengthen them as women.
- Feminist practice values diversity among women and men and the relations between them, validating a wide variety of non-exploitative relationships in clients' lives.
- It also seeks opportunities to use groups to promote an awareness and understanding of oppression, as well as strategies to respond to it. This is the traditional feminist

approach of 'consciousness-raising' – more broadly a social pedagogical approach of increasing women's understanding and awareness through using learning opportunities and gaining experience of a wide range of social relations.

Additional resources

Further reading

Dominelli, L. (2002) *Feminist Social Work Theory and Practice* (Basingstoke: Palgrave Macmillan).

This is the only comprehensive social work text offering a feminist model of social work practice – its position is socialist feminist.

Freedberg, S. (2008) *Relational Theory for Social Work Practice: A Feminist Perspective* (London: Routledge).

This book provides a good account of feminist theory applied to a psychodynamic model of interpersonal social work practice.

Orme, J. (2000) *Gender and Community Care: Social Work and Social Care Perspectives* (Basingstoke: Palgrave Macmillan).

Although written more than a decade ago, and exploring the provision of adult services in the UK, Orme's book provides a good example of a feminist analysis of many factors relevant to caring for people with long-term conditions and mental illness that is still relevant.

White, V. (2006) *The State of Feminist Social Work* (London: Routledge).

Good theoretical analysis and research on feminist practice.

Journal

AFFILIA: *Journal of Women and Social Work* – Sage; see http://aff.sagepub.com/

Websites

For up-to-date general information about issues of concern to women, relevant news and links, see, from the US, the Feminist Majority Foundation http://feminist.org/ and from the UK, the feminism pages from *The Guardian* http://www.guardian.co.uk/world/feminism

http://feminism.eserver.org/

For materials on the academic study of feminism, with good links.

http://www.cddc.vt.edu/feminism/

The Feminist Theory Website at Virginia Tech University.

http://fwsa.org.uk/

The website for the Feminist and Women's Studies Association (UK & Ireland).

Anti-oppressive and multicultural sensitivity approaches to practice

14

Main contribution

Ideas on anti-oppressive and multicultural sensitivity approaches to practice help practitioners to understand the cultural and ethnic barriers, conflicts and differences in societies so that they may practise in ways that respect people's individual and social identities and respond to oppression by dominant social groups. Cultural and ethnic differences have important consequences for people's personal development and social experience, and these ideas help practitioners to incorporate these factors into their practice.

Main points

- Anti-oppressive practice focuses on combating the oppressive effects of discrimination, in which the powerful groups in society maintain power by creating negative stereotypes. Anti-oppressive practice seeks particularly to combat the exclusion of some social groups from social equality, from full participation as citizens and from social justice. Anti-oppressive practice may be distinguished from anti-discriminatory practice because it concentrates on processes of oppression and exclusion rather than on the discrimination itself, but the two terms are often used interchangeably.
- Multicultural sensitivity approaches, which include ideas such as cultural competence and cultural diversity, promote responses to the cultural and ethnic diversity that is found in societies.
- Anti-oppressive and multicultural sensitivity practice both emerge from widespread concern about racism and ethnic conflict.
- Multiculturalism affirms ethnic diversity and aims to improve societies by valuing their many different cultural contributions.
- Racism comprises ideologies and social processes that discriminate on the grounds of assumed differences in ethnicity and culture between racial groups. All human beings

are of the same biological race, so using 'race' and similar terms to refer to ethnicity is incorrect. Some writers therefore enclose such terms in quotation marks to show that it is not a valid descriptive and analytical term. Talking about race is, however, a widely accepted usage, and I do not use quotation marks.

▪ Alternative anti-racist perspectives are assimilation, liberal and cultural pluralism, structuralism and black perspectives.

▪ Anti-discriminatory practice combats discrimination on grounds of race, gender, disability, sexuality and age. Bringing such issues together draws on an overarching explanation that discrimination comes from social structures rather than individual or group processes. Anti-discriminatory practice may be distinguished from anti-oppressive practice because it concentrates on preventing and combating discrimination, rather than working on the oppression that may result from it; however, the two terms are often used interchangeably (see the first bullet point above).

▪ Including in one practice oppression or discrimination on multiple grounds of race, gender, disability, sexual orientation and age may be criticized. First, it may not reflect the views of those who experience a particular form of discrimination, and second, it may not help to set practice priorities between different forms of discrimination.

▪ Personal, cultural and social factors are all relevant to discrimination. Where there is a focus on language and culture as a basis for reducing discrimination, there have been accusations of 'political correctness'.

▪ The theory of anti-oppressive and anti-discriminatory practice focuses on structural explanations of discrimination, while multicultural sensitivity approaches focus on the role of cultural and ethnic differences in stimulating discrimination.

Practice ideas

☐ *Discrimination* and *oppression* are important aspects of people's experience of social relations and should therefore be a focus of social work practice.

☐ A focus on people's personal identity and the way in which *ethnicity and cultural experience constructs identity* is also relevant to social work practice.

☐ The idea of *sensitivity* to or *competence* in dealing with social and cultural difference can be an important part of practice.

☐ Taking a *black and oppressed people's perspective* can be a guiding factor in practice.

Major statements

The major anti-discrimination statements build upon Thompson's (2012) introductory text *Anti-discriminatory Practice*, now in its fifth edition. Okitikpi and Aymer (2010) provide a broad introduction focusing on contemporary concerns but carrying less historical baggage. Another introductory book, Dalrymple and Burke's (2006) *Anti-*

oppressive Practice, offers a practical account of practice related to social work responsibilities in welfare states, focusing on legal and professional responsibilities, and is used as an example text in this chapter. Dominelli's (2002b) *Anti-oppressive Social Work Theory and Practice* provides a practice guide, although it is not as well informed by interpersonal practice as is Dalrymple and Burke's book. Dominelli's text is more theoretically comprehensive and more internationally focused than Thompson's, and builds on her work in anti-racism, an area for which her introductory text *Anti-racist Social Work* (2008) remains well used.

Devore and Schlesinger's (1999) *Ethnic-sensitive Social Work Practice* remains an important statement of sensitivity practice. Another contribution is from O'Hagan (2001), who offers a British research-based discussion of cultural competency – the idea that practitioners should gain competence in understanding and dealing with people from different cultures. However, it does not, except by implication, provide comprehensive practice guidance. Recent accounts by Marsiglia and Kulis (2009) and Sisneros et al. (2008) are examples of attempts to incorporate a critical and structural analysis of oppression that have been informed by multicultural sensibilities into prescriptions of practice. Sisneros et al.'s (2008) account is used as an example text illustrating this trend.

The debate summary

These areas of theory emerged from growing concern, during the 1980s, about ethnic conflict in many Western societies. Debates within social work and broader social movements raised the need for and possibility of practice that responds to ethnic and cultural division. I discuss what brought this about more fully later in the chapter.

I deal in this account with three main areas of debate in this area:

- the two distinct approaches to practice dealing with this issue – anti-oppression and multiculturalism – and the differing explanatory frameworks that underlie these approaches;
- the consequences of using a social construction approach to social change around these issues; some argue that this leads to a restrictive 'political correctness' that, in neo-liberal thinking, conflicts with people's right to 'think the unthinkable' and exercise freedom of thought and autonomy of action;
- whether the main concern is diversity, particularly of culture, or social division; what are the consequences for practice of the balance that we draw between these two factors?

Figure 14.1 represents some of the relationships and oppositions in this group of theories. The starting point – concern about racism and ethnic conflict – generated both anti-oppressive and multiculturalism approaches, both of which include elements of pluralist, structural and black perspectives.

These concerns broadened to incorporate wider forms of social exclusion and discrimination against other social groups. Anti-oppressive theories take a primarily social change view, while multiculturalism approaches emphasize empowerment objectives; however, they also incorporate some elements of the structural perspectives that we met in Chapter 12, particularly in American critical race theory. Multicultural ideas leading to cultural competence or sensitivity practice do not focus on oppression. Their main aim is to help people build upon positive aspects of cultural and other differences in society. Intersectionality in particular addresses issues of plural concerns. It proposes an intersection of people who experience multiple oppressions on grounds of, for example, racism, ageism or disability, gender and other discriminations. We cannot therefore give priority to one form of oppression: race, for example, does not trump ageism or disability. Neither do oppressions accumulate, so that the more you have, the more oppressed you are. Instead, it is important to explore how they interact in each instance, because the social circumstances and personal experiences of the people affected will have varying effects (Murphy et al., 2009).

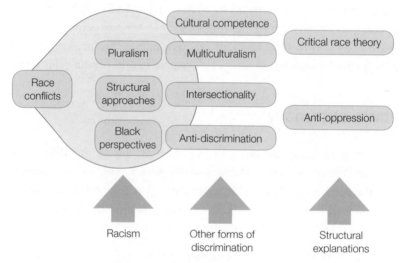

Figure 14.1 The development of theories and practices from racial conflicts

The main source of debate between these two groups of theories is between two different views about the origin of discrimination and oppression, which lead to different views about how to tackle it. Anti-oppressive views say that much of the problem arises because of a conflict or tension between the interests of social groups whose members have social identities linked to devalued characteristics. Because they have little choice about this, for example, being black in a white society or female in a patriarchal society, the response should be to deal with the conflicts of interest through social change. Multicultural sensitivity views, and related ideas such as cultural competence and cultural awareness, argue that the main problem is in our ability to understand and value the social identities that are linked to devalued characteristics. Accordingly, we should educate people to value diversities in society and improve relationships between different social groups, with the aim of reducing the impact, and removing the sources, of misunderstanding and conflict. Practitioners would do this by understanding the implications arising from the different cultures associated with different ethnicities and increasing their competence in responding more appropriately to those cultural differences, so that interventions were more appropriate to the different cultures.

Both views are concerned about how we use language. Anti-oppressive and anti-discriminatory practices often take a social construction view about our use of language (see Chapter 9): if we avoid using devaluing language, we can create a new narrative about the differences that are of concern to us. Multicultural sensitivity views argue that we should use courteous language that respects people's differences. Language has changed in several aspects of life to avoid terms that have become stigmatizing or disrespectful. For example, in British law, people with learning disabilities were once described in legal terms such as 'idiots' or 'feeble-minded', and the study of learning disability is still called 'defectology' in some Eastern European countries. Professions involved with people moved to talking about 'mental handicap', and there have been further shifts to a use of 'learning disabilities' and the medical terminology 'intellectual disabilities'. Concern about discrimination, oppression and a lack of cultural competence leads people to be sensitive about how language is used. Practitioners often feel that they have to keep up with the latest changes in language in order to remain respectful. In turn, different terms proliferate and come to be associated with particular points of view in the debate.

Case example: Confusion about the nature of Nia's disability

Nia's parents knew that she had been slow to develop but were confused when a doctor they consulted described her as having 'intellectual disabilities'. They said to their social worker: 'We never expected her to be an intellectual.' They were used to the social worker and education staff talking about 'learning difficulties' and had accepted this:

'It seems to mean that she will be able to learn, even if not as much as other children'. The social worker explained that 'intellectual disabilities' was the internationally accepted medical jargon for the same thing and meant that Nia was less good at using her thought processes; this would also have an effect on other aspects of her life.

This is an example of the consequences for clients of the different approaches of the range of professions working with clients and their families.

Overconcern with language use is sometimes called 'political correctness', and there has been significant conflict about this issue affecting social work, among other walks of life. Philpot (1999) points out that 'political correctness' is often used indiscriminately as a term of abuse, with very little meaning or in jokes that criticize anti-discrimination practices. Fairclough (2003), reviewing the issue, points out that social construction ideas sought to achieve political change by trying to promote the correct use of language; this led to accusations of political correctness, aiming to change cultural attitudes rather than social institutions, law or policy. This attempt to change social behaviour and structure by changing the use of language was new and was experienced as an arrogant personal attack rather than a valid way of achieving social change. Moreover, Fairclough argues, the campaigners did not campaign strategically, but presented the changes as a matter of justice requiring immediate and practicable action. This meant that they did not establish the case fully and work to change social institutions before the backlash emerged. Dent (1999) argues that effective service provision is a more important focus of anti-discrimination than language use or procedural caution, although these may disguise inadequacies in service provision.

While most people agree that sensitive language is an appropriate courtesy, complaining about political correctness often reveals hidden prejudice because it is a soft target for what would otherwise be unacceptable attacks on anti-discriminatory practice. Practitioners need similarly to consider whether focusing only on multicultural sensitivity may be avoiding the issue of prejudice; some sensitivity views, however, acknowledge that abusive language is oppressive.

Another language issue is the distinction between 'discrimination' and 'oppression'. The word 'discrimination' may have positive connotations: it means the capacity to draw distinctions between people or things with discernment and good judgement. Used negatively, however, discrimination means putting individuals and identifiable groups into categories according to personal characteristics that people often devalue, and treating them less well than other people or groups with valued characteristics. Oppression, on the other hand, sees discrimination as part of the use of social power by the dominant social groups in a society. The point of making a distinction between anti-discriminatory and anti-oppressive practice is that oppression always arises because of the misuse of social power, while discrimination might result from misunderstanding or conflict in particular social relationships.

Pause and reflect *Thinking about issues of culture and oppression*

Consider what issues of culture and oppression might be at work in the following situation.

Case example: Gang fights in the social housing scheme

Police and social workers were concerned that two gangs of teenagers, the Rams and the Goats, had established different territories in a social housing scheme. This had led to street fighting and knife attacks on young people from the other part of the scheme who strayed into the wrong territory. In conferences about this issue, police officers saw this as mainly about territory for the distribution of illegal drugs. Social workers saw some of the conflict as stemming from a large group of migrants from the Caribbean in the Goats' area: the name 'Goats' had originally come from a favourite dish of these families, goat stew, which had appeared in local shops when this ethnic group became significant customers. People from the indigenous white population often talked about the way the Caribbean men were taking jobs away from skilled white workers because they would accept lower wages for semi-skilled work.

Some suggestions

Part of the source of gang violence might have stemmed from racist stereotypes about migrants 'taking work away' from indigenous people, although there is little evidence that this happens in most advanced economies. Other sources of the drug abuse might also be explored: there might be alienation because of poor opportunity for education and social mobility. It is often necessary to explore a range of social conflicts before arriving at a view about which social issues to tackle.

There is a particular debate about multiculturalism. This concept affirms cultural diversity, allowing individuals to keep much that is distinctive about their cultural traditions. It also works to integrate diverse cultural traditions into society, thus avoiding a single, dominant culture (Sanders, 1978). The difficulty with this is that the variety of cultures available in a diverse community or nation may lead to only a partial understanding of each. It might also lead to a lack of commitment to any cultural or religious identity. For example, schools successively teaching the features of several religions may not adequately support each child in a commitment to the religion that their parents would prefer.

Case example: Celebrating cultural diversity in residential care

Children in a group of private sector children's residential care homes were encouraged to celebrate the festivals of Diwali (Hindu/Jain), Christmas (Christian), Passover (Jewish) and Ramadan (Islamic), which were relevant to some of the children in the home. However, there was no education about their importance in different cultural and historical contexts, and no attempt to ensure that children from different backgrounds realized the significance of a particular festival for their own cultural heritage. As a result, many of the children merely saw the celebrations as a disconnected series of occasional celebrations, rather like birthday parties.

Because multicultural policies may lead to this kind of disconnected treatment of important cultural or religious events, people may enjoy the exoticism of a cultural idea that is new to them, or find it distasteful, without thinking about its implications for their personal system of thought or for practice within existing social structures. Another example is the debate about adopting elements or procedures of Islamic *sharia* law into Western legal systems. To do so may seem respectful to the traditions of important ethnic and religious minorities in society, but the ideas may also conflict with important tenets of the majority religion and culture. Thus, multiculturalism finds itself valuing and respecting alterative cultures, but resisting their acceptance into established legal or cultural traditions. This can seem ambivalent or dismissive of the importance of all of the traditions that are represented in the society.

Wider theoretical perspectives

A variety of terms are used in this field. The first to emerge was 'anti-racism'. This refers to attempts to combat racial prejudice. Later, anti-discriminatory and anti-oppressive practice emerged to broaden the scope of concern about discrimination, taking in other common grounds for discrimination such as gender, disability, sexuality and age. To the proponents of action on these broader issues, referring only to anti-racism may seem to prioritize racial discrimination above other kinds of discrimination. When referring to measures aimed at particular issues, however, it is reasonable to talk about racism, gender discrimination, disableism, discrimination against gay, lesbian, bisexual or transgender people and ageism. Therefore, making this distinction may be important when looking at the circumstances of a particular client or category of people. Talking about discrimination only as negative is sometimes criticized (perhaps trying to avoid, a bit pedantically, the negative implications of discrimination) because, as I have already said, the word has a broader meaning of drawing distinctions with discernment and good judgement.

In addition, individuals or interest groups affected by particular circumstances sometimes dispute the idea of rolling up their concerns about, for example, disability or sexuality into these omnibus terms because they see the source of discrimination against them as being more specific. Some people also question the implication of anti-oppressive practice that the issue and the focus of practice should be not discriminatory attitudes but the social oppression that results. Part of the reason for these doubts is sometimes political dissent from the idea of oppression because of its association with political and social opinion that is radical or critical.

Anti-discriminatory practice derives from the sociological and psychological study of the processes by which some social groups and individuals devalue particular characteristics and discriminate against others on these grounds in social relations. Anti-oppressive practice derives from an analysis of how such difference and discrimination leads to social divisions – the way in which divisions create social identities that generate oppression is central to anti-oppressive theory (Dominelli, 2002b). Multicultural sensitivity practice, on the other hand, is built on the study of cultures and their interaction with behaviour and relationships in societies. The two practices overlap but have different primary aims: anti-oppressive practice intends to transform social structures to achieve greater equality and social justice, while multicultural sensitivity practice intends to manage and respond effectively to the conflicts in individual group and community social relationships.

An important source of ideas is research and commentary on the social issues concerned with race and ethnicity. Feminist theory and work on disability and sexuality are also contributors. Anti-oppressive practice brings together these areas of concern into an overarching theory and practice covering any people inappropriately discriminated against or oppressed. Multicultural sensitivity focuses more on ethnicity, race and spirituality, although it is increasingly applied to other social divisions where sensitivity is required. Devore and Schlesinger (1999) point out that many minority ethnic groups do not accept the association with wider oppressions that is implied by adopting anti-oppressive practice, since there are particular factors involved in the oppression of black and minority ethnic groups, particularly slavery in the USA. Other groups included in anti-oppressive practice theory often feel similarly – that oppression on grounds of gender, disability, sexuality or age stems from different sources and requires a range of responses. However, the main thrust of anti-oppression theory derives from critical social science analysis (see Chapter 12) rather than the views of oppressed people themselves. This view holds that oppression comes from inequalities that are part of the structure of societies as a result of the power of the ruling elites. Because of this, anti-oppression theory argues that excluded groups are affected by similar social processes.

Anti-racist perspectives and discrimination

Racism is a range of ideologies and social processes that discriminate against others using assumptions of different racial membership (Solomos, 2003: 11). Dominelli (2008) identifies personal, institutional and cultural racism as elements of such processes and ideologies. Racism has been a worldwide phenomenon throughout history (Bowser, 1995) and affects different societies differently. Evidence from contemporary social science has shifted conventional norms from assumptions that white people are biologically superior to black 'races' towards a focus on discriminatory behaviour that is a consequence of feelings or attitudes of cultural superiority.

Reviewing the history of racist ideas, Banton (1987) showed that, in colonial times, different racial types, often associated with skin colour, were distinguished. In the nineteenth century, these types became connected with evolutionary ideas in biology, so that different types were related to different evolutionary lines of development. This became associated with social status, and more successful and dominant societies claimed superiority over others. As races came into contact with one another, superiority and inferiority became associated with class positions in societies where different races were in contact. There was then a movement away from assumptions that biological differences between 'races' (which do not exist biologically in human beings) justified superiority to a position of justification on grounds of cultural and social differences.

Social change from 1980 onwards accentuated this (Pilkington, 2003). As global travel and communication became quicker and more comprehensive, migration because of disasters and wars became more widespread, and cultures and ethnic groups came into contact more extensively. Significant minority groups with different physical appearances and cultures formed in many countries (Payne and Askeland, 2008).

Many countries, in their own way, face problems of conflict between different ethnic and cultural groups. In some, there are indigenous peoples, such as native Americans in Canada and the USA, Inuit people in Canada, Sami people in Nordic countries, Roma peoples (formerly called gypsies) in Southern Europe and Aborigines and Maoris in Australia and New Zealand. Difficulties have often arisen because of an inward migration by other powerful ethnic groups and a record of oppression and conflict, as in O'Hagan's (2001) example of Northern Ireland; another example might be Israel/Palestine.

Responding to such situations has often led to an emphasis on respect for ethnic diversity or multiculturalism (Isajiw, 1997) and, in social work, to approaches involving sensitivity and cultural competence. Multiculturalism refers to attempts to incorporate groups different from the dominant population into a nation or community by valuing their cultural contribution to the whole and emphasizing the value of diversity and pluralism (Rex, 1997). In particular, multiculturalism opposes separatism; this idea was particularly influential at the time of campaigns opposing social policies based on a separation of ethnic and cultural groups. Examples include the American civil rights movement, South African apartheid and, in Canada, Australia and New Zealand, concern about the rights and cultural identity of, respectively, the 'first nation', Aboriginal and Maori populations. These concerns pressed social workers and their agencies to make services more appropriate and responsive. Much of the literature focuses on culture, but a significant element of cultural diversity arises from religious and spiritual diversity. There has as a result been growing interest in understanding different religious and spiritual experiences (see Chapter 10). Rising concern with the impact of Islam in international conflicts has also affected this (Ashencaen Crabtree et al., 2008).

Inequalities in housing provision and employment markets were the first focus of concern about racial discrimination; it became associated with discrimination in all large organizations, often using the idea of *institutional racism*. This proposes that indirect discrimination arises because established patterns of social relations privilege majority ethnic groups. Such privilege is part of the structure of organizations such as the police, health and social care agencies, schools and government bodies in societies, and the assumptions of their workforces, managers and political leadership. As social institutions, organizations may become oppressive because they are 'institutionally racist' in their ordinary functioning, and members of the organization may not be aware of this. For example, a social work agency may place a strong emphasis on confidentiality as a principle of practice – this is part of many social work codes of ethics or practice. To some minority ethnic groups, however, this may exclude family, community or religious groups from participating in active involvement in making family or community decisions.

Minority groups may be excluded from the main economic and social systems, and may become concentrated in economically and socially deprived geographical communities that are eventually associated with that minority. Consequently, minority ethnic groups become associated with the economic and social problems of deprived communities. Cultural representations, through the media, literature and films, also connect deprivation with minorities. Because of its knowledge base in social science, social work was among the first professions to develop an awareness of these issues and incorporate anti-oppressive and sensitivity practice into its corpus of knowledge and skills.

Figure 14.2 identifies a number of perspectives in anti-racism, which you can extend to apply to most oppressed groups; most are, for example, similar to the feminist perspectives identified in Chapter 13. The interaction and role of each are debated.

Assimilation assumes that migrants to a new country will assimilate to the culture and lifestyle of that country. Where there is a native population and dominant incomers, assimilation will be to the incomers (as happened, for example, in Australia; see LeSueur, 1970). This demonstrates that the power of the dominant culture, rather than who was present first, is at issue. Small (1989) suggests that immigrants start by identifying with the culture and lifestyle of their country of origin and then *substitute* the new country's culture and way of life. Isajiw (1997) refers to an interweaving of minority and majority social structures, cultures and identities, leading to reciprocity between the minority group and the majority society, both of which gain economically and culturally. In gender, disability, sexuality, age or other discrimination, assimilation views assume that different groups can adapt to a society that includes these differences.

Figure 14.2 Anti-racist perspectives

Perspective	Explanation
Assimilation	Migrants or minorities will assimilate to the majority culture and lifestyle
Liberal pluralism	All groups should co-exist, and equal opportunities, but not necessarily equal outcomes, are assured by legal and administrative means
Cultural pluralism	There is a focus on diversity: all groups should co-exist, maintaining their cultural traditions
Structuralist/ critical perspective	Ethnic and cultural divisions are strengthened by economic and cultural domination by elite groups
Black perspectives	Black and minority ethnic groups develop particular perspectives on societies because of their history and experience

Source: Denney (1991), Ely and Denney (1987), Dominelli (2008), Gould (1994), Jenkins (1988) and Sisneros et al. (2008, pp. 5–6).

An important issue with assimilation perspectives is that they assume a *cultural deficit* with the minority's original culture not developing the skills and knowledge to cope with the new environment. This may assume that the minority culture is deficient. For example, people might think that child care skills are lacking, or that the oppression of female members of Muslim families is inappropriate in a Western society. As a result, services may *pathologize* black people (Singh, 1992), an example of 'blaming the victim'. In this way, the power to define the culturally acceptable behaviour of the minority community as a problem is used to remove oppression on grounds of this behaviour from the agenda, so that agencies do not recognize this aspect of the problem.

Most anti-racist approaches are structuralist; see, for example, Dominelli's (2008) anti-racist work. Multicultural sensitivity and black perspectives often include elements of explanation from structural perspectives but focus on cultural and social domination, rather than economic and class analysis. Consequently, structural theorists often regard them as providing inadequate accounts of racism.

One aspect of sensitivity is to emphasize black people's contribution to the history of social work (Carlton-LaNey, 1994, 2001; Martin and Martin, 1995). These may have been hidden by racist assumptions, which devalue such contributions. Views from black perspectives propose that practitioners should be sensitive to black perspectives and experiences of the world, and sensitive in their attempts to adapt the skills of conventional practice to this perspective. Practice methods can contribute to this. For example, Martin (1995) shows how a process of exploring the 'oral history' of an individual in family and community contexts can include black and community perspectives in professional assessment. Graham (2007) argues, however, that we must be careful to avoid assuming that black people's lives involve only struggle and reaction to white oppression: black perspectives offer creative and original views of the world. Efforts should be made to develop and make use of social science information about black people, which responds to the understandings that black people have about the world (Robinson, 1995). We should avoid assuming that there is only one minority culture, or that each group has a single culture, but explore the range of views in each case (Gross, 1995).

In the USA, *critical race theory* (CRT; Delgado and Stefancic, 2012) incorporates both multicultural and oppression perspectives, and has been influential in professional education (Abrams and Moio, 2009). Arising from the American civil rights movement of the 1970s, it particularly emphasizes the role of legal interventions to correct racial oppression. It criticizes 'colour-blind' policies and practice, because trying to treat people of all ethnicities as the same evades the reality that some ethnic groups are historically oppressed and need additional support to take up opportunities so they can realize their potential. CRT also emphasizes black people's perspectives and criticizes the American focus on cultural competence as a way of dealing with racism, because cultural competence fails to deal with structural oppression. Marxist analysis proposes that CRT does not sufficiently recognize structural oppression in neo-liberal and liberal economies (Cole, 2009).

Discrimination and oppression

Anti-oppressive approaches to social work developed in the late 1980s and 90s because of policy concerns in Western democratic states. These arose partly from serious social conflict, such as the inner city riots in the UK in the early 1980s, which were largely ascribed to alienation among young black people, similar riots and a high level of crime among black people in the USA, and conflict in Germany and Italy over refugees from Eastern Europe and in France over refugees from North Africa. Official responses to this were largely socially liberal. That is, they focused on reducing inequalities and marginalization by policies and practice that promoted social inclusion (Barry and Hallett, 1998). Anti-oppressive practice also springs from the concerns of critical theory about groups of people within societies who suffer from inequality and consequent injustice. Critical theory questions the existing social order, so it sees the problem as one of social order and structures rather than one of individual or group problems or disadvantages.

As I described earlier in the chapter, discrimination involves treating individuals or groups with identifiable characteristics less well than people and groups that are not identified as having those characteristics because those characteristics are devalued. An important strand in thinking about anti-discriminatory work comes from the influence of feminist thinking (see Chapter 13). The oppression of black women, whose problems may combine racism and sexism, has led to a approach that is distinctive from broader feminist perspectives. An important wider debate that has relevance to social work is the issue of the role of psychoanalysis and its approach to women (see Chapter 4). Other influences on anti-discriminatory thought have been lesbian and gay rights work, and ideas on disability, mental illness, learning disabilities and the political economy of ageing (Phillipson, 1982; Laczko and Phillipson, 1991; Bytheway, 1995). Many of these factors interrelate (for example, age and ethnicity, Blakemore and Boneham, 1994; age and gender, Arber and Ginn, 1991), so that problems occurring where two or more aspects of identity lead to social oppression may be magnified, or may lead to conflicts in response and attitude.

Theoretical approaches in relation to other oppressed groups are less well developed, but it is possible to position them within these perspectives. *Normalization* and *social role valorization* (Wolfensberger, 1972, 1984; Race, 2003; see Chapter 11) take, in many ways, an assimilationist position. This is because this approach seeks to include people with learning disabilities as far as possible into 'ordinary life' (Towell, 1988), so that their social roles can be, as far as possible, equivalent to those that are widely valued in society. However, this also has elements of a perspectives position, because it seeks to take up and promote disabled people's own perspectives on their situation.

A *social model of disability* view (Oliver, 2009) is a pluralist position with structural elements arguing that medical models concentrate on disabled people's impairment. Instead, we must recognize that social definitions of what is normal lead to society being organized in ways that create disability. For example, if there were no steps in buildings, a person with a walking impairment would not be disabled. Society should be changed so that all groups can coexist on an equal basis. The recognition of 'communities' among disabled people suggests the possibility of a perspectives position as well. One example is a Deaf community of people born deaf whose language and culture derives from sign language – the capitalization of 'D' in 'Deaf' denotes participation in that community.

A *political economy of ageing* view (Laczko and Phillipson, 1991) is mainly structuralist. It argues that assumptions about ageing derive from the exclusion of older people from the labour market, making them economically and socially dependent. A *disabled living* view (Morris, 1993) is related to perspectives positions. It argues that disabled individuals and communities should direct and manage the services designed to support them towards independence. More recently, *citizenship practice* with older people has stressed the importance of emphasizing the rights of older people and people with dementia to participate in and contribute to society through as many normal processes as possible (Marshall and Tibbs, 2006; Payne, 2011b). Matthies (2010) argues that social work values promote participation and citizenship in society more broadly, although we noted in Chapter 8 that a critique of knee-jerk participation exists.

Discrimination is created and maintained by personal beliefs and behaviour, reinforced by ideologies that develop from the power exerted by groups in order to sustain and strengthen their dominant position within social structures. This is an increasingly important concept in critical theory, as we saw in Fook's account of critical practice in Chapter 12. Wilson and Beresford (2000) go further, to argue that the way in which social work has given importance to anti-oppressive practice allows social workers to appropriate the ideas of oppressed service users while retaining the power to define what is oppressive. Service users still lose control of how their lives are defined, and this in itself is oppressive. One of the ways in which discrimination is maintained through cultural means is by the use of language and social assumptions to support conventions that are discriminatory. This makes important connections with social construction theory. Denney (1992) argues that poststructuralist theory provides a method for exploring, through an analysis of court or agency reports, how people have moved from assumptions to making discriminatory decisions. Another example is using the words 'spastic' and 'idiot' as terms of abuse, when they were originally technical terms referring to a particular form or severity (respectively) of physical and learning (respectively) disabilities.

Pause and reflect *Your life experience*

Think about the categories of race and ethnicity, gender, disability, sexuality and ageism, and if possible compare your thinking with that of others. At what age and in what circumstances did you become aware that you were different from others in each of these categories? What were social assumptions about such differences in your family or among your peers? How would you describe your present attitudes?

Some suggestions

We tend to take for granted such assumptions about ourselves. For example, I am white and grew up without meeting any black people until my late teens, so I find it hard not to think of being white as normal and being black as out of the ordinary. Another example is Owusu-Bempah's (1994) research showing that social workers assume that self-identity in black children will be problematic, when they do not make the same assumptions about white children. This suggests that we need to be open and flexible in our views about all ethnic groups and listen carefully to their own perspective, rather than taking any issue for granted in relation to ethnic identity.

Connections

Concerns about social conflict led to attempts to frame an approach to combating racism within social work and to a lesser extent other related occupational groups. Impetus was given to many of these developments by the curriculum development activities of the UK and US education authorities for social work (for example, Norton, 1978; CCETSW, 1991; CD Project Steering Group, 1991; Patel, 1994, all on race). Some reviews of theory do not refer to anti-discrimination or feminism (for example, Lishman, 2007; Teater, 2010). This may reflect the debate about whether anti-discrimination is a separable theory of practice, since it does not refer to many social problems faced by social workers and might be better regarded as a value principle that should 'permeate' all approaches to social work. Clifford and Burke (2009) take this permeation approach in a recent text framing anti-oppressive practice as ethics and values applicable to all social work theory, rather than as a separate practice model.

Social work in India interprets conflict between existing social groups as a problem of *communalism*. Chandra (1987) defines this as the belief that people following a particular religion consequently have common social, political and economic interests. This belief leads to conflicts between different language, religious and caste communities (Miri, 1993; Kumar, 1994). Five conflict strategies have been identified (by Oomen, quoted by Kumar, 1994: 65–6):

- *assimilationist communalism*, in which particular interests try to recruit others to their cause;
- *welfarist communalism*, where social services and benefits are limited to one community;
- *retreatist communalism*, where groups withdraw from interaction with others;
- *retaliatory communalism*, in which communities act violently against others when they perceive threats or acts against them;
- *separatist communalism*, where language or culture is used to create enclaves away from others.

Here, the issue is constructed by defining it as excessive separation or conflict. The social work role might be to reduce conflict and achieve a fair distribution of resources. Applying this to some Western countries might raise a concern for anti-oppressive strategies that focus on extreme separatism, and suggest that it is important to understand and respond to the specific perspectives and needs of minority groups.

Analyses of anti-discrimination

A creation of the 1990s is an approach that includes all forms of discrimination in a generic anti-discriminatory (Thompson, 2012) or anti-oppressive (Dalrymple and Burke, 2006) approach. Both make an analysis of discrimination – in Dalrymple and Burke's case drawing on Norton's (1978) earlier work – that takes a concentric view of the relevant social forces. Figure 14.3 compares the terminology and approach of each.

Norton's position sees the individual and their family and immediate community as being 'embedded' (1978: 4) in a wider social system. The individual's primary identification is to the nurturing or immediate system. The wider or sustaining system is seen as 'taking on the attitude of the wider society in regard to oneself' (1978: 4).

Thompson's (2012) anti-discriminatory theory links the personal/psychological, cultural and structural levels of analysis of social issues. Here, the personal (P) level is about interpersonal relationships and the personal or psychological feelings, attitudes and actions between people; this includes social work practice, which is mainly carried out at this level. This takes place within a cultural context (C), which influences and forms individual thought and action; that is, the C level refers to shared ways of thinking, feeling and acting. It is thus about commonalities between people within different groups, an assumed consensus about normality and the assumption that people conform to the social norms created within particular cultures, cultural norms that we internalize. These levels are in turn embedded in a structural level (S), which is an established social order and a set of accepted social divisions. This established social order and its structures, as well as the cultural norms and assumptions and personal behaviour that result, come from an acceptance of the social order and its divisions. Social workers have a good deal of influence over the personal level but decreasing influence over matters at the cultural and then structural levels.

Dalrymple and Burke's (2006) analysis develops a practice model involving the practitioner and client in a partnership committed to change in order to achieve greater equality in society. This operates at three levels: at the level of feelings, reflecting the client's and social worker's biographies; at the level of ideas, working to achieve a changed consciousness of both feelings and society; and at the level of political action in wider society

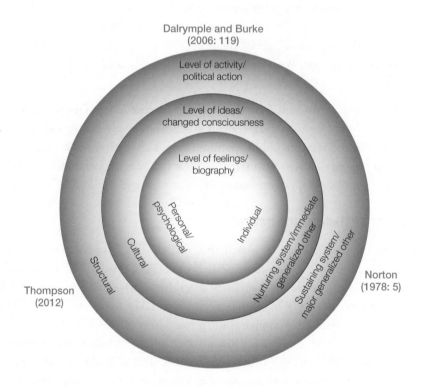

Figure 14.3 Three concentric formulations of anti-oppressive practice
Source: Dalrymple and Burke (2006: 119), Thompson (2012).

There are, however, problems with a concentric view, because it may assume that wider social ideas and structures are always mediated in their effect on individuals' ideas and feelings by a more immediate culture. Against this, the immediate culture may be in conflict with the wider society, and may support individuals against wider ideas and structures. Alternatively, individuals may be in conflict with their culture and more in touch with wider ideas.

The politics of anti-oppression and sensitivity

Anti-oppressive practice is an alternative perspective to ideas of multicultural sensitivity that contribute to cultural competence or awareness practice. Competition between them derives from different emphases:

- an emphasis on structural explanation in anti-oppression theory;
- an emphasis on cultural and social inclusion in sensitivity theory.

While both perspectives include both elements, structural explanations would logically obstruct the inclusion and empowerment strategies that sensitivity theory focuses on. Sensitivity perspectives see themselves as a legitimate alternative, encouraging an awareness and acceptance of structural explanations but leading to an empowerment objective, which does not prioritize them to focus on social change. Sensitivity perspectives may also be taken up as an aspect of relational social work in complex therapeutic work, since cultural and ethnic issues are often important aspects of the issues faced by such clients (Ganzer and Ornstein, 2002). American accounts of anti-racism (for example, Pinderhughes, 1988, 1989) attach great significance to power but see this in relation to its interpersonal effects and its consequences for behaviour and experience. Similarly, Dietz (2000) argues for a clinical practice that assesses the impact of oppression but works on strengths and personal social and political contexts. The increasing emphasis on different cultural expressions of spirituality is another aspect of this approach (see Chapter 10). Gould (1995) argues that we should develop multiculturalism to offer a framework for all groups to integrate thinking across cultures.

Black perspectives propose a more experiential and political understanding of the black experience. We should focus on understanding and working with power differentials and value opportunities to achieve power for black perspectives, black participation and black influence, and control in services and attitudes. Black perspectives connect with the approach of the disabled living perspective and some aspects of normalization and ordinary life perspectives. This leads us to the possibility of an oppressed groups' perspective, with a detailed analysis and understanding of the views and experience of oppressed groups. This is the basis for social work action and for promoting the involvement of members of those groups in managing and developing services.

O'Hagan (2001) presents a multicultural critique of anti-discrimination as follows:

- In analysing racism, it ignores important cultural aspects of discrimination, such as religion.
- It focuses on 'black/white' distinctions, referring to such ideas as 'black tradition', 'black experience' and 'black perspectives'. This is contrary to the wishes of many people within the groups so labelled, who prefer to distinguish different histories, cultures and religions as aspects of their personal and social identity.
- Anti-discrimination uses terms such as 'ethnicity', with a meaning in historical derivation implying 'not us', that are associated with pejorative terms such as 'ethnic cleansing' and have come to be used offensively, as in referring to people from minority groups as

'ethnics'. Since O'Hagan was writing, the abbreviation BME (black and minority ethnic group) and reference to BMEs in daily practice is sometimes seen as similarly offensive.

In addition, Clarke (2003) proposes that the structural origins of racism interact with emotional responses to it to create a complex mixture of factors; neither the internal and emotional nor the external can be ignored. Robinson (1999) argues that the stage a person has reached in the development of their racial identity is more important than the mere fact of their race. Thus, in general, the picture is of a more complex set of social interactions than simple discrimination would suggest. Even so, Robinson (2001) argues that there is a shared experience of discrimination and racism.

Attempts to create an overall theoretical model of anti-discriminatory and anti-oppressive practice seek to subsume anti-racist concerns and concerns about other groups with feminism's focus on gender discrimination. However, the strong ideological and theoretical roots of feminism in wider political, social and cultural ideology, and its many distinctive features, make it a separate force.

Anti-discriminatory and anti-oppressive practice theory sees the interaction between various oppressions as complex and requiring analysis, for example through intersectionality. This, however, presents practical and ideological problems. Macey and Moxon (1996) criticize anti-racism because it emphasizes racism as an explanation of discrimination in the context of high levels of poverty and poor environments. Poor education, crime and disorder, unemployment and inequality are due to many other factors, and anti-discrimination exaggerates the importance of racism in its interaction with other sources of inequality. An agency or social workers may specialize in ways that make it impossible for them to accord equal weight to all the oppressions. The needs of clients may present in one area, and social workers may resist dealing with other areas. Both practitioners and clients may, at the level of ideas, have difficulty in accepting the equivalence of oppression of, say, elderly people or lesbians and gays with that of, say, people from other cultures. This may be due to their own prejudice or their reasonable assessment that ageism, for example, has far less serious consequences than racism for particular clients or in general.

Values issues

Both anti-oppressive and multicultural sensitivity theory implement the shared value principles of critical practice and a concern for rights (see Figure 1.7). Recent accounts of anti-oppressive practice (Clifford and Burke, 2009; Gray and Webb, 2010) make a strong connection with social justice and human rights. Gray and Webb's (2010) analysis sees anti-racism, anti-oppression and participatory actions in practice as being connected with human rights and social justice objectives and as part of a set of social rather than moral values. Clifford and Burke (2009) see such social objectives alongside the interpersonal values, such as feminist relationship ethics, that caring derives from interpersonal connectedness rather than justice perspectives.

Applications

Anti-oppressive, sensitivity and other social work practices

We have seen that anti-oppressive perspectives are critical of all social work practice and organization in their failure to incorporate major social change to achieve equality and social justice for oppressed groups. Multicultural sensitivity approaches question this structuralist focus on inequalities and social change, suggesting that other issues are just as important in practice. The choice presented for practitioners is to embrace the structural critique completely (a social change theoretical strategy) or focus on the perspectives of cultural and black or oppressed groups as a way of being committed to meeting oppressed minorities' needs within interpersonal and therapeutic practice (a theoretical strategy of empowerment).

Anti-discriminatory practice theory seeks to incorporate into social work practice a concern for combating discrimination against all groups. Thompson's (2012) analysis of anti-discriminatory practice is important as being the first account to attempt to provide a theoretical rationale for practice across a range of discriminatory behaviour. Its current theoretical emphasis connects the issues of quality, diversity and social justice as principles of anti-discrimination. Thompson includes gender, ethnicity, ageing, disability, sexuality and spirituality. All forms of discrimination are seen as important, with each form of discrimination strengthening the adverse effects of others.

Some American writers (for example, Sisneros et al. 2008; Marsiglia and Kulis, 2009) emphasize diversity and ideas of cultural pluralism and multiculturalism, and more recent formulations combine this with elements of critical theory and oppression. This approach stems from literature accentuating the cultural element of ethnic difference, for example different dress, social customs, artistic and musical contributions and diet and cuisine. The education of children in religious and social customs is an important strategy, and in the 1980s multiculturalism played a part in influencing education.

Forte (1999) proposes that social workers develop 'toolkits' of information about the values associated with different cultures. A characteristic of 1990s American literature (for instance, Jacobs and Bowles, 1988; Ryan, 1992; Kim, 1995) is the exploration of detailed information about different minority groups. This appears to be at least partly because of the presence in the USA of large groups of indigenous native American ethnic groups and recent migrants, raising specific language, cultural and practical issues. Dungee-Anderson and Beckett (1995) argue that we need to understand other cultures with which we work to avoid mistakes in intervention caused by a misunderstanding of our own or our clients' reactions. Developing from this is the idea of workers having 'cultural competence' (O'Hagan, 2001; Lum, 2011) or being 'culturally grounded' (Marsiglia and Kulis, 2009), practising with respect for maintaining diversity and understanding the main cultures they would have contact with.

Emphasizing culture presents difficulties. Culture may imply a relatively unchanging, dominating collection of social values, and assumes that members of an identified group will always accept all of these. Against this assumption, the source of influences on an individual or a social or ethnic group may be variable. Multiculturalism in education is criticized for encouraging people to gain a smattering of other cultures without an in-depth appreciation of the origins and reasons for the differences. Applied to social work, anti-oppression theorists argue that multiculturalism may encourage a surface appreciation of visible diversities without dealing with substantial social inequalities and discrimination. This risks ignoring diversity within categories, subordinating alternative cultures to Western interpretations of them, or simplifying them and denying real philosophical and practical differences in cultural views (Gross, 1995). In this way, multiculturalism does not address inequality, discrimination and the depth of cultural diversity. Fellin (2000) argues that multiculturalism also fails to address diversity within white communities, focusing instead on the differences within minority ethnic groups and between minority ethnic and white groups.

Taking a rather different approach to diversity, Cox and Ephross (1998), like Lee (2001; see also Chapter 11), highlight the 'lens' through which practitioners see clients and their social situations, arguing that we must identify aspects of homogeneity and heterogeneity in the ethnic groups we deal with. So, faced with a situation in which ethnicity is an issue, practitioners should assess where there are connections with wider issues of inequality and structural racism; they should also identify issues that particularly affect the group, including diversities such as those of gender and sexuality. We would identify that an African-Caribbean man suffers structural inequality in Western societies, for example, but also work on the specific issues raised by his oppressive gender relations with his wife and the personal and social issues raised by his increasing awareness that he is gay. Seeley (2004) suggests that, in short-term work with people from cultural minorities, it is important to focus on their own interpretations of their cultural experience so that they can grasp issues that are important to the client.

The practice benefits for workers in diverse societies have ensured the continued use and development of approaches involving ethnic and cultural sensitivity and competence. However, their pragmatism and their emphasis on the contested concept of culture means that the ideological and theoretical elements of anti-discrimination theory have in many respects become a theoretical position that competes with ethnic sensitivity.

Because the range of opinion and terminology is considerable, I have selected two example texts that take different viewpoints in illustrating how writers from different theoretical traditions have applied anti-oppressive and cultural sensitivity approaches in inclusive accounts of practice.

Example text: Dalrymple and Burke (2006) on anti-oppressive practice

Dalrymple and Burke (2006) place many of the ideas discussed here in a comprehensive account of anti-oppressive practice. Their focus is on how the legal and professional responsibilities of social workers may be implemented either oppressively or in an empowering way. They have thus developed their model in an extremely difficult area for social work – the use of power and authority derived from legal responsibilities – in search of protection for both the public and clients. It makes their formulation all the more powerful for focusing on an area of social work that sometimes seems to conflict with the approach of attacking discrimination and developing empowerment for clients. Dalrymple and Burke see anti-oppressive practice as part of the critical tradition of social work, including radical, structural, feminist and black perspectives and anti-racist practice. They also view it as being informed by movements of oppressed people such as gay and lesbian people, people with learning disabilities, survivors of psychiatric care, individuals living with AIDS and disabled people. The book has a strong emphasis on black feminist perspectives.

As with all forms of critical social work, three important theoretical approaches in anti-oppressive practice are:

- an emphasis on the structural origins of the issues faced by clients;
- social change as an important aspect of practice;
- the critical analysis of practice relationships, and trying to transform those relationships accordingly.

The aims of anti-oppressive practice are:

- overcoming barriers to clients achieving greater control of their lives;
- working in partnership with clients and including them in decision-making;
- minimal intervention, to reduce the impact of the oppressive and disempowering aspects of social work;
- critical reflection and reflexivity of our self to understand how our values and biographies affect our practice relationships.

One of the issues currently faced by social workers is the managerialist and technicist approach of many social work agencies to social work practice, associated with a loss of professional autonomy and discretion. By emphasizing measurements of the efficiency of delivery of services, rather than the inner world of clients and the practitioner–client relationship, clients may be denied a voice in how decisions are made and services provided. To counteract these processes, practitioners need to maintain a critical engagement with a range of theories.

Powerlessness arises from people taking on a self-image and identity of being unable to achieve their objectives. This happens because of the experience they have of external limitations, and because social systems constantly block powerless groups from taking effective action. Consequently, powerlessness goes with economic insecurity, poverty and the inability to think critically about their position. Poverty generates that inability through a lack of training and opportunity and through the physical and emotional stress that arises from economic insecurity.

People experience oppression as the pervasive but fluid impact of political and economic structures through interpersonal relations that leads to social control by the dominant groups in society. It may be specifically related to a particular factor in their identity or life, such as ethnicity, gender or disability, but this usually interconnects with other factors such as poverty and lack of opportunity for self-expression and social mobility. Identity is an important element of oppression and therefore of anti-oppressive practice. Some identities are constructed as being superior to others.

Using the law is not the first resort in social work, and it usually presents contradictions that require critical analysis. It may offer rights, require practitioners or clients to accept duties, or impose obligations – 'a morally binding relationship between individuals based on reciprocal biographies' (Dalrymple and Burke, 2006, p. 75).

Anti-oppressive practice comprises four main elements, set out in Figure 14.4. Values are often expressed in codes of ethics or practice and in declarations of human rights. Such statements often point to areas of contradiction and uncertainty. The law can help to resolve these and to support social work values, for example of self-determination and informed consent; alternatively, it may oversimplify or harden conflicts that are inherent in people's value systems. An important aspect of anti-oppressive practice is, therefore, identifying and working out value conflicts and their effects on people's lives and decisions.

Figure 14.4 Four main elements of anti-oppressive practice

Element	Explanation
Values	Practice is informed by competing discourses within the sets of beliefs, ideas and assumptions that individuals and groups hold about themselves and the society they live in
Empowerment	Practice assists people through a process of gaining greater control of their personal lives, and a greater capacity to engage with the local personal and cultural factors that influence their lives, as well as with political and social change
Partnership	Practice aims to achieve an alliance between practitioners and clients, with other agencies in the public, private and voluntary or third sectors and between different professionals
Minimal intervention	Practice aims to intervene with as little intrusion as possible in people's rights and freedom to make their own decisions

Source: Dalrymple and Burke (2006, pp. 81–178).

Empowerment is a process of understanding the links between people's personal positions and structural inequality. This enables people to see that the problems they face are not wholly individual, and they may be able to find increased power to gain increasing control over aspects of their lives. In this way, they may come to see themselves as having increased psychological efficacy (the belief that they can have an impact on their problems) and social agency (the capacity to join with others to make a difference). This may involve exploring the three elements of oppression identified in Figure 14.3: their feelings and personal biography, their ideas and consciousness and understanding about the world, and their activity or political action in a wider social context.

Partnership involves commitment to common objectives, a shared responsibility to develop aims and strategy, a negotiation of commitments to work together, sharing risks, resources and skills, and aiming to achieve mutual benefit and synergy (energy to take action that could not be achieved alone).

Minimal intervention involves a careful consideration of where there are legal duties to intervene and legal responsibilities to respect people's freedoms. Within those requirements, practitioners have a wide choice over how to intervene, including whether to intervene with individuals, families or more widely. In addition, it is important that they consider ways in which their intervention may be limiting or empowering and act accordingly.

Anti-oppressive work means reframing practice in five different areas, set out in Figure 14.5.

Figure 14.5 Reframing practice as anti-oppressive

Reframe practice around...	Explanation
Prevention	Look for ways of preventing difficulties arising and avoid making things worse
Assessment	Use assessment to involve people in identifying their needs and to enhance their rights and service provision
Planning	Forward-looking practice obtains better outcomes, and shared planning generates agreed aims
Involvement	Seek ways of involving people in the decisions that affect them, offering a range of opportunities that respond to their needs and the situation
Evaluation	Engage people and colleagues in reflection and more formal evaluations of the practice and services provided

The first area is to have a strong focus on preventing difficulties from arising by diverting people from problematic situations, intervening early to prevent situations from worsening, focusing on the most serious situations to ensure that they are dealt with and using restorative intervention to reduce any adverse impacts of intervention. An important aim is to improve people's quality of life.

Assessment is a universal aspect of social work roles. Anti-oppressive assessment involves the people who are being assessed, making clear the decisions and issues to be addressed and sharing values and concerns. Practitioners should incorporate the narratives and perspectives of everyone involved, and reflect the complexity of the whole of the client's situation, looking at alternative explanations, perspectives and courses of action.

Planning is a way of working towards positive outcomes, rather than focusing on deficits and problems, thus attaining one of the shared principles (see Figure 1.7). As with assessment, anti-oppressive planning aims to involve relevant people in the process and seeks to build on strengths and positives in their lives.

Anti-oppressive practice sees clients' involvement in decisions as a citizen's democratic right. That right builds on and extends clients' rights as the consumers of services so that they can access services, information, choice, redress when things go wrong and representation through advocacy within the service system. Agencies sometimes structure involvement as a representative process for influencing service planning, but practitioners can look for an involvement of different people in their work in a variety of ways, in a range of situations and in many different aspects of practice.

Evaluation is often seen as something done in a formal way by practitioners and managers. Involving clients and carers in the process can gain a range of different perspectives and respect people's rights to influence how they are dealt with in the present and in the future.

Example text: Sisneros et al. (2008) on critical multicultural social work

Sisneros et al. (2008) provide an example of an interpretation of sensitivity practice that reflects some incorporation of wider cultural issues than ethnicity and race, as well as ideas such as intersectionality and (racial) identity development. It covers ethnicity and race, gender and disabilities. I have not summarized their account of problems in each of these areas, but have instead focused on their analysis of practice. Sisneros et al.'s account concentrates solely on the USA, and I have generalized this material to refer more broadly to a wider range of societies.

This text sees societies as patchworks 'of overlapping stories, perspectives and world-views' (p. 1), and practitioners need to engage with this variety and complexity. Critical multiculturalism implies a move beyond simply acknowledging diversity to engaging with the variety of differences between people and social groups and accepting that power, dominance and socioeconomic class shape social structures and interactions. Practitioners need to analyse these systems and understand how they maintain and perpetuate inequality, with the value objective of taking action for greater equality (see Figure 1.7). Oppression is pervasive and universal and operates simultaneously at the individual, institutional and societal levels; this tells us that change must also operate at each of these levels. Oppression is maintained by five processes:

- *exploitation*, one group appropriating the benefits gained by others;
- *marginalization*, in which individuals and groups are denied participation in social life and relations;
- *powerlessness*, where social groups lack power, status and a sense of self;
- *cultural imperialism*, in which the culture and experience of one group is the norm;
- *violence*, where some groups are subjected to physical and emotional violence, ridicule, harassment and stigma.

Diversity is presented in some social perspectives as frightening and threatening, causing alarm and hostility. Multiple threads in people's stories are ignored in favour of one account of a society's history and culture; political and economic systems are then organized to follow that dominating story. To respond to this, critical multicultural practice seeks to develop self-awareness in people's understanding of their life and social relations. Critical reflection is required so that they can analyse their present position and become aware of potentialities and opportunities. It is important not to be 'empty of assumptions' (p. 26). That is, we must be aware of the social assumptions that we take for granted, learning and accepting misinformation and myths.

It is important for people to develop a clear personal and social identity on which we can build the acceptance of multiple worldviews. Ideas about the development of racial identity (Helms, 1993, 1995) suggest that people move through a series of stages in encountering and internalizing an identity that is focused on their race and ethnicity. Similarly, white people develop an identity of difference from black people and need to develop a non-racist identity, immersing themselves in alternative cultures and developing a commitment to opposing racism.

However, alternative conceptions of identity development propose that people have a variety of simultaneous experiences of differences that intersect and influence each other, rather than going through a developmental sequence. People's experience includes differences in and group history, language, culture, traditions and spirituality. Other factors may include the experience of hostility, stigma and social injustice and inequality and their impact on our lives and relationships. Gender identity and sexual orientation may include biological factors and alternative views of well-being, for example that gay or lesbian life preferences might legitimately be different from heterosexual life aims.

Our understanding of identity development needs therefore to be multidimensional, including the results of experiencing privilege and disadvantage. Each individual's self-identity and how it interacts with others around them needs to be explored. It is also necessary to understand how relationships and patterns of behaviour generate the capacity to understand and respond to multidimensional worldviews for both practitioners and clients. Understanding how multiple identifies intersect in individuals, families and communities is an important aspect of this.

Sisneros et al. (2008: 82–94) express understanding and practice in this model as 'creating a web' of the various dimensions of someone's identity, understanding their position and then shifting it through providing additional or alternative experiences. This involves interweaving various aspects of privilege and marginalization.

Case example: Selma's life develops from profound Deafness

Selma was born Deaf to two Deaf parents; as described earlier in the chapter, the capitalization of 'D' in 'Deaf' denotes her position as part of a community of 'Deaf' people who see themselves as having a shared culture informed by the shared use of sign language.

Until her teenage years, most of Selma's social life took place in organizations of Deaf people. Although she went to a mainstream school, alongside other children who were not deaf or Deaf, and learned some lip-reading skills, most of her friends were Deaf young people. During her teens, she became interested in gymnastics and took part in competitions and teams. This gave her the motivation to improve her lip reading, and she gained a number of friends who were not deaf or Deaf, who became increasingly important to her. However, her parents were concerned that she was cutting herself off from the supports available in the Deaf community. She herself regretted some of the losses in convenient social relationships, and she spent some time discussing these issues with the social worker for the Institute for Deaf People.

In this case example, we can see strengths that may be derived from the support of the Deaf community, and from social engagement in it, but also marginalization from other communities. An alternative experience stimulated reflection on Selma's position in this 'web', and her work with the social worker was concerned with 'shifting' her position so that she was able to draw strength from both social situations with which she was engaged. The practitioner could see that this repositioning might also strengthen her capacity to make better use of her school experiences and help with the development of her education.

Sisneros et al. (2008: 87) developed a diagram of the web of intersecting identities that may be relevant, and I have presented a simplified and generalized form of this in Figure 14.6. This diagram defines a variety of factors that contribute towards a personal identity; it is this identity that defines access to privilege, power, access and resources or limitations on them. We can look at this web in individual cases historically, as the situation is now or in order to provide aims for the future. Exploring this shifting web in our lives can be transformative, allowing us to see strengths that we have not previously identified. Cultural competence allows us to understand our own worldview, based on this shifting web, and to help others identify and value their own worldview.

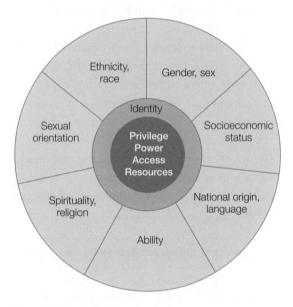

Figure 14.6 Web of intersecting identities
Source: Sisneros et al. (2008, p. 87). Reprinted with permission from Lyceum Books.

Pause and reflect *Using the web of intersecting identities*

Review Selma's situation from the previous case example and identify where identity strengths were in her childhood and her teenage years. Also think through how to work on positive identity shifts for the future.

Some suggestions

Thelma's early identity strengths were with her family and the Deaf community, while her 'ability' at school and in non-Deaf language was not strong. However, her growing ability in gymnastics enabled her to shift those identities. Further shifts might include shifts in possible employment and socioeconomic status coming from improvements in her education and language. Since the development of gender and sexual orientation identities are often important in the teenage years, it would be useful to explore how these changes in identity affected Thelma's development in these areas.

Conclusion: using anti-oppressive and multicultural sensitivity approaches

Anti-oppressive and multicultural sensitivity are useful because many societies and agencies face pressures from the consequences of population migration through an increasingly global economy and refugee population movements. In addition, attitudes among groups such as women, disabled people and people with diverse sexualities have become less deferential, less accepting of present patterns of power. These theoretical perspectives help to analyse and respond to these social issues. Perspectives from black and other oppressed groups and multicultural understanding have also helped practitioners to use knowledge about various minority ethnic groups and women, disabled individuals and older people in social relations.

Anti-oppressive theories also make an important theoretical contribution to other social work approaches. They contribute to critical theory an analysis of the different bases for the oppression of groups and the production of inequalities and divisions in society, and thus provide a more effective account of issues that critical practice must face. The focus on oppression raised important social issues that draw on and make important use of critical theory. They draw attention to the weaknesses of many psychological and individualistic theories of social work in dealing with discrimination and the issues facing minority groups and women in present-day society, and offer a way of understanding these issues. They thus strengthen the sociological basis of social work.

The perspectives of oppressed groups and those of black people do not permit a wholly structural response. They require careful attention to be paid to the wishes and needs of the groups affected, in all their variety, and do not accept just one structural explanation of oppression. Nonetheless, the shared experience of oppression requires a response from services and workers.

Multicultural sensitivity approaches and those of black and oppressed people reject the alignment of all members of a group together as victims of oppression, and seek a more diversified, complex analysis of their needs. Sensitive plural responses will be required, while acknowledging the importance of structural analyses of power as partly conditioning the appropriate response. As a result, a variety of services involving and fitting the needs of particular minorities and oppressed groups would grow up. Sensitivity approaches focus on building up a range of social workers with detailed and specialized understanding. All social workers would take responsibility for a sensitive response to the expressed needs and wishes of the people they worked with. If these required specialized understanding, there would be referral to someone with the appropriate knowledge and experience.

While these two approaches represent values and demand understanding that should permeate social work, it is not clear that either can form the only basis of practice – other service and therapeutic objectives will usually also be required. Both approaches seek to influence all forms of social work, rather than create specific models of practice. They therefore often call for an empowerment approach, although this may not be consonant with the structural focus of anti-oppression theory. Structural explanations of oppression are central to anti-oppression and offer a clear view of the social objectives of such a theory. Multicultural sensitivity approaches mainly help by providing an understanding of the diversities that practitioners will have to deal with in practice.

Additional resources

Further reading

Clifford, D. and Burke, B. (2009) *Anti-oppressive Ethics and Values in Social Work* (Basingstoke: Palgrave Macmillan).

Dalrymple, J. and Burke, B. (2006) *Anti-oppressive Practice: Social Care and the Law* (2nd edn) (Maidenhead: Open University Press).

Useful recent presentations of values and practice views of anti-oppressive practice.

Devore, W. and Schlesinger, E. G. (1999) *Ethnic-sensitive Social Work Practice* (5th edn) (Boston, MA: Allyn & Bacon).

A significant text presenting a sensitivity approach, although it is now somewhat elderly.

Sisneros, J., Stakeman, C., Joyner, M. C. and Schmitz, C. L. (2008) *Critical Multicultural Social Work* (Chicago: Lyceum).

A more recent account of cultural sensitivity approaches incorporating some critical elements.

Dominelli, L. (2008) *Anti-racist Social Work* (3rd edn) (Basingstoke: Palgrave Macmillan).

Dominelli, L. (2002) *Anti-oppressive Social Work Theory and Practice* (Basingstoke: Palgrave Macmillan).

Two examples of Dominelli's many ideologically informed books in this area.

O'Hagan, K. (2001) *Cultural Competence in the Caring Professions* (London: Jessica Kingsley).

A good account of the cultural competence approach to responding to diverse ethnicities.

Thompson, N. (2012) *Anti-discriminatory Practice: Equality, Diversity and Social Justice* (5th edn) (Basingstoke: Palgrave Macmillan).

The latest edition of Thompson's important introductory text.

Journal

Journal of Ethnic and Cultural Diversity in Social Work – Taylor & Francis.

Websites

http://www.saifscotland.org.uk/fileuploads/low-res-saif-social-model-8338.pdf

The Scottish Accessible Information Forum has a downloadable brief account of the social model of disability: Carson, G. (2009) *The Social Model of Disability* (Norwich: TSO).

http://socialworkandoppression.blogspot.co.uk/

The Anti-oppressive Social Work Practice Theory blog has not been kept up to date but contains a useful collection of quotations from international writing, as well as references lists.

http://news.bbc.co.uk/1/hi/uk/3600791.stm

This BBC News website offers a number of interviews presenting alternative views of multicultural society and useful links for further information.

Bibliography

Abrams, L. J. and Moio, J. A. (2009) 'Critical race theory and the cultural competence dilemma in social work education', *Journal of Social Work Education* 45(2): 245–61.

Adam, B., Beck, U. and van Loon, J. (eds) (2000) *The Risk Society and Beyond: Critical Issues for Social Theory* (London: Sage).

Adams, R. (2008) *Empowerment, Participation and Social Work* (4th edn) (Basingstoke: Palgrave Macmillan).

Adler, R. B., Rodman, G. and Cropley Hutchinson, C. (2011) *Understanding Human Communication* (11th edn) (New York: Oxford University Press).

Ahmad, B. (1990) *Black Perspectives in Social Work* (Birmingham: Venture).

Ainsworth, M. D., Blehar, M. C., Waters, E. and Wall, S. (1978) *Patterns of Attachment* (New Jersey: Erlbaum).

Aldgate, J. (2007) 'The place of attachment theory in social work with children and families', in Lishman, J. (ed.) *Handbook for Practice Learning in Social Work and Social Care: Knowledge and Theory* (2nd edn) (London: Jessica Kingsley): 57–73.

Allan, J. (2003) 'Theorising critical social work', in Allan, J., Pease, B. and Briskman, L. *Critical Social Work: An Introduction to Theories and Practices* (Crows Nest, NSW: Allen & Unwin): 52–72.

Allan, J., Briskman, L. and Pease, B. (2009) *Critical Social Work: Theories and Practices for a Socially Just World* (2nd edn) (Crows Nest, NSW: Allen & Unwin).

Allen, T. and Thomas, A. (eds) (2000) *Poverty and Development into the 21st Century* (Oxford: Oxford University Press).

Alter, S. K. (2006) 'Social enterprise models and their mission and money relationships', in Nicholls, A. (ed.) *Social Entrepreneurship: New Models of Sustainable Social Change* (Oxford: Oxford University Press): 205–32.

American Psychiatric Association (2013) *Diagnostic and Statistical Manual of Mental Disorders* (5th edn). Arlington, VA: American Psychiatric Association.

Angell, G. B. (2011) 'Neurolinguistic programming theory and social work treatment', in Turner, F. J. (ed.) *Social Work Treatment: Interlocking Theoretical Approaches* (5th edn) (New York: Oxford University Press): 327–42.

Applegate, J. S. and Shapiro, J. R. (2005) *Neurobiology for Clinical Social Work: Theory and Practice* (New York: Norton).

Arber, S. and Ginn, J. (1991) *Gender and Later Life: A Sociological Analysis of Resources and Constraints* (London: Sage).

Archer, M. S. (1995) *Realist Social Theory: The Morphogenetic Approach* (Cambridge: Cambridge University Press).

Archer, M. S. (2000) *Being Human: the Problem of Agency* (Cambridge: Cambridge University Press).

Argyris, C. and Schön, D. A. (1974) *Theory in Practice: Increasing Professional Effectiveness* (San Francisco: Jossey-Bass).

Armelius B.-Å. and Andreassen T. H. (2007) *Cognitive-behavioural Treatment for Antisocial Behaviour in Youth in Residential Treatment* (Oslo: Campbell Collaboration).

Ashencaen Crabtree, S., Husain, F. and Spalek, B. (2008) *Islam and Social Work: Debating Values, Transforming Practice* (Bristol: Policy Press).

Ashton, R. (2010) *How To Be a Social Entrepreneur: Make Money and Change the World* (Chichester: Capstone).

Atherton, C. R. (1993) 'Empiricists versus social constructionists: time for a cease-fire', *Families in Society* 74: 617–24.

Atherton, C. R. (1994) 'Atherton's response', *Families in Society* 75(5): 315–17.

Atherton, J. S. (1989) *Interpreting Residential Life: Values to Practise* (London: Tavistock/Routledge).

Bailey, R. and Brake, M. (1975) 'Introduction: social work in the welfare state', in Bailey, R. and Brake, M. (eds) *Radical Social Work* (London: Edward Arnold): 1–12.

Bailey, R. and Brake, M. (1980) 'Contributions to a radical practice in social work', in Brake, M. and Bailey, R. (eds) *Radical Social Work and Practice* (London: Edward Arnold): 7–25.

Baldwin, M. (2004) 'Critical reflection: opportunities and threats to professional learning and service development in social work organizations', in Gould, N. and Baldwin, M. (eds) *Social Work, Critical Reflection and the Learning Organization* (Aldershot: Ashgate): 41–55.

Bandura, A. (1977) *Social Learning Theory* (Englewood Cliffs, NJ: Prentice-Hall).

Banks, S. (2003) 'Conflicts of culture and accountability: managing ethical dilemmas and problems in community practice', in Banks, S., Butcher, H., Henderson, P. and Robertson, J. (eds) *Managing Community Practice: Principles, Policies and Programmes* (Bristol: Policy Press): 103–20.

Banton, M. (1987) *Racial Theories* (Cambridge: Cambridge University Press).

Barnes, C. and Mercer, G. (2006) *Independent Futures: Creating User-led Disability Services in a Disabling Society* (Bristol: Policy Press).

Barry, M. and Hallett, C. (eds) (1998) *Social Exclusion and Social Work: Issues of Theory, Policy and Practice* (Lyme Regis: Russell House).

Bateman, N. (2005) *Practising Welfare Rights* (London: Routledge).

Bayley, M. (1997) 'Empowering and relationships', in Ramcharan, P., Roberts, G., Grant, G. and Borland, J. (eds) *Empowerment in Everyday Life: Learning Disabilities* (London: Jessica Kingsley): 15–34.

BBC (2010) *Panorama – unseen Tracey Connelly interview reveals missed opportunity to save Baby P.* Retrieved 27th October 2011 from: http://www.bbc.co.uk/pressoffice/pressreleases/stories/2010/12_december/13/panorama.shtml.

Beck, A. T. (1989) *Cognitive Therapy and the Emotional Disorders* (Harmondsworth: Penguin).

Beck, J. S. and Beck, A. T. (2011) *Cognitive Behavior Therapy: Basics and Beyond* (2nd edn) (New York: Guilford).

Beckett, C. (2006) *Essential Theory for Social Work Practice* (London: Sage).

Becvar, R. J., Canfield, B. S. and Becvar, D. S. (1997) *Groupwork: Cybernetic, Constructivist and Social Constructionist Perspectives* (Denver, CO: Love).

Behrman, G. and Reid, W. J. (2005) 'Posttrauma intervention: basic tasks', in Roberts, A. R. (ed.) *Crisis Intervention Handbook* (3rd edn) (New York: Oxford University Press): 291–302.

Bell, L. (2011) 'Divorce', in Bell, L. *... and they lived happily ever after.* Retrieved 28th October 2011 from: http://andtheylivedhappilyeverafter.com/5.htm.

Bellamy, J. L., Bledsoe, S. E. and Mullen, E. J. (2009) 'The cycle of evidence-based practice', in Otto, H.-U., Polutta, A. and Ziegler, H. (eds) *Evidence-based Practice – Modernising the Knowledge Base of Social Work?* (Opladen/Farmington Falls, MI: Barbara Budrich): 21–9.

Bellinger, A. and Fleet, F. (2012) 'Counselling and contemporary social work', in Stepney, P. and Ford, D. (eds) *Social Work Models, Methods and Theories* (2nd edn) (Lyme Regis: Russell House): 152–65.

Belsky, J. and Rovine, M. J. (1988) 'Nonmaternal care in the first year of life and the security of infant-parent attachment', *Child Development* 59(1): 157–67.

Beresford, P. and Croft, S. (1993) *Citizen Involvement: A Practical Guide for Change* (Basingstoke: Macmillan – now Palgrave Macmillan).

Beresford, P. and Croft, S. (2001) '"Service users" knowledges and the social construction of social work', *Journal of Social Work* 1(3): 295–316.

Berger, P. L. and Luckmann, T. (1971) *The Social Construction of Reality* (Harmondsworth: Penguin) (original American publication, 1966).

Berne, E. (1961) *Transactional Analysis in Psychotherapy* (New York: Grove Press).

Berne, E. (1964) *Games People Play* (Harmondsworth: Penguin).

Bertens, H. (1995) *The Idea of the Postmodern: A History* (London: Routledge).

Berzoff, J. (2003) 'Psychodynamic theories in grief and bereavement', *Smith College Studies in Social Work* 73(3): 273–98.

Besthorn, F. H. and McMillen, D. P. (2002) 'The oppression of women and nature: ecofeminism as a framework for an expanded ecological social work', *Families in Society* 83(3): 221–32.

Bettelheim, B. (1950) *Love is Not Enough* (Glencoe: IC Free Press).

Bhaskar, R. (1979) *A Realist Theory of Science* (2nd edn) (Brighton: Harvester).

Bhaskar, R. (1989) *Reclaiming Reality* (London: Verso).

Bion, W. R. (1961) *Experiences in Groups and Other Papers* (London: Tavistock).

Blakemore, K. and Boneham, M. (1994) *Age, Race and Ethnicity: A Comparative Approach* (Buckingham: Open University Press).

Blewitt, J. (2008) *Community, Empowerment and Sustainable Development* (Totnes: Green Books).

Blom, B. (1994) 'Relationem socialarbetare – klient ur ett Sartre anskt perspektiv', *Nordisk Sosialt Arbeid* 4: 265–76.

Blom, B. (2002) 'The social worker–client relationship – a Sartrean approach', *European Journal of Social Work* 5(3): 277–85.

Boeck, T., McCullogh, P. and Ward, D. (2001) 'Increasing social capital to combat social exclusion', in Matthes, A.-L., Närhi, K and Ward, D. (eds) *The Eco-social Approach in Social Work* (Jyväskylä: SoPhi): 4–107.

Boehm, A. and Staples, L. H. (2002) 'The functions of the social worker in empowering: the voices of consumers and professionals', *Social Work* 47(14): 449–60.

Bonner, C. E. (2002) 'Psychoanalytic theory and diverse populations: reflections of old practices and new understandings', *Psychoanalytic Social Work* 9(2): 61–70.

Borden, B. (2009) *Contemporary Psychodynamic Theory and Practice* (Chicago: Lyceum).

Borden, W. (2010a) 'Taking multiplicity seriously: pluralism, pragmatism and integrative perspectives in clinical social work', in Borden, W., *Reshaping Theory in Contemporary Social Work: Toward a Critical Pluralism in Clinical Practice* (New York: Columbia University Press): 3–27.

Borden, W. (ed.) (2010b) *Reshaping Theory in Contemporary Social Work: Toward a Critical Pluralism in Clinical Practice* (New York: Columbia University Press).

Borton, T. (1970) *Reach, Touch, Teach* (London: Hutchinson).

Bottomore, T. B. (1993) *Elites and Society* (2nd edn) (London: Routledge).

Bourdieu, P. (1977) *Outline of a Theory of Practice* (Cambridge: Cambridge University Press).

Bowell, T. and Kemp, G. (2002) *Critical Thinking: A Concise Guide* (London: Routledge).

Bowes, A. and Sim, D. (2006) 'Advocacy for black and minority ethnic communities: understanding and expectations', *British Journal of Social Work* 36(7): 1209–26.

Bowlby, J. (1951) *Maternal Care and Mental Health* (Geneva: World Health Organization).

Bowlby, J. (1969) *Attachment and Loss*, vol. I: *Attachment* (London: Hogarth Press).

Bowlby, J. (1973) *Attachment and Loss*, vol. II: *Separation* (London: Hogarth Press).

Bowlby, J. (1980) *Attachment and Loss*, vol. III: *Loss* (London: Hogarth Press).

Bowlby, J. (1988) *A Secure Base: Clinical Applications of Attachment Theory* (London: Routledge).

Bowser, B. P. (ed.) (1995) *Racism and Anti-racism in World Perspective* (Thousand Oaks, CA: Sage).

Boylan, J. and Dalrymple, J. (2009) *Understanding Advocacy for Children and Young People* (Maidenhead: Open University Press).

Brandell, J. R. (2004) *Psychodynamic Social Work* (New York: Columbia University Press).

Brandell, J. R. (ed.) (2011) *Theory and Practice in Clinical Social Work* (2nd edn) (Los Angeles: Sage).

Brandon, D. (1976) *Zen and the Art of Helping* (London: Routledge & Kegan Paul).

Brandon, D. (2000) *Tao of Survival: Spirituality in Social Care and Counselling* (Birmingham: Venture).

Brandon, D., Brandon, A. and Brandon, T. (1995) *Advocacy: Power to People with Disabilities* (Birmingham: Venture).

Braye, S. (2000) 'Participation and involvement in social care: an overview', in Kemshall, H. and Littlechild, R. (eds) *User Involvement and Participation in Social Care: Research Informing Practice* (London: Jessica Kingsley): 9–28.

Brearley, J. (2007) 'A psychodynamic approach to social work', in Lishman, J. (ed.) *Handbook for Practice Learning in Social Work and Social Care: Knowledge and Theory* (2nd edn) (London: Jessica Kingsley): 86–98.

Brechin, A. and Sidell, M. (2000) 'Ways of knowing', in Gomm, R. and Davies, C. (eds) *Using Evidence in Health and Social Care* (London: Sage): 3–25.

Bremble, A. and Hill, J. (2004) 'A model of multi-agency psychology consultation', *Clinical Psychology* 34 (February): 29–33.

Bricker-Jenkins, M., Hooyman, N. R. and Gottlieb, N. (eds) (1991) *Feminist Social Work Practice in Clinical Settings* (Newbury Park, CA: Sage).

Brigham, T. M. (1977) 'Liberation in social work education: applications from Paulo Freire', *Journal of Education for Social Work* 13(3): 5–11.

Bronfenbrenner, U. (1979). *The Ecology of Human Development: Experiments by Nature and Design* (Cambridge, MA: Harvard University Press).

Brookfield, S. (1990) *The Skilful Teacher: On Technique, Trust and Responsiveness in the Classroom* (San Francisco: Jossey-Bass).

Brown, A. (1992) *Groupwork* (3rd edn) (Aldershot: Arena).

Brown, A., Caddick, B., Gardiner, M. and Sleeman, S. (1982) 'Towards a British model of groupwork', *British Journal of Social Work* 12(6): 587–603.

Brown, E., Bullock, R., Hobson, C. and Little, M. (1998) *Making Residential Care Work: Structure and Culture in Children's Homes* (Aldershot: Ashgate).

Brown, H. and Smith, H. (eds) (1992) *Normalisation: A Reader for the Nineties* (London: Routledge).

Burghardt, S. (2011) *Macro Practice in Social Work for the 21st Century* (Thousand Oaks, CA: Sage).

Burr, V. (2003) *Social Constructionism* (2nd edn) (London: Routledge).

Bytheway, B. (1995) *Ageism* (Buckingham: Open University Press).

Callahan, M. (1996) 'A feminist perspective on child welfare', in Kirwin, B. (ed.) *Ideology, Development and Social Welfare: Canadian Perspectives* (Toronto: Canadian Scholars Press): 111–126.

Cameron, C., Petrie, P., Wigfall, V., Kleipoedszus, S. and Jasper, A. (2011) *Final Report of the Social Pedagogy Pilot Programme: Development and Implementation* (London: Thomas Coram Research Unit, Institute of Education, University of London).

Canda, E. R. and Furman, L. (2009) *Spiritual Diversity in Social Work Practice: The Heart of Helping* (2nd edn) (New York: Oxford University Press).

Canda, E. R. and Smith, E. D. (2001) *Transpersonal Perspectives on Spirituality in Social Work* (New York: Haworth).

Cannan, C. (1972) 'Social workers: training and professionalism', in Pateman, T. (ed.) *Counter Course: A Handbook for Course Criticism* (Harmondsworth: Penguin): 247–63.

Caplan, G. (1965) *Principles of Preventive Psychiatry* (London: Tavistock).

Caplan, G. (1974) *Support Systems and Community Mental Health: Lectures on Concept Development* (New York: Behavioral Publications).

Caplan, G. and Killilea, M. (eds) (1976) *Support Systems and Mutual Help: Multidisciplinary Explorations* (New York: Grune & Stratton).

Carkhuff, R. R. and Berenson, B. C. (1977) *Beyond Counseling and Therapy* (2nd edn) (New York: Holt, Rinehart & Winston).

Carlton-LaNey, I. (ed.) (1994) *The Legacy of African-American Leadership in Social Welfare.* Special issue of *Journal of Sociology and Social Welfare* 21(1).

Carlton-LaNey, I. P. (ed.) (2001) *African American Leadership: An Empowerment Tradition in Social Welfare History* (Washington, DC: NASW Press).

Carr, A. (2006) *The Handbook of Child and Adolescent Clinical Psychology: A Contextual Approach* (2nd edn) (London: Routledge).

Carr, W. (1986) 'Theories of theory and practice', *Journal of the Philosophy of Education* 20(2): 177–86.

Carson, G. (2009) *The Social Model of Disability* (Norwich: TSO).

Cassidy, J. and Shaver, P. R. (eds) (2008) *Handbook of Attachment: Theory, Research and Clinical Applications* (2nd edn) (New York: Guilford).

Cavanagh, K. and Cree, V. E. (eds) (1996) *Working with Men: Feminism and Social Work* (London: Routledge).

CCETSW (1991) *One Small Step Towards Racial Justice: The Teaching of Antiracism in Diploma in Social Work Programmes* (London: CCETSW).

CD Project Steering Group (1991) *Setting the Context for Change* (London: CCETSW).

Chambon, A. S. and Irving, A. (eds) (1994) *Essays on Postmodernism and Social Work* (Toronto: Canadian Scholars' Press).

Chambon, A. S., Irving, A. and Epstein, L. (eds) (1999) *Reading Foucault for Social Work* (New York: Columbia University Press).

Chandra, B. (1987) *Communalism in Modern India* (2nd edn) (New Delhi: Vikas).

Chatterjee, P. and Brown, S. (2012) 'Cognitive theory and social work treatment', in Turner, F. J. (ed.) *Social Work Treatment: Interlocking Theoretical Approaches* (5th edn) (New York: Oxford University Press): 103–16.

Christie, A. (2006) 'Negotiating the uncomfortable intersections between gender and professional identities to social work', *Critical Social Policy* 26(2): 390–411.

Cigno, K. and Bourn, D. (eds) (1998) *Cognitive Behavioural Social Work in Practice* (Aldershot: Ashgate).

Clark, D. H. (1974) *Social Therapy in Psychiatry* (Harmondsworth: Penguin).

Clark, J. J. (2010) 'Social work, psychobiography, and the study of lives', in Borden, W. (ed.) *Reshaping Theory in Contemporary Social Work: Toward a Critical Pluralism in Clinical Practice* (New York: Columbia University Press): 81–113.

Clark, M. (2009) *The Social Entrepreneur Revolution: Doing Good by Making Money, Making Money by Doing Good* (London: Marshall Cavendish).

Clarke, I. and Wilson, H. (eds) (2009) *Cognitive Behaviour Therapy for Acute Inpatient Mental Health Units: Working with Clients, Staff and the Milieu* (London: Routledge).

Clarke, J. and Newman, J. (1997) *The Managerial State: Power, Politics and Ideology in the Remaking of Social Welfare*. London: Sage.

Clarke, S. (2003) *Social Theory, Psychoanalysis and Racism* (Basingstoke: Palgrave).

Clasen, J. and Clegg, D. (2006) 'Beyond activation: reforming European unemployment protection systems in post-industrial labour markets', *European Societies* 8(4) 2006: 527–53.

Clifford, D. and Burke, B. (2009) *Anti-oppressive Ethics and Values in Social Work* (Basingstoke: Palgrave Macmillan).

Clough, R. (2000) *The Practice of Residential Work* (Basingstoke: Macmillan – now Palgrave Macmillan).

Clutterbuck, D. and Oates, D. (1995) *The Power of Empowerment: Release the Hidden Talents of Your Employees* (London: Kogan Page).

Cnaan, R. A. (1996) 'Empowerment under capitalism: the case of the United States', in Parsloe, P. (ed.) *Pathways to Empowerment* (Birmingham: Venture): 27–39.

Cnaan, R. A., Boddie, S. C., Handy, F., Yancey, G. and Schneider, R. (2002) *The Invisible Caring Hand: American Congregations and the Provision of Welfare* (New York: New York University Press).

Coates, J. (2003) *Ecology and Social Work: Towards a New Paradigm* (Halifax, NS: Fernwood).

Collins, B. G. (1986) 'Defining feminist social work', *Social Work* 31(3): 214–19.

Corcoran, J. and Pillai, V. (2009) 'A review of the research on solution-focused therapy', *British Journal of Social Work* 39(2): 234–42.

Cohen, S., Underwood, L. G., and Gottlieb, B. H. (2000) *Social Support Measurement and Intervention: A Guide for Health and Social Scientists* (New York: Oxford University Press).

Cole, M. (2009) *Critical Race Theory and Education: A Marxist Response* (Basingstoke: Palgrave Macmillan).

Collins, P. H. (2000) *Black Feminist Thought: Knowledge, Consciousness, and the Politics of Empowerment* (2nd edn) (New York: Routledge).

Compton, B. R., Galaway, B. and Cournoyer, B. R. (2005) *Social Work Processes* (7th edn) (Pacific Grove, CA: Brooks/Cole).

Cooke, B. and Kothari, U. (eds) (2001) *Participation: The New Tyranny?* (London: Zed).

Corden, J. and Preston-Shoot, M. (1987) 'Contract or con trick?; a reply to Rojek and Collins', *British Journal of Social Work* 17(5): 535–43.

Corden, J. and Preston-Shoot, M. (1988) 'Contract or con trick?; a postscript', *British Journal of Social Work* 18(6): 623–34.

Corrigan, P. and Leonard, P. (1978) *Social Work Practice under Capitalism: A Marxist Approach* (London: Macmillan – now Palgrave Macmillan).

Cort, E., Monroe, B., Hansford, P., Moorey, S., Hotopf, M. and Kapari, M. (2009) 'Palliative care nurses' experiences of training in cognitive behaviour therapy and taking part in a randomized controlled trial', *International Journal of Palliative Nursing* 15: 290–8.

Costa, M. das Dores (1987) 'Current influences on social work in Brazil: practice and education', *International Social Work* 30(2): 115–28.

Coulshed, V., Mullender, A. and McGlade, M. (2013) *Management in Social Work* (4th edn) (Basingstoke: Palgrave Macmillan).

Cox, C. B. and Ephross, P. H. (1998) *Ethnicity and Social Work Practice* (New York: Oxford University Press).

Craig, G., and Mayo, M. (eds) (1995) *Community Empowerment: A Reader in Participation and Development* (London: Zed Books).

Crane, R. (2009) *Mindfulness-based Cognitive Therapy* (London: Routledge).

Craven, S. M. (2009) 'No fault divorce is institutionalized evil', in *Anti Misandry: Curing feminist indoctrination*. Retrieved 28th October 2011 from: http://antimisandry.com/a/no-fault-divorce-institutionalized-evil-22972.html.

Crawford, F., Dickinson, J. and Leitmann, S. (2002) 'Mirroring meaning making: narrative ways of reflecting on practice for action', *Qualitative Social Work* 1(2): 170–90.

Cree, V. E. and Macaulay, C. (eds) (2000) *Transfer of Learning in Professional and Vocational Education* (London: Routledge).

Croft, S. and Beresford, P. (1994) 'A participatory approach to social work', in Hanvey, C. and Philpot, T. (eds) *Practising Social Work* (London: Routledge): 49–66.

Cummins, K. K., Byers, K. V. and Pedrick, L. (2011) *Policy Practice for Social Workers: New Strategies for a New Era* (updated edn) (Boston, MA: Allyn & Bacon).

Curry, J. F. (1995) 'The current status of research into residential treatment', *Residential Treatment for Children and Youth* 12(3): 1–17.

D'Cruz, H. (2009) 'Social work knowledge-in-practice', in D'Cruz, H., Jacobs, S. and Schoo, A. (eds) *Knowledge-in-Practice in the Caring Professions: Multidisciplinary Perspectives* (Farnham: Ashgate): 61–92.

Dalrymple, J. and Burke, B. (2006) *Anti-oppressive Practice: Social Care and the Law* (2nd edn) (Maidenhead: Open University Press).

Danto, E. A. (2011) 'Psychoanalysis and social work: a practice partnership', in Turner, F. J. (ed.) (2011) *Social Work Treatment: Interlocking Theoretical Approaches* (5th edn) (New York: Oxford University Press): 374–86.

Dattilio, F. M. and Freeman, A. (eds) (2007) *Cognitive-Behavioral Strategies in Crisis Intervention* (3rd edn) (New York: Guilford).

Davis, L. V. (1985) 'Female and male voices in social work', *Social Work* 30(2): 106–13.

de Maria, W. (1992) 'On the trail of a radical pedagogy for social work education', *British Journal of Social Work* 22(3): 231–52.

de Maria, W. (1993) 'Exploring radical social work teaching in Australia', *Journal of Progressive Human Services* 4(2): 45–63.

de Shazer, S. (1985) Keys to Solution in Brief Therapy (New York: Norton).

de Shazer, S. and Berg, I. K. (1997) 'What works?', *Journal of Family Therapy* 19(2): 1221–5.

Delgado, M. (2011) *Latino Small Businesses and the American Dream: Community Social Work Practice and Economic and Social Development* (New York: Columbia University Press).

Delgado, R. and Stefancic, J. (2012) *Critical Race Theory: An Introduction* (2nd edn) (New York: New York University Press).

Denney, D. (1991) 'Antiracism, probation training and the criminal justice system', in CCETSW, *One Small Step Towards Racial Justice: The Teaching of Antiracism in Diploma in Social Work Programmes* (London: CCETSW): 58–80.

Denney, D. (1992) *Racism and Anti-Racism in Probation* (London: Routledge).

Dent, H. (1999) 'PC pathway to positive action', in Philpot, T. (ed.) *Political Correctness and Social Work* (London: IEA Health and Welfare Unit): 27–41.

Dent, H. R. and Golding, K. S. (2006) 'Engaging the network: consultation for looked after and adopted children', in Golding, K. S., Dent, H. R., Nissim, R. and Stott, L. (eds) *Thinking Psychologically About Children who Are Looked After and Adopted: Space for Reflection* (Chichester: Wiley): 164–94.

Devore, W. and Schlesinger, E. G. (1999) *Ethnic-sensitive Social Work Practice* (5th edn) (New York: Allyn & Bacon).

Dewey, J. (1933) *How We Think* (New York: Heath).

Dickinson, D. (2000) 'Consultation: assuring the quality and outcomes', *Educational Psychology in Practice* 16(1): 19–23.

Dietz, C. A. (2000) 'Reshaping clinical practice for the new millennium', *Journal of Social Work Education* 36(3): 503–20.

Dobson, D. and Dobson, K. S. (2009) *Evidence-based Practice of Cognitive-Behavioral Therapy* (New York: Guilford).

Doel, M. and Marsh, P. (1992) *Task-centred Social Work* (Aldershot: Ashgate).

Dominelli, L. (2002a) *Feminist Social Work Theory and Practice* (Basingstoke: Palgrave Macmillan).

Dominelli, L. (2002b) *Anti-oppressive Social Work Theory and Practice* (Basingstoke: Palgrave Macmillan).

Dominelli, L. (2008) *Anti-racist Social Work* (3rd edn) (Basingstoke: Palgrave Macmillan).

Dominelli, L. (2009) 'Anti-oppressive practice: the challenges of the twenty-first century', in Adams, R., Dominelli L. and Payne, M. (eds) *Social Work: Themes, Issues and Critical Debates* (3rd edn) (Basingstoke: Palgrave Macmillan): 49–64.

Dominellli, L. (2012) *Green Social Work: from Environmental Crises to Environmental Justice* (Cambridge: Polity).

Dominelli, L. and McCleod, E. (1989) *Feminist Social Work* (Basingstoke: Macmillan – now Palgrave Macmillan).

Donnison, D. (2009) *Speaking to Power: Advocacy for Health and Social Care* (Bristol: Policy Press).

Dore, M. M. (1990) 'Functional theory: its history and influence on contemporary social work', *Social Service Review* 64(3): 358–74.

Douglas, H. and Brennan, A. (2004) 'Containment, reciprocity and behaviour management: preliminary evaluation of a brief early intervention (the Solihull Approach) for families with infants and young children', *International Journal of Infant Observation* 7(1): 89–107.

Dungee-Anderson, D. and Beckett, J. O. (1995) 'A process model for multicultural social work practice', *Families in Society* 76(8): 459–66.

Dunham, A., Furbey, R. and Lownes, V. (eds) (2009) *Faith in the Public Realm: Controversies, Policies and Practices* (Bristol: Policy Press).

Eamon, M. K. (2008) *Empowering Vulnerable Populations: Cognitive-Behavioral Interventions* (Chicago: Lyceum).

Earnshaw Smith, E. (1990) 'Editorial: The hospice social worker in the multiprofessional team', *Palliative Medicine* 4(2): i–iii.

Elliott, D. (1993) 'Social work and social development: towards an integrative model for social work practice', *International Social Work* 36(1): 21–36.

Ellis, A. (1962) *Reason and Emotion in Psychotherapy* (Secaucus, NJ: Lyle Stuart).

Ellis, A. and MacLaren, C. (2005) *Rational Emotive Behavior Therapy: A Therapist's Guide* (2nd edn) (Atascadero, CA: Impact).

Ely, P. and Denney, D. (1987) *Social Work in a Multi-racial Society* (Aldershot: Gower).

England, H. (1986) *Social Work as Art* (London: Allen & Unwin).

Epstein, L. and Brown, L. B. (2002) *Brief Treatment and a New Look at the Task-Centered Approach* (3rd edn) (Boston: Allyn & Bacon).

Erikson, E. (1965) *Childhood and Society* (2nd edn) (London: Hogarth Press).

Estes, R. J. (1993) 'Toward sustainable development: from theory to praxis', *Social Development Issues* 15(3): 1–29.

Evans, D. and Kearney, J. (1996) *Working in Social Care: A Systemic Approach* (Aldershot: Arena).

Evans, E. N. (1992) 'Liberation theology, empowerment theory and social work practice with the oppressed', *International Social Work* 35(2): 135–47.

Eyrich, K. M., Pollio, D. E. and North, C. S. (2003) 'An exploration of alienation and replacement theories of social support in homelessness', *Social Work Research* 27(4): 222–31.

Ezell, M. (1993) 'The political activity of social workers: a post-Reagan update', *Journal of Sociology and Social Welfare* 20(4): 81–7.

Ezell, M. (1994) 'Advocacy practice of social workers', *Families in Society* 75(1): 36–46.

Fairclough, N. (1992) *Discourse and Society* (Cambridge: Polity).

Fairclough, N. (2003) '"Political correctness": the politics of culture and language', *Discourse and Society* 14(1): 17–28.

Farmer, R. (2009) *Neuroscience and Social Work Practice: The Missing Link* (Thousand Oaks, CA: Sage).

Fawcett, B. (2009) 'Postmodernism', in Gray, M. and Webb, S. A. (eds) *Social Work Theories and Methods* (Los Angeles: Sage): 119–28.

Fawcett, B. and Featherstone, B. (2000) 'Setting the scene: an appraisal of notions of postmodernism, postmodernity and postmodern feminism', in Fawcett, B., Featherstone, B., Fook, J. and Rossiter, A. (eds) *Practice and Research in Social Work: Postmodern Feminist Perspectives* (London: Routledge): 5–23.

Fawcett, B., Featherstone, B., Fook, J. and Rossiter, A. (eds) (2000) *Practice and Research in Social Work: Postmodern Feminist Perspectives* (London: Routledge).

Fellin, P. (2000) 'Revisiting multicultural social work', *Journal of Social Work Education* 36(12): 261–75.

Ferguson, I. and Lavalette, M. (1999) 'Social work, postmodernism, and Marxism', *European Journal of Social Work* 2(1): 27–40.

Ferguson, I. and Woodward, R. (2009) *Radical Social Work in Practice: Making a Difference* (Bristol: Policy Press).

Finlay, L. (2003) 'The reflexive journey: mapping multiple routes', in Finlay, L. and Gough, B. (eds) *Reflexivity: A Practical Guide for Researchers in Health and Social Sciences* (Oxford: Blackwell): 3–20.

Finlay, L. and Gough, B. (eds) (2003) *Reflexivity: A Practical Guide for Researchers in Health and Social Sciences* (Oxford: Blackwell).

Fischer, J. (1973) 'Is casework effective? A review', *Social Work* 18(1): 5–20.

Fischer, J. (1976) *The Effectiveness of Social Casework* (Springfield, IL: Charles C. Thomas).

Fischer, J. and Gochros, H. L. (1975) *Planned Behavior Change: Behavior Modification in Social Work* (New York: Free Press).

Fisher, M. (1994) 'Man-made care: community care and older male carers', *British Journal of Social Work* 24(6): 659–80.

Fisher, R. and Kling, J. (1994) 'Community organization and new social movement theory', *Journal of Progressive Human Services* 5(2): 5–23.

Flannery, R. B. and Everly, G. S. (2000) 'Crisis intervention: a review', *International Journal of Emergency Mental Health* 2(2): 119–26.

Fook, J. (2012) *Social Work: A Critical Approach to Practice* (2nd edn) (Los Angeles: Sage).

Fook, J. and Gardner, F. (2007) *Practising Critical Reflection: A Resource Handbook* (Maidenhead: Open University Press).

Fook, J., Ryan, M. and Hawkins, L. (2000) *Professional Expertise: Practice, Theory and Education for Working in Uncertainty* (London: Whiting & Birch).

Forcey, L. R. and Nash, M. (1998) 'Rethinking feminist theory and social work therapy', *Women and Therapy* 21(4): 85–99.

Ford, P. and Postle, K. (2012) 'Task-centred practice in challenging times', in Stepney, P and Ford, D. (eds) *Social Work Models, Methods and Theories: A Framework of Practice* (2nd edn) (Lyme Regis: Russell House): 102–22.

Forte, J. A. (1999) 'Culture: the tool-kit metaphor and multicultural social work', *Families in Society* 80(1): 51–62.

Fortune, A. E. (2012) 'Development of the task-centered model', in Rzepnicki, T. L., McCracken, S. G. and Briggs, H. E. (eds) *From Task-centered to Evidence-Based and Integrative Practice: Reflections on History and Implementation* (Chicago: Lyceum): 15–39.

Foucault, M. (1972) *The Archaeology of Knowledge and the Discourse on Language* (New York: Pantheon).

Foulkes, S. H. (1964) *Therapeutic Group Analysis* (London: Allen & Unwin).

Frankl, V. E. (1964 [1946]) *Man's Search for Meaning: An Introduction to Logotherapy* (rev. edn) (London: Hodder & Stoughton).

Frankl, V. E. (2011 [1948]) *Man's Search for Ultimate Meaning* (rev. edn) (London: Rider).

Franklin, M. E. (1968) 'The meaning of planned environment therapy', in Barron, A. T. (ed.) *Studies in Environment Therapy*, vol. 1 (Worthing: Planned Environment Therapy Trust).

Fraser, S. and Matthews, S. (eds) (2008) *The Critical Practitioner in Social Work and Health Care* (London: Sage).

Freddolino, P. O., Moxley, D. M. and Hyduk, C. A. (2004) 'A differential model of advocacy in social work practice', *Families in Society* 85(1): 119–28.

Freedberg, S. (2008) *Relational Theory for Social Work Practice: A Feminist Perspective* (New York: Routledge).

Freire, P. (1972) *Pedagogy of the Oppressed* (Harmondsworth: Penguin).

Froggett, L. (2002) *Love, Hate and Welfare: Psychosocial Approaches to Policy and Practice* (Bristol: Policy Press).

Furman, R. (2009) 'Ethical consideration of evidence-based practice', *Social Work* 54(1): 82–4.

Gambrill, E. (1994) 'What's in a name? Task-scentred, empirical, and behavioral practice', *Social Service Review* 68(4): 578–99.

Gambrill, E. (1995) 'Behavioral social work: past, present and future', *Research on Social Work Practice* 5(4): 460–84.

Gambrill, E. (2006) *Social Work Practice: A Critical Thinker's Guide* (2nd edn) (New York: Oxford University Press).

Ganzer, C. and Ornstein, E. D. (2002) 'A sea of trouble: a relational approach to the culturally sensitive treatment of a severely disturbed client', *Clinical Social Work Journal* 30(2): 127–44.

Garber, B. (1992) 'Countertransference reactions in death and divorce: comparison and contrast', *Residential Treatment for Children and Youth* 9(4): 43–60.

Gardner, F. (2003) 'Critical reflection in community-based evaluation', *Qualitative Social Work* 2(2): 197–212.

Garfinkel, H. (1967) *Studies in Ethnomethodology* (Englewood Cliffs, NJ: Prentice Hall).

Garvin, C. D. (2011) 'Group treatment with adults', in Brandell, J. R. (ed.) (2011) *Theory and Practice in Clinical Social Work* (2nd edn) (Los Angeles: Sage): 323–44.

Garvin, C. D., Gutierrez, L. M. and Galinsky, M. J. (eds) (2004) *Handbook of Social Work with Groups* (New York: Guilford).

George, E. (2005) 'Consultation: a solution-focussed approach', in Southall, A. (ed.) *Consultation in Child and Adolescent Mental Health Services* (Oxford: Radcliffe).

George, V. and Wilding, P. (1994) *Welfare and Ideology* (London: Harvester Wheatsheaf).

Gergen, K. J. (1994) *Realities and Relationships: Soundings in Social Construction* (Cambridge, MA: Harvard University Press).

Gergen, K. J. (1999) *An Invitation to Social Construction* (London: Sage)

Gergen, M. and Gergen, K. J. (2003) *Social Construction: A Reader* (London: Sage).

Germain, C. B. (ed.) (1979) *Social Work Practice: People and Environments – an Ecological Perspective* (New York: Columbia University Press).

Gerth, H. H. and Mills, C. W. (1948) *From Max Weber: Essays in Sociology* (London: Routledge & Kegan Paul).

Gibbons, J., Bow, I., Butler, J. and Powell, J. (1979) 'Clients' reactions to task-centred casework: a follow-up study', *British Journal of Social Work* 10(2): 203–15.

Gibbs, G. (1988) *Learning by Doing: A Guide to Teaching and Learning Methods* (Oxford: Oxford Polytechnic).

Gibbs, L. and Gambrill, E. (2002) 'Evidence-based practice: counterarguments to objectives', Research in Social Work Practice 12(3): 452–76.

Gibson, A. (2007) 'Erikson's life cycle approach to development', in Lishman, J. (ed.) (2007) *Handbook for Practice Learning in Social Work and Social Care: Knowledge and Theory* (2nd edn) (London: Jessica Kingsley): 74–85.

Gibson, F. (2011) Reminiscence and Life Story Work: A Practice Guide (4th edn) (London: Jessica Kingsley).

Giddens, A. (1998) *The Third Way: The Renewal of Social Democracy* (Cambridge: Polity Press).

Giddens, A. (2000) *The Third Way and its Critics*. (Cambridge Polity Press).

Gilchrist, A. (2004) *The Well-connected Community: A Networking Approach to Community Development* (Bristol: Policy Press).

Gilgun, J. F. (1994) 'Hand in glove: The grounded theory approach and social work practice research', in Sherman, E. and Reid, W. J. (eds) *Qualitative Research in Social Work* (New York: Columbia University Press): 115–25.

Gilligan, C. (1982) *In a Different Voice: Psychological Theory and Women's Development* (Cambridge, MA: Harvard University Press).

Gitterman, A. and Germain, C. B. (2008) *The Life Model of Social Work Practice: Advances in Theory and Practice* (3rd edn) (New York: Columbia University Press).

Gitterman, A. and Shulman, L. (eds) (2005) *Mutual Aid Groups, Vulnerable and Resilient Populations, and the Life Cycle* (3rd edn) (New York: Columbia University Press).

Glaister, A. (2008) 'Introducing critical practice', in Fraser, S. and Matthews, S. (eds) *The Critical Practitioner in Social Work and Health Care* (London: Sage): 8–26.

Glasser, W. (1965) *Reality Therapy: A New Approach to Psychiatry* (New York: Harper & Row).

Glassman, U. (2009) *Group Work: A Humanistic and Skills Building Approach* (2nd edn) (Los Angeles: Sage).

Goffman, E. (1968) *The Presentation of Self in Everyday Life* (Harmondsworth: Penguin).

Golan, N. (1986) 'Crisis theory', in Turner, F. J. (ed.) *Social Work Treatment: Interlocking Theoretical Approaches* (3rd edn) (New York: Free Press): 296–340.

Goldberg, E. M. (1987) 'The effectiveness of social care: a selective exploration', *British Journal of Social Work* 17(6): 595–614.

Golding, K. S. (2004) 'Providing specialist psychological support to foster carers: a consultation model' *Child and Adolescent Mental Health* 9(2): 71–6.

Golding, K. S. (2008) *Nurturing Attachments: Supporting Children Who Are Fostered or Adopted* (London: Jessica Kingsley).

Golding, K. S. and Hughes, D. A. (2012) *Creating Loving Attachments: Parenting with PACE to Nurture Confidence and Security in the Troubled Child* (London; Jessica Kingsley).

Golding, K. S., Dent, H. R., Nissim, R. and Stott, L. (eds) (2006) *Thinking Psychologically About Children Who are Looked After and Adopted: Space for Reflection* (Chichester: Wiley).

Goldstein, E. G. (1995) *Ego Psychology and Social Work Practice* (2nd edn) (New York: Free Press).

Goldstein, E. G. (2002) *Object Relations Theory and Self Psychology in Social Work Practice* (New York: Free Press).

Goldstein, E. G. and Noonan, M. (1999) *Short-Term Treatment and Social Work Practice: An Integrative Perspective* (New York: Free Press).

Goldstein, E., Miehls, D. and Ringel, S. (2009) *Advanced Clinical Social Work Practice: Relational Principles and Techniques* (New York: Columbia University Press).

Goldstein, H. (1973) *Social Work Practice: A Unitary Approach* (Columbia, SC: University of South Carolina Press).

Goldstein, H. (1981) *Social Learning and Change: A Cognitive Approach to Human Services* (Columbia, SC: University of South Carolina Press).

Goldstein, H. (ed.) (1984) *Creative Change: a Cognitive-humanistic Approach to Social Work Practice* (New York: Tavistock).

Goleman, D. (1996) *Emotional Intelligence: Why It Matters More than IQ* (London: Bloomsbury).

Goodman, J. (1984) 'Reflection and teacher education: a case study and theoretical analysis', *Interchange* 15: 9–26.

Gorey, K. M. (1996) 'Social work intervention effectiveness research: comparison of the findings from internal versus external evaluations', *Social Work Research* 20(2): 119–28.

Gould, K. H. (1995) 'The misconstruing of multiculturalism: the Stanford debate and social work', *Social Work* 40(2): 198–205.

Gould, N. (1994) 'Anti-racist social work: a framework for teaching and action', *Issues in Social Work Education* 14(1): 2–17.

Gould, N. and Baldwin, M. (eds) (2004) *Social Work, Critical Reflection and the Learning Organization* (Aldershot: Ashgate).

Graham, M. (2002) *Social Work and African-centred Worldviews* (Birmingham: Venture).

Graham, M. (2007) *Black Issues in Social Work and Social Care* (Bristol: Policy Press).

Graversen, B. K. and van Ours, J. C. (2009) *How a Mandatory Activation Program Reduces Unemployment Durations: The Effects of Distance* (Bonn: Forschungsinstitutzur Zukunft der Arbeit).

Gray, M. (2011) 'Back to basics: a critique of the strengths perspective in social work', *Families in Society* 92(1): 5–11.

Gray, M. and Bernstein, A. (1994) 'Pavement people and informal communities: lessons for social work', *International Social Work* 37(2): 149–63.

Gray, M. and Webb, S. A. (2009) 'Introduction', in Gray, M. and Webb, S. A. (eds) *Social Work Theories and Methods* (London: Sage): 1–10.

Gray, M. and Webb, S. A. (2010) 'Introduction: ethics and value perspectives in social work' in Gray, M. and Webb, S. A. (eds) *Ethics and Value Perpsectives in Social Work*, Basingstoke: Palgrave Macmillan: 1–16.

Gray, M. and Webb, S. A. (eds) (2013) *Social Work Theories and Methods* (2nd edn). (London: Sage).

Gray, M., Plath, D. and Webb, S. A. (2009) *Evidence-based Social Work: A Critical Stance* (London: Routledge).

Greene, G. J. and Lee, M. Y. (2011) *Solution-oriented Social Work Practice: An Integrative Approach to Working with Client Strengths* (New York: Oxford University Press).

Greene, R. R. (2008) 'General systems theory', in Green, R. R. (ed.) *Human Behavior Theory and Social Work Practice* (3rd edn) (New Brunswick, NJ: Aldine Transaction): 165–97.

Greene, R. R. (ed.) (2008a) *Human Behavior Theory and Social Work Practice* (3rd edn) (New Brunswick, NJ: Aldine Transaction).

Greene, R. R. (2008b) 'Human behaviour theory, person-in-environment, and social work method', in Greene, R. R. (ed.) *Human Behavior Theory and Social Work Practice* (3rd edn) (New Brunswick, NJ: Aldine Transaction): 1–26.

Greene R. R. (ed.) (2012) *Resiliency: An Integrated Approach to Practice, Policy, and Research* (2nd edn) (Washington, DC: NASW Press).

Gross, E. R. (1995) 'Deconstructing politically correct practice literature: the American Indian case', *Social Work* 40(2): 206–13.

Guidry, J. D., Kennedy, M. D. and Zald, M. N. (2003) *Globalisations and Social Movements: Culture, Power and the Transnational Public Sphere* (Ann Arbor, MI: University of Michigan Press).

Gutiérrez, G. (1973) *A Theology of Liberation* (Maryknoll: Orbis Books).

Gutiérrez, G. (1992) 'Poverty from the perspective of liberation theology', in Campfens, H. (ed.) *New Reality of Poverty and Struggle for Social Transformation* (Vienna: International Association of Schools of Social Work): 19–24.

Gutiérrez, L. M. (1995) 'Understanding the empowerment process: does consciousness make a difference?', *Social Work Research* 19(4): 229–37.

Gutiérrez, L. M., DeLois, K. A. and GlenMaye, L. (1995) 'Understanding empowerment practice: building on practitioner-based knowledge', *Families in Society* 76(8): 534–42.

Gutiérrez, L. M., Parsons, R. J. and Cox, E. O. (2003) *Empowerment in Social Work Practice: A Sourcebook* (2nd edn) (Pacific Grove, CA: Brooks/Cole).

Habermas, J. (1986 [1971]) *The Theory of Communicative Action: Reason and the Rationalization of Society*, vol. 1: *Reason and the Rationalization of Society* (Cambridge: Polity).

Hall, C., Juhila, K., Parton, N. and Pösö, T. (2003) *Constructing Clienthood in Social Work and Human Services: Interaction, Identities and Practices* (London: Jessica Kingsley).

Hall, N. (1993a) 'The social workers of tomorrow and fieldwork today: poverty and urban social work in Africa in the 1990s', in Hall, N. (ed.) *Social Development and Urban Poverty* (Harare: School of Social Work): 7–14.

Hall, N. (ed.) (2012) *Social Work around the World V: Building the Global Agenda for Social Work and Social Development* (Geneva: International Federation of Social Workers).

Hämäläinen, J. (1989) 'Social pedagogy as a meta-theory of social work education', *International Social Work* 32(2): 117–28.

Hämäläinen, J. (2003) 'The concept of social pedagogy in the field of social work', *Journal of Social Work* 3(1): 69–80.

Hanmer, J. and Statham, D. (1999) *Women and Social Work: Towards a More Woman-centred Practice* (Basingstoke: Macmillan – now Palgrave Macmillan).

Hanson, B. G. (1995) *General Systems Theory: Beginning with Wholes* (Washington, DC: Taylor & Francis).

Hardiker, P. and Barker, M. (2007 [1991]) 'Towards social theory for social work', in Lishman, J. (ed.) *Handbook for Practice Learning in Social Work and Social Care* (2nd edn) (London: Jessica Kingsley): 39–56.

Hardiman, M. and Midgley, J. (1989) *The Social Dimensions of Development: Social Policy and Planning in the Third World* (rev. edn) (Aldershot: Gower).

Harrington, R. (2003) 'Cognitive behaviour therapies', in Garralda, E. and Hyde, C. (eds) *Managing Children with Psychiatric Problems* (2nd edn) (London: BMJ Books).

Harris, T. A. (1973) *I'm OK – You're OK* (London: Pan).

Harrison, W. D. (1991) *Seeking Common Ground: A Theory of Social Work in Social Care* (Aldershot: Avebury).

Hartley, N. and Payne, M. (eds) (2008) *The Creative Arts in Palliative Care* (London: Jessica Kingsley).

Hawkins, C. A. (2010) 'Sustainability, human rights, and environmental justice: critical connections for contemporary social work', *Critical Social Work* 11(3). Retrieved 25th August 2011 from: http://www.uwindsor.ca/criticalsocialwork/the-nexus-of-sustainability-human-rights-and-environmental-justice-a-critical-connection-for-contemp

Healy, K. (2000) *Social Work Practices: Contemporary Perspectives on Change* (London: Sage).

Healy, K. (2005) *Social Work Theories in Context: Creating Frameworks for Practice* (Basingstoke: Palgrave Macmillan).

Heap, K. (1992) 'The European groupwork scene: where were we? where are we? where are we going?', *Groupwork* 5(1): 9–23.

Hearn, G. (1958) *Theory-building in Social Work* (Toronto: University of Toronto Press).

Hearn, G. (ed.) (1969) *The General Systems Approach: Contributions toward an Holistic Conception of Social Work* (New York: Council on Social Work Education).

Hearn, J. (1982) 'The problem(s) of theory and practice in social work and social work education', *Issues in Social Work Education* 2(2): 95–118.

Helms, J. E. (ed.) (1993) *Black and White Racial Identity* (Westport, CT: Praeger).

Helms, J. E. (1995) 'An update of Helms's white and people of color racial identity models', in Ponteroto, J. G., Cases, J. M., Suzuki, L. A. and Alexander, C. M. (eds) *Handbook of Multicultural Counseling* (Thousand Oaks, CA: Sage): 181–98.

Herbert, M. (1999) *Clinical Child Psychology: Social Learning, Development and Behaviour* (Chichester: Wiley).

Hettne, B. (1990) *Development Theory and the Three Worlds* (London: Longman).

Hick, S. F. (ed.) (2009) *Mindfulness and Social Work* (Chicago: Lyceum).

Hill, R. (1965) 'Generic features of families under stress', in Parad, H. (ed.) *Crisis Intervention: Selected Readings* (New York: Family Service Association of America): 32–52.

Hindmarsh, J. H. (1992) *Social Work Oppositions: New Graduates' Experiences* (Aldershot: Avebury).

Hinshelwood, R. D. (1999) 'Psychoanalytic origins and today's work: the Cassel Heritage', in Campling, P. and Haigh, R. (eds) *Therapeutic Communities: Past, Present and Future* (London: Jessica Kingsley): 39–49.

Hirschman, O. (1970) *Exit, Voice and Loyalty* (Cambridge, MA: Harvard University Press).

Hodge, D. R. (2001) 'Spiritual assessment: a review of major qualitative methods and a new framework for assessing spirituality', *Social Work* 46(3): 213–14.

Hodge, D. R. (2003a) 'Differences in worldviews between social workers and people of faith', *Families in Society* 82(2): 285–95.

Hodge, D. R. (2003b) 'The challenge of spiritual diversity: can social work facilitate an inclusive environment?', *Families in Society* 84(3): 348–58.

Hodge, D. R. and Limb, G. (2007) 'Developing spiritual lifemaps as a culture-centered pictorial instrument for spiritual assessments with native American clients', *Research on Social Work Practice* 17(2): 296–304.

Hodge, D. R. and Williams, T. R. (2002) 'Assessing African-American spirituality with spiritual ecomaps', *Families in Society* 83(5): 585–95.

Hoefer, R. (2012) *Advocacy Practice for Social Justice* (2nd edn) (Chicago: Lyceum).

Holloway, M. and Moss B. (2010) *Spirituality and Social Work* (Basingstoke: Palgrave Macmillan).

House, R. and Loewenthal, D. (2008) 'Introduction: an exploration of the criticisms of CBT', in House, R. and Loewenthal, D. (eds) *Against and for CBT: Towards a Constructive Dialogue?* (Ross-on-Wye: PCCS Books): 7–18.

Houston, S. (2001) 'Beyond social constructionism: critical realism and social work', *British Journal of Social Work* 31(6): 845–61.

Houston, S. (2002) 'Reflecting on habitus, field and capital: towards a culturally sensitive social work', *Journal of Social Work* 2(2): 149–67.

Houston, S. (2013) 'Jürgen Habermas', in Gray, M. and Webb, S. A. (eds) *Social Work Theories and Methods* (2nd edn) (London: Sage): 13–24.

Howard, J. (1971) 'Indian society, Indian social work: identifying Indian principles and methods for social work practice', *International Social Work* 14(4): 16–31.

Howe, D. (1989) *A Consumer's View of Family Therapy* (Aldershot: Ashgate).

Howe, D. (1995) *Attachment Theory for Social Work Practice* (Basingstoke: Macmillan – now Palgrave Macmillan).

Howe, D. (2005) *Child Abuse and Neglect: Attachment, Development and Intervention* (Basingstoke: Palgrave Macmillan).

Howe, D. (2008) *The Emotionally Intelligent Social Worker* (Basingstoke: Palgrave Macmillan).

Howe, D. (2009) *A Brief Introduction to Social Work Theory* (Basingstoke: Palgrave Macmillan).

Howe, D. (2011) *Attachment Across the Lifecourse: A Brief Introduction* (Basingstoke: Palgrave Macmillan).

Howe, D., Brandon, M., Hinings, D. and Schofield, G. (1999) *Attachment Theory, Child Maltreatment and Family Support* (Basingstoke: Macmillan – now Palgrave Macmillan).

Hudson, B. and Macdonald, G. (1986) *Behavioural Social Work: An Introduction* (Basingstoke: Macmillan – now Palgrave Macmillan).

Hudson, C. G. (2009) 'Decision making in evidence-based practice: science and art', *Smith College Studies in Social Work* 79(2): 155–74.

Hugen, B. and Scales, T. L. (eds) (2008) *Christianity and Social Work: Readings on the Integration of Christian Faith and Social Work Practice* (3rd edn) (Botsford, CT: North American Association of Christians in Social Work).

Hughes, D. A. (2006) *Building the Bonds of Attachment: Awakening Love in Deeply Troubled Children* (2nd edn) (New York: Jason Aronson).

Hughes, D. A. (2009) *Principles of Attachment-focused Parenting: Effective Strategies to Care for Children* (New York: Norton).

Hujo, K. and McClanahan, S. (2011) 'Introduction and overview', in Hujo, K. and McClanahan, S. (eds) *Financing Social Policy: Mobilizing Resources for Social Development* (Basingstoke: Palgrave Macmillan): 1–24.

Hulme, D. and Turner, M. (1990) *Sociology and Development: Theories, Policies and Practices* (Hemel Hempstead: Harvester Wheatsheaf).

Humphries, B. (1996) 'Contradictions in the culture of empowerment', in Humphries, B. (ed.) *Critical Perspectives on Empowerment* (Birmingham: Venture): 1–16.

Hunter, M. (2001) *Psychotherapy with Young People in Care* (Hove: Brunner-Routledge).

Hunter, S. and Ritchie, P. (eds) (2007) *Co-production and Personalisation in Social Care: Changing Relationships in the Provision of Social Care* (London: Jessica Kingsley).

Illich, I., Zola, I. K., McKnight, J., Caplan, J. and Shaiken, H. (1977) *Disabling Professions* (London: Marion Boyars).

International Federation of Social Workers (2000) *Definition of social work*. Retrieved 18th August 2012 from: http://ifsw.org/policies/definition-of-social-work/.

International Federation of Social Workers (2012) *The global agenda for social work and social development*. Retrieved 28th August 2012 from: http://ifsw.org/tag/global-agenda-for-social-work-and-social-development/.

Irvine, E. E. (1956) 'Transference and reality in the casework relationship', *British Journal of Psychiatric Social Work* 3(4): 1–10.

Irving, A. (2009) 'Michel Foucault', in Gray, M. and Webb, S. A. (eds) *Social Work Theories and Methods* (London: Sage): 43–52.

Isajiw, W. W. (1997) 'On the concept and theory of social incorporation', in Isajiw, W. W. (ed.) *Multiculturalism in North American and Europe: Comparative Perspectives on Interethnic Relations and Social Incorporation* (Toronto: Canadian Scholars' Press): 79–102.

Jacobs, C. and Bowles, D. D. (eds) (1988) *Ethnicity and Race: Critical Concepts in Social Work* (Silver Spring, MD: National Association of Social Workers).

Jacobs, S. (2009) 'Ideas of knowledge in practice', in D'Cruz, H., Jacobs, S. and Schoo, A., *Knowledge-in-Practice in the Caring Professions: Multidisciplinary Perspectives* (Farnham: Ashgate): 13–28.

James, R. K. (2008) *Crisis Intervention Strategies* (6th edn) (Belmont, CA: Thomson Brooks/Cole).

Jansson, B. S. (1994) *Social Policy: From Theory to Policy Practice* (2nd edn) (Belmont, CA: Brooks/Cole).

Jansson, B. S. (2011a) *Becoming an Effective Policy Advocate: From Policy Practice to Social Justice* (6th edn) (Belmont, CA: Brooks/Cole).

Jansson, B. S. (2011b) *Improving Healthcare through Advocacy: A Guide for the Health and Helping Professions* (Hoboken, NJ: Wiley).

Jasper, M. (2003) Beginning Reflective Practice (Cheltenham: Nelson Thornes).

Jehu, D. (1967) *Learning Theory and Social Work* (London: Routledge & Kegan Paul).

Jehu, D. (ed.) (1972) *Behaviour Modification in Social Work* (Chichester: John Wiley).

Jenkins, R. (2008) *Social Identity* (3rd edn) (London: Routledge).

Jenkins, S. (1988) 'Ethnicity: theory base and practice link', in Jacobs, C. and Bowles, D. D. (eds) *Ethnicity and Race: Critical Concepts in Social Work* (Silver Spring, MD: NASW).

Jenson, J. M. (2005) 'Connecting science to intervention: advances, challenges, and the promise of evidence-based practice', *Social Work Research* 29(3) 131–5.

Jenson, J. M. (2007) 'Evidence-based practice and the reform of social work education: a response to Gambrill and Howard and Allen-Meares', *Research on Social Work Practice* 19(5): 569–73.

John, M. and Trevithick, P. (2012) 'Psychodynamic thinking in social work practice', in Stepney, P. and Ford, D. (eds) *Social Work Models, Methods and Theories: A Framework for Practice* (2nd edn) (Lyme Regis: Russell House): 62–79.

Johnson, Y. M. (1999) 'Indirect work: social work's uncelebrated strength', *Social Work* 44(4): 323–34.

Jokinen, A., Juhila, K. and Pösö, T. (1999) *Constructing Social Work Practices* (Aldershot: Ashgate).

Jones, H. (1990) *Social Welfare in Third World Development* (Basingstoke: Macmillan – now Palgrave Macmillan).

Jones, J. F. (1981) 'An introduction to social development: an international perspective', in Jones, J. F. and Pandey, R. S. (eds) *Social Development: Conceptual, Methodological and Policy Issues* (Delhi: Macmillan India).

Jones, J. F. and Pandey, R. S. (eds) (1981) *Social Development: Conceptual, Methodological and Policy Issues* (Delhi: Macmillan India).

Jones, K., Cooper, B. and Ferguson, H. (eds) (2007) *Best Practice in Social Work: Critical Perspectives* (Basingstoke: Palgrave Macmillan).

Jones, M. (1968) *Social Psychiatry in Practice: The Idea of the Therapeutic Community* (Harmondsworth: Penguin).

Jones-Devitt, S. and Smith, L. (2007) *Critical Thinking in Health and Social Care* (London: Sage).

Juhila, K. (2003) 'Creating a "bad" client: disalignment of institutional identities in social work interaction', in Hall, C., Juhila, K., Parton, N. and Pösö, T. (2003) *Constructing Clienthood in Social Work and Human Services: Interaction, Identities and Practices* (London: Jessica Kingsley): 83–95.

Kadushin, G. (1998) 'Adaptations of the traditional interview in the brief-treatment context', *Families in Society* 79(4): 346–57.

Kanel, K. (2012) *A Guide to Crisis Intervention* (5th edn) (Belmont, CA: Brooks/Cole Cengage Learning).

Karls, J. M. and Wandrei, K. E. (eds) (1994) *Person-in-Environment System: The PIE Classification System for Social Functioning Problems* (Washington, DC: NASW Press).

Karvinen, S., Pösö, T. and Satka, M. (1999) *Reconstructing Social Work Research* (Jyväskylä: SoPhi).

Kazi, M. A. F. (1998) *Single-case Evaluation by Social Workers* (Aldershot: Ashgate).

Kazi, M. A. F. (2003) *Realist Evaluation in Practice: Health and Social Work* (London: Sage).

Keefe, T. (2011) 'Meditation and social work practice', in Turner, F. J. (ed.) *Social Work Treatment: Interlocking Theoretical Approaches*

(5th edn) (New York: Oxford University Press): 293–314.

Kelly, G. (1955) *The Psychology of Personal Constructs* (2 vols) (New York: Norton).

Kemp, S. P. (2010) 'Place matters: toward a rejuvenated theory of environment for direct social work practice', in Borden, W. (ed.) *Reshaping Theory in Contemporary Social Work: Toward a Critical Pluralism in Clinical Practice* (New York: Columbia University Press): 114–45.

Kennard, D. (1998) *An Introduction to Therapeutic Communities* (2nd edn) (London: Jessica Kingsley).

Khandwalla, P. N. (ed.) (1988) *Social Development: A New Role for the Organizational Sciences* (New Delhi: Sage).

Kim, Y.-O. (1995) 'Cultural pluralism and Asian-Americans: culturally sensitive social work practice', *International Social Work* 38(1): 69–78.

Kirke, D. M. (2009) 'Social network analysis', in Gray, M. and Webb, S. A. (eds) *Social Work Theories and Methods* (London: Sage): 131–41.

Klein, M. (1959) 'Our adult world and its roots in infancy', in Segal, H. (ed.) (1988) *Envy and Gratitude* (London: Virago).

Koggel, C. and Orme, J. (eds) (2010, 2011) 'Care ethics: new theories and applications: 2 parts', *Ethics and Social Welfare* (Special issue) 4(2): 109–216; 5(2): 107–227.

Kornbeck, J. and Jensen, N. R. (eds) (2009) *The Diversity of Social Pedagogy in Europe* (Bremen: Europäischer Hochschulverlag).

Krill, D. F. (1978) *Existential Social Work* (New York: Free Press).

Kübler-Ross, E. (1969) *On Death and Dying* (New York: Macmillan).

Kumar, H. (1994) *Social Work: An Experience and Experiment in India* (New Delhi: Gitanjali).

Kumar, H. (1995) *Theories in Social Work Practice* (Delhi: Friends).

Laczko, F. and Phillipson, C. (1991) *Changing Work and Retirement* (Buckingham: Open University Press).

Laing, R. D. (1965) *The Divided Self: An Existential Study in Sanity and Madness* (Harmondsworth: Penguin).

Laing, R. D. (1971) *Self and Others* (2nd edn) (Harmondsworth: Penguin).

Lavalette, M. (ed.) (2011) *Radical Social Work Today: Social Work at the Crossroads* (Bristol: Policy Press).

Lavalette, M. and Ferguson, I. (eds) (2007) *International Social Work and the Radical Tradition* (Birmingham: Venture).

Lavalette, M. and Ioakimidis, V. (eds) (2011) *Social Work* In Extremis: *Lessons for Social Work Internationally* (Bristol: Policy Press).

Ledwith, M. (2011) *Community Development: A Critical Approach* (2nd edn) (Bristol: Policy Press).

Lee, J. A. B. (2001) *The Empowerment Approach to Social Work Practice: Building the Beloved Community* (2nd edn) (New York: Columbia University Press).

Lee, M. Y., Ng, S.-M., Leung, P. P. Y. and Chan, C. L. W. (2009) *Integrative Body-Mind-Spirit Social Work: An Empirically Based Approach to Assessment and Treatment* (New York: Oxford University Press).

Lehmann, P. and Coady, N. (2007) *Theoretical Perspectives for Direct Social Work Practice: A Generalist-Eclectic Approach* (2nd edn) (New York: Springer).

Leonard, P. (1984) *Personality and Ideology: Towards a Materialist Understanding of the Individual* (London: Macmillan – now Palgrave Macmillan).

Leonard, P. (1993) 'Critical pedagogy and state welfare: intellectual encounters with Freire and Gransci, 1974–86', in McLaren, P and Leonard, P. (eds) *Paulo Friere: A Critical Encounter* (London; Routledge): 155–68.

Leonardsen, M. (2007) 'Empowerment in social work: an individual vs. a relational perspective', *International Journal of Social Welfare* 16: 3–11.

LeSueur, E. (1970) 'Aboriginal assimilation: an evaluation of some ambiguities in policy and services', *Australian Journal of Social Work* 23(2): 6–11.

Levy, A. and Kahan, B. (1991) *The Pindown Experience and the Protection of Children: the Report of the Staffordshire Child Care Inquiry* (Stafford: Staffordshire County Council).

Liddle, R. (2009) '"Solution Focused Therapy" is only the worst of the delusions in the Baby P case', *The Spectator* 6th May 2009. Retrieved 27th May 2011 from: http://www.spectator. co.uk/essays/3592051/solution-focused-therapy-is-only-the-worst-of-the-delusions-in-the-baby-p-case.thtml.

Lindemann, E. (1944) 'Symptomatology and management of acute grief', in Parad, H. J. (ed.) (1965) *Crisis Intervention: Selected Readings* (New York: Family Service Association of America): 7–21.

Lindsay, C. and Mailand, M. (2004) 'Different routes, common directions? Activation policies for young people in Denmark and the UK', *International Journal of Social Welfare* 13(3): 195–207.

Lindsay, T. (ed.) (2009) *Social Work Intervention* (Exeter: Learning Matters).

Lishman, J. (ed.) (2007) *Handbook for Practice Learning in Social Work and Social Care: Knowledge and Theory* (2nd edn) (London: Jessica Kingsley).

Lohmann, R. A. and Lohmann, N. (2005) 'Epilogue: what is rural practice?', in Lohmann, N. and Lohmann, R. A. (eds) *Rural Social Work Practice* (New York: Columbia University Press): 313–18.

Loney, M. (1983) *Community Against Government: The British Community Development Project 1968–1978: A Study of Government Incompetence* (London: Heinemann).

Longres, J. F. and McCleod, E. (1980) 'Consciousness raising and social work practice', *Social Casework* 61(5): 267–76.

Lorenz, W. (1994) *Social Work in a Changing Europe* (London: Routledge).

Loughran, H. (2011) *Understanding Crisis Therapies: An Integrative Approach to Crisis Intervention and Post-traumatic Stress* (London: Jessica Kingsley).

Lukes, S. (2005 [1974]) *Power: A Radical View* (2nd edn) (Basingstoke: Palgrave Macmillan).

Lum, D. (2011) *Culturally Competent Practice: A Framework for Understanding Diverse Groups and Justice Issues* (4th edn) (Pacific Grove, CA: Brooks/Cole).

Lusk, M. W. (1981) 'Philosophical changes in Latin American social work', *International Social Work* 24(2): 14–21.

Lusk, M. W. and Hoff, M. D. (1994) 'Sustainable social development', *Social Development Issues* 16(3): 20–31.

Lyon, K. (1993) 'Why study roles and relationships?', in Walmsley, J., Reynolds, J., Shakespeare, P. and Woolfe, R. (eds) *Health Welfare and Practice: Reflecting on Roles and Relationships* (London: Sage): 231–9.

Macdonald, G. (2007) 'Cognitive behavioural social work', in Lishman, J. (ed.) *Handbook for Practice Learning in Social Work and Social Care* (London: Jessica Kingsley): 169–87.

Macdonald, G. and Sheldon, B., with Gillespie, J. (1992) 'Contemporary studies of the effectiveness of social work', *British Journal of Social Work* 22(6): 615–43.

Mace, C. (2008) *Mindfulness and Mental Health: Therapy, Theory and Science* (Hove: Routledge).

Macey, M. and Moxon, E. (1996) 'An examination of anti-racist and anti-oppressive theory and practice in social work education', *British Journal of Social Work* 26(3): 297–314.

Maguire, L. (1991) *Social Support Systems in Practice* (Silver Spring, MD: NASW Press).

Mansell, W. (2008) 'What is CBT *really*, and how can we enhance the impact of effective psychotherapies such as CBT?', in House, R. and Lowenthal, D. (eds) *Against and For CBT: Towards a Constructive Dialogue?* (Ross-on-Wye: PCCS Books): 19–32.

Manthorpe, J., Moriarty, J., Rapaport, J., Clough, R., Cornes, M., Bright, L., Iliffe, S. and OPRSI (2008) '"There are wonderful social workers but it's a lottery": older people's views about social workers', *British Journal of Social Work* 38(6): 1132–50.

Maroda, K. J. (2010) *Psychoanalytic Techniques: Working with Emotion in Therapeutic Relationships* (New York: Guilford).

Marsh, P. (2007) 'Task-centred practice', in Lishman, J. (ed.) *Handbook for Practice Learning in Social Work and Social Care* (London: Jessica Kingsley): 188–200.

Marsh, P. and Crow, G. (1997) *Family Group Conferences in Child Welfare* (Oxford: Blackwell).

Marsh, P. and Doel, M. (2005) *The Task-centred Book* (London: Routledge).

Marshall, J. (2009) 'Motivational interviewing', in Lindsay, T. (ed.) *Social Work Intervention* (Exeter: Learning Matters): 78–89.

Marshall, M. and Tibbs, M.-A. (2006) *Social Work with People with Dementia: Partnerships, Practice and Persistence* (Bristol: Policy Press).

Marsiglia, F. F. and Kulis, S. (2009) *Diversity, Oppression and Change: Culturally Grounded Social Work* (Chicago: Lyceum).

Martin, E. P. and Martin, J. M. (1995) *Social Work and the Black Experience* (Washington, DC: NASW Press).

Martin, E. P. and Martin, J. M. (2002) *Spirituality and the Black Helping Tradition in Social Work* (Washington, DC: NASW Press).

Martin, G. (2001) 'Social movements, welfare and social policy: a critical analysis', *Critical Social Policy* 21(3): 361–83.

Martin, R. R. (1995) *Oral History in Social Work: Research, Assessment, and Intervention* (Thousand Oaks, CA: Sage).

Mary, N. L. (2008) *Social Work in a Sustainable World.* (Chicago: Lyceum).

Maslow, A. (1970) *Motivation and Personality* (2nd edn) (New York: Harper & Row).

Mathews, I. and Crawford, K. (eds) (2011) *Evidence-based Practice in Social Work* (Exeter: Learning Matters).

Mattaini, M. A. and Lowery, C. T. (eds) (2007) *Foundations of Social Work Practice: A Graduate Text* (4th edn) (Washington, DC: NASW Press).

Matthies, A.-L. (2010) 'Participation and citizenship', in Gray, M. and Webb, S. A. (eds) *Ethics and Value Perspectives in Social Work* (Basingstoke: Palgrave Macmillan): 173–82.

Matthies, A.-L., Närhi, K. and Ward, D. (eds) (2000a) *From Social Exclusion to Participation: Explorations Across Three European Cities.* Working Papers in Social Policy 106 (Jyväskylä: University of Jyväskylä).

Matthies, A.-L., Järvelä, M. and Ward, D. (2000b) 'An eco-social approach to tackling exclusion in European cities: a new comparative research project in progress', *European Journal of Social Work* 3(1): 43–51.

Matthies, A.-L., Närhi, K. and Ward, D. (eds) (2001) *The Eco-social Approach in Social Work* (Jyväskylä: SoPhi).

Mawson, A. (2008) *The Social Entrepreneur: Making Communities Work* (London: Atlantic).

McCracken, S. G. and Marsh, J. C. (2008) 'Practitioner expertise in evidence-based practice decision-making', *Research on Social Work Practice* 18(4): 301–10.

McDonald, C. (2006) *Challenging Social Work: The Context of Practice* (Basingstoke: Palgrave Macmillan).

McGlynn, P. (ed.) (2006) *Crisis Resolution and Home Treatment: A Practical Guide* (London: Sainsbury Centre for Mental Health).

McIntyre, D. (1982) 'On the possibility of "radical" casework: a "radical" dissent', *Contemporary Social Work Education* 5(3): 191–208.

McLaughlin, J. (2003) *Feminist Social and Political Theory: Contemporary Debates and Dialogues* (Basingstoke: Palgrave Macmillan).

Mead, G. H. (1934) Mind, Self and Society (Chicago: University of Chicago Press).

Meichenbaum, D. (1985) *Stress Inoculation Training* (New York: Pergamon).

Menzies-Lyth, I. (1988) *Containing Anxiety in Institutions* (London: Free Association).

Meyer, W. S. (2000) 'The psychoanalytic social worker/the social work psychoanalyst: what shall be our message?', *Clinical Social Work Journal* 28(4): 355–67.

Mezirow, J. (1981) 'A critical theory of adult learning and education', *Adult Education* 32: 3–24.

Mezirow, J. (1991) *Transformative Dimensions of Adult Learning* (San Francisco: Jossey-Bass).

Midgley, J. (1981) *Professional Imperialism: Social Work in the Third World* (London: Heinemann).

Midgley, J. (1987) 'Popular participation, statism and development', *Journal of Social Development in Africa* 2(1): 5–15.

Midgley, J. (1989) 'Social work in the Third World: crisis and response', in Carter, P., Jeffs, T. and Smith, M. (eds) *Social Work and Social Welfare Yearbook 1* (Milton Keynes: Open University Press): 33–45.

Midgley, J. (1993) 'Ideological roots of social development strategies', *Social Development Issues* 15(1): 1–13.

Midgley, J. (1995) *Social Development: The Developmental Perspective in Social Welfare* (London: Sage).

Midgley, J. (1997) *Social Welfare in Global Context* (Thousand Oaks, CA: Sage).

Midgley, M. and Conley, A. (eds) (2010a) *Social Work and Social Development: Theories and Skills for Developmental Social Work* (New York: Oxford University Press).

Midgley, J. and Conley, A. (2010b) 'Limitations and prospects of developmental social work', in Midgley, M. and Conley, A. (eds) *Social Work and Social Development: Theories and Skills for Developmental Social Work* (New York: Oxford University Press): 193–204.

Miehls, D. (2011) 'Neurobiology and clinical social work', in Brandell, J. R. (ed.) *Theory and Practice in Clinical Social Work* (Los Angeles: Sage): 81–98.

Milkman, H. and Wanberg, K. (2007) *Cognitive-behavioral Treatment: A Review and Discussion for Corrections Professionals* (Washington, DC: National Institute of Corrections, US Department of Justice).

Miller, W. and Rollnick, S. (2002) *Motivational Interviewing: Preparing People to Change Addictive Behaviour* (2nd edn) (New York: Guilford).

Milner, J. (2001) *Women and Social Work: Narrative Approaches* (Basingstoke: Palgrave Macmillan).

Milner, J. (2004) 'From "disappearing" to "demonised": the effects on men and women of professional interventions based on challenging men who are violent', *Critical Social Policy* 24(1): 79–101.

Mills, C. Wright (1999 [1956]) *The Power Elite* (Oxford: Oxford University Press).

Miri, S. (1993) *Communalism in Assam: A Civilisational Approach* (New Delhi: Har-Anand).

Mitchell, J. (1975) *Psychoanalysis and Feminism* (Harmondsworth: Penguin).

Mokate, K. M. (2004) *Women's Participation in Social Development: Experiences from Asia, Latin America, and the Caribbean* (Washington DC: Inter-American Development Bank).

Mondros, J. B. and Wilson, S. M. (1994) *Organizing for Power and Empowerment* (New York: Columbia University Press).

Moorey, S., Cort, E., Kapari, M., Monroe, B., Hansford, P., Mannix, K., Henderson, M., Fisher, L. and Hotopf, M. (2009) 'A cluster randomized controlled trial of cognitive behaviour therapy for common mental disorders in patients with advanced cancer', *Psychological Medicine* 39: 713–23.

Moreau, M. J. (1979) 'A structural approach to social work practice', *Canadian Journal of Social Work Education* 5(1): 78–94.

Moreau, M. J. (1990) 'Empowerment through advocacy and consciousness-raising: implications of a structural approach to social work', *Journal of Sociology and Social Welfare* 17(2): 53–68.

Morén, S. and Blom, B. (2003) 'Explaining human change: on generative mechanisms in social work practice', *Journal of Critical Realism* 2(1): 37–61.

Morgan, R. T. T. and Young, G. C. (1972) 'The conditioning treatment of childhood enuresis', *British Journal of Social Work* 2(4): 503–10.

Morris, J. (1993) *Disabled Lives: Community Care and Disabled People* (Basingstoke: Macmillan – now Palgrave Macmillan).

Morrison, T. (2007) 'Emotional intelligence: emotion and social work: context, characteristics, complications and contribution', *British Journal of Social Work* 37(2): 245–63.

Muldoon, A. (2006) 'Environmental efforts: the next challenge for social work', *Critical Social Work* 7(2). Retrieved 25th August 2011 from: http://www.uwindsor.ca/criticalsocialwork/environmental-efforts-the-next-challenge-for-social-work.

Mullaly, B. (R. P.) (2007) *The New Structural Social Work* (4th edn) (Ontario: Oxford University Press).

Mullaly, B. (R. P.) (2010) *Challenging Oppression and Confronting Privilege* (Ontario: Oxford University Press).

Mullaly, R. P. and Keating, E. F. (1991) 'Similarities, differences and dialectics of radical social work', *Journal of Progressive Human Services* 2(2): 49–78.

Mullen, E. J. and Dumpson, J. R. (1972) *Evaluation of Social Intervention* (San Francisco: Jossey-Bass).

Mullender, A. and Ward, D. (1991) *Self-directed Groupwork: Users Take Action for Empowerment* (London: Whiting & Birch).

Mullin, A. (2011) 'Gratitude and caring labour', *Ethics and Social Welfare* 5(2): 110–22.

Murdach, A. D. (2010) 'What good is soft evidence?', *Social Work* 55(4): 309–16.

Murphy, M. (2009) *Critical Hermeneutics for Social Work: Theory, Research and Practice in Preventative Child Welfare* (Saarbrücken: VDM Verlag Dr Müller).

Murphy, Y., Hunt, V., Zajicek, A. M., Norris, A. N. and Hamilton, L. (2009) *Incorporating Intersectionality in Social Work Practice, Research, Policy and Education* (Washington, DC: NASW Press).

Muzumdar, A. M. (1964) *Social Welfare in India: Mahatma Gandhi's Contributions* (London: Asia Publishing House).

Myers, S. (2008) *Solution-focused Approaches* (Lyme Regis: Russell House).

Närhi, K (2002) 'Transferable and negotiated knowledge: constructing social work expertise for the future', *Journal of Social Work* 2(3): 317–36.

Närhi, K. and Matthies, A.-L. (2001) 'What is the ecological (self-)consciousness of social work?', in Matthies, A.-L., Närhi, K and Ward, D. (eds) *The Eco-social Approach in Social Work* (Jyväskylä: SoPhi): 16–53.

Nash, M. and Stewart, B. (eds) (2002) *Spirituality and Social Care: Contributing to Personal and Community Well-being* (London: Jessica Kingsley).

Nash, M., O'Donoghue, K. and Munford, R. (2005a) 'Introduction: integrating theory and practice', in Nash, M., O'Donoghue, K. and Munford, R. (eds) *Social Work Theories in Action* (London: Jessica Kingsley): 15–28.

Nash, M., Munford, R. and O'Donoghue, K. (eds) (2005b) *Social Work Theories in Action* (London: Jessica Kingsley).

Neary, M. (1992) 'Some academic freedom', *Probation Journal* 39(8): 200–2.

NHS Health Advisory Service Report (1995) *Together We Stand: Thematic review of the Commissioning, Role and Management of*

Child and Adolescent Mental Health Services (London: TSO).

Nicholls, A. (2006) 'Introduction', in Nicholls, A. (ed.) Social Entrepreneurship: New Models of Sustainable Social Change (Oxford: Oxford University Press): 1–35.

Nkunika, A. I. Z. (1987) 'The role of popular participation in programmes of social development', *Journal of Social Development in Africa* 2(1): 17–28.

Norton, D. G. (1978) *The Dual Perspective: Inclusion of Ethnic Minority Content in the Social Work Curriculum* (Washington, DC: Council on Social Work Education).

Nursing and Midwifery Council (2008) *The Code: Standards of Conduct, Performance and Ethics for Nurses and Midwives* (London: NMC).

O'Brien, D. and Pace, J. (1988) 'The role of social work development theory in informing social work degree programs for indigenous native people: a critique of the Canadian experience', in Guzzetta, C. and Mittwoch, F. (eds) *Social Development and Social Rights* (Vienna: International Association of Schools of Social Work): 89–99.

O'Hagan, K. (1994) 'Crisis intervention: changing perspectives', in Hanvey, C. and Philpot, T. (eds) *Practising Social Work* (London: Routledge): 134–45.

O'Hagan, K. (2001) *Cultural Competence in the Caring Professions* (London: Jessica Kingsley).

Okitikpi, T. and Aymer, C. (2010) *Key Concepts in Anti-discriminatory Social Work* (London: Sage).

Oldfield, M. (2002) 'What works and the conjunctural politics of probation: effectiveness, managerialism and neoliberalism', *British Journal of Community Justice* 1(1): 79–88.

Oliver, M. (2009) *Understanding Disability: From Theory to Practice* (2nd edn) (Basingstoke: Palgrave Macmillan).

Olsson, E. and Ljunghill, J. (1997) 'The practitioner and "naive theory" in social work intervention processes', *British Journal of Social Work* 27(6): 931–50.

Orme, J. (2000) *Gender and Community Care: Social Work and Social Care* (Basingstoke: Palgrave Macmillan).

Orme, J. (2003) '"It's feminist because I say so!" Feminism, social work and critical practice in the UK', *Qualitative Social Work* 2(2): 131–53.

Orme, J. (2009a) 'Feminist social work', in Adams, R., Dominelli, L. and Payne, M. (eds) *Critical Practice in Social Work* (2nd edn) (Basingstoke: Palgrave Macmillan): 199–208.

Orme, J. (2009b) 'Feminist social work', in Gray, M. and Webb, S. A. (2009) *Social Work Theories and Methods* (London: Sage): 65–75.

Orme, J. and Shemmings, D. (2010) *Developing Research Based Social Work Practice* (Basingstoke: Palgrave Macmillan).

Osei-Hwedie, K. (1990) 'Social work and the question of social development in Africa', *Journal of Social Development in Africa* 5(2): 87–99.

Osmo, R. and Landau, R. (2003) 'Religious and secular belief systems in social work: a survey of Israeli social work professionals', *Families in Society* 84(3): 359–66.

Otto, H.-U., Polutta, A. and Ziegler, H. (eds) (2009) *Evidence-based Practice – Modernising the Knowledge Base of Social Work?* (Opladen/Farmington Falls, MI: Barbara Budrich).

Owusu-Bempah, J. (1994) 'Race, self-identity and social work', *British Journal of Social Work* 24(2): 123–36.

Paiva, J. F. X. (1977) 'A conception of social development', *Social Service Review* 51(2): 327–36.

Paiva, J. F. X. (1993) 'Excuse me, I wish to be unboxed…', *Social Development Issues* 15(1): 22–3.

Pandey, R. S. (1981) 'Strategies for social development: an analytical approach', in Jones, J. F. and Pandey, R. S. (eds) *Social Development: Conceptual, Methodological and Policy Issues* (Delhi: Macmillan India): 33–49.

Papell, C. P. and Rothman, B. (1966) 'Social group work models: possession and heritage', *Journal of Education for Social Work* 2(2): 66–73.

Parad, H. J. (1965) 'Introduction', in Parad, H. J. (ed.) *Crisis Intervention: Selected Readings* (New York: Family Service Association of America): 1–4.

Parad, H. J. and Parad, L. G. (1990) *Crisis Intervention Book 2: The Practitioner's Sourcebook for Brief Therapy* (Milwaukee, WI: Family Service America).

Parker, G. (1993) *With This Body: Caring and Disability in Marriage* (Buckingham: Open University Press).

Parker, I. (ed.) (1998) *Social Constructionism, Discourse and Realism* (London: Sage).

Parkes, C. M. and Prigerson, H. G. (2010) *Bereavement: Studies in Adult Life* (London: Penguin).

Parkes, C. M., Stevenson-Hinde, J. and Marris, P. (eds) (1993) *Attachment Across the Life Cycle* (London: Routledge).

Parton, N. (ed.) (1996) *Social Theory, Social Change and Social Work* (London: Routledge).

Parton, N. (2003) 'Rethinking professional practice: the contributions of social constructionism and the feminist "ethics of care"', *British Journal of Social Work* 33(1): 1–16.

Parton, N. and O'Byrne, P. (2000) *Constructive Social Work: Towards a New Practice* (Basingstoke: Macmillan – now Palgrave Macmillan).

Patel, N. (1994) 'Establishing a framework for anti-racist social work education in a multi-racial society – the UK experience from a statutory body, CCETSW', in Dominelli, L., Patel, N. and Bernard, W. T., *Anti-Racist Social Work Education: Models for Practice* (Sheffield: University of Sheffield Department of Sociological Studies): 7–21.

Pawson, R. and Tilley, N. (1997) *Realistic Evaluation* (London: Sage).

Payne, C. (1977) 'Residential social work', in Specht, H. and Vickery, A. (eds) *Integrating Social Work Methods* (London: Allen & Unwin): 195–216.

Payne, M. (1991) 'Relationships between theory and practice in social work: educational implications', *Issues in Social Work Education* 10(1/2): 3–23.

Payne, M. (1992) 'Psychodynamic theory within the politics of social work theory', *Journal of Social Work Practice* 6(2): 141–9.

Payne, M. (1993) 'Routes to and through clienthood and their implications for practice', *Practice* 6(3): 169–80.

Payne, M. (1996) 'The politics of social work theory and values', in IASSW (ed.) *Proceedings of the 27th Congress* (Hong Kong: IASSW): 73–6.

Payne, M. (1998) 'Task-centred practice within the politics of social work theory', *Issues in Social Work Education* 17(2): 48–65.

Payne, M. (1999a) 'Social construction in social work and social action', in Jokinen, A., Juhila, K. and Pösö, T. (eds) *Constructing Social Work Practices* (Aldershot: Ashgate): 25–65.

Payne, M. (1999b) 'The moral bases of social work', *European Journal of Social Work* 2(3), 247–58.

Payne, M. (2000) *Teamwork in Multiprofessional Care* (Basingstoke: Palgrave Macmillan).

Payne, M. (2002) 'The politics of systems theory within social work', *Journal of Social Work* 2(3): 269–92.

Payne, M. (2005) *The Origins of Social Work: Continuity and Change* (Basingstoke: Palgrave Macmillan).

Payne, M. (2006) *What is Professional Social Work?* (2nd edn) (Bristol: Policy Press).

Payne, M. (2009a) *Social work theories table.* Retrieved 18th August 2012 from http://www.scribd.com/doc/13917703/Social-work-theories-table.

Payne, M. (2009b) 'Understanding social work process', in Adams, R., Dominelli, L. and Payne, M. (eds) *Social Work: Themes, Issues and Critical Debates* (3rd edn) (Basingstoke: Palgrave Macmillan): 159–74.

Payne, M. (2009c) 'Critical reflection and social work theories', in Adams, R., Dominelli, L. and Payne, M. (eds) *Critical Practice in Social Work* (2nd edn) (Basingstoke: Palgrave Macmillan): 91–104.

Payne, M. (2009d) *Social Care Practice in Context* (Basingstoke: Palgrave Macmillan).

Payne, M. (2009e) 'Social work practice: struggling to be a wise person', in Agius, A., Cole, M., Naudi, M. and Xuereb J. (eds) *Social Work and Social Cohesion in Europe* (Malta: Maltese Association of Social Workers/University of Malta): 180–91.

Payne, M. (2011a) *Humanistic Social Work: Core Principles in Practice* (Basingstoke: Palgrave Macmillan).

Payne, M. (2011b) *Citizenship Social Work with Older People* (Chicago: Lyceum).

Payne, M. and Askeland, G. A. (2008) *Globalization and International Social Work: Postmodern Change and Challenge* (Aldershot: Ashgate).

Payne, M., Adams, R. and Dominelli, L. (2009) 'On being critical in social work', in Adams, R., Dominelli, L. and Payne, M. (eds) *Critical Practice in Social Work* (Basingstoke: Palgrave Macmillan): 1–15.

Pearson, G. (1975) *The Deviant Imagination: Psychiatry, Social Work and Social Change* (London: Macmillan – now Palgrave Macmillan).

Pease, B. (2002) 'Rethinking empowerment: a postmodern reappraisal for emancipatory practice', *British Journal of Social Work* 32(2): 135–47.

Pease, B. (2009) 'From radical to critical social work: progressive transformation or mainstream incorporation?', in Adams, R., Dominelli, L. and Payne, M. (eds) *Critical Social Work Practice* (2nd edn) (Basingstoke: Palgrave Macmillan): 189–98.

Pease, B. and Fook, J. (1999) *Transforming Social Work Practice: Postmodern Critical Perspectives* (London: Routledge).

Penketh, L. (2011) 'Social work and women's oppression today', in Lavalette, M. (ed.) *Radical Social Work Today: Social Work at the Crossroads* (Bristol: Policy Press): 45–58.

Perlman, F. T. and Brandell, J. R. (2011) 'Psychoanalytic theory', in Brandell, J. R. (ed.) *Theory and Practice in Clinical Social Work* (2nd edn) (Los Angeles: Sage): 41–79.

Perlman, H. H. (1957a) *Social Casework: A Problem-Solving Process* (Chicago: University of Chicago Press).

Perlman, H. H. (1957b) 'Freud's contribution to social welfare', *Social Service Review* 31(2): 192–202.

Petrie, P. (2011) *Communication Skills for Working with Children and Young People: Introducing Social Pedagogy* (London: Jessica Kingsley).

Phillips, D. (2011) 'What produces successful interventions?', in Shemmings, D. and Shemmings, Y. (eds) *Understanding Disorganized Attachment: Theory and Practice for Working with Children and Adults* (London: Jessica Kingsley): 173–97.

Phillipson, C. (1982) *Capitalism and the Construction of Old Age* (London: Macmillan – now Palgrave Macmillan).

Philp, M. (1979) 'Notes on the form of knowledge in social work', *Sociological Review* 27(1): 83–111.

Philpot, T. (1999) 'The modern mark of Cain', in Philpot, T. (ed.) *Political Correctness and Social Work* (London: IEA Health and Welfare Unit): 1–15.

Pilkington, A. (2003) *Racial Disadvantage and Ethnic Diversity in Britain* (Basingstoke: Palgrave Macmillan).

Pincus, A. and Minahan, A. (1973) *Social Work Practice: Model and Method* (Itasca, IL: Peacock).

Pinderhughes, E. B. (1988) 'Significance of culture and power in the human behavior curriculum', in Jacobs, C. and Bowles, D. D. (eds) *Ethnicity and Race: Critical Concepts in Social Work* (Silver Spring, MD: National Association of Social Workers): 152–66.

Pinderhughes, E. B. (1989) *Understanding Race, Ethnicity and Power: The Key to Efficacy in Clinical Practice* (New York: Free Press).

Pitman, E. (1982) 'Transactional analysis: an introduction to its theory and practice', *British Journal of Social Work* 12(1): 47–64.

Pitman, E. (1983) *Transactional Analysis for Social Workers* (London: Routledge & Kegan Paul).

Pitts, J. (1992) 'The end of an era', *Howard Journal of Criminal Justice* 31(2): 133–49.

Polsky, H. (1968) *Cottage Six: The Social System of Delinquent Boys in Residential Treatment* (Chapel Hill, NC: University of North Carolina Press).

Potter, C. and Brough, F. (2004) 'Systemic capacity building: a hierarchy of needs', *Health Policy and Planning* 19(5): 336–45.

Prior, V. and Glaser, D. (2006) *Understanding Attachment and Attachment Disorders: Theory, Evidence and Practice* (London: Jessica Kingsley).

Pružinská, J. (2011) *Reflexia poradenských prístupov v priamej práci s klientom sociálneho pracovníka*. Paper presented to the conference *Realita a Vízia Sociálnej Práca*, Comenius University, Bratislava, 10th February 2011.

Pugh, R. and Cheers, B. (2010) *Rural Social Work: International Perspectives* (Bristol: Policy Press).

Race, D. G. (ed.) (2003) *Leadership and Change in Human Services: Selected Readings from Wolf Wolfensberger* (London: Routledge).

Ramcharan, P., Roberts, G., Grant, G. and Borland, J. (eds) (1997) *Empowerment in Everyday Life: Learning Disabilities* (London: Jessica Kingsley).

Ramon, S. (1989) 'The value and knowledge bases of the normalization approach: implications for social work', *International Social Work* 32(1): 11–23.

Rapoport, L. (1970) 'Crisis intervention as a mode of brief treatment', in Roberts, R. W. and Nee, R. H. (eds) *Theories of Social Casework* (Chicago: University of Chicago Press): 265–311.

Rapp, C. A. and Goscha, R. J. (2006) *The Strengths Model: Case Management with People with Psychiatric Disabilities* (2nd edn) (New York: Oxford University Press).

Rawlinson, D. (1999) 'Group analytic ideas: extending the group matrix into TC', in Campling, P. and Haigh, R. (eds) *Therapeutic Communities: Past, Present and Future* (London: Jessica Kingsley): 50–62.

Raynor, P. (2003) 'Evidence-based probation and its critics' *Probation Journal* 50(4): 334–45.

Raynor, P. and Vanstone, M. (1994) 'Probation practice, effectiveness and the non-treatment paradigm', *British Journal of Social Work* 24(4): 387–404.

Raynor, P. and Vanstone, M. (1998) 'Adult probationers and the STOP programme', in Cigno, K. and Bourn, D. (eds) *Cognitive-behavioural Social Work in Practice* (Aldershot: Ashgate): 143–62.

Raynor, P., Smith, D. and Vanstone, M. (1994) *Effective Probation Practice* (Basingstoke: Macmillan – now Palgrave Macmillan).

Redmond, B. (2006) *Reflection in Action: Developing Reflective Practice in Health and Social Services* (Farnham: Ashgate).

Rees, S. (1991) *Achieving Power* (Sydney: Allen & Unwin).

Reid, W. J. (1978) *The Task-Centered System* (New York: Columbia University Press).

Reid, W. J. (1985) *Family Problem-solving* (New York: Columbia University Press).

Reid, W. J. (1992) *Task Strategies: An Empirical Approach to Clinical Social Work* (New York: Columbia University Press).

Reid, W. J. (2000) *The Task Planner: An Intervention Resource for Human Service Professionals* (New York: Columbia University Press).

Reid, W. J. and Epstein, L. (1972a) *Task-centered Casework* (New York: Columbia University Press).

Reid, W. J. and Epstein, L. (eds) (1972b) *Task-centered Practice* (New York: Columbia University Press).

Reid, W. J. and Hanrahan, P. (1982) 'Recent evaluations of social work: grounds for optimism', *Social Work* 27: 328–40.

Reid, W. J. and Shyne, A. W. (1969) *Brief and Extended Casework* (New York: Columbia University Press).

Reid, W. J., Kenaley, B. D. and Colvin, J. (2004) 'Do some interventions work better than others? A review of comparative social work experiments', *Social Work Research* 28(2): 71–81.

Reith, M. (2011) 'Helping individual caregivers of people who are dying using a groupwork intervention', in Brągiel, J., Dąbrowska-Jabłońska, I. and Payne, M. (eds) *Social Work in Adult Services in the European Union: Selected Issues and Experiences* (London: College Publications): 200–7.

Reith, M. and Payne, M. (2009) *Social Work in End-of-life and Palliative Care* (Bristol: Policy Press).

Rex, J. (1997) 'Multiculturalism in Europe and North America', in Isajiw, W. W. (ed.) *Multiculturalism in North American and Europe: Comparative Perspectives on Interethnic Relations and Social Incorporation* (Toronto: Canadian Scholars' Press): 5–33.

Reynolds, J. (1993) 'Feminist theory and strategy in social work', in Walmsley, J., Reynolds, J., Shakespeare, P. and Woolfe, R. (eds) *Health, Welfare and Practice: Reflecting on Roles and Relationships* (London: Sage): 74–82.

Rhodes, M. L. (1985) 'Gilligan's theory of moral development as applied to social work', *Social Work* 30(2): 101–5.

Righton, P. (1975) 'Planned environment therapy: a reappraisal', *Association of Workers with Maladjusted Children Journal*, Spring; reprinted in Righton, P. (ed.) *Studies in Environment Therapy*, vol. 3 (Teddington: Planned Environment Therapy Trust): 9–16.

Roberts, A. R. (ed.) (2005a) *Crisis Intervention Handbook: Assessment, Treatment, and Research* (3rd edn) (New York: Oxford University Press).

Roberts, A. R. (2005b) 'Bridging the past and present to the future of crisis intervention and crisis management', in Roberts, A. R. (ed.) *Crisis Intervention Handbook: Assessment, Treatment, and Research* (3rd edn) (New York: Oxford University Press): 3–34.

Roberts, A. R. and Yeager, K. R. (eds) (2004) *Evidence-Based Practice Manual: Research and Outcome Measures in Health and Human Services* (New York: Oxford University Press).

Roberts, B. (2006) *Micro Social Theory* (Basingstoke: Palgrave).

Roberts, R. (1990) *Lessons from the Past: Issues for Social Work Theory* (London: Tavistock/Routledge).

Roberts, R. W. and Nee, R. H. (eds) (1970) *Theories of Social Casework* (Chicago: University of Chicago Press).

Robinson, L. (1995) *Psychology for Social Workers: Black Perspectives* (London: Routledge).

Robinson, L. (1999) 'Racial identity attitudes and interracial communication: implications for social work practice in Britain', *European Journal of Social Work* 2(3): 315–26.

Robinson, L. (2001) 'A conceptual framework for social work practice with black children and adolescents in the United Kingdom: some first steps', *Journal of Social Work* 1(2): 165–85.

Rogers, C. R. (1951) *Client-centered Therapy: Its Current Practice, Implications and Theory* (London: Constable).

Rogers, C. R. (1961) *On Becoming a Person: A Therapist's View of Psychotherapy* (London: Constable).

Rogers, C. R. (1977) *Carl Rogers on Personal Power* (London: Constable).

Rojek, C. (1986) 'The "Subject" in social work', *British Journal of Social Work* 16(1): 65–77.

Rojek, C. and Collins, S. (1987) 'Contract or con trick?', *British Journal of Social Work* 17(2): 199–211.

Rojek, C. and Collins, S. (1988) 'Contract or con trick revisited: comments on the reply by Corden and Preston-Shoot', *British Journal of Social Work* 18(6): 611–22.

Rojek, C., Peacock, G. and Collins, S. (1989) *Social Work and Received Ideas* (London: Routledge).

Ronen, T. (1998) 'Direct clinical work with children', in Cigno, K. and Bourn, D. (eds) *Cognitive-behavioural Social Work in Practice* (Aldershot: Ashgate): 39–59.

Ronen, T. and Freeman, A. (2007) *Cognitive Behavior Therapy in Clinical Social Work Practice*. New York: Springer.

Ronnby, A. (1992) 'Praxiology in social work', *International Social Work* 35(3): 317–26.

Rose, S. M. (1990) 'Advocacy/empowerment: an approach to clinical practice for social work', *Journal of Sociology and Social Welfare* 17(2): 41–52.

Rose, S. M. and Black, B. L. (1985) *Advocacy and Empowerment: Mental Health Care in the Community* (Boston: Routledge & Kegan Paul).

Ross, R. R., Fabiano, E. A. and Ewles, C. D. (1988) 'Reasoning and rehabilitation', *International Journal of Offender Therapy and Comparative Criminology* 32(1): 29–35.

Ross, R. R., Fabiano, E. A. and Ross, R. (1989) *Reasoning and Rehabilitation: A Handbook for Teaching Cognitive Skills* (Ottawa: Cognitive Centre).

Royse, D. D. (2008) *Research Methods in Social Work* (5th edn) (Belmont, CA: Thomson).

Rubin, A. (1985) 'Practice effectiveness: more grounds for optimism', *Social Work* 30: 469–76.

Rubin, A. and Parrish, D. (2007) 'Views of evidence-based practice among faculty in Master of Social Work programs: a national survey', *Research on Social Work Practice* 17(1): 110–22.

Ruch, G., Turney, D. and Ward, A. (2010) *Relationship-based Social Work: Getting to the Heart of Practice* (London: Jessica Kingsley).

Rutter, M. (1981) *Maternal Deprivation Reassessed* (Harmondsworth: Penguin).

Ryan, A. S. (ed.) (1992) *Social Work with Immigrants and Refugees* (New York: Haworth Press).

Ryant, J. C. (1969) 'The revolutionary potential of social work', *Social Worker* 37(3): 151–6.

Rzepnicki, T. L., McCracken, S. G. and Briggs, H. E. (eds) (2012) *From Task-centered to Evidence-based and Integrative Practice: Reflections on History and Implementation* (Chicago: Lyceum).

Sage, N., Sowden, M., Chorlton, E. and Edeleanu, A. (2008) *CBT for Chronic Illness and Palliative Care: A Workbook and Toolkit* (Chichester: Wiley).

Saleebey, D. (ed.) (2009a) *The Strengths Perspective in Social Work Practice* (5th edn) (Boston: Pearson).

Saleebey, D. (2009b) 'Introduction: power in the people', in Saleebey, D. (ed.) *The Strengths Perspective in Social Work Practice* (5th edn) (Boston: Pearson): 1–23.

Salzberger-Wittenberg, I. (1970) *Psychoanalytic Insights and Relationships: A Kleinian Approach* (London: Routledge & Kegan Paul).

Sanders, D. S. (1978) 'Multiculturalism: implications for social work', in IFSW (ed.) *Social Work and the Multi-cultural Society* (Geneva: International Federation of Social Workers): 33–41.

Sands, R. G. (1996) 'The elusiveness of identity in social work practice with women: a postmodern feminist perspective', *Clinical Social Work Journal* 24(2): 167–86.

Sands, R. G. and Nuccio, K. (1992) 'Postmodern feminist theory and social work', *Social Work* 37(6): 489–94.

Schön, D. A. (1983) *The Reflective Practitioner: How Professionals Think in Action* (New York: Basic Books).

Schön, D. A. (1987) *Educating the Reflective Practitioner* (San Francisco: Jossey-Bass).

Scourfield, J. B. (2002) 'Reflections on gender, knowledge and values in social work', *British Journal of Social Work* 32(1): 1–15.

Scourfield, J. (2006) 'Gendered organizational culture in child protection social work', *Social Work* 51(1): 80–2.

Secker, J. (1993) *From Theory to Practice in Social Work: The Development of Social Work Students' Practice* (Aldershot: Avebury).

Seed, P. (1990) *Introducing Network Analysis in Social Work* (London: Jessica Kingsley).

Seeley, K. M. (2004) 'Short-term intercultural psychotherapy: ethnographic inquiry', *Social Work* 49(1): 121–30.

Seligman, M. E. P. (1998) *Learned Optimism* (2nd edn) (New York: Knopf).

Sellick, M. M., Delaney, R. and Brownlee, K. (2002) 'The deconstruction of professional knowledge: accountability without authority', *Families in Society* 83(5): 493–8.

Sharry, J. (2007) *Solution-Focused Groupwork* (2nd edn) (London: Sage).

Sheldon, B. (1987) 'Implementing findings from social work effectiveness research', *British Journal of Social Work* 17(6): 573–86.

Sheldon, B. (1995) *Cognitive-behavioural Therapy: Research, Practice and Philosophy* (London: Routledge).

Sheldon, B. (1998) 'Research and theory', in Cigno, K. and Bourn, D. (eds) *Cognitive-Behavioural Social Work in Practice* (Aldershot: Ashgate): 1–38.

Sheldon, B. (2012) 'Cognitive-behavioural methods in social care: a look at the evidence', in Stepney, P. and Ford, D. (eds) *Social Work Models, Methods and Theories: A Framework for Practice* (Lyme Regis: Russell House): 123–51.

Sheldon, B. and Macdonald, G. (2009) *A Textbook of Social Work* (London: Routledge).

Shemmings, D. and Shemmings, Y. (2011) *Understanding Disorganized Attachment: Theory and Practice for Working with Children and Adults* (London: Jessica Kingsley).

Sheppard, M. and Ryan, K. (2003) 'Practitioners as rule using analysts: a further development of process knowledge in social work', *British Journal of Social Work* 33(2): 157–76.

Sheppard, M., Newstead, S., di Caccavo, A. and Ryan, K. (2000) 'Reflexivity and the development of process knowledge in social work: a classification and empirical study', British Journal of Social Work 30(4): 465–88.

Shier, M. L. (2011) 'Problem-solving and social work', in Turner, F. J. (ed.) *Social Work Treatment: Interlocking Theoretical Approaches* (5th edn) (New York: Oxford University Press): 364–73.

Sibeon, R. (1990) 'Comments on the structure and forms of social work knowledge', *Social Work and Social Sciences Review* 1(1): 29–44.

Simon, B. L. (1995) *The Empowerment Tradition in American Social Work: A History* (New York: Columbia University Press).

Sinclair, E. (1988) 'The formal evidence', in National Institute for Social Work, *Residential Care: a Positive Choice* (London: HMSO).

Singh, G. (1992) *Race and Social Work from 'Black Pathology' to 'Black Perspectives'* (Bradford: Race Relations Research Unit, University of Bradford).

Singh, K. (1999) *Rural Development: Principles, Policy and Management* (New Delhi: Sage).

Sinha, D. and Kao, H. S. R. (eds) (1988a) *Social Values and Development: Asian Perspectives* (New Delhi: Sage).

Sinha, D. and Kao, H. S. R. (1988b) 'Introduction: values-development congruence', in Sinha, D. and Kao, H. S. R. (eds) *Social Values and Development: Asian Perspectives* (New Delhi: Sage): 10–27.

Siporin, M. (1975) *Introduction to Social Work Practice* (New York: Macmillan).

Sisneros, J. Stakeman, C., Joyner, M. C. and Schmitz, C. L. (2008) *Critical Multicultural Social Work* (Chicago: Lyceum).

Skeith, P. (1992) 'Liberation theology and social development', in Estes, R. J. (ed.) *Internationalizing Social Work Education: A Guide to Resources for a New Century* (Philadelphia, PA: University of Pennsylvania School of Social Work): 262–6.

Small, J. (1989) 'Towards a black perspective in social work: a trans-cultural exploration', in Langan, M. and Lee, P. (eds) *Radical Social Work Today* (London: Unwin Hyman): 279–91.

Smalley, R. E. (1967) *Theory for Social Work Practice* (New York: Columbia University Press).

Smid, G. and van Krieken, R. (1984) 'Notes on theory and practice in social work: a comparative view', *British Journal of Social Work* 14(1): 11–22.

Smith, P. (2001) *Cultural Theory: An Introduction* (Oxford: Blackwell).

Smith, S. R. (2007) 'Applying theory to policy and practice: methodological problems and issues', in Smith, S. R. (ed.) *Applying Theory to Policy and Practice: Issues for Critical Reflection* (Aldershot: Ashgate): 1–18.

Soares, H. H., Rose, M. and Feiger, R. (2011) 'Clinical practice with older adults', in Brandell, J. R. (ed.) (2011) *Theory and Practice in Clinical Social Work* (2nd edn) (Los Angeles: Sage): 407–34.

Sociaaliportti (2009) The Good Practice website – good practices in the field of social welfare and health care. Retrieved 20th February 2012 from: http://www.sosiaaliportti.fi/en-GB/goodpractice/.

Social Care Institute for Excellence (2011) *Dignity in Care* (SCIE Guide 15) (London: Social Care Institute for Excellence).

Solomos, J. (2003) *Race and Racism in Britain* (3rd edn) (Basingstoke: Palgrave Macmillan).

Speer, P. W. and Peterson, N. A. (2000) 'Psychometric properties of an empowerment scale: testing cognitive, emotional, and behavioral domains', *Social Work Research* 24(2): 109–18.

Spong, S. (2007) 'Scepticism and belief: unraveling the relationship between theory and practice in counseling and psychotherapy', in Smith, S. R. (ed.) *Applying Theory to Policy and Practice: Issues for Critical Reflection* (Aldershot: Ashgate): 55–70.

Stallard, P. (2005) *A Clinicians Guide to Think Good, Feel Good: Using CBT with Children and Young People* (Chichester: Wiley).

Stark, C. (2010) 'The neoliberal ideology and the challenges for social work ethics and practice', *Revista de Assitenţă Socială* 9(1): 9–19.

Stewart, C. and MacNeil, G. (2005) 'Crisis intervention with chronic school violence and volatile situations' in Roberts, A. R. (ed.) *Crisis Intervention Handbook* (3rd edn) (New York: Oxford University Press): 519–40.

Stirrat, R. (1997) 'The new orthodoxy and old truths: participation, empowerment and other buzzwords', in Bastian, S., Bastian, N. and Nivaran, D. (eds) *Assessing Participation: A Debate from South Asia* (Delhi: Konark): 67–92.

Strean, H. S. (1979) *Psychoanalytic Theory and Social Work Practice* (New York: Free Press).

Stroebe, M. and Schut, H. (1999) 'The dual process model of coping with bereavement: rationale and description', *Death Studies* 23(3): 197–224.

Tattersall, R. (2002) 'The expert patient: a new approach to chronic disease management for the twenty-first century', *Clinical Medicine* 2: 227–9.

Taylor, C. and White, S. (2000) *Practising Reflexivity in Health and Welfare: Making Knowledge* (Buckingham: Open University Press).

Taylor, P. and Daly, C. (eds) (1995) *Gender Dilemmas in Social Work: Issues Affecting Women in the Profession* (Toronto: Canadian Scholars' Press).

Teater, B. (2010) *An Introduction to Applying Social Work Theories and Methods* (Maidenhead: Open University Press).

Thomas, E. J. (1968) 'Selected sociobehavioral techniques and principles: an approach to interpersonal helping', *Social Work* 13(1): 12–26.

Thomas, E. J. (1971) 'The behavior modification model and social casework', in Strean, H. S. (ed.) *Social Casework: Theories in Action* (Metuchen, NJ: Scarecrow Press): 267–96.

Thomlison, R. and Thomlison, B. (2011) 'Cognitive behaviour theory and social work treatment', in Turner, F. J. (ed.) *Social Work Treatment: Interlocking Theoretical Approaches* (5th edn) (New York: Oxford University Press): 77–102.

Thomlison, R. J. (1984) 'Something works: evidence from practice effectiveness studies', *Social Work* 29(1): 51–7.

Thompson, N. (1992) *Existentialism and Social Work* (Aldershot: Avebury).

Thompson, N. (2002) 'Social movements, social justice and social work', *British Journal of Social Work* 32(6): 711–22.

Thompson, N. (2010) *Theorizing Social Work Practice* (Basingstoke: Palgrave Macmillan).

Thompson, N. (2011a) *Crisis Intervention* (Lyme Regis: Russell House).

Thompson, N. (2011b) *Effective Communication: A Guide for the People Professions* (2nd edn) (Basingstoke: Palgrave Macmillan).

Thompson, N. (2012) *Anti-discriminatory Practice: Equality, Diversity and Social Justice* (5th edn) (Basingstoke: Palgrave Macmillan).

Thyer, B. A. (1994) 'Empiricists versus social constructionists: more fuel on the females', *Families in Society* 75(5): 308–12.

Thyer, B. A. and Kazi, M. A. F. (eds) (2004) *International Perspectives on Evidence-based Practice in Social Work* (Birmingham: Venture).

Thyer, B. A. and Myers, L. L. (2011) 'Behavioral and cognitive theories', in Brandell, J. R. (ed.) *Theory and Practice in Clinical Social Work* (Los Angeles: Sage): 21–40.

Tolman, R. M. and Molidor, C. E. (1994) 'A decade of social group work research: trends in methodology, theory, and program development', *Research on Social Work Practice* 4(2):142–59.

Tolson, E. R., Reid, W. and Garvin, C. D. (2003) *Generalist Practice: A Task-centered Approach* (2nd edn) (New York: Columbia University Press)

Towell, D. (ed.) (1988) *An Ordinary Life in Practice* (London: King Edward's Hospital Fund for London).

Trevillion, S. (1999) *Networking and Community Partnership* (2nd edn) (Aldershot: Arena).

Trevithick, P. (2012) 'Groupwork theory and practice', in Stepney, P. and Ford, D. (eds) *Social Work Models, Methods and Theories* (2nd edn) (Lyme Regis: Russell House): 236–54.

Truax, C. B. and Carkhuff, R. J. (1967) *Toward Effective Counseling and Psychotherapy: Training and Practice* (Chicago: Aldine).

Turner, F. J. (ed.) (2011) *Social Work Treatment: Interlocking Theoretical Approaches* (5th edn) (New York: Oxford University Press).

Urban Dictionary (2012) *Freudian slip*, 1. Retrieved 13th March 2012 from: http://www.urbandictionary.com/define. php?term=Freudian%20slip.

Valentich, M. (2011) 'Feminist theory and social work practice', in Turner, F. J. (ed.) *Social Work Treatment: Interlocking Theoretical Approaches* (5th edn) (New York: Oxford University Press): 205–24.

van de Luitgaarden, G. M. J. (2009) 'Evidence-based practice in social work: lessons from judgment and decision-making theory', *British Journal of Social Work* 39(2): 243–60.

van den Bergh, N. (ed.) (1995) *Feminist Practice in the 21st Century* (Washington, DC: NASW Press).

van Elst, T. (1994) 'Gender-specific social work with men and boys', in Hesser, K.-E. and Koole, W. (eds) *Social Work in the Netherlands: Current Developments* (Utrecht: SWP): 24–34.

van Wormer, K. (1999) *Social Welfare: A World View* (Belmont, CA: Wadsworth).

van Wormer, K., Besthorn, F. H. and Keefe, T. (2007) *Human Behavior and the Social Environment: Macro Level: Groups, Communities and Organizations* (New York: Oxford University Press).

Videka-Sherman, L. (1988) 'Meta-analysis of research on social work practice in mental health', *Social Work* 33: 325–38.

Wakefield, J. C. (1996) 'Does social work need the eco-systems perspective? Part 1: Is the perspective clinically useful?', *Social Service Review* 70(1): 1–31; 'Does social work need the eco-systems perspective? Part 2: Does the perspective save social work from incoherence?', *Social Service Review*, 70(2): 183–213.

Walker, B. G. (1994) 'Science: feminists' scapegoat?', *Research on Social Work Practice* 4(4): 510–14.

Walker, S. (2007) 'Family therapy and systemic practice', in Lishman, J. (ed.) *Handbook for Practice Learning in Social Work and Social Care: Knowledge and Theory* (2nd edn) (London: Jessica Kingsley): 216–34.

Wallen, J. (1982) 'Listening to the unconscious in case material: Robert Langs' theory applied', *Smith College Studies in Social Work* 52(3): 203–33.

Walsh, F. (2011) *Strengthening Family Resilience* (2nd edn) (New York: Guilford).

Walsh, J. (2010) *Theories of Direct Social Work Practice* (2nd edn) (Belmont, CA: Wadsworth).

Walsh, J. and Corcoran, J. (2010) 'Motivational interviewing', in Walsh, J., *Theories for Direct Social Work Practice* (2nd edn) (Belmont, CA: Wadsworth Cengage): 253–72.

Walter, I., Nutley, S., Percy-Smith, J., McNeish, D. and Frost, S. (2004) *Improving the Use of Research in Social Care Practice* (London: Social Care Institute for Excellence).

Walter, U. M. (2003) 'Toward a third space: improvisation and professionalism in social work', *Families in Society* 84(3): 317–22.

Walton, R. G. and el Nasr, M. M. A. (1988) 'Indigenization and authentization in terms of social work in Egypt', *International Social Work* 31(2): 135–44.

Watson, D. (1980) *Caring for Strangers* (London: Routledge & Kegan Paul).

Webb, D. (1981) 'Themes and continuities in radical and traditional social work', *British Journal of Social Work* 11(2): 143–58.

Webb, S. A. (2001) 'Some considerations on the validity of evidence-based practice in social work', British Journal of Social Work 31(1): 57–79.

Weber, M. (1930) *The Protestant Ethic and the Spirit of Capitalism* (London: Allen & Unwin).

Weick, A. (1981) 'Reframing the person-in-environment perspective', *Social Work* 26(2): 140–3.

Wetherell, M. and Maybin, J. (1996) 'The distributed self: a social constructionist perspective', in Stevens, R. (ed.) *Understanding the Self* (London: Sage): 219–79.

Whitaker, D., Archer, L. and Hicks, L. (1998) *Working in Children's Homes: Challenges and Complexities* (Chichester: Wiley).

White, M. (2007) *Maps of Narrative Practice* (New York: Norton.)

White, M. and Epston, D. (1990) *Narrative Means to Therapeutic Ends* (New York: Norton).

White, S. (1997) 'Beyond retroduction? Hermeneutics, reflexivity and social work practice', *British Journal of Social Work* 275: 739–53.

White, S. (2006) 'Unsettling reflections: the reflexive practitioner as "trickster" in interprofessional work', in White, S., Fook, J. and Gardner, F. (eds) *Critical Reflection in Health and Social Care* (Maidenhead: Open University Press): 21–39.

White, S., Fook, J. and Gardner, F. (eds) (2006) *Critical Reflection in Health and Social Care* (Maidenhead: Open University Press).

White, V. (1995) 'Commonality and diversity in feminist social work', *British Journal of Social Work* 25(2): 143–56.

White, V. (2006) *The State of Feminist Social Work* (London: Routledge).

Whyte, W. F. (ed.) (1991) *Participative Action Research* (Newbury Park, CA: Sage).

Wilks, T. (2012) *Advocacy and Social Work Practice* (Maidenhead: Open University Press).

Wilkinson, R. and Pickett, K. (2010) *The Spirit Level: Why Equality is Better for Everyone* (rev. edn) (London: Penguin).

Wills, D. (1973) 'Planned environment therapy – what is it', in Klare, H. and Wills, D. (eds) *Studies in Environment Therapy*, vol. 2 (London: Planned Environment Therapy Trust): 9–21.

Wilson, A. and Beresford, P. (2000) '"Anti-oppressive practice": emancipation or appropriation?' *British Journal of Social Work* 30(5): 553–73.

Winkels, D. (1994) 'Social work and community development work', in Hesser, K.-E. and Koole, W. (eds) Social Work in the Netherlands: Current Developments (Utrecht: SWP): 105–11.

Winnicott, D. W. (1964) *The Child, the Family and the Outside World* (Harmondsworth: Penguin).

Witkin, S. L. (1992) 'Empirical clinical practice or Witkin's revised views: which is the issue?', *Social Work* 37(5): 465–8.

Witkin, S. L., & Saleebey, D. (eds) (2007). *Social Work Dialogues: Transforming the Canon in Inquiry, Practice, and Education* (Alexandria, VA: Council on Social Work Education).

Wodarski, J. S. and Thyer, B. A. (1998) *Handbook of Empirical Social Work Practice*, two vols (Hoboken, NJ: Wiley).

Wolfensberger, W. (1972) *The Principle of Normalisation in Human Services* (Toronto: National Institute on Mental Retardation).

Wolfensberger, W. (1984) 'A reconceptualisation of normalisation as social role valorization', *Mental Retardation* 34: 22–5.

Wood, K. M. (1971) 'The contribution of psychoanalysis and ego psychology to social work', in Strean, H. S. (ed.) *Social Casework: Theories in Action* (Metuchen, NJ: Scarecrow Press): 45–122.

Woods, M. E. and Hollis, F. (1999) *Casework: A Psychosocial Therapy* (5th edn) (New York: McGraw-Hill).

World Bank (2012) *World Development Report 2012: Gender Equality and Development* (Washington, DC: World Bank).

World Health Organization/World Bank (2011) *World Report on Disability* (Geneva: World Health Organization).

Yasas, F. M. and Mehta, V. (eds) (1990) *Exploring Feminist Visions: Case Studies on Social Justice Issues* (Pune: Streevani/Ishvani Kendra).

Yelloly, M. A. (1980) *Social Work Theory and Psychoanalysis* (Wokingham: Van Nostrand Reinhold).

York, A. S. (1984) 'Towards a conceptual model of community social work', *British Journal of Social Work* 14(3): 241–55.

Young, K. P. H. (1983) *Coping in Crisis* (Hong Kong: Hong Kong University Press).

Zapf, M. K. (2010) 'Social work and the environment: understanding people and place', *Critical Social Work* 11(3). Retrieved 25th August 2011 from: http://www.uwindsor. ca/criticalsocialwork/social-work-and-the-environment-understanding-people-and-place.

Zimmerman, S., Scott, A. C., Park, N. S., Hall, S. A., Wetherby, M. M., Gruber-Baldini, A. L. and Morgan, L. A. (2003) 'Social engagement and its relationship to service provision in residential care and assisted living', *Social Work Research* 27(1): 6–18.

Author index

Subject index

In the subject index, major discussions of a listed topic are shown in **bold**.